Teach Yourself®

XML™

Sandra E. Eddy and John E. Schnyder

One CD-ROM included in back of
book.

IDG Books Worldwide, Inc.
An International Data Group Company

Foster City, CA • Chicago, IL • Indianapolis, IN • New York, NY

Teach Yourself® XML™
Published by
IDG Books Worldwide, Inc.
An International Data Group Company
919 E. Hillsdale Blvd., Suite 400
Foster City, CA 94404
`www.idgbooks.com` (IDG Books Worldwide Web site)

ISBN: 0-7645-7513-9

Printed in the United States of America

10 9 8 7 6 5 4 3 2 1

1P/RQ/QY/ZZ/IN

Distributed in the United States by IDG Books Worldwide, Inc.

Distributed by CDG Books Canada Inc. for Canada; by Transworld Publishers Limited in the United Kingdom; by IDG Norge Books for Norway; by IDG Sweden Books for Sweden; by IDG Books Australia Publishing Corporation Pty. Ltd. for Australia and New Zealand; by TransQuest Publishers Pte Ltd. for Singapore, Malaysia, Thailand, Indonesia, and Hong Kong; by Gotop Information Inc. for Taiwan; by ICG Muse, Inc. for Japan; by Norma Comunicaciones S.A. for Colombia; by Intersoft for South Africa; by Eyrolles for France; by International Thomson Publishing for Germany, Austria and Switzerland; by Distribuidora Cuspide for Argentina; by LR International for Brazil; by Galileo Libros for Chile; by Ediciones ZETA S.C.R. Ltda. for Peru; by WS Computer Publishing Corporation, Inc., for the Philippines; by Contemporanea de Ediciones for Venezuela; by Express Computer Distributors for the Caribbean and West Indies; by Micronesia Media Distributor, Inc. for Micronesia; by Grupo Editorial Norma S.A. for Guatemala; by Chips Computadoras S.A. de C.V. for Mexico; by Editorial Norma de Panama S.A. for Panama; by American Bookshops for Finland. Authorized Sales Agent: Anthony Rudkin Associates for the Middle East and North Africa.

For general information on IDG Books Worldwide's books in the U.S., please call our Consumer Customer Service department at 800-762-2974. For reseller information, including discounts and premium sales, please call our Reseller Customer Service department at 800-434-3422.

For information on where to purchase IDG Books Worldwide's books outside the U.S., please contact our International Sales department at 317-596-5530 or fax 317-596-5692.

For consumer information on foreign language translations, please contact our Customer Service department at 1-800-434-3422, fax 317-596-5692, or e-mail rights@idgbooks.com.

For information on licensing foreign or domestic rights, please phone +1-650-655-3109.

For sales inquiries and special prices for bulk quantities, please contact our Sales department at 650-655-3200 or write to the address above.

For information on using IDG Books Worldwide's books in the classroom or for ordering examination copies, please contact our Educational Sales department at 800-434-2086 or fax 317-596-5499.

For press review copies, author interviews, or other publicity information, please contact our Public Relations department at 650-655-3000 or fax 650-655-3299.

For authorization to photocopy items for corporate, personal, or educational use, please contact Copyright Clearance Center, 222 Rosewood Drive, Danvers, MA 01923, or fax 978-750-4470.

Library of Congress Cataloging-in-Publication Data
Eddy, Sandra E.
    Teach Yourself XML / Sandra E. Eddy and John E. Schnyder.
        p.   cm.
    Includes index.
    ISBN 0-7645-7513-9 (alk. paper)
    1. XML (Document markup lnaguage) I. Schnyder, John E.
II. Title.
QA76.76.H94E34 1999
005.7'2--dc21   99–11877
                                                            CIP

 is a registered trademark or trademark under exclusive license to IDG Books Worldwide, Inc. from International Data Group, Inc. in the United States and/or other countries.   7/9/99

ABOUT IDG BOOKS WORLDWIDE

Welcome to the world of IDG Books Worldwide.

IDG Books Worldwide, Inc., is a subsidiary of International Data Group, the world's largest publisher of computer-related information and the leading global provider of information services on information technology. IDG was founded more than 30 years ago by Patrick J. McGovern and now employs more than 9,000 people worldwide. IDG publishes more than 290 computer publications in over 75 countries. More than 90 million people read one or more IDG publications each month.

Launched in 1990, IDG Books Worldwide is today the #1 publisher of best-selling computer books in the United States. We are proud to have received eight awards from the Computer Press Association in recognition of editorial excellence and three from Computer Currents' First Annual Readers' Choice Awards. Our best-selling ...*For Dummies*® series has more than 50 million copies in print with translations in 31 languages. IDG Books Worldwide, through a joint venture with IDG's Hi-Tech Beijing, became the first U.S. publisher to publish a computer book in the People's Republic of China. In record time, IDG Books Worldwide has become the first choice for millions of readers around the world who want to learn how to better manage their businesses.

Our mission is simple: Every one of our books is designed to bring extra value and skill-building instructions to the reader. Our books are written by experts who understand and care about our readers. The knowledge base of our editorial staff comes from years of experience in publishing, education, and journalism — experience we use to produce books to carry us into the new millennium. In short, we care about books, so we attract the best people. We devote special attention to details such as audience, interior design, use of icons, and illustrations. And because we use an efficient process of authoring, editing, and desktop publishing our books electronically, we can spend more time ensuring superior content and less time on the technicalities of making books.

You can count on our commitment to deliver high-quality books at competitive prices on topics you want to read about. At IDG Books Worldwide, we continue in the IDG tradition of delivering quality for more than 30 years. You'll find no better book on a subject than one from IDG Books Worldwide.

John Kilcullen
Chairman and CEO
IDG Books Worldwide, Inc.

Steven Berkowitz
President and Publisher
IDG Books Worldwide, Inc.

WINNER

*Eighth Annual
Computer Press
Awards 1992*

WINNER

*Ninth Annual
Computer Press
Awards 1993*

WINNER

*Tenth Annual
Computer Press
Awards 1994*

WINNER

*Eleventh Annual
Computer Press
Awards 1995*

Credits

Acquisitions Editor
Debra Williams Cauley

Development Editor
Laura E. Brown

Technical Editor
Michael P. Corning

Copy Editors
Corey Cohen, Suki Gear, Don St. John,
Nicole LeClerc

Book Designers
Daniel Ziegler Design, Cátálin Dulfu,
Kurt Krames

Production
IDG Books Worldwide Production

Proofreading and Indexing
York Production Services

About the Authors

Sandra E. Eddy specializes in writing both how-to and reference books about the Internet, Windows, and Windows applications. Until she became a full-time freelance writer in 1993, Ms. Eddy was a documentation manager and technical writer for a major software company. From 1984 to 1993, she wrote and edited user and technical manuals for both PC- and mainframe-based computer programs. Ms. Eddy is a senior member of the Society for Technical Communications. She is the author of the following books from IDG Books Worldwide: *HTML in Plain English*, *XML in Plain English*, and *The GIF Animator's Guide*.

John E. Schnyder is a software trainer and technical writer. He has co-authored four other computer books.

For our fathers, Edwyn A. Eddy and E. A. Schnyder

Welcome to
Teach Yourself

Welcome to *Teach Yourself*, a series read and trusted by millions for nearly a decade. Although you may have seen the *Teach Yourself* name on other books, ours is the original. In addition, no *Teach Yourself* series has ever delivered more on the promise of its name than this series. That's because IDG Books Worldwide recently transformed *Teach Yourself* into a new cutting-edge format that gives you all the information you need to learn quickly and easily.

Readers told us that they want to learn by doing and that they want to learn as much as they can in as short a time as possible. We listened to you and believe that our new task-by-task format and suite of learning tools deliver the book you need to successfully teach yourself any language or technology topic. Features such as our Personal Workbook, which lets you practice and reinforce the skills you've just learned, help ensure that you get full value out of the time you invest in your learning. Handy cross-references to related topics and online sites broaden your knowledge and give you control over the kind of information you want, when you want it.

More Answers . . .

In designing the latest incarnation of this series, we started with the premise that people like you, who are beginning to intermediate computer users, want to take control of their own learning. To do this, you need the proper tools to find answers to questions so you can solve problems now.

In designing a series of books that provide such tools, we created a unique and concise visual format. The added bonus: *Teach Yourself* books actually pack more information into their pages than other books written on the same subjects. Skill for skill, you typically get much more information in a *Teach Yourself* book. In fact, *Teach Yourself* books, on average, cover twice the skills covered by other computer books — as many as 175 skills per book — so they're more likely to address your specific needs.

...In Less Time

We know you don't want to spend twice the time to get all this great information, so we provide lots of timesaving features:

▶ A modular task-by-task organization of information: Any task you want to perform is easy to find and includes simple-to-follow steps.

▶ A larger size than standard makes the book easy to read and convenient to use at a computer workstation. The large format also enables us to include many more code listings and illustrations.

▶ A Personal Workbook at the end of each chapter reinforces learning with extra practice, real-world applications for your learning, and questions and answers to test your knowledge.

▶ Cross-references appearing at the bottom of each task page refer you to related information, providing a path through the book for learning particular aspects of the software thoroughly.

▶ A Find It Online feature offers valuable ideas on where to go on the Internet to get more information or to download useful files.

▶ Take Note sidebars provide added-value information from our expert authors for more in-depth learning.

▶ An attractive, consistent organization of information helps you quickly find and learn the skills you need.

These *Teach Yourself* features are designed to help you learn the essential skills about a language or technology in the least amount of time, with the most benefit. We've placed these features consistently throughout the book, so you quickly learn where to go to find just the information you need — whether you work through the book from cover to cover or use it later to solve a new problem.

You will find a *Teach Yourself* book on almost any technology subject — from Windows to XML to C++. Take control of your learning today, with IDG Books Worldwide's *Teach Yourself* series.

Teach Yourself
More Answers in Less Time

Go to this area if you want special tips, cautions, and notes that provide added insight into the current task.

Search through the task headings to find the topic you want right away. To learn a new skill, search the contents, chapter opener, or the extensive index to find what you need. Then find — at a glance — the clear task heading that matches it.

Learn the concepts behind the task at hand and why the task is relevant in the real world. Timesaving suggestions and advice show you how to make the most of each skill.

After you learn the task at hand, you may have more questions, or you may want to read about other tasks related to the topic. Use the cross-references to find different tasks to make your learning more efficient.

Including Sections

You can create sections in a document type declaration and then explicitly include or exclude their contents. In the XML specification, these are known as conditional sections. According to the specification, "conditional sections are portions of the [DTD] external subset which are included in, or excluded from, the logical structure of the DTD based on the keyword which governs them." A conditional section can be made up of a variety of components — declarations, processing instructions, comments, and other conditional sections. As you can see on the next page, conditional sections can have one of two keywords: INCLUDE indicates that the section is included in the DTD (that is, an XML parser will process its contents); IGNORE indicates that the section is not presently part of the DTD. By changing these single keywords, you can activate or inactivate an entire section. Note that the parser reads through both types of sections to determine the section start and section end.

An XML parser processes only INCLUDE sections. Remember that conditional sections can include other conditional sections. This means that an INCLUDE section can contain an IGNORE section and vice versa. If an IGNORE section encloses an INCLUDE section, both sections are ignored.

The examples on the facing page both contain INCLUDE and IGNORE sections that define elements for a paper. In the first example, the INCLUDE section consists of three elements, and the IGNORE section adds a new element. A writer or editor testing the document might want to parse the document without the newly developed ABSTRACT element and then switch the INCLUDE and IGNORE keywords, thereby including the ABSTRACT element, its child elements, and its contents in processing. If the first version of the document "passes" the parser test and the second does not, the writer or editor can concentrate on correcting the ABSTRACT element, its child elements, and contents.

In the second example, the INCLUDE section allows the members of a team developing a document to enter comments throughout the document. The other elements (INTRO, ABSTRACT, BODY, and APPENDIX) must be entered in a particular order. When the INCLUDE and IGNORE section keywords are switched for the final draft, the COMMENTS element has disappeared: No comments are allowed. Note the addition of the INDEX element. An index should not be added until the document is at or near the final draft.

TAKE NOTE

▶ MIXING CONDITIONAL SECTIONS AND PARAMETER-ENTITY REFERENCES

You can use parameter-entity references to identify and process particular conditional sections. Thus, if a conditional section's keyword (INCLUDE or IGNORE) is a parameter-entity reference, an XML processor should replace the section's content — as it would any parameter-entity reference — before processing the section. For more information about parameter-entity references, refer to Chapter 10.

CROSS-REFERENCE
Chapter 7, which covers the first steps in creating a DTD, emphasizes the contents of the prolog.

FIND IT ONLINE
XML Tutorials (**http://www.hypermedic.com/style/xml/xmlindex.htm**) contains tutorial and other links.

84

Use the Find It Online element to locate Internet resources that provide more background, take you on interesting side trips, and offer additional tools for mastering and using the skills you need. (Occasionally you'll find a handy shortcut here.)

The current chapter name and number always appear in the top right-hand corner of every task spread, so you always know exactly where you are in the book.

PLANNING A DTD

Including Sections

CHAPTER
6

XML 1.0: THE CONDITIONAL SECTION PRODUCTIONS

```
[61]    conditionalSect ::= includeSect | ignoreSect  ①
[62]        includeSect ::= '<![' S? 'INCLUDE' S? '[' extSubsetDecl ']]>'  ③
[63]         ignoreSect ::= '<![' S? 'IGNORE' S? '[' ignoreSectContents* ']]>'  ②
[64]  ignoreSectContents ::= Ignore ('<![' ignoreSectContents ']]>' Ignore)*
[65]             Ignore ::= Char* - (Char* ('<![' | ']]>') Char*)
```

① A conditional section can be either an INCLUDE or IGNORE section.
② Start either type of section with the <![string.
③ End either section with the]]> string.

Listing 6-3: AN INCLUDE-IGNORE EXAMPLE

```
<![INCLUDE[
<!ELEMENT THISWAY (INTRO,BODY,APPENDIX)>
    <!ELEMENT INTRO (#PCDATA)>
    <!ELEMENT BODY (#PCDATA)>
    <!ELEMENT APPENDIX (#PCDATA)>
]]>
<![IGNORE[
<!ELEMENT THATWAY
(INTRO,ABSTRACT,BODY,APPENDIX)>
    <!ELEMENT INTRO (#PCDATA)>
    <!ELEMENT ABSTRACT (#PCDATA)>
    <!ELEMENT BODY (#PCDATA)>
    <!ELEMENT APPENDIX (#PCDATA)>
]]>
```

▲ Both sections contain identical element declarations, but the IGNORE section adds the ABSTRACT element, which might be used to summarize a document.

Listing 6-4: ANOTHER INCLUDE-IGNORE EXAMPLE

```
<![INCLUDE[
<!ELEMENT DRAFT
(COMMENTS|(INTRO,ABSTRACT,BODY,APPENDIX))>
    <!ELEMENT COMMENTS (#PCDATA)>
    <!ELEMENT INTRO (#PCDATA)>
    <!ELEMENT ABSTRACT (#PCDATA)>
    <!ELEMENT BODY (#PCDATA)>
    <!ELEMENT APPENDIX (#PCDATA)>
]]>
<![IGNORE[
<!ELEMENT FINAL
(INTRO,ABSTRACT,BODY,APPENDIX,INDEX)>
    <!ELEMENT INTRO (#PCDATA)>
    <!ELEMENT ABSTRACT (#PCDATA)>
    <!ELEMENT BODY (#PCDATA)>
    <!ELEMENT APPENDIX (#PCDATA)>
    <!ELEMENT INDEX (#PCDATA)>
]]>
```

▲ In the DRAFT section, you can insert comments throughout the document. The FINAL section does not allow comments but adds an INDEX element.

85

Learn by example: Review the annotated listings on the right-hand page of every task to understand the concepts more clearly and avoid errors and pitfalls.

Who This Book Is For

This book is written for you, an intermediate PC user who isn't afraid to take charge of his or her own learning experience. You don't want a lot of technical jargon; you *do* want to learn as much about a language as you can in a limited amount of time. You need a book that is straightforward, easy to follow, and logically organized, so you can find answers to your questions easily. And you appreciate simple-to-use tools such as handy cross-references and visual step-by-step procedures that help you make the most of your learning. We have created the unique *Teach Yourself* format specifically to meet your needs.

Personal Workbook

It's a well-known fact that much of what we learn is lost soon after we learn it if we don't reinforce our newly acquired skills with practice and repetition. That's why each *Teach Yourself* chapter ends with your own Personal Workbook. Here's where you can get extra practice, test your knowledge, and discover ideas for using what you've learned in the real world. There's even a Visual Quiz to help you remember your way around the topic's software environment.

Feedback

Please let us know what you think about this book, and whether you have any suggestions for improvements. You can send questions and comments to the *Teach Yourself* editors on the IDG Books Worldwide Web site at **www.idgbooks.com.**

Personal Workbook

Q&A

❶ Can you use an internal DTD subset to define the components of a set of documents?

_____

_____

_____

❷ What sort of planning goes into designing a DTD?

_____

_____

_____

❸ What is the best way to start a DTD outline?

_____

_____

_____

❹ Why should you not use a component for more than one purpose?

_____

_____

_____

❺ Name five ways in which information from an XML document can be output.

_____

_____

_____

❻ What is a *conditional section*, and what are the two types of condition sections for DTDs?

_____

_____

_____

❼ What is the difference between an INCLUDE section and an IGNORE section?

_____

_____

_____

❽ What are the two main differences between creating DTDs for individual documents and for sets of documents?

_____

_____

_____

ANSWERS: PAGE 452

90

After working through the tasks in each chapter, you can test your progress and reinforce your learning by answering the questions in the Q&A section. Then check your answers in the Personal Workbook Answers appendix at the back of the book.

Another practical way to reinforce your skills is to do additional exercises on the same skills you just learned without the benefit of the chapter's visual steps. If you struggle with any of these exercises, it's a good idea to refer to the chapter's tasks to be sure you've mastered them.

PLANNING A DTD
Personal Workbook

CHAPTER 6

Read the list of Real-World Applications to get ideas on how you can use the skills you've just learned in your everyday life. Understanding a process can be simple; knowing how to use that process to make you more productive is the key to successful learning.

EXTRA PRACTICE

1. Write an outline for a memorandum DTD.

2. Create the memorandum DTD with the root element and the first level of child elements.

3. Using the memorandum DTD as the basis, create a template for a standard memorandum document.

4. Write an instruction-sheet DTD containing (1) an INCLUDE section with document components for telling time using an analog clock, and (2) an IGNORE section for telling time using a digital clock.

5. Write a DTD for an all-purpose business letter. Use INCLUDE and IGNORE sections to enclose elements for two types of letters: formal and informal.

6. Plan and design a cover sheet that will be attached to all XML documents and used to track them as they are circulated among your workgroup.

REAL-WORLD APPLICATIONS

✔ Plan the document standards for a series of user manuals to be published by your company. Each manual includes an introduction, table of contents, several chapters, two appendixes, and an index.

✔ Outline a DTD for the user manuals based on the standards you developed in the previous exercise.

✔ Your company is planning its first intranet and you have been named the chief developer. Create a DTD that will convert your current Web pages to the same structure and design.

✔ You are the coordinator of a group of 10 DTD developers. Plan and schedule a cycle for the development of five new corporate DTDs. Each DTD will be worked on for three months. After it's completed, it should receive biweekly maintenance for the first year and on a monthly basis after that.

Visual Quiz

How would you design a DTD to duplicate the structure and formats of this sample fax cover sheet? Don't forget the margins.

91

Take the Visual Quiz to see how well you're learning your way around the language. Our Visual Quiz helps you find your way.

Acknowledgments

Creating an Internet or computer book requires many hands — from the editors who lead the way to those who lay out the pages. We would like to thank those people whose help has been so important in producing this book.

A special thank you to acquisitions editor Debra Williams Cauley for her continuing support.

Thanks also to development editor Laura Brown for her patience throughout these months.

Thanks to the other people at IDG Books for making this a rewarding experience. Thanks to copy editors Corey Cohen, Suki Gear, Don St. John, and Nicole LeClere. And thanks very much to Regina Snyder and all the other members of the design/production team.

For his technical knowledge and great attention to detail, thanks very much to the technical editor, Michael Corning.

Thanks to Matt Wagner of Waterside Productions.

For their support and understanding during the writing of this book, a special thank you to Kathe and Maddie.

For their continued encouragement, thanks to our family and friends.

For their important and continuing contributions — Toni and Eli. And in loving memory of Indy and Bart.

Finally, thanks to the readers of *Teach Yourself XML*. Please let us know what you think of the book and how we can make the next edition even better.

Sandra E. Eddy
eddygrp@sover.net

Contents at a Glance

Contents

Contents

CONTENTS

CONTENTS

CONTENTS

CONTENTS

Teach Yourself
XML ™

PART

I

XML Basics

In this part, you'll be introduced to the Extensible Markup Language (XML). XML is a subset of Standard Generalized Markup Language (SGML), which is the parent of other markup languages, such as HyperText Markup Language (HTML). HTML is the popular language used to create pages on the World Wide Web. Now, with XML, you can develop sophisticated Web pages *and* create custom languages for your company or industry. In addition, you will be able to structure page layout, format paragraphs, and enhance text using style sheets.

A *markup language* is composed of commands that instruct a program such as a word processor, text editor, or even an Internet browser how to publish its output — on the printed page or onscreen. The term *markup* comes to us from typesetting: editors "mark up" manuscripts with corrections and instructions for page and paragraph layout.

After you have completed this part, you'll be familiar with the various components of an XML document and how they work together. You'll also get an overview of the current XML software for editing, parsing, and styling XML documents and browsing XML documents online.

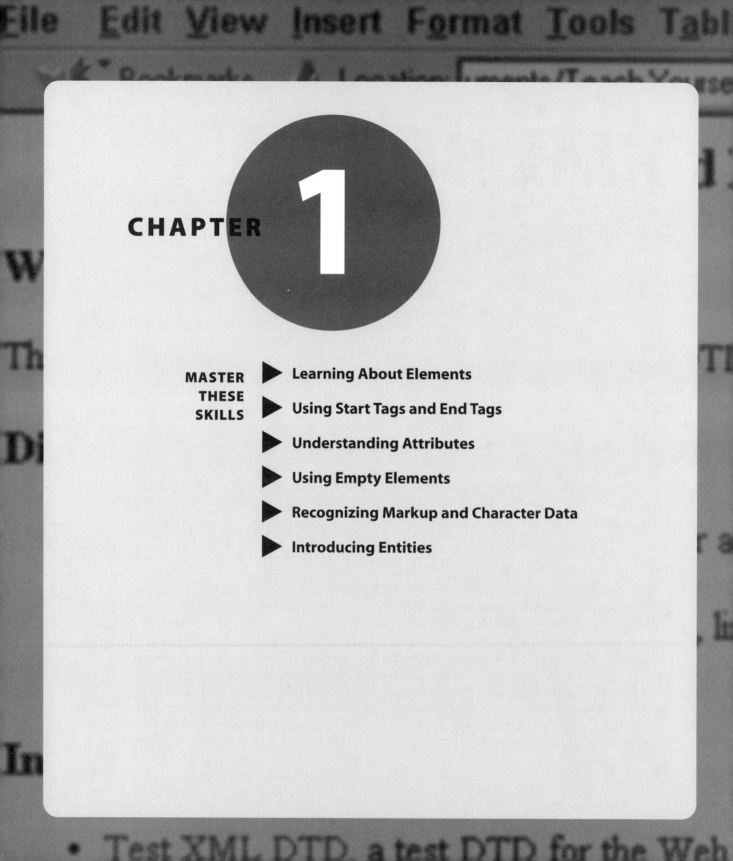

CHAPTER 1

MASTER THESE SKILLS

- Learning About Elements
- Using Start Tags and End Tags
- Understanding Attributes
- Using Empty Elements
- Recognizing Markup and Character Data
- Introducing Entities

XML Building Blocks

XML enables you to issue instructions that combine text, images, and white space to present sophisticated and aesthetically pleasing Web pages from XML documents. In this chapter, you'll learn all about the basics of XML and get an overview of its most important components.

Here you'll find out about elements, the fundamental building blocks of XML documents. In documents, elements identify individual components to be processed in certain ways.

In this chapter, you'll also get an overview of attributes, with which you can specify characteristics of elements. With attributes, you can set the look of an element (such as its height and width, or color) or an initial value (such as your home city or the name of your documents' primary editor). You can also require that an element be used or make its use optional.

XML also provides empty elements, a special type of element that is a placeholder for a future component of a Web page. In this chapter, you'll get an overview of empty elements and how to create them in an XML document.

XML documents are made up of markup and character data. XML *markup* is the instructions to the programs that process and build XML documents; *character data* is everything else. Character data is also known as *content* (all the text and images that appear on the page).

Finally, you'll learn about entities, which allow an XML processor to replace a reference (an entity) with replacement text (a single character, a phrase, a paragraph, or even an entire file). This enables you to structure your documents — especially long ones — logically. You can also use entities to save typing time. Simply declare a set of entities giving three- or four-character shortcut names for long commonly used phrases, technical terms, or corporate names. Then, whenever you want to use the long phrase, term, or name in a document, enter an entity reference that contains the shortcut. When the XML parser processes the document, it replaces all the entity references with the appropriate phrases, terms, and names.

As you read through the remaining chapters in this book, you will build on the foundation information you have learned here.

Learning About Elements

If you analyze an electronic or word-processing document — be it a Web page, a report, or long reference guide — you'll find that it is made up of common components, which can include titles, headings, and paragraphs. All of these are elements of the document. In the XML markup language, these elements actually define the document and mark the boundaries of the components for future processing.

Elements can contain other elements. For example, an element that identifies a chapter can contain elements that set the bounds of several heading levels as well as standard body text. Or a paragraph element can contain elements that enhance or format text elements. Look at some of the levels of elements that comprise a typical book:

```
book
    chapter
        paragraph
            sentence
                word
                    character
```

In XML, the top element in a document is the *root element*, or the *document element*. All other elements are nested under the root. Some are child elements, the first generation under the root, while others are child elements of child elements. As a document grows more complex, the number of elements and the number of generations increase. The document structure is like a tree, with its trunk (root element) and branches (child elements). At the end of the branches are elements that contain *character data*, which is the content that will be formatted and output. In fact,

some elements can contain both child elements and character data. XML documents do not always follow a formal and predictable structure. For example, *empty elements* do not contain any child elements or character data: These elements refer to future contents (such as image files, sound files, or video files) or mark a change in a document (such as a line break).

XML didn't spring forth without the laying of some groundwork. Table 1-1 lists some events that led up to the current status of XML.

TAKE NOTE

▶ DISCOVERING THE MAIN DIFFERENCES BETWEEN HTML AND XML

With its predefined elements and attributes, HTML not only includes character data, but also instructs Web browsers how to display the data. Using XML, you can define sets of custom elements to organize and describe the data, and then use style sheets to display it.

▶ UNDERSTANDING PRODUCTIONS AND PRODUCTION NUMBERS

The official XML 1.0 specification contains *productions*, or rules that make up the XML *grammar*, or language. When you browse through the specification, notice the numbers ([30]) to the left of the name of each production. A *production number* shows the order of its production within its group of related productions. For example, in the first listing on the facing page, the production number for the `element` production is 39.

CROSS-REFERENCE

Chapter 7 describes how to define the first element in an XML document.

FIND IT ONLINE

You can find the official XML specification at **http://www.w3.org/TR/1998/REC-xml-19980210**.

XML 1.0: THE ELEMENT PRODUCTION

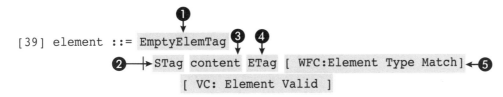

```
[39] element ::= EmptyElemTag
                  STag content ETag [ WFC:Element Type Match]
                  [ VC: Element Valid ]
```

1 *An empty element is a placeholder for a future component.*
2 *Mark the beginning of an element with a start tag.*
3 *A non-empty element can contain a variety of content.*
4 *Mark the end of an element with an end tag.*
5 *WFC alerts you to a constraint on a document being well-formed; VC indicates a validity constraint.*

Listing 1-1: YOUR FIRST XML DOCUMENT

```
<?xml version="1.0"?>        1
<!DOCTYPE first [            2
<!ELEMENT first (#PCDATA)>   3
]>                           4
<first>
This is the first XML document in
"Teach Yourself XML."
</first>
```

1 *Enter the <?xml?> processing instruction, which starts the document.*
2 *Enter <!DOCTYPE, the document name, and type [.*
3 *Start an element definition with the < and the !ELEMENT keyword.*
4 *Mark the end of the document type definition with a]>.*

Table 1-1: A TIMELINE OF XML-RELATED EVENTS

Year	Event
1980	First draft of SGML is issued.
1986	SGML is made an international standard (ISO 8879: 1986).
1989	Tim Berners-Lee proposes the World Wide Web.
1996	The XML Working Group starts up early in the year. By the end of the year, the first draft of XML is released.
1996	Cascading Style Sheets, Level 1, specification is released.
1997	HTML 4.0, the latest recommendation, appears.
1998	Extensible Markup Language (XML) 1.0 becomes a World Wide Web Consortium (W3C) Recommendation. Working drafts for the XML Linking Language (XLink) and XML Pointer Language (Xpointer) are released. Cascading Style Sheets, Level 2, specification adds media-specific style sheets.

Using Start Tags and End Tags

In an XML document, an element starts with a start tag (for example, `<element>`) and ends with an end tag (for example, `</element>`). The less-than (<) character marks the beginning of both start and end tags, and the greater-than (>) character marks the end of them. Both the < and > characters are known as *delimiters*: they mark the "limits" of the tags. The only difference between the start tag and end tag is the slash (/), which identifies the end tag and is placed between the less-than character and the first character in the element name. Then, between the start tag and end tag is the content, if any. For example:

```
<text>This is one sentence.</text>
```

The example starts with the `<text>` start tag, contains content of one sentence, and ends with the `</text>` end tag.

In XML, start tags and end tags come in matching sets: for every start tag, there must be an end tag. The pairing of tags enables you (and XML processors) to track the proper construction of a document, element by element. In addition to their other work, XML processors check to ensure that all elements consist of pairs of start tags and end tags and that the tags have all the required delimiters and characters.

Most non-empty elements contain other elements, character data, or both, between the start tag and end tag. However, if you add attributes and attribute values to a document, they are located within the start tag. The sample element with an added attribute and an attribute value looks like this:

```
<text font="12pt">This is one
sentence.</text>
```

The `font` attribute, within the start tag, sets the text size to 12 points.

TAKE NOTE

▶ USING END TAGS IN XML

In HTML, some elements allow you to omit the end tag. In XML, the end tag is *always* present. So, if you currently work with HTML documents but plan to convert to XML in the future, adding both required and optional end tags to your HTML documents is a good idea, for future compatibility with XML.

▶ ELEMENT TERMINOLOGY

As you read through the XML specification and XML books that are more technical than this one, you'll encounter new terms. The meaning of *element name* is quite obvious; it's the name that you or someone else has given to an element. An element name is also known as a *generic identifier*. An *element* is the actual physical occurrence of the element, its start tag, end tag, and content in one location in a document (for example, a highlighted section starting with `<text color="red">` and ending with `</text>`). An *element type* is the named element (for example, `text`), which can occur numerous places in a document.

CROSS-REFERENCE
Chapter 13 shows how to insert content in an XML document.

FIND IT ONLINE
The Extensible Markup Language (XML), at **http://www.w3.org/XML/**, is the official XML home page.

XML 1.0: THE STAG AND ETAG PRODUCTIONS

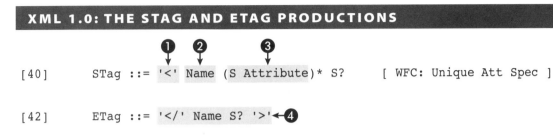

```
[40]      STag ::= '<' Name (S Attribute)* S?      [ WFC: Unique Att Spec ]

[42]      ETag ::= '</' Name S? '>'
```

❶ The STag production begins with the < character.
❷ An element name must start with a letter or underscore character.
❸ A start tag can contain whitespace and attributes.
❹ The end tag begins with the </ characters and matches the start tag.

Listing 1-2: AN UNFORMATTED XML DOCUMENT

```
<text font="12pt"><bold>
This is one bold sentence.</bold></text>
<text font="9pt"><italics>
This is an italicized
sentence.</italics></text>
<text font="16pt"><bold><italics>
This sentence is bold and
italicized.</italics></bold></text>
```

▲ This example demonstrates that you do not have to spend much time formatting an XML document. The example is inelegant and difficult to understand, but it saves space.

Listing 1-3: A FORMATTED XML DOCUMENT

```
<text font="12pt">
  <bold>
    This is one bold sentence.
  </bold>
</text>
<text font="9pt">
  <italics>
    This is an italicized sentence.
  </italics>
</text>
<text font="16pt">
  <bold>
    <italics>
      This sentence is bold and italicized.
    </italics>
  </bold>
</text>
```

▲ On the other hand, the same code is easier to read and clearly shows the nested <bold> and <italics> elements. However, this example is composed of many more lines.

Understanding Attributes

Some elements — even empty elements — also have associated *attributes*, which specify their characteristics (such as size, color, or dimensions), limitations (such as whether their use is required or optional), or initial values or list of possible values. In XML, you can use child elements to define the characteristics of higher-level elements, thereby eliminating some attributes. You can also use style sheets (see Part V) to set characteristics of certain elements. As a result, XML documents usually have fewer attributes than HTML documents.

Attributes enable you to define values for elements. For example, you can start a numbered list with a particular value or incorporate color, boldface, and so on, for text controlled by a particular element type. Or you can add an identifier to a graphic so that you can find it in a document (for linking purposes or to specify the start/end of an area to be formatted or enhanced). Elements with attributes look something like this:

```
<element option1="value1" option2="value2">
</element>
```

Notice that the start tag, within the less-than and greater-than symbols, includes all the attributes. For example:

```
<box border width="70"></box>
```

where:

- ▶ < marks the beginning of the start tag.
- ▶ box is the element name.
- ▶ border is an attribute that turns on a border.

- ▶ width="70" is an attribute that sets the box width to 70 pixels. Notice that the value is surrounded by quotation marks. You can also surround the value by single quotes ('). Do not mix quotation marks and single quotes when entering a value.
- ▶ > marks the completion of the start tag.
- ▶ < marks the beginning of the end tag.
- ▶ / makes it clear that this is an end tag, not a start tag.
- ▶ box is the element name.
- ▶ > marks the completion of the end tag.

TAKE NOTE

▶ LEARNING ABOUT HYPERTEXT

Hypertext, which represents a variety of media, is the factor that differentiates both HTML and XML documents from many other types of documents. Under HTML, hypertext includes one-directional, simple links to locations in the current document or to external documents. In addition to providing simple links, XML offers other types of links. *Extended links* enable links to one or more locations within the current document and/or to one or more locations in external documents. *Extended link groups* store lists of links to other documents. *Extended pointers* (*XPointers*) use elements, identifiers (IDs), and other document elements to point to a particular location in a document.

CROSS-REFERENCE

Chapter 9 shows how to add attributes to elements you declare in a DTD.

FIND IT ONLINE

XML.com, at **http://www.xml.com/**, provides links to articles and news about XML.

XML 1.0: THE ATTRIBUTE PRODUCTION

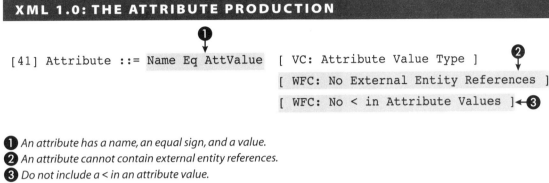

```
[41] Attribute ::= Name Eq AttValue    [ VC: Attribute Value Type ]
                                        [ WFC: No External Entity References ]
                                        [ WFC: No < in Attribute Values ]
```

❶ *An attribute has a name, an equal sign, and a value.*
❷ *An attribute cannot contain external entity references.*
❸ *Do not include a < in an attribute value.*

Listing 1-4: AN EXAMPLE OF GOOD NESTING

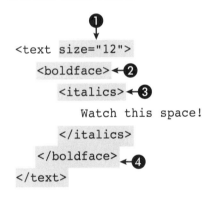

```
<text size="12">
   <boldface>
      <italics>
         Watch this space!
      </italics>
   </boldface>
</text>
```

❶ *The attribute* `size` *changes the size of the text to 12 points.*
❷ *Indent the* `<boldface>` *tag to show that it's nested under* `<text>`.
❸ *Indent* `<italics>` *under* `<boldface>`.
❹ *Align the end tags under their respective start tags.*

Listing 1-5: AN EXAMPLE OF BAD NESTING

```
<text size="12">
   <boldface>
      <italics>
         Watch this space!
      </boldface>
   </italics>
</text>
```

▲ *In this example, the* `<boldface>` *and* `</boldface>` *tags are not at the same level of indention, nor are the* `<italics>` *and* `</italics>` *tags. No doubt, processing will end prematurely with a warning message.*

Using Empty Elements

XML provides empty-element tags, which are elements that have no current content. An empty-element tag refers to an object, such as an image or a line break, that will be added to a document when it is output. One syntax for empty elements has no end tag and has a slightly different syntax:

```
<image/>
```

or

```
<br/>
```

Notice that the slash associated with a typical end tag appears at the end of the tag. The empty-element syntax actually combines a start tag and end tag. Because of this different syntax, HTML-based browsers that have not been updated recently do not recognize empty-element tags.

Empty elements usually have attributes. If actual content, such as an image, will be included in the document after it is processed, there must be a reference, such as a Uniform Resource Identifier (URI). For example:

```
<image src="flower.gif"/>
```

You can also have a start tag and an end tag with no content:

```
<br></br>
```

or

```
<image src="flower.gif"></image>
```

In these examples, the slash resumes its normal position in the end tag.

TAKE NOTE

COMPARING XML WITH ITS PARENT, SGML

XML is a subset of SGML, so XML has many SGML features — in a much smaller package. Both SGML and XML forcefully encourage document structure by tagging sections. Both languages concentrate on elucidating document content rather than style, and both allow you to define your own custom languages. In addition, because both SGML and XML keep content separate from style, document output can vary, depending on the style sheets currently used. It is easy to maintain document standards, in which every particular component of your documents can look exactly the same.

There are important differences between SGML and XML, however. XML is designed with electronic documents in mind, while SGML is suited for maintaining large sets of long documents over extended periods of time. Most importantly, because XML is a subset of SGML, there are fewer rules to keep in mind.

LEARNING ABOUT DTDS AND OTHER XML DOCUMENTS

There are two main categories of XML documents: external DTD subsets and documents that will be output in some way. External DTD subsets, to which you will be introduced in Chapter 2, are used purely for defining elements, attributes, and so on that will be used in one or more "output" documents. *DTDs* are document type definitions. Output documents can also contain DTDs — in this case, known as internal DTD subsets; however, the primary purpose of output documents is to produce output.

CROSS-REFERENCE

"Declaring an Empty Element" in Chapter 8 provides more information about empty elements.

FIND IT ONLINE

Check out XML: A Professional Alternative to HTML, at **http://www.heise.de/ix/artikel/E/1997/06/106/**.

XML 1.0: THE EMPTYELEMTAG PRODUCTION

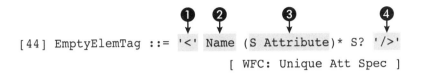

```
[44] EmptyElemTag ::= '<' Name (S Attribute)* S? '/>'
                        [ WFC: Unique Att Spec ]
```

1 *Start an* EmptyElemTag *with the < delimiter.*
2 *Add a valid XML name.*
3 *If you want to, add one or more attributes.*
4 *End the empty element with the unique /> end tag. To have a well-formed document, each attribute must be unique.*

Listing 1-6: AN EXAMPLE OF A MEMORANDUM DTD

```
<?xml version="1.0"?>
<!DOCTYPE MEMO [
<!ELEMENT MEMO (LOGO, TO, FROM, SUBJECT, BODY)>
<!ELEMENT LOGO    EMPTY>
<!ELEMENT TO      (#PCDATA)>
<!ELEMENT FROM    (#PCDATA)>
<!ELEMENT SUBJECT (#PCDATA)>
<!ELEMENT BODY    (#PCDATA)>
]>
```

1 *Define the root element* MEMO *and list its child elements.*
2 *Insert the* LOGO *element, which is a placeholder for a graphic.*
3 *Enter the* EMPTY *keyword to declare the empty element.*

Listing 1-7: AN EXAMPLE OF A MEMORANDUM DOCUMENT

```
<LOGO src="smalllogo.gif"/>
<TO>Charles Smith</TO>
<FROM>Tess Curtis</FROM>
<SUBJECT>Christmas Party</SUBJECT>
<BODY>
The first planning session for the
Christmas party will take place on Friday
at 2 PM. See you there.
</BODY>
```

1 *The* <LOGO> *start tag contains the source (*src*) attribute.*
2 *The file name refers to a GIF file.*
3 *End the empty element with the /> delimiting characters.*

Recognizing Markup and Character Data

XML documents are made up of two types of components: markup and character data. *Markup*, which comprises the skeleton of the document, instructs XML processors and browsers on how to treat the content — how to store it and how it is organized. Markup consists of the prolog and the document type declaration, start tags, end tags, empty elements, comments, processing instructions, CDATA sections, and references to entities and characters. Markup represents the *logical structure* of the document. All of the non-markup content of a document is *character data*. The character data is what you will see on a printed or displayed page — the *physical structure* of the document. The combination of markup and character data is *XML text*.

Markup contains delimiters such as < and >, as well as reserved keywords such as !ELEMENT and !DOCTYPE. Delimiters and reserved keywords are the most important differences between markup and character data.

Processing Instructions

Processing instructions, which start with the <? delimiters and end with the ?> delimiters, are an important type of markup. Processing instructions tell programs such as XML parsers and browsers how to process the "delimited" part of an XML document. For example:

```
<?tailormade black border?>
```

instructs a formatting program called `tailormade` to apply a `black border` to the selected page.

You have already learned about the most common XML processing instruction, `<?xml?>`, which states to an XML parser or browser, "This is an XML document." In fact, this processing instruction can tell a program not only that this is a valid XML document, but also that it uses a particular character set and/or is a standalone document:

```
<?xml version "1.0" encoding="UTF-8"
      standalone="yes"?>
```

Dividing Documents into Sections

XML uses CDATA sections to mark the beginning and end of blocks of character data. Use the <![CDATA[markup to indicate the start of a section, and use]]> to indicate the end. Within a CDATA section, all XML text, including markup, is considered to be character data. This means that delimiters such as < and > are regarded as literals and will not be processed. You cannot nest CDATA sections.

TAKE NOTE

INCLUDING AND IGNORING SECTIONS IN XML DOCUMENTS

XML also provides INCLUDE and IGNORE sections, which are used to include or ignore, respectively, particular sections in your documents. For more information about INCLUDE and IGNORE sections, refer to Chapter 6.

CROSS-REFERENCE

Chapter 3 covers the rules of entering markup in an XML document.

FIND IT ONLINE

See **http://sunsite.unc.edu/pub/sun-info/ standards/xml/why/xmlapps.htm** for XML and future Web information.

XML 1.0: THE PROCESSING INSTRUCTIONS PRODUCTION

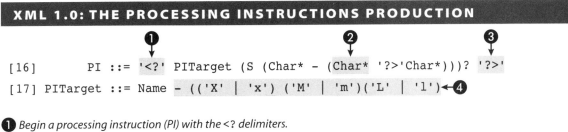

```
[16]        PI ::= '<?' PITarget (S (Char* - (Char* '?>'Char*)))? '?>'
[17] PITarget ::= Name - (('X' | 'x') ('M' | 'm')('L' | 'l'))
```

1 Begin a processing instruction (PI) with the <? delimiters.
2 You can enter any number of valid characters in a PI.
3 End a PI with the ?> delimiters.
4 Do not start a PI name with XML or xml.

XML 1.0: THE CDATA SECTION

```
[18]  CDSect ::= CDStart CData CDEnd
[19] CDStart ::= '<![CDATA['
[20]  CData ::= (Char* - (Char* ']]>' Char*))
[21]  CDEnd ::= ']]>'
```

1 Insert three components in a CDATA section.
2 Start a CDATA section with <![CDATA[.
3 Insert any characters but]]> in a CDATA section.
4 CDATA sections end with the]]> delimiters.

Listing 1-8: AN IMPROVED MEMORANDUM

```
<?xml version="1.0"?>
<!DOCTYPE MEMO [
<!ELEMENT MEMO (TO, FROM, SUBJECT, BODY)>
<!ELEMENT TO      (#PCDATA)>
<!ELEMENT FROM    (#PCDATA)>
<!ELEMENT SUBJECT (#PCDATA)>
<!ELEMENT BODY    (#PCDATA)
]>
<TO>Charles Smith</TO>
<FROM>Tess Curtis</FROM>
<SUBJECT>Christmas Party</SUBJECT>
<BODY>
```

1 Start markup in an XML document with the XML declaration.
2 End the markup section with the]> delimiters.
3 Use start tags to mark the start of character data.
4 End a block of character data with end tags.

Introducing Entities

In XML, it is possible to insert a reference in a document to an *entity*, one or more characters from the ISO 10646 standard—up to and including an entire document—that will replace the reference. The characters that replace the reference are known as *replacement text*. Entity references and entities work in the same way as a word processor's search-and-replace function; the program searches for a word or phrase (the entity reference) and replaces it with another word or phrase (the entity).

If you use a particular technical term or a long name many times in a document, use an entity reference as a shortcut. For example, the entity reference wmc could represent `The Widget Manufacturing Corporation, Inc.`:

```
<!ENTITY wmc  "The Widget Manufacturing
         Corporation, Inc."
```

Then, when you specify wmc in a document:

```
<text>Buy from &wmc;—the world's
best!<text>
```

the XML processor replaces it:

Buy from The Widget Manufacturing Corporation, Inc.—the world's best!

Another use for entities is to insert several documents (such as individual chapters, Web pages, or other components such as graphs and sound files) into a single document. For example:

```
<!ELEMENT busplan (#PCDATA)
<!ENTITY  execsumm  PUBLIC "execsum.doc">
<!ENTITY  busdescrp PUBLIC "describe.doc">
<!ENTITY  competit  PUBLIC "compete.doc">
```

```
<!ENTITY  marktpln  PUBLIC "mplan.doc">
<!ENTITY  markgrph  PUBLIC "graf1.gif
```

Using entities, you can assign members of your team to create pieces of the document. Then, you can incorporate all the pieces into a single large document.

XML provides several types of entities:

▶ A *parsed entity*, which is parsed only if it is used in a document. These entities can include both character data and markup. In contrast, an *unparsed entity* will never be parsed.

▶ An *internal entity*, which is declared in the same document from which it is referenced. In contrast, an *external entity* is in an external document and is referred to by using a URL.

▶ A *general entity*, which is named within the character data in an XML document. In contrast, a *parameter entity* (PE) is named within DTD markup.

XML enables you to differentiate among entity references by preceding each type with one or more special characters. Table 1-2 gives a list of various entity references and the delimiting characters used to precede their names. All end with a semicolon (;).

XML reserves the general entities shown in Table 1-3. In the table, the first column lists the reserved characters, and the second column shows the entity that replaces the character in well-formed documents.

CROSS-REFERENCE

Chapter 10 shows the variety of entities supported by XML and how to use them.

FIND IT ONLINE

Robin Cover's XML site, at **http://www.oasis-open. org/cover/xml.html**, is a well-organized XML directory.

Table 1-2: SPECIAL CHARACTERS FOR XML ENTITY REFERENCES

Entity References	Start With	Refers To	Example
Decimal character	&#	a decimal character inserted in the instance	&#250;
Hexadecimal character	&#x	a hexadecimal character inserted in the instance	&#x00C4;
Parsed general	&	alphanumeric characters inserted in the instance	&wmc;
Parameter entity (PE)	%	alphanumeric characters inserted in the DTD	%wmc;

TAKE NOTE

LEARNING ABOUT NUMBER SYSTEMS

XML's general entities can use the decimal number system or the hexadecimal number system. The *decimal system*, also known as the base-10 system, consists of the numbers 0 through 9. In a decimal number, each digit position is a power of 10. The *hexadecimal system*, also known as the base-16 system, consists of the numbers 0 through 9 and the letters A through F (10 through 15). The advantage of using the hexadecimal system is that two hexa-decimal digits can fit into a single 8-bit byte, thereby saving storage space on a computer.

Table 1-3: RESERVED XML ENTITIES

To produce this character	Insert this entity
ampersand (&)	&amp;
apostrophe (!)	&apos;
greater-than (>)	&gt;
less-than (<)	&lt;
quotation mark (")	&quot;

Listing 1-9: EXAMPLES OF ENTITIES

```
<!ENTITY copyrt_info
    "Copyright 1998, The Eddy Group, Inc.">
<text>Insert &copyrt_info; here.</text>

<text>Frick &amp; Frack,
 Tweedledee &amp; Tweedledum</text>

<!ENTITY eacute "&#233;">
<text>A r&eacute;sum&eacute; describes
 your job history.</text>

<!ENTITY % copyrt_info
    "http://www.eddygrp.com/copyright.txt">
<text>Insert %copyrt_info; here.</text>
```

❶ *Name a general entity and enclose replacement text in quotation marks.*

❷ *Use the default general entity* & *to represent an ampersand.*

❸ *Replace the e's in résumé with the* é *decimal character reference.*

❹ *For an external entity reference, state a URL.*

Personal Workbook

Q&A

1 What is the history of the term *markup*?

_____

_____

_____

2 What is *XML markup*?

_____

_____

_____

3 What is the difference between *character data* and *XML text*?

_____

_____

_____

4 What are *elements*?

_____

_____

_____

5 What is the character that marks the difference between start tags and end tags?

_____

_____

_____

6 How can you describe the characteristics of a particular element?

_____

_____

_____

7 Show two ways to write an empty element.

_____

_____

_____

8 What is an *entity*?

_____

_____

_____

ANSWERS: PAGE 447

EXTRA PRACTICE

① Write one or two lines of XML code that includes an element that encloses some character data.

② Write one or two lines of XML code that includes a "Do Not Disturb" message surrounded by a red border that is 25 pixels high and 50 pixels long. The name of the element is `message`, and the names of the attributes are `border` and `width`.

③ Write an empty element for an image titled `rainbow.gif`. Use the `align` attribute to center the image between the left and right margins.

④ Write a processing instruction to tell the `pageformatter` program to insert a red box on the current page.

REAL-WORLD APPLICATIONS

✔ You are writing a short letter inviting some friends to a party. Create an XML document that includes the following elements: DATE, NAME, ADDRESS, CITY, STATE, ZIP, and BODY.

✔ You are creating a flyer to be distributed at a local mall. Develop a document containing a short sales pitch that is emphasized with boldface, italics, and underlines in various combinations. Hint: Be sure to follow the proper rules for nesting elements.

✔ You are designing an XML document used to display a library of images — three images per row. Develop a document that inserts the images and aligns them on the left side of the page, in the center, and on the right side. Hint: Use attributes to specify alignment.

Visual Quiz

Circle the markup on this page, and underline the character data.

_____

_____

_____

_____

_____

_____

```
memo - Notepad
File  Edit  Search  Help
<?xml version="1.0"?>
<!DOCTYPE MEMO [
<!ELEMENT MEMO (TO, FROM, SUBJECT, BODY)>
<!ELEMENT TO      (#PCDATA)>
<!ELEMENT FROM    (#PCDATA)>
<!ELEMENT SUBJECT (#PCDATA)>
<!ELEMENT BODY    (#PCDATA)>
]>
<TO>Charles Smith</TO>
<FROM>Tess Curtis</FROM>
<SUBJECT>Christmas Party</SUBJECT>
<BODY>
The first planning session for the Christmas party
will take place on Friday at 2 PM. See you there.
</BODY>
```

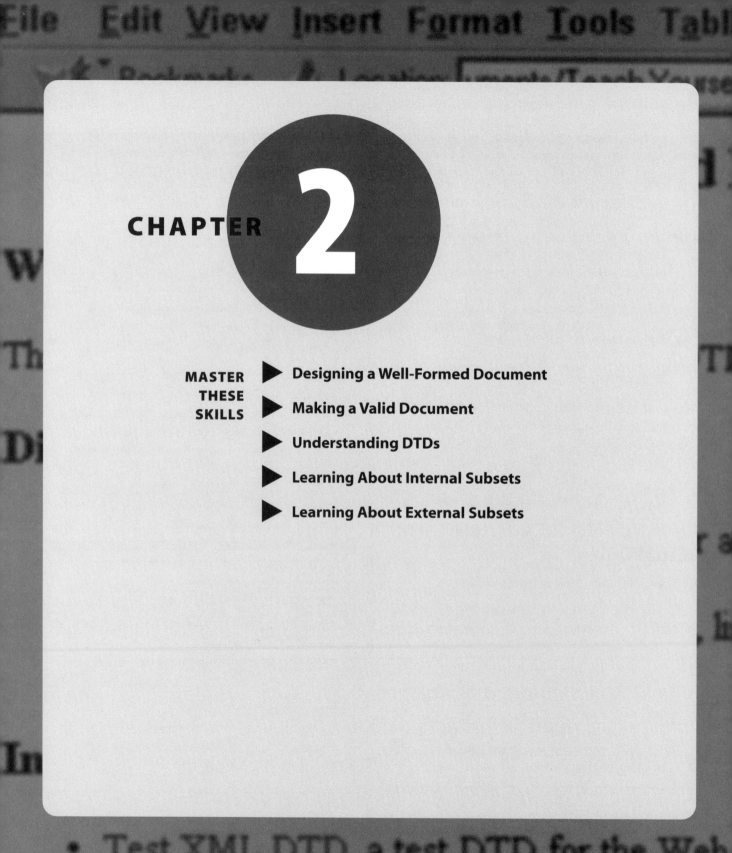

CHAPTER

2

MASTER
THESE
SKILLS

▶ Designing a Well-Formed Document

▶ Making a Valid Document

▶ Understanding DTDs

▶ Learning About Internal Subsets

▶ Learning About External Subsets

Examining an XML Document

This chapter looks at the two different types of XML documents; well-formed and valid. It also covers the structure of a document and how the components fit together to form an accurate, well-organized document.

You'll also get your first look at *document type definitions* (DTDs), which define elements and their attributes, entities, and notation. As the foundation of XML documents, DTDs enable a developer to create elements that set the structure, content, and format of an XML document. DTDs permit companies and departments to set document standards for various types of documents, ranging from memos to reports to user/technical manuals. DTDs also allow the creation of custom markup languages for particular industries and occupations.

Well-formed documents must be well-organized and are checked for accuracy by a nonvalidating XML parser. These documents must contain one root element under which all other elements are nested and meet other basic rules. For example, well-formed documents must have matching start and end tags. In HTML, the paragraph element (`<P>`) does not require an end tag: HTML browsers assume that the beginning of the next paragraph marks the end of the current paragraph. However, well-formed documents do not have DTDs. Without a DTD, XML processors can't figure out when elements end, how they are formatted, and so on.

Valid documents are well-formed documents that go a step further: they include DTDs. DTDs come in two flavors — internal and external. Valid XML documents include internal DTD subsets, external DTD subsets, or a combination of both. An *internal DTD subset* is a DTD completely enclosed within the XML document whose elements, attributes, entities, and notation the DTD is defining. An internal DTD subset can also consist only of a reference to an external DTD file. *External DTD subsets* are XML documents that are used purely for defining elements, attributes, and so on that will be used in one or more "output" documents. An internal DTD subset defines the components of one document — the one in which it is enclosed. External DTD subsets define the components of a set of documents.

Designing a Well-Formed Document

Well-formed XML documents should be well-organized and accurate but are not required to meet some of the extra criteria for validity. The difference between well-formed and valid documents is that a valid document requires a document type (`!DOCTYPE`) declaration, which includes a document type definition (DTD). A well-formed document does not. A *DTD* defines the elements, attributes, entities, and rules for creating one or more documents in a markup language such as SGML, HTML, or XML.

Although a well-formed document does not require a DTD, it must be accurate and must meet certain rules. All elements must begin with start tags and end with end tags. All elements but the root element must be completely nested within a higher-level element. Well-formed documents must not contain reserved characters in any other context but their defined purpose. (See the "Rules for Well-Formed Documents" sidebar on the facing page.)

Well-formed documents provide a convenient means of converting your HTML documents to XML without having to write, or conform to, a DTD. However, many HTML documents are not well-organized, because HTML browsers forgive lack of organization; and some HTML documents contain syntax errors that must be corrected, because HTML browsers often forgive these types of errors. This means that you may have to edit a converted document more than once before a nonvalidating XML

processor will produce accurate, error-free results. On the plus side, this means that your edited documents will be better — both structurally and syntactically. You'll find out more about converting HTML documents in Chapter 16.

What factors do you use to decide whether a document should be well-formed or valid? Both well-formed and valid documents should be carefully and accurately constructed. In general, if you are working with a single document or a small group of unlike documents, you can try to work without a DTD and create a well-formed document. However, if you are developing or maintaining a set of documents, you should strive toward validity. Producing valid documents allows you to set and apply document standards. Then you can create documents more easily; you won't have to invent a set of elements for each new document.

CROSS-REFERENCE
In Chapter 11 you learn how to test a well-formed XML document for accuracy.

FIND IT ONLINE
http://www.ucc.ie/xml/ displays a comprehensive list of questions and answers about XML.

Some Rules for Well-Formed Documents

▶ The first line of a well-formed XML document must be an XML declaration.

▶ All non-empty elements must have start tags and end tags with matching element names.

▶ All empty elements must end with />.

▶ A document must contain one root element.

▶ Nested elements must be completely nested within their higher-level elements.

▶ The only reserved entity references are &, ', >, <, and ".

Listing 2-1: A WELL-FORMED DOCUMENT

```
<?xml version="1.0"?>  ①
<title>A Well-Formed Document</title>
<first>  ②
This is a simple
<bold>well-formed</bold>  ④
document.
</first>
```
③

① Start a well-formed document with an XML declaration.
② Begin each element with a start tag.
③ End each element with an end tag.
④ Nest child elements completely within higher-level elements.

Listing 2-2: A WELL-FORMED DOCUMENT WITH PROBLEMS

```
<?xml version="1.0"?>
<TO>Charles Smith</TO>
<FROM>Tess Curtis</FROM>
<SUBJECT>Christmas Party</SUBJECT>
<BODY>
   The
      <italics>first</italics>
   planning session for the Christmas party
   will take place on Friday at
      <boldface>2 PM.</boldface>
   See you there.
</BODY>
```

▲ *Although this document is well-structured and uses indentions to show child elements, there is no way of defining the elements. Where does the XML developer define the enhancements for the boldface and italics elements?*

Listing 2-3: ANOTHER WELL-FORMED DOCUMENT

```
<?xml version = "1.0"?>
<TITLE>Memo with Logo</TITLE>
<LOGO src="smalllogo.gif"/>
<TO>Charles Smith</TO>
<FROM>Tess Curtis</FROM>
<SUBJECT>Christmas Party</SUBJECT>
<BODY>
The first planning session for the
Christmas party
will take place on Friday at 2 PM. See you
there.
</BODY>
```

▲ *This example of a well-formed XML document shows that you can include an empty element.*

Making a Valid Document

The main difference between well-formed and valid documents is the absence or presence of a document type declaration; this declaration also includes a DTD, which defines the elements, attributes, entities, notations, and so on contained in the current document (and possibly others). A *valid document* is well-formed (that is, it is accurate and can be parsed by a nonvalidating parser), but must include a DTD. The structure of a valid document must match the structure defined by the DTD. XML supports two types of DTDs: internal and external.

An XML document can access its own *internal DTD*, or *internal DTD subset*, which is completely contained within the document. An internal DTD defines the components of only one document — the one in which it is included. You'll learn more about internal DTDs later in this chapter.

A separate file that defines elements and other document components of the current document is known as an *external DTD*, or *external DTD subset*. The "Learning About External Subsets" task, also in this chapter, describes external DTDs in more detail. In fact, all valid XML documents include an internal DTD subset; if a document has an external DTD, the internal subset refers to the external file. Some XML documents contain internal subsets and external subsets — and they both define elements.

Nonvalidating XML parsers check well-formed documents; the counterpart for valid documents is a validating XML parser. Because DTDs define the elements by their generations, a validating parser builds an element tree, with the root element on top, followed by the root's children, their children, and down through the remaining levels of descendant elements. XML extended links (XLinks) and extended pointers (XPointers) rely on the element tree for proper linking; style sheets rely on the element tree for proper styling. A non-validating XML parser builds an element tree based on the well-formed tags in the document and checks that start tags and end tags match properly, that attributes are enclosed within the start tags, that entities and entity references are well-written, and so on.

CROSS-REFERENCE

Chapter 11 shows you how to test a valid XML document for accuracy.

FIND IT ONLINE

The Case for XML, at **http://www.mcs.net/~dken/ xmlcase.htm**, discusses the use of SGML, HTML, and XML.

Listing 2-4: A BRIEF VALID DOCUMENT

```
<?xml version="1.0"?>
<!DOCTYPE demodoc [
<!ELEMENT demodoc (title, first)>
<!ELEMENT TITLE (#PCDATA)>
<!ELEMENT FIRST (#PCDATA)>]>
<title>A Valid Document</title>
<first>This is a simple <bold>valid</bold>
document.</first>
```

① Start a document type declaration with the !DOCTYPE keyword.
② Make sure that the !DOCTYPE and root element names match.
③ Begin the DTD with a left bracket ([).
④ End the DTD with a right bracket (]).

Listing 2-5: A VALID DOCUMENT WITH A LONGER INTERNAL DTD

```
<?xml version = "1.0"?>
<!DOCTYPE MEMO [
<!ELEMENT MEMO (TO, FROM, SUBJECT, BODY)>
    <!ELEMENT TO        (#PCDATA)>
    <!ELEMENT FROM      (#PCDATA)>
    <!ELEMENT SUBJECT (#PCDATA)>
    <!ELEMENT BODY      (italics|boldface)>
        <!ELEMENT italics  (#PCDATA)>
        <!ELEMENT boldface (#PCDATA)>]>
<TO>Charles Smith</TO>
<FROM>Tess Curtis</FROM>
<SUBJECT>Christmas Party</SUBJECT>
<BODY>The <italics>first </italics>
planning session for the Christmas party
will take place on Friday at <boldface>
2 PM. </boldface>See you there.</BODY>
```

① Define the root element and list its child elements.
② Then declare each of the child elements.
③ Use the #PCDATA keyword for elements that accept parsed character data, which a parser processes.
④ List and declare the child elements of the child elements.

Listing 2-6: A VALID DOCUMENT WITH AN EMPTY-ELEMENT DECLARATION

```
<?xml version = "1.0"?>
<!DOCTYPE MEMO [
<!ELEMENT MEMO (LOGO, TO, FROM, SUBJECT,
BODY)>
<!ELEMENT LOGO      EMPTY>
<!ELEMENT TO        (#PCDATA)>
<!ELEMENT FROM      (#PCDATA)>
<!ELEMENT SUBJECT (#PCDATA)>
<!ELEMENT BODY      (#PCDATA)>
]>
<TITLE>Memo with Logo</TITLE>
<LOGO src="smalllogo.gif"/>
<TO>Charles Smith</TO>
<FROM>Tess Curtis</FROM>
<SUBJECT>Christmas Party</SUBJECT>
<BODY>
The first planning session for the
Christmas party
will take place on Friday at 2 PM. See you
there.
</BODY>
```

▲ This example (as well as Listings 2-4 and 2-5) is related to Listings 2-1, 2-2, and 2-3 in the previous task. To get an idea of the differences between well-formed and valid documents, review all six examples.

Understanding DTDs

In the previous task, you learned that DTDs are required parts of valid documents. You also discovered that a DTD can be completely within the current document, a separate document that is referred to from within the current document, or a combination of both. This task describes the general concept of the DTD more thoroughly.

For all valid XML documents, the line starting with the !DOCTYPE reserved keyword specifies a particular type of document. For example, all memoranda fall into a single class of documents that look very similar, with *To*, *From*, and *Subject* headings at the top of the first page and content taking up the rest of the pages. Of course, an individual memo can differ from others. For example, some have a centered company name, some number the pages, some add a corporate logo, and some use different fonts and point sizes. Other document classes include user manuals, letters, reports, invoices, forms, and so on.

A document type definition (DTD), which is included or referred to in the document type declaration, writes all of the rules for a named document type. In the DTD, you will define all the elements that control the structure, content, and some formats for the document type. If you do a good job, each of the documents of one type will look almost identical. Then, if the DTD is well-written and well-organized, an XML processor, such as a parser or browser, will be able to interpret the document's elements based on the DTD's definitions.

In a way, using a !DOCTYPE declaration encourages the use of external DTDs because you are actually defining elements and other such components for a class of documents. External DTDs allow you to specify a set of elements, attributes, entities, notations, and so on for a set of document types. So, if your department or company produces sets of documents using document standards, DTDs are bound to make your life easier.

TAKE NOTE

ANALYZING THE DOCUMENT INSTANCE AND THE DOCUMENT PROLOG

XML is so new that its terminology is still being developed as you read this book. For example, there are differing opinions about how to define the terms *document instance* and *document prolog*. Some say that the instance is the entire document and the prolog is part of the instance (the definition that we use in this book). Other people — especially those from the HTML world — say that the prolog is analogous to the HEAD section of an HTML document and that the instance is comparable to the BODY section. Yet others with an SGML background state definitively that the prolog defines the structure of the document, and the instance is the part of the document that is output. Stay tuned!

CROSS-REFERENCE

Part II explains how to create DTDs and their components.

FIND IT ONLINE

You can find a variety of links to XML resources at **http://www.xmlinfo.com/**.

Listing 2-7: STARTING AN XML DOCUMENT

```
<?xml version = "1.0"?>◄❶
<!DOCTYPE sampdoc [ ◄❸

❷

]>◄❹
```

❶ As always, start an XML document with an XML declaration.
❷ Declare a document type (!DOCTYPE) and its name.
❸ Insert a left bracket ([) to start an internal DTD.
❹ Mark the end of the DTD with a right bracket (]).

Listing 2-8: DECLARING THE ROOT ELEMENT

```
<?xml version = "1.0"?>
<!DOCTYPE sampdoc [
<!ELEMENT sampdoc ANY>◄❽
]>  ❺      ❻      ❼
```

❺ Begin an element declaration with < and the !ELEMENT keyword.
❻ Insert the root element name, which matches the document type.
❼ Enter the ANY keyword to allow any type of content.
❽ End every element declaration with the greater-than (>) character.

Listing 2-9: ADDING ANOTHER ELEMENT AND ITS CHILD ELEMENTS

```
<?xml version = "1.0"?>
<!DOCTYPE sampdoc [
<!ELEMENT sampdoc ANY>            ❿
<!ELEMENT metadata (editor, date, keywords)>
❾  <!ELEMENT editor (#PCDATA)>
    <!ELEMENT date (#PCDATA)>    ◄⓫
    <!ELEMENT keywords (#PCDATA)>
]>                               ⓬
```

❾ Declare a metadata element.
❿ Insert three child elements within parentheses.
⓫ Indent and define each child element.
⓬ Allow parsed character data to be entered.

Listing 2-10: REFINING THE DTD

```
<?xml version = "1.0"?>
<!DOCTYPE sampdoc [
<!ELEMENT sampdoc ANY>                    ⓭
<!ELEMENT metadata (editor|date|keywords)>
   <!ELEMENT editor (#PCDATA)>
⓮►<!ATTLIST editor id    ID   #REQUIRED>
⓯►<!ATTLIST editor name NAME #REQUIRED>
   <!ATTLIST editor dept
        ⓰►writing | support ) "writing">
   <!ELEMENT date (#PCDATA)>
   <!ELEMENT keywords (#PCDATA)> ]>
```

⓭ Replace commas with pipes to allow any order of entry.
⓮ Indent and define the identifier for the editor element.
⓯ Specify a required editor name.
⓰ Allow a choice of the writing and support departments.

Learning About Internal Subsets

All DTDs are internal subsets in one way or another. Internal DTD subsets range from an entire DTD that defines all the components of the containing document to a simple Uniform Resource Identifier (URI) that refers to an external DTD.

An internal DTD, which is located in the document prolog, starts after the !DOCTYPE declaration and ends with a right bracket and greater-than symbol (]>), followed immediately by the start of the content that will be output. For example:

```
<?xml version="1.0"?>
<!DOCTYPE doc [
<!ELEMENT doc (#PCDATA)>
]>
<doc>
This document contains its own DTD
starting with the left bracket and
ending with the right bracket and
greater-than symbol.
</doc>
```

The DTD (the internal subset) is contained completely within the brackets. After the end of the DTD, the information to be output is placed within the <doc> start tag and the </doc> end tag. If you used components not defined in the DTD, a validating parser would display a message and possibly stop processing.

Note that an internal DTD only defines elements for the document in which it is contained. You cannot use an internal DTD to specify the elements for a set of documents. So, if you must spend a great deal of time writing a long, complex DTD, using it for a single document would be a waste of your time. Consider using an external DTD instead.

Why use an internal DTD at all?

▶ XML documents that do not fall into a standard document type may not need to use one of your standard external DTDs. If you know that a document will never be part of a document set, you may decide to use an internal DTD instead. Another example of a nonstandard document is one that contains many unique graphics that you will refer to using entity declarations.

▶ If you are dashing off a short document — even if it will eventually become part of a document set — the quick-and-dirty approach may be the best approach. In this situation, be prepared to edit the document later so that it will conform to one of your standard external DTDs.

▶ You can use a temporary internal DTD to validate a new XML document for the first time. Then, when the document is completely accurate and all its elements have been tested, you can replace the internal DTD with an external DTD.

TAKE NOTE

▶ STICKING WITH THE STANDARDS

A properly written DTD can force an individual writing an XML document to use certain elements in a certain order. In addition, the DTD can restrict the values of a particular element.

CROSS-REFERENCE

Learn more about internal DTDs in Chapter 7's "Declaring an Internal DTD" task.

FIND IT ONLINE

XML Resources, at **http://www.finetuning.com/xml.html**, provides many well-described XML-related links.

Listing 2-11: A VERY SHORT INTERNAL DTD

```
<?xml version = "1.0" standalone="yes"?>
<!DOCTYPE sampdoc [
<!ELEMENT sampdoc (#PCDATA)>
]>
```
❶ ❷ ❸ ❹

❶ *In the XML declaration,* standalone = "yes" *indicates an internal DTD.*

❷ *Enter a left bracket (*[*) to start the DTD.*

❸ *Declare the* sampdoc *root element, which can contain parsed character data.*

❹ *Enter (*]>*) symbols to end the DTD.*

Listing 2-12: ADDING DOCUMENT CONTENT

```
<?xml version = "1.0" standalone="yes"?>
<!DOCTYPE sampdoc [
<!ELEMENT sampdoc (#PCDATA)>
]>
<sampdoc>
You can include any parsed character data
in this space!
</sampdoc>
```
❺ ❻ ❼

❺ *Begin the data that will be output with a start tag.*

❻ *Type any parsed character data after the start tag.*

❼ *Close the document with an end tag.*

Listing 2-13: DECLARING AN ENTITY

```
<?xml version = "1.0" standalone="yes"?>
<!DOCTYPE sampdoc [
<!ELEMENT sampdoc (#PCDATA)>
<!ENTITY fwi "Flammis Widgets, Inc.">
]>
<sampdoc>
You can include any parsed character data
in this space!
</sampdoc>
```
❽ ❾ ❿ ⓫

❽ *To add an entity reference, start with* <!ENTITY.

❾ *Enter the name of the entity reference.*

❿ *Within quotation marks, type the replacement text.*

⓫ *Close the entity reference with* >.

Listing 2-14: ADDING AN ENTITY REFERENCE

```
<?xml version = "1.0" standalone="yes"?>
<!DOCTYPE sampdoc [
<!ELEMENT sampdoc (#PCDATA)>
<!ENTITY fwi "Flammis Widgets, Inc.">
]>
<sampdoc>
Buy your widgets from &fwi;--your
widget source!
</sampdoc>
```
⓬ ⓭ ⓮

⓬ *Enter a start tag to begin the data that will be output.*

⓭ *Type any* #PCDATA, *including the entity, after the start tag.*

⓮ *Close the document with an end tag.*

Learning About External Subsets

As you have already learned, you can use an internal DTD subset to define elements, attributes, entities, and other components for a particular document, or you can use an external DTD subset to define components for one or more documents. External DTDs enable entire sets of documents to share a single set of components, thereby enabling corporate or departmental standards.

If you use an external DTD subset, you call it from within an XML document by using a `!DOCTYPE` declaration with the option of a few variations:

```
<?xml version = "1.0" standalone="no"?>
<!DOCTYPE MANUAL SYSTEM
"/storage/manual.dtd"
```

or

```
<?xml version = "1.0"?>
<!DOCTYPE MANUAL PUBLIC
"http:/www/storage/manual.dtd"
```

Note the first example includes the `standalone="no"` component. This indicates that external DTDs may be associated with the current document. The value `standalone="no"` is the default if there is an external DTD. Therefore, you can consider `standalone="no"` a document comment.

Notice also that the `!DOCTYPE` line is very similar to that of an internal DTD subset. Since element declarations are in the external DTD, you don't have to include the brackets (`[` and `]`).

You can also use external and internal DTDs in a XML document. For example, if you are creating a document that generally conforms to a standard document type but has special sections that require additional elements, you can define those elements in an internal DTD.

TAKE NOTE

▶ USING SYSTEM OR PUBLIC KEYWORDS

External DTDs can be stored on a local-area network (LAN) where they are accessible within a department or corporation, or on a wider network available to more people. To access a DTD file stored locally, use the `SYSTEM` keyword, which indicates that the Uniform Resource Identifier of a system identifier follows. To access a widely available DTD file, use the `PUBLIC` keyword, which indicates that a public identifier follows. Valid public identifiers can include uppercase and lowercase characters in the current alphabet, numbers from 0 to 9, spaces, carriage-return characters, line-feed characters, and several special characters (– ' ( ) + , . / : = ? ; ! * # @ $ _ %).

▶ DIFFERENTIATING AMONG URIS, URLS, AND URNS

A Uniform Resource Identifier (URI) is the address of an external file in its storage location. A URI can be an absolute Uniform Resource Locator (URL), which is a complete address (for example, **http://www. eddygrp.com/dtds/file.dtd**) or a relative address (such as **/dtds/file.dtd**). Because it is *relative* to the current file address, the URL doesn't require a full address.

CROSS-REFERENCE

Chapter 7's "Declaring an External DTD" task reveals more about external DTDs.

FIND IT ONLINE

You can find many links to XML resources at What Is XML?, located at **http://www.gca.org/conf/xml/xml_what.htm**.

Listing 2-15: A DOCUMENT WITH A LOCAL EXTERNAL SUBSET

```
<?xml version = "1.0"?>
<!DOCTYPE DOCUMENT SYSTEM ◀❷        ❸
                "/storage/document.dtd">
        ❶
<TITLE>A Sample Document</TITLE>        ❹
<BODYTEXT>
This document refers to a DTD that defines
at least three elements: the DOCUMENT root
element and the TITLE and BODYTEXT child
elements.
</BODYTEXT>
```

❶ *Enter the* !DOCTYPE *keyword and type* DOCUMENT, *the name.*
❷ *Enter the* SYSTEM *keyword if the DTD is stored on your LAN.*
❸ *Enter the file location and name within quotation marks.*
❹ *Fill in the output text within the start tags and end tags.*

Listing 2-16: A DOCUMENT WITH A PUBLIC EXTERNAL SUBSET

```
<?xml version = "1.0"?>
<!DOCTYPE DOCUMENT PUBLIC ◀❶
                        ❷
"ftp://ftp.eddygrp.com/docs/document.dtd">
<TITLE>A Sample Document</TITLE>
<BODYTEXT>This document refers to a DTD
that is stored at a publicly accessibleL ◀❸
FTP site.</BODYTEXT>
```

❶ *Enter the* PUBLIC *keyword if the DTD is stored at a public site.*
❷ *Enter the file location and name within quotation marks.*
❸ *Enter the output text below the document prolog.*

Listing 2-17: ANOTHER EXAMPLE OF A LOCAL EXTERNAL DTD

```
        ❶                                    ❷ ❸
<?xml version="1.0"? standalone="no">
<!DOCTYPE special SYSTEM "document.dtd" [
<!ELEMENT special (specintro, specbody,
specindex)>
<!ELEMENT specintro (#PCDATA)>
<!ELEMENT specbody (headlev1 | headlev2 |
italpara |normpara)>
<!ELEMENT headlev1 (#PCDATA)> ◀❹
<!ELEMENT headlev2 (#PCDATA)>
<!ELEMENT italpara (#PCDATA)>
<!ELEMENT normpara (#PCDATA)>
<!ELEMENT specindex (#PCDATA)>
]>
```

❶ *Enter the* !DOCTYPE *keyword and* special, *the document type.*
❷ *Enter the* SYSTEM *keyword, and specify the* document.dtd *file.*
❸ *Enter* [*to start the internal DTD.*
❹ *Define elements, ending with the*]> *characters.*

Personal Workbook

Q&A

1 What is a *document type definition (DTD)*?

_____

_____

_____

2 What is the difference between a well-formed XML document and a valid XML document?

_____

_____

_____

3 Name the possible contents of an internal DTD subset.

_____

_____

_____

4 What components make up a document type declaration?

_____

_____

_____

5 What are the rules for start tags and end tags in elements that are not empty?

_____

_____

_____

6 What are the three categories of XML elements?

_____

_____

_____

7 What is a *document type*?

_____

_____

_____

8 What characters do you use to "delimit" an internal DTD?

_____

_____

_____

ANSWERS: PAGE 448

EXTRA PRACTICE

1 Write a well-formed document for a business letter.

2 Convert the well-formed document to a valid document.

3 Create a DTD that includes elements that enhance text. The name of the root element is `text`. Child elements, which can be used in any order, include `boldface`, `italics`, and `underline`.

4 Write any type of external DTD and refer to it from an XML document.

5 Plan and write an external DTD using the look of your company's memoranda.

6 Plan and write an external DTD using the look of your company's reports.

REAL-WORLD APPLICATIONS

✔ You have decided to convert your HTML documents to well-formed XML documents. Applying the rules of well-formed documents, convert one document to XML.

✔ The general belief is that the typical XML document is better organized than the typical HTML document. With that thought in mind and using an HTML document, draw a hierarchical diagram of its elements. Then redraw the diagram as it should be under XML. Hint: Be sure to show a proper hierarchy of root element/child elements.

✔ Your company allows employees to design in-house user manuals without centralized standards. Plan a set of standards and then create a DTD that enforces those standards.

Visual Quiz

Identify components in this XML document. Where is the XML declaration? Where is the document type declaration? Mark the symbol that starts the DTD and the symbol that ends the DTD. What is the name of the root element? Circle the output text. Mark one start tag and one end tag. Identify the empty element and show its location in the output text.

```
valid3 - Notepad
File  Edit  Search  Help
<?xml version = "1.0"?>
<!DOCTYPE MEMO [
<!ELEMENT MEMO (LOGO, TO, FROM, SUBJECT, BODY)>
<!ELEMENT LOGO     EMPTY>
<!ELEMENT TO       (#PCDATA)>
<!ELEMENT FROM     (#PCDATA)>
<!ELEMENT SUBJECT  (#PCDATA)>
<!ELEMENT BODY     (#PCDATA)>
]>
<TITLE>Memo with Logo</TITLE>
<LOGO src="smalllogo.gif"/>
<TO>Charles Smith</TO>
<FROM>Tess Curtis</FROM>
<SUBJECT>Christmas Party</SUBJECT>
<BODY>
The first planning session for the Christmas party
will take place on Friday at 2 PM. See you there.
</BODY>
```

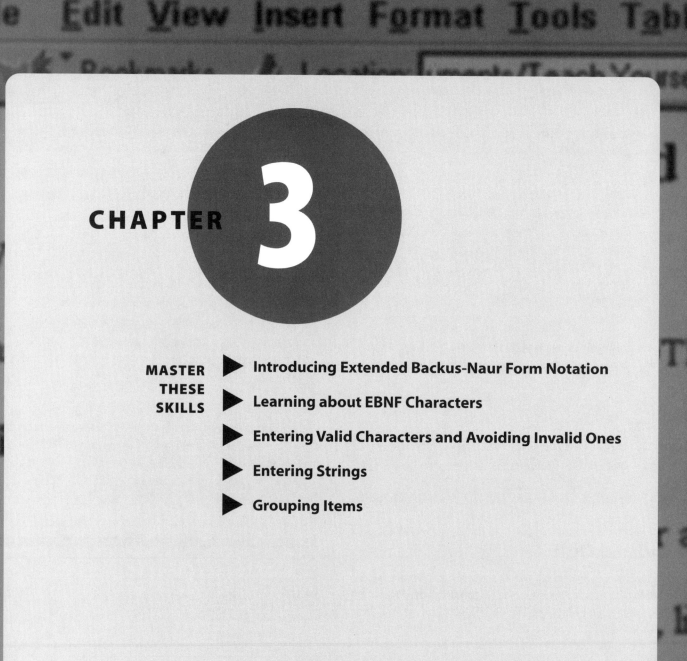

CHAPTER 3

MASTER
THESE
SKILLS

▶ Introducing Extended Backus-Naur Form Notation

▶ Learning about EBNF Characters

▶ Entering Valid Characters and Avoiding Invalid Ones

▶ Entering Strings

▶ Grouping Items

The Anatomy of XML Syntax

In this chapter, you learn about how to use the *Extended Backus-Naur Form* (EBNF) notation. EBNF is the standard syntax that comprises XML and its official specification. You also use EBNF syntax to define the elements, attributes, entities, and other components that comprise XML DTDs and other XML documents. EBNF enables you to specify ranges of values, valid values, valid elements and entities, the location of particular elements in the hierarchy of elements, and much more. Before you declare your first XML element or write your first entity, you should take the time to learn EBNF. EBNF is the International Standard ISO/IEC 14977: 1996 of the International Standardization Organization (ISO) and the International Electrotechnical Commission (IEC).

Among EBNF's unique terminology are three new terms: rule, production, and grammar. A *rule* is a statement that defines a *production*. An entire set of productions is a *grammar*, which comprises every rule for a language. In addition, because it is a technical syntax, EBNF uses programming and mathematical terms such as symbol, expression, operator, and operand.

EBNF uses special characters to delimit or connect components in XML documents. Each character has a unique meaning. For example, the less-than symbol (<) marks the beginning of components, such as declarations, start tags, and end tags. Quotation marks (") and single-quote marks (') indicate the beginning and end of strings, and sets of parentheses (( )) group parts of expressions. Sets of brackets ([ ]) group optional ranges of characters or other components.

Within statements, other characters connect components. For example, the pipe (|) connects components from which you can choose or specifies the order in which elements can be used. EBNF enables a custom-language developer to specify whether certain characters are permitted as element values. Simply use the not symbol (^) to precede characters that are not allowed.

Introducing Extended Backus-Naur Form Notation

Extended Backus-Naur Form (EBNF) notation is the syntax that defines the elements, entities, notation, and other components comprising an XML document. Consequently, you can use EBNF syntax to impose control over document creation. For example, you can require the use of specific elements, define attributes for those elements, limit the attribute values that can be entered, specify default attribute values, and set the order in which elements are used.

EBNF is known as a syntactic metalanguage, where *syntactic* means *of syntax* and a *metalanguage* is data about language (analogous to metadata, which is data about data). Thus, EBNF is a syntax with which you can create languages.

Backus-Naur Form (BNF), EBNF's predecessor, was developed in 1960 by John Backus and Peter Naur to specify the syntax of the Algol programming language. As new programming languages appeared, their developers used variations of BNF to show their commands and other syntax. This led to the definition of an international standard.

For many of us, the XML specification introduces new terms: rule, production, and grammar. A *rule* is a statement, a line of markup. Each rule defines a *production*, or *symbol*, the name given to an operator, value, or other component. A *grammar* comprises all of the productions in a syntax; it is the set of rules for a language.

Each XML production follows this general syntax:

```
Symbol ::= expression
```

or

```
symbol ::= expression
```

Note that when inserting an XML rule in a document, do not enter the `symbol` or `::=`; enter the expression only.

XML is a case-sensitive language; symbols that have an initial uppercase letter indicate a *regular expression* (a way of grouping characters or options); all other symbols are completely lowercase.

Most XML productions are composed of two or more components, which in most cases are other productions in the specification. This allows components used by two or more productions to be defined once — concisely and simply.

TAKE NOTE

▶ XML CASE-SENSITIVITY

Supported Unicode alphabets contain both upper- and lowercase letters, all of which have different decimal or hexadecimal values. As an XML parser processes a document, its interpretation of individual characters can result in errors or strange output. This importance of case means that you have to be very careful about writing declarations and other markup in XML documents.

CROSS-REFERENCE

Chapter 1 discusses XML basics.

FIND IT ONLINE

Get XML links at **http://www.cs.caltech.edu/ ~adam/local/xml.html.**

The Anatomy of XML Syntax
Introducing Extended Backus-Naur Form Notation

CHAPTER 3

Table 3-1: EBNF NOTATION

Syntax	Description
#xN	Enter #x and N, a hexadecimal integer matching any UCS-4 code value in ISO/IEC 10646 standard (see Chapter 4).
[ ]	Brackets indicate that the grouped content within is optional.
[a-zA-Z], [#xN-#xN]	Enter one of the characters within the range a to z, A to Z, or #xN to #xN.
[^a-z], [^#xN-#xN]	Do *not* enter any of the characters within the range adjacent to the NOT character.
[^abc], [^#xN#xN#xN]	Do *not* enter any of the characters adjacent to the NOT character.
"string"|'string'	Enter the literal string enclosed within the quotation marks or single quote marks. Do *not* mix quotation marks and single quote marks in an expression.
( )	Parentheses contain an expression in the same way that you would write a mathematical expression.
(expression)	Enter an expression consisting of a combination of the previously listed parts of XML syntax and using the syntax in Table 3-2, where A represents an expression:

Table 3-2: EBNF EXPRESSION SYNTAX

Syntax	Description
A?	An expression followed by a question mark indicates that the expression is optional.
A B	One expression followed by another must be matched exactly
A|B	Expressions separated by pipe symbols indicate ORs. Choose one expression OR the other — in other words, just choose one. In this book, pipes appear in a larger point size to differentiate them from pipe characters within elements.
A - B	The first expression must be present, and the expression following the minus sign must be absent. Note that a range (for example, A-B) contains no spaces, but the minus sign indicating an absent expression (A - B) is both preceded and succeeded by a space.
A+	An expression followed by a plus sign indicates that the expression *must* appear one or more times.
A*	An expression followed by an asterisk indicates that the expression *may* appear one or more times.

Learning About EBNF Characters

EBNF syntax for XML contains a variety of characters that indicate the start or end of components such as tags, entities, or strings. These characters are known as *delimiters*. For example, start tags are delimited by the less-than (<) symbol and the greater-than (>) symbol, and end tags are delimited by the combination of less-than and slash (</) and the greater-than (>) symbol. Strings are delimited by matching pairs of either quotation marks (`"string"`) or single quote marks (`'string'`).

EBNF also uses *connectors*, symbols that join like components, such as items within lists. The pipe (|) connector specifies a choice list of *content particles* (the names of individual components), and the comma (,) connector specifies a sequence list of content particles. To create a choice list of elements or attributes in an XML DTD, use the `choice` production; to create a sequence list, use the `seq` production.

In the XML specification, the `choice` and `seq` productions look like this:

```
[49] choice ::= '(' S? cp ( S? '|' S? cp )*
S?                      ')'
[50] seq ::= '(' S? cp ( S? ',' S? cp )* S?
                        ')'
```

In these productions, the `'('`, `'|'`, `')'`, and `','` literals are surrounded by single quote marks. Notice that (and) are actually part of the production: they enclose expressions. Within the productions, the `'|'` and `','` literals represent the | and , connectors.

The following examples show how these productions are expressed:

```
(  boldface  |  italics  |  underline  )
( intro, chapter*, appendix*, index )
```

The | connector indicates an OR condition. Someone developing an XML document can select the `boldface` OR `italics` OR `underline` element in any order. On the other hand, the , indicates a distinct order. A developer must choose `intro`, followed by `chapter`, followed by `appendix`, and concluding with `index`. The S in the productions represents whitespace; you can separate list items by as much or as little whitespace as you wish.

TAKE NOTE

INDICATING THE NUMBER OF TIMES A CONTENT PARTICLE CAN APPEAR

Indicators tell an XML parser the number of times that a particular component is allowed to appear in a document. The XML specification includes three main indicators: ?, *, and +. The ? indicator states that a content particle is optional and can occur up to one time. For example, S? indicates that white space can optionally appear wherever it is specified in the `choice` and `seq` productions. The * indicator states that a content particle is optional and can occur any number of times. (See `chapter*` and `appendix*` in the prior example.) The third indicator, +, states that a content particle must occur one or more times.

CROSS-REFERENCE

Chapter 4 covers characters.

FIND IT ONLINE

Review EBNF at **http://www.cs.man.ac.uk/~pjj/ bnf/ebnf_rjb93a_xbnf.mth.**

Table 3-3: EBNF SYMBOLS

Symbols	Description
< and >	Delimits the start and end of a declaration or tag.
/	With < (i.e., </), indicates the beginning of an end tag. With > (i.e., />), indicates the end of an empty-element tag.
::=	Represents the formula for a production: `symbol|Symbol ::= expression`
!	Indicates that a reserved keyword follows.
–	Indicates a range if the expressions (A-B) do not include spaces *or* subtraction if the expressions (A - B) include spaces.
^	Indicates that you must not select any of the characters that follow.
&	Starts a parsed general entity.
&#	Starts a decimal character reference.
&#x	Starts a hexadecimal character reference.
%	Starts a parameter entity or parameter entity reference.
;	Ends an entity.
?	Indicates that a content particle can occur up to one time.
+	Indicates that a content particle *must* occur one or more times.
*	Indicates that a content particle can occur an unlimited number of times.
|	Connects content particles and states that an XML developer can select the listed content particles in any order. Within brackets, indicates a choice.
,	Connects content particles and states that an XML developer *must* select the listed content particles in the order in which they appear.
/* and */	Delimits the start and end of a comment.
(and)	Delimits the start and end of an expression to be evaluated as a whole.
" and '	Delimits the start and end of a string. Do not mix quotation marks and single quote marks for the same string.
<? and ?>	Delimits the start and end of a processing instruction.
[and]	Delimits the start and end of a range; [delimits the start of an internal DTD.
]>	Delimits the end of an internal DTD.
<![and]]>	Delimits the start and end of a CDATA section.

Entering Valid Characters and Avoiding Invalid Ones

Every XML document is composed of characters—all supported by the ISO/IEC 10646 international standard. (See Chapter 4.) EBNF provides syntax that lists the valid and invalid characters for a specific production. Look at these XML productions:

```
[75]    ExternalID ::= 'SYSTEM'
            S SystemLiteral
            | 'PUBLIC' S PubidLiteral S
            SystemLiteral
[11] SystemLiteral ::= ('"' [^"]* '"')
            | ("'" [^']* "'")
[12]  PubidLiteral ::= '"' PubidChar* '"'
            | "'" (PubidChar* - "'")* "'"
[13]    PubidChar ::= #x20 | #xD | #xA
            | [a-zA-Z0-9]
            | [-'()+,./:=?;|*#@$_%]
```

The names to the left of the ::= are simply names; they will not be part of your lines of XML code. However, the names are shortcut terms that tell you the meaning of the production. For example, ExternalID means external identifier, SystemLiteral represents SYSTEM identifier literal, and PubidChar symbolizes PUBLIC identifier character. Notice that some productions are components of other productions. For example, use SystemLiteral and PublicLiteral in the ExternalID production, and PubidChar within the PubidLiteral production. This use of productions within other productions occurs throughout the XML specification.

Items within single quote marks (') or quotation marks (") are strings; for example, SYSTEM and

PUBLIC are both keywords. Remember that XML is case sensitive, so these strings must be uppercase. Also remember that S is a production that represents whitespace. Therefore, SYSTEM and its system literal can be separated by any amount of whitespace.

The pipe symbol (|) has two meanings: Within the brackets ([ ]), the pipe is a literal; outside the brackets, it is part of the EBNF syntax and represents a logical OR. For example, you can enter SYSTEM and a system identifier literal *or* PUBLIC and a public identifier literal. You can place strings inside sets of single quote marks *or* quotation marks. The not character (^) indicates that you *cannot* select the bracketed character or characters preceded by the ^. Thus, you cannot use the quotation mark in a string enclosed by a set of quotation marks, and you cannot use a single quote mark in a string enclosed by a set of single quote marks.

CROSS-REFERENCE

Chapter 4 discusses converting characters.

FIND IT ONLINE

Read about symbols at **http://www.cs.upe.ac.za/staff/csabhv/slim/ebnf.html**.

The Anatomy of XML Syntax
Entering Valid Characters and Avoiding Invalid Ones

XML 1.0: USING SYMBOLS IN AN XML LINE

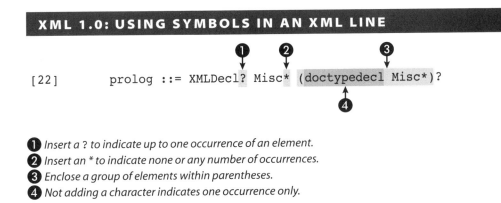

[22]   prolog ::= XMLDecl? Misc* (doctypedecl Misc*)?

❶ *Insert a ? to indicate up to one occurrence of an element.*
❷ *Insert an * to indicate none or any number of occurrences.*
❸ *Enclose a group of elements within parentheses.*
❹ *Not adding a character indicates one occurrence only.*

XML 1.0: BUILDING THE PROLOG

[22]   prolog ::= XMLDecl? Misc* (doctypedecl Misc*)?

[23]   XMLDecl ::= '<?xml' VersionInfo EncodingDecl? SDDecl? S? '?>'
[24]   VersionInfo ::= S 'version' Eq (' VersionNum ' | " VersionNum ")
[25]   Eq ::= S? '=' S?
[26]   VersionNum ::= ([a-zA-Z0-9_.:] | '-')+
[27]   Misc ::= Comment | PI | S
[28]   doctypedecl ::= '<!DOCTYPE' S Name (S ExternalID)?
                        S? ('[' (markupdecl | PEReference
                        | S)* ']' S?)? '>'

❶ *(Optional) Use the XMLDecl production to write one XML declaration.*
❷ *Insert VersionInfo into the XML declaration.*
❸ *(Optional) Add any amount of miscellaneous information.*
❹ *(Optional) Insert a document type declaration, including miscellaneous information.*

Entering Strings

A *string* is a group of one or more characters or words, usually text, enclosed within delimiters and sometimes given a unique name as identification. In EBNF, a string can be a keyword (such as "PUBLIC" or 'SYSTEM') or character references (such as '&' or "<"). Throughout the XML specification, you'll even find the single-quote-mark and quotation-mark strings enclosed within sets of quotation marks or single quote marks (" ' " and ' " ') serving as delimiters. The following example shows strings enclosed within single quote marks or quotation marks:

```
[32]     SDDecl :: S 'standalone' Eq
            (("'" ('yes' | 'no') "'")
            | ('"' ('yes' | 'no') '"')
```

The SDDecl production indicates that a standalone declaration within an XML declaration is composed of the lowercase standalone string, an equal sign (=), and a yes or no answer. Note that EBNF indicates that standalone, yes, and no are strings by enclosing them within single quote marks. However, when you write the standalone declaration, you do not enter those single quote marks. The single quote marks and quotation marks are also enclosed within quotation marks and single quote marks, respectively. The enclosed marks are also strings, so you add them to the declaration. All the following declarations are correct:

```
standalone = "yes"
standalone = 'yes'
standalone = "no"
standalone = 'no'
```

You'll find that other strings are *not* allowed within a production. For example:

```
[17] PITarget ::= Name - (('X' | 'x')
                 ('M' | 'm')('L' | 'l'))
```

Remember that the dash symbol (-) preceded and succeeded by a space *subtracts* the following values from the values that are allowed in a production. So the PITarget (processing instruction target) production allows any valid XML name but XML or xml, which are reserved.

For future reference, a valid XML name starts with a letter or underscore character and can include letters, digits, periods, dashes, underscores, colons, combining characters, and extenders. A *combining character* is a character such as an accent or circumflex that is added to a letter. An *extender* is one of a variety of punctuation marks.

TAKE NOTE

▶ USING QUOTE SYMBOLS FOR QUOTATIONS

What happens when you incorporate a quotation within a string? Entities provide the best example of this usage:

```
<!ENTITY twain1 'Mark Twain said,
"Always do right. This will gratify
some people, and astonish the
rest."'>
```

CROSS-REFERENCE

Chapter 10 covers entities.

FIND IT ONLINE

Learn about BNF at **http://lem.stud.fh-heilbronn. de/doc/ada/lovelace/bnf.html**.

XML 1.0: WRITING AN ENCODING DECLARATION

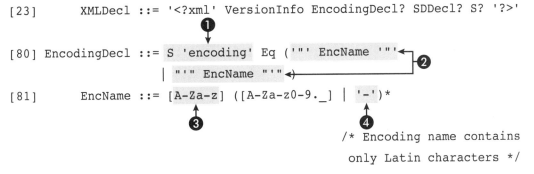

```
[23]      XMLDecl ::= '<?xml' VersionInfo EncodingDecl? SDDecl? S? '?>'

[80] EncodingDecl ::= S 'encoding' Eq ('"' EncName '"'
                      | "'" EncName "'"

[81]      EncName ::= [A-Za-z] ([A-Za-z0-9._] | '-')*
```

/* Encoding name contains
only Latin characters */

❶ *Start an encoding declaration with whitespace and the string* encoding.
❷ *Enclose the encoding name within sets of ' or ".*
❸ *The* EncName *starts with an upper- or lowercase Latin character.*
❹ *The EncName can contain a dash (–) string.*

XML 1.0: WRITING A COMMENT

```
[2]     Char ::= #x9 | #XA | #xD | [#x20-#xD7FF]
                 | [#xE000-#xFFFD]          /* any Unicode character,
                 | [#x10000-#x10FFFF]          excluding the surrogate
                                               blocks, FFFE, and FFF. */
```

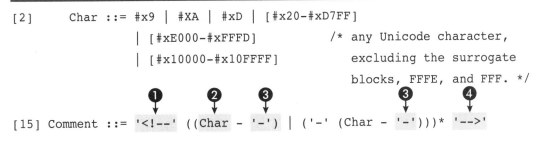

```
[15] Comment ::= '<!--' ((Char - '-') | ('-' (Char - '-')))* '-->'
```

❶ *Start a comment with the string* <!--.
❷ *Comment text can begin with a valid character.*
❸ *The string or character following the minus sign is invalid.*
❹ *End a comment with the string* -->.

Grouping Items

EBNF groups items using two sets of characters: brackets ([ ]) and parentheses (( )). As you have seen in previous tasks in this chapter, brackets group ranges of characters or other components. For example, [A-Za-z0-9] lists ranges of valid characters, and [^%&"] lists a range of characters that are invalid. In mathematics and programming, including EBNF, you can group items to change their order of precedence. Note that in programming syntax, including the official EBNF standard, brackets can also indicate optional material. In the XML version of EBNF, brackets include ranges only. The items within the parentheses ((and)) are processed before items outside the parentheses are. The difference between the contents of brackets and parentheses is that brackets contain ranges and parentheses include expressions.

An expression combines symbols (which include other symbols, values, functions, other expressions, and operators) that are evaluated to produce a result. For example:

```
[3] S ::= (#x20 | #x9 | #xD | #xA)+
```

The white space production is an expression that allows one of four values: the space (#x0020) character or the tab (#x0009) character or the carriage return (#x000D) character or the line feed (#x000A) character. The parentheses enclose the expression. Remember that the plus sign indicates that a content particle (such as one space or one character) *must* occur one or more times.

The following production for an entity value is more complicated:

```
[9] EntityValue ::= '"' ([^%&"]
           | PEReference | Reference)* '"'
           | "'" ([^%&']
           | PEReference | Reference)* "'"
```

The ranges of invalid characters [^%&"] and [^%&'] are enclosed along with the PEReference and Reference productions within parentheses. The sets of parentheses form expressions that are controlled by the *. Remember, the * indicates that the enclosed expression is optional but can occur any number of times. Notice also that you can enclose an entity value within quotation marks or single quote marks. This is the reason for the near duplication of the two expressions within the production.

TAKE NOTE

ACCEPTABLE ATTRIBUTE VALUES

Another use for parentheses in XML documents is to contain a list of valid values for a particular attribute. You can write an attribute list to define types of allowable lists for the list element:

```
<!ATTLIST list type ( number | bullet
| simple )
```

In the example, number represents a numbered list, bulleted indicates a bulleted list, and simple stands for an unnumbered, unbulleted list.

CROSS-REFERENCE
Chapter 9 shows attributes.

FIND IT ONLINE
Learn about EBNF parsers at **http://www.cs.man. ac.uk/~pjj/bnf/ebnf_kern_hill_young.html**.

Listing 3-1: A GROUP OF ORDERED ELEMENTS

```
<?xml version="1.0"?>  ←❶
<!DOCTYPE sampdoc [  ←❷                    ❸
<!ELEMENT sampdoc (begin, middle, end)>
]>  ←❹
```

❶ Surround the XML declaration with the <? and ?> delimiters.
❷ Start the internal DTD with the left bracket ([) delimiter.
❸ Enclose begin, middle, and end child elements within parentheses.
❹ End the internal DTD with the]> delimiters.

Listing 3-2: A GROUP OF ATTRIBUTES

```
<!ATTLIST border
          id ID #REQUIRED
          type ( bold | solid | dashed )
          color ( red | green | blue )>
```

▲ This example shows choices for two of the three listed attributes. The type attribute allows a border to be bold, solid, or dashed. The color attribute enables the choice of a red, green, or blue border.

Listing 3-3: A GROUP OF UNORDERED ELEMENTS

```
<?xml version = "1.0"?>
<!DOCTYPE sampdoc [
<!ELEMENT sampdoc ANY>          ❶
<!ELEMENT metadata (editor|date|keywords)>
    <!ELEMENT editor (#PCDATA)>  ←❷
      <!ATTLIST editor id    ID    #REQUIRED>
      <!ATTLIST editor name NAME #REQUIRED>
      <!ATTLIST editor dept (writing | ←❸
support ) "writing">
    <!ELEMENT date (#PCDATA)>  ←❷
    <!ELEMENT keywords (#PCDATA)>  ←❷
]>
```

❶ The metadata element groups three child elements within parentheses.
❷ The #PCDATA expression within parentheses is replaced by parsed character data.
❸ The writing and support attribute values are grouped within parentheses.

Listing 3-4: A COMPLEX SET OF ELEMENT CHOICES

```
<?xml version="1.0"?>
<!DOCTYPE customer [
<!ELEMENT customer (name+, address*,
 city+, state+, zip+, telephone*, fax?,
 email?)>
]>
```

▲ This example shows the definition of the root element and, within the set of parentheses, several child elements.

Personal Workbook

Q&A

1 What does *EBNF* stand for?

_____

_____

_____

2 What is a *grammar*?

_____

_____

_____

3 What is the general syntax for an XML production?

_____

_____

_____

4 Is XML sensitive or insensitive to the case of its symbols? Why?

_____

_____

_____

5 What do brackets represent in XML syntax?

_____

_____

_____

6 Can you use a combination of quotation marks and single quote marks to delimit an expression? Within an expression?

_____

_____

_____

7 What does an exclamation point mean in an XML statement?

_____

_____

_____

8 What does the *not* character mean in an XML statement?

_____

_____

_____

ANSWERS: PAGE 448

EXTRA PRACTICE

❶ Write an expression that indicates a range from I to G. Then write an expression that indicates that M must be present but N may not be present.

❷ Write an expression that indicates that S must appear one or more times. Change the expression to indicate that S is entirely optional.

❸ Write an expression that indicates a choice of apple, orange, or plum.

❹ Write a start tag and end tag for the non-empty planet element. Then write a start tag and end tag for the empty jupiterimg element.

❺ Make your favorite quote an XML entity.

❻ Write an XML comment. (Hint: Look at the [15] Comment production in the XML specification.)

REAL-WORLD APPLICATIONS

✔ You live in a world in which the tilde (~), braces ({ }), dollar sign ($) and all odd numbers are illegal. Write an EBNF statement that ensures that these characters and digits do not appear in any of your XML documents.

✔ You have decided to create an XML version of your grocery list. Based on your accumulated knowledge of the first three chapters of this book, create a DTD with the root element grocery, a level of child elements that categorize types of groceries by aisle, and a lower level of child elements listing individual grocery items. Make sure that grocery categories must appear in a set order, whereas individual items can appear in any order.

✔ Using the previous application and the elements that you declared, prepare an XML document that produces a grocery list.

Visual Quiz

The Language Identification productions in the XML specification enable an individual to declare the code of the language in which an XML document will be written. For the ISO639Code, IanaCode, UserCode, and Subcode productions, specify the characters that are valid and the order in which they can appear. Then combine the appropriate productions to form the three possible versions of the LanguageID production.

_____

_____

_____

```
visualquiz - Notepad
File  Edit  Search  Help
Language Identification

[33] LanguageID ::= Langcode ('-' Subcode)*

[34]   Langcode ::= ISO639Code | IanaCode | UserCode

[35] ISO639Code ::= ([a-z] | [A-Z]) ([a-z] | [A-Z])

[36]    IanaCode ::= ('i' | 'I') '-' ([a-z] | [A-Z])+

[37]    UserCode ::= ('x' | 'X') '-' ([a-z] | [A-Z])+

[38]     Subcode ::= ([a-z] | [A-Z])+
```

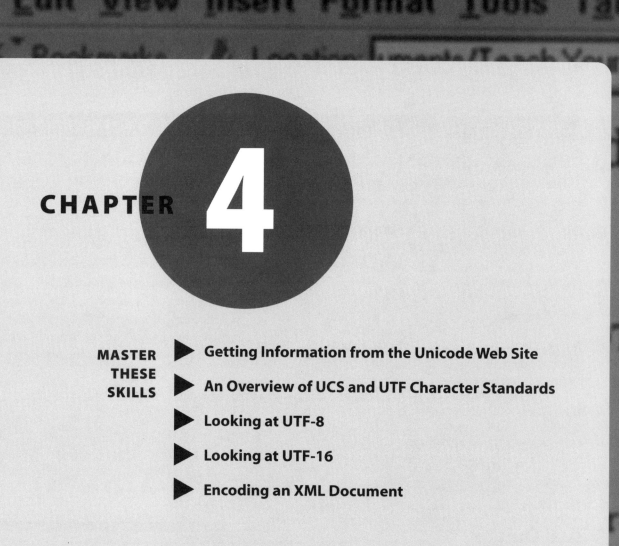

CHAPTER **4**

Supported Characters and Character Sets

As you know, the World Wide Web is an international phenomenon. However, up to this point in its development, most Web documents have been written in English. In the early days of the Web, the creation of non-English-language documents was a challenge. Characters in other languages often are not part of the traditional Latin-based alphabet, and some languages display or print in a direction other than the European and American languages' left-to-right.

All XML documents are composed of characters. If a document is to be well-formed or valid, all of its characters — including both markup and content — must be supported by the Unicode Standard, which is maintained and supported by the Unicode Consortium. Founded in 1991, the Consortium is an international group of software companies and researchers. The Unicode Standard, which is a subset of the International Standard ISO/IEC 10646-1: 1993, consists of scripts and other character sets. A *script* is the set of character codes for a particular language. Other character sets include punctuation marks, technical and mathematical characters, arrows, dingbats, and

diacritics, or marks that are added to a letter. Diacritics include acute and grave accents, breves, cedillas, circumflexes, macrons, tildes, and so on.

According to the Unicode Consortium, the Unicode Standard, which is currently at Version 2.1, provides codes for almost 39,000 characters. The latest revision of Version 2.1, which is dated September 4, 1998, includes two new characters: the Object Replacement character (`U+FFFC`), which marks an insertion point, and the Euro Sign (`U+20AC`), which is the new currency of the European Monetary Union (EMU). Version 2.1 also corrects Version 2.0 errors.

This chapter shows you how to use the Unicode Web site to get up-to-date information about the supported XML characters, character sets, and scripts. It also provides an overview of various supported character standards, and teaches you how to convert character codes. You also learn how to evaluate the characters in an XML document.

For an extensive list of the Unicode characters supported by the XML specification, refer to my book *XML in Plain English* (also published by IDG Books Worldwide).

Getting Information from the Unicode Web Site

The Unicode Consortium's Web site provides all the information you'll ever need about XML-supported character sets, characters, and scripts. From the Unicode home page (**http://www.unicode.org/**), you can link to several important pages, including a text-only alternate to the default graphical home page. You can find out how to join the Unicode Consortium, browse a table of contents for the Unicode Standard Book (and order it), and access technical reports and publications.

From the home page (and most other pages at the site), you can link to six pages: Contents, Unicode Standard, Updates and Errata, Technical Work, Online Data, and Conferences. The first two are perhaps the most important: the Contents link brings you to a long, two-column list of links at the site; and the Unicode Standard link is the entry to pages of information, including extensive charts of all the coded characters. Table 4-1, on the facing page, lists many of the pages at the Unicode site and provides a short description and URL for each.

XML AROUND THE WORLD

As the Web has grown in scope and popularity, the developers of HTML realized that they had to address the issue of *internationalization*, the support of non-English alphabets and special characters. In both HTML 2.0 and HTML 3.2, the supported character code was the International Standard ISO-8859, which consisted of Latin character sets and special characters; international character sets and symbols were not supported. By the time HTML 4.0 was being developed, its Working Group decided to support the International Standard ISO 10646-1. This standard includes ISO 8859-1 while adding international characters and symbols — and it enables programmers to set the direction of text output.

From the very start, the XML Working Group stated support for ISO 10646-1. The World Wide Web Consortium (W3C), which sets the standards for both XML and HTML, provides a home page (**http://www.w3.org/International/**) offering discussions and links to information about international and local character sets.

TAKE NOTE

SPECIFYING UNPARSED AND PARSED CHARACTER ATTRIBUTES IN XML

XML supports two character-data types with the CDATA and #PCDATA attributes. CDATA is unparsed character data, which an XML parser passes straight through to document output without interpreting or processing it in any way. With CDATA, what you see in the original XML document is what you get in the output. #PCDATA, on the other hand, represents parsed character data: An XML parser processes #PCDATA by removing all delimiters and other markup. The end result is all non-markup character data. Chapter 9 talks more about CDATA, #PCDATA, and other XML attributes.

CROSS-REFERENCE

Learn about the basics of XML markup and character data in Chapter 1.

FIND IT ONLINE

The ISO home page, at **http://www.iso.ch/**, contains links to ISO standards and related standards sites.

Table 4-1: SELECTED PAGES AT THE UNICODE WEB SITE

Page	Description	URL
Unicode Home Page (graphical version)	A graphical home page	**http://www.unicode.org/**
Unicode Home Page (text version)	A text-only home page	**http://www.unicode.org/textonly.html**
Unicode Copyright	Copyright information about the pages at the Unicode site	**http://www.unicode.org/ unicode/copyright.html**
Contents	A list of page links at the Unicode site	**http://www.unicode.org/ unicode/contents.html**
What's New?	A list of new or changed features, arranged from newest to oldest	**http://www.unicode.org/ unicode/wnew.html**
The Unicode Consortium	Information about the Unicode Consortium and its members	**http://www.unicode.org/ unicode/consortium/consort.html**
The Unicode Standard	Links to information about the Unicode Standard, scripts, code charts, proposed scripts and codes, and related publications	**http://www.unicode.org/ unicode/standard/standard.html**
Unicode 2.1 Character Charts	The home page for code charts: names lists and glyphs	**http://charts.unicode.org/charts.html**
Supported Scripts	A list of scripts (such as alphabets and character sets) supported in the Unicode Standard	**http://www.unicode.org/ unicode/standard/supported.html**
The Unicode Standard: A Technical Introduction	Eight pages of concise information about the Unicode Standard	**http://www.unicode.org/unicode/ standard/principles.html**
Online Data	Links at the Unicode site and other sources, including the Unicode FTP site, language codes, and country codes	**http://www.unicode.org/unicode/ onlinedat/online.html**
Unicode Publications	Links to information about printed and electronic publications	**http://www.unicode.org/unicode/ publications.html**
Updates & Errata	An index of updates to the Unicode Standard, Version 2.0	**http://www.unicode.org/unicode/ uni2errata/UnicodeErrata.html**

An Overview of UCS and UTF Character Standards

According to information at the Unicode Web site: "The Unicode Worldwide Character Standard is a character coding system designed to support the interchange, processing, and display of the written texts of the diverse languages of the modern world. In addition, it supports classical and historical texts of many written languages." Table 4-2, on the facing page, lists the scripts supported by the Unicode Standard and the URL of the code chart for each script at the Unicode Web site.

As you have learned in previous chapters, XML documents are made up of markup and character data, all of which are composed of individual characters. However, computer programs such as XML parsers do not actually read characters; they read bits and bytes made up of 0's and 1's. *Character encoding* is this representation of characters.

UTF-8 is basically an 8-bit version of a character set specified by the Unicode Technical Committee (UTC). This is the default encoding for XML documents. Other popular supported encodings include UTF-16, (an extended version that varies from 16 to 32 bits) and UCS-2 (a 4-byte encoding that conforms completely to the ISO/IEC 10646 standard). The acronym *UCS* represents universal coded character set or Universal Character Set, and *UTF* represents UCS transformation format. You'll learn more about these and other encodings in the following pages.

TAKE NOTE

▶ REVIEWING ASCII BASICS

ASCII, which is an acronym for the American Standard Code for Information Interchange, is either a 128- or 256-character system — depending on whether it is in its original or extended form. ASCII is arranged in four 32-character groups. The first group consists of the uppercase alphabet and commonly used punctuation characters. The second group contains digits, spaces, and more punctuation symbols. The third group is composed of the lowercase alphabet and the less common punctuation characters. The fourth group features control characters, such as line feeds (known as LF) and carriage returns (CR).

ASCII coincides with the ANSI (American National Standards Institute) coding standard for characters, numbers, and other symbols — whether they're on your keyboard or not. ANSI is a U.S. organization related to the International Organization for Standardization, which you know as ISO (remember ISO-8859 and ISO/IEC 10646). ASCII, which is the International Standard ISO/IEC 646, is an integral part of computing.

▶ INTEGRATING ASCII INTO XML

UTF-8, ASCII, ANSI, and several versions of ISO 8859 (that is, Latin scripts) are completely intertwined. UTF-8, the XML encoding default, contains the first 128 characters of the ASCII character set. The various versions of ISO 8859 also include ASCII in conjunction with characters from various languages.

CROSS-REFERENCE

Chapter 3 covers the proper syntax for valid and invalid characters.

FIND IT ONLINE

The American National Standards Institute (ANSI), **http://www.ansi.org/**, is the U.S. standards organization.

Table 4-2: SOME OF THE CODE PAGES AT THE UNICODE WEB SITE

Code	Enter http://charts.unicode.org/Unicode.charts/normal/ and:	Code	Enter http://charts.unicode.org/Unicode.charts/normal/ and:
C0 Controls and Basic Latin	U0000.html	Arrows	U2190.html
C1 Controls and Latin-1 Supplement	U0080.html	Mathematical Operators	U2200.html
Latin Extended-A	U0100.html	Miscellaneous Technical	U2300.html
Latin Extended-B	U0180.html	Control Pictures	U2400.html
IPA Extensions	U0250.html	Optical Character Recognition	U2440.html
Spacing Modifier Letters	U02B0.html	Enclosed Alphanumerics	U2460.html
Combining Diacritical Marks	U0300.html	Box Drawing	U2500.html
Greek	U0370.html	Block Elements	U2580.html
Cyrillic	U0400.html	Geometric Shapes	U25A0.html
Armenian	U0530.html	Miscellaneous Symbols	U2600.html
Hebrew	U0590.html	Dingbats	U2700.html
Arabic	U0600.html	CJK Symbols and Punctuation	U3000.html
Devanagari	U0900.html	Hiragana	U3040.html
Bengali	U0980.html	Katakana	U30A0.html
Gurmukhi	U0A00.html	Bopomofo	U3100.html
Gujarati	U0A80.html	Hangul Compatibility Jamo	U3130.html
Oriya	U0B00.html	Kanbun	U3190.html
Tamil	U0B80.html	Enclosed CJK Letters and Months	U3200.html
Telugu	U0C00.html	CJK Compatibility	U3300.html
Kannada	U0C80.html	CJK Ideographs	U4E00.html
Malayalam	U0D00.html	Hangul Syllables	UAC00.html
Thai	U0E00.html	High Surrogates	UD800.html
Lao	U0E80.html	High Private Use Surrogates	UDB80.html
Tibetan	U0F00.html	Low Surrogates	UDC00.html
Georgian	U10A0.html	Private Use Area	UE000.html

Looking at UTF-8

Every XML document is associated with one character set, or encoding. The default encoding is UTF-8, which is a compressed character representation supported by the XML specification and the Unicode Consortium. UTF-8 is an amendment of ISO/IEC 10646. It contains the entire US-ASCII character set and the UCS universal coded character set, and is documented in RFC 2044.

UTF-8 compresses each of the common 7-bit ASCII 0-127 characters into eight bits (one byte or one octet) and uses the same code values as ASCII. However, the non-ASCII characters are three bytes long. So if you use ASCII characters to develop your XML documents, UTF-8 can save storage space. Conversely, if your documents are non-Latin (for example, Chinese, Japanese, or Korean), your storage requirements will increase a great deal. UTF-8 allows a range of 0 to 255 bytes.

In XML, you can express UTF-8 character codes as character references by using the decimal or hexadecimal number system. The decimal number system consists of the numbers 0 through 9. The hexadecimal number system consists of 0 through 9 and the letters A through F (which represent 10 through 15). The main advantage of using hexadecimal numbers is that you can fit two hexadecimal digits into one byte.

If you use a decimal code, its format is

`&#code;`

If you use a hexadecimal code, its format is

`&#xcode;`

where `code` represents a supported character code.

Because UTF-8 is compatible with ASCII, you can use a text editor to create your XML documents. UTF-8 also makes it more likely that software developed from the days before XML will be able to read your output.

Computing with Non-Latin Languages

Those of us who use Latin-based languages with their limited alphabets take our keyboards and fonts for granted. And to enter special non-keyboard characters into a document, we can use software built into our word processors or our operating systems.

Those who use other languages — especially Chinese, Japanese, and Korean (in Unicode terminology, known as CJK) — must choose from tens of thousands of characters, most of which are not on their keyboards. The CJK languages are made up of *ideographs*, which are symbols that represent entire words, ideas, or objects. Some CJK ideographs are shared among the Chinese, Japanese, and Korean alphabets.

All of them are in the ISO/IEC 10646 standard. That means you can specify a CJK character set in order to create an XML document, or you can embed CJK characters into your document. Remember that you and those who view your document must have software that can understand your characters and a font that can display or print the document output.

CROSS-REFERENCE

In Chapter 7 you'll learn about adding an encoding set to an XML declaration.

FIND IT ONLINE

SGML: Related Standards (**http://www.sil.org/sgml/related.html**) links to SGML and XML standards.

Table 4-3: SELECTED ISO 639 LANGUAGE CODES

Language	Code	Language	Code	Language	Code
Afar	aa	Greenlandic	kl	Quechua	qu
Afrikaans	af	Hausa	ha	Romanian	ro
Albanian	sq	Hebrew	iw, he	Russian	ru
Arabic	ar	Hindi	hi	Samoan	sm
Armenian	hy	Hungarian	hu	Sanskrit	sa
Azerbaijani	az	Icelandic	is	Scots Gaelic	gd
Basque	eu	Indonesian	in, id	Serbian	sr
Bengali	bn	Irish	ga	Serbo-Croatian	sh
Bulgarian	bg	Italian	it	Spanish	es
Burmese	my	Japanese	ja	Sindhi	sd
Byelorussian	be	Korean	ko	Slovak	sk
Cambodian	km	Kurdish	ku	Slovenian	sl
Chinese	zh	Laotian	lo	Somali	so
Corsican	co	Latin	la	Swahili	sw
Croatian	hr	Latvian	lv	Swedish	sv
Czech	cs	Lithuanian	lt	Tagalog	tl
Danish	da	Macedonian	mk	Telugu	te
Dutch	nl	Malay	ms	Thai	th
English	en	Malayalam	ml	Tibetan	bo
Esperanto	eo	Maltese	mt	Tonga	to
Estonian	et	Moldavian	mo	Turkish	tr
Fiji	fj	Mongolian	mn	Turkmen	tk
Finnish	fi	Nauru	na	Ukrainian	uk
French	fr	Nepali	ne	Vietnamese	vi
Galician	gl	Norwegian	no	Oromo	om
Georgian	ka	Polish	pl	Welsh	cy
German	de	Portuguese	pt		
Greek	el	Punjabi	pa		

Looking at UTF-16

UTF-16 is a 16-bit (two bytes/two octets) character representation, or encoding form, supported by the XML specification and the Unicode organization. This form, which is an amendment of ISO/IEC 10646, allows characters outside the Basic Multilingual Plane (BMP) of ISO/IEC 10646 to be encoded. In other words, UTF-16 has the capability of being an extension to ISO/IEC 10646 — 16 planes more than the BMP. UTF-16 allows the definition of up to 65,536 characters. Because this encoding is relatively new, older software may have problems reading your output.

UTF-16 characters are represented on character charts by a U prefix followed by four hexadecimal numbers, two for each octet. For example, U+00D9 represents a U character with a accent grave (Ù). In an XML document, you would insert the Ù by inserting the following character reference:

`&#x00D9;`

The `&#x` characters indicate that this character reference uses the hexadecimal number system. Remember that you end any character reference with a semicolon.

Because the number of bytes in both UTF-8 and UTF-16 vary, the first byte indicates the number of bytes that follow.

You can easily convert UTF-8 to UTF-16 and UTF-16 to UTF-8.

CROSS-REFERENCE

Chapter 13 discusses adding character data content to a document.

FIND IT ONLINE

Learn about the ISO/IEC 10646 standard at **http://www.nada.kth.se/i18n/ucs/ unicode-iso10646-oview.html**.

Table 4-4: SELECTED ISO 3166 COUNTRY CODES

Country	Code	Country	Code	Country	Code
Afghanistan	AF	Guatemala	GT	Pakistan	PK
Algeria	DZ	Haiti	HT	Panama	PA
Argentina	AR	Hong Kong	HK	Peru	PE
Australia	AU	Hungary	HU	Philippines	PH
Austria	AT	Iceland	IS	Poland	PL
Bangladesh	BD	India	IN	Portugal	PT
Belarus	BY	Indonesia	ID	Puerto Rico	PR
Belgium	BE	Iran	IR	Romania	RO
Bolivia	BO	Iraq	IQ	Russian Federation	RU
Brazil	BR	Ireland	IE	Saudi Arabia	SA
Bulgaria	BG	Israel	IL	Singapore	SG
Cambodia	KH	Italy	IT	Slovakia	SK
Canada	CA	Jamaica	JM	Somalia	SO
Chile	CL	Japan	JP	South Africa	ZA
China	CN	Jordan	JO	Spain	ES
Colombia	CO	Kenya	KE	Sweden	SE
Costa Rica	CR	Korea, North	KP	Switzerland	CH
Croatia	HR	Korea, South	KR	Syria	SY
Cuba	CU	Kuwait	KW	Taiwan	TW
Czech Republic	CZ	Latvia	LV	Ukraine	UA
Denmark	DK	Lebanon	LB	United Kingdom	GB
Ecuador	EC	Libya	LY	United States	US
Egypt	EG	Mexico	MX	Venezuela	VE
El Salvador	SV	Morocco	MA	Vietnam	VN
Finland	FI	Netherlands	NL	Yugoslavia	YU
France	FR	New Zealand	NZ	Zimbabwe	ZW
Germany	DE	Nicaragua	NI		
Greenland	GL	Norway	NO		

Encoding an XML Document

When you create an XML document, your character data can include any character in the International Standard ISO/IEC 10646 (except for FFFE and FFFF, which are reserved as surrogate blocks that Unicode may use in the future to help define many more characters). You define a document's character set by including an encoding declaration in the XML declaration. The syntax of the XML encoding declaration is as follows:

```
[80] EncodingDecl ::= S 'encoding' Eq
                      ('"' EncName '"'
                      | "'" EncName "'" )
[81]      EncName ::= [A-Za-z]
                      ([A-Za-z0-9._] | '-')*
             /* Encoding name contains
                only Latin characters */
```

In the declaration, `EncName` starts with any character from a Latin character set and includes any combination of Latin characters, the digits from 0 to 9, the period (.), and the underscore (_), or can contain a dash string (-).

An XML declaration with an encoding declaration included looks something like this:

```
<?xml version="1.0" encoding="UTF-8"?>
```

Remember that UTF-8 is the default encoding system, so this encoding declaration is not required. According to the XML specification, "[An] XML processor is required to read only entities in the UTF-8 and UTF-16 encodings; it is recognized that other encodings are used around the world, and it may be desired for XML processors to read entities that use them." So, if you use any encoding other than UTF-8 or UTF-16, the particular processor that you are using may not recognize the "foreign" encoding and may result in strange output:

```
<?xml version="1.0" encoding="EUC-JP"?>
```

In this example, if your processor does not support the EUC-JP Japanese/UNIX encoding (and the computer with which you look at the output does not include a Japanese screen font), many garbage characters will appear on your screen.

TAKE NOTE

▶ DECLARING A NOTATION

In Chapter 10 you learn how to declare notations, which specify that a document includes some non-XML information that may not be valid to an XML parser. Notation specifies a formalized set of symbols or an alphabet (such as graphics, audio or other multimedia files, Java applets, and so on). A notation declaration states the notation name, which means that the notation can appear in entity declarations, attribute-list declarations, attribute specifications, and in some external identifiers. When an XML parser encounters notation information, it doesn't process it: it passes the information's location to the target application for processing.

CROSS-REFERENCE

In Chapter 27 you'll learn how to manipulate content: characters and words.

FIND IT ONLINE

Browse through European characters and scripts at **http://www.indigo.ie/egt/standards/mes.html.**

Table 4-5: SELECTED ENCODING NAMES FOR XML DOCUMENTS

Name	Character Set
US-ASCII	ASCII
ANSI_X3.4-1968	Same as US-ASCII
UTF-8	8-bit UCS transformation format
UTF-16	16- to 32-bit UCS transformation format
ISO-10646-UCS-2	ISO/IEC 10646 16-bit
ISO-10646-UCS-4	ISO/IEC 10646 31-bit
ISO-8859-1	ASCII and western European
ISO-8859-2	ASCII and central European
ISO-8859-3	ASCII and various European
ISO-8859-5	ASCII and Cyrillic
ISO-8859-6	ASCII and Arabic
ISO-8859-7	ASCII and Greek
ISO-8859-8	ASCII and Hebrew
ISO-8859-9	Latin-1 and some Turkish
ISO-8859-10	ASCII and Nordic
ISO-8859-11	ASCII and Thai
ISO-8859-12	ASCII and Celtic
ISO-8859-13	ASCII and some Baltic
ISO-8859-14	ASCII and Sami
ISO_5427	Cyrillic
ISO646-PT2	Portuguese
Big5	Chinese (Taiwan)
GB2312	Chinese (Mainland)
BS_4730	United Kingdom
Shift_JIS	Katakana, Kanji, and Windows
EUC-JP	Fixed-width Japanese and UNIX

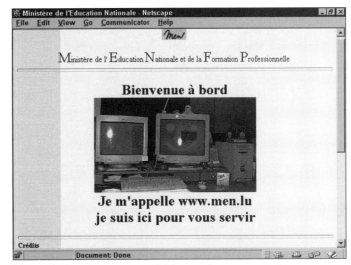

■ *This French government Web page demonstrates that a character set such as French — a Latin-based language — consists of familiar letters, which are supported by the default font.*

■ *This Japanese-language page has many missing characters (represented by rectangles) and incorrect characters (represented in Latin characters). That's because a Japanese font is not on the computer on which the page is displayed — not because the character set is incorrectly encoded.*

Personal Workbook

Q&A

1 What is the URL of the Unicode Consortium's home page?

_____

_____

_____

2 What is the name of the international XML-supported standard for character sets? What is its alternate name?

_____

_____

_____

3 What is the main difference between CDATA and #PCDATA?

_____

_____

_____

4 Name the URL of the Contents page at the Unicode site.

_____

_____

_____

5 What is *UTF-8*?

_____

_____

_____

6 What does *UCS* represent? What does *UTF* represent?

_____

_____

_____

7 Under UTF-8, how many bytes long are common ASCII characters? How many bytes long are non-ASCII characters?

_____

_____

_____

8 What production do you use to represent the name of an encoding?

_____

_____

_____

ANSWERS: PAGE 449

EXTRA PRACTICE

1. Go to the Unicode Consortium site and find the Combining Diacritical Marks code chart.

2. Locate the Unicode chart on which you can find the U+1E7A character.

3. What is the Unicode code for the lowercase letter *q*? (Hint: This is an ASCII character.)

4. At the Unicode site, learn about the history of the Consortium.

5. From the World Wide Web Consortium home page, jump to the Internationalization home page. Then browse through the other Internationalization pages.

6. Research bits and bytes. What do 7-bit, 8-bit, and 16-bit actually mean?

REAL-WORLD APPLICATIONS

✔ You are preparing a list of documents that your company distributes worldwide. Although the list is written in English, many document titles include letters with accents and other diacritical marks. Make sure that every title is completely accurate.

✔ For an algebra class that you are teaching, create an XML DTD that defines character references for the mathematical symbols and specifies appropriate elements for a test template.

✔ You are currently taking a German course, and you will have to write German-language papers. Explore the ways in which you can prepare XML documents in German.

Visual Quiz

This XML document is a DTD that lists 10 character references. Go to the Unicode Consortium site and identify each of the character references. Then write an XML document that includes all 10 characters.

_____

_____

_____

_____

```
charactersDTD - Notepad                    _ B X
File  Edit  Search  Help
<?xml version = "1.0"?>
<!DOCTYPE sampdoc [
<!ELEMENT sampdoc (#PCDATA)>
<!ENTITY symbol-0 "&#x0040;">
<!ENTITY symbol-1 "&#x00A1;">
<!ENTITY symbol-2 "&#x00A2;">
<!ENTITY symbol-3 "&#x00AE;">
<!ENTITY symbol-4 "&#x00A9;">
<!ENTITY symbol-5 "&#x00D8;">
<!ENTITY symbol-6 "&#x00F7;">
<!ENTITY symbol-7 "&#x00B6;">
<!ENTITY symbol-8 "&#x00A7;">
<!ENTITY symbol-9 "&#x01C1;">
]>
```

CHAPTER 5

MASTER THESE SKILLS

▶ Downloading and Installing XML Software

▶ Running XML Software

▶ Using an XML Editor

▶ Parsing an XML Document

▶ Styling an XML Document

An Overview of XML Software

In this chapter, you learn about the software that you can use to create, edit, parse, and style XML documents. Each task covers a particular category of software.

You can use XML editors to create and edit documents. Editing software ranges from simple editors that ensure that the resulting document will be well-formed (for example, that you enter pairs of elements that match) to sophisticated publishing systems that show you how your document will look as you type its contents and provide many extra tools with which you can enhance a document.

You can also use text editors and word processors to construct your documents.

XML parsers come in two varieties — those that check documents that are well-formed and those that validate documents. In this chapter, you'll get an overview of how to parse a document. You'll learn more about parsing an XML document in Chapter 11.

Typical XML documents collect and contain information and are not automatically formatted for output. Styling software helps you create style sheets with which you can format and enhance document output.

You can find links to software in several directories of XML information, including the following: SGML & XML Tools — Parsers and Engines (**http://www.infotek.no/sgmltool/sdk.htm**), SGML & XML Tools — By Tool Category (**http://www.infotek.no/sgmltool/products.htm**), James Tauber's XML INFORMATION: Software (**http://www.xmlinfo.com/**), XML Tools (**http://www.microsoft.com/xml/xmltools.asp**), Software (**http://www.megginson.com/Software/software.html**), Parser Central (**http://www.finetuning.com/parse.html**), Public SGML/XML Software (**http://www.sil.org/sgml/publicSW.html**), XML Software (**http://www.w3.org/xml/#software**), Free XML Software (**http://birk105.studby.uio.no/liner/XMLtool.html**), and The Whirlwind Guide to SGML Tools (**http://www.falch.no/people/pepper/sgmltool**).

Downloading and Installing XML Software

Most downloads involve finding the appropriate page, selecting a platform (for example, Windows, Mac, or UNIX), and clicking on a link or a Download button. After you specify the folder in which you want the program to be stored, simply wait for the executable (.EXE) or compressed (say, .ZIP) file to download completely.

Many programs, particularly commercial versions, prompt you through a series of dialog boxes that help you choose from various installation options. For example, in the early stages of installation, you may have to select the type of installation. The three common choices are

- ▶ **Default Installation:** This is usually the recommended choice; the installation program installs the application and selects the most appropriate options for most users. This selection may not install every available file.
- ▶ **Customized Installation:** If you are an experienced user, you can select the options or files that you want to install. This choice gives you control over every aspect of the installation.
- ▶ **Minimum Installation:** If you select this option, the installation program installs a minimum number of files. If you want to save space on your computer, choose this option.

You install a program in one of several ways. If you have downloaded a compressed file, you will have to "uncompress" it. Then, before installing the program, make sure that your operating system is completely installed and read through any minimum requirements to ensure that your computer is compatible with the software. In addition, close all active applications—especially virus-protection software.

To install a downloaded program using the Default installation on a Windows computer, follow these steps:

1. Find the executable file.
2. Click the Start button, select Run, and type *d:\folder\install* in the Open text box, where *d* represents the identifier of the drive and *folder* represents the folder in which the file is located. Click OK. The installation program displays a preliminary screen. Note that you can usually double-click on the name of the executable file to start the installation process.
3. Follow the prompts to move from screen to screen.

TAKE NOTE

▶ **ABIDING BY COPYRIGHTS**

Unless specifically stated, software programs are copyrighted. Copyright laws protect creative people from infringement of their work. To learn about U. S. copyright law and to link to related sites, go to the United States Copyright Office (**http://lcweb. loc.gov/copyright/**).

CROSS-REFERENCE

Chapter 6 helps you design DTDs for both single documents and document sets.

FIND IT ONLINE

An Introduction to XML (**http://www.ifi/uio.no/ ~larsga/download/xml/xml_eng.html**) covers XML and its features.

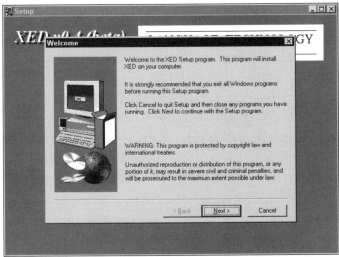

The first screen in a Windows installation program usually tells you
to close other Windows programs and click Next to continue.

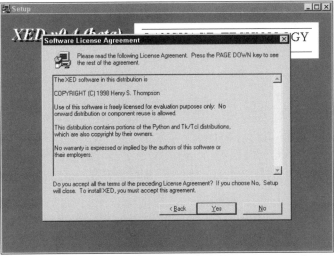

To protect the developer from copyright infringement, you often
have to agree to accept the terms of the software's License
Agreement. Click Yes to agree.

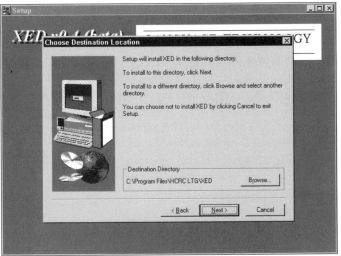

You can accept the suggested folder or directory, or click the
Browse button to choose a different folder or directory. After you
select, click Next to continue.

At the end of the installation, you often have the choice of
immediately starting the program or ending the installation.

Running XML Software

When you use XML software, it behaves like any other software. So, if you are *not* a novice, feel free to skip this task. If you are a beginner, read on.

You can start an XML program on a Windows computer in several ways:

► Click the Start button, select Programs, and select the appropriate name from the list of programs.

► Open the My Computer window or Windows Explorer, find the folder in which the application file is located, and double-click on the program's filename.

► Create a shortcut on the Desktop and then double-click on the shortcut icon.

Once you have started a Windows program, its *user interface* (the part of the program that you see on your computer screen) usually looks very much like another Windows program. For example, a typical Windows program has a title bar and menu bar at the top of the screen and a large area in which you can work. The title bar displays the name of the program and contains buttons with which you can resize the application window or exit the program. Most Windows menu bars display these familiar menu names: File, Edit, Options, and Help. With the File menu, you can create a new file, open an existing one, and so on, and exit the program. The Edit menu allows you to manipulate (usually copy, cut, paste, and such) the contents of the work area. The Options menu enables you to control the program (for example, set preferences and issue random commands).

A help system can vary from a single page of command references to an extensive number of pages with hypertext links to other pages. To get help, open the Help menu and select a Topics or Contents command. Then click or double-click on a topic or type a search keyword. You may have to browse through several topics to finally find the desired one.

Creating a Shortcut Icon

To create a shortcut icon on your Desktop, find the folder in which the application file is located. Select the application file and choose the Create Shortcut command from the File menu. Then drag the shortcut onto the Desktop.

You can quickly make a shortcut icon by dragging the application onto the Desktop. (This action makes a copy and does not actually move the original file.)

To edit the name below the shortcut icon, click twice slowly, and then edit as you would any filename. Note that if you click too quickly, Windows will think that you have double-clicked and will start the program.

CROSS-REFERENCE

Chapter 12 shows how to modify DTDs — both ones you create and those you download from the Web.

FIND IT ONLINE

At **http://www.venus.co.uk/omf/cml/doc/ tutorial/xml.html**, read a paper on XML and custom languages.

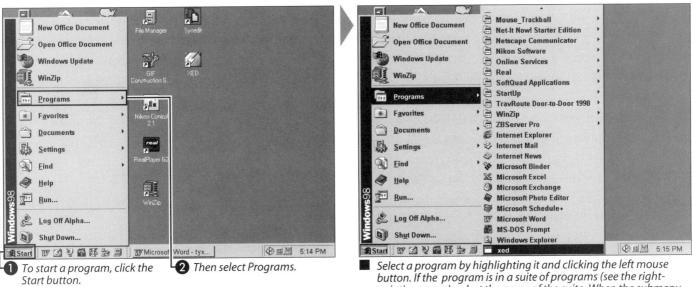

1 To start a program, click the Start button.

2 Then select Programs.

■ Select a program by highlighting it and clicking the left mouse button. If the program is in a suite of programs (see the right-pointing arrow), select the name of the suite. When the submenu opens, highlight the program and click.

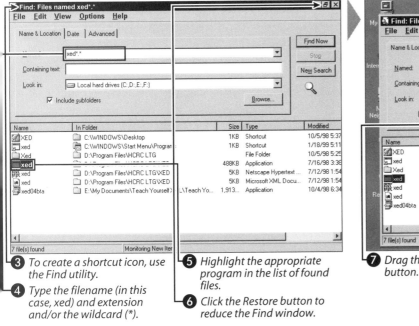

3 To create a shortcut icon, use the Find utility.

4 Type the filename (in this case, xed) and extension and/or the wildcard (*).

5 Highlight the appropriate program in the list of found files.

6 Click the Restore button to reduce the Find window.

7 Drag the program icon onto the Desktop and release the mouse button.

Using an XML Editor

You can create an XML document using a standard word processor or text editor, or you can use a program that is specially created to edit XML documents.

Creating an XML document using a word processor or text editor is similar to creating a standard word-processing document or text file. Simply start the program and start typing both XML markup and content. When you have finished, save the document as a text file or ASCII file. (If you save the document as a word-processing file, hidden formats will be built in and will result in odd characters here and there.) Don't worry about document format. To produce good-looking output, you'll use a style sheet, which is a separate document referred to in the XML document.

XML editors can be parts of suites or text editors dedicated to XML. For example, Adobe FrameMaker+SGML is a sophisticated commercial program that includes multiplatform publishing features and formatting and behaves like a full-featured word processor. Originally created for SGML documents, FrameMaker+SGML now supports XML and checks document validity as you enter content. When you work with FrameMaker+SGML, you won't see the underlying XML statements; as you enter information into the document, the program formats it so that you can see how the document will look when displayed onscreen or printed. You can also look at the structure of the document as you create it. You'll find trial versions of Frame Maker and SGHL on the CD-ROM bundled with this book.

In contrast, an editor such as the freeware XED shows the XML markup and content as you enter it; you cannot see the document's structure. When you type an element, XED automatically adds matching start tags and end tags to the document. As you enter markup and content, XED ensures that the document is well-formed.

Using XML DTD Editors

You can also use an editor to construct a DTD. For example, ezDTD (**http://www.geocities.com/ SiliconValley/Haven/2638/ezDTD.htm**) is a freeware Windows DTD editor whose work area has five main sections (Document, Heading, Elements, Parameter Entities, and Others). In each section, you'll find labeled text boxes that you fill in with the appropriate markup, letting ezDTD fill in the delimiters. ezDTD displays valid markup in color and invalid markup in black. After launching the program, you can use the File menu to create a file or open an existing file. Then fill in the text boxes, letting ezDTD fill in the delimiters. After you complete the DTD, you can save the file (with an .ezd extension) or you can export it to a file with a .dtd or .htm extension. Note that commercial suites of XML tools sometimes include DTD editors. The CD-ROM that is bundled with this book lists other DTD editors. For more information, see Appendix B.

CROSS-REFERENCE
Chapter 13 helps you construct an effective XML document, step by step.

FIND IT ONLINE
Extensible Markup Language (**http://www.qucis. queensu.ca/achallc97/papers/p050.html**) covers XML history.

An Overview of XML Software

Using an XML Editor

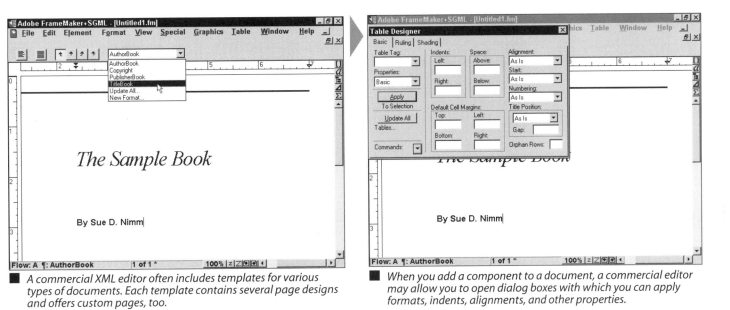

■ A commercial XML editor often includes templates for various types of documents. Each template contains several page designs and offers custom pages, too.

■ When you add a component to a document, a commercial editor may allow you to open dialog boxes with which you can apply formats, indents, alignments, and other properties.

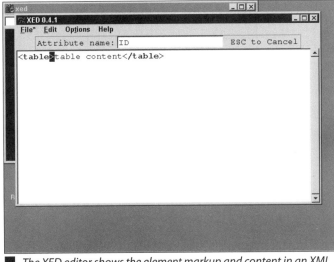

■ A freeware XML editor may allow you to customize the program with your preferences.

■ The XED editor shows the element markup and content in an XML document.

Parsing an XML Document

Parsing is the act of analyzing the text in a document, both markup and content, using the information in the document prolog as a guide. An XML parser locates the XML rules and encoding specified in the XML declaration and uses the information in the document type declaration to find a DTD (if one exists and if the document will be tested for validity) and other referred-to external files, such as style sheets. The parser ensures that a document follows the rules set in the DTD (if it is a validating parser) or makes sure the document is well-formed (if it is a nonvalidating parser).

The parser also creates an element tree that shows the root, its child elements, and other generations of elements. The parser is programmed to recognize the delimiters that mark the beginning and end of start and end tags and entities, and to process parsed character data or ignore character data. At the end of processing, the parser passes the interpreted document to a target application to create output after further processing and interpretation of elements, entities, attributes, and so on. Output can include printed material, Web pages, and even information stored for processing by other programs.

The previous paragraph points out the importance of DTDs. Without a DTD to define markup, the parser and target application can only go so far in interpreting a document. For example, if an XML processor encounters an element named <RULE>, it has no way of understanding the meaning of the element. Will the contents of the element eventually be formatted as a horizontal rule or as the text of a regulation?

As you read through the remaining chapters, you'll see examples of XML parsers at work.

Browsing XML Documents

Browsers that support XML are in short supply because XML is in the early stages of development. The current XML browser is JUMBO (Java Universal Molecular or Markup Browser for Objects), which was developed to read documents written in the Chemistry Markup Language (CML). You can use JUMBO (whose home page is at **http://www. vsms.nottingham.ac.uk/vsms/java/jumbo**) as a standalone browser or as a set of applets running under Netscape Navigator or Internet Explorer. You can also use it as an XML parser, and it supports XSL style sheets.

Another browser that supports XML is Amaya (**http://www.w3.org/Amaya/User/BinDist.html**), from the World Wide Web Consortium. Amaya is an HTML browser that can read documents written in the Mathematical Markup Language (MathML). Plume (**http://www.zveno.com/**) is another Web browser that supports XML. In addition, Microsoft Internet Explorer (**http://www.microsoft.com/ie/**) supports XML, and Netscape (**http://home. netscape.com/**) has announced that the upcoming version of Netscape Navigator (v. 5.0) will support XML. To check on the progress of this software, go to **http://www.mozilla.org/**.

CROSS-REFERENCE

Part IV teaches you how to create XML documents with functional links.

FIND IT ONLINE

XML Hacking is Fun (**http://www.w3.org/XML/ 9705/hacking.html**), by Dan Connolly, discusses creating XML parsers.

Listing 5-1: A BADLY NESTED XML DOCUMENT AND PARSING ERRORS

```
<?xml version = "1.0"?>
<text size="12">
    <boldface>
        <italics>
            Watch this space!
        </boldface>
        <picture/>
    </italics>
</text>
```

```
c:\lark>jview
  Driver c:\xmlsamp\badnest.xml
Hello Tim
Lark V1.0 final beta Copyright © 1997-98
Tim Bray.
 All rights reserved; the right to use
 these class files for any purpose
 is hereby granted to everyone.
Parsing...
Lark:c:\xmlsamp\badnest.xml:8:13:E:Fatal:
Encountered </boldface> expected </italics>
...assumed </italics>
Lark:c:\xmlsamp\badnest.xml:8:13:E:Fatal:
Encountered </italics> with no start tag.
Done.
```

❶ *The boldface end tag occurs before* `</italics>`.
❷ *Start lark and enter a command line.*
❸ *The parser finds* `</italics>` *instead of* `</boldface>`.
❹ *The parser also does not recognize the* `<italics>` *start tag.*

Listing 5-2: A VALID XML DOCUMENT AND ITS PARSING RESULTS

```
<?xml version = "1.0"?>
<!DOCTYPE ANNOUNCE [
<!ELEMENT ANNOUNCE (FROM, BODY)>
<!ELEMENT FROM     (#PCDATA)>
<!ELEMENT BODY     (#PCDATA)>]>
<ANNOUNCE>
<FROM>Tess Curtis</FROM>
<BODY>
The first planning session for the
Christmas party will take place on Friday
at 2 PM. See you there.
</BODY></ANNOUNCE>
```

```
c:\xml4j> jre -cp xml4j_1_1_9.jar;
xml4jSamples_1_1_9.jar samples.XJParse
.XJParse -d c:\XMLSamp\valid3.xml
<?xml version = "1.0"?>
<!DOCTYPE ANNOUNCE [
<!ELEMENT ANNOUNCE (FROM, BODY)>
<!ELEMENT FROM     (#PCDATA)>
<!ELEMENT BODY     (#PCDATA)>]>
<ANNOUNCE>
<FROM>Tess Curtis</FROM>
<BODY>
The first planning session for the
Christmas party will take place on Friday
at 2 PM. See you there.
</BODY></ANNOUNCE>
```

❶ *A valid XML document must include a DTD.*
❷ *Start XML for Java and enter a command line.*
❸ *The parser processes the DTD and document and finds no errors.*

Styling an XML Document

If you have developed HTML documents, you know that certain formats are built into the standard. For example, you can use the `<B>` element to apply boldface and `<U>` to underline selected text. When you create XML documents, you can add formatting attributes. However, the trend in both HTML and XML is moving toward using attached style sheets to format and enhance selected text.

Those of us who have used computers for many years — especially for processing words and documents — are familiar with style sheets, which are used to define *rules* (formats and enhancements) for selected text, paragraphs, or entire documents. On May 5, 1996, the World Wide Web Consortium (W3C) announced *cascading style sheets* (CSS), which are sets of document style sheets that enable XML (and HTML) developers to change a document's format and look — just as they would change a word-processing document. You can attach multiple cascading style sheets to a single document and define several styles for a single element. Currently, some browsers support style sheets — completely or partially — while many other browsers will support style sheets soon.

To create a style sheet for an XML document, you can either enter the commands via a text editor or use styling software that automates some of the functions. XML Styler, from ArborText, is an example of a styling application. This program leads you through the development of an Extensible Stylesheet Language (XSL) style sheet, with an emphasis on the tree structure of the elements. With XML Styler, you can create one or more styles for a particular element. Other software, such as Adobe FrameMaker+SGML, implicitly styles a document as you enter it. FrameMaker+SGML includes templates for various types of documents. In addition, you can use the commands on the Format menu to apply custom formats and enhancements without ever seeing a style sheet. Appendix B lists the styling software that is included on the CD-ROM bundled with this book.

TAKE NOTE

DEVELOPING XSL

The Extensible Stylesheet Language (XSL) Version 1.0 is under development at the World Wide Web Consortium. XSL, which is being designed to style XML documents, uses an XML-like language. For more information about XSL, refer to Chapter 30.

LEARNING ABOUT WORD-PROCESSOR STYLE SHEETS

All word-processing programs format paragraph and character output using style sheets. Each program has a default style sheet that automatically applies predefined formats to all new documents, their paragraphs, and text. For example, in Microsoft Word for Windows, the default is called *Normal*; its predefined formats include a Normal font (Times New Roman) a 10-point font size, and a default paragraph that is left-aligned and single-spaced. Users can also define custom style sheets.

CROSS-REFERENCE

Part V teaches you how to style pages, page elements, lists, tables, and text.

FIND IT ONLINE

Extensible Markup Language JumpStart (**http://www.jeremie.com/JS/XML/all.html**) is a table of XML links.

Listing 5-3: A SAMPLE DTD AND A RELATED CSS STYLE SHEET

```
<?xml version="1.0"?>
<!DOCTYPE MEMO [
<!ELEMENT MEMO (TO, FROM, SUBJECT, BODY)>
<!ELEMENT TO        (#PCDATA)>
<!ELEMENT FROM      (#PCDATA)>
<!ELEMENT SUBJECT (#PCDATA)>
<!ELEMENT BODY      (#PCDATA)>

]>
```

➊

```
<!doctype style-sheet
  SYSTEM "-//Sandra Eddy//DTD
  CSS Style Sheet//EN">
```

➋

➌

```
MEMO
      { font-family: "Times New Roman",
        "Book Antigua", serif;
        font-size: 12pt;
        background-color: silver;
        color: navy;
        margin: 1in;
        border-top: block solid medium;
        border-bottom: block solid medium }
```

```
TO, FROM, SUBJECT
      { font-family: "Helvetica",
        sans-serif;
        font-size: 14pt;
        font-weight: bold }
```

➍

➊ Declare the elements of a memorandum.
➋ Declare the style-sheet document type.
➌ Set styles for the entire memo.
➍ Define specific styles for the TO, FROM, and SUBJECT elements.

Listing 5-4: A SAMPLE XSL STYLESHEET

```
<xsl:stylesheet>   ➊
  xmlns:xsl="http://www.w3.org/TR/WD-xsl"
  xmlns:fo="http://www.w3.org/TR/WD-xsl/FO"
  result-ns="fo">
<!-- A pattern identifies a source
            element. -->
    <xsl:template match= "redtext">   ➋

    <!-- The action identifies a paragraph
            formatting object. -->
  <fo:block-level-box>   ➌
    <fo:block color="red">
      <xsl:apply-templates/>
    </fo:block>
  </fo:block-level-box>
</xsl:stylesheet>   ➍
```

➊ Begin the stylesheet with this start tag.
➋ Match the redtext element.
➌ Style the matched element (formatting object) in a block format.
➍ Conclude the stylesheet with this end tag.

Personal Workbook

Q&A

1 What steps do you take to download a program?

_____

_____

_____

2 What are the three common installation options?

_____

_____

_____

3 If you download a file with a .ZIP extension, what do you have to do to it?

_____

_____

_____

4 What U.S. government office provides information on copyright laws? What is the URL of its Web site?

_____

_____

_____

5 What are the three common ways of starting a program?

_____

_____

_____

6 How do you get help in learning about a program?

_____

_____

_____

7 What types of software can you use to create an XML document?

_____

_____

_____

8 What is _parsing_?

_____

_____

_____

ANSWERS: PAGE 451

EXTRA PRACTICE

1 Using a directory of XML tools, find an XML editor, and then download and install it.

2 Start the XML editor that you just installed. Either open a sample document (if one is provided) or create a document.

3 Save the document using a unique name. (Hint: Find the Save As command.)

4 In the XML editor, open the help menu and find out about the program's version number and copyright information. (Hint: Use the About command.)

5 From the XML editor's help window, get information about commands.

6 In the XML editor, open the File menu and exit the program.

REAL-WORLD APPLICATIONS

✔ You are in charge of training a staff that will produce all of your company's XML documents. Write a user's guide that covers starting, using, and exiting each of the programs that the staff will use.

✔ For the previous application, prepare a compact command reference guide.

✔ Your company or department will use a commercial suite of XML programs and tools for all of its business documents. Design a system of folders and subfolders under which your work will be organized.

✔ Your company or department has assigned you to evaluate XML software. Decide whether it's best to use a commercial developer's suite of programs or individual shareware or freeware programs.

Visual Quiz

This is a typical Adobe FrameMaker+SGML application window. Identify each of the following elements: title bar, work area, and menu bar. Identify the two buttons that resize the application window and the button that closes the application. Name the menu under which you will find a command that saves files. In what drive will you find the program files for FrameMaker+SGML?

_____

_____

_____

PART

II

Working with DTDs

In this part, we focus on document type definitions (DTDs), which represent the main difference between well-formed and valid XML documents. Using a DTD, you define the elements, attributes, entities, notation, and other components that make up the structure, content, and format of one or more valid XML documents.

In Chapter 2, you learned that a DTD comes in two flavors: an internal subset (embedded in the prolog of an XML document) and an external subset (a separate document). An external DTD is actually an XML document that follows the guidelines with which you set up any XML document. However, an external DTD sets the rules under which you construct other XML documents. In contrast, "non-DTD" documents combine markup and XML text to produce displayed or printed output or information exported to programs. The only way to define elements and other components for a set of XML documents is to use an external DTD. An internal DTD can only set the rules for the document in which it is located.

In the next seven chapters, you learn how to plan DTDs — for a single document or for a document set — and find out how to construct them, component by component.

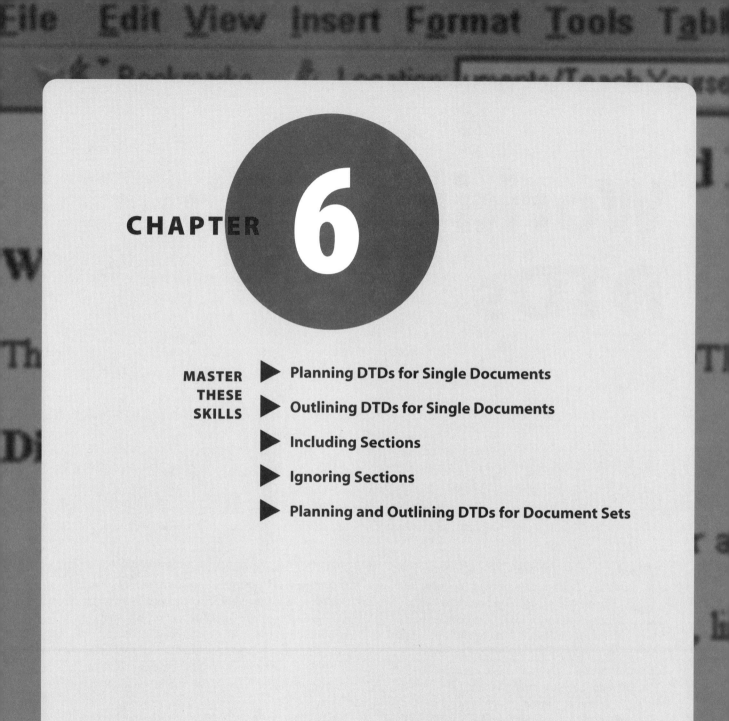

CHAPTER 6

MASTER THESE SKILLS

▶ Planning DTDs for Single Documents

▶ Outlining DTDs for Single Documents

▶ Including Sections

▶ Ignoring Sections

▶ Planning and Outlining DTDs for Document Sets

Planning a DTD

The first five chapters of this book introduced you to XML's various components in a rather generalized way. This chapter is the first to touch on the finer points of a particular part of XML — how to plan a DTD for one document or an entire document set. A DTD gives a document or set of documents their identity; using a DTD, you can not only define components, but also specify how they behave and set limits.

Every version of HTML is associated with a predefined DTD. In many ways, HTML's DTD is a compromise that has had input from many sources — from highly technical programmers to Web writers and editors. Examples of this accommodation to various interests include alternate ways of formatting selected text as quotes (<BLOCKQUOTE> and <Q>) and of italicizing selected text (<I> and <EM>, if the current browser interprets <EM> by using italics).

When you use XML, you start with a blank slate: You can plan, design, and define your own custom DTD. This means that you can specify just one element for italics. If you seldom use quotations, you can omit explicit quotation elements and use your italics element instead.

If you're part of an industry with a unique vocabulary, you can go a step further and define elements that are counterparts to industry terms. You can also specify a set of entities as shortcuts to long technical terms or even company names (for detailed information, see Chapter 10).

Using one custom XML DTD, you can set standards for classes of documents within your organization. This means that all memoranda, for instance, will have the same look — regardless of the author. If your Web pages are the responsibility of a workgroup, your custom DTD can compel each group member to use particular document parts in a particular order — for example, starting with a certain level heading, following with an introductory paragraph and several paragraphs of body text, and concluding with links to the prior page, home page, and following page.

Planning DTDs for Single Documents

All internal DTD subsets and selected external DTD subsets are suitable for use for a single XML document. In fact, if you define an internal DTD subset, it *must* be used for the document in which it is enclosed; it cannot define elements, attributes, entities, and so on for other documents. Use external DTD subsets to define components of both individual documents and sets of documents.

As you have learned, a DTD formally defines all the rules that control a document. DTDs enable you — indeed, encourage you — to design well-organized, valid XML documents that will stand the test of time. In contrast, if you slap together a document and create its DTD as an afterthought, errors are bound to happen.

Designing a DTD requires a certain amount of planning. For example, you must decide on the structure, content, and formats of the future document and evaluate one or more applications that will control the output.

Try to think of every possible component of the document that you will write, and try to specify an appropriate set of elements. But don't stop at elements. Consider entities, for instance: If a regularly used company name is long and difficult to type, specify an entity that allows you to use a shortcut name to refer to the longer name.

You can specify the order in which elements are used in a document. For example, a long document may be composed of a title page, preface, table of contents, several chapters, one or two appendixes, and an index. In a DTD, you can list elements in a certain order and make sure that they are used in that order, thereby preventing an appendix from being nested between two chapters.

You should design your DTDs to be understood. When you name elements, attributes, and so on, be sure that you use names that are discernible. You can call plain-vanilla paragraphs `<P>` (to conform to HTML, if you are accustomed to that standard), `<PARA>`, or even `<PARAGRAPH>`. Or you can name a bulleted list `<BUL_LIST>`, `<B-LIST>`, or `<BUL-LETED_LIST>`. The clearer a name, the better it will be to others who will use or edit the DTD in the future.

If you think that a particular line of a DTD will be obscure, it's easy to insert a comment. You can also use comments to separate parts of a DTD from others. You'll learn about how to insert comments in the next chapter.

CROSS-REFERENCE

Chapter 2 introduces you to valid documents and both types of DTDs — internal and external DTD subsets.

FIND IT ONLINE

XML Activity (**http://www.w3.org/XML/Activity.html**) enables you to keep up to date with XML.

Asking the Right Questions

Before you make the first declaration in a DTD, ask yourself the following questions:

▶ What is the purpose of this document? Will it be output on a computer screen or on paper? Will it be output to an intermediate application?

▶ What information will the XML parser need to successfully process this document?

▶ What will this document's tree of elements look like? How many generations of elements will be required?

▶ What kind of content will this document have? Will the document contain much more text than graphics?

▶ How will you format and enhance various components of the document? Will you use the DTD to define styles, or will you use a style sheet?

▶ How should each defined element behave? Are you going to provide a list of values from which to choose? Will you require the use of certain elements and make others optional? Will you require that some elements be entered in a particular order?

▶ What types of entities will you define? Will some entities be used to specify shortcuts for technical terms, company names, or regularly used terms? Will you use other entities to refer to certain characters (such as accented letters, and so on) by "nicknames"?

Listing 6-1: TYPICAL COMPONENTS OF A MANUAL

```
Read Me First ◀❶
Title Page
    Book Title ◀❷
    Author's Name
Copyright Page
Table of Contents
Introduction
Chapters ◀❸
    Chapter Title
    Introduction
    Sections
    Figures
    Summary
Appendixes
Glossary ◀❹
    Terms
    Descriptions
Index
```

❶ *A Read Me First section points the buyer to important information.*

❷ *You can force the Book Title to come before the Author's Name.*

❸ *You can allow a user to write any number of chapters.*

❹ *The Glossary contains a list of terms and descriptions.*

Outlining a DTD for Single Documents

The best way to outline a DTD is to enter the highest-level components first. Then, fill in components for the next level down, the level below that, and so on. For example, in the manual example illustrated in the last task, the Read Me First, Title, Copyright, Table of Contents, Introduction, Chapters, Appendixes, Glossary, and Index pages are all at the highest level. The second-level elements are indented under the highest-level components.

To decide if a component is indeed a top-level component, ask yourself whether any other component is at a higher level. For example, in most books, a chapter is at the highest level: no other component comes between a chapter and the entire book. However, some larger books consist of parts under which sets of chapters are organized. (See Listing 6-2 on the facing page.) When you insert a new top-level component, you may have to move some components down a level.

After you set the highest-level components in place, you should consider each of them. How many components will become children? Looking at the manual example, you can see that each chapter consists of a chapter title, introduction, several sections, figures spotted throughout, and a summary. How many of these items should occur in a particular order?

Determine components that may not be children. For example, if you want to restrict figures to chapters, they may be children of chapters. However, if you place figures in other locations within the book, you may want to move them to a higher level.

Continue to evaluate components and add more children as needed. Table 6-1 lists some of the declarations that can or must be included in a DTD. Note that boldface in the example column indicates the applicable part.

You may be inclined to reduce the number of components and have some of them serve more than one purpose (such as using one element for all the body text, whether it's an italicized introduction paragraph or a bulleted summary). If you do this, make sure that all of these components are styled identically. If you overuse a particular component, you may have to insert styles in certain parts of the document. This means that you may defeat the purpose of spending extra time organizing the DTD and ensuring that all the pieces of the document are properly defined.

TAKE NOTE

EVALUATING XML OUTPUT

Those who tend to equate XML with HTML don't realize one special benefit of working with XML: its output is not restricted to onscreen displays and printed pages. Using XML, you can write documents that produce output that you'll never see — the information is sent to an intermediate program for further processing. For example, you can load fields into a database, or send information to a program that converts text to audio, updates an inventory system, or even controls the behavior of a metal-working machine or robot.

CROSS-REFERENCE

Chapter 3 discusses the Extended Backus-Naur Form, with which you "code" DTDs.

FIND IT ONLINE

Read about markup languages, HTML, and XML at http://www.cs.caltech.edu/~adam/papers/xml/ascent-of-xml.html.

Table 6-1: SELECT XML DECLARATION PRODUCTIONS

Production Name	Declares:	Example (boldface marks the component)
XMLDecl	An XML document	**<?xml version="1.0"?>**
doctypedecl	A document's type	**<!DOCTYPE manual [**
extSubsetDecl	An external subset	<!DOCTYPE tst **SYSTEM "tst.dtd">**
SDDecl	A standalone document	<?xml version="1.0" **standalone="yes"?>**
elementdecl	An element type	**<!ELEMENT hello (#PCDATA)>**
AttlistDecl	An element's list of attributes	**<!ATTLIST text id ID #REQUIRED>**
EntityDecl	A general or parameter entity	**<!ENTITY egi "Eddy Group, Inc.">**
PEDecl	A parameter entity	**<!ENTITY % chap01 SYSTEM "chap01.doc">**
NDataDecl	An unparsed external entity	**<!ENTITY fimg SYSTEM "fish.gif" NDATA gif>**
TextDecl	Information about an external parsed entity	**<?xml version="1.0" encoding="UTF-8"?>**
EncodingDecl	An encoding name	<?xml version="1.0" **encoding="UTF-8"?>**

Listing 6-2: ADDING A HIGHER-LEVEL COMPONENT

Read Me First
Title Page
  Book Title
  Author's Name
Copyright Page
Table of Contents
Introduction
Parts
  Part Introduction
  Chapters
    Chapter Title
    Introduction
    Sections
    Figures
    Summary
Appendixes
Glossary
  Terms
  Descriptions
Index

▲ *When you add a higher-level component (such as* Parts*), elements that are newly defined as child elements (see* Chapters*) are further indented.*

Including Sections

You can create sections in a document type declaration and then explicitly include or exclude their contents. In the XML specification, these are known as conditional sections. According to the specification, "conditional sections are portions of the [DTD] external subset which are included in, or excluded from, the logical structure of the DTD based on the keyword which governs them." A conditional section can be made up of a variety of components — declarations, processing instructions, comments, and other conditional sections. As you can see on the next page, conditional sections can have one of two keywords: INCLUDE indicates that the section is included in the DTD (that is, an XML parser will process its contents); IGNORE indicates that the section is not presently part of the DTD. By changing these single keywords, you can activate or inactivate an entire section. Note that the parser reads through both types of sections to determine the section start and section end.

An XML parser processes only INCLUDE sections. Remember that conditional sections can include other conditional sections. This means that an INCLUDE section can contain an IGNORE section and vice versa. If an IGNORE section encloses an INCLUDE section, both sections are ignored.

The examples on the facing page both contain INCLUDE and IGNORE sections that define elements for a paper. In the first example, the INCLUDE section consists of three elements, and the IGNORE section adds a new element. A writer or editor testing the

document might want to parse the document without the newly developed ABSTRACT element and then switch the INCLUDE and IGNORE keywords, thereby including the ABSTRACT element, its child elements, and its contents in processing. If the first version of the document "passes" the parser test and the second does not, the writer or editor can concentrate on correcting the ABSTRACT element, its child elements, and contents.

In the second example, the INCLUDE section allows the members of a team developing a document to enter comments throughout the document. The other elements (INTRO, ABSTRACT, BODY, and APPENDIX) must be entered in a particular order. When the INCLUDE and IGNORE section keywords are switched for the final draft, the COMMENTS element has disappeared: No comments are allowed. Note the addition of the INDEX element. An index should not be added until the document is at or near the final draft.

TAKE NOTE

MIXING CONDITIONAL SECTIONS AND PARAMETER-ENTITY REFERENCES

You can use parameter-entity references to identify and process particular conditional sections. Thus, if a conditional section's keyword (INCLUDE or IGNORE) is a parameter-entity reference, an XML processor should replace the section's content — as it would any parameter-entity reference — before processing the section. For more information about parameter-entity references, refer to Chapter 10.

CROSS-REFERENCE

Chapter 7, which covers the first steps in creating a DTD, emphasizes the contents of the prolog.

FIND IT ONLINE

XML Tutorials (http://www.hypermedic.com/style/xml/xmlindex.htm) contains tutorial and other links.

XML 1.0: THE CONDITIONAL SECTION PRODUCTIONS

```
[61]    conditionalSect ::= includeSect | ignoreSect  ←❶
[62]       includeSect ::= '<![' S? 'INCLUDE' S? '[' extSubsetDecl ']]>'
                        ❷
[63]        ignoreSect ::= '<![' S? 'IGNORE' S? '[' ignoreSectContents* ']]>'
[64] ignoreSectContents ::= Ignore ('<![' ignoreSectContents ']]>' Ignore)*
[65]            Ignore ::= Char* - (Char* ('<![' | ']]>') Char*)
```

❶ *A conditional section can be either an* INCLUDE *or* IGNORE *section.*
❷ *Start either type of section with the* <![*string.*
❸ *End either section with the*]]> *string.*

Listing 6-3: AN INCLUDE-IGNORE EXAMPLE

```
<![INCLUDE[
<!ELEMENT THISWAY (INTRO,BODY,APPENDIX)>
   <!ELEMENT INTRO (#PCDATA)>
   <!ELEMENT BODY (#PCDATA)>
   <!ELEMENT APPENDIX (#PCDATA)>
]]>
<![IGNORE[
<!ELEMENT THATWAY
(INTRO,ABSTRACT,BODY,APPENDIX)>
   <!ELEMENT INTRO (#PCDATA)>
   <!ELEMENT ABSTRACT (#PCDATA)>
   <!ELEMENT BODY (#PCDATA)>
   <!ELEMENT APPENDIX (#PCDATA)>
]]>
```

▲ *Both sections contain identical element declarations, but the* IGNORE *section adds the* ABSTRACT *element, which might be used to summarize a document.*

Listing 6-4: ANOTHER INCLUDE-IGNORE EXAMPLE

```
<![INCLUDE[
<!ELEMENT DRAFT
(COMMENTS|(INTRO,ABSTRACT,BODY,APPENDIX))>
   <!ELEMENT COMMENTS (#PCDATA)>
   <!ELEMENT INTRO (#PCDATA)>
   <!ELEMENT ABSTRACT (#PCDATA)>
   <!ELEMENT BODY (#PCDATA)>
   <!ELEMENT APPENDIX (#PCDATA)>
]]>
<![IGNORE[
<!ELEMENT FINAL
(INTRO,ABSTRACT,BODY,APPENDIX,INDEX)>
   <!ELEMENT INTRO (#PCDATA)>
   <!ELEMENT ABSTRACT (#PCDATA)>
   <!ELEMENT BODY (#PCDATA)>
   <!ELEMENT APPENDIX (#PCDATA)>
   <!ELEMENT INDEX (#PCDATA)>
]]>
```

▲ *In the* DRAFT *section, you can insert comments throughout the document. The* FINAL *section does not allow comments but adds an* INDEX *element.*

Ignoring Sections

Why would you use IGNORE sections? You can use them when you test a DTD — especially a very long and/or complex one. As you edit the DTD, enclose one part at a time (or several parts) within an IGNORE section. After the DTD parses cleanly, move the IGNORE delimiters to another part of the DTD and reparse. When the parser shows that every part of the DTD is valid, remove the IGNORE section altogether. This technique is also useful for SGML or XML DTDs that you are adapting, or for multiple DTDs that you are combining into one.

Another reason for using INCLUDE and IGNORE sections in a DTD is to produce successive drafts of a document. Using INCLUDE and IGNORE sections, you can add or remove elements for different versions of the document. The examples on the previous page demonstrate the addition and deletion of elements.

You can also modify the attributes elements as a document progresses from the first draft through the final version. For example, when a writer submits an early draft of a book manuscript, he or she usually increases the size of body text to 12 points and double-spaces lines so that others can read and mark up the draft more easily. After editing is complete and the final draft is due, the writer may reduce the font size to 10 points and make the lines single-spaced. So, when a first draft is underway, the writer may enclose first-draft elements and attributes within an

INCLUDE section and final-draft elements and attributes within an IGNORE section. In the final draft, all the writer has to do is switch the INCLUDE and IGNORE keywords and section delimiters. The first example on the facing page shows an INCLUDE section for a draft and an IGNORE section for the final version of a document. Note that you can accomplish the same purpose by using alternate style sheets. For more information about using style sheets for XML documents, see Part V.

TAKE NOTE

▶ USING OTHER SECTIONS IN AN XML DOCUMENT

In a non-DTD XML document, the counterpart of the INCLUDE and IGNORE sections is a CDATA section. These sections, which start with the string <![CDATA[and end with the]]> string, treat markup as character data: A parser reads the contents of the section (and recognizes the purpose of the start and end strings) but doesn't process the section. And if you insert]]> within the section, the parser will consider it a string — not markup. You cannot nest CDATA sections.

▶ USING CONDITIONAL SECTIONS IN SGML

SGML also supports INCLUDE and IGNORE sections. However, SGML does not limit conditional sections to the DTD; you can use them in any part of a document.

CROSS-REFERENCE

In Chapter 8, you learn how to declare root and child elements and specify their content.

FIND IT ONLINE

Browse through an introduction to SGML DTDs at **http://www.livepage.com/lpdocs/sgmled/ .node-6602**.

Listing 6-5: IGNORING AND INCLUDING DOCUMENT DRAFTS

```
<![INCLUDE[
<!ELEMENT DRAFT (HEADING|BODYTEXT)>
<!ELEMENT HEADING (#PCDATA)>
   <!ATTLIST HEADING
       fontsize    CDATA #FIXED "14pt"
       linespacing CDATA #FIXED "12pt">
<!ELEMENT BODYTEXT (#PCDATA)>
   <!ATTLIST BODYTEXT
       fontsize    CDATA #FIXED "12pt"
       linespacing CDATA #FIXED "12pt">
]]>
<![IGNORE[
<!ELEMENT FINAL (HEADING|BODYTEXT)>
<!ELEMENT HEADING (#PCDATA)>
   <!ATTLIST HEADING
       fontsize    CDATA #FIXED "12pt"
       linespacing CDATA #FIXED "6pt">
<!ELEMENT BODYTEXT (#PCDATA)>
   <!ATTLIST BODYTEXT
       fontsize    CDATA #FIXED "10pt"
       linespacing CDATA #FIXED "6pt">
]]>
```

▲ *This segment of a DTD changes the font size and line spacing for a first draft and for a final version of a document.*

Listing 6-6: INCLUDING AND IGNORING PARAMETER ENTITIES

```
<!ENTITY % hello   "INCLUDE" >
<!ENTITY % goodbye "IGNORE" >
<![%hello; [
<!ELEMENT histate (#PCDATA)>]]>
<![%goodbye; [
<!ELEMENT byestate (#PCDATA)>]]>
```

▲ *This example contains* INCLUDE *and* IGNORE *sections with parameter-entity references. The* INCLUDE *section contains an element named* histate, *and the* IGNORE *section contains the* byestate *element.*

Listing 6-7: AN IMPLICIT INCLUDE SECTION

```
<!ELEMENT DRAFT
(COMMENTS|(INTRO,ABSTRACT,BODY))>
   <!ELEMENT COMMENTS (#PCDATA)>
   <!ELEMENT INTRO (#PCDATA)>
   <!ELEMENT ABSTRACT (#PCDATA)>
   <!ELEMENT BODY (#PCDATA)>
<![IGNORE[
<!ELEMENT FINAL
(INTRO,ABSTRACT,BODY,INDEX)>
   <!ELEMENT INTRO (#PCDATA)>
   <!ELEMENT ABSTRACT (#PCDATA)>
   <!ELEMENT BODY (#PCDATA)>
   <!ELEMENT INDEX (#PCDATA)>]]>
```

▲ *An* INCLUDE *section is always processed, so you can choose to remove its start and end delimiters — unless you have another reason to mark the section. (See the following example.)*

Listing 6-8: IGNORING AND INCLUDING AN ENTIRE DTD

```
<?xml version = "1.0" standalone="yes"?>
<!ENTITY % everything "IGNORE">
<![ %everything;
   <!DOCTYPE sampdoc [
   <!ELEMENT sampdoc (#PCDATA)>
   <!ENTITY fwi "Flammis Widgets, Inc.">
   ]>
   <sampdoc>Add parsed character data here!
   </sampdoc>
]]>
```

▲ *You can ignore an entire DTD by using a parameter-entity reference. To include the DTD, simply change the keyword from* IGNORE *to* INCLUDE.

Planning and Outlining DTDs for Document Sets

There are two main differences between creating DTDs for individual documents and for sets of documents: You should spend more time planning standards for the document sets, and must ensure that elements and other document components work for all the documents in the set.

Document standards are rules that control the structure, content, and formats of individual documents in a set. For example, all the business letters for a business or department use the same letterhead, paper and envelope styles; include the corporate logo in a particular place within the letterhead or elsewhere on the page; use the same font, font sizes, and margin settings; have the same numbering style for the pages after the first; and so on. And all Web pages might contain a black title and black text; red active links to the home page, previous page, following page, and a central e-mail address; left-aligned graphics surrounded by a blue border; and more. Standards should be developed, maintained, and improved by a committee of managers, XML developers, writers, designers, and artists. Those setting the standards should address every detail of a document type but allow a little latitude for individual creativity.

After developing a robust set of standards for a document type, the DTD developers should take over. They should design elements, attributes, entities, and such that echo every part of the standards.

For example, if the document type (say, a report) consists of a cover page, table of contents, three levels of headings, standard body text, and figures with captions, elements should completely echo that structure and follow the order of document elements. Where a document developer must use a particular value for an element, no other values should be offered. On the other hand, if there are several available choices, the DTD should list them. Of course, if the developers find an incompatibility between the standards and the DTD, they should consult with the standards committee and find a mutually agreeable solution.

Setting document standards will save a company or department both time and money. Once a standard is set for a particular document type, there is no need to go back and redesign it from scratch. Writers and editors can simply use the DTD as a template and fill in the blanks.

Using a Single DTD for All Types of Documents

If you decide to use an all-purpose DTD to develop all types of documents — from memos to business plans — parsing time may increase precipitously: Your XML processor will be forced to go through lines of markup that do not apply to a particular document. Note that maintaining a large DTD is also very time-consuming.

CROSS-REFERENCE

Chapter 12 discusses how to find an XML or SGML DTD, and then modify it to suit the current document or document set.

FIND IT ONLINE

Read a long paper on SGML DTD structure at **http://etext.virginia.edu/bin/ tei-tocs?div=DIV1&id=ST.**

Planning a Document Type

When standardizing a document type, consider the following questions:

- ▶ How many heading levels are required?
- ▶ What size margins are needed on all four sides of the page?
- ▶ Will the first page of the document be different from the remaining pages?
- ▶ Will all the headers and footers be the same for all the pages? For all but the first page? For the odd-numbered pages? For the even-numbered pages? What content will you include in headers? In footers?
- ▶ How will you style page numbers? Will the page number appear on the first page? Will page numbers be continuous, or will they restart at the beginning of a document part? Will you precede page numbers with chapter or section numbers?
- ▶ How will text be aligned? (Your choices are left-aligned, centered, right-aligned, and justified.)
- ▶ How will you present figures and other graphics? Will you choose a default height and width? Will graphics be surrounded by a border? Will they be numbered? Where will the caption be located? Will you include a table of figures at the front of the document?
- ▶ How will you present tables? Will you choose a default height and width? Will tables be surrounded by a border? Will they be numbered? Where will the caption be located? Will you include a table of tables at the front of the document?

- ▶ Will you require a table of contents? An index? How will you format them?
- ▶ Will you include footnotes and/or endnotes? What numbering format will you use? Will numbering be continuous, or will numbers restart at the beginning of a chapter or section?

Checking the Review Cycle

Whether your workgroup is setting standards or producing a document, the most efficient way of completing a task is to develop a list of review tasks, such as the following:

- ▶ Plan overall schedules for the entire group and for each member. Consider graphing the schedules.
- ▶ Maintain a paper trail of all meetings and editorial changes. Make sure that each document contains the creation date, modification date, or both.
- ▶ Set up editing guidelines. How detailed or superficial do you want the review?
- ▶ Who decides to accept or reject suggestions?
- ▶ Make sure that each group member has a unique method of identifying his or her comments.
- ▶ Schedule timely group meetings.
- ▶ Communicate with every member of the group regularly.
- ▶ Develop a system of circulating drafts of the standards or document, ensuring that everyone uses the most current version. For example, insert the revision date and, optionally, the revision number in the footer. Or circulate the version through the group, one member at a time.
- ▶ When you incorporate changes, immediately update the revision date. When changes are based on oral comments, it's best to modify the standards or document as quickly as possible.

Personal Workbook

Q&A

1 Can you use an internal DTD subset to define the components of a set of documents?

_____

_____

_____

2 What sort of planning goes into designing a DTD?

_____

_____

_____

3 What is the best way to start a DTD outline?

_____

_____

_____

4 Why should you not use a component for more than one purpose?

_____

_____

_____

5 Name five ways in which information from an XML document can be output.

_____

_____

_____

6 What is a *conditional section*, and what are the two types of condition sections for DTDs?

_____

_____

_____

7 What is the difference between an INCLUDE section and an IGNORE section?

_____

_____

_____

8 What are the two main differences between creating DTDs for individual documents and for sets of documents?

_____

_____

ANSWERS: PAGE 452

EXTRA PRACTICE

① Write an outline for a memorandum DTD.

② Create the memorandum DTD with the root element and the first level of child elements.

③ Using the memorandum DTD as the basis, create a template for a standard memorandum document.

④ Write an instruction-sheet DTD containing (1) an INCLUDE section with document components for telling time using an analog clock, and (2) an IGNORE section for telling time using a digital clock.

⑤ Write a DTD for an all-purpose business letter. Use INCLUDE and IGNORE sections to enclose elements for two types of letters: formal and informal.

⑥ Plan and design a cover sheet that will be attached to all XML documents and used to track them as they are circulated among your workgroup.

REAL-WORLD APPLICATIONS

✔ Plan the document standards for a series of user manuals to be published by your company. Each manual includes an introduction, table of contents, several chapters, two appendixes, and an index.

✔ Outline a DTD for the user manuals based on the standards you developed in the previous exercise.

✔ Your company is planning its first intranet and you have been named the chief developer. Create a DTD that will convert your current Web pages to the same structure and design.

✔ You are the coordinator of a group of 10 DTD developers. Plan and schedule a cycle for the development of five new corporate DTDs. Each DTD will be worked on for three months. After it's completed, it should receive biweekly maintenance for the first year and on a monthly basis after that.

Visual Quiz

How would you design a DTD to duplicate the structure and formats of this sample fax cover sheet? Don't forget the margins.

_____

_____

_____

_____

_____

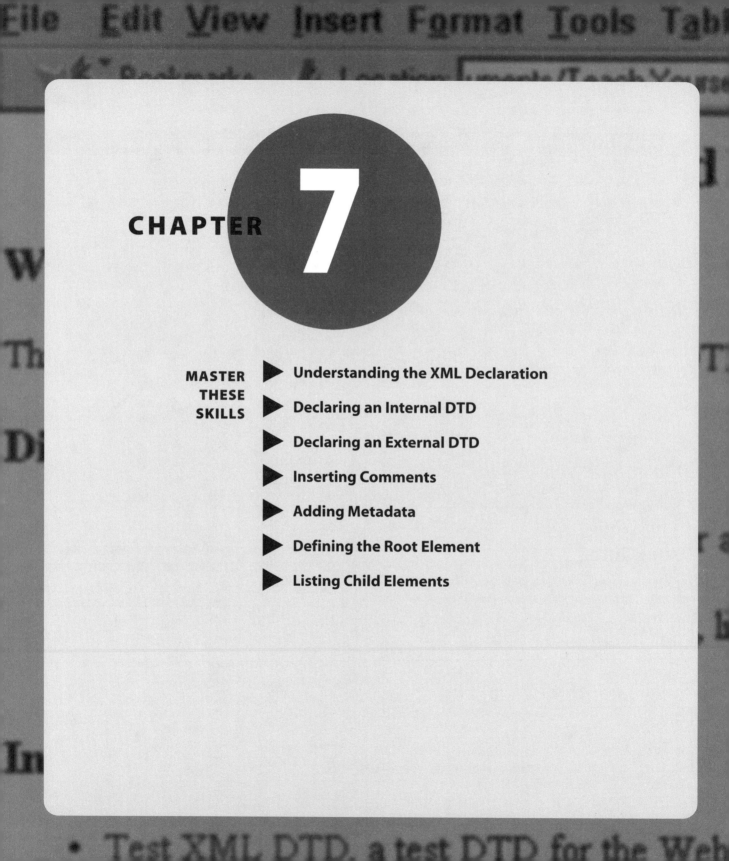

CHAPTER

7

MASTER
THESE
SKILLS

▶ Understanding the XML Declaration

▶ Declaring an Internal DTD

▶ Declaring an External DTD

▶ Inserting Comments

▶ Adding Metadata

▶ Defining the Root Element

▶ Listing Child Elements

Starting a DTD

In this chapter, you start to fill in the *document prolog*, the top part of any XML *document instance*, which is the entire document. The prolog includes the introduction to the document, or *document type declaration* (the *DOCTYPE*). The DOCTYPE points to an external or internal *document type definition* (*DTD*) that specifies the elements, attributes, entities, and notations for one or more XML documents.

The longer and more complex a DTD is, the more important it is to document it in the same way that you probably have added comments to the programs and scripts that you have written. Comments help those who will maintain an XML document in the future to understand why you have inserted certain statements.

If you have developed HTML documents for the Web, you know how important it is to incorporate metadata by using the META tag. To enable search indexes and robots to find a particular Web document, its developer should provide information about the document's content, including keywords and its history. In addition, metadata is a valuable commenting tool for XML documents.

Also in this chapter, you will learn how to define the *root element*, also known as the *document element*, within which all other XML elements in the current document are nested. All elements under the root element are collectively known as *child elements*. The last task of this chapter teaches you how to list the first level of child elements. In Chapter 8 you will find out about other generations of elements and how to add them to a DTD.

A DTD can be completely enclosed within an XML document, can be a separate document, or can be composed of both internal and external components. The part of a DTD that is within the source document is known as an *internal DTD subset*. It follows that the part of a DTD that is stored in a separate document is an *external DTD subset*. An external DTD subset can be referred to by more than one XML document. So, if you want to set standards for all of your company's or department's XML documents, it is best to develop one or two external DTDs that your documents can use to define common elements, attributes, and values.

Understanding the XML Declaration

The XML declaration is the first line in every XML document whether the document is a DTD or another document. A typical XML declaration looks like this:

```
<?xml version = "1.0" standalone = "yes"?>
```

The entire line is a *processing instruction*, which is enclosed within the `<?` and `?>` delimiters and which tells the XML processor how to interpret the document that follows. The processing instruction states that this is an XML document and that it uses XML Version 1.0, the current default. Thus, if you omit the version number from the processing instruction, an XML parser automatically processes the document against XML version 1.0. XML supports other processing instructions, most of which refer the current document to an external document. Table 7-1 lists other XML processing instructions.

The sample XML declaration also states that the current document is a *standalone document*: it stands alone without referring to an external DTD. If all of the document's elements and attributes are defined completely within the document, the default value is `standalone="yes"`. If an external DTD is declared in the document, the default value is `standalone ="no"`.

Look at the following XML declaration:

```
<?xml version="1.0" encoding="UTF-8"
standalone="yes"?>
```

The XML declaration can include an *encoding declaration* (typically `encoding="UTF-8"`) that states the supported Unicode character set for this document. For more Unicode information, see Chapter 4.

Although well-formed XML documents do not require an XML declaration, you should use one. Valid XML documents always require an XML declaration. The prolog can also contain comments and other processing instructions. See the XML prolog productions on the facing page.

TAKE NOTE

VERSION NUMBER PITFALLS

According to the current XML specification, the version number "1.0" indicates conformance to this version of this specification; it is an error for a document to use the value "1.0" if it does not conform to this version. In other words, when you create an XML document, it is important to follow the XML specification to the letter: "cross every *t* and dot every *i*."

RESERVING THE ?XML CHARACTERS

The combination of the `?xml` characters is reserved for current and future versions of XML. This means that you can use any processing instructions that do *not* start with `?xml` within XML documents. However, XML parsers will not necessarily understand and process a random processing instruction. It is important to note that processing instructions that begin with `?xml` must be supported by the following current specifications: XML, XLink, XPointer, and other future XML-supported specifications.

CROSS-REFERENCE

For an introduction to DTDs, see "Learning About DTDs" in Chapter 2.

FIND IT ONLINE

Learn about SGML topics at **http://www. oasis-open.org/cover/topics.html**.

Table 7-1: OTHER XML PROCESSING INSTRUCTIONS

Processing Instruction	Instructs the XML processor to:
xml:alternate style sheet	Use the referred-to alternate style sheet
xml:attributes	Rename XML-defined attribute names in order to make them unique
xml:lang	Process the referred-to XML language code
xml:link	Process the referred-to XLinking elements
xml:space	Preserve the whitespace in the XML document
xml:style sheet	Use the referred-to style sheet

Listing 7-1: A SHORT XML DOCUMENT

```
<?xml version="1.0"?>     ← 1
<!DOCTYPE welcome         ← 2
<!ELEMENT welcome (#PCDATA)>  ← 3
]>
<welcome>
Welcome Earthling!        4
</welcome>
```

1 On the first line, enter the ?xml processing instruction, which states the version number.

2 In most XML documents, enter a document type declaration (!DOCTYPE) next.

3 Use the document type definition to define the root element welcome.

4 The <welcome> and </welcome> tags enclose a greeting.

XML 1.0: THE PROLOG PRODUCTIONS

```
[22]        prolog ::= XMLDecl? Misc* (doctypedecl Misc*)?  ← 1
[23]       XMLDecl ::= '<?xml' VersionInfo EncodingDecl? SDDecl? S? '?>'  ← 2
[24]   VersionInfo ::= S 'version' Eq (' VersionNum ' | " VersionNum ")  ← 3
[25]            Eq ::= S? '+' S?
[26]    VersionNum ::= ([a-zA-Z0-9_.:] | '-')+  ← 4
[27]          Misc ::= Comment | PI | S
```

1 The productions in the XML specification are stated in Extended Backus-Naur Form.

2 The prolog production defines all the components in the prolog.

3 The XML declaration, which includes the ?xml processing instruction, opens every XML document.

4 The encoding declaration names the character set.

Declaring an Internal DTD

In addition to the XML declaration, the document prolog includes the document type declaration (see the facing page). The document type declaration must precede the first start tag in an XML document that starts with the !DOCTYPE reserved keyword, and that includes the DTD. The DTD can consist of an internal DTD subset, an external DTD subset, or a combination of both. The *internal DTD subset* is the part of a DTD that is located within its source document. In fact, the internal DTD subset can include an entire DTD. The DTD is composed of markup that can include elements, attributes, entities, and notation—all parts of an internal DTD subset—as well as references to external DTDs. When the DTD is completely located in the internal subset, it is *local*. The source document contains both the DTD markup and the defined XML, which will be processed and output by the XML processor.

The document type declaration must precede the first start tag in an XML document. A !DOCTYPE declaration is required for an XML document to be valid; otherwise, the document is well-formed at best. Note that internal DTD subsets are higher in precedence than external DTD subsets. In other words, if an XML processor detects both types of DTD subsets in the same document, it processes the internal subset rather than the external subset.

It is best to use internal DTD subsets to define elements, attributes, notation, and entities for a single, unique XML document. When your business or department sets standards for document output, produces many of the same type of document (such as corporate memos or letters), or creates long, complex documents (for example, user or technical manuals), it is a good idea to develop external DTD subsets. This way, one external DTD can define the elements, attributes, entities, and notation for sets of documents.

TAKE NOTE

▶ USING PARAMETER ENTITY REFERENCES IN INTERNAL DTD SUBSETS

If you include a parameter entity reference in an internal subset, it must follow supported syntax: it must start with a percent sign and end with a semicolon. In addition, the name of the entity reference must match the same name in the entity declaration. If you declare the entity reference in an internal DTD subset, the parameter entity reference must be defined completely within the brackets but cannot be nested within markup declarations. An XML processor parses parameter entity references first, resulting in replacement text being placed in the markup declarations.

▶ THE DOCUMENT TYPE *DECLARATION* VS. THE DOCUMENT TYPE *DEFINITION* (DTD)

The document type declaration is *never* known as the DTD; it *contains* the DTD. The document type definition, which is *always* known as the DTD, is the actual location of element, attribute, notation, and entity definitions.

CROSS-REFERENCE

For an introduction to internal subsets, see "Learning About Internal Subsets" in Chapter 2.

FIND IT ONLINE

The paper at **http://www.arbortext.com/ sgmlxept.html** explains why XML does not allow exceptions.

XML 1.0: THE DOCUMENT TYPE DECLARATION PRODUCTIONS

```
XML 1.0: The Document Type Declaration Productions
[28] doctypedecl ::= '<!DOCTYPE' S Name (S ExternalID)?    [ VC: Root Element
                     S? ('[' (markupdecl | PEReference      Type ]
                     | S)* ']' S?)? '>'
[29]   markupdecl ::= elementdecl | AttlistDecl             [ VC: Proper
                      | EntityDecl | NotationDecl | PI        Declaration/PE
                      | Comment                               Nesting ]
                                                            [ WFC: PEs in Internal
                                                              Subset ]
```

❶ *The* !DOCTYPE *reserved keyword starts a DTD.*
❷ *A valid XML name must begin with a letter or underscore.*
❸ *The declaration can include an external DTD filename.*
❹ *A DTD can contain markup and entities, too.*

Listing 7-2: A ONE-ELEMENT DOCUMENT

```
<?xml version="1.0"? standalone="yes">←❶
<!DOCTYPE anytext [ ❷
<!ELEMENT anytext (#PCDATA)> ]>←❸
<anytext>                    ❹
#PCDATA stands for parsed character data.
It can include character data, entities,
and elements--in fact, any nonmarkup data.
</anytext>
```

❶ *First, enter the* <?xml?> *processing instruction to start an XML document.*
❷ *The document type declaration starts with the* !DOCTYPE *keyword.*
❸ *End the DTD by entering the*]> *delimiters.*
❹ *Type the body of the document within the* <anytext> *and* </anytext> *tags.*

Listing 7-3: A DOCUMENT WITH AN INTERNAL DTD

```
<?xml version="1.0"?>←❶
<!DOCTYPE EXAMPLE [←❷
<!ELEMENT EXAMPLE (#PCDATA)>←❸          ❹
<!ENTITY Commentary "This is an example of
a short XML document with an internal
DTD."> ]>
<EXAMPLE>Insert the commentary here:
&Commentary;</EXAMPLE>
```

❶ *Enter the* <?xml?> *processing instruction.*
❷ *Type* !DOCTYPE, *its name, and start the DTD with* [.
❸ *Enter the* EXAMPLE *element declaration, which can contain parsed character data.*
❹ *Declare the* Commentary *entity.*

Declaring an External DTD

An *external DTD subset* is the part of a DTD that is stored in a separate document, completely outside the source document. An external subset can be referred to by more than one XML document. XML documents can include internal DTDs, can refer to external DTDs, or both. Either or both types of DTDs can contain markup declarations that define XML elements, their attributes, values, and constraints, and can also define entities and notations. Both types of DTDs can be short or long, simple or complex. In general, internal DTD subsets should be relatively short and contain few definitions, and external DTD subsets can be long and more complicated. For example, you can use an external DTD subset to define the root element and several generations of nested child elements and related attributes, as well as lists of entities. If you define elements with the same level of complexity in an internal DTD subset, its source document will be more difficult to review and maintain because it contains both the DTD and the information to be output.

An internal DTD subset is contained within brackets ([and]), whereas an external DTD subset is not. To refer to an external DTD subset from within an XML document, the document type declaration contains a uniform resource identifier (URI), which is the Internet address of the DTD. The URI can be an absolute address (an entire address such as **http://www.eddygrp.com/storage/entire.dtd**) or a relative address (a partial address such as **entire.dtd** or **/storage/entire.dtd**).

When you declare an external DTD subset, you can use the SYSTEM keyword or the PUBLIC keyword to indicate that you can find the DTD file on a system (such as your local server or a small corporate network restricted to a relatively small population), or a public resource (for example, on a large industrial or governmental internet accessible by a large population).

Note that you can use an internal DTD subset temporarily to test an XML document; then, after successful testing, you can replace it with an external DTD subset.

If an XML document is associated with a DTD, it does not necessarily have to be valid. For example, you can use a nonvalidating XML processor on the document. A nonvalidating processor not only does not validate the document, but also is not even required to read the external subset.

TAKE NOTE

TEXT DECLARATIONS IN EXTERNAL DTD SUBSETS

An external DTD subset can include a *text declaration*, which is a stripped-down version of a document's opening XML declaration. Although a text declaration looks like an XML declaration, it is a string that identifies the external subset. For example, the text declaration can specify the XML version and the encoding. Identifying the encoding is especially important if the DTD refers to an international alphabet or a character set that is not the default UTF-8.

CROSS-REFERENCE

For an introduction to external subsets, see "Learning About External Subsets" in Chapter 2.

FIND IT ONLINE

The XML-Tagged Religion Set (**http://sunsite.unc.edu/pub/sun-info/xml/eg/religion.1.10.xml.zip**) is a well-known XML DTD.

XML 1.0: THE EXTERNAL SUBSET PRODUCTIONS

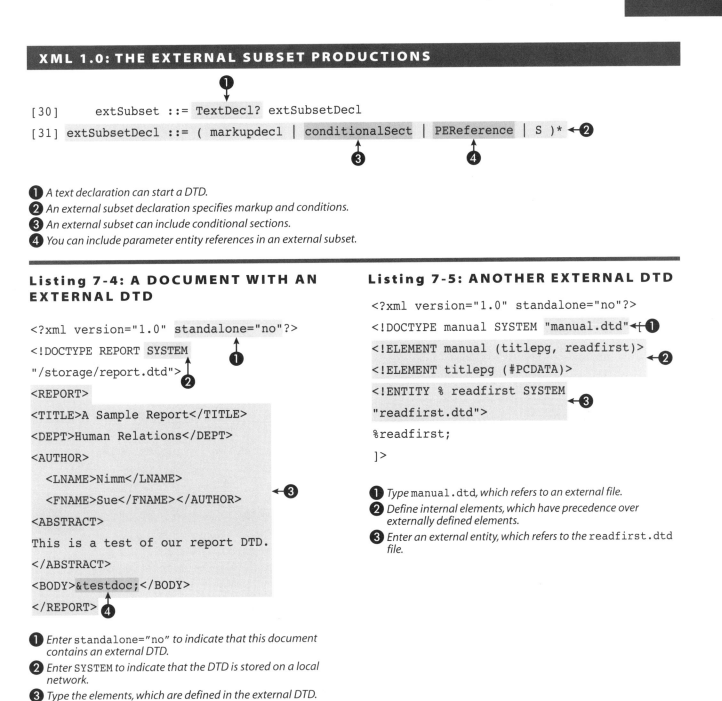

```
[30]        extSubset ::= TextDecl? extSubsetDecl
[31]  extSubsetDecl ::= ( markupdecl | conditionalSect | PEReference | S )*
```

❶ *A text declaration can start a DTD.*
❷ *An external subset declaration specifies markup and conditions.*
❸ *An external subset can include conditional sections.*
❹ *You can include parameter entity references in an external subset.*

Listing 7-4: A DOCUMENT WITH AN EXTERNAL DTD

```
<?xml version="1.0" standalone="no"?>
<!DOCTYPE REPORT SYSTEM
"/storage/report.dtd">
<REPORT>
<TITLE>A Sample Report</TITLE>
<DEPT>Human Relations</DEPT>
<AUTHOR>
   <LNAME>Nimm</LNAME>
   <FNAME>Sue</FNAME></AUTHOR>
<ABSTRACT>
This is a test of our report DTD.
</ABSTRACT>
<BODY>&testdoc;</BODY>
</REPORT>
```

❶ *Enter* standalone="no" *to indicate that this document contains an external DTD.*
❷ *Enter* SYSTEM *to indicate that the DTD is stored on a local network.*
❸ *Type the elements, which are defined in the external DTD.*
❹ *Enter* &testdoc;, *an external entity defined in the external DTD.*

Listing 7-5: ANOTHER EXTERNAL DTD

```
<?xml version="1.0" standalone="no"?>
<!DOCTYPE manual SYSTEM "manual.dtd"
<!ELEMENT manual (titlepg, readfirst)>
<!ELEMENT titlepg (#PCDATA)>
<!ENTITY % readfirst SYSTEM
"readfirst.dtd">
%readfirst;
]>
```

❶ *Type* manual.dtd, *which refers to an external file.*
❷ *Define internal elements, which have precedence over externally defined elements.*
❸ *Enter an external entity, which refers to the* readfirst.dtd *file.*

99

Inserting Comments

Comments are an important part of XML documents — especially DTDs. Imagine what it would be like if you were a newly hired XML developer suddenly responsible for maintaining a complex, multipage company-wide DTD loaded with element declarations, many lists of attributes and values, and custom entities. Without comments explaining the purpose of blocks of code, you could have problems interpreting the meanings of certain elements and other markup.

Note that another way of clarifying an XML document is to use descriptive names for elements, attributes, entities, and so on. For example, you can name the element that will contain the top-level heading text tophead, headingone, or even H1, which is identical to the name of HTML's top-level heading.

Identify XML comments by their delimiters: comments are preceded by `<!--` and end with `-->` (see Listing 7-6). When XML processors interpret XML documents, comments should not appear in the output.

Because double hyphens (`--`) are reserved in comment delimiters, do not place them within the comment text. Embedded double hyphens may cause an XML processor to misinterpret the remaining part of a comment.

You can insert comments almost anywhere in an XML document. However, do not place comments at the very top of the document: the XML declaration must always be the first line in a document. Do not use comments within a character data section: an XML processor will interpret the comments and their delimiters as standard character data. Do not embed comments within tags or in declarations.

Comments can be composed of a few words, like this:

```
<!-- Root element definition -->
```

Or they can wrap over more than one line, like so:

```
<!-- This DTD defines the elements for a
corporate memo standard. -->
```

TAKE NOTE

► COMMENTS WITHIN THE XML SPECIFICATION

When you review the EBNF syntax of productions in the XML specification, comments are preceded by `/*` and succeeded by `*/`. XML, HTML, and their parent, SGML, use the `<!--` and `-->` delimiters.

► NAMING ELEMENTS TO COMMENT ON THEM

In the not-so-distant past of computing, PC filenames were restricted to eight characters and a three-character extension. It has been difficult for many people to get away from that convention and use longer filenames. One convincing reason for using longer filenames is that these names are more understandable: A long filename actually documents the file. You can apply the same logic when naming XML elements. For example, is it easier to understand the meaning of an element named S or one named STRIKETHROUGH?

CROSS-REFERENCE

Chapter 23 shows how to point to an XML comment.

FIND IT ONLINE

ftp://navycals.dt.navy.mil/pub/dtd/81927.dtd has a DTD written in SGML for the U.S. Navy.

XML 1.0: THE COMMENTS PRODUCTION

❶ **❷** **❸**

[15] Comment ::= '<!--' ((Char - '-') | ('-' (Char - '-')))* '-->'

❶ *Start a comment by typing the <!-- delimiters.*
❷ *Insert any number of characters and dashes.*
❸ *End a comment by typing the --> delimiters.*

Listing 7-6: USING COMMENTS PROPERLY

```
<?xml version="1.0"?> ❶
<!-- The root element accepts all data. -->
<!DOCTYPE EXAMPLE [
<!ELEMENT EXAMPLE (#PCDATA)> ❷
<!-- The entity replaces &Commentary; with
the Commentary text. -->
<!ENTITY Commentary "This is an example of
a short XML document with an internal DTD.":
]>
<EXAMPLE>Insert the commentary here: &Commentary
</EXAMPLE>
<!-- End of the document --> ❸
```

❶ *Type comments after the first line, the XML declaration.*
❷ *Enter comments after markup is complete.*
❸ *You can indicate the end of a document with a comment.*

Listing 7-7: USING COMMENTS IMPROPERLY

```
<!-- start of document --> ❶
<?xml version="1.0"?>
<!DOCTYPE EXAMPLE [
<!ELEMENT EXAMPLE <!-- The entity replaces
&Commentary;                              ❷
with the Commentary text. -->
(#PCDATA)>
<!ENTITY Commentary "This is an example of
a short XML document with an internal
DTD.">
]>
<EXAMPLE>Insert the commentary here:
&Commentary;
</EXAMPLE>
```

❶ *Do not start a document with a comment.*
❷ *Do not embed a comment within markup.*

Adding Metadata

Metadata is information about the current XML document. For example, you can create and use one or more metadata elements to name the author, those who edit the document, and the dates on which the document was created and edited.

A metadata element can also contain keywords that can help search indexes match the keywords that users enter. When the metadata and user-entered keywords match, search indexes assign a rank to a document and include it in a list that users can browse.

Resource Description Framework

The Worldwide Web Consortium (W3C) supports XML metadata as described in two working drafts: the Resource Description Framework (RDF) Model and Syntax Specification and the Resource Description Framework (RDF) Schema Specification. The Resource Description Framework (RDF) home page states that RDF will enable XML developers to support a wide variety of metadata. RDF uses XML elements to define metadata properties (see the following example). Properties include a general description, an identifier (ID), property name and property value, a resource, and an about element containing a URI reference. With a future RDF specification, it will be easier for search-tools developers to enable successful searches for XML documents: the developers will use the same terms and syntax. Metadata that can be used repeatedly enables developers to save time.

A sample RDF metadata section in an XML document looks like this:

```
<rdf:RDF
  <rdf:Description
  about="http://www.eddy.com/sci_book.html>
  <y:Creator>Sandra E. Eddy</s:Creator>
    <y:Date>1999-10-13</y:Date>
    <y:Email>eddygrp@sover.net</y:Email>
  </rdf:Description>
</rdf:RDF>
```

In the preceding example, the `<rdf:RDF>` and `</rdf:RDF>` tags enclose the RDF code, and `<rdf:Description>` and `</rdf:Description>` are predefined tags containing nested elements from a referred-to namespace file. The `y` is a legal namespace prefix. As you can see, the description contains a variety of descriptive metadata.

TAKE NOTE

▶ USING XML NAMESPACES

When you create RDF code, you can use qualified names that are defined using XML *namespaces*, which are predefined names for elements, attributes, entities, and so on. XML namespaces allow XML document developers to stay on the same page with their peers. Throughout the world, developers can use the same set of names — each name in the set has the same meaning. For more information about XML namespaces, go to the "Namespaces in XML" page at **http://www.w3.org/TR/WD-xml-names/**.

CROSS-REFERENCE
Chapter 8 provides detailed information on how to declare elements and specify or restrict content.

FIND IT ONLINE
The W3C's Metadata Activity site (**http://www.w3.org/Metadata/Activity.html**) has the latest metadata standards.

Because XML is still in the early stages of development, its metadata standards are works in process. Table 7-2 lists and provides the URLs for Resource Description Framework (RDF) and other notes and drafts related to metadata in XML.

Table 7-2: XML METADATA NOTES AND DRAFTS

Document Title	URL
Resource Description Framework (RDF)	http://www.w3.org/RDF
Resource Description Framework (RDF) Schema Specification	http://www.w3.org/TR/WD-rdf-schema/
Resource Description Framework (RDF) Model and Syntax Specification	http://www.w3.org/TR/WD-rdf-syntax/
Channel Definition Format (CDF)	http://www.microsoft.com/standards/cdf/default.asp
Document Content Description for XML	http://www.w3.org/TR/NOTE-double-clicked
PICS Signed Labels (DSig) 1.0 Specification	http://www.w3.org/TR/REC-DSig-label/
PICSRules 1.1	http://www.w3.org/TR/REC-PICSRules
Meta Content Framework Using XML	http://www.w3.org/TR/NOTE-MCF-XML/
W3C Data Formats	http://www.w3.org/TR/NOTE-rdfarch
XML-Data	http://www.w3.org/TR/1998/NOTE-XML-data-0105/

Listing 7-8: A DOCUMENT WITH METADATA

```
<?xml version="1.0" standalone="no"?>
<!DOCTYPE SCIENCE SYSTEM
"/storage/science.dtd">
<SCIENCE>
<!-- The metadata section -->
<ID>0-9999-1111-1</ID>          ←❶
<EDITOR>Sandra E. Eddy</EDITOR>  ←❷
<REVISE-DATE>10/13/99</REVISE-DATE>  ←❸
<KEYWORDS>
books, book, weather book, children's books,
elementary school books, tornadoes, weather,
storms, tornado books, weather books, storm books
</KEYWORDS>
                                ↑
<!-- The body -->               ❹
<TITLE>Learning about Tornadoes</TITLE>
<ABSTRACT>
This illustrated book, for 8-12 year olds,
introduces readers to tornadoes and what
causes them.
</ABSTRACT>
```

❶ Enter the ID element's metadata information, the ISBN identification number.

❷ Enter the EDITOR's name within the start and end tags.

❸ Insert a date for the REVISE-DATE element or accept the default.

❹ Separate each keyword or keyword phrase with a comma.

Defining the Root Element

The document instance contains definitions of elements and attributes, as well as entities, notation, other markup, and content. Typically, DTDs contain more markup than content; other XML documents — especially those with external DTD subsets — usually contain more content than markup.

Use the element declaration to list the root element and its first generation of child elements. Generations of elements are similar to generations of human families: they include parents (that is, roots), ancestors (all elements above the parents), descendants (all elements below the parents), and children.

Several generations of child elements can exist. For example, the first generation of child elements are immediately under the root, the second generation of child elements (analogous to grandchildren) are under the first generation of child elements, the third generation of child elements (analogous to great-grandchildren) are under the second generation, and so on. Table 7-3 summarizes generations of XML elements.

The element declaration starts with the uppercase keyword !ELEMENT followed by the element name and the content type specification. The element name must be a valid XML name, starting with a letter or underscore character. The content type specification can be one of four values: EMPTY (a reserved keyword stating that there is no content), ANY (a reserved keyword stating that the content includes any defined elements, including itself), Mixed (a production that represents a combination of character data and child elements), or children (a production that represents a list of one or more child elements). Because the element declaration occurs within the DTD, actual character data is not included in the declaration; the declaration allows character data to be contained within the element tags in the future XML document. For more information, refer to Chapter 8.

For the future XML document to be valid, the root element must follow the declaration: an EMPTY element must be empty, an ANY element must contain at least one child element, a children element must declare at least one child element. Note that you cannot declare the same element type more than once in a DTD; however, you can declare attributes and entities more than once.

TAKE NOTE

▶ POLISHING AN XML DOCUMENT

When you browse through the XML specification, you'll notice that many productions include the S component, which represents whitespace. This means that you can decide how much whitespace to add to each line of an XML document; there is no effect to the document when it is processed. For example, some individuals like to indent certain lines in a document in the same way that they indent lines of programming code — to indicate lines that are subordinate to other lines. Other XML developers like to line up portions of several lines; for example, names aligned in one column and default values in another.

CROSS-REFERENCE

To learn much more about elements, see Chapter 8.

FIND IT ONLINE

Basic XML (http://www.hypermedic.com/style/xml/xmltut.txt) discusses how to write well-formed documents.

Table 7-3: XML GENERATIONS OF ELEMENTS

Generation	Description
root	The top-level element in an XML document; the *document element* within which all other XML elements for the current document are nested.
child	An element that is nested under a parent element. In an XML document, all elements other than the root are child elements.
parent	An element under which its child elements are nested.
ancestor	A higher-level element, such as a parent element or the root, in a family tree of elements.
descendant	All the generations of elements that are nested under a parent element or the root.

Listing 7-9: FOUR EXAMPLES OF ROOT ELEMENT

```
<?xml version="1.0"?>
<!DOCTYPE customer [ ❶
<!ELEMENT customer (name, address, city, state,
zip, telephone, fax, email)>]>


<!DOCTYPE image [ ❷
<!ELEMENT image (EMPTY)>]>


<!DOCTYPE ksink [ ❸
<!ELEMENT ksink (ANY)>]>


<!DOCTYPE mixed [ ❹
<!ELEMENT mixed (#PCDATA|list)>]>
```

❶ Insert child elements within the parentheses.
❷ Declare an empty element by using the EMPTY keyword.
❸ Use the ANY keyword to indicate any type of content.
❹ Enter mixed content within the parentheses.

XML 1.0: THE ELEMENT TYPE DECLARATION PRODUCTIONS

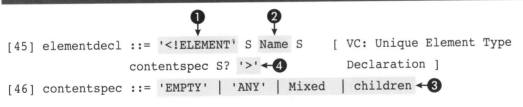

```
[45] elementdecl ::= '<!ELEMENT' S Name S    [ VC: Unique Element Type
                     contentspec S? '>'          Declaration ]
[46] contentspec ::= 'EMPTY' | 'ANY' | Mixed | children
```

❶ Start an element declaration with < and the !ELEMENT keyword.
❷ Enter a valid XML element name, which starts with a letter or underscore.
❸ Enter one of four contentspec types.
❹ End the element declaration with >.

Listing Child Elements

After you have declared the root element, it's usually time to list the root's child elements. Many of those child elements will probably have child elements of their own. Thus is formed the tree of elements — from the root to the first generation of children to each succeeding generation. For example:

```
root-element
   generation 1
      generation 2
      generation 2
         generation 3
            generation 4
            generation 4
         generation 3
            generation 4
   generation 1
   generation 1
      generation 2
         generation 3
      generation 2
      generation 2
   generation 1
```

As you list child elements, you can use special characters to indicate certain behaviors. If you use commas (,) to separate all or some child elements, the comma indicates that each element *must* appear in the order in which it was defined in the element declaration. If you separate all or some elements with pipe (|) symbols, you allow more latitude: each element may occur one or more times and can appear in any order. You can use a combination of commas and pipes to control strictly the use of some elements

and allow relaxation in the use of others. You can also place lists of elements, separated by pipes or commas, within parentheses. Parentheses group like elements in the same way that you can group mathematical expressions to move them up in the order of calculating precedence. Table 7-4 lists and briefly describes the special characters that indicate the behavior of child elements.

Other special characters control each element or group of elements. Close the name of a child element with a ? (`elementname?`) to indicate that it may appear; follow the element with * (`elementname*`) to indicate that it may not appear at all or may appear any number of times; or follow the element with a + to indicate that it must appear at least once or any number of times. If the element name is not followed by one of these three characters, it must appear just once.

CROSS-REFERENCE

Chapter 3 reviews the use of special characters and symbols used in XML syntax.

FIND IT ONLINE

The Extensible Markup Language site (**http://www. microsoft.com/workshop/c-frame. htm#/sml/ default.asp**) covers a variety of XML topics.

Table 7-4: SPECIAL CHARACTERS IN CHILD ELEMENT LISTS

Special Character	Purpose
(	Indicates the start of a list of elements
)	Indicates the end of a list of elements
,	Separates two elements that *must* be entered in a particular order
|	Separates two elements that can be entered in any order
?	Specifies that an element or group of elements can occur none or one time
*	Specifies that an element or group of elements can occur none or an unlimited number of times
+	Specifies that an element or group of elements *must* occur one or more times
No symbol	Specifies that an element or group of elements *must* occur just once.

Listing 7-10: EXAMPLES OF DOCUMENT ELEMENTS

```
<!ELEMENT report (cover, title, abstract, intro,
❶→ section1, section2, section3, summary)>


<!ELEMENT manual (cover, title, abstract, TOC,
intro,        ❷
      chapter*, appendix*, index)>
                           ❸
<!ELEMENT paper (title, abstract, intro,
      section*, appendix*, footnotes)>


<!-- bodytext child elements -->  ❹
<!ELEMENT bodytext (normal|bold|italics|
      underline|strikethrough)>
```

❶ *Type child elements within the parentheses.*
❷ *Enter an asterisk (*) to allow an element to occur more than once.*
❸ *Separate elements with commas (,) to force a strict order of entry.*
❹ *Separate elements with pipes (|)to allow entry in any order.*

XML 1.0: THE ELEMENT CONTENT PRODUCTIONS

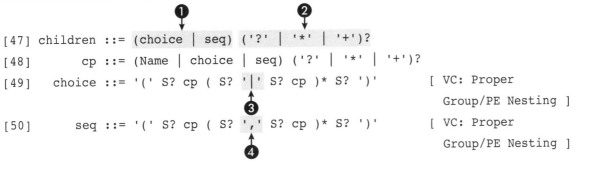

```
              ❶                  ❷
[47] children ::= (choice | seq) ('?' | '*' | '+')?
[48]       cp ::= (Name | choice | seq) ('?' | '*' | '+')?
[49]   choice ::= '(' S? cp ( S? '|' S? cp )* S? ')'      [ VC: Proper
                                 ❸                           Group/PE Nesting ]
[50]      seq ::= '(' S? cp ( S? ',' S? cp )* S? ')'      [ VC: Proper
                                 ❹                           Group/PE Nesting ]
```

❶ *Enclose a list of child elements within parentheses.*
❷ *Separate child elements with |s for any order.*
❸ *Use commas to signal a strict order of child elements.*
❹ *Control an element's occurrences with ?, *, and +.*

107

Personal Workbook

Q&A

1 What are the *document prolog* and the *document instance*?

_____

_____

_____

2 What is a *DTD*?

_____

_____

_____

3 Explain the difference between a document type declaration and a document type definition.

_____

_____

_____

4 What is the difference between an internal DTD subset and an external DTD subset?

_____

_____

5 What three places can you *not* put comments in an XML document?

_____

_____

_____

6 What is *metadata*?

_____

_____

_____

7 What is the *root element*?

_____

_____

_____

8 Write an element declaration for the root element TALK, which can hold parsed character data.

_____

_____

ANSWERS: PAGE 453

EXTRA PRACTICE

1 Write an XML document that says "Hello World." (Hint: You do not need to write a DTD.)

2 Write an XML document that defines a root element that accepts parsed character data.

3 Write an XML document that defines a root element with five child elements. Each child element can be entered once and in the order in which you listed them.

4 Change the XML document so that all of the child elements can be entered in any order.

5 Change the XML document so that the first child element is optional, the second must be entered at least once, and the third can occur any number of times or not at all.

REAL-WORLD APPLICATIONS

✔ You have been using internal DTD subsets to declare elements, attributes, and entities for your XML documents. You convert to external DTD subsets.

✔ You want as many search indexes as possible to find your XML documents. Without using RDF code, you declare elements to provide metadata information.

✔ You're writing an XML document that tracks your library of videotapes. You declare a root element and the first level of child elements.

✔ You are leaving your XML development job at XMLDocs International one week from Friday, and your best friend is your replacement. Use comments to document your XML documents.

Visual Quiz

Name the eight things that are wrong with this DTD.

_____

_____

_____

_____

_____

_____

```
visualquiz - Notepad
File  Edit  Search  Help
<!-- a new document -->
<?xml version="2.0" standalone="no"
<!DOCTYPE badnews [
    <!ELAMENT badnews (cover,
    <-- declare a child -->
    headline, para%, pullquote*)
]>>
```

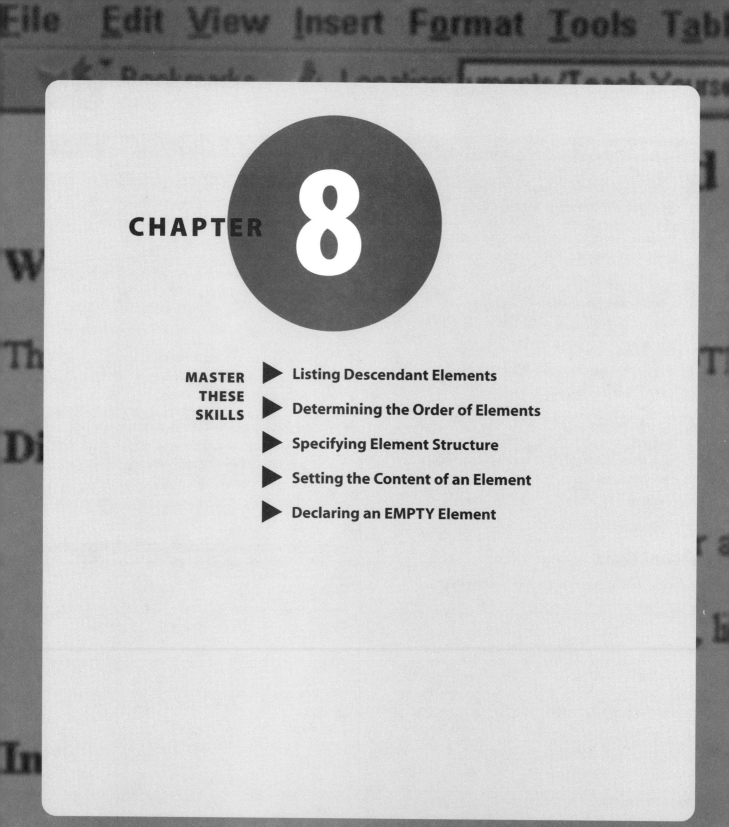

CHAPTER 8

MASTER THESE SKILLS

▶ Listing Descendant Elements

▶ Determining the Order of Elements

▶ Specifying Element Structure

▶ Setting the Content of an Element

▶ Declaring an EMPTY Element

Declaring Elements

In the prior chapter, you learned how to start a DTD by filling in the prolog, defining the root element, and listing the first generation of child elements. Most DTDs do not stop there: they usually include a complex element tree of elements with many generations.

In this chapter, you discover a great deal more about declaring elements and enabling them to accept certain contents. First, you learn more about declaring additional generations beyond the root element and the first level of child elements. A DTD can contain any number of generations — whatever is required to produce the best possible XML document or document set. In this chapter and in the remaining chapters in Part II, you see a DTD as it evolves from the minimal root element and the first generation of child elements to additional levels. For example, the sample DTD (for a mail-order company) can generate catalogs. Of course, by using XML, the company could develop one or more interfaces that would allow the catalog to be constructed with fields from a database.

This chapter also teaches you more about managing the order in which elements are used.

For example, as you have learned in previous chapters, you can force a specific arrangement of element use, allow elements to be used in any order, or a combination of both.

A typical element can contain other elements, character data, or a mix of elements and data. Other *empty* elements can be containers for contents (such as graphics or line breaks) that will be furnished during processing. The other tasks in this chapter demonstrate how to set the content of elements. You will learn how to specify no value at all or any value. You have already found out how to list the child elements for a particular element and allow parsed character data (#PCDATA). As the catalog DTD develops, you will see examples of all these types of element content.

Once you have defined elements, you aren't finished. To produce a first-rate DTD, your elements should include attributes with which you can allow certain values and disallow others. You'll learn about attributes in the next chapter. And of course, most DTDs also comprise other components, such as entities and notation. Chapter 10 covers these subjects.

Listing Descendant Elements

DTDs can be quite complex and can incorporate several generations of elements. For example, an outline listing a Web site's current and future elements may start with a set of diverse pages (home page, site map, company information, employment opportunities, and so on), and each page can contain several child elements — some shared with other pages and some unique. In turn, many of those child elements may have child elements of their own. Or a computer manual can consist of chapter-level elements — some sharing the same set of elements and others (such as glossaries or indexes) quite unique. Then, each chapter or appendix can contain its own set of child elements, such as several levels of headings and various defined sections (including plain body text, notes, tips, and cautions). Each of the section components can have its own set of child elements and attributes. Every time you add a new layer of elements, the DTD can control more of the input, thereby enabling you to enforce your corporate XML standards.

If you are an experienced HTML document developer, you know that HTML browsers are quite forgiving: Incomplete nesting of one element under another in HTML does not always result in an error. However, mismatched elements do not make for a robust document — especially if you will eventually convert to valid XML documents. You have probably realized by now that the elements that make up valid XML documents are strictly organized — from the root element to one or more generations of child elements. The more control you wish to apply to a document or document set and the individuals who write and maintain it, the greater chance there is that you will define more elements covering a complex structure of several generations. For example, a database can be simple, with fields such as the following: `Name`, `Address`, `City`, `State`, and `ZIP`. These fields are all at the same high level. Here's a more complex structure: `Name` and its children (`First`, `Middle Initial`, and `Last`) and `Address` and its children (`Street`, `Post Office Box`, `Suite`, `City`, `State`, and `ZIP`).

When you work with more complex documents, such as contact management databases and business plans, the level of complexity will increase rapidly.

TAKE NOTE

CONTROLLING THE USE OF ELEMENTS

As you have discovered in earlier chapters, declaring an element is just the beginning of defining it. In XML DTDs, you can specify the relationship of one element to another. Is a particular element another element's peer? Is it a child of the root element or of another child element? If it is a child, its use is limited to its location under its parent element. As you have learned, you can also determine whether an element is required or optional, is used just once, is used in a particular order or in any order, and so on. This extra control represents one of the powers of XML.

CROSS-REFERENCE

Chapter 1 introduces you to elements and other XML building blocks.

FIND IT ONLINE

The SGML Primer (**http://www.sw.com/ sgmlinfo/primbody.html**) discusses DTDs, declarations, entities, and more.

XML 1.0: THE ELEMENT DECLARATION AND RELATED PRODUCTIONS

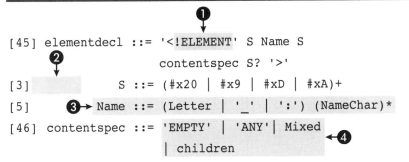

```
[45] elementdecl ::= '<!ELEMENT' S Name S
                        contentspec S? '>'
[3]          S ::= (#x20 | #x9 | #xD | #xA)+
[5]    Name ::= (Letter | '_' | ':') (NameChar)*
[46] contentspec ::= 'EMPTY' | 'ANY'| Mixed
                        | children
```

[VC: Unique Element Type
 Declaration]

❶ *The element declaration must start with the* !ELEMENT *keyword.*
❷ *Insert any amount of whitespace between declaration components.*
❸ *An element name must begin with a letter, underscore, or colon.*
❹ *An element can have four types of content.*

Listing 8-1: A SIMPLE DTD

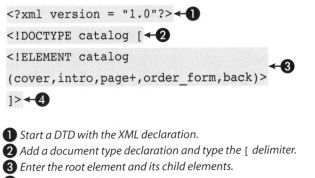

```
<?xml version = "1.0"?>
<!DOCTYPE catalog [
<!ELEMENT catalog
(cover,intro,page+,order_form,back)>
]>
```

❶ *Start a DTD with the XML declaration.*
❷ *Add a document type declaration and type the* [*delimiter.*
❸ *Enter the root element and its child elements.*
❹ *Type*]> *to end the DTD.*

Listing 8-2: A CATALOG DTD

```
<?xml version = "1.0"?>
<!DOCTYPE catalog [
<!ELEMENT catalog
(cover,intro,page+,order_form,back)>
  <!ELEMENT cover (#PCDATA)>
  <!ELEMENT intro (#PCDATA)>
  <!ELEMENT page
(letter,graphic,blurb,id,code,price)>
  <!ELEMENT order_form (#PCDATA)>
  <!ELEMENT back (#PCDATA)>
]>
```

❺ *Indent to start the list of child elements.*
❻ *Declare child elements that accept parsed character data.*
❼ *Declare a child element and list its own child elements.*
❽ *Declare the last two child elements of the root element.*

Determining the Order of Elements

Chapter 3 introduced you to Extended Backus-Naur Form (EBNF) notation. Using EBNF, you can specify how often you can use a particular component and the order in which it appears (among many other options). For example, you can use EBNF to set up a book that allows an introduction, table of contents, glossary, and index (each of which will appear just once), and to enable one, two, or more chapters and zero, one, or two appendixes. And rather than permit an appendix to appear before the table of contents, or an introduction to be inserted after the index, you can make sure that a document conforms to a strict order of elements.

When you declare two or more elements, you can separate them by using a comma (,) or a pipe (|) symbol. The format of the symbols is determined by the `choice` and `seq` productions, respectively. Both productions say, via their notation, that a list of child elements must be enclosed within parentheses (( )), can contain any amount of white space, and must use a comma or pipe to separate one element from the next.

The comma symbol compels the use of the listed elements in a particular order. For example:

`name,address`

indicates that you must use `name` before using `address`.

The pipe symbol allows the use of the elements in any order. For example:

`name|address`

allows `name` to be used before or after `address`.

You can also combine commas and pipes, to allow some elements to be selected in any order and to force the selection of other elements in a particular order. When you combine these symbols, group like elements within parentheses. For example:

`name,address, (telephone|fax|e-mail)`

forces you to use name and address in that order, and follow with telephone *or* fax *or* e-mail, in any order.

TAKE NOTE

▶ LEARNING ABOUT SGML'S & SYMBOL

If you are an SGML developer, you are probably wondering why the ampersand (&), the logical AND, is not included in the XML specification. In SGML, you can use & to ensure that two elements are present, in any order. In XML, you can simulate the ampersand by appending the asterisk and/or plus sign to an element, ensuring that a particular element must appear. Table 3-3 lists all of the symbols supported by the XML specification.

▶ SHARING COMPONENTS AMONG DTDS

When you develop several DTDs for various types of documents, you can share declarations. For example, if all of your documents present your company name, address, and logo in the same way (regardless of the location of that information in a particular document), you can write a module that defines appropriate elements, entities, and so on. Then, simply copy and paste the module into the proper DTDs. You can also share common entities within DTDs so you can insert commonly used terms, chunks of text, or entire files of boilerplate text.

CROSS-REFERENCE

In Chapter 3, you can learn about Extended Backus-Naur Form notation, with which you can declare elements.

FIND IT ONLINE

A List of SGML Reference Sites (**http://www.cdc. com/DocSvc/sgmlref.htm**) provides many DTD and SGML resources.

XML 1.0: THE CHOICE AND SEQ PRODUCTIONS

```
  ❶              ❷
[49] choice ::= '(' S? cp ( S? '|' S? cp )*S? ')' [VC: Proper Group/PE Nesting]
[50]    seq ::= '(' S? cp ( S? ',' S? cp )*S? ')' [VC: Proper Group/PE Nesting]
        ❸
```

❶ *From a* choice *list, choose any element in any order.*
❷ *Enter a content particle (*cp*) — an element name or list of elements.*
❸ *A* seq *list forces a specific sequence of elements.*

Listing 8-3: ORDERING ELEMENT SELECTIONS IN A BUSINESS-PLAN DOCUMENT

```
<?xml version = "1.0"?>
<!DOCTYPE busplan [
<!ELEMENT busplan
(fixed_info,(marketing|operations|team
|financials))>
  <!ELEMENT fixed_info (#PCDATA)>
  <!ELEMENT marketing (#PCDATA)>
  <!ELEMENT operations (#PCDATA)>
  <!ELEMENT team (#PCDATA)>
  <!ELEMENT financials (#PCDATA)>
]>
<fixed_info>You must use fixed_info
  first.</fixed_info>
<financials>Optionally, you can enter
  financial statements here.</financials>
<team>List the members of the management
  team in one of four places.</team>
<marketing>This doesn't have to be first
  anymore.<marketing>
<operations>Discuss business operations
  almost anywhere.</operations>
```

▲ *In this example, you must use the* fixed_info *element first. Then you can use the remaining elements in any order.*

Listing 8-4: ADJUSTING ELEMENT SELECTION IN THE BUSINESS-PLAN DOCUMENT

```
<?xml version = "1.0"?>
<!DOCTYPE busplan [
<!ELEMENT busplan (fixed_info,team,
(marketing|operations),financials)>
  <!ELEMENT fixed_info (#PCDATA)>
  <!ELEMENT marketing (#PCDATA)>
  <!ELEMENT operations (#PCDATA)>
  <!ELEMENT team (#PCDATA)>
  <!ELEMENT financials (#PCDATA)>
]>
<fixed_info>You must use fixed_info
first.</fixed_info>
<team>List the members of the management
  team next.</team>
<operations>Discuss business operations
  third or fourth.</operations>
<marketing>Cover marketing third or
fourth.</marketing>
<financials>Financial statements must be
  in last place.</financials>
```

▲ *This example forces you to use* fixed_info *followed by* team. *You can use the* marketing *and* operations *elements in the third or fourth place. You must use the* financials *element last.*

Specifying Element Structure

Novice developers learn that the best-written computer programs and those that run without errors have the same characteristics: they are designed to run from the top line to the bottom (in other words, no disorganized messes of statements branching here and there); they often consist of modules of related lines of code; and they're well-documented. Writing a DTD is analogous to writing a program. When you write a DTD, it is equally important to organize the entire document and the elements within it in a logical order, to group related components, and to include a liberal dose of comments throughout. Consider the development of a program or a DTD a combination of the logical and creative. A well-organized and well-documented DTD allows for easy maintenance, thereby saving time and tempers. And an innovative approach allows the developer to have fun and almost always ensures an outstanding document.

When you develop a DTD, you should also borrow document formats from computer programmers. You should indent lines to indicate the level of elements and other components. For example, indent — by two or three spaces — to indicate child elements and indent further when you declare child elements of those child elements.

You can also insert blank lines between sections of related markup. For example, you can group all entities and separate them from preceding and following lines. As a DTD grows in both size and complexity, proper organization and formatting will enable you and others to maintain it.

Specifying Required and Optional Tags in SGML

As you know, XML requires both start tags and end tags. In SGML DTDs, including the DTD for HTML, end tags can be optional. For example, in the HTML 4.0 specification (and in previous versions), the end tag for the paragraph element (P) is not required. So in the HTML 4.0 DTD, the element declaration for P looks like this:

```
<!ELEMENT P - O (%inline)*>
```

In this example, the dash (–) indicates a required start tag (a start tag is always required in HTML), and the letter O (which stands for *omit*) indicates an optional end tag. (NONE means that the end tag is not allowed.) Notice the %inline, which is an entity that includes four "subentities" representing four categories of inline elements. The asterisk at the end of the declaration indicates that you can use any number of this element — including none.

Two dashes represent required start and end tags:

```
<!ELEMENT SELECT - - (OPTION+)>
```

The SELECT element requires the use of the start tag and the end tag. Note that the plus sign indicates that the child element OPTION must be used at least once.

CROSS-REFERENCE

Chapter 9 provides detailed information about attributes, attribute types, and attribute values.

FIND IT ONLINE

XML for Managers (http://www.arbortext.com/xmlwp.html) is a white paper for those planning to convert from SGML to XML.

Listing 8-5: AN UNINDENTED DTD

```
<?xml version = "1.0"?>
<!DOCTYPE MEMO [
<!ELEMENT MEMO (LOGO|(TO, FROM, SUBJECT,
BODY))>
<!ELEMENT LOGO     EMPTY>
<!ELEMENT TO      (#PCDATA|DISTLIST)>
<!ELEMENT DISTLIST (#PCDATA)>
<!ELEMENT FROM    (#PCDATA)>
<!ELEMENT SUBJECT (#PCDATA)>
<!ELEMENT BODY    (INTRO,PARA+,SUMMARY)>
<!ELEMENT INTRO (#PCDATA)>
<!ELEMENT PARA (#PCDATA)>
<!ELEMENT SUMMARY (#PCDATA)>
]>
```

▲ *This valid DTD is not easy to read: all of its lines start at the left margin.*

Listing 8-6: AN INDENTED DTD

```
<?xml version = "1.0"?>
<!DOCTYPE MEMO [
<!ELEMENT MEMO (LOGO|(TO, FROM, SUBJECT,
   BODY))>
   <!ELEMENT LOGO     EMPTY>
   <!ELEMENT TO      (#PCDATA|DISTLIST)>
   <!ELEMENT DISTLIST (#PCDATA)>
   <!ELEMENT FROM    (#PCDATA)>
   <!ELEMENT SUBJECT (#PCDATA)>
   <!ELEMENT BODY    (INTRO,PARA+,SUMMARY)>
   <!ELEMENT INTRO (#PCDATA)>
   <!ELEMENT PARA (#PCDATA)>
   <!ELEMENT SUMMARY (#PCDATA)>
]>
```

▲ *Now the child elements, regardless of generation, are indented.*

Listing 8-7: ANOTHER INDENTED DTD

```
<?xml version = "1.0"?>
<!DOCTYPE MEMO [
<!ELEMENT MEMO (LOGO|(TO, FROM, SUBJECT,
                 BODY))>
    <!ELEMENT LOGO          EMPTY>
    <!ELEMENT TO          (#PCDATA|DISTLIST)>
        <!ELEMENT DISTLIST  (#PCDATA)>
    <!ELEMENT FROM         (#PCDATA)>
    <!ELEMENT SUBJECT      (#PCDATA)>
    <!ELEMENT BODY (INTRO,PARA+,SUMMARY)>
        <!ELEMENT INTRO      (#PCDATA)>
        <!ELEMENT PARA       (#PCDATA)>
        <!ELEMENT SUMMARY    (#PCDATA)>
]>
```

▲ *In this version, you can easily identify the generations by the level of indention.*

Listing 8-8: PART OF A COMMENTED DTD

```
<?xml version = "1.0"?>
<!DOCTYPE MEMO [
<!— Enter all but the logo in a set
 order. —>
<!ELEMENT MEMO (LOGO|(TO, FROM, SUBJECT,
                 BODY))>
<!— LOGO is a container for a graphic. —>
<!ELEMENT LOGO          EMPTY>
<!— You can enter parsed character data
    or select a distribution list. —>
    <!ELEMENT TO
(#PCDATA|DISTLIST)>
        <!ELEMENT DISTLIST   (#PCDATA)>
```

▲ *The best version of the DTD includes comments to explain some of the element declarations.*

Setting the Content of an Element

Each declared element in a DTD can have one of four possible content types: EMPTY, ANY, Mixed, or children. You have already learned about the children type in previous tasks, and you will find out about the EMPTY type in the next task. Here are the other types.

The ANY Type

The ANY type of element content does just what it says: It can include any type of content—both unparsed and parsed data, as well as any type of markup. As you might guess, ANY is a good type to use when you have to convert SGML DTDs, HTML documents, or well-formed XML documents to valid XML, if you are working under a rapidly approaching deadline.

You can also use ANY when you start developing a new XML DTD and want to parse it as you add statements. Declare all elements, giving them all the ANY type. After making sure that the DTD parses properly, change each element to its final type, repeatedly parsing every few edits. However, you shouldn't get into the habit of using ANY to avoid thinking about the true contents of an element and structure of a DTD.

A typical element declaration with the ANY type looks like this:

```
<!ELEMENT shebang ANY>
```

The Mixed Type

The Mixed element type comprises either parsed character data or combines parsed character data (#PCDATA) with any number of child elements—

a little less encompassing than the ANY type. For example, you might want to provide a choice of using an element or entering a comment. When you specify mixed content, you cannot use the comma separator; thus, you cannot set the order in which an element or #PCDATA is used. Some XML developers suggest that using the Mixed type is only a little better than using the ANY type: Combining child elements and #PCDATA within an element allows too much flexibility in the content of a document. In other words, you should declare child elements *or* #PCDATA.

A typical Mixed element declaration with two elements looks like this:

```
<!ELEMENT this_or_that
((this|that)|#PCDATA)>
```

> ### TAKE NOTE
>
> #### LEARNING ABOUT #PCDATA AND ASSOCIATED ENTITY REFERENCES
>
> In virtually all DTDs, you'll see the keyword #PCDATA enclosed within parentheses next to many elements. Parsed character data represents any text that is not markup, as well as entity references, which you might think of as markup. However, keep in mind that entity references should have been declared separately (in a statement starting with the !ENTITY keyword). When an entity reference is associated with #PCDATA, it has already been declared, so it is no longer considered markup.

CROSS-REFERENCE

In Chapter 12, you learn how to modify an existing DTD and to revise the document to which it will be attached.

FIND IT ONLINE

Learn how to define SGML document structures using DTDs at **http://www.ua.ac.be/MAN/WP31/t14.html**.

XML 1.0: THE CONTENT SPECIFICATION PRODUCTIONS

```
            ❶          ❷
[46] contentspec ::= 'EMPTY' | 'ANY' | Mixed
            ❸              | children
[47]    children ::= (choice | seq) ('?' | '*' | '+')?
[48]         cp ::= (Name | choice | seq) ('?' | '*'
            ❹                | '+')?
[51]      Mixed ::= '(' S? '#PCDATA' (S? '|' S? Name)*
                     S? ')*'
                   | '(' S? '#PCDATA' S? ')' [VC: Proper Group/PE Nesting]
                                            [VC: No Duplicate Types]
```

❶ An EMPTY element is a container for future content.
❷ The ANY type allows any content.
❸ The children type lists child elements of the declared element.
❹ The Mixed type enables a combination of #PCDATA and child elements.

Listing 8-9: AN EARLY DRAFT OF A DTD

```
<?xml version = "1.0"?>
<!DOCTYPE document [
<!ELEMENT document
(title,abstract,page+,end_notes)>
  <!ELEMENT title (#PCDATA)>
  <!ELEMENT abstract (ab_text|#PCDATA)>
    <!ELEMENT ab_text (#PCDATA)>
  <!ELEMENT page (#PCDATA)>
  <!ELEMENT end_notes (#PCDATA)>
  ]>
```

▲ After parsing to check the document and element structure, start changing from ANY to mixed content consisting of #PCDATA and child elements. Note the addition of the first third-generation child element.

Listing 8-10: CONTINUING TO DEVELOP THE DTD

```
<?xml version = "1.0"?>
<!DOCTYPE document [
<!ELEMENT document
(title,abstract,page+,end_notes)>
  <!ELEMENT title (#PCDATA)>
  <!ELEMENT abstract (ab_text|#PCDATA)>
    <!ELEMENT ab_text (#PCDATA)>
  <!ELEMENT page ((head1|head2|pg_text))
                  |#PCDATA>
    <!ELEMENT head1 (#PCDATA)>
    <!ELEMENT head2 (#PCDATA)>
    <!ELEMENT pg_text (#PCDATA)>
  <!ELEMENT end_notes (end_text|#PCDATA)>
      <!ELEMENT end_text (#PCDATA)> ]>
```

▲ As you develop the DTD, continue to change from the ANY type to mixed content. Also, add other third-generation child elements.

119

Declaring an EMPTY Element

An empty element is either a container for future content (such as HTML's `<IMG>` element, which imports graphic images into a document) or an element that needs no content (such as HTML's `<BR>` element). In the case of the `<IMG>` element (or the `<OBJECT>` element, which imports graphics and other multimedia files such as audio or video files), you specify the URL of the image file that will be included in the final output; there is no reason or logical way to include the graphic or file in the XML document before it is processed and sent on to a target application for further processing. As you know, `<BR>` just places a line break within a file being output. The `<BR>` element is a formatting tool that does not add content to the file. Therefore, a `<BR>` element is empty.

An empty element can have attributes (such as the URL of an image to be imported, alignment information, height and width, or a name), but cannot have contents between its start tag and end tag.

When you declare an empty element, use the following format:

```
<!ELEMENT linebreak EMPTY>
<!ELEMENT image EMPTY>
```

You could also use one of these two formats to declare empty elements:

```
<!ELEMENT linebreak ANY>
<!ELEMENT image (#PCDATA)>
```

If you want the elements to be empty, simply don't include any contents. However, declaring any content other than `EMPTY` means that you could insert unwanted content accidentally — and an XML parser may not discover your error.

TAKE NOTE

SPECIFYING AN EMPTY ELEMENT IN AN XML DOCUMENT

Because all XML elements must have both start tags and end tags, you can format an empty element as follows:

```
<linebreak></linebreak>
```

However, you can also use the following special shortcut format:

```
<linebreak/>
```

This format combines the start tag and the end tag into one, saving you extra keystrokes. When an empty element includes one or more attributes, you can format it as follows:

```
<image url="/pictures/tree001.gif"
id="firstgraf" height="60px"
width="60px" align="center"/>
```

or

```
<multi url="/sounds/train.wav"
id="whistle"/>
```

Note that you will probably use style sheets to format your documents, so the only important attributes in the prior example are the URL and the identifier.

The shortcut format of an empty element serves an important purpose: It signals those maintaining the XML document that this particular element is and should remain empty.

CROSS-REFERENCE

Chapter 13 teaches you how to set up an XML document and how to add both empty elements and elements with content to it.

FIND IT ONLINE

MIL-M-38784C, at **ftp://navycals.dt.navy.mil/pub/dtd/3878c.dtd**, is a 16-page U.S. Navy SGML DTD.

Listing 8-11: PART OF AN EXPANDED CATALOG DTD

```
<?xml version = "1.0"?>
<!DOCTYPE catalog [
<!ELEMENT catalog (logo
❶→ |(cover,intro,page+,order_form,back))>
    <!ELEMENT logo EMPTY>←❷
    <!ELEMENT cover (#PCDATA)>
    <!ELEMENT intro (#PCDATA)>  ❸
    <!ELEMENT page (letter,graphic,blurb,
                    id,code,price)>
      <!ELEMENT letter (#PCDATA)>
      <!ELEMENT graphic EMPTY>←❹
      <!ELEMENT blurb (#PCDATA)>
      <!ELEMENT id (#PCDATA)>
      <!ELEMENT code (#PCDATA)>
      <!ELEMENT price (#PCDATA)>
```

❶ *A pipe symbol allows the* logo *element to be selected any time.*
❷ *Declare the* logo *element to be the* EMPTY *type.*
❸ *The* graphic *element must appear after* letter *and before* blurb.
❹ *Declare the* graphic *element to be* EMPTY.

Listing 8-12: A DTD FOR A MEMO DOCUMENT

```
<?xml version="1.0"?>
<!DOCTYPE MEMO [
<!ELEMENT MEMO ((TO, FROM, SUBJECT,
BODY)|linebreak|image|hrule)>
<!ELEMENT TO         (#PCDATA)
<!ELEMENT FROM       (#PCDATA)
<!ELEMENT SUBJECT    (#PCDATA)
<!ELEMENT BODY       (#PCDATA)
<!ELEMENT linebreak EMPTY>
<!ELEMENT image      EMPTY>
<!ELEMENT hrule      EMPTY>
]>
```

▲ *This internal DTD subset includes three empty elements. The* image *element inserts an image. And after you define attributes or add styles, the* hrule *and linebreak elements will format the XML output.*

Listing 8-13: A FORM-LETTER DTD

```
<?xml version="1.0"?>
<!DOCTYPE customer [
<!ELEMENT customer ((name+, address*,
                    city+, state+,
 zip+, email?)|hrule|linebreak|spaces))>
    <!ELEMENT name       (#PCDATA)>
    <!ELEMENT address    (#PCDATA)>
    <!ELEMENT city       (#PCDATA)>
    <!ELEMENT state      (#PCDATA)>
    <!ELEMENT zip        (#PCDATA)>
    <!ELEMENT email      (#PCDATA)>
    <!ELEMENT hrule      EMPTY>
    <!ELEMENT linebreak EMPTY>
    <!ELEMENT spaces     EMPTY>
]>
```

▲ *This internal DTD subset, which includes three empty elements, defines a mailing label separated from the next label with a horizontal rule. After you style it, the* spaces *element will insert a set number of spaces.*

Personal Workbook

Q&A

1 How do you add a list of child elements to an element declaration?

_____

_____

_____

2 What does a *comma symbol* indicate? What does a *pipe symbol* mean?

_____

_____

_____

3 Name three ways to make a DTD more understandable to those who will maintain it.

_____

_____

_____

4 What are the four types of content for an element?

_____

_____

_____

5 What content can the ANY type of element include?

_____

_____

_____

6 What content can the Mixed type of element include?

_____

_____

_____

7 What trait of an entity reference allows it to be included in #PCDATA?

_____

_____

_____

8 What content can the EMPTY type of element include?

_____

_____

_____

ANSWERS: PAGE 453

EXTRA PRACTICE

1 For a DTD that will control an instruction-sheet document for assembling a bookcase, list the elements — root, child elements, and additional generations.

2 Write the instruction-sheet DTD based on the elements that you listed.

3 Assign types for each of the elements in the instruction-sheet DTD.

4 For a DTD that will structure an employment page at your Web site, list the elements — root, child elements, and additional generations. Include a page title, two heading levels, body text, and a footer with links to your home page.

5 Write the employment-page DTD based on the elements that you listed.

REAL-WORLD APPLICATIONS

✔ Your company has assigned you the task of creating a letterhead module to be inserted into all corporate DTDs. Design and create an external DTD subset that includes the appropriate elements.

✔ You have volunteered to put a local nonprofit organization on the Web. Your first task is to develop the organization's home page, which will include links to five future pages of your choice. Plan and write a DTD that includes elements for the home page.

✔ You are teaching a course in elementary PC use. Plan and write a DTD that includes name, address, and grade information that can be plugged into a database program and can also be printed in a report format.

Visual Quiz

What elements would you write for this database input form? What would you do to convert the information in this database to a DTD that would produce printed reports?

_____

_____

_____

_____

_____

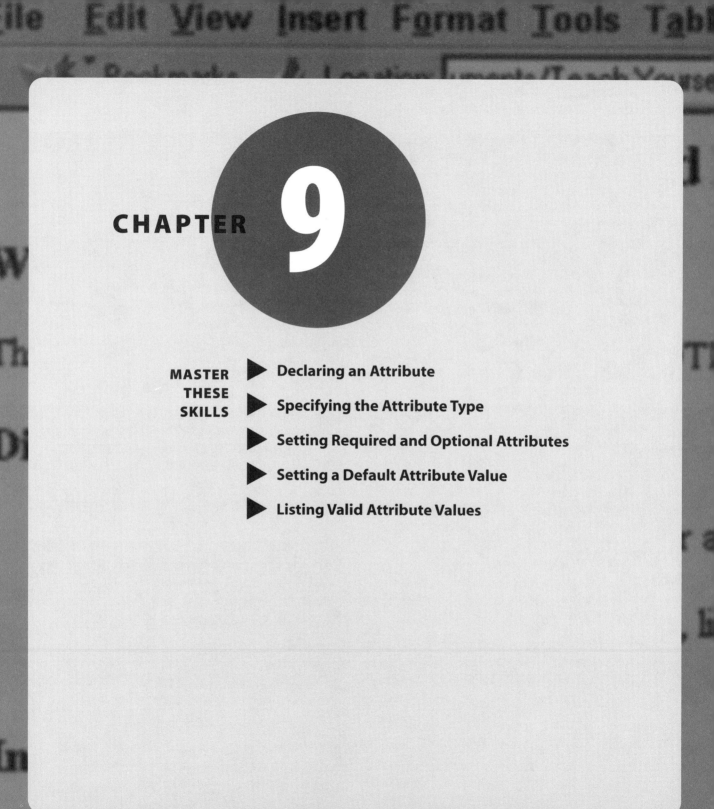

CHAPTER 9

MASTER
THESE
SKILLS

▶ Declaring an Attribute

▶ Specifying the Attribute Type

▶ Setting Required and Optional Attributes

▶ Setting a Default Attribute Value

▶ Listing Valid Attribute Values

Defining Attributes

In this chapter, you will get detailed information about attribute-list declarations and each of their components. An *attribute* is an option that affects the behavior of and further defines an element. Attributes can change or specify formats, alignments, text enhancements, paragraphs, or other parts of an XML document.

When you declare an attribute list for an element, you provide additional information that will upgrade the element in some way. For example, you can give the element an identifier that allows extended linking—one of the great advantages of using XML. Or you can format or enhance an element by aligning it, changing its color, adding a border, and so on. In a DTD, the ATTLIST keyword signals an attribute-list declaration, a list of attributes and their values for a particular element. Because an attribute list appears in a DTD, attributes are important only to valid XML documents. Typically, each element in a DTD has an associated list of several attributes—all contributing in their own way to the element.

When you assign an attribute type to a particular attribute in the attribute-list declaration, you control both the attribute value and the type of value that is allowed. For example, CDATA, the most common attribute type, enables you to limit the attribute value of a string to character data only. So, by giving an attribute a CDATA attribute type, you are actually stating that the attribute value is both a string and that it is character data. The XML specification provides 10 attribute types in three categories: string, *tokenized* (a basic unit of XML, such as a name), and *enumerated* (one or more notations).

The default declaration, which is at the end of an attribute-list declaration, enables you to make an attribute's use required or optional. You can also fix one valid value, set a default value that can be changed, or list a set of valid values.

XML reserves several attributes, all starting with xml: or xml-. For example, you can use xml:space to state whether white space is preserved, or you can use xml-stylesheet to associate a style sheet with the current document. (Thus, when you name attributes, do not start the name with xml.) As you read through the book, you'll find more of these predefined xml: attributes.

Declaring an Attribute

Attributes build on the element structure defined in a DTD. In a way, attributes are the icing on the element cake. For example, if you define a horizontal-rule element, you can add attributes that control the font, font size, and color; align the rule with the left margin, the right margin, or both margins; and identify the rule so that you can link to it.

As you declare elements or after you complete all the element declarations in a DTD, you can specify attributes for each element. The order in which you specify attributes is up to you. An attribute-list declaration includes the `ATTLIST` keyword, the name of the element with which it is associated, the attribute name, its attribute type or one or more values, and its default declaration. An attribute list is located under the element with which it is associated. For example:

```
<!ELEMENT HRULE EMPTY>
<!ATTLIST HRULE
    id        ID                  #IMPLIED
    align     (left|right|center) #IMPLIED
    noshade   (noshade)           #IMPLIED
    size      CDATA               #IMPLIED
    width     CDATA               #IMPLIED
>

    or

<!ELEMENT HRULE EMPTY>
<!ATTLIST HRULE id    ID
                                #IMPLIED>
<!ATTLIST HRULE align (left|right|center)
                                #IMPLIED>
<!ATTLIST HRULE noshade  (noshade)
                                #IMPLIED>
<!ATTLIST HRULE size        CDATA
                                #IMPLIED>
```

```
<!ATTLIST HRULE width      CDATA
                                #IMPLIED>
```

Note that these examples, which show the two valid ways of declaring attributes, are based on the horizontal rule (`HR`) element declaration in the HTML 4.0 DTD. (See the original HTML 4.0 declaration on the facing page.) The name of the attribute list is the same as the element name. The first column of the list (starting with `id` and ending with `width`) is the individual attribute name. The second column contains the attribute type or one or more values from which you can choose. (For more information about the 10 XML attribute types, see the next task.) The final column contains the default declaration. (Table 9-1 lists the XML attribute defaults.) The default `#IMPLIED` indicates that the attribute is optional.

CROSS-REFERENCE

Chapter 1 contains information about understanding and including attributes in an XML document.

FIND IT ONLINE

To browse through an online book about SGML declarations, go to **http://www.omnimark.com/white/dec/**.

XML 1.0: THE ATTRIBUTE-LIST DECLARATION AND RELATED PRODUCTIONS

[52]   AttlistDecl ::= '<!ATTLIST' S Name AttDef* S? '>' ←❶

[53]   AttDef ::= S Name S AttType S DefaultDecl ←❷
                        ❸   ❹

❶ *Start an attribute-list declaration with the* !ATTLIST *keyword.*
❷ *Use the same valid name for the element and attribute list.*
❸ *Name an individual attribute.*
❹ *End with the attribute type and the default declaration.*

HTML 4.0: THE HR ELEMENT AND ATTRIBUTE DECLARATION

[52]   AttlistDecl ::= '<!ATTLIST' S Name AttDef* S? '>' ←❶

[53]   AttDef ::= S Name S AttType S DefaultDecl ←❷
                        ❸   ❹

❶ *This empty element has a start tag and no end tag.*
❷ *Both the element and the attribute list are named* HR.
❸ *The* %coreattrs; *and* %events; *entities include regularly used attributes.*
❹ %Pixels; *and* %Length; *represent commonly used values.*

Specifying the Attribute Type

ttribute types control the values of particular attributes. For example, the CDATA type limits an attribute in two ways: it must be a string, and it must contain character data. As mentioned earlier, XML supports 10 attribute types in three categories: string, tokenized, and enumerated. Obviously, the string type refers to an attribute that is a string. The tokenized types apply to a *token*, which is a basic unit that cannot be broken down into smaller pieces. Tokens include reserved words, entities, operators, and variable names. The enumerated type is either a *notation* (a formalized set of symbols or an alphabet) or a list of notation values.

CDATA, the only string type, indicates that the attribute contains character data. This is the default attribute type. An example of an attribute list item with a CDATA type is

```
<!ATTLIST logo height CDATA #IMPLIED>)
```

In this case, the height attribute (for the logo element) will be expressed as a string (for example, "10" in the default unit of measure). Notice that the value of the string is enclosed within quotation marks. You can also enclose strings within single quote marks.

The ID type, one of several tokenized types, is a unique identification value: no other attribute for this element type can have this particular value. In addition, an ID must be a valid XML name and it must have a default value of #IMPLIED or #REQUIRED. An example of the ID type is

```
<!ATTLIST logo id ID #REQUIRED>
```

You should almost always require an identifier for all of your elements — primarily to take advantage of XML's support for extended links and extended pointers. For more information about XLinks and XPointers, see Part IV.

The tokenized types IDREF and IDREFS are a cross-reference to one or more ID values that occur somewhere in the XML document. Both IDREF and IDREFS must be valid XML names. An attribute list with an IDREF type might look like this:

```
<!ATTLIST LABEL for IDREF #IMPLIED>
```

This example is for the for attribute of HTML 4.0's LABEL element. The IDREFS type is a list of IDREF values. For example:

```
<!ATTLIST TH headers IDREFS #IMPLIED>
```

When you list IDREFS names in an XML document, separate each one with a space.

Continued

TAKE NOTE

▶ DIFFERENT CDATAS

Do not confuse the CDATA attribute type with a CDATA section in an XML document. Although they both represent character data, they have completely different reasons for existing. The CDATA attribute type, like all other attributes types, never represents markup of any kind. The markup within a CDATA section is interpreted as character data.

CROSS-REFERENCE

In Chapter 13, you learn how to enter elements, attributes, and content in an XML document.

FIND IT ONLINE

RFC 1738: Uniform Resource Locators (**http://www.w3.org/Addressing/rfc1738.txt**) discusses URLs.

XML 1.0: THE STRINGTYPE AND TOKENIZEDTYPE PRODUCTIONS

```
[52]     AttlistDecl ::= '<!ATTLIST' S Name AttDef* S? '>'  ①
[53]        AttDef ::= S Name S AttType S DefaultDecl  ②
[54]       AttType ::= StringType | TokenizedType | EnumeratedType
[55]    StringType ::= 'CDATA'  ③
[56]  TokenizedType ::= 'ID' | 'IDREF' | 'IDREFS' | 'ENTITY' | 'ENTITIES'
                   ④  | 'NMTOKEN' | 'NMTOKENS'
```

① *The attribute-list declaration includes any number of attribute definitions.*
② *An attribute definition includes a name, attribute type, and default declaration.*
③ *The keyword for the StringType production is* CDATA.
④ *The TokenizedType production lists seven choices.*

Listing 9-1: PART OF A CATALOG DTD

```
<?xml version = "1.0"?>
<!DOCTYPE catalog [
<!ELEMENT catalog (logo |(cover,intro,page+,
order_form,back))>
  <!ELEMENT logo EMPTY>
  <!ELEMENT cover (#PCDATA)>
    <!ATTLIST intro
    id        ID          #IMPLIED  ①
    border  (on|off)  "on"  ②
                                     ③
    company CDATA       #FIXED "Acme"
    phone   CDATA       #FIXED "800-555-5555"
```

① *Include an identifier attribute for almost every element.*
② *Set the default value for* border *to "on."*
③ *Fix the* company *and* phone *attributes to particular values.*

Listing 9-2: MORE OF THE CATALOG DTD

```
<!ELEMENT page
    (letter, graphic, blurb, id, price)>
  <!ELEMENT letter (#PCDATA)>
  <!ELEMENT graphic EMPTY>
  <!ELEMENT blurb (#PCDATA)>
    <!ATTLIST blurb id    ID    #IMPLIED  ⑧
      lang   CDATA    "EN"  ⑨
      align    (left|right|center) #IMPLIED>
  <!ELEMENT id (#PCDATA)>                 ⑩
  <!ELEMENT price (#PCDATA)>
```

⑧ *Add an* id *attribute to the* blub *element.*
⑨ *Set the value of the* lang *(language) attribute to "*EMN*" (English).*
⑩ *A developer can choose from three align values.*

Specifying the Attribute Type

Continued

Another set of tokenized types, ENTITY and ENTITIES, refers to one or more general entities. ENTITY refers to a single general entity. An example of the ENTITY type is:

```
<!ATTLIST logo src ENTITY #REQUIRED>
```

The src attribute refers to a URI in an entity declared elsewhere in the DTD. The ENTITIES type refers to a list of general entities, also declared in this DTD. For example:

```
<!ATTLIST pics src ENTITIES #REQUIRED>
```

In this case, ENTITIES indicates that there will be a list of pictures (pics), each separated by a space. Note that you do not precede the general entities with the & and ; delimiters.

The last set of tokenized attribute types is NMTOKEN and NMTOKENS, which refer to one or more valid XML name tokens. *Name tokens* are names that start with any letter, digit, or valid character. An example of an attribute list declaration for the NMTOKEN type is

```
<!ATTLIST macintosh model NMTOKEN #IMPLIED>
```

The model attribute of the macintosh element refers to a computer model name, which might contain both letters and numbers. The NMTOKENS type is a list of valid XML name tokens (in this case, a list of computer models), each separated by one space. For example:

```
<!ATTLIST macintosh models NMTOKENS
#IMPLIED>
```

XML names and name tokens serve the same purpose. However, valid XML names must start with a letter or an underscore, and valid XML name tokens can start with any letter, digit, and many other characters. (Note that the XML specification also allows valid names to start with colons; however, the colon is actually reserved for future use.)

The enumerated attribute types, NOTATION and enumerated NOTATION, indicate that the attribute has one or more values specified by a notation declaration in the current DTD. For example:

```
<!ATTLIST audio play NOTATION #REQUIRED>
```

To use the enumerated version of NOTATION, enter the keyword NOTATION followed by notation values separated by the pipe symbol and enclosed within parentheses. For example:

```
<!ATTLIST audio play NOTATION (jp | ra)
#REQUIRED>
```

TAKE NOTE

▶ LEARNING ABOUT NOTATION

Notation is a system of defining a means of communication using an authorized set of symbols or characters. It can identify Braille, musical notes, dance steps, and even computer file formats.

CROSS-REFERENCE
Chapter 3 discusses EBNF, with which you can create well-formed or valid XML documents, including DTDs.

FIND IT ONLINE
RFC 1808: Relative Uniform Resource Locators (**http://www.w3.org/Addressing/rfc1808.txt**) covers relative URLs.

XML 1.0: THE ENUMERATEDTYPE AND RELATED PRODUCTIONS

```
[54]        AttType ::= StringType | TokenizedType
                    | EnumeratedType

[57] EnumeratedType ::= NotationType | Enumeration   ←❶

[58]    NotationType ::= 'NOTATION' S '(' S? Name (S? '|'   [ VC: Notation
                    ❷  S? Name) * S? ')'                ❸        Attributes ]

[59]      Enumeration ::= '(' S? Nmtoken (S? '|' S?        [VC: Enumeration ]
                    Nmtoken)* S? ')' ❹
```

❶ The EnumeratedType *production allows two choices:* NotationType *and* Enumeration.
❷ The NotationType *production starts with the* NOTATION *keyword.*
❸ *A notation list consists of XML names separated by pipe symbols.*
❹ *An enumeration list comprises XML name tokens separated by pipes.*

Listing 9-3: AN UNORDERED-LIST ELEMENT

```
<!ELEMENT ulist (listitem)+>  ←❶

<!ATTLIST ulist ←❷

lang      CDATA                    ❸→"EN"
id        ID                    #IMPLIED
type      (disc|square|circle)  #IMPLIED
compact (compact) ❹             #IMPLIED
>
```

❶ *The ulist element includes any number of list items.*
❷ *Start the attribute list with the* !ATTLIST *keyword.*
❸ *The default language is English.*
❹ *Choose a value from within the set of parentheses.*

Listing 9-4: A SAMPLE TABLE ELEMENT AND ITS ATTRIBUTES

```
<!ELEMENT table (caption?, (col*|colgroup*),
thead?, tfoot?, tbody+)>
<!ATTLIST table
        id          ID          #IMPLIED
        align       (left|center|right)
                                #IMPLIED
        bgcolor     CDATA       #IMPLIED
        width       CDATA       #IMPLIED
        border      CDATA       #IMPLIED
        frame       (none|top|bottom
         |topbottom|left|right|leftright
         |all)                  #IMPLIED
        rules       (none|groups|rows
         |cols|all)             #IMPLIED
>
```

▲ *The attribute list for this sample* table *element is a simplified version of HTML's* TABLE *attribute list.*

Setting Required and Optional Attributes

The last item on an attribute list is the default declaration. This item enables you to further control the attribute by making it required or optional; by setting a default value that is the only allowable value; by supplying one default value that can be changed; or by listing a set of valid values. In a default declaration, you can select from the following options:

► Use the #REQUIRED keyword to require that the XML document developer supply a value for a particular attribute.

► Use the #IMPLIED keyword to allow the XML document developer to decide whether to supply a value, accept the default value, or let the processing application choose a default value that may or may not be identical to the default value that you set in the DTD.

► Use the #FIXED keyword to fix a default value that you include in the attribute definition. If the XML document developer enters a value that is not the fixed value, the XML processor should issue a warning. If the developer does not enter a value, the processing application takes the default value.

► You can supply a value. If the developer enters a value other than that you entered in the DTD, the XML processor accepts that value. If the developer does not enter a value, the processing application uses the default value.

► You can supply a set of valid values from which the developer can choose.

When you specify a value for an attribute, it cannot contain the less-than (<) symbol or the ampersand (&).

The XML specification includes certain rules for using the #REQUIRED and #IMPLIED keywords in XML documents. For instance, for an XML document to be valid, an attribute that is #REQUIRED must include the attribute name and an attribute value. If the XML document developer has not included a value for an #IMPLIED attribute, the XML parser must report on the missing value and continue processing.

TAKE NOTE

► QUESTIONING THE #IMPLIED TERM

As you have learned, the #IMPLIED attribute value means that the value is optional. So, why isn't the #IMPLIED attribute value named #OPTIONAL instead? After all, the term *optional* seems to be much more popular among the computer-literate. The value of #IMPLIED *implies* that the processing application will supply a default value. In other words, an attribute should always have a user- or application-supplied value: the value is not really optional.

► USING THE POUND SIGN (#) IN DTDS

Why do keywords such as #REQUIRED, #IMPLIED, and #FIXED start with the pound sign? The answer is that this symbol distinguishes these keywords from valid XML names. In other words, when you create a DTD you can use uppercase or lowercase required, implied, and fixed to name components in the DTD.

CROSS-REFERENCE

Chapter 16 includes a task on correcting attributes in an HTML document that you are converting to XML.

FIND IT ONLINE

For a list of SGML and other resources, go to http://www.NCSA.uiuc.edu/SDG/Software/ Mosaic/WebSGML.html.

Table 9-1: XML ATTRIBUTE DEFAULTS

Default	Description
#IMPLIED	This default is optional. If the document developer does not supply an attribute value, the processing application should.
#REQUIRED	This default requires that the attribute be used.
#FIXED default_value	This default provides a fixed attribute value. The individual working on the document cannot enter a different value. If no value is entered, the attribute takes the default value.
default_value	This default provides a default value for the attribute. If no value is entered, the attribute takes the default value.

Listing 9-5: A SAMPLE FRAMESET ELEMENT AND ATTRIBUTES

①

```
<!ELEMENT frameset ((frameset|frame)+
                            |noframes)>
<!ATTLIST frameset
rows            CDATA           #IMPLIED  ←②
cols            CDATA           #IMPLIED
>
<!ELEMENT frame EMPTY>
<!ATTLIST frame
name            CDATA           #IMPLIED
url             CDATA           #IMPLIED
frameborder     (1|0)           "1"  ←③
marginwidth     CDATA           #IMPLIED
marginheight    CDATA           #IMPLIED
```

① *You can include another frameset or a frame in a frameset.*
② *#IMPLIED indicates that the attribute value is optional.*
③ *The value "1" is the default value for the frameborder attribute.*

XML 1.0: THE DEFAULT DECLARATION AND RELATED PRODUCTIONS

```
[52]     AttlistDecl ::= '<!ATTLIST' S Name AttDef*S? '>'
[53]          AttDef ::= S Name S AttType S DefaultDecl
[60] DefaultDecl    ::= '#REQUIRED' | '#IMPLIED' | (('#FIXED' S)? AttValue)
                                        [VC: Required Attribute ]
                                        [VC: Attribute Default Legal ]
                                        [WFC: No < in Attribute Values ]
                                        [VC: Fixed Attribute Default ]
[10]        AttValue ::= '"' ([^<&"] | Reference)* '"'
                       | "'" ([^<&'] | Reference)* "'"
```

▲ *A default declaration can consist of the #REQUIRED keyword, the #IMPLIED keyword, the #FIXED keyword with an attribute value, or the attribute value alone.*

Setting a Default Attribute Value

You can set a default attribute value in two ways: You can suggest the value or insist on it. The difference is the `#FIXED` keyword. Look at the following two examples:

```
<!ATTLIST info company CDATA "Acme">
<!ATTLIST info company CDATA #FIXED
"Acme">
```

In the first example, although "`Acme`" is the default value for the company attribute, an XML document developer can override that value by typing a different company name. The second example forces the developer to accept the default company name. In both cases, however, the XML processor uses the default value if the company name is not entered.

The value of an attribute can be an entity reference, which must be preceded by a # symbol. The entity reference cannot contain a & (because this symbol represents an entity-reference delimiter) or a less-than symbol (because it indicates the beginning of a start tag or end tag). The attribute value must follow other rules of the attribute type and rules stated in the XML specification. For example, if the type is `CDATA`, the value must be treated as a string.

Keep in mind that when you use an attribute in an XML document, it is inserted completely within the start tag. If the element is not empty, the attribute looks something like this:

```
<table id="table1" height="30" width="60">
insert table contents here
</table>
```

However, if the element is empty, the attribute might look like this:

```
<image url="/pictures/sample1.gif/>
```

Remember that the end tag symbol is inserted at the end of the start tag.

Choosing Between Attributes and Elements

As you develop a DTD, sometimes you may have to choose between adding one or more attributes to an existing element or declaring a new element. In making a decision, you should know the basic difference between elements and attributes. Elements usually specify part of a document's structure (say, the body or a title) or a type of content (such as a list). Attributes usually add information about an element (for example, its size, its look, or an identifier). Sometimes, the choice is obvious, as in adding a high-level structural element (which would not make a good attribute) or a formatting attribute. (Elements don't work well as formatting components.)

Other times — especially when you are working in the content area or in elements that define small areas of a document, it's a tossup between elements and attributes. When you set up a short paper with a title, byline, and creation date — none of which contribute to the document structure — either choice is appropriate, but declaring an attribute is probably better. However, note that attributes are not as flexible as elements: they cannot have attributes of their own. The bottom line is that the choice should usually be left to the DTD developer. He or she may be more comfortable declaring elements or attributes.

CROSS-REFERENCE

Chapter 23 shows you how to use an extended pointer to find an attribute to which you can create a link.

FIND IT ONLINE

Read about XML history and more at **http://www. csclub.uwaterloo.ca/u/relander/Academic/XML/ xml_mw.html.**

XML 1.0: THE ATTVALUE DECLARATION AND RELATED PRODUCTIONS

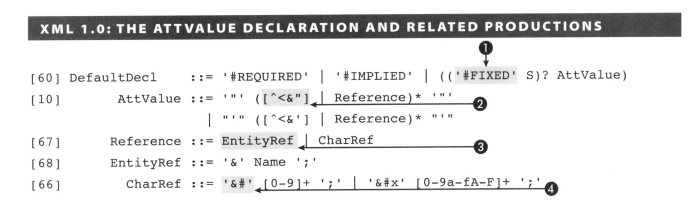

```
[60] DefaultDecl    ::= '#REQUIRED' | '#IMPLIED' | (('#FIXED' S)? AttValue)
[10]        AttValue ::= '"' ([^<&"] | Reference)* '"'
                       | "'" ([^<&'] | Reference)* "'"
[67]       Reference ::= EntityRef | CharRef
[68]       EntityRef ::= '&' Name ';'
[66]         CharRef ::= '&#' [0-9]+ ';' | '&#x' [0-9a-fA-F]+ ';'
```

❶ *The #FIXED keyword is optional.*
❷ *The* AttValue *production does not include the* < *or* &.
❸ *The attribute value can be an entity reference (*&name;*).*
❹ *The attribute value can be a character reference, preceded by* &#.

Listing 9-6: A TEXTFONT ELEMENT AND ITS ATTRIBUTES

```
<!ELEMENT textfont EMPTY>
<!ATTLIST textfont
lang   CDATA                        "EN"
size   (10|12)                      "10"
color  (black|red|blue)             "black"
face   (Times New Roman|Courier New)
                        "Times New Roman"
>
```

▲ *The* textfont *attribute list is based on HTML's* BASEFONT
attributes.

Listing 9-7: PART OF A PRESS RELEASE DTD

```
<?xml version = "1.0"?>
<!DOCTYPE pr [
<!ELEMENT pr (logo|(title,para+, info))>
  <!ELEMENT    logo  EMPTY>
    <!ATTLIST logo
        url      CDATA        #REQUIRED>
  <!ELEMENT    title (#PCDATA)>
    <!ATTLIST title
        font    CDATA        "Helvetica"
        size    CDATA        "14">
```

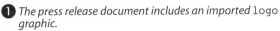

❶ *The press release document includes an imported* logo *graphic.*
❷ *The* title *attribute list includes defaults for the* font *and* size.

Listing Valid Attribute Values

As some of the examples in this chapter have shown, you are not limited to supplying individual attribute values. The attribute value production also allows XML document developers to choose from a list of valid values.

```
[10] AttValue ::= '"' ([^<&"]
                 | Reference)* '"'
                 | "'" ([^<&']
                 | Reference)* "'"
```

Remember that the asterisk (*) indicates that the expression within the parentheses can be used any number of times. Thus, an attribute list can include single values

```
<!ATTLIST title size CDATA        "14">
```

and lists of values. These values can be followed by an attribute value default declaration (which specifies a default value)

```
<!ATTLIST title size (12|14|16|24) "14">
```

or they can be followed by a keyword type of default declaration (which allows the user to choose from the list):

```
<!ATTLIST title size (12|14|16|24)
                              #IMPLIED>
```

If you have any questions about the default declaration syntax, refer to the AttValue Declaration and Related Productions listing on the previous page.

Introducing XML-Data

XML-Data, which is currently a note at the World Wide Web Consortium (W3C), is a vocabulary: a set of predefined XML elements, attributes, entities, and relationships. This vocabulary allows XML document developers to specify *schema*, which set the characteristics of object types. You can use XML-Data to define a syntax, such as XML itself, or relationships, such as the connection between databases and graphs that illustrate those databases. Obviously, you can use a DTD to define a syntax, but defining a relationship is another matter. Using XML-Data, you can manipulate a database to produce a series of reports — all based on various relationships that you define.

The W3C note on XML-Data suggests the elementType declaration, with which you can declare an element and add attributes (and which is considered the cornerstone of XML-Data). XML-Data also includes a syntax for adding child elements and specifying relationships within the specific element (and to other classes of elements as well). Earlier chapters in this book discuss how to control the content of elements using the EMPTY and ANY keywords as well as the Mixed and children productions. XML-Data extends and enriches these element-declaration components.

To track the "official" development of XML-Data, read the note at **http://www.w3.org/TR/1998/ NOTE-XML-data/**, which includes a copy of the XML-Data DTD. Microsoft employee Andrew Layman wrote the initial proposal for XML-Data.

CROSS-REFERENCE

Chapter 30 introduces the Extended Stylesheet Language, an XML-like language for styling documents.

FIND IT ONLINE

Go to **http://www.w3.org/XML/Activity.html** to read about using generic SGML in Web documents.

Listing 9-8: ENHANCED PRESS RELEASE ELEMENTS

```
<!ELEMENT    title (#PCDATA)>
    <!ATTLIST title
            name    CDATA               #REQUIRED
            id      ID                  #REQUIRED
            font    (Helvetica|Arial Black)
                                    "Helvetica"
            size    (12|14|16|24)       "14">


  <!ELEMENT    para (#PCDATA)>
    <!ATTLIST para
            id      ID                  #REQUIRED
            font    (Times New Roman
            |Book Antigua) "Times New Roman"
            size    (10|12)             "10">
```

▲ The enhanced title and para elements enable the
document developer to choose from lists of fonts and sizes.

Listing 9-9: AN IMPROVED UNORDERED-LIST EXAMPLE

```
<!ELEMENT ulist (listitem)+>
<!ATTLIST ulist
lang    (en|fr|es|de)           "en"
id      ID                      #IMPLIED
type    (disc|square|circle)    "disc"
compact (compact)               #IMPLIED
>
```

▲ The up-to-date version of the unordered-list attributes
example offers a choice of four languages: English, French,
Spanish, and German. Note that you must have a font that
supports the alphabet of the chosen language.

Listing 9-10: AN IMPROVED TABLE ELEMENT EXAMPLE

```
<!ELEMENT table (caption?, (col*|colgroup*), thead?, tfoot?, tbody+)>
  <!ATTLIST table
  id          ID                                                      #IMPLIED
  align       (left|center|right)                                     #IMPLIED
  bgcolor     CDATA                                                   #IMPLIED
  width       CDATA                                                   #IMPLIED
  border      CDATA                                                   #IMPLIED
  frame       (none|top|bottom|topbottom|left|right|leftright|all)    #IMPLIED
  rules       (none|groups|rows|cols|all)                             #IMPLIED
  cellpadding CDATA                                                   #IMPLIED
  cellspacing CDATA                                                   #IMPLIED
>
```

▲ The table attributes example, shown earlier in this chapter, now includes defaults for each list of values.

Personal Workbook

Q&A

1 What is an *attribute*?

_____

_____

_____

2 What signals an attribute-list declaration?

_____

_____

_____

3 What is the most common attribute type? What is its purpose?

_____

_____

_____

4 Where do you place an attribute-list declaration in a DTD?

_____

_____

_____

5 List the tokenized types of attributes.

_____

_____

_____

6 What purpose does the default declaration serve?

_____

_____

_____

7 What is the basic difference between elements and attributes?

_____

_____

_____

8 When you list valid values in an attribute-list declaration, what can you include in the default declaration?

_____

_____

_____

ANSWERS: PAGE 454

EXTRA PRACTICE

❶ Compile a list of attributes that you could declare for a text element.

❷ Look at the last catalog DTD example in this chapter. How would you change the default language from English to German?

❸ In the last catalog DTD example, how would you specify the Book Antiqua font as the default value?

❹ In the catalog DTD example, insert an attribute list for the `graphic` element. (Hint: Look at the logo attributes example.)

❺ In the catalog DTD example, add a fixed fax attribute at an appropriate place.

❻ In the catalog DTD example, declare an attribute list for the order-form page, which is a table. Include table attributes as well as font and size attributes.

REAL-WORLD APPLICATIONS

✔ You like the press release DTD and want to adapt it for your business letters. Add appropriate elements, modify existing elements, add and edit attributes, and save it as a business letter DTD.

✔ Your company wants to add a telephone directory to its intranet. Write a DTD that produces a well-formatted Web page that includes employee telephone extensions and e-mail addresses.

✔ As you know, you can place predefined modules in DTDs. Write modules for an ordered (numbered) list and a definition list. (Hint: You can start with the syntax for the HTML OL and DL elements.)

✔ You manufacture and sell five models of bicycles for men, women, girls, and boys through a mail-order catalog. Write a DTD for an online catalog. Be sure to include elements and attributes for model, illustrations, order number, price, color, and size.

Visual Quiz

These are the XML productions that control the syntax of attribute declarations. Using the XML specification (http://www.w3.org/XML/) and this book, evaluate each of the VC comments for the TokenizedType production. Look at the Name and Nmtoken productions in the XML specification and decide which characters are valid and invalid in each production.

```
W Microsoft Word - attribute productions - fg09vq

File  Edit  View  Insert  Format  Tools  Table  Window  Help

[52]    AttlistDecl ::= '<!ATTLIST' S Name AttDef* S? '>'
[53]       AttDef ::= S Name S AttType S DefaultDecl
[54]      AttType ::= StringType | TokenizedType | EnumeratedType
[55]   StringType ::= 'CDATA'
[56] TokenizedType ::= 'ID'                        [VC: ID ]
                                                   [VC: One ID per
                                                        Element Type]
                                                   [VC: ID Attribute
                                                        Default ]
               | 'IDREF'                           [VC: IDREF ]
               | 'IDREFS'                          [VC: IDREF ]
               | 'ENTITY'                          [VC: Entity Name ]
               | 'ENTITIES'                        [VC: Entity Name ]
               | 'NMTOKEN'                         [VC: Name Token ]
               | 'NMTOKENS'                        [VC: Name Token ]
[57] EnumeratedType ::= NotationType | Enumeration
[58]  NotationType ::= 'NOTATION' S '(' S? Name (S? '|' S? Name)* S? ')'
                                                   [VC: Notation Attributes ]
[59]    Enumeration ::= '(' S? Nmtoken (S? '|' S? Nmtoken)* S? ')'
                                                   [VC: Enumeration ]
[60] DefaultDecl   ::= '#REQUIRED' | '#IMPLIED' | (('#FIXED' S)? AttValue)
                                                   [VC: Required Attribute ]
                                                   [VC: Attribute Default Legal ]
                                                   [WFC: No < in Attribute Values ]
                                                   [VC: Fixed Attribute Default ]

Page 1  Sec 1    1/1    At 4.9"  Ln 26  Col 1    REC TRK EXT OVR WPH
```

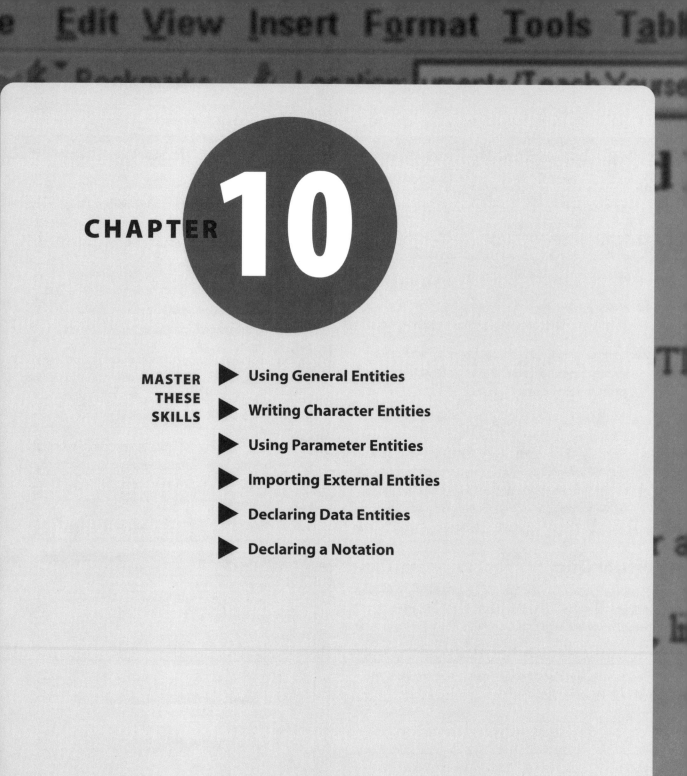

CHAPTER **10**

MASTER
THESE
SKILLS

▶ **Using General Entities**

▶ **Writing Character Entities**

▶ **Using Parameter Entities**

▶ **Importing External Entities**

▶ **Declaring Data Entities**

▶ **Declaring a Notation**

Using Entities

An *entity* is simply a named chunk of information — ranging in size all the way from a single character to an entire book consisting of one file. An *entity reference* refers to an entity from within an XML document. When an XML parser processes the document, it identifies each entity reference and replaces it with the content of the entity — that is, the replacement text.

You can use entities to represent long or technical words, commonly used but difficult-to-type text, or text (such as a product name) that you think will change in the final document. For example, an entity allows you use the nickname *fram* to avoid typing *The Frammis Manufacturing Organization, Inc.* too many times throughout a business plan or long report. You can compile a book using a series of chapter entities and other external documents. This has certain advantages: you can create boilerplate pages or documents that you can plug into all your books (and you can store the files in a central location), and you can show the underlying structure of the book without obstructing it with a great deal of text.

The two main categories of XML entities are general and parameter. A *general entity* occurs anywhere in the document, including some parts of the DTD, whereas a *parameter entity* occurs only within the DTD.

XML supports two combinations of general and parameter entities — and unparsed, internal and external:

▶ An *unparsed entity* contains information that has not been processed by an XML parser. The information is not tested for validity, but is sent to the target application in its original condition. An unparsed entity consists of a named *notation* (formal set of symbols). A *parsed entity* contains information that has been parsed and converted into replacement text. A parsed entity has a name and is called by an entity reference.

▶ An *internal entity* is a parsed literal that is declared and stored completely within the current DTD. Any other entity is an external entity. An *external entity* has its content stored in a separate file that is completely outside the XML document.

Using General Entities

Entities give XML document developers power over their documents. Obviously, developers can control the structure and content. However, a single document can continue for many pages. With entities, long documents can be made up of smaller files organized logically — somewhat like chapters in a book. Each of the files can be edited or even printed separately.

A *general entity* is a string usually named within the non-DTD part of a document; that is, its replacement text will become part of the document content. If a general entity will become part of the content, it can occur in the DTD. In an XML document, a general entity is preceded by an ampersand (&) and succeeded by a semicolon (;), using the format of the `EntityRef` production:

```
[68]    EntityRef ::= '&' Name ';'
```

Valid general-entity categories are internal parsed general, external parsed general, and external unparsed general. As you can see, a general entity comes in almost every flavor (except internal unparsed).

Here's a typical internal general entity declaration:

```
<!ENTITY copyright "This document is
    copyrighted by the Eddy Group, Inc.">
```

In this example, `copyright` is the name of the entity. When the XML parser finds the entity reference `&copyright;` in the document, it replaces the reference with the text `This document is copyrighted by the Eddy Group, Inc.`

You can embed an entity within an entity, like so:

```
<!ENTITY eddy "Eddy Group, Inc.">
<!ENTITY copyright "This document is
    copyrighted by the &eddy;">
```

Just make sure that you declare the entity that is to be embedded before the entity that contains it.

TAKE NOTE

USING ENTITY AND ENTITIES ATTRIBUTES IN A DTD

In Chapter 9, you learned about writing attribute-list declarations. Part of this type of declaration is the attribute type, which controls the value of a particular attribute. One of the three kinds of attribute types is the tokenized type. Tokens, which are the basic units (like the atoms) of markup, include entities, reserved words, operators, and variable names. The ENTITY and ENTITIES attribute types refers to one or a list of several general entities, respectively.

ENTITY DECLARATIONS IN DTDS

An XML parser processes an XML document from top to bottom. If an entity declaration is located after a mixed-content element in which that entity appears, the parser cannot correctly interpret the element's contents. Therefore, consider declaring all entities at the top of the DTD, above all element declarations. This ensures that all the entities included in mixed-content elements are processed before the XML parser interprets the elements.

CROSS-REFERENCE

Chapter 1 introduces you to XML and its building blocks — elements, tags, attributes, and entities.

FIND IT ONLINE

Read about markup and XML history at **http://www.cs.caltech.edu/~adam/papers/xml/x-marks-the-spot.html**.

Table 10-1: XML ENTITIES

Entity	Parsed/Unparsed	Internal/External	Description
General	Parsed	Internal	An embedded string that will appear as document content
General	Parsed	External	An imported file that will appear as document content
Character	Parsed	Internal/External	A type of general entity used to represent special characters
Data	Unparsed	External	A type of general entity used to import a non-XML file defined as binary
Parameter (PE)	Parsed	Internal	An embedded string used to enhance a DTD
Parameter (PE)	Parsed	External	An imported file used to enhance a DTD

XML 1.0: THE GENERAL ENTITY PRODUCTIONS

```
[70]    EntityDecl ::= GEDecl | PEDecl

[71]       GEDecl ::= '<!ENTITY' S Name S EntityDef S? '>'

[73]    EntityDef ::=  EntityValue | (ExternalID NDataDecl?)

[75]    ExternalID ::= 'SYSTEM' S SystemLiteral | 'PUBLIC' S PubidLiteral
                       S SystemLiteral

[76]    NDataDecl ::= S 'NDATA' S Name

[9]    EntityValue ::= '"' ([^%&"] | PEReference | Reference)* '"'
                       | "'" ([^%&'] | PEReference | Reference)* "'"
```

1 *A general entity starts with the* !ENTITY *keyword.*
2 *An entity definition can include a value, identifier, or data entity.*
3 *An external ID can be a* SYSTEM *or* PUBLIC *identifier.*
4 *A data entity includes the* NDATA *keyword.*

Writing Character Entities

Character entities are a particular type of general entity used to enter non-keyboard characters into an XML document. Say you're creating a cover letter in English and you want to incorporate accented *e*'s into the word *resume* to make *résumé*. Rather than incorrectly omit the accented *e*'s or use a utility such as Windows Character Map to insert the accented *e*'s (which the parser will probably misinterpret), you can declare entities for the character, as in this example:

```
<!ENTITY accent_e    "&#233;">
```

In an XML document, the character entity reference might look like this:

```
<para>
Enclosed is my r&#233;sum&#233;.
</para>
```

Remember that XML supports the entire Unicode character set. When you use a predefined entity name for the accented *e* (in this case, `&eacute;`), you can incorporate the accented *e*'s into the word without declaring an entity. For example:

```
<para>
Enclosed is my r&eacute;sum&eacute;.
</para>
```

If you use a certain special character constantly, consider explicitly declaring it in the DTD for the current document or for a set of documents. You can either look it up at the Unicode site or find it in one of the International Standards Organization (ISO) character sets. If you compile an entire set of commonly used character entities (or any other list of entities), either paste them into each of your DTDs or refer to them by using an external identifier.

Remember that XML reserves five predefined character entities. For a detailed list, see Table 10-3. Note also that Table 10-2 shows special characters used in XML entity references — mainly as starting delimiters.

Using Predefined Sets of ISO Entities

Many SGML DTDs refer to entity sets that are international standards from the ISO. You can do the same thing in your XML DTDs. For instance, you can specify the Latin 1 set using this type of entity declaration:

```
<!ENTITY % ISOlat1 PUBLIC
  "-//W3C//ENTITIES Full Latin
1//EN//HTML">
```

(Note that the `%` is a starting delimiter that indicates a parameter entity, which will be described in detail in the following task.) You can find the ISO standard entity sets at several Web or FTP sites. The Union of All ISO 8879 Entity Sets is located at **http://www.bbsinc.com/iso8879b.html.** To locate individual sets in the ISO 8879: 1986 standard, enter **ftp://ftp.ucc.ie/pub/sgml/entities/** and add the name of the entity group (such as isoamsa). If you know the name of the set, you can find both ISO 8879: 1986 and ISO 9573-13 or 15 ISO character sets. Enter **ftp://ftp.ucc.ie/pub/sgml/entities/** and the name of the entity group (say, isoamsa) followed by the **ent** extension. Table 10-2 lists the character entity sets in the ISO 8879 and 9573 standards.

CROSS-REFERENCE

In Chapter 4, you learn about XML-supported Unicode characters, including those used in entities.

FIND IT ONLINE

Go to an Introduction to XML (**http://www.arbortext.com/nwalsh.html**) to read a technical introduction.

Table 10-2: ISO 8879 AND 9573 CHARACTER ENTITY SETS

Character Entity Set	(ISO *nnnn*)	Title
ISOamsa	8879 and 9573-13	Added Math Symbols: Arrow Relations
ISOamsb	8879 and 9573-13	Added Math Symbols: Binary Operators
ISOamsc	8879 and 9573-13	Added Math Symbols: Delimiters
ISOamsn	8879 and 9573-13	Added Math Symbols: Negated Relations
ISOamso	8879 and 9573-13	Added Math Symbols: Ordinary
ISOamsr	8879	Added Math Symbols: Relations
ISObox	8879	Box and Line Drawing
ISOchem	9573-13	Chemistry
ISOcyr1	8879	Russian Cyrillic
ISOcyr2	8879	Non-Russian Cyrillic
ISOdia	8879	Diacritical Marks
ISOgrk1	8879	Greek Letters
ISOgrk2	8879	Monotoniko Greek
ISOgrk3	8879	Greek Symbols
ISOgrk4	8879	Alternative Greek Symbols
ISOgrk5	9573-15	Extra Classical Greek Letters
ISOlat1	8879	Added Latin 1
ISOlat2	8879	Added Latin 2
ISOmfrk	9573-13	Math Alphabets: Fraktur
ISOmopf	9573-13	Math Alphabets: Open Face
ISOmscr	9573-13	Math Alphabets: Script
ISOnum	8879	Numeric and Special Graphic
ISOpub	8879	Publishing
ISOtech	8879	General Technical

Using Parameter Entities

A parameter entity (PE) is a string that is named in the DTD only. A PE is always parsed because it is part of the document markup. Use a PE to enhance the current DTD by inserting a chunk of another DTD or by importing a DTD that is a standard either for your industry or the type of document on which you are working. For example, if you develop a document that combines a standard set of elements defined in your main DTD and elements declared especially for this document, use a PE to import the standard DTD. You could copy and paste, but this would increase the size of the current DTD unnecessarily. Using a PE to import the DTD limits the number of lines; the PE serves as a comment, too.

A PE's syntax differs slightly from that of a general entity. For example,

```
<!ENTITY % fontstyle "TT | I | B | BIG
                    | SMALL">
```

is declared by using the syntax in the XML PEReference production:

```
[69] PEReference ::= '%' Name ';'
```

Note that the only syntax difference between a general entity and a PE is the starting delimiter: The general entity begins with an ampersand (&). The PE's entity name *must* be preceded by a percent symbol and a space (%). (Note that in the document itself, you omit the space.)

The following example shows the parameter-entity declaration within the HTML INPUT element:

```
<!ENTITY % InputType
"(TEXT | PASSWORD | CHECKBOX | RADIO
       | SUBMIT | RESET | FILE | HIDDEN
       | IMAGE | BUTTON)"
>
```

When an HTML processor reads the % InputType entity in the INPUT element declaration, it replaces % InputType with the list of 10 attributes. In other words, without the InputType entity, the number of lines in this very large element declaration would increase by 10.

Learning About Entities from the HTML 4.0 DTD

You can learn a great deal about using entities — especially PEs — by studying the HTML 4.0 DTD. At the top of the DTD are pages of PEs, which either categorize child elements or name lists of attributes. For example, the events entity lists 10 dynamic HTML attributes (see the facing page). When you specify one of these attributes in an HTML document, you can link an event, such as clicking a mouse or pressing a key, with a particular action, such as changing a color. Many entities in the HTML DTD contain other entities. For example, the inline entity includes four subcategories of formatting entities (and allows an HTML developer to enter #PCDATA as well).

CROSS-REFERENCE

Chapter 7 teaches you how to start both internal and external DTD subsets and add to their contents.

FIND IT ONLINE

http://www.jeremie.com/JS/XML/all.html contains a well-documented directory of links to XML sites.

XML 1.0: THE PARAMETER ENTITY DECLARATION AND RELATED

```
[70]    EntityDecl ::= GEDecl | PEDecl
[72]       PEDecl ::= '<!ENTITY' S '%' S Name S PEDef S? '>'
[74]        PEDef ::= EntityValue | ExternalID
[9]    EntityValue ::= '"' ([^%&"] | PEReference | Reference)* '"'
                     | "'" ([^%&'] | PEReference | Reference)* "'"
[75]     ExternalID ::= 'SYSTEM' S SystemLiteral
                     | 'PUBLIC' S PubidLiteral S SystemLiteral
```

❶ *Start the PE declaration with the* !ENTITY *keyword.*
❷ *The PE definition is either a value or an external identifier.*
❸ *Enclose an entity value within quotation marks or single quotes.*
❹ *An external identifier can be either* SYSTEM *or* PUBLIC.

HTML 4.0: THE HTML EVENTS DECLARATION

```
<!ENTITY % events
"onclick       %Script;    #IMPLIED -- a pointer button was clicked --
 ondblclick    %Script;    #IMPLIED -- a pointer button was double clicked --
 onmousedown   %Script;    #IMPLIED -- a pointer button was pressed down --
 onmouseup     %Script;    #IMPLIED -- a pointer button was released --
 onmouseover   %Script;    #IMPLIED -- a pointer button was moved onto --
 onmousemove   %Script;    #IMPLIED -- a pointer button was moved within --
 onmouseout    %Script;    #IMPLIED -- a pointer button was moved away --
 onkeypress    %Script;    #IMPLIED -- a key was pressed and released --
 onkeydown     %Script;    #IMPLIED -- a key was pressed down --
 onkeyup       %Script;    #IMPLIED -- a key was released --
```

❶ *The event name appears in the first column.*
❷ *The* Script *entity specifies a* CDATA *script expression.*
❸ *Each of these events is optional.*
❹ *In SGML, you can enclose comments within two-dash (- -) delimiters.*

147

Importing External Entities

oth general entities and PEs support external entities: To use an external entity in an XML document or a DTD, simply refer to a URI for a standalone file that contains one or more entity declarations. An external general entity refers to content that will be inserted in the non-DTD part of an XML document, whereas an external PE refers to markup that will be inserted in a DTD.

These productions enable you to declare an external general entity:

```
[71]        GEDecl ::= '<!ENTITY' S Name S
                       EntityDef S? '>'
[73]    EntityDef ::= EntityValue
                     | (ExternalID
                        NDataDecl?)
[75]   ExternalID ::= 'SYSTEM' S
                       SystemLiteral
                     | 'PUBLIC' S
                       PubidLiteral
                       S SystemLiteral
```

These productions let you declare an external PE:

```
[72]        PEDecl ::= '<!ENTITY' S '%' S
                       Name S PEDef S? '>'
[74]        PEDef ::= EntityValue
                     | ExternalID
[75]   ExternalID ::= 'SYSTEM' S
                       SystemLiteral
                     | 'PUBLIC' S
                       PubidLiteral
                       S SystemLiteral
```

You can see that the syntax of an external PE is almost identical to that of an external general entity.

The only difference is that the external PE includes a percent sign (%) separated by at least one space (S).

Creating Well-Formed, Valid External Entity Documents

Any type of external document referred to from within an XML document must be a standalone XML document. Thus, external parsed entity documents must start with a text declaration (the TextDecl production), which is actually an XML declaration; for example:

```
<?xml version = "1.0"?>
```

After the text declaration, general entity documents and PE documents differ. The general entity document follows the syntax of the content production:

```
[43] content ::= (element | CharData
                 | Reference | CDSect |
PI               | Comment)*
```

A PE document uses the syntax of the extSubsetDecl production:

```
[31] extSubsetDecl ::= ( markupdecl
                       |
conditionalSect        | PEReference
                       | S )*
```

Thus, it can combine markup declaring elements, attribute lists, entities, and notation declarations; INCLUDE and IGNORE sections; PEs; and whitespace.

CROSS-REFERENCE

Chapter 12 discusses how to modify SGML and XML DTDs and how to revise a document to fit a particular DTD.

FIND IT ONLINE

Peruse a long document about SGML DTDs at http://etext.virginia.edu/bin/tei-tocs?div=DIV1&id=ST.

Listing 10-1: PART OF A USER GUIDE DOCUMENT

```
<!ELEMENT uguide (intro,chap+)>
<!ENTITY  ch01       SYSTEM "ch01.doc">
<!ENTITY  ch02       SYSTEM "ch02.doc">
<!ENTITY  ch03       SYSTEM "ch03.doc">

<uguide>
  <intro>***insert some text ***</intro>
  <chap>
     &chap01;
     &chap02;
     &chap03;
  </chap>
</uguide>
```

▲ *This XML document for a short user's guide includes entities for three chapters and six glossaries. To "assemble" a guide, insert an introduction and the chapters.*

Listing 10-2: AN EXAMPLE OF A LONG DOCUMENT

```
<?xml version="1.0"?>
<!DOCTYPE manual [
<!ELEMENT manual (#PCDATA)>
<!ENTITY  intro      SYSTEM "intro.doc">
<!ENTITY  chap01     SYSTEM "chap01.doc">
<!ENTITY  chap02     SYSTEM "chap02.doc">
<!ENTITY  chap03     SYSTEM "chap03.doc">
<!ENTITY  appxa      SYSTEM "appxa.doc">
]>
<manual>
&chap01;
&chap02;
&chap03;
&appxa;
</manual>
```

▲ *You can construct a long document from entities only. This example shows an XML document made up of several entities: an introduction, six chapters, a glossary, and two appendixes. Entities enable you to plug in interchangeable boilerplate files.*

HTML 4.0: EXTERNAL PARAMETER ENTITIES

```
<!ENTITY % HTMLlat1 PUBLIC
   "-//W3C//ENTITIES Latin1//EN//HTML"
   "http://www.w3.org/TR/1998/REC-html40-19980424/HTMLlat1.ent">
%HTMLlat1;

<!ENTITY % HTMLsymbol PUBLIC
   "-//W3C//ENTITIES Symbols//EN//HTML"
   "http://www.w3.org/TR/1998/REC-html40-19980424/HTMLsymbol.ent">
%HTMLsymbol;

<!ENTITY % HTMLspecial PUBLIC
   "-//W3C//ENTITIES Special//EN//HTML"
   "http://www.w3.org/TR/1998/REC-html40-19980424/HTMLspecial.ent">
%HTMLspecial;
```

▲ *This example shows three PE declarations from the HTML 4.0 DTD. Each of the three declarations is followed by the related entity reference.*

Declaring Data Entities

The XML specification supports the inclusion of unparsed external general entities in your documents. Unparsed external entities, also known as data entities, are truly external: they are produced by applications that have nothing to do with creating, editing, or processing XML. For example, you can declare a graphic, audio, or video file — anything that you don't intend the XML parser to process. Typically, these files are binary. You can also use this type of declaration to import text (ASCII) files that would normally be parsed but that you don't want to parse in this case.

When you declare a data entity, you must include the NDATA keyword and the file type (such as gif, avi, pdf, doc, jpeg or jpg, mpeg, and so on):

```
<!ENTITY robin-pic
    SYSTEM "../grafix/robin.gif" NDATA gif >
```

This example declares a GIF file called `robin.gif`.

As you know, you can usually place general-entity references anywhere in an XML document. The location of data entities is more restricted; they must be declared as element attributes, and the attribute type must be ENTITY or ENTITIES. For example, use the following declarations in a DTD for a document that contains illustrations of birds:

```
<!ELEMENT bird EMPTY>
<!ATTLIST bird url ENTITY #IMPLIED>
```

Then, insert the following line in the XML document:

```
<bird url="&robin-pic;"/>
```

TAKE NOTE

REVIEWING BINARY FILES AND TEXT FILES

Binary files, which are composed of series of 8-bit data, are usually readable by certain computer programs. In contrast, text files, also known as ASCII files, are made up of 7-bit data and are readable by humans and many more programs. Binary files usually include formatting and control characters; text files include alphabet characters, digits, punctuation, and a few control characters (primarily the carriage return), and do not include formatting information.

LEARNING ABOUT THE VARIETY OF GENERAL ENTITY VALUES IN SGML

One way to demonstrate the streamlined size of XML compared to its SGML parent is to compare the number of general entity values in both markup languages. In XML, a general-entity declaration can comprise three types of internal entity values (parameter-entity reference, general entity reference, or character reference), a parsed external entity located on SYSTEM or PUBLIC storage, or an unparsed external entity.

In contrast, SGML allows you to select from over 10 values, including tags, character data from within marked sections or that will be interpreted as a processing instruction, and two flavors each of PUBLIC and SYSTEM data.

CROSS-REFERENCE

In Chapter 13, you learn how to insert entities, elements, graphics, and other components in an XML document.

FIND IT ONLINE

What the ?XML! Home Page (**http://www. geocities.com/SiliconValley/Peaks/5957/ xml.html**) has several XML links.

XML 1.0: THE DATA ENTITY DECLARATION AND RELATED PRODUCTIONS

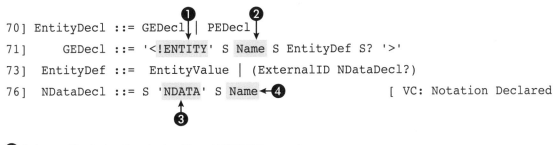

```
70]  EntityDecl ::= GEDecl | PEDecl
71]     GEDecl ::= '<!ENTITY' S Name S EntityDef S? '>'
73]  EntityDef ::=  EntityValue | (ExternalID NDataDecl?)
76]  NDataDecl ::= S 'NDATA' S Name ←❹              [ VC: Notation Declared
```

❶ A data-entity declaration starts with an !ENTITY keyword.
❷ Follow the keyword with a valid XML name.
❸ Enter the NDATA keyword in the declaration.
❹ Include a valid XML name in the declaration.

Listing 10-3: AN ABBREVIATED DTD FOR AN ILLUSTRATED BIRD LIBRARY

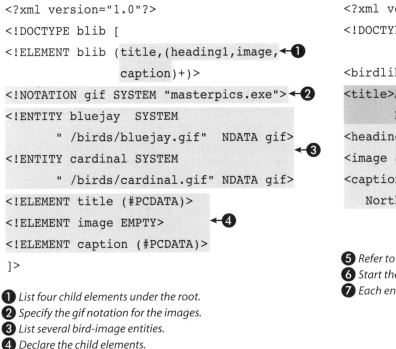

```
<?xml version="1.0"?>
<!DOCTYPE blib [
<!ELEMENT blib (title,(heading1,image, ←❶
                caption)+)>
<!NOTATION gif SYSTEM "masterpics.exe"> ←❷
<!ENTITY bluejay  SYSTEM
       " /birds/bluejay.gif"  NDATA gif>
                                          ←❸
<!ENTITY cardinal SYSTEM
       " /birds/cardinal.gif" NDATA gif>
<!ELEMENT title (#PCDATA)>
<!ELEMENT image EMPTY>                     ←❹
<!ELEMENT caption (#PCDATA)>
]>
```

❶ List four child elements under the root.
❷ Specify the gif notation for the images.
❸ List several bird-image entities.
❹ Declare the child elements.

Listing 10-4: PART OF THE BIRD LIBRARY DOCUMENT

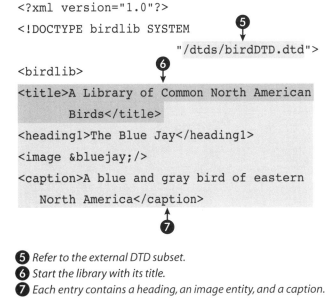

```
<?xml version="1.0"?>
<!DOCTYPE birdlib SYSTEM
                    "/dtds/birdDTD.dtd">
<birdlib>
<title>A Library of Common North American
       Birds</title>
<heading1>The Blue Jay</heading1>
<image &bluejay;/>
<caption>A blue and gray bird of eastern
   North America</caption>
```

❺ Refer to the external DTD subset.
❻ Start the library with its title.
❼ Each entry contains a heading, an image entity, and a caption.

Declaring a Notation

In the previous chapter, you were introduced to notation, a system of defining a means of communication using a formalized set of symbols or an alphabet. Remember that examples of notation are Braille, musical notes, dance steps, and even computer file formats. (Note that markup languages such as XML, SGML, and HTML are considered notations, too.) In XML, you can declare one or more notations for use in the current document or document set.

Notation declarations are connected to data entities (which are covered in the previous task) because they are both involved with importing external non-XML data into one or more documents with which the current DTD is associated. In fact, before declaring a data entity, you must declare the notation for its file type. Notation declarations specify the names of notations that are valid in the current XML document and data entity declarations identify an actual file. Note that the XML parser does not process the non-XML data referred to in the notation declaration.

In the last task, you saw these lines of XML code:

```
<!ENTITY robin-pic
   SYSTEM "../grafix/robin.gif" NDATA gif>
<!ELEMENT bird EMPTY>
<!ATTLIST bird url ENTITY #IMPLIED>
```

Before writing those lines, you might have to declare the `gif` notation as follows:

```
<!NOTATION gif SYSTEM "masterpics.exe">
```

This declaration could name an application with which you could create or edit `gif` graphics.

TAKE NOTE

USING NOTATIONS AND PROCESSING INSTRUCTIONS TOGETHER

You can use notation declarations along with processing instructions (PIs), which instruct an application on how to process the information embedded within the PI. Some PIs (such as `<?xml version="1"?>`) tell any XML parser processing a document that the XML version is 1.0. XML parsers ignore other PIs, but may pass the instructions to an external application, which may or may not abide by the instructions. For example, if you include a PI such as `<?Biltron run prograt?>` in an XML document and the target application is not named Biltron, it will probably ignore the `run prograt` instruction. On the other hand, if you issue a PI such as `<?wizstil text black foreground gray?>` and the target application, wizstil, is programmed to understand text and foreground color styling commands, the likelihood of successful processing will improve dramatically.

USING NOTATION ATTRIBUTES IN A DTD

When you wrote attribute-list declarations in Chapter 9, you learned about components of the declarations, including attribute type. Remember that the attribute type controls the value of a particular attribute. One of the three kinds of attribute types is the enumerated type, which contains one or more notations. The NOTATION and Enumerated NOTATION attribute types refer to one or a list of several notations, respectively.

CROSS-REFERENCE

Chapter 20 demonstrates how to write simple link statements in order to link to target resources.

FIND IT ONLINE

Find a library of U.S. Navy SGML tags at **http://navycals.dt.navy.mil/dtdfosi/tag_library.html**.

XML 1.0: THE NOTATION DECLARATION AND RELATED PRODUCTIONS

❶

```
[82]   NotationDecl ::= '<!NOTATION' S Name S (ExternalID | PublicID) S? '>'
[75]     ExternalID ::= 'SYSTEM' S SystemLiteral | 'PUBLIC' S PubidLiteral
                         S SystemLiteral                              ◀❷
[83]       PublicID ::= 'PUBLIC' S PubidLiteral ◀❸
[11] SystemLiteral ::= ('"' [^"]* '"') | ("'" [^']* "'")
[12]  PubidLiteral ::= '"' PubidChar* '"' | "'" (PubidChar - "'")* "'"
[13]     PubidChar ::= #x20 | #xD | #xA | [a-zA-Z0-9] | [-'()+,./:=?;!*#@$_%]
```

❶ *Start a notation declaration with the* !NOTATION *keyword.*
❷ *The external identifier can be* SYSTEM *or* PUBLIC.
❸ *The public identifier must be* PUBLIC.

Listing 10-5: THE NOTATION OF SELECTED WINDOWS FILE TYPES

```
<!NOTATION doc SYSTEM "d:\Program Files
    \Microsoft Office\Office\winword.exe">
<!NOTATION txt SYSTEM
                "c:\Windows\notepad.exe">
<!NOTATION pdf SYSTEM
               "d:\lotus\doc\acrord32.exe">
<!NOTATION aud SYSTEM
                "c:\pcaudio\audiorec.exe">
<!NOTATION crd SYSTEM
                "c:\Windows\cardfile.exe">
<!NOTATION cda SYSTEM
                "c:\Windows\cdplayer.exe">
```

▲ *This example shows the notation for some of the file types on a Windows computer.*

Listing 10-6: SAMPLE NOTATIONS FOR GRAPHICS FILES

```
<!NOTATION gif SYSTEM "masterpics.exe">
<!NOTATION tif SYSTEM "masterpics.exe">
<!NOTATION jpg SYSTEM "masterpics.exe">
<!NOTATION bmp SYSTEM "masterpics.exe">
<!ELEMENT   picture EMPTY>
<!ATTLIST   picture
    url         CDATA                   #REQUIRED
    filetype    NOTATION
            ( gif | tif | jpg | bmp ) "gif"
    align       (left | center | right)
```

▲ *The notation in this example shows that the masterpics program supports four types of graphic files (gif, tif, jpg, and bmp). The* filetype *attribute lists the same file types.*

Personal Workbook

Q&A

1 What is an *entity?*

_____

_____

_____

2 What is an *entity reference?*

_____

_____

_____

3 What are the two main categories of XML entities?

_____

_____

_____

4 Describe the difference between unparsed and parsed entities.

_____

_____

_____

5 Describe the difference between internal and external entities.

_____

_____

_____

6 Describe a general entity.

_____

_____

_____

7 Describe a parameter entity.

_____

_____

_____

8 What delimiters precede and succeed general entities and PEs?

_____

_____

_____

ANSWERS: PAGE 455

EXTRA PRACTICE

① Declare an entity that provides a nickname for your company.

② Declare an entity that contains your e-mail signature information.

③ Create a DTD that contains entities that declare each of the symbols on your keyboard. Use the Unicode codes in each declaration.

④ Using the DTD that contains keyboard-symbol entities, write an XML document.

⑤ Create a DTD that includes notation declarations for your word processor, spreadsheet, database, and graphics programs. Also, write a set of data entities matching the notation declarations.

⑥ Edit the DTD created in the previous exercise to include elements that can contain files from all the programs that you use once a week.

REAL-WORLD APPLICATIONS

✔ Your company wants to list some of its customers in its XML-based marketing literature. Write entity declarations for each of your company's customers.

✔ Most of your XML documents will eventually contain some French phrases. After reviewing a French-English dictionary, write entity declarations for each accented letter in French.

✔ You have volunteered to create a contact document for a charity in your hometown. Write a DTD that uses internal general entities to contain your local business addresses.

✔ Your company's employee manual contains chapters that rarely change and ones that constantly change. The chapters cover many human resources topics. Write a human resources DTD.

Visual Quiz

This DTD includes many mistakes, not all concerning entity declarations. Identify all the errors.

_____

_____

_____

_____

_____

```
visual quiz 10 - Notepad
File   Edit   Search   Help
<?XML VERSION="1.0"?>
<!DOCTYPE mistakes [
<!ELEMENT misteaks (#DATA)>
<!ENTITY  intr     SYSTEM "intro.doc">
<!ENTITY  ch01     SYSTEM "ch01.doc">
<!entity  ch02     SYSTEM "ch02.doc"
<!ENTITY  ch03     SYSTEM "ch03.doc">
<!ENTITY  ch03     SYSTEM "ch04.doc">
]>
<book>
  <intro>
  This is a small section that introduces the book.
  </intro>
    &chap01;
    &chap02;
    &chap03;
    &chap04;
</mistakes>
```

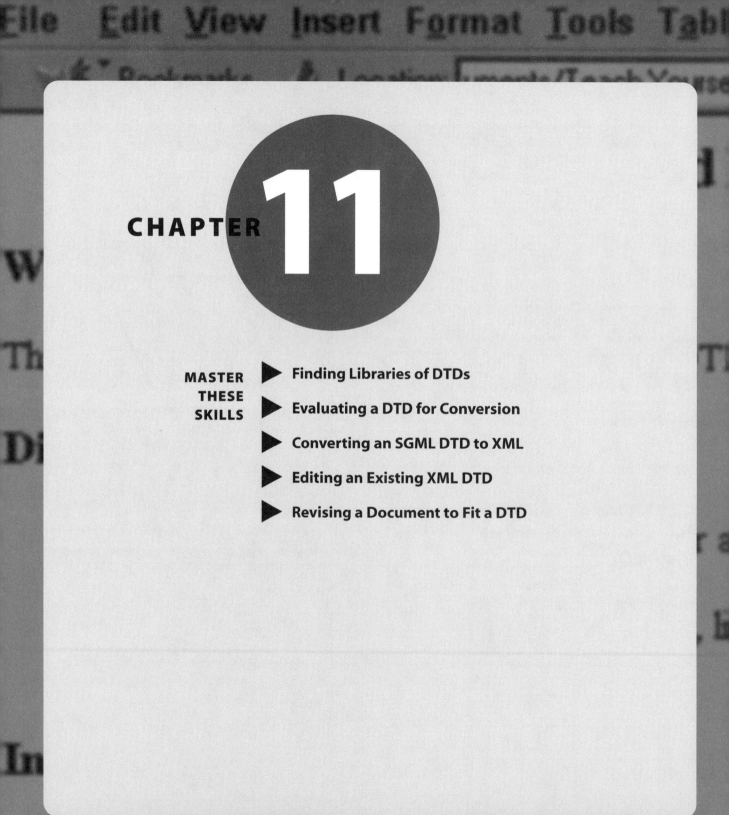

CHAPTER **11**

MASTER
THESE
SKILLS

▶ **Finding Libraries of DTDs**

▶ **Evaluating a DTD for Conversion**

▶ **Converting an SGML DTD to XML**

▶ **Editing an Existing XML DTD**

▶ **Revising a Document to Fit a DTD**

Modifying an Existing DTD

You don't always have to build a new DTD from scratch. Sometimes you can find a DTD that you can either use in its current condition or adapt to your XML document or document set. If you find an XML DTD or an SGML DTD on the Internet, you should determine whether it fits the XML document or document set with which it will be associated. If you find both an XML DTD and an SGML DTD, note that you will have to make fewer changes to the structure and content of an XML DTD. However, if you locate an SGML DTD whose elements and other components more closely match your document, that DTD may be your best choice — even if you have to work a little more to convert it to XML.

You can find many XML and SGML DTDs on the Internet — on the World Wide Web or at FTP sites. In addition, if you can find an XML-based custom markup language for your industry or technology, the underlying DTD may fit your XML documents very well. Look for a DTD that matches your document type, that contains the elements and other components

with which you can construct a solid document, and that appears to be accurate.

After you choose a DTD, you will have to modify it — especially if it is an SGML DTD. SGML contains many more productions and options than XML does, so you will have to add, modify, and/or delete certain components so the DTD conforms to the XML specification. Sometimes you will have to approach the document-DTD relationship in the opposite direction: edit the document to fit the DTD. If a DTD is well-written and the XML-related document or document sets are in the early stages of creation, you might want to write the document so it matches the DTD.

In this chapter, you learn how to locate the increasing number of DTDs and DTD libraries posted on the Internet and how to evaluate DTDs for adaptation to your documents. Then, based on the information in previous chapters in this book, you learn how to modify the DTDs you download, how to edit your documents or document sets to fit the DTDs with which they will be associated, or both.

Finding Libraries of DTDs

Because XML is in its early development, you will not always find an XML DTD that is suitable for your documents and document sets on the Internet. However, the number of posted XML DTDs and XML DTD libraries is growing every day (see Table 11-1). Your best source of DTDs still may be SGML (see Table 11-2). Note that you can also evaluate the XML-based custom markup languages on the Web (see Tables 11-3 and 11-4), whose underlying DTDs may also fit your document type.

To find an existing DTD, start up your favorite search engine, such as one of the following:

- ▶ Altavista (**http://www.altavista.com/**)
- ▶ Excite (**http://www.excite.com/**)
- ▶ HotBot (**http://www.hotbot.com/**)
- ▶ Infoseek (**http://www.infoseek.com/**)
- ▶ LookSmart (**http://www.looksmart.com/**)
- ▶ Lycos (**http://www.lycos.com/**)
- ▶ Metacrawler (**http://www.metacrawler.com/**)

In the text box on the search engine's home page, enter a keyword, such as **dtd**, or a keyword phrase, such as **"xml dtd"**, **"sgml dtd"**, or **"dtd library"**. (Note that a keyword phrase should be enclosed within quotation marks or single quotes.) Finally, run the search by clicking a Search button or pressing Enter. For the best results, the keywords you enter should be all-lowercase: many search engines find combinations of uppercase and lowercase text only if you enter all-lowercase text.

CROSS-REFERENCE

Chapter 2 introduces you to external DTD subsets, some of which you can find and download from the Internet.

Table 11-1: SELECTED XML DTDS

Name	URL	Description
Test XML DTD	http://www.lists.ic.ac.uk/archives/xml-dev/9704/0061.html	A test DTD for the Web from the DocBook standard: a catalog , test file, and four entity files
DocBook DTD	http://www.oreilly.com/davenport/	Another DocBook DTD
XML for HR	http://pw2.netcom.com/%7Ece_allen/hrxml.htm	Links to several DTDs to generate HTML pages for a job bank Web site, including job postings, addresses, and telephone numbers
XML DTD for v2.1 LOM Specification	http://www.manta.ieee.org/p1484/xml/intro.htm	Links to two DTDs for the Learning Object Metadata (LOM) draft, including element declarations and the data type, obligation, and list properties
Terminal Aerodrome Forecasts (TAF)	http://zowie.metnet.navy.mil/~spawar/JMV-TNG/XML/OMF.dtd	The Weather Observation Definition Format DTD: a DTD for weather forecasts and observation
WebDAV Protocol	http://www.ics.uci.edu/~ejw/authoring/protocol/webdav3.dtd	A DTD with commented links to WebDAV protocol documents
ibtwsh: Itsy Bitsy Teeny Weeny Simply Hypertext DTD	http://www.schema.net/general	A DTD that describes a subset of HTML 4.0 for use as an entity within XML DTD

Evaluating a DTD for Conversion

A DTD should match your XML document or document set in three ways: the DTD should have been designed for the particular type of document; its elements, attributes, entities, and other components should measure up to the components of, and your desires for, the document; and the DTD should be well-constructed and accurate. Make sure the DTD meets all three criteria. Otherwise, you will have defeated the purpose of finding and downloading it.

There are two ways to discover the purpose of a DTD. If you access the DTD from the Web, the page on which the link is located usually includes a description. Also, many publicly available DTDs are nicely commented. If the DTD and your document seem to complement each other (for example, the DTD formats a computer manual and your XML document is a computer manual), continue assessing the DTD.

The next step is to read through the DTD to learn if you can use the elements and entities, and whether other declarations and components work with your document or document set. Obviously, you are not going to find a complete match, but if the DTD fits in many ways, consider yourself lucky.

The make-or-break portion of your examination is whether you find the DTD well written. Turnoffs include misspellings, obvious errors in syntax, poor use or lack of indentions, and lack of comments.

Converting an Internal DTD Subset to an External DTD Subset

What if one of your XML documents has an internal DTD subset that you want to use for other documents? It's easy to convert an internal DTD subset to a standalone external DTD and to "repair" the document from which you remove the internal DTD. As you know, the top lines of an XML document with an internal DTD look something like this:

```
<?xml version = "1.0"?>
<!DOCTYPE document [
```

The left bracket ([) indicates the start of an internal DTD subset. The declarations for entities, child elements, attributes, and other components appear, followed by the]>, which signal the end of the internal DTD:

```
<!ELEMENT document (intro,chap+)>
    <!ELEMENT intro (#PCDATA)>
    <!ELEMENT chap (#PCDATA)>]>
```

Your first step is to copy the entire internal DTD subset, from the [to the]>, to a new XML document. Insert an XML declaration at the top of the document. Then, save the document as a DTD, using a valid XML name and the .dtd extension. Change the document type declaration in the original document so it refers to the newly created external DTD subset. The edited line will look something like this:

```
<!DOCTYPE document SYSTEM
"/dtds/document.dtd">
```

CROSS-REFERENCE

Chapter 6 can help you format a DTD and help ensure that it conforms to the XML specification.

FIND IT ONLINE

SGML, XML, DTD Development (http://www.techbooks.com/sgml.html) presents an overview of these topics and provides links.

Table 11-2: SELECTED SGML DTDS

Name	URL	Description
TEI P3 DTDs, Declarations, and Entity Sets	http://www.uic.edu/orgs/tei/p3/dtd/dtd.html	Links to many DTDs for presenting electronic text
\<TAG> Article DTD	ftp://www.sgml.com/article.dtd	A DTD for a newspaper or magazine article, which not only provides article elements but also author information and contact data
Information Mapping SGML DTDs	http://www.imap.dk/sgmdtd01.htm	Links to three DTDs from Information Mapping Europe. Two DTDs create information-mapped (a technical document-creation standard) documents and a third encodes tables
CALS DTD Index	http://www.ornl.gov/sgml/dtd/	Links to several general, scientific, and mathematical DTDs: general elements, tables, lists, mathematics, chemistry, technical reports, and more
SGML DTD for Internet Explorer 3.0 Markup	http://microsoft.com/workshop/author/ie3 html/ie3dtd.asp	Links to three DTDs that define HTML markup for Internet Explorer 3.0: headers and document bodies, tables, and strict HTML
American Memory DTD for Historical Documents	http://lcweb2.loc.gov/ammem/amdtd.html	Links to DTD files used to mark up full texts of historical documents as well as finding aids
Elsevier Science DTDs	http://www.elsevier.nl/homepage/about/sgml/	Links to an article, subject-index, and glossary DTD from a scientific publisher
Humanities Text Initiative	ftp://ftp.hti.umich.edu/pub/panorama/12083/	Links to four DTDs (article, book, mathematics, and serials) from the University of Michigan

Converting an SGML DTD to XML

Because XML is a subset of SGML, it does not support every feature of SGML. So, when you find an SGML DTD, you will have to convert it. When you edit an SGML DTD, be sure to use these conversion rules:

▶ At the top of the DTD, insert an XML declaration.

▶ Modify the document type declaration to fit the `doctypedecl` production (see the following sidebar).

▶ XML is case-sensitive. Make sure all declarations are lowercase, and all reserved keywords are uppercase. When in doubt, refer to the XML specification.

▶ XML always requires both start tags and end tags and does not include the required (–) and omit (O) symbols in element declarations. So, remove these symbols from element declarations.

▶ Look for and edit declarations with keywords (for example, NUMBER, NUMBERS, RCDATA, SDATA, NUTOKEN, NUTOKENS, #CONREF, #CURRENT, and so on). XML does not support these keywords.

▶ Pay special attention to the CDATA keyword. You cannot use CDATA in element declarations in XML DTDs. Change occurrences of CDATA to #PCDATA.

▶ Modify statements that include the ampersand (&) connector. XML does not support logical ANDs.

▶ XML does not support SGML public-identifier naming conventions (see the following note). So, edit all public identifiers to conform to the XML specification.

Using SGML Public-Identifier Naming Conventions

If you look at the top of HTML documents, you'll find a public identifier that refers to the HTML version and other information:

```
<!DOCTYPE HTML PUBLIC
          "-//W3C//DTD HTML 4.0//EN">
```

Because HTML is based on an SGML DTD, its public identifiers conform to the official SGML specification. For example, the dash (–) immediately after the first quotation mark indicates that this particular DTD is *not* an approved ISO standard (a plus sign would indicate approval). Other information included in the line is as follows: W3C is the creator of the DTD, DTD is the document type, HTML 4.0 is the document name, and EN is English.

Look at the following syntax for the document type declaration:

```
[28] doctypedecl ::= '<!DOCTYPE' S
Name
                 (S ExternalID)? S?
                 ('[' (markupdecl
                 | PEReference
                 | S)* ']' S?)? '>'
```

Note the absence of the dash, plus sign, double slashes, and so on, in the production.

CROSS-REFERENCE

In Chapter 3, you can explore Extended Backus-Naur Form (EBNF) notation with which you can write accurate DTDs.

FIND IT ONLINE

Go to http://nwalsh.com/articles/xmldtd/index.html to learn about converting an SGML DTD to XML.

Table 11-3: SELECTED CUSTOM MARKUP AND RELATED LANGUAGES (W3C WORKING DRAFTS AND NOTES)

Name	URL	Subject
Extensible Forms Description Language (XFDL)	http://www.w3.org/TR/NOTE-XFDL	Complex forms, including precision layout and digital signatures (W3C note)
Extensible Stylesheet Language (XSL)	http://www.w3.org/TR/1998/WD-xsl-19980818	XML-related style sheets (W3C working draft)
Handheld Device Markup Language (HDML)	http://www.w3.org/TR/NOTE-Submission-HDML-spec.html	Handheld devices acting as Web clients (W3C note)
Mathematical Markup Language (MathML)	http://www.w3.org/TR/WD-math/	Mathematics (Appendix A includes the DTD text) (W3C working draft)
Precision Graphics Markup Language (PGML)	http://www.w3.org/TR/1998/NOTE-PGML/	Two-dimensional scalable graphics (W3C note)
Signed Document Markup Language	http://www.w3.org/TR/1998/NOTE-SDML/	Document structuring and signing (W3C note)
Vector Markup Language (VML)	http://www.w3.org/TR/1998/NOTE-VML	Vector information and display (W3C note)
XML Linking Language (XLink)	http://www.w3.org/TR/WD-xlink	XML-related link language (W3C working draft)
XML-QL	http://www.w3.org/TR/NOTE-xml-ql/	XML-based query language (W3C note)

Editing an Existing XML DTD

If you have selected an existing XML DTD using the criteria described in the previous task, you start with a big advantage: The DTD is already constructed properly, should have been tested sufficiently, and is closely related to your document or document set. You may have to add or remove elements, entities, and other components and change attributes and their values, but you do not have to check each line of the DTD to ensure it meets the XML specifications. However, as you work on the DTD, make sure you become thoroughly familiar with it.

When you planned your document, you should have listed document components, defaults, and values. Before you start editing, have a fairly good idea of the changes you will make. Once you open the DTD file, carefully go through each of the declarations following these guidelines:

▶ Change the structure of the DTD as needed. For example, consider moving all the entities above the child elements, or consider grouping them in one place.

▶ Rename elements, entities, or attributes to comply with your corporate naming standards.

▶ Change default attribute values or lists of values to agree with the values you decide are valid.

▶ If your document will include a variety of links and extended pointers, add an identifier or name attribute for each element.

▶ When an attribute default declaration is #REQUIRED or #IMPLIED, decide whether you want to provide a default value instead.

▶ Although having an element accept #PCDATA is a good starting point, you may want to specify child elements to better control input.

▶ Decide whether to change the look of the DTD to make it easier for those who will maintain the document in the future. For example, add indents or change the number of spaces certain lines are indented.

▶ Insert comments so others can understand the DTD.

After you complete your modifications, make sure you store the DTD in the appropriate place — the location at which you store all your DTDs. You want to ensure that each of the XML documents that refer to the DTD can locate it.

TAKE NOTE

▶ LEARNING ABOUT THE LIGHTER SIDE OF MARKUP LANGUAGES

When you search for markup languages (see the previous Take Note), you will run across a few surprises. For example, you might find the Irritating Text Markup Language (**http://www.digicrime. com/~mccurley/humorritml.html**), which contains tags such as <ADVERTISING> and <DRIVEL>. The ITML page also features links to the Mind Reading Markup Language (MRML) (**http://www.oxy.edu/~ashes/mrml.html**) and the Real Aroma Text Markup Language (RATML) (**http://www.realaroma.com/Docs/develop. html**) sites.

CROSS-REFERENCE

Because of its information about planning and outlining DTDs, Chapter 6 can help you edit an imported DTD.

FIND IT ONLINE

XML Under the Hood (**http://preview.thesphere. com/CNethtml/Travis/**) is a series of presentation pages.

Table 11-4: SELECTED CUSTOM MARKUP LANGUAGES (NOT AT W3C)

Name	URL	Subject
Chemical Markup Language (CML)	http://www.xml-cml.org.uk/	Chemistry, enabling the conversion of files and structuring documents
Conceptual Knowledge Markup Language (CKML)	http://wave.eecs.wsu.edu/WAVE/Ontologies/CKML/CKML15.html	*Ontology*, a branch of metaphysics
Development Markup Language (DML)	http://resources.bellanet.org/xml/	An Internet-protocol and information-sharing standards for developers
Electronic Data Markup Language (EDML)	http://www.edml.com/	The NAME component of name/value pairs in an HTML form
Human Resources Markup Language	http://www.hrml.com/	Human resources transactions for electronic (online) recruitment (HRML)
Java Speech Markup Language (JSML)	http://java.sun.com/java-media/speech/forDevelopers/JSML/	Text input to Java Speech API speech synthesizers
MatseML	http://macke.wiwi.hoc/MatSeML/u-berlin.de/matse/d	Definition of file formats for scheduling problems using Java classes
Speech Synthesis Markup Language (SSML)	http://www.cstr.ed.ac .k/projects/ssml_details. html	Text pronunciation aid
Theological Markup Language (ThML)	http://ccel.wheaton.edu/ThML/	Christian Classics Ethereal Library texts
Tutor Domain Markup Language	http://www.bovik.org/tdml-pt.html	Multimedia instructional systems
Tutorial Markup Language (TML)	http://www.ilrt.bris.ac.uk/mru/netquest/tml/	Searchable online question banks

Revising a Document to Fit a DTD

O ccasionally, you will find a DTD that fits the purpose of your document or document set so well that you decide to write or convert the documents to fit the DTD. This usually happens very early in the development of your document, possibly even before you write a single word. Otherwise, you will have to edit the document — sometimes extensively.

Locating and using a well-designed and accurate DTD actually strengthens the structure — and sometimes the content — of your documents. Those who have developed the DTD have already spent a great deal of time and energy working on the DTD and testing it against one or more documents.

If you have found the DTD in the library of an organization or association that sets standards for your document type, you can make those prototypes and rules your own. Most standard-setting bodies name committees of experienced and skilled experts to create document standards over months or even years. Regardless of how you get the DTD, your documents will most likely be better for the association with a robust, well-developed DTD.

Online Writing and Editing Help

Many Web sites aid in solving writing and editing problems for documents of all types. Here are four resources that can help you get started:

The Editorial Eye (**http://www.eeicom.com/eye/ eyeindex.html**) provides 10 pages of links to articles and references resources. Subjects include E-mail Etiquette, Essential Home Page Details, Editing All the Legalese the Law Allows, and several articles under the heading "Untangling the Web." The University of Illinois at Urbana-Champaign offers the Online Writing Guide (**http://www.english.uiuc.edu/cws/ wworkshop/mainmenu.html**), which contains links to The Grammar Handbook, The Writing Techniques Handbook, and The Bibliography Handbook.

The Purdue On-line Writing Lab's (OWL's) Writing Resources page (**http://owl.english.purdue.edu/ writers/introduction.html**) includes links to over 120 online writing handouts as well as other online resources, under 10 categories, at OWL and elsewhere. The California Lutheran University's Virtual Library (**http://robles.callutheran.edu/iss/vlib2. html**) is a directory of links to Internet search tools, reference information, and links to resources arranged by subject — ranging from arts and humanities and business and economics to government and medical information.

CROSS-REFERENCE

Chapter 16 instructs you on how to convert an HTML document and its components to an accurate XML document.

FIND IT ONLINE

The page at http://www.cis.ohio-state.edu/hypertext/information/rfc.html links to RFCs for the Internet.

Table 11-5: PROPOSED AND EXISTING STANDARDS FOR XML

Name	URL	Purpose
Channel Definition Format (CDF)	http://www.w3.org/TR/NOTE-CDFsubmit.html	Prepares grouped collections of pushing or content for streaming
Document Content Description for XML of XML-Data and RDF	http://www.w3.org/TR/NOTE-dcd	Specifies rules for XML document structure and content using a subset
Document Object Model (DOM)	http://www.w3.org/TR/REC-DOM-Level-1	Enables programs and scripts to access and update documents dynamically
Meta Content Framework Using XML	http://www.w3.org/TR/NOTE-MCF-XML/	Describes machine-usable metadata for channels (collections of networked information)
Namespaces in XML	http://www.w3.org/TR/WD-xml-names	Associates qualifying XML names with URI namespaces
Resource Description Framework (RDF)	http://www.w3.org/TR/WD-rdf-schema/	Processes metadata between applications that exchange Web information
Scalable Vector Graphics (SVG)	http://www.w3.org/TR/WD-SVGReq	Replaces some raster graphics with an XML tag set and namespace
Schema for Object-Oriented XML checking	http://www.w3.org/TR/NOTE-SOX/	Defines XML documents for proper validation and automated content checking

Personal Workbook

Q&A

1 What are the three types of DTDs you can convert for an XML document?

_____

_____

_____

2 What parts of the Internet provide DTDs and libraries of DTDs?

_____

_____

_____

3 How do you search for a DTD on the Internet?

_____

_____

_____

4 When you enter a keyword phrase in a text box, how do you format it?

_____

_____

_____

5 How do you use multiple external DTDs in your documents?

_____

_____

_____

6 What are the three ways in which a DTD should match an XML document or document set?

_____

_____

_____

7 How do you convert an internal DTD subset to an external DTD subset?

_____

_____

_____

8 Does XML ever accept optional end tags?

_____

_____

_____

ANSWERS: PAGE 456

EXTRA PRACTICE

1 Get online and find an XML DTD that does not appear in one of the tables in this chapter.

2 Using the list in "Converting an SGML DTD to XML" as a guide, mark the changes you must make to an SGML DTD to convert it to XML.

3 Download one of the DocBook DTDs listed in Table 11-1. Compare its markup to any computer manual.

4 Download the XML-Tagged Shakespeare Set (**http://sunsite.unc.edu/pub/sun-info/xml/eg/ shakespeare1.10.xml.zip**). Edit the DTD so it can be applied to any play.

5 Compile a list of keywords and keyword phrases you can use to search for DTDs.

REAL-WORLD APPLICATIONS

✔ You are responsible for writing and maintaining XML-based press releases for your organization. Find an online DTD for press releases.

✔ In the past, your company's CEO has written a weekly report for employees. Now that the company has an intranet, your department has been charged with converting the reports to Web pages. Because of a tight deadline, search the Internet for a DTD to be edited.

✔ Using the list of elements and entities you composed in the previous application, search the Internet for a DTD that meets your requirements.

✔ You are a volunteer at an organization that helps high school students learn advanced mathematics. Find and download the Mathematical Markup Language recommendation. Decide whether you can use that language for your Web site.

Visual Quiz

This Web page lists individual DTDs and DTD directories. Identify DTDs you can use for weather observation. Find a file that refers to HTML 4.0. Find an electronic newsletter.

_____

_____

_____

_____

_____

A Page of DTDs - Netscape

File   Edit   View   Go   Communicator   Help

XML and SGML DTDs

Welcome

This page contains links to XML and SGML DTDs.

Directories

- <TAG>, an electronic SGML newsletter and resource directory.
- XML for HR, links to several DTDs
- XML DTD for v2.1 LOM Specification, links to two DTDs for the Learning Object Metadata (LOM) draft

Individual DTDs

- Test XML DTD, a test DTD for the Web from the Docbook standard
- DocBook DTD, a Docbook DTD
- Terminal Aerodrome Forecasts, a Weather Observation Definition Format DTD
- WebDAV Protocol, a DTD with commented links to WebDAV protocol documents
- ibtwsh, a DTD that describes a subset of HTML 4.0

You are offline. Choose "Go Online..." to connect

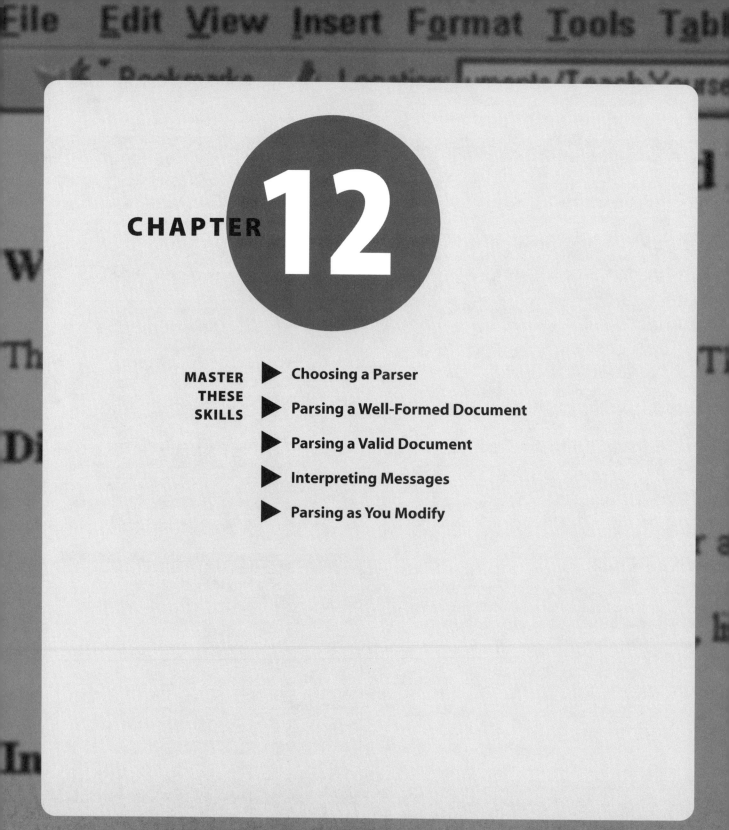

CHAPTER **12**

MASTER
THESE
SKILLS

▶ Choosing a Parser

▶ Parsing a Well-Formed Document

▶ Parsing a Valid Document

▶ Interpreting Messages

▶ Parsing as You Modify

Parsing an XML Document

An XML parser analyzes a document, determining what is markup and what is content. As the parser processes the document, it reduces the document to its smallest parts, examining each character for its meaning. For example, when the parser reads a less-than symbol (<), it is programmed to know the beginning of some markup — such as a start tag, end tag, declaration, processing instruction, or a comment. And when the parser recognizes a greater-than symbol (>), it knows it has reached the end of that markup. Of course, the parser also interprets pipes (|), ampersands (&), percent signs (%), parentheses (( )), and so on — in the same way we are taught to understand punctuation as we read through text.

XML parsers evaluate XML documents to determine if they are well-formed, valid, or both. As you learned in Chapter 2, an XML document must be well-formed at the very least. A parser that is programmed to read through a DTD is called a *validating* parser. Otherwise, it is a *non-validating* parser. The greatest factor in selecting a parser is whether it

validates documents. You might find a non-validating parser you really like, but it won't work because it can only check whether a document is well-formed. In most real-world situations, you must also be able to create valid documents.

This chapter covers the basics of using parsers to check XML documents for errors and how to use information from a parser to fix those errors. The first thing you must do is choose a parser. Try using different parsers; you'll like some and use them often. As you use parsers, you need to become familiar with their error codes. Some parsers have very good error codes, while others frustrate you with their obfuscation. This affects your decision about which parser to use. (If you can't figure out the errors, how are you going to fix them?)

The final task discusses some of the basic techniques of fixing errors. Learning to use tools to find those errors will help you wade through some of those frustrating moments when you are trying to figure out what the %@$#* is wrong with your XML document.

Choosing a Parser

A parser is a program that processes some sort of input (such as XML markup and content) and converts that input into output for another application (such as a browser). While parsers do this processing and conversion, they check to see that the structure of the input is correct. In this chapter, you use parsers to check both well-formed and valid XML documents.

XML parsers check syntax, elements, and URLs by using programmed criteria. An XML parser evaluates each line of a document and creates a tree of elements and sometimes creates a diagram of the root element, its child elements, and their children.

XML parsers fall into two main categories. Non-validating parsers simply check how well-formed a document is. Validating parsers check whether an XML document is valid, which means it evaluates both the DTD and the document. XML parsers are available from many different online sources. Most are freeware: you don't have to pay for them.

When you create an HTML document, you use either the HTML editor or the browser to test the document for appropriate syntax, supported HTML elements and attributes, and properly named URLs for links and graphics. You also check how your page looks under various browsers. With XML, very few browsers are available. So, when you create an XML document, you can run your document through an XML parser to check for accuracy. Depending on the parser and the condition of your document, you will see warning and error codes, so you can find and correct problems with your XML document before you release it to the world.

As you start to use XML parsers, don't rush into choosing one over another. You might even want to install and test out multiple parsers on your computer. Note that some XML parsers require that you have some form of Java installed. For a list of XML parsers and the site from which you can download Java, see Table 12-1, Appendix B, and the Find It Online notes in this chapter.

TAKE NOTE

▶ JAVA AND PARSING XML

When you start to look for parsers, you will find they are written in different languages. A good number of them are written in Java (and others are written in C++). If you decide to go with a Java-based parser; you need to make sure you have the capability to run Java. Two of the more popular Java loaders for Windows-based computers are Sun's Java Runtime Loader, also known as Java Runtime Environment (JRE), and Microsoft's Command-line Loader for Java (JVIEW). This chapter includes examples using both loaders. As with the parsers, try different loaders and find out which one you're more comfortable using. You can download JRE from **http://java.sun.com/products/ jdk/1.1/jre/index.html**. JVIEW.EXE should be in your main Windows folder.

CROSS-REFERENCE

In Chapter 2, you learn the difference between well-formed and valid XML documents.

FIND IT ONLINE

Parser Central (**http://www.finetuning.com/ parse.html**) lists XML programs of all types, including parsers.

Table 12-1: SELECTED XML PARSERS

Parser Name	URL	Description
Ælfred	**http://www.microstar.com/XML/ Aelfred/aelfred.html**	A validating parser for Java programmers who want to add XML support to their applets
DataChannel-Microsoft Java XML Parser	**http://www.datachannel.com/xml_ resources/developers/tools.shtml**	A validating Java-based parser that checks for well-formed documents and optionally checks for validity
expat (EXtensible markup language PArser Toolkit)	**http://www.jclark.com/xml/ expat.html**	A non-validating C-based XML browser
Lark	**http://www.textuality.com/Lark/**	A non-validating XML parser
Larval	**http://www.textuality.com/Lark/**	A validating XML parser that has the characteristics and features of Lark
NXP	**http://www.edu.uni-klu.ac.at/ ~nmikula/NXP/**	A validating Java-based parser in the public domain
PaxSyntactica	**http://208.204.84.117/ XMLTreeViewer/**	An Xapi-J-compliant XML parser
SP	**http://www.jclark.com/sp/**	A C++-based SGML parser that can parse well-formed XML documents
Tcl (Tool Command Language) Toolkit	**http://tcltk.anu.edu.au/XML/**	A toolkit for parsing XML documents and DTDs
XAF	**http://www.megginson.com/ XAF/home.html**	A Java-based, SAX-conformant XML parser
XML for Java	**http://www.alphaworks.IBM.com/ formula/xml/**	A validating XML parser written in Java
xmlproc	**http://www.stud.ifi.uio.no/~larsga/ download/python/xml/index**	A Python-based validating XML parser
XP	**http://www.jclark.com/xml/xp/ index.html**	A Java-based parser that tests for well-formed documents
XParse	**http://www.jeremie.com/Dev/XML/**	A JavaScript-based XML parser that tests for well-formed documents

Parsing a Well-Formed Document

As you begin to learn XML, you may find that you want to check whether the documents you create are well-formed. One of the tools currently available is a non-validating parser. These parsers are useful if you only want to check the structure of an XML document without checking for validity.

One non-validating parser is Lark. Tim Bray, one of the editors of the XML standard, wrote Lark (and its validating counterpart, Larval). To download Lark, go to **http://www.textuality.com/Lark/**; you'll find the download link at the bottom of the page. Lark is also on the CD-ROM bundled with this book.

After completing the download, unzip the file. WinZip and PKZip will both unzip this file, but make sure the filename hasn't been truncated during the download (the filename should be `lark.tar.gz`). You can place the unzipped files anywhere on your computer. In the examples in this chapter, Lark is installed in the `c:\lark` directory.

Lark is a command-line utility. The text shown in the following example is from a command prompt in an MS-DOS window. The example shows Lark run against an XML document:

```
c:\lark>jview Driver c:\xmlsamp\text1.xml
Hello Tim
Lark V1.0 final beta Copyright (c) 1997-98
Tim Bray.
 All rights reserved; the right to use
these class files for any purpose
 is hereby granted to everyone.
Parsing...
Done.
```

The capitalization of the `D` in the word `Driver` is important. Without it, Lark won't run because jview is case-sensitive. The parsing of the document `text1.xml` was uneventful. Lark parsed the document and finished with no errors to report. Of course, the first XML document is simple. This is what `text1.xml` looks like:

```
<?xml version ="1.0"?>
<text>This is text</text>
```

Now if there is a problem, Lark reports the error. You can also modify Lark so it shows you the structure of the document. Look at the Lark documentation to find the method you must modify to show the structure of a parsed XML document.

Learning to Run a Parser

When you start to work with parsers, sometimes the hardest step is figuring out how to run them. Start with smaller XML documents, those documents with structures you thoroughly understand. Some parsers may not come with much instruction. In these cases, try running the parser without any arguments; you will see options for using the parser.

If you are not familiar with Java, don't worry: you will be able to run many Java-based parsers without any knowledge of Java. The downside is you won't be able to customize them to better suit your needs. If you are having problems, try to run your applications incrementally. Start by trying the Java loader. If this works, try to run the parser.

CROSS-REFERENCE
Chapter 13 instructs you on creating a basic XML document with properly used markup.

FIND IT ONLINE
James Tauber's XML INFORMATION: Software (**http://www.xmlinfo.com/**) lists XML software and links.

Listing 12-1: A SIMPLE XML DOCUMENT

```
<?xml version = "1.0"?>
<text size="12">
    <boldface>
        <italics>
            Watch this space!
        </boldface>←❶
        <picture/>
    </italics>
</text>
```

❶ *Italics should end before boldface.*

Listing 12-2: PARSING LISTING 12-1

```
c:\lark>jview Driver c:\xmlsamp\badnest.xml
Hello Tim
Lark V1.0 final beta Copyright © 1997-98
Tim Bray.
 All rights reserved; the right to use
 these class files for any purpose
 is hereby granted to everyone.
Parsing...
Lark:c:\xmlsamp\badnest.xml:8:13:E:Fatal:
Encountered </boldface> expected </italics>
...assumed </italics>←❹
Lark:c:\xmlsamp\badnest.xml:8:13:E:Fatal:
Encountered </italics> with no start tag.
Done.
```

❷ Lark finds the boldface end tag before italics.

❸ The italics end tag must come first: italics is a child of boldface.

❹ Lark assumes </boldface> is actually </italics>.

❺ Lark finds extra </italics> because of its assumption.

Listing 12-3: ANOTHER SAMPLE XML DOCUMENT

```
<?xml version = "1.0"?>
<!DOCTYPE TURTLE [
<!ELEMENT TURTLE (PICTURE, DESC)>
<!ELEMENT PICTURE    EMPTY>←❶
<!ELEMENT DESC    (#PCDATA)>
]>
<TURTLE>
   <PICTURE>A picture goes here</PICTURE>
   <DESC>This is Freddy</DESC>
</TURTLE>
```

❶ *The element* PICTURE *is supposed to be empty.*

Listing 12-4: PARSING LISTING 12-3

```
c:\lark>jview Driver c:\xmlsamp\turtle.xml
Hello Tim
Lark V1.0 final beta Copyright © 1997-98
Tim Bray.
 All rights reserved; the right to use
 these class files for any purpose
 is hereby granted to everyone.
Parsing...←❷
Done.←❸
```

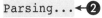

❷ *The parser parses the document.*

❸ *The parser finds no errors because it doesn't know to check the DTD.*

Parsing a Valid Document

Eventually — sooner rather than later — you'll want to see how your DTD works in conjunction with your XML document. That's when you'll start using a validating parser. A validating parser checks to see that a document is not only well-formed but is also valid.

For this chapter, use IBM's XML Parser for Java, which is a validating parser. You can download this parser from the **http://www.alphaworks.ibm.com/formula/xml** page. This file, which is written for Windows systems, is compressed in the familiar `zip` file type. After you download, you can place the files anywhere. For example, the directory used for this book is `c:\xml4j`.

XML Parser for Java is also a command-line utility. Depending on the version you download, you may not type everything exactly as shown here. For example, the sequence `_1_1_9` will change. Look at the following example:

```
c:\xml4j> jre -cp
xml4j_1_1_9.jar;xml4jSamples_1_1_9.jar
samples.XJParse.XJParse
c:\XMLSamp\sample.xml [Just fine - JES]

c:\xml4j>
```

There is no output to the MS-DOS window when the parser is run without any switches associated with a valid argument. This parser provides many switches. For instance, if you add a **–d** to the command line before the XML document name, the parser prints the document in its XML format. That command would look something like this:

```
c:\xml4j> jre -cp
xml4j_1_1_9.jar;xml4jSamples_1_1_9.jar
samples.XJParse.XJParse -d
c:\XMLSamp\sample.xml [Ditto right back -
JES]
```

The output of this command is simply the XML document, including its tags.

Using XML Editors

Running XML parsers can be frustrating. Depending on the parser, you need to spend some time figuring out why errors occur. An easier approach is to use an XML editor. Most editors enable you to create XML documents and also check the syntax for both your DTD and document. Some editors also show the tree structure of an XML document. The features of an editor depend on its developer.

XML editors range in price from nothing (freeware) to $2,000 (for a commercial suite of programs). Get more information and try out some XML editors at the following sites: **http://wvinter.softseek.com/Programming/Java/Review_18699_index.html**, **http://www.vervet.com/**, and **http://www.pierlou.com/visxml/**. In addition, the CD-ROM accompanying this book contains XML editors.

CROSS-REFERENCE

In Chapter 7, you can learn about the XML declaration and how to declare an internal or external DTD.

FIND IT ONLINE

Software (**http://www.megginson.com/Software/software.html**) is a page of programs, patches, and classes.

Listing 12-5: A SAMPLE XML DOCUMENT

```
<?xml version = "1.0"?>
<!DOCTYPE ANNOUNCE [
<!ELEMENT ANNOUNCE (FROM, BODY)>
<!ELEMENT FROM      (#PCDATA)>
<!ELEMENT BODY      (#PCDATA)>]>
<ANNOUNCE>
<FROM>Tess Curtis</FROM>
<BODY>
The first planning session for the
Christmas party will take place on Friday
at 2 PM. See you there. </BODY></ANNOUNCE>
```

❶ *The DTD makes this a valid XML document.*

Listing 12-6: PARSING THE DOCUMENT

```
c:\xml4j> jre -cp xml4j_1_1_9.jar;
xml4jSamples_1_1_9.jar samples.XJParse
.XJParse -d c:\XMLSamp\valid3.xml ❷
<?xml version = "1.0"?>
<!DOCTYPE ANNOUNCE [
<!ELEMENT ANNOUNCE (FROM, BODY)>
<!ELEMENT FROM      (#PCDATA)>
<!ELEMENT BODY      (#PCDATA)>]>
<ANNOUNCE>
<FROM>Tess Curtis</FROM>
<BODY>The first planning session for the
Christmas party will take place on Friday
at 2 PM. See you there. </BODY></ANNOUNCE>
```

❷ *The −d switch causes the parser to print the XML document.*

Listing 12-7: ANOTHER SAMPLE XML DOCUMENT

```
<?xml version = "1.0"?>
<!DOCTYPE TURTLE [
<!ELEMENT TURTLE (PICTURE, DESC)>
<!ELEMENT PICTURE    EMPTY> ❶
<!ELEMENT DESC     (#PCDATA)>
]>
<TURTLE>
   <PICTURE>A picture goes here</PICTURE>
   <DESC>This is Freddy</DESC>
</TURTLE>
```

❶ *The PICTURE element should be empty.*

Listing 12-8: PARSING THE DOCUMENT

```
c:\xml4j> jre -cp xml4j_1_1_9.jar;
xml4jSamples_1_1_9.jar samples.XJParse
.XJParse c:\XMLSamp\turtle.xml
c:\xmlsamp\turtle.xml: 8, 40: Element
"<PICTURE>" is not valid because it does ❷
not follow the rule, "EMPTY".
```

❷ *The parser finds an error: <PICTURE> is not empty. This result differs from that in Listing 12-4 because a validating parser checked the DTD and the document.*

Interpreting Messages

There is no universal directory for interpreting messages. Each parser is designed differently. If you are having problems making well-formed or valid documents, find a parser with well-documented error descriptions, easy-to-understand error descriptions, or both.

This following XML document is similar to the example used in the "Parsing a Well-Formed Document" section. The difference is the end tag is not properly formed.

```
<?xml version ="1.0"?>
<text>This is text<text>
```

Running Lark:

```
c:\lark>jview Driver c:\xmlsamp\text1.xml
Hello Tim
Lark V1.0 final beta Copyright (c) 1997-98
 Tim Bray.
 All rights reserved; the right to use
 these class files for any purpose
 is hereby granted to everyone.
Parsing...
Lark:c:\xmlsamp\badsamp.xml:2:24:E:Fatal:
 End of document entity before end of
 root element.
Done.
```

Running IBM's parser:

```
c:\xml4j> jre -cp
xml4j_1_1_9.jar;xml4jSamples_1_1_9.jar
 samples.XJParse.XJParse
c:\XMLSamp\badsamp.xml
c:\xmlsamp\badsamp.xml: 3, 1: "</text>"
 expected.
c:\xmlsamp\badsamp.xml: 3, 1: "</text>"
 expected.
```

Both parsers are describing the same error: Lark basically tells you it ran out of content before it came across the end of the root element. IBM's parser says it expected `</text>` twice. That's why the error message appears to be repeated; IBM's parser expects both `<text>` tags — correct and incorrect — to have their own end tags. Both parsers interpret the reason for the error differently.

Now look at the numbers listed in the error reports. Lark uses 2:24 and IBM's parser uses 3,1. Lark's usage refers to the second line, character 24, to describe the location of the error (that's the end of the second line). IBM's parser reports the first character of the third line.

CROSS-REFERENCE
Chapter 11 instructs you on finding DTD libraries and editing both DTDs and XML documents.

FIND IT ONLINE
SGML & XML Tools — Parsers and Engines (**http://www.infotek.no/sgmltool/sdk.htm**) lists software development kits.

Listing 12-9: AN INVALID XML DOCUMENT

```
<?xml version="1.0"?>
<!DOCTYPE birdlib [
<!ELEMENT birdlib
(title,(heading1,image,caption)+)>
<!NOTATION gif SYSTEM "masterpics.exe">
<!ENTITY bluejay  SYSTEM
"http://eddygrp.com/birds/bluejay.gif"
  NDATA gif>
<!ENTITY chickdee SYSTEM
"http://eddygrp.com/birds/chickdee.gif" >
<!ELEMENT title (#PCDATA)>
<!ELEMENT heading1 (#PCDATA)>
<!ELEMENT image EMPTY>
<!ATTLIST image pic ENTITY #REQUIRED>
<!ELEMENT caption (#PCDATA)>
]>
<birdlib>
<title>A Library of Common North American
 Birds<title/>
<heading1>The Blue Jay</heading1>
<image pic="&bluejay;"/>
<caption>A blue and gray bird of eastern
North America</caption>
<heading>The Chickadee</heading1>
<image />
<Caption>A small white and gray bird with a
black head</Caption>
</birdlib>
```

▲ *This is not a valid XML document. Try to find the mistakes.*

Listing 12-10: PARSING THE DOCUMENT

```
c:\xml4j> jre -cp xml4j_1_1_9.jar;
xml4jSamples_1_1_9.jar samples.XJParse
.XJParse -d c:\XMLSamp\birdlib3.xml
c:\xmlsamp\birdlib3.xml: 16, 21: NDATA
reference, "&bluejay;", is invalid in this
context.
c:\xmlsamp\birdlib3.xml: 16, 24: Invalid
character
'?' in attribute value.
c:\xmlsamp\birdlib3.xml: 16, 24: Attribute
value, "?", is not binary external entity.
c:\xmlsamp\birdlib3.xml: 18, 32:"</heading>
expected.
c:\xmlsamp\birdlib3.xml: 18, 33: Element
"<heading>" is not valid in this context.
c:\xmlsamp\birdlib3.xml: 19, 9: Required
attribute
"pic", is not specified.
c:\xmlsamp\birdlib3.xml: 20, 64: Element
"<Caption>" is not valid in this context.
c:\xmlsamp\birdlib3.xml: 21, 9: "</title>"
expected.
c:\xmlsamp\birdlib3.xml: 21, 10: Element
"<title>"
is not valid because it does not follow the
rule, "(#PCDATA)".
c:\xmlsamp\birdlib3.xml: 22, 0: Element
"<birdlib>" is not valid because it does
not follow the rule,"(title,(heading1,
image,caption)+)".
```

▲ *Parsing this document shows a large number of errors for a short document. Some errors (for example, </title/>) caused the parser to generate multiple error messages.*

Parsing as You Modify

Now that you've had a basic introduction to parsers, you're ready to jump into XML. You won't have to worry about making mistakes and not being able to find them. However, parsing doesn't solve all your XML problems. Just because a parser has pointed out a problem doesn't mean you know how to fix it. Correcting errors requires an understanding of the XML document's structure.

Take a look at the example shown in the last "Interpreting Messages" task. Recall that the two parsers produced two different types of messages: The Lark message states that it cannot find an end tag for the root element, and IBM's XML Parser for Java says it cannot find end tags for the two elements `<text>` and `<text>`. How do you correct the error?

To correct the error, you need to know the structure of the element. In most cases, you will be the author of the XML document, and you should understand its structure because you planned and designed it. When you understand the structure of the document, you also know the degree that something needs to be corrected. Whenever you find errors in a document, you should not fix all the errors at once. Often when you try to fix everything, you wind up adding unnecessary changes — in effect, fixing problems more than once, or even introducing new errors.

Referring back to the `badsamp.xml` example, look at the results from IBM's parser. The parser lists two errors, but are there actually two errors in the document? In this case, the author of the document forgot to insert a slash in an end tag. This inadvertently created a second start tag. If you tried to fix both errors at once, you might have changed the entire structure of the document!

Repairing errors is a process that does not come easy for many people — especially novices to a new technology. When you find yourself in that situation, take your time and repair one error at a time. Keep running a parser against your document. You'll eventually correct all of those errors.

TAKE NOTE

TOOLS THAT CONVERT XML TO HTML

As you read through this book, you will notice how similar the XML and HTML statements are. One tool that appears in some XML parsers and editors is an XML-to-HTML converter. Converters are useful because not all current browsers can properly evaluate XML documents. Depending on the tool you use, some information from the XML document may be lost when it is converted to HTML. Evaluate the conversion tool to find out how it handles the structural information from an XML document. Some tools save this information as attributes within the HTML document; other tools ignore the information and create an HTML document for display.

CROSS-REFERENCE

In Chapter 16, you find out how to convert HTML documents to XML and create associated DTDs.

FIND IT ONLINE

1998 XML News (**http://sunsite.unc.edu/xml/news1998.html**) lists many news events as well as links.

Listing 12-11: CORRECTING LINES IN AN INVALID XML DOCUMENT

```
<?xml version = "1.0"?>
<!DOCTYPE SAMPLE [
<!ELEMENT SAMPLE (HEADER, BODY)>
<!ELEMENT HEADER (#PCDATA)>
<!ELEMENT BODY (#PCDATA)>
]>

<SAMPLE>
<HEADER>This is the title<HEADER/>
<BODY>Here is the body</body>
</SAMPLE>

jre -cp xml4j_1_1_9.jar;xml4jSamples_1_1_9.jar samples.XJParse.XJParse -d
c:\xmlsamp\sample.xml
c:\xmlsamp\sample.xml: 3, 26: Element content sequence token expected. (':',
',', or ')')
c:\xmlsamp\sample.xml: 4, 0: '>' expected.
c:\xmlsamp\sample.xml: 10, 28: "</BODY>" expected.
c:\xmlsamp\sample.xml: 11, 8: "/HEADER>" expected.
c:\xmlsamp\sample.xml: 11, 9: Element "Header" is not valid because it does not
follow the rule, "(#PCDATA)".
c:\xmlsamp\sample.xml: 12, 0: Element "<SAMPLE>" is not valid in this context.
<?xml version="1.0"?>
<!DOCTYPE SAMPLE [
<!ELEMENT HEADER (#PCDATA)>
<!ELEMENT BODY (#PCDATA)>
]>

<SAMPLE>
<HEADER>This is the title<HEADER/>
<BODY>Here is the body</BODY>
</HEADER>
</SAMPLE>
```

▲ *The parser processes the entire document and finds problems you must fix. For example, in line 3, change the period to a comma. In line 9, move the slash in front of* HEADER. *In line 10, capitalize* body.

Personal Workbook

Q&A

1 What is a *parser*?

_____

_____

_____

2 What types of document components do parsers check?

_____

_____

_____

3 What are the two parser categories? What do they do?

_____

_____

_____

4 When a parser finds a problem in a DTD or document, what does it do?

_____

_____

_____

5 How should you run a parser for the first time?

_____

_____

_____

_____

6 If you have problems running a parser, what are some of the ways that you can find the problem?

_____

_____

_____

_____

7 How do you run a command-line utility?

_____

_____

_____

8 What is the main advantage of using an XML editor?

_____

_____

_____

ANSWERS: PAGE 457

EXTRA PRACTICE

① Install and test the Java Runtime Environment (JRE) or the Java Development Kit (JDK).

② Install a non-validating parser from the accompanying CD-ROM or download and install it from a Web site.

③ Test the parser on a small XML document with or without a DTD.

④ Evaluate and correct the results of your test and rerun the parser, if necessary.

⑤ Install a validating parser from the accompanying CD-ROM or download and install it from a Web site.

⑥ Test both parsers on a medium-sized XML document with an internal or external DTD.

REAL-WORLD APPLICATIONS

✔ In the previous chapter, you found and converted a DTD to use for your company press releases. Parse the DTD against two or three press releases to ensure you can use it properly.

✔ You are in charge of converting your company's intranet to XML. As you convert each document, parse it and correct it.

✔ In the previous chapter, you were assigned to convert reports to Web pages stored in an archive folder. Test the DTD you found and edited to ensure it is accurate.

✔ You are the human resources employee who will design and write a DTD to convert your employee handbook to a set of Web documents. Write a DTD and a dummy document. Then parse the DTD until the dummy document is accurate.

Visual Quiz

Find all the errors in this XML document using an XML parser. Correct the document and rerun the parser until the document is completely accurate.

_____

_____

_____

_____

_____

```
W Microsoft Word - visual quiz 12                          _ 8 X
 File Edit View Insert Format Tools Table Window Help      _ 8 X
<?xml version="1.0" standalone="no"?>
<!DOCTYPE science [
<!ELEMENT science (title|para)>
<!ELEMENT title (#PCDATA)>
<!ELEMENT para (#PCDATA)>
]>
<science>
<title>Learning about Tornadoes<title>
<para id="0001">
This illustrated book, for 8-12 year olds,
introduces readers to tornadoes and what
causes them.
</para>
<para Align="left"
Don't search for tornadoes without permission.
</para>

Page 1    Sec 1        1/1    At      Ln      Col      REC TRK EXT OVR WPH
```

PART

III

Contents of 'Desktop'

Name

My Computer

Network Neigh

Internet Explore

Microsoft Outlo

Recycle Bin

My Briefcase

3252-9

3259-6

3261-8

3262-6

3281-2

3286-3

DE Phone List

Device Manager

In

Iomega Tools

Writing an XML Document

In this part, you start to create XML documents. By now, you know how to define the elements, attributes, entities, notation, and other components that compose the structure, content, and format of valid XML documents. Now it's time to put those components into your first set of XML documents. In other words, you have learned all about the structure and how to put it into play; now you will be adding content to documents. As you read this section, you'll return from time to time to the DTD — only because the contents of the DTD provide structural information about your XML document.

The next six chapters show you how to create basic XML documents by assembling components and content, by importing content from an outside source, or both. You'll learn how to build basic XML documents using the basic components that you learned in previous chapters of this book. You'll also discover how to convert an HTML document and import database information into XML. This part finishes by teaching you the basics of constructing forms for your documents.

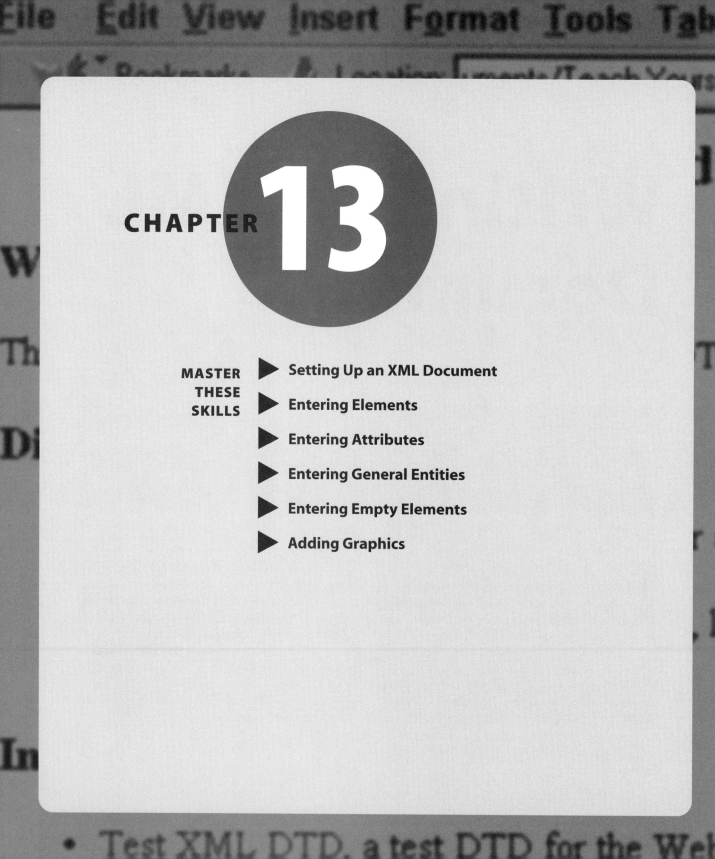

CHAPTER **13**

MASTER
THESE
SKILLS

▶ Setting Up an XML Document

▶ Entering Elements

▶ Entering Attributes

▶ Entering General Entities

▶ Entering Empty Elements

▶ Adding Graphics

Creating a Basic XML Document

In this chapter, you learn how to create a basic XML document. The tasks in this chapter use information from the first two parts of this book. In Part II, you learned about the all-important DTD, which defines the structure of the document, including the data storage components. But a DTD is meant to produce XML documents, not to actually provide the information. However, as is the case with any foundation, you should not ignore the DTD. This point cannot be emphasized enough: Whenever you construct an XML document, remember its foundation. You cannot expect to build a *valid* XML document without knowing its DTD completely.

This chapter also shows you how to use the components introduced and explained in the first part of this book. As a matter of fact, if you examine the task headings in this chapter, you see that it could almost be entitled *Elements, Elements, Everywhere*. The basic building block of an XML document is the element. As you have learned, an XML document must have at least one element, the root element, to be considered well-formed.

As you also know, attributes are modifiers of elements. If you have developed HTML documents, you are familiar with attributes that control the font of a particular element or define whether a specific piece of text should be bold, blue, or larger. In this chapter, the discussion of attributes covers more than text formatting; you'll get a more general point of view.

You will also find out about how to use entities and empty elements in your XML documents. Entities, again, are containers of data, ranging from one character to an entire document to a complete file. They are either parts of attributes or parts of elements. Remember that empty elements are just elements without any current content. Empty elements are placeholders or bookmark areas of an XML document.

The chapter ends with a sample document that shows how all the elements and related components might be used together, and it introduces a new and important component — imported graphics.

Speaking of XML documents, of course, you've heard about how important it is to know all about your DTD. . . .

Setting Up an XML Document

When you actually reach the task of constructing an XML document (and you're probably more than ready at this point), you should have spent a great deal of time and effort planning and preparing. In fact, by the time you add content to a document, you should only have to concern yourself with the content and not have to worry at all about the underlying structure of the document. If you structure the document (that is, write the DTD) at the same time that you write the document, it will probably be well formed — at best — due to the lack of initial planning. Whenever you create a valid XML document, you should have a clear idea of the contents of the DTD. You should have tested the DTD thoroughly and completed it before you start writing the XML document. All the tasks in this chapter assume that you have already developed a DTD.

Remember that XML browsers are not programmed to be as forgiving as browsers that only read HTML. If you code the XML statements inaccurately, these mistakes will probably result in the browser showing the errors or even stopping altogether. Even if a well-formed document does not look pretty (although we're sure that anything you create will), it must follow a specific set of rules. Throughout this chapter, you will find out about the features of both well-formed and valid documents.

The top line of any XML document should be an XML declaration:

```
<?xml version="1.0"?>
```

Basically, the declaration tells browsers that this is an XML document, and the supported XML version is 1.0. This means that the XML document follows the rules in the XML 1.0 specification. Without the version information, some browsers may signal an error.

The remaining tasks discuss how the rest of an XML document is put together.

TAKE NOTE

USING HTML AS A GUIDE FOR CREATING XML DOCUMENTS

XML documents and HTML documents follow essentially the same design and structure. So, you can take advantage of the many Web coding and design resources that you'll find online. For example, you can use the HTML 4.0 specification as the basis for many of the custom XML elements that you'll declare, or you can get an idea of the elements, attributes, and entities that make up a particular document type — such as a home page, a white paper, or even a manual. You can also find a particular Web document that you like and view the underlying source code to see what makes it tick. Throughout this chapter and other chapters in this part, most of the Find It Onlines feature HTML resources.

USING WORD-PROCESSING TEMPLATES AS A GUIDE FOR CREATING XML DOCS

Another source of ideas for creating XML documents demonstrates excellent document design. The templates provided with any of today's word processors show you what a particular document type should look like. The only disadvantage is that these documents don't have underlying DTDs.

CROSS-REFERENCE

In Chapter 6, you'll learn how to plan and outline DTDs — both internal and external — and mark sections.

FIND IT ONLINE

The HTML home page (http://www.w3.org/MarkUp/) links to Web design help and the HTML specification.

XML 1.0: DOCUMENT PROLOG PRODUCTIONS

```
[22]        prolog ::= XMLDecl? Misc* (doctypedecl Misc*)?


[23]       XMLDecl ::= '<?xml' VersionInfo EncodingDecl? SDDecl? S? '?>'◄─❶

[24]   VersionInfo ::= S 'version' Eq (' VersionNum ' | " VersionNum ")◄─❷

[25]            Eq ::= S? '=' S?

[26]    VersionNum ::= ([a-zA-Z0-9_.:] | '-')+

[27]          Misc ::= Comment | PI | S ◄─❸

[28]   doctypedecl ::= '<!DOCTYPE' S Name (S ExternalID)?

                       S? ('[' (markupdecl | PEReference ◄─❹

                       | S)* ']' S?)? '>'
```

❶ Use the XMLDecl production to write one XML declaration.
❷ Insert the VersionInfo into the XML declaration.
❸ Optionally, add any amount of miscellaneous information.
❹ Optionally, insert a document type declaration, including miscellaneous information.

Listing 13-1: SAMPLE XML DECLARATIONS

```
<?xml version="1.0"?>◄─❶


<?xml version="1.0" standalone="no"?>◄─❷


<?xml version="1.0" encoding="UTF-8"?>◄─❸


<?xml version="1.0" standalone="yes"
  encoding="UTF-16"?>            ◄─❹
```

❶ This declaration relies on the defaults.
❷ Add standalone="no" to indicate that the DTD is external.
❸ This declaration uses the default encoding.
❹ This is a standalone document with UTF-16 encoding.

Listing 13-2: SAMPLE DOCUMENT PROLOGS

```
<?xml version="1.0" encoding="UTF-8"
  standalone="no"?>                    ◄─❶
<!DOCTYPE CDjacket SYSTEM "CDjacket.DTD">


<?xml version="1.0" standalone="no"?>
                                       ◄─❷
<!DOCTYPE CDjacket SYSTEM "CDjacket.DTD">


<?xml version="1.0"?>
<!DOCTYPE PAPER [
                                  ◄─❸
<!ELEMENT PAPER (#PCDATA)>
]>
```

❶ This prolog refers to an external DTD.
❷ This equivalent prolog doesn't include encoding information.
❸ This prolog includes a short internal DTD.

Entering Elements

Elements are the basic building blocks of your document. When you create a DTD, you declare elements and define how to use them. Then, when you build a document based on the DTD, you will have to recall the elements declared in the DTD and use them as directed in the DTD. This is a perfect argument for adding numerous comments to your DTD. Without comments, the individuals responsible for maintaining the XML documents that you created will not always know exactly how to use the declared elements or even what elements to use in particular situations.

Remember that all XML documents contain one or more elements. At the highest level is the root element; all other elements are children of this root element, with some child elements of the original child elements, and so on. Also remember that elements are nested within each other; elements should never overlap. Lastly, when you start an element, you always need to finish it — each element must have both a start tag and an end tag.

Following is a simple example of an element from Chapter 1. There is a start tag, followed (in this case) by content, and finished with an end tag.

```
<text>This is one sentence.</text>
```

Whenever a document is composed of multiple elements (and this is almost always the case), you will have to be careful about how the elements are nested. This becomes complicated as you add elements. Look at the following example of nesting:

```
<sentence>This <verb>is</verb> one
sentence<punctuation>.</punctuation>
</sentence>
```

Now, without seeing the DTD in which it is declared, it's hard to say whether `<sentence>` is a root element or a child element. The first example on the facing page demonstrates how to add an internal DTD subset to the XML document.

CROSS-REFERENCE

Chapter 1 introduces you to elements and other building blocks of DTDs and other XML documents.

FIND IT ONLINE

Use the tutorial at **http://www.w3.org/MarkUp/Guide** as a guide to creating your first XML documents.

Listing 13-3: A SMALL, VALID DOCUMENT

```
<?xml version="1.0"?>
<!DOCTYPE sentence [
<!ELEMENT sentence (verb|punctuation)>
  <!ELEMENT verb (#PCDATA)>
  <!ELEMENT punctuation (#PCDATA)>
]>
<sentence>
This <verb>is</verb> one
sentence<punctuation>.</punctuation>
</sentence>
```

▲ *Now you know definitely that the <sentence> element is the root element. Note the importance of changing the format to be able to read the nested structure more easily.*

Listing 13-4: INVALID NESTING EXAMPLES, PART 1

```
<?xml version="1.0"?>
<!DOCTYPE house [
<!ELEMENT house (address|price|offer+)>
  <!ELEMENT address (#PCDATA)>
  <!ELEMENT price (#PCDATA)>
  <!ELEMENT offer (#PCDATA)>
]>
<house>
  <address>1235 Oak Drive<address>  ◀❶
<price>$130,000</price>
</house>  ◀❷
<offer>$120,000</offer>  ◀❸
```

❶ *This line should end with the </address> end tag.*
❷ *The </house> end tag appears prematurely.*
❸ *The offer child element is outside its root element, house.*

Listing 13-5: INVALID NESTING EXAMPLES, PART 2

```
<?xml version="1.0"?>
<!DOCTYPE house [
<!ELEMENT house (address|price|offer+)>
  <!ELEMENT address (#PCDATA)>
  <!ELEMENT price (#PCDATA)>
  <!ELEMENT offer (#PCDATA)>
]>
<house>
  <address>1235 Oak Drive</address>
  <price>$130,000
  <offer>$120,000</price></offer>
</house>
```

❹ *The offer start tag starts too soon.*
❺ *To nest properly, move the </price> end tag up one line.*

Listing 13-6: AN EXAMPLE OF GOOD NESTING

```
<?xml version="1.0"?>
<!DOCTYPE house [
<!ELEMENT house (address|price|offer+)>
  <!ELEMENT address (#PCDATA)>
  <!ELEMENT price (#PCDATA)>
  <!ELEMENT offer (#PCDATA)>
]>
<house>
  <address>1235 Oak Drive</address>
  <price>$130,000</price>
  <offer>$120,000</offer>
</house>
```

▲ *The example is finally accurate. There is a single root element, the tags are valid and correctly matched, and the elements are properly nested.*

Entering Attributes

You have learned that you can find attributes in two places within your document — in start tags and in empty-element tags. As discussed in Chapter 9, attributes are pairs of names and values associated with an element. An attribute adds important information that refines its element. Sometimes, an attribute helps format or enhance an element for an end user; at other times, the information is completely invisible to the end user and is passed directly to another application.

Remember that you declare attributes in the DTD. This serves as a reminder that you should be aware of all the declarations in the DTD before you add values to your elements. Adding an attribute to a document is easy; however, problems may occur when you have to remember specifically what to add.

In the following example, the attribute is in the correct location — within the start tag:

```
<text sentence id="001">
This is one sentence.
</text>
```

Notice that there is a space between `sentence` and `id`. You can include spaces as part of the attribute name; this is one important difference between naming elements and naming attributes.

An element can have more than one attribute. The only thing to remember is that each attribute must be followed by its value, enclosed within quotation marks or single quote marks. (When an XML processor issues warning messages or does not display certain attribute values, look for missing quotes.) For example:

```
<text sentence id="001" author="Madeleine
S."
length="21" color="red">This is one
sentence.</text>
```

The above example also shows that it is very possible to include so many attributes that content is not easily seen. In this case, you might want to reformat your code to make the XML document easier to read. For example:

```
<text
    sentence id="001"
    author="Madeleine S."
    length="21"
    color="red">
This is one sentence.
</text>
```

The above example shows how an element with many attributes might be organized in an XML document. The start tag begins in the one column; the attributes are each on their own line and indented from the start tag. The content is on the last line, separate from the attributes and followed by the end tag.

TAKE NOTE

▶ **USING A PARSER TO CHECK A DOCUMENT AS YOU DEVELOP IT**

Remember that parsing a document is a great way to test and keep track of the document's organization. It's never too early to use a parser as you build a document. Although you may think that a document is well-organized, running the parser against it may point out weaknesses and errors.

CROSS-REFERENCE

Chapter 9 discusses how attributes are defined.

FIND IT ONLINE

The HTML specification (**http://www.w3.org/TR/REC-html40/**) can help in defining XML elements.

Listing 13-7: MISSING QUOTES

```
<?xml version="1.0"?>
<!DOCTYPE house [
<!ELEMENT house (address|price|offer+)>
  <!ATTLIST house id    ID   #IMPLIED>
  <!ELEMENT address (#PCDATA)>
      <!ATTLIST address taxmap CDATA
        #REQUIRED>
  <!ELEMENT price (#PCDATA)>
  <!ELEMENT offer (#PCDATA)>]>
<house>
  <address taxmap=Lot 5T>1235 Oak Drive
  </address>
  <price>$130,000</price>
  <offer>$120,000</offer></house>
```

▲ The `taxmap` *attribute should be "quoted." You can enclose values within quotation marks or single quote marks. Do not combine quotation marks and single quote marks to enclose a single value.*

Listing 13-8: MISPLACED ATTRIBUTE

```
<?xml version="1.0"?>
<!DOCTYPE house [
<!ELEMENT house (address|price|offer+)>
  <!ATTLIST house id    ID   #IMPLIED>
  <!ELEMENT address (#PCDATA)>
      <!ATTLIST address taxmap CDATA
            #REQUIRED>
  <!ELEMENT price (#PCDATA)>
  <!ELEMENT offer (#PCDATA)>]>
<house>
  <address taxmap="Lot 5T">1235 Oak Drive
  </address>
  <price>$130,000</price>
  <offer>$120,000</offer>
</house   id='125A'>
```

▲ The `id` *attribute is incorrectly located in the end tag for the* house *element. Attributes may only be placed in start tags.*

Listing 13-9: A MISSING ATTRIBUTE

```
<?xml version="1.0"?>
<!DOCTYPE house [
<!ELEMENT house (address|price|offer+)>
  <!ATTLIST house id    ID   #IMPLIED>
  <!ELEMENT address (#PCDATA)>
      <!ATTLIST address taxmap CDATA
            #REQUIRED>
  <!ELEMENT price (#PCDATA)>
  <!ELEMENT offer (#PCDATA)>
]>
<house id='125A'>
  <address>1235 Oak Drive</address>
  <price>$130,000</price>
  <offer>$120,000</offer>
</house>
```

▲ The required attribute, `taxmap`, *is missing from the* address *element. Either add the attribute or remove the requirement.*

Listing 13-10: A CORRECTED EXAMPLE

```
<?xml version="1.0"?>
<!DOCTYPE house [
<!ELEMENT house (address|price|offer+)>
  <!ATTLIST house id    ID   #IMPLIED>
  <!ELEMENT address (#PCDATA)>
      <!ATTLIST address taxmap CDATA
            #REQUIRED>
  <!ELEMENT price (#PCDATA)>
  <!ELEMENT offer (#PCDATA)>
]>
<house id='125A'>
  <address taxmap="1501C">1235 Oak Drive
  </address>
  <price>$130,000</price>
  <offer>$120,000</offer>
</house>
```

▲ The attributes are now in the correct places. Note the value for `id` *is surrounded by single quote marks and the value for* `taxmap` *is surrounded by quotation marks.*

Entering General Entities

As you have learned in this book, entities are storage containers for information, ranging from a single character to an entire file. Remember that the XML specification supports the use of two basic categories of entities: general entities and parameter entities (PEs), which can be internal or external. General entities can be parsed or unparsed, whereas PEs are always parsed. (The following Take Note summarizes the available variations of general entities.) General entities place non-markup information into document content at the location of an entity reference, and PEs place information into the DTD, also at the location of a reference. For more information about using PEs, refer to the "Using Parameter Entities" task in Chapter 10.

This task reviews how to use general entities — both internal and external — and their entity references. The syntax for a general entity starts with an ampersand and ends with a semicolon. Take a look at the following internal general entity declaration, which is located within the current XML document:

```
<!ENTITY name "Waterdogs Miss Madeleine">
<!ENTITY callname "Maddie">
```

Here, too, is the entity reference also within the XML document:

```
<MyDog>
  <text>
    My dog's full name is &name;.
    I call her &callname;.
  </text>
</MyDog>
```

The following examples show how an external general entity works. Let's say that you have created the following XML statements:

```
<weather><skies>Partly Cloudy</skies>
  <temp>40-50</temp>
  <precip>Rain</precip></weather>
```

After creating this information, assume that you save it on your local network in a file titled **weather.xml** and store the file at **http://www.joesweather.com/NewPaltz/weather.xml**. You can declare the **weather.xml** file in a DTD using the following syntax:

```
<!ENTITY wthr SYSTEM
"http://www.jweather.com/NewPaltz/wthr.xml"
```

In an XML document, refer to the entity as

```
<MyWeather>
  <title>My Weather</title>
  &wthr;
</MyWeather>
```

TAKE NOTE

OTHER GENERAL ENTITIES

XML supports two variations of general entities: character and data. A character entity, which is parsed and either internal or external, represents special characters in a document. For more information about using this type of entity, see the "Writing Character Entities" task in Chapter 10. A data entity, which is unparsed and external, represents an imported non-XML file defined as binary. For more information about using this type of entity, see "Declaring Data Entities" in Chapter 10.

CROSS-REFERENCE

Chapter 1 introduces you to entities, along with elements, tags, attributes, and other XML components.

FIND IT ONLINE

The HTML Activity page (http://www.w3.org/MarkUp/Activity.html) tracks HTML news and plans.

Listing 13-11: INCORRECT SYNTAX FOR VALID ENTITIES

```
<!ENTITY main "Main Street">        ①
<!ENTITY oak   "Oak Drive">
<!ENTITY offer SYSTEM "offerletter.xml">  ②

<house id='125A'>
  &offer      ←③            ④
  <address taxmap="1501C">1235 oak;
  </address>
  <price>$130,000</price>
  <offer>$120,000</offer>
</house>
```

① These are correctly formatted internal general entities.
② This external general entity is properly formatted.
③ Remember to enter a semicolon after an entity name.
④ Remember to precede a general entity name with an ampersand.

Listing 13-12: CORRECT SYNTAX FOR GENERAL ENTITIES

```
<!ENTITY main "Main Street"
<!ENTITY oak   "Oak Drive"
<!ENTITY offer SYSTEM "offerletter.xml"

<house id='125A'>
  &offer;
  <address taxmap="1501C">1235 &oak;
  </address>
  <price>$130,000</price>
  <offer>$120,000</offer>
</house>
```

▲ Now the entities are correctly preceded by the ampersand and succeeded by a semicolon.

Listing 13-13: AN ENTITY FOR AN ATTRIBUTE

```
<house id='Jerry&apos;s'>
  &offer;
  <address taxmap="1501C">1235 &oak;
  </address>
  <price>$130,000</price>
  <offer>$120,000</offer>
</house>
```

▲ This is an example of an entity used within the value of the id attribute.

Listing 13-14: THE OFFERLETTER.XML DOCUMENT

```
<?xml version="1.0"?>
<!DOCTYPE letter [
<!ELEMENT letter (#PCDATA)>
]>

<letter>
Dear Homeowner(s),
  We are pleased to submit this anonymous
  bid for the property listed below.

  Please respond to our office with your
decision.
</letter>
```

▲ This is the external document offerletter.xml, which is used with the other documents on this page.

Entering Empty Elements

As you know, empty elements contain no text content; they serve as containers for future content. However, empty elements can have attributes, which might mark a particular location in a document or point to a file, such as a picture or a sound file, to be contained at the location of the empty element.

You can specify empty elements in two ways: You can use start tags and end tags as you would with any non-empty element, or you can use a shortcut form that combines start tags and end tags into a single tag. Look at the following example:

```
<elevenmonths/>
```

The empty `<elevenmonths>` element consists of a single tag with no attributes. You might use `<elevenmonths>` to mark a section of the document.

In the example below, `<picture>` is the empty element, which has separate start tags and end tags.

```
<statistics>
  <shoulderheight>22.25 inches
  </shoulderheight>
  <weight>65 pounds</weight>
  <nose>Still black</nose>
  <picture pict="11months.gif"></picture>
<statistics/>
```

This element contains no textual data but does have an attribute. You can also express `<picture>` as follows:

```
<picture pict="11months.gif"/>
```

It is important to note that when using empty elements, both types of syntaxes work with attributes. One difference, however, is that people looking at the tags in the XML document will be able to immediately tell that an element is empty when you use the combined start tag-end tag syntax.

Marking Spans of Document Content

If you are familiar with HTML 4.0, you know that one of its new elements is SPAN, which marks a section or a location in a document (in the same way that you would use a bookmark in a word-processing document). You can use SPAN within a paragraph to identify a new sentence or within a list to mark a new list item. Also, you can use SPAN to apply styles to a particular section in a document — even a single character or word — or to apply a dynamic HTML script.

How would you span part of a document in XML? Simply define an empty element and use it as follows:

```
<para>I don't want to mark every
character
 in this paragraph but I would like to
 take some future action on
<span/>this location.</para>
```

You could also declare two empty elements to span characters or words:

```
<para>I don't want to mark every
character
 in this paragraph but I would like to
take
 some future
<spnbegin/>action<spnend/> on
 this location.</para>
```

CROSS-REFERENCE

Among other important topics, Chapter 8 instructs you on how to declare an empty element.

FIND IT ONLINE

Learn about plans to make the Web accessible to all types of users at **http://www.w3.org/WAI/GL/**.

Listing 13-15: INVALID EMPTY ELEMENTS

```
<?xml version="1.0"?>
<!DOCTYPE house [
<!ELEMENT house
(bookmark|address|price|offer+|image)>
<!ATTLIST house id    ID    #IMPLIED>

<!ELEMENT bookmark (mark1|mark2) EMPTY>◄─❶
<!ELEMENT address (#PCDATA)>
<!ATTLIST address taxmap CDATA #REQUIRED>
<!ELEMENT price (#PCDATA)>
<!ELEMENT offer (#PCDATA)>
<!ELEMENT image EMPTY (#PCDATA)>◄─❷
<!ATTLIST picture ENTITY #REQUIRED>
```

❶ The empty bookmark element is invalid because it has child elements.
❷ The invalid empty image element must not contain text.

Listing 13-16: VALID EMPTY ELEMENTS

```
<!ELEMENT bookmark EMPTY>
<!ELEMENT address (#PCDATA)>
<!ATTLIST address taxmap CDATA #REQUIRED>
<!ELEMENT price (#PCDATA)>
<!ELEMENT offer (#PCDATA)>
<!ELEMENT image EMPTY>
<!ATTLIST picture CDATA #REQUIRED>

<bookmark></bookmark>

<image picture="Jerryshouse.gif"/>
```

▲ The declared empty elements are empty, but bookmark should have an attribute that marks different houses (assuming that more houses will be added in the future).

Listing 13-17: A DTD WITH EMPTY ELEMENTS

```
<?xml version="1.0"?>
<!DOCTYPE house [
<!ELEMENT house
     (listdate,address,price,offer+,image)>
<!ATTLIST house
          id        ID            #IMPLIED>
<!ELEMENT listdate (#PCDATA)>
<!ELEMENT address (#PCDATA)>
<!ATTLIST address
          taxmap    CDATA         #REQUIRED>
<!ELEMENT price (#PCDATA)>
<!ELEMENT offer (#PCDATA)>
<!ELEMENT image EMPTY>
<!ATTLIST image    CDATA         #REQUIRED
          type    NOTATION  (jpg|gif) "jpg">
]>
```

▲ Here, the empty bookmark element has been replaced with a listing-date element. The empty picture element allows two notations, with the JPEG format the default.

LISTING 13-18: A SAMPLE XML DOCUMENT

```
<?xml version="1.0"?>
<!DOCTYPE house SYSTEM "/dtds/house.dtd">
<house id="98032201>Beautiful Ranch
<address>123 Main Street</address>
<price>125000</price>
<offer>97000</offer>
<image picture="123main.jpg"/>
</house>
<house id="98122201>Back to Nature
<address>60 Bronco Road</address>
<price>377000</price>
<offer>none</offer>
<image picture="60bronco.jpg"/>
</house>
```

▲ This document is associated with the DTD in Listing 13-17. Each entry can be exported to a database, displayed online, or printed.

Adding Graphics

For the last task of this chapter, we'll review most of what we have learned and apply it to adding graphics to XML documents.

To add graphics to XML documents, simply declare an empty element using the following syntax:

```
<!ELEMENT image EMPTY>
```

As you can see, a graphic element is empty: It has no current contents but is a placeholder for future contents. Remember that empty elements can have attributes such as those shown in the following attribute list:

```
<!ATTLIST image
        id    ID                  #IMPLIED
        uri   CDATA               #REQUIRED
        type  NOTATION  (jpg|gif) "jpg">
```

You've seen the first two attributes, `id` and `uri`, in other chapters. The id attribute enables you to identify this element, primarily for future linking. (See Part IV for information about XML links.) The required `uri` attribute enables you to insert a graphic into the `image` element. The third attribute, `type`, deserves a more extensive discussion.

In the last task of Chapter 10, you learned about notation and how to declare it in a DTD. The last line in the attribute list is a real-life example of notation. As mentioned in Chapter 10, a notation is a formalized set of symbols or an alphabet. Notations include computer file formats. Perhaps the two most popular file types for Web-based graphics are jpg and gif. JPEG files are ideal for photographic images, such as a picture of a dog or a flower, and GIF files are suitable for 256-color illustrations and animations. (See the following sidebar.) In the example, the `type` attribute declaration states that you can use two types of graphic formats, JPEG and GIF, in any document associated with this DTD. However, the default format is JPEG.

When you use a graphic in an XML document, you can import it into an empty element. You also have the choice of declaring the graphic as an entity and inserting that into your document. The choice is up to you. As you will see in the two document examples on the right side of the facing page, you can save yourself some time when you use entities.

Learning About JPEG and GIF Graphic Formats

The most popular graphic formats for Web pages are JPEG and GIF. Developed by the Joint Photographic Experts Group, JPEG is the best format for photographic 24-bit images, with over 16 million colors possible. JPEG files compress very efficiently and lose very little image quality. However, every time you compress a JPEG file, it loses some of its quality.

GIF files are 8-bit files, which means that they are limited to 256 colors. However, GIFs have some definite advantages. You can make parts of GIF files transparent, so you are not limited to rectangular images. GIF files can be *interlaced*: An image can load onto a page in stages. You can also animate GIF files.

CROSS-REFERENCE
Look through the other tasks of this chapter for more information about the components discussed above.

FIND IT ONLINE
Integrating Web and television technologies is the subject of the **http://www.w3.org/TV/** page.

Listing 13-19: DTD COMBINING TEXT AND AN IMAGE

```
<?xml version="1.0"?>
<!DOCTYPE maddie [
<!-- Declare root element-->
<!ELEMENT maddie (bodytext|figure)>
<!-- Set up the entity for image-->        ❶
<!ENTITY pict SYSTEM "/cute/maddie.jpg">

<!-- Define child elements-->        ❷
<!ELEMENT bodytext (intro,para*,summary)>
<!ELEMENT intro (#PCDATA)>
<!ELEMENT para (#PCDATA)>
<!ELEMENT summary (#PCDATA)>
<!ELEMENT figure (image, caption?)>
<!ELEMENT image EMPTY>   ◀❸
<!-- Set up the image attribute list -->    ❹
<!ATTLIST image  pict ENTITY    #REQUIRED
              type  NOTATION  (jpg|gif) "jpg">
<!ELEMENT caption (#PCDATA)>
```

❶ *Declare an entity for the image.*
❷ *For future styling differences, declare three children of* bodytext.
❸ *Declare an empty* image *element.*
❹ *Allow JPEG and GIF file formats.*

Listing 13-20: DOCUMENT COMBINING TEXT AND AN IMAGE

```
<?xml version="1.0"?>
<!DOCTYPE maddie SYSTEM "/m/maddie.dtd">  ❶
<intro>My dog Maddie is a Newfoundland who
loves her toys and gnawing on the molding
on my stairway. To learn more about my
girl, read on.</intro>
<image pict="&maddie;"/>   ❷
<caption>Look at those buggy eyes! ◀❸
</caption>
<para>Newfoundlands are large dogs that
are usually black and originate in
Newfoundland, Canada. They are renowned as
rescue dogs who love the water.</para>
```

❶ *Use the* intro *element to contain an introduction.*
❷ *Insert the* &maddie; *entity.*
❸ *Add a caption, which can be styled in a unique way.*

Listing 13-21: ANOTHER DOCUMENT THAT TAKES A SHORTCUT

```
<?xml version="1.0"?>
<!DOCTYPE maddie SYSTEM "/m/maddie.dtd">
<intro>My dog Maddie is a Newfoundland who
loves her toys and gnawing on the molding
on my stairway. To learn more about my
girl, read on.</intro>
<figure file="/cute/maddie.gif">
Look at those buggy eyes!</figure>
<para>Newfoundlands are large dogs that
are usually black and originate in
Newfoundland, Canada. They are renowned as
rescue dogs who love the water.</para>
```

▲ *This example shows a way to streamline your work: You no longer need to define an entity or declare the* caption *element.*

Personal Workbook

Q&A

1 What declaration needs to be placed at the beginning of an XML document?

_____

_____

_____

2 When you use elements in a valid XML document, what should determine the choice of possible elements?

_____

_____

_____

3 What element must all XML documents have?

_____

_____

_____

4 What are *attributes*?

_____

_____

_____

5 Where do you place attributes?

_____

_____

_____

6 What are the basic types of entities to use in an XML document?

_____

_____

_____

7 What are *external entities*?

_____

_____

_____

_____

8 What is the advantage of using a combined start tag and end tag for an empty element?

_____

_____

_____

ANSWERS: PAGE 458

EXTRA PRACTICE

1 How would you add graphics to the code shown in Listing 13-17?

2 How would you add a graphic to the weather example in the "Entering General Entities" task?

3 In the MyDog example in the "Entering General Entities" task, how would you italicize the name "Maddie"?

4 If the Valid Empty Elements example listed in the Empty Elements section were to be passed to another application, how could you reorganize that example?

5 How could you change the code of a document that would display graphic images to enable someone to change a figure and its corresponding caption more easily?

REAL-WORLD APPLICATIONS

✔ Your aunt has spent a lot of time researching your family history. Create a basic family tree document to show her how she might use XML.

✔ You want to publish recipes on the Internet. Create an XML document that visually shows users the finished dish. How could you modify the application so that for certain recipes, you can add pictures to certain instructional steps?

✔ You are a cartoonist and want to publish your own creations. Create an XML document for publishing cartoons.

✔ You manufacture and sell five models of bicycles for men, women, girls, and boys through a mail-order catalog. Create an XML document for an online catalog. (The DTD was a real world application in Chapter 9.)

Visual Quiz

What is wrong with this section of an XML document?

_____

_____

_____

_____

```
PotatoWedges - Notepad                                        _ |8|X
File  Edit  Search  Help
<cookbook>
  <Recipe title="John&aposs Baked Wedges'/>

    <quantity>1 serving</quantity>

    <ingredients>
      <name>potato
        <quantity>1 potato</qunatity>
        <preparation>6 wedges</name></preparation>

      <name>paprika
        <quantity>1 teaspoon</quantity>

      <name>garlic powder</name>
        <quantity>2 teaspoons</quantity>

      <name>olive oil
        <quantity="1 tablespoon"></quantity>

      <Instructions>Take potato wedges. Place in bag with oil</instructions>
      <instructions>Place on baking pan. Sprinkle with spices</instructions>

      <Baking Temperature="450 degrees">Bake 45 minutes in oven</Baking>
      <picture image="wedges.gif">

  </Recipe>
```

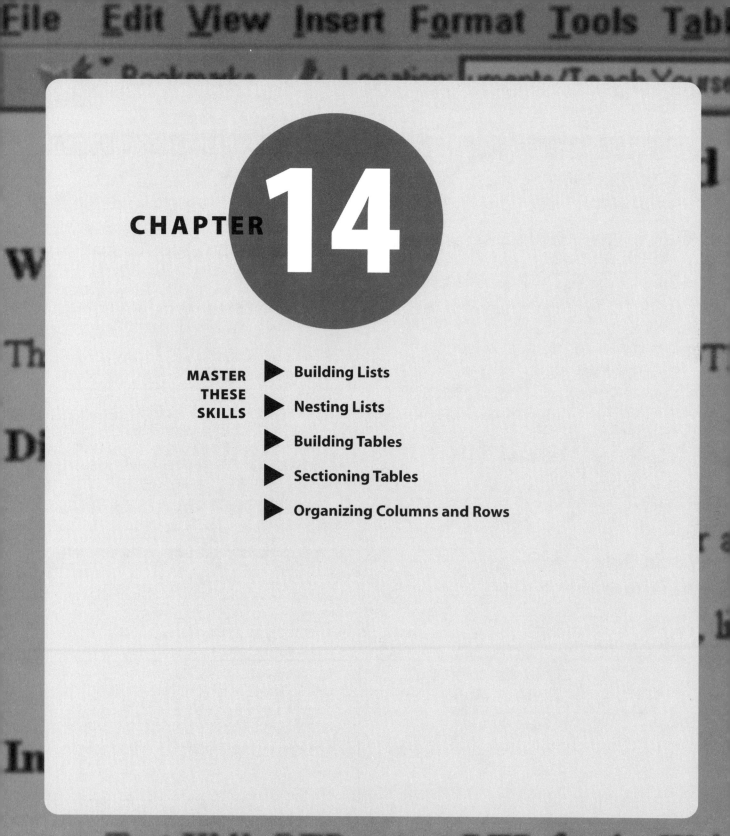

CHAPTER **14**

MASTER
THESE
SKILLS

▶ Building Lists
▶ Nesting Lists
▶ Building Tables
▶ Sectioning Tables
▶ Organizing Columns and Rows

Using Lists and Tables in an XML Document

This chapter discusses lists and tables, two features that enable a designer to organize and present data. This chapter isn't a discussion of the presentation of lists and tables; rather, it covers the underlying structure of elements. The presentation of lists and tables is covered in Chapter 28.

In HTML, lists and tables have a specific structure that cannot be modified very much by the designer. HTML presents certain types of lists, as well as specific components that form tables. With XML, the structure of lists and tables depends on the designer. Your lists and tables can mimic those of HTML, or you can create your own list and table designs.

The first topic discussed in this chapter is the basic construction of lists. Lists are either ordered or unordered. The only difference between ordered lists and unordered lists is that ordered lists are numbered and the items on ordered lists appear in a particular order. The underlying structure of basic unordered and ordered lists are the same. The next topic is a discussion of how lists are used with other lists. This topic includes nesting of lists as well as a special form called the definition list. Basically, a definition list consists of a pair of list items: a term and a description of that term.

The second part of this chapter covers the subject of tables. Tables consist of rows and columns of data. The intersection of a row and column is called a cell. The first table task covers the basic structure of a table and compares the structure with that of the list. The following task is a discussion of sectioning a table and how you can structure a table so that it is a more flexible object. Even though a table is flexible, it has a format that makes it easy to extract data as a row or a column but not as both a row and a column. The final task in the chapter is a basic strategy for making it easier to extract data from rows and columns in the same table.

Up through this chapter, you have seen information about making DTDs and using elements. This is the first chapter in which you will really see how some of the structures in XML are created. After completing this chapter, you will understand two of the basic structures that you can create in XML.

Building Lists

In HTML, there are two basic types of lists: unordered and ordered. An *unordered list* is a collection of items that have no particular sequence. Items in an unordered list typically are preceded by a bullet, which you can change through style sheets. The items in an *ordered list* are arranged in a specific sequence and are preceded by numbers. One item in an ordered list is supposed to follow another that follows another, and so on. The visual difference between unordered and ordered lists essentially comes to formatting.

Both unordered and ordered lists consist of list items. In HTML, a list item, whether it's for an unordered or ordered list, is marked with the start tag <LI> and the optional end tag </LI>. Obviously, when you define a list item in a custom XML language, you can give it any name. But remember that XML *always* requires the use of both start tags and end tags.

Essentially, to create a list, you must have the following structure. A list is marked with a start tag followed by a number of items and, at some point, an end tag. Basically, translated into markup, this means that a list is an element containing a repeating embedded child element. In a DTD, you can set up the element structure for a list as follows:

```
<!ELEMENT topten (item+)>
<!ELEMENT item (#PCDATA)>
```

The CLASS and TYPE attributes in HTML control formatting, but you can also use CLASS and TYPE to differentiate one list from another in the same document. In XML, you can do the same thing — either through the use of formatting attributes or identifying attributes (such as ID or TITLE). For an XML developer or designer, consider defining several list-related elements, each using the name of the list type. The alternative, which probably takes more of your time and resources, is to define one list element and use attributes to differentiate among the list types. Which of the following list examples is easier to understand?

```
<top10lst>
  <item>this</item>
  <item>that</item>
</top10lst>
```

or

```
<ol CLASS="top10lst">
  <item>this</item>
  <item>that</item>
</ol>
```

TAKE NOTE

ORDERING LISTS

The true difference between unordered and ordered lists is whether order actually is important. Take, for example, instructions for maintaining a lawn. Some might say that it is very important to mow the lawn before edging it, and arrange those tasks in a particular numerical order. Others might create a bulleted list of lawncare tasks, in which the bullets might imply (and not demand) the order. To others, order might not matter at all.

CROSS-REFERENCE

In Chapter 28, you learn how to add style to your lists, ordered unordered, definition, and plain.

FIND IT ONLINE

Read an article on XML in electronic commerce at
http://www.anywhere.co.uk/papers.html.

HTML 4.0: THE OL AND LI ELEMENT DECLARATIONS

```
<!ENTITY % OLStyle "CDATA">          -- constrained to: "(1|a|A|I|I)"  -->

<!ELEMENT OL - - (LI)+               -- ordered list -->

<!ATTLIST OL
  &attrs;                            -- %coreattrs, %i18n, %events -->
  type             %OLStyle;  #IMPLIED  -- numbering style --
  compact          (compact)  #IMPLIED  -- reduced interitem spacing --
  start            NUMBER     #IMPLIED  -- starting sequence number -->


<!ENTITY % LIStyle "CDATA">          -- constrained to: "(%ULStyle;|%OLStyle;)" -->

<!ELEMENT LI - O (%flow;)            -- list item -->

<!ATTLIST LI
  &attrs;                            -- %coreattrs, %i18n, %events --
  type             %LIStyle;  #IMPLIED  -- numbering style --
  value            NUMBER     #IMPLIED  -- reset sequence number -->
```

➊ *Use the* OL *element to mark an ordered list.*
➋ *The* LI *element specifies a list item.*

HTML 4.0: THE TRANSITIONAL DTD'S VERSION OF THE HTML UL ELEMENT

```
<!ENTITY % ULStyle "(disc|square|circle)">

<!- Unordered Lists (UL) bullet styles ->
<!ELEMENT UL - - (LI)+               - unordered list ->
<!ATTLIST UL
  &attrs;                            - %coreattrs, %i18n, %events -
  type      %ULStyle;   #IMPLIED     - bullet style --
  compact   (compact)   #IMPLIED     - reduced interitem spacing ->
```

▲ *The HTML* UL *element declaration resembles the declaration of both the* OL *and* LI *elements. Obviously, the only change is within the type attribute, which provides a bullet style rather than a number style.*

Nesting Lists

In an HTML document, you can embed one list within another. In fact, you can nest several layers of ordered lists and unordered lists. HTML also provides a special kind of nested list: The *definition list* is a form of unordered list that contains two nested elements: a term and a description. A glossary is the most common example of a definition list.

Nesting a list in HTML is easy enough: Simply place a list completely within the start tags and end tags of another list. You can embed ordered lists within other ordered lists or within unordered lists, and you can nest unordered lists within both unordered and unordered lists.

Since you define list elements in XML and can declare additional elements to differentiate among list types, you can produce more readable nested listings. For example, think about creating an outline composed of nested lists. First, define a series of list elements as follows: the top-level list under which all other lists are nested is named `nest1`; the second, which is nested within `nest1` lists, is `nest2`; the third, which is nested within `nest2` lists, is `nest3`; and so on. Then, you style each list to indent it properly and to apply other distinctive formats and enhancements. Of course, this can work against you, too. When you create lists using different element names, you may have to make sure that you keep track of nesting levels. Every time you add or remove a nesting level or change the order of nesting, you have to edit the tags carefully.

An HTML definition list consists of three elements: `DL`, `DT`, and `DD`. The `DL` element encloses the entire definition list, the `DT` element defines the term component, and the `DD` element describes that term. To create a similar set of tags in XML, define an element and two child elements under it. In the following DTD segment, the child elements are required and appear in a particular order:

```
<!ELEMENT deflist (term,definition)+>
<!ELEMENT term (#PCDATA)>
<!ELEMENT definition (#PCDATA)>
```

The + at the end of the first line indicates that one or more sets of child elements must be present in a document. Without the +, you would be limited to a single set. That's hardly a definition list.

TAKE NOTE

ANALYZING CROSSWORD PUZZLES

How do you view crossword puzzles? Some see them as tables and others think of them as a series of lists. As a table, you might imagine them typically as a square where every cell of the table is either a letter or a blank space. The clues are associated with a series of horizontal or vertical cells that begin and end with either a blank space or the border of the table. Another way to look at a crossword puzzle is to imagine it as a series of lists. The lists have some common letters between them where a horizontal list intersects with a vertical list. Each list is associated with a clue.

CROSS-REFERENCE

In Chapter 23, you can learn about extended pointers to be used with extended links.

FIND IT ONLINE

http://www.poet.com/xml/xml_lib.html links to a library of XML documents and resources.

HTML 4.0: DL, DT, AND DD ELEMENTS

```
<!ELEMENT DL - - (DT|DD)+              -- definition list -->
<!ATTLIST DL                                                    ←❶
  &attrs;                             -- %coreattrs, %i18n, %events -->
<!ELEMENT DT - 0 (%inline;)*          -- definition term -->
<!ELEMENT DD - 0 (%flow;)*            -- definition description -->
<!ATTLIST DT|DD)                                                ←❷
  &attrs;                             -- %coreattrs, %i18n, %events -->
<!ENTITY % inline "#PCDATA | %fontstyle; | %phrase; | %special; | %formctrl;">
<!ENTITY % flow "%block; | %inline; ">
```

❶ The DL element encloses all the term-definition pairs.
❷ The DT and DD elements specify terms and definitions, respectively.

Listing 14-1: UNORDERED AND ORDERED NESTING

```
<!ELEMENT numberlist (li+, bulletlist*)>
<!ELEMENT bulletlist (li+)>←❶
<!ELEMENT li (#PCDATA)>←❷
<numberlist>
  <li>Clean garage</li>
  <bulletlist>
    <li>Sweep floor</li></bulletlist>←❸
  <li>Fix kitchen sink</li><bulletlist>←❹
    <li>Replace faucet gasket</li>
  </bulletlist></numberlist>
```

❶ The bulletlist element is a child element of numberlist.
❷ The li element is a child of bulletlist and numberlist.
❸ Sweep floor is nested under Clean garage.
❹ Replace faucet gasket is nested under Fix kitchen sink.

Listing 14-2: DEFINITION LIST

```
<!ELEMENT deflist(term, describe)+>
<!ELEMENT term (#PCDATA)>
<!ELEMENT describe (#PCDATA)>
<deflist>←❶
  <term>Maddie</term>←❷
  <describe>A big black dog with a pink
tongue. Hard to see at night.</describe>←❸
</deflist>←❹
```

❶ The <deflist> start tag begins the definition list.
❷ The term element contains the name being described.
❸ The describe element contains the description.
❹ The </deflist> end tag marks the conclusion of the list.

Building Tables

A table is composed of horizontal rows and vertical columns. The cells, which are the intersections of rows and columns, contain the actual data.

In HTML, you make an elementary table using five elements; each sets a distinctive table structure.

- ▶ The TABLE element defines a table.
- ▶ The TR element defines a single row in the table.
- ▶ The TH element defines a single heading cell. By default, a table-heading is formatted in boldface. Under HTML rules, you must nest a TH element within a TR element.
- ▶ The TD element defines a single data cell. Under HTML rules, you must nest a TD element within a TR element.
- ▶ The CAPTION element specifies a table's title.

You can see that the elements are defined so that a table is *row-centric*: you add data one row at a time. This is great for people who look at data on a row by row basis, but not everyone does that. Some tables, like accountants' balance sheets, are based on a columnar layout; they are *column-centric*. Other tables, such as multiplication tables or the periodic table, are neutral; they are neither row-centric nor column-centric.

In XML, you can go your own way: You can define tables so they are assembled on a row-by-row basis or on a column-by-column basis. In XML, element declarations for a table can be this simple:

```
<!ELEMENT table (row+)>
<!ELEMENT row (cell+)>
<!ELEMENT cell (#PCDATA)>
```

This table is very basic. It consists of one or more rows, each containing one or more cells. As usual, the cells contain the data. This table is little more than a series of lists. You can also define the table so that it is column-centric. Simply change the name of one element:

```
<!ELEMENT table (col+)>
<!ELEMENT col (cell+)>
<!ELEMENT cell (#PCDATA)>
```

Compare the last two lines of both of these examples with the two lines of the DTD from the previous task. In both examples, elements are composed of multiple instances of child elements.

TAKE NOTE

▶ USING TABLES TO LAY OUT PAGES

In some electronic documents, tables are useful for formatting text. Tables are a convenient way to format data and keep the data organized within the confines of row and column borders. For example, you can use a two-column table to create a page composed of a long narrow column of a given color and a long wide column of white. Or you can make sure that a graphic is located in the upper right corner of a page and that a link to corporate information stretches across the bottom of the page. Of course, if you become proficient with styling your documents, you can use cascading style sheets to accomplish the same purpose.

CROSS-REFERENCE

Chapter 24 describes how to style and place page elements, which can include lists and tables.

FIND IT ONLINE

Find an XML directory at **http://www.arbortext. com/Think_Tank/XML_Resources/xml_resources .html**.

HTML 4.0: THE TABLE ELEMENT

```
<!ELEMENT TABLE - - (CAPTION?, (COL*|COLGROUP*), THEAD?, TFOOT?, TBODY+)>
<!ATTLIST TABLE                        -- table element --
  %attrs;                              -- %coreattrs, %i18n, %events --
  summary      %Text;     #IMPLIED     -- purpose/structure for speech output --
  width        %Length;   #IMPLIED     -- table width --
  border       %Pixels;   #IMPLIED     -- controls frame width around table --
  frame        %TFrame;   #IMPLIED     -- which parts of frame to render --
  rules        %TRules;   #IMPLIED     -- rulings between rows and cols --
  cellspacing  %Length;   #IMPLIED     -- spacing between cells --
  cellpadding  %Length;   #IMPLIED     -- spacing within cells --
>
```

❶ *The* TABLE *element contains several child elements.*
❷ *All the attributes of the* TABLE *element are optional.*

HTML 4.0: THE TR ELEMENT

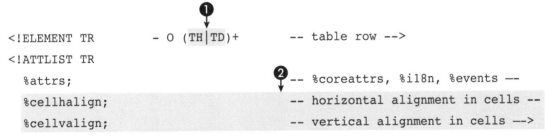

```
<!ELEMENT TR        - O (TH|TD)+        -- table row -->
<!ATTLIST TR
  %attrs;                               -- %coreattrs, %i18n, %events --
  %cellhalign;                          -- horizontal alignment in cells --
  %cellvalign;                          -- vertical alignment in cells -->
```

❶ *The* TR *element has two child elements,* TH *and* TD.
❷ *You can align the contents of cells horizontally or vertically.*

Sectioning Tables

As you know, tables are collections of rows and columns. Typically, the top row of a table and its leftmost column indicate the type of content stored in the rest of the table. These indications are clues for those interpreting your data. If an individual doesn't know what the data means, he or she won't understand the table. One clarifying solution is to use the first row and/or the first column of a table to label the remaining content of the table. However, this heading information can get lost among the other data — especially if its format is the same as the other rows or columns.

In HTML, the TH element defines a table's heading cells. You can define heading cells in the first row of a table to label each of the table's columns, or as the first element of each row to label each of the table's columns. The TD element, which stands for *table data*, specifies all non-heading cells in a table. Both the TH and TD elements are child elements of the TR (table row) element.

Another piece of identifying information is the table caption, represented in HTML by the CAPTION element. A caption displays a table title or summary information. In HTML, this tag is nested within the <TABLE> start tag and the </TABLE> end tag.

In defining a table in XML, the following example shows that a caption is optional but may only appear once. Headings can be placed anywhere within the row of a table and don't have to be used. So far, the definition of elements for our table looks like this:

```
<!ELEMENT table (row+ caption?)>
<!ELEMENT row (heading* cell+)>
<!ELEMENT caption (#PCDATA)>
<!ELEMENT heading (#PCDATA)>
<!ELEMENT cell (#PCDATA)>
```

This is a pretty good start to organizing a table. There are other table-sectioning methods to examine. For example, some tables are longer than a single page. For these tables, it makes sense to repeat information about columns at the top of each page. For this reason, you might add an element that contains this page header information.

There are many other ways to section a table. You might divide the body of a table, or add other pieces such as additional information about footnotes. Sectioning a table depends on your requirements.

TAKE NOTE

FINDING INSPIRATION FROM SPREADSHEETS

If you ever get stuck thinking of ideas for how to present data in a table, start your spreadsheet program. Simply take a look at sheets that contain information similar to your future table. The more complex the table, the better it is to find reference points in a related sheet. The developers of spreadsheet programs design and bundle all types of sheets, ranging from check registers to time sheets, with their newest releases.

CROSS-REFERENCE

In Chapter 29, you can learn how to apply styles to tables — from the smallest to the most complex.

FIND IT ONLINE

CommerceNet's XML Exchange (**http://www.xmlx. com/**) provides a forum, reference guide, and more.

HTML 4.0: TH, TD, AND CAPTION ELEMENTS

```
<!ELEMENT (TH|TD)     - O (%flow;)*      -- table header cell, table data cell -->
<!ATTLIST (TH|TD)                        -- header or data cell --
  %attrs;                                -- %coreattrs, %i18n, %events --
  abbr              %Text;   #IMPLIED    -- default number of columns in group --
  axis              CDATA    #IMPLIED    -- names groups of related headers --
  headers           IDREFS   #IMPLIED    -- list of ids for header cells --
  scope             %Scope;  #IMPLIED    -- scope covered by header cells --
  rowspan           NUMBER   1           -- number of rows spanned by cell --
  colspan           NUMBER   1           -- number of columns spanned by cell --
  %cellhalign;                           -- horizontal alignment in cells --
  %cellvalign;                           -- vertical alignment in cells --
>
```

← **1**

```
<!ELEMENT CAPTION  - - (%inline;)*>
<!ATTLIST CAPTION
  %attrs;                                -- %coreattrs, %i18n, %events -->
```

← **2**

1 The TH and TD elements share all the same characteristics.

2 The CAPTION element shares many attributes with other HTML elements.

Listing 14-3: TABLE WITH COLUMN LABELS

```
<register>Fred's bank account
  <columns>
    <cell>Date</cell>
    <cell>Supplier</cell>
    <cell>Price</cell>
    <cell>Category</cell>
  </columns>
```

← **1**

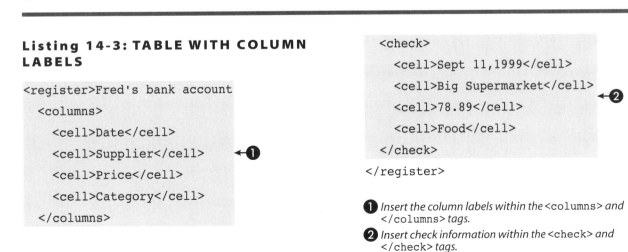

```
  <check>
    <cell>Sept 11,1999</cell>
    <cell>Big Supermarket</cell>
    <cell>78.89</cell>
    <cell>Food</cell>
  </check>
</register>
```

← **2**

1 Insert the column labels within the `<columns>` and `</columns>` tags.

2 Insert check information within the `<check>` and `</check>` tags.

Organizing Columns and Rows

As you have learned, HTML tables are completely row-centric; an HTML table is a collection of rows. However, in XML, nothing prevents you from changing the rows into columns and presenting the information in a column-centric way — but that isn't quite the point. From a design point of view, when you look at a table — whether it is created using HTML elements or XML elements — the data contained within is very easy to read when you look at it from a single direction. Looking at the data from another direction is harder because you may not be able to see how the data is organized. The following example shows the table elements shown earlier in this chapter:

```
<!ELEMENT table (row+ caption?)>
<!ELEMENT row (heading* cell+)>
<!ELEMENT caption (#PCDATA)>
<!ELEMENT header (#PCDATA)>
<!ELEMENT cell (#PCDATA)>
```

One method to define columns is to use attributes. Look at the following example of an attribute declaration:

```
<!ATTLIST cell column (column1|column2
                      |column3) #REQUIRED>
```

It is possible to define a different element for each column, but unless you always used the same number of columns, you'd have to always return to your DTD to add or subtract individual column elements.

You can also apply styles to a table to make it easier to read. For example, you can go the route of old computer printout paper with its alternating stripes of light green and offwhite. Or you can experiment with various weights of borders or an easier-to-read typeface or point size.

Viewing Tables in Different Ways

The end result of the combined elements that define an HTML or XML table is similar to the format of a table or a relation in a relational database. The tables in a relational database are organized by row, which is sometimes called an *instance*. The columns mark the different types of data found in the instance. Accountants use tables in different ways; for example, consider the balance sheet, which is organized into vertical instances. In this case, each instance is a year or other measure of time. The rows in a balance sheet define the type of data stored in the instance. Other tables are not as easily divided into instances and data types. The mileage charts between cities on some road maps is a good example. Here, the important data is the intersection of a row and a column. People don't generally look at the mileage chart as a row or column of numbers. Another example of a table not easily divided into instances is a table of trigonometric functions, which is used either to find the sine, cosine, or tangent of a particular angle or to find the angle given a particular value for a cosine, sine, or tangent.

CROSS-REFERENCE

In Chapter 30, you find out about XSL, a styling language specifically designed to work with XML.

FIND IT ONLINE

http://www.quadzilla.com/ contains many links to HTML authoring and design resources.

Using Lists and Tables in an XML Document

Organizing Columns and Rows

Listing 14-4: A TABLE WITH COLUMNS MARKED BY ELEMENTS

```
<!ELEMENT multiplication (row+)>
<!ELEMENT columns (factor,one,two,three)>
<!ELEMENT row (factor,one,two,three)>
<!ELEMENT factor (#PCDATA)
<!ELEMENT one (#PCDATA)>
<!ELEMENT two (#PCDATA)>
<!ELEMENT three (#PCDATA)>
```
← ❶
```
<multiplication>
```
← ❷
```
  <columns>
    <factor>factor</factor>
    <one>1</one>
    <two>2</two>
    <three>3</three>
  </columns>
```
← ❸
```
  <row>
    <factor>1</factor>
    <one>1</one>
    <two>2</two>
    <three>3</three>
  </row>
  <row>
    <factor>2</factor>
    <one>2</one>
    <two>4</two>
    <three>6</three>
  </row>
```
← ❹
```
</multiplication>
```

❶ *Declare elements for the table.*
❷ *Start the table with the* `<multiplication>` *start tag.*
❸ *Label the columns.*
❹ *Fill two rows.*

Listing 14-5: A TABLE WITH COLUMNS MARKED BY ATTRIBUTES

```
<!ELEMENT balance (year+)>
<!ELEMENT year (cell+)>
<!ELEMENT cell (#PCDATA)>
```
← ❶
```
<!ATTLIST cell
    type (assets|liabil|equity|total)>
```
← ❷
```
<balance>
  <year>1998
    <cell type="assets">1500
    <cell type="liabil">250
    <cell type="equity">1250
    <cell type="total">1500
  </year>
  <year>1997
    <cell type="assets">1200
    <cell type="liabil">400
    <cell type="equity">800
    <cell type="total">1200
  </year>
  <year>1996
    <cell type="assets">1000
    <cell type="liabil">400
    <cell type="equity">600
    <cell type="total">1000
  </year>
</balance>
```

❶ *Nest one element under another.*
❷ *Declare an attribute list for the* cell *element.*
❸ *Name each type of cell.*

Personal Workbook

Q&A

1 What are the basic components of a list?

_____

_____

_____

2 Can you nest a combination of ordered and unordered lists?

_____

_____

_____

3 What are the two child elements of a definition list?

_____

_____

_____

4 What is a *cell*?

_____

_____

_____

5 How is a basic table similar to a list?

_____

_____

_____

6 Does a table have to contain elements that represent rows?

_____

_____

_____

7 What is the advantage of creating a heading element separate from the main body element of a table?

_____

_____

_____

8 In a table composed of rows and cells in the row, how can you visually track the column to which the cells belong?

_____

_____

_____

ANSWERS: PAGE 459

EXTRA PRACTICE

1. Create a template for a basic recipe using an unordered list for the ingredients and an ordered list for the instructions.

2. Use nested elements to prepare a note card to organize your thoughts about why your boss should give you a raise.

3. Build a table to hold bibliography listings.

4. Section the bibliography so that different body elements contain listings of different types of media (books, web pages, articles, and so on).

5. Create a table showing the prices of computers from different vendors. Include general specifications about the computer.

REAL-WORLD APPLICATION

✔ You are searching for a new job. Write and lay out your résumé in XML using lists, tables, or both.

✔ You are publishing a dictionary of slang terms. Create an element for the dictionary entries. Remember that some words have multiple definitions.

✔ You work at a radio station that does not have a catalog for its music collection. Create an XML table to help organize the collection of music so you can find a particular song title.

✔ You are working on a big consulting project as a project manager. Make a table to track the status of various stages of the project.

Visual Quiz

How would you structure this table in XML?

_____

_____

_____

_____

_____

_____

W Microsoft Word - visual quiz 14

File Edit View Insert Format Tools Table Window Help

Person	Location	Distance		
		Theresa	Jim	Susan
Theresa	Main Street	-	1 mile	4 miles
Jim	Oak Lane	1 mile	-	3.5 miles
Susan	BC Way	4 miles	3.5 miles	-

Page 1   Sec 1   1/1   At 2.1"   Ln 7   Col 1   REC   TRK   EXT   OVR   WPH

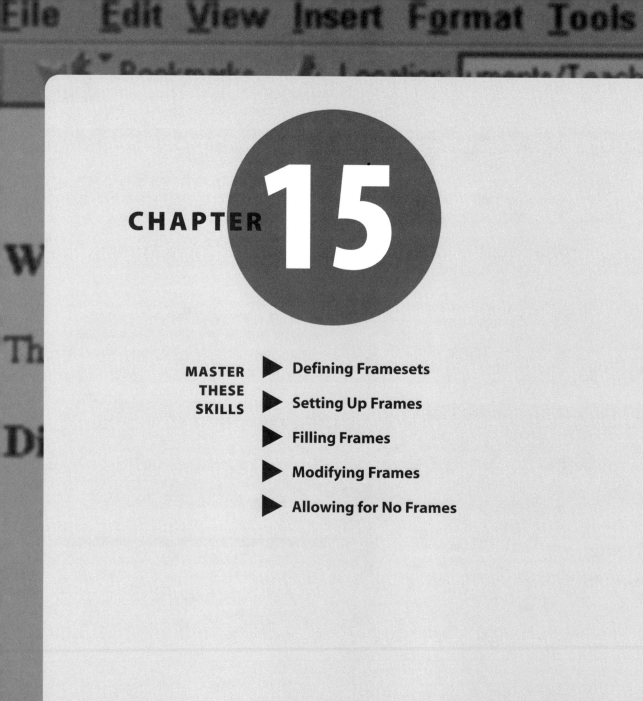

CHAPTER 15

MASTER
THESE
SKILLS

▶ Defining Framesets

▶ Setting Up Frames

▶ Filling Frames

▶ Modifying Frames

▶ Allowing for No Frames

Adding Frames to an XML Document

The topic for this chapter is frames, which is a recent addition to the HTML language and not yet recognized in the XML world. Using frames, you can divide the window in which your online documents appear into one or more smaller windows, each with its own content. Until a future XML specification adds the capability to divide windows into frames, a developer at your company will have to write a custom frames application or applet. In the meantime, this chapter gives you an overview of frames based on the HTML 4.0 recommendation and its DTD. Once your XML documents can appear in frames, you'll have a headstart.

In this chapter, you learn how to define framesets, which are the containers for individual frames. Using the HTML FRAMESET element, you can specify in the frameset the dimensions for individual frames or the percentage of the window devoted to each of the frames. Frames contain the contents of a document. The HTML FRAME element specifies the URI for the document that will appear in the frame. The FRAME element also has attributes with which you can affect the look and content of a particular frame.

After you specify the appearance of a particular frame, you should fill it with some type of content. In the third task, you will learn about the order in which frames are filled and in which content is added. This task also includes a discussion about the relationship of documents that are placed in each of the frames in a single frameset. The fourth task describes the way that you can control the size, behavior, and appearance of a frame. As you'll see, the content of one frame can actually control the content of another frame. For example, you can click on a link in a table of contents frame to place the target resource document into its neighboring frame.

Finally, in an uncertain world in which some browsers support certain elements and ignore others, you have to allow for the fact that certain browsers are not programmed to recognize frames. When this happens, you should include alternate content in your documents. In HTML, the NOFRAMES element marks the information to be displayed when a browser does not support frames.

Defining Framesets

Frames are a feature of the HTML 4.0 standard. At this time, there is no direct support for frames in XML. This doesn't mean that you can't use frames; it just means that an experienced programmer will have to write a large application or an applet to support their use in XML.

Use frames to split a full-screen window into two or more windows in order to show parts of one or more documents. In HTML, the FRAMESET element controls frame setup and the size of frames on a page. Under HTML, FRAMESET has many attributes. (See the element declaration and attribute list on the facing page.) The two most important are ROWS and COLS. ROWS controls the number of rows of frames, and COLS determines the number of columns. Take a look at the following example of HTML code:

```
<frameset rows="33%,*,33%" cols="50%,*">
```

This example, which shows the start tag and attributes for FRAMESET, sets up a frameset composed of three rows that are each approximately one-third of a page. Each row is divided into two columns. (The asterisks in the rows and cols attributes represents the remaining space — in rows, * represents 33%, and in cols, * represents 50%.) A complete list of the attributes for the HTML 4.0 FRAMESET element appears on the facing page.

In XML, to pass this information to the frames application or applet, you need to declare an element that instructs the application about how to process the frameset and how to organize its frames onscreen. The type and amount of information that you provide depends on the way in which the application or applet is written. Use the HTML descriptions and examples provided in this chapter as your guide. In fact, the frame application or applet will probably determine the amount of information that you have to provide as well as the element and attribute declarations that you have to write.

TAKE NOTE

USING TABLES TO SIMULATE FRAMES

An alternate approach to frames is to create tables composed of one row and one column — one big cell. Because a table is an object on an XML page, you can use styles to control its appearance. For example, you can add a border, set margins, and specify a background color. Of course, you can style textual contents with the font and text properties. When you design a set of tables for a single page, you must specify the dimensions manually, and very carefully. You can also use Dynamic HTML to simulate frames. For more information, see "An Overview of Dynamic HTML" in Chapter 17. However, be aware that creating frames with Dynamic HTML is beyond the scope of this book.

THE NEW HTML'S RELATIONSHIP TO XML

The upcoming version of HTML, which is currently being planned, will be reformulated as an application of XML. The new version of HTML will also support frames. To follow the development of HTML, go to the HTML Home Page (**http://www.w3. org/MarkUp/**) and the HTML Activity Statement (**http://www.w3.org/MarkUp/Activity.html**).

CROSS-REFERENCE

In Chapter 13, you can learn how to start a basic XML document and enter its components.

FIND IT ONLINE

Look for many Java links at its home, the Java Technology Home Page (**http://java.sun.com/**).

HTML 4.0: THE FRAMESET ELEMENT

```
<![ %HTML.Frameset; [◄①
<!ELEMENT FRAMESET - - ((FRAMESET|FRAME)+ & NOFRAMES?) -- window subdivision-->◄②
<!ATTLIST FRAMESET
    %coreattrs;                          -- id, class, style, title --
    rows         %MultiLengths; #IMPLIED  -- list of lengths,
                                             default: 100% (1 row) --    ◄③
    cols         %MultiLengths; #IMPLIED  -- list of lengths,
                                             default: 100% (1 col) --    ◄④
    onload       %Script;      #IMPLIED  -- all the frames have been loaded --
    onunload     %Script;      #IMPLIED  -- all the frames have been removed --
>
]]>
```

① *The* %HTML.Frameset; *entity implicitly specifies an* INCLUDE *section.*
② *A frameset can be composed of another frameset, frames, or no frames.*
③ *The* rows *attribute specifies the layout of horizontal frames.*
④ *The* cols *attribute specifies the layout of vertical frames.*

Listing 15-1: A FRAMESET EXAMPLE

```
<doc>
<title>Chapter 5 Examples</title>
<frameset cols=20%,60%,*>◄①
   <frame href="frame1.xml"/>◄②
   <frameset rows=40%,*>
③►    <frame href="frame2.xml"/>
       <frame href="frame3.xml" scrolling="yes"/>
   </frameset>
   <frameset cols=100%>
       <frame href="frame4.xml"/>◄④
   </frameset>
</frameset>
</doc>
```

① *Define three columns, at 20%, 60%, and 20% widths.*
② *Insert the* frame1.xml *document as content.*
③ *Set two frames within the next frameset.*
④ *The final frameset contains* frame4.xml.

219

Setting Up Frames

Frames are components of — and are nested within — framesets. However, the size and location of the frames is determined by the attributes and values used in the FRAMESET element. The HTML FRAME element actually controls the content shown in the frame and the appearance of the frame. For example:

```
<frameset rows=40%,*>
    <frame href="frame2.xml"/>
    <frame href="frame3.xml"
        scrolling="yes"/>
</frameset>
```

Frames are windows within windows — or more accurately, within framesets. In this example, the frameset includes two frames: one takes 40% of the horizontal space, and the other takes the remaining horizontal space, 60%. (A complete list of the attributes for the HTML 4.0 FRAME element appears on the facing page.)

In HTML, the order of frames for formatting and adding content is row-centric — across the top row, down to the next row, across that row, down to the next, and so on. However, in XML — depending on the frames application or applet — you might be able to make frames either row-centric or column-centric.

CROSS-REFERENCE

Chapter 14 instructs you on using tables to hold content and to layout your XML documents.

FIND IT ONLINE

Link to many Java programming resources and tutorials at **http://www.apl.jhu.edu/~hall/java/**.

HTML 4.0: THE FRAME ELEMENT

```
<![ %HTML.Frameset; [
<! — reserved frame names start with "_" otherwise starts with letter -->
<!ELEMENT FRAME — O EMPTY ←❶          -- subwindow -->
<!ATTLIST FRAME
    %coreattrs;                       -- id, class, style, title —-
    longdesc      %URI;      #IMPLIED  -- link to long description
                                          (complements title) --
    name          CDATA      #IMPLIED  -- name of frame for targetting --←❷
    src           %URI;      #IMPLIED  -- source of frame content --
    frameborder   (1|0)      1         -- request frame borders? --←❸
    marginwidth   %Pixels;   #IMPLIED  -- margin widths in pixels --
    marginheight  %Pixels;   #IMPLIED  -- margin height in pixels --←❹
    noresize      (noresize) #IMPLIED  -- allow users to resize frames? --
    scrolling     (yes|no|auto) auto   -- scroll bar or none --
    >
]]>
```

❶ *In HTML, the* FRAME *element is empty.*
❷ *You can name a frame so that you can activate it.*
❸ *Turn on (1) a border, or suppress it (0).*
❹ *Set the width and/or height of a frame margin.*

Filling Frames

The most important attribute for frames is the one that specifies the content. That's the whole point of a frame: It displays content. In HTML, the content displayed in frames includes HTML documents, images, or other objects. The SRC attribute points to the URI of the object to be displayed in the frame.

One thing to consider when filling in frames is the order in which they get filled. In HTML, successive frames are filled starting with the top leftmost frame followed by the next frame in that row. After the first row is filled, the next <FRAME> start tag controls the content of the leftmost column in the following row. This continues until all the defined frames are filled. If a frameset is nested within another, the nested framesets are filled completely before the parent frameset is.

With XML, the frame application or applet would determine how frames get filled. For example, the application or applet might follow the HTML model or might be column-centric. Examine the application to determine how frames are filled.

Whether you use HTML or XML, there should be some sort of relationship among the documents within the frames. When you plan the content of frames that will be displayed simultaneously, you should treat the entire display on your Desktop as a single object. Probably the more common use of frames is to display various documents that are related in some way. One document (a table of contents is a good example) might control the other documents (such as chapters) that are displayed in the other frames. Another configuration is the same document — perhaps using different formats — displayed in different frames. For example, you might want to show a document before and after formatting in side-by-side frames. In XML, you will control document and text formats and enhancements by using CSS or XSL style sheets (see Chapters 24 through 30).

Another use of style sheets is to change the typeface and point size for the content to fit it all in one window. For example, you could display an entire table of contents in a frame on the left side of the screen in a narrow column that stretches from the top to the bottom.

TAKE NOTE

DESIGNING FRAMESETS CAREFULLY

Many users — particularly those with small-screen monitors — dislike frames. If frames are not carefully designed, they can annoy rather than inform. For example, if a bar of linking buttons at the bottom of a window cannot be resized, it may take up too much room onscreen. And if it is too small, part of its contents may be out of sight, off the bottom of the screen. Another potential problem is subsidiary frames that seem to take over the computer screen. In general, one frame should dominate the window, and the rest — such as tables of contents, site titles, and navigation buttons — should be less important.

CROSS-REFERENCE

Chapter 16 shows you how to convert your HTML documents to accurate XML documents.

FIND IT ONLINE

Go to **http://www.progsource.com/java.html** to link to Java FAQs, tools, tutorials, and online manuals.

Listing 15-2: EXAMPLES OF THREE SIDE-BY-SIDE FRAMES

❶ ❷ ❸

```
<frameset cols=30%,20%,*>
    <frame href="framea.xml"/>
    <frame href="frameb.xml"/>  ←❹
    <frame href="framec.xml"/>
</frameset>
```

❶ *Set the first column's width to 30% of the screen.*
❷ *Set the second column's width to 20% of the screen.*
❸ *Set the third column's width to the remaining part.*
❹ *Specify the content of each of the frames.*

Listing 15-4: ONE VERTICAL AND TWO HORIZONTAL FRAMES

```
<frameset cols=20%,*>                ←❶
    <frame href="frame1.xml"/>
❷<frameset rows=40%,*>  ←❸
        <frame href="frame2.xml"/>
        <frame href="frame3.xml"/>   ←❹
    </frameset></frameset>
```

❶ *Set the first frame at 20% and add its content.*
❷ *Set the top row's height to 40% of the screen.*
❸ *Set the bottom row's height to the remaining part.*
❹ *Specify the content of each of the frames.*

Listing 15-3: EXAMPLES OF THREE TOP-TO-BOTTOM FRAMES

❶ ❷ ❸

```
<frameset rows=50%,40%,*>
    <frame href="framea.xml"/>
    <frame href="frameb.xml"/>  ←❹
    <frame href="framec.xml"/>
</frameset>
```

❶ *Set the first row's height to 50% of the screen.*
❷ *Set the second row's height to 40% of the screen.*
❸ *Set the third row's height to the remaining part.*
❹ *Specify the content of each of the frames.*

Listing 15-5: TWO SCROLLING AND TWO NON-SCROLLING FRAMES

```
<frameset cols=20%,60%,*>  ←❶
    <frame href="frame1.xml"
           scrolling="yes"/>     ←❷
    <frameset rows=40%,*>
        <frame href="frame2.xml"/>   ←❸
        <frame href="frame3.xml"
               scrolling="yes"/>
    </frameset>              ❹
    <frameset cols=100%>
        <frame href="frame4.xml"/>
    </frameset></frameset>
```

❶ *Split the screen into three columns.*
❷ *Insert content into the leftmost scrolling frame.*
❸ *Split the screen into two rows and add content.*
❹ *Give the last frame the full column height.*

Modifying Frames

In some documents—especially dynamic electronic documents—appearance and content should change. Any examination of frames should include information about if, when, and how frames change. This task discusses how you can control the behavior of frames. Frames can be resized, and their content and the way an individual views the content can change.

In HTML, you can prevent individuals from resizing frames by entering the NORESIZE attribute. Because individual frames are part of a frameset, in some cases, the effect of setting NORESIZE on a frame prevents other frames in the frameset from being resized. For example, suppose you have a frameset consisting of three frames. Assuming that the frameset used 100 percent of the available space, you can resize frames one and two, but you cannot resize frame three. The border between frames one and two can be moved because you can resize both frames. However, the border between frames two and three cannot be moved because frame three cannot be resized. And, if you change frame two to NORE-SIZE, no border can be resized: there isn't a common border between two sizable frames.

Scrolling allows a user to look at content that cannot be completely displayed in a frame. The SCROLLING attribute either displays or hides scroll bars on a frame. The difference is in the value of the SCROLLING attribute. Setting SCROLLING="yes" indicates that the current frame always has scroll bars, and SCROLLING="no" states that the current frame never has scroll bars. When SCROLLING="auto", the content determines whether the scroll bar is displayed or hidden.

You can use frames to specify the content of other frames. A common application of these frames is a document that is divided into two frames: one with a table of contents and the other with the actual contents. Clicking on a link in the table of contents controls the contents of the second frame. This allows you to display certain sections of a document while having the table of contents onscreen and always visible as a guide to the entire document.

TAKE NOTE

TARGETING FRAMES

In the "Comparing the show Attribute with the HTML TARGET Attribute" sidebar in Chapter 20, you learned how HTML targets a window for the display of new content. The frames counterpart to TARGET is NAME, which offers the same five choices as TARGET, but for frames rather than windows. You can name the frame into which content is loaded or use a reserved keyword: _blank, which loads the contents into a blank window; _parent, which loads the contents into the frame that is one level above the current frame; _self, which replaces the contents of the current frame; or _top, which loads the content into the original frame.

CROSS-REFERENCE

Chapter 17 explains how to build XML databases and import information from existing databases.

FIND IT ONLINE

The Java Tutorial (**http://java.sun.com/docs/books/tutorial/**) is a comprehensive online resource.

Listing 15-6: THREE FRAMES

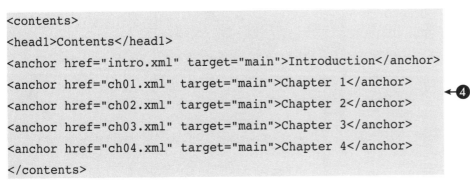

```
<frameset cols=30%,70%>          ◄──❶

    <frame="toc.xml" noresize name="toc" scrolling="no"/>

        <frameset rows=17%,*>                                    ◄──❷
            <frame href="title.xml" noresize scrolling="no"/>

        </frameset>

    <frame="intro.xml" name="main"/>      ◄──❸

</frameset>


<bar>
<title>Welcome to Our Site</title>
</bar>


<contents>
<head1>Contents</head1>
<anchor href="intro.xml" target="main">Introduction</anchor>
<anchor href="ch01.xml" target="main">Chapter 1</anchor>
<anchor href="ch02.xml" target="main">Chapter 2</anchor>          ◄──❹
<anchor href="ch03.xml" target="main">Chapter 3</anchor>
<anchor href="ch04.xml" target="main">Chapter 4</anchor>
</contents>
```

❶ *Specify the table of contents and body frame.*
❷ *Create a welcoming frame — 17% at the top of the screen.*
❸ *Load the introduction into the main frame.*
❹ *Make a table of contents with links to the main frame.*

225

Allowing for No Frames

In the HTML world, some browsers do not support the use of frames. The same may be true of some future XML browsers. If you use frames to present your XML documents, a custom-written application or applet will control frame behavior. However, you cannot control your visitors' choice of XML browsers. So, you should declare an element to present alternate content to visitors whose browsers do not support frames.

The HTML NOFRAMES element solves the problem of browsers that do not support frames. After defining framesets and frames in an HTML document, the developer adds a section marked by a <NOFRAMES> start tag at the top and a </NOFRAMES> end tag at the end. When a particular browser does not support frames, it is not programmed to understand the FRAMESET and FRAME elements or their attributes. The HTML 4.0 recommendation says that "user agents that support frames must only display the contents of a NOFRAMES declaration when configured not to display frames," and adds the following: "User agents that do not support frames must display the contents of NOFRAMES in any case." It may completely ignore the content of the frames, too. When this happens, the browser drops through the FRAMESET and FRAME statements, immediately goes to the NOFRAMES section, and displays its content. For example:

```
<frameset statement>
    <frame content/>
    <frame content/>
</frameset>
<noframes>
```

```
    content
</noframes>
```

Whether developers are designing "framed" XML or HTML documents, they should offer individuals visiting their site the opportunity to choose between frames and no frames. For example, an individual with a small-screen monitor might prefer no frames rather than viewing a clutter of several windows at once.

Leaving a Frames Site without Taking the Frames

Occasionally, after visiting a frames site, you'll find that subsequent sites you visit will be inserted into the frame: The only way to get out of the frame is to click on the Back button until you finally reach the page immediately preceding the culprit frames site.

The way to solve this problem is to always have a nonframes page at the top of your site's hierarchy of framed pages. Since a home page is usually the first page a visitor sees, it's a good idea to make that the nonframes page. Then, on every page, provide an escape route. Insert a statement that looks something like this:

```
<para><anchor href="homepage.xml"
               target="_top"/>
```

The href attribute points to the home page document, and the _top keyword targets the top page at the site. When you declare the element, you should also declare an attribute that enables visitors to jump to one of several types of pages.

CROSS-REFERENCE

Chapter 18 demonstrates how to use forms and their components in your XML documents.

FIND IT ONLINE

Link to all types of official Java platform documentation at **http://java.sun.com/docs/index.html**.

HTML 4.0: THE NOFRAMES ELEMENT

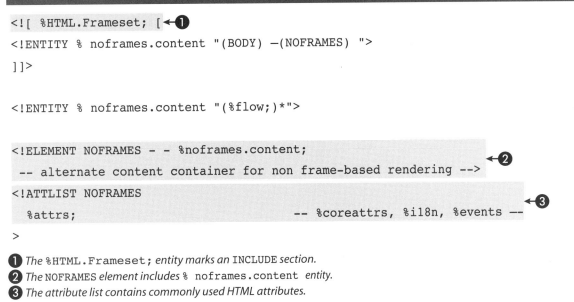

```
<![ %HTML.Frameset; [
<!ENTITY % noframes.content "(BODY) —(NOFRAMES) ">
]]>


<!ENTITY % noframes.content "(%flow;)*">


<!ELEMENT NOFRAMES - - %noframes.content;
 -- alternate content container for non frame-based rendering -->
<!ATTLIST NOFRAMES
  %attrs;                                -- %coreattrs, %i18n, %events --
>
```

❶ The `%HTML.Frameset;` *entity marks an* INCLUDE *section.*
❷ The NOFRAMES *element includes* `% noframes.content` *entity.*
❸ *The attribute list contains commonly used HTML attributes.*

Listing 15-7: A NOFRAMES EXAMPLE

```
<frameset rows=50%,50%>
    <frame href="frame2.xml"/>
    <frame href="frame3.xml"/>
</frameset>
<noframes>
<head2>You Should Be Looking at Two Frames!</head2>
<para>If you are reading this message, you are using an XML browser
that does not support frames. Try again with a different browser.
</para>
<img href=/pics/blah.gif/>
</noframes>
```

❶ *The* <noframes> *start tag marks the beginning of alternate content.*
❷ *The* </noframes> *end tag marks the end.*

Personal Workbook

Q&A

1 Does the current version of XML support frames and framesets?

_____

_____

_____

2 How can you use frames now?

_____

_____

_____

3 What does the HTML FRAMESET element do?

_____

_____

_____

4 What does the HTML FRAME element do?

_____

_____

_____

5 What two attributes control the splitting of window into frames?

_____

_____

_____

6 What does the asterisk represent in the COLS or ROWS attribute?

_____

_____

_____

7 What attribute do you use to control the content of a particular frame?

_____

_____

_____

8 When you have a frames site, how do you deal with browsers that do not support frames?

_____

_____

_____

ANSWERS: PAGE 460

EXTRA PRACTICE

❶ Create a frames site that displays illustrations of birds in one frame, and information about a clicked-on bird link in the other.

❷ Plan a third frame for the bird site.

❸ Create a frameset for a four-frames site. One corner of each of the frames should meet in the middle of the screen.

❹ Go online and find a frames site that you like. What factors contribute to your positive feelings?

❺ Go online and find a frames site that has design problems. How would you correct it?

❻ If the documents available to a two-frame site include an illustration of a ping pong ball, can you simulate a game of Pong?

REAL-WORLD APPLICATIONS

✔ For your corporate site, you have been assigned to design and create a three-frame site. The top frame always contains the name of your company, the large middle frame displays the current page, and the bottom frame has links to the site's copyright information, the home page, and a site map.

✔ Your catalog company sells children's toys, books, and clothing online. Your new site features two uneven frames that divide the screen vertically. On the left is a narrow frame that serves as a table of contents to your site. On the left is the current page.

✔ You are designing an online yearbook for your class or organization, and have decided to create a three-frame site. One frame displays the title of the yearbook. Another frame contains photographs of each individual. The third frame contains an autobiography of the active photograph.

Visual Quiz

How would you define these frames?

_____

_____

_____

_____

_____

_____

CHAPTER **16**

MASTER
THESE
SKILLS

▶ Inserting an XML Declaration

▶ Specifying a Root Element

▶ Establishing Proper Tag Structures

▶ Correcting Attributes

▶ Modifying Entities

Converting HTML Documents to XML

Right now, there are many HTML documents in the world. XML won't replace HTML in all applications, but it will in some, mainly to take advantage of XML's features.

Converting a typical HTML document to an XML document takes some planning. HTML browsers do not require strict adherence to HTML syntax, and even HTML syntax isn't structured in the same manner as XML's. Anyone converting from HTML to XML has to be wary of HTML code, whether it's created by machine or by hand.

This chapter discusses some of the factors you have to take into account during this process. It begins with a discussion of the XML declaration. There's a lot more to the HTML-to-XML conversion than placing an XML declaration at the top of the HTML document. The process is something that needs to be carefully planned. The plan must include the new structure of the document. A lot of HTML is formatted to give a document the appearance of structure, but the underlying structure is missing. XML can provide that.

The rest of the chapter is a discussion of the use of elements, attributes, and entities in the conversion process. Though there are direct correlations between each of the XML and HTML components, it is not necessarily in your best interest to use the HTML format or information. Organize elements in your document. Don't just list them: use them to their fullest extent. Attributes don't need to be used in XML to format a document. Use them in XML as identifiers or to store other information about an element. Take advantage of entities. In many HTML documents, entities are just character replacements. Use entities to replace sections of text or to speed the conversion process.

This chapter doesn't cover all aspects of the conversion process. The formatting of the converted data is done via style sheets; XML formatting is discussed in Chapters 24 through 30. However, this chapter is a good introduction to the basic steps needed to convert an HTML document to XML.

Inserting an XML Declaration

By this time, you should be familiar with the basic XML declaration and its three basic components. When you convert an HTML document to XML, the most important aspect of the declaration is the `standalone` attribute. The HTML document is based on a DTD that you will probably not use when you create your XML document. Why bother to convert to XML if you will use it exactly as HTML? The conversion process should add more information to the document and not be a simple translation from HTML to XML. When you use XML, parts of the document are organized into more informative elements rather than generic elements such as `body`.

Converting an HTML document is the reverse of building an XML document from scratch. When you create an XML document from scratch, you have ideas about the content, but you should concentrate on the structure of the document first. When you convert an existing HTML document, you know about the content: it's already in place. In this case, you must carefully examine the content and then determine the best structure for it.

For some documents, the choice to use the HTML DTD as a basis is tempting. The only real work might be to update or omit some attributes and make sure that there are matching end tags for every start tag. However, using the HTML DTD limits the benefits of converting to XML in the first place. In HTML, the content is held in tags that are not particularly descriptive. Custom XML tags allow you to organize

content and search more easily for information about the content.

Obviously, when you decide whether the document should have a standalone DTD, you should either add internal DTD information to the XML document or develop an external DTD. For conversions of several HTML documents with the same general format and structure, it is easier to associate one external DTD with all the documents. For a single document, the choice is yours.

At the point at which you add the internal DTD or refer to an external DTD, you probably have reviewed the original HTML document and may or may not have determined the elements to use in the document. You may not be ready to include the DTD information yet, but remember that it is necessary for validity.

TAKE NOTE

ADDING COMMENTS

Throughout the process of converting a document to XML, be sure to add comments to your XML document. Comments aren't as important for simple documents as they are for complex documents. With simple documents, it's easy to remember the elements that you changed and why. When a document is large or you convert multiple HTML documents simultaneously, understanding why you made changes is critical. Comments also help you to remember to declare elements, attributes, and entities in the XML document's DTD. Comments won't be covered in the rest of this chapter. You decide how to best use them for the HTML conversion process.

CROSS-REFERENCE

Chapter 2 reviews the requirements for making well-formed and valid XML documents.

FIND IT ONLINE

The Faqfiles.com page (**http://www.faqfiles.com/**) provides links to tutorials, articles, and more.

Listing 16-1: SAMPLE HTML DOCUMENT TO CONVERT TO XML

```
<HTML>
<HEAD><TITLE>Pat's Food Room</TITLE></HEAD>
<H1>Menu for Tuesday</H1>
<H2>Breakfast</H2>
<B>Get off to a great start!</B><P>
Eggs, Toast, Home Fries, Small Orange Juice and Coffee<BR>
All for $7.95<P>
<H2>Lunch</H2>
<H4>Keep your energy up!</H4>
Tuna fish or roast beef sandwich, potato chips, choice of soda<BR>
For the low price of $9.95<P>
<H2>Dinner</H2>
<B>Keep eating, you're almost done for the day!</B>
Chicken Florentine served over rice with assorted side veggies, choice of water<BR>
For the price of $17.95<P>
<FONT SIZE=6>Wine available for the price of $27.95 per bottle</FONT><P>
<H2>Dessert</H2>
<B>Finish this and you can go to bed</B><P>
Vanilla Ice Cream<BR>
$4.95<P>
Cookies<FONT SIZE=3><I>Ask for today's
Selection</I></FONT><BR>
$3.95<P>
<FONT SIZE=2>All meals subject to 18% service charge</FONT><P>
</HTML>
```

▲ *This HTML document will gradually be converted to an XML document as the chapter continues.*

Specifying a Root Element

The root element, of course, is required for an XML document to be well-formed or valid. Choosing a root element is not difficult. The document designer defines the root element, and it can be any valid element name. Once you have selected the root element, you can begin to design its child elements.

Selecting the root element for an HTML-to-XML conversion is the same process as selecting a root element for any XML document. Simply choose a root element that makes sense within the document. Once you select the name of the root element, replace the `<HTML>` start tag and `</HTML>` end tag with the new root element. At this point, you have the first element that you need to define in the DTD. Of course, you can use `HTML` as the root element. However, the name certainly does not describe a document as an element that you might name yourself.

The rest of the document takes more planning. The structure that you select for the new document depends on the document's purpose. For most HTML documents — particularly those that are a few years old — document designers will not use cascading style sheets, relying instead on the basic HTML elements for styling. The basic HTML elements do not define very much of the document structure. You will have to interpret the structure of the HTML document so that you can define the structure of the resulting XML document. Remember the basic XML rules: only one root element, and child elements nest but do not overlap.

Creating a Well-Formed XML Document from HTML

Every HTML document can be a well-formed XML document. First, change the top of an HTML document from the following:

```
<!DOCTYPE HTML PUBLIC
        "-//W3C//DTD HTML 4.0//EN">
<HTML>
```

to this:

```
<?xml version="1.0"?>
```

Then, go through each line of the document, checking for the following:

▶ Every start tag must have a matching end tag.
▶ All attribute values are enclosed within quotation marks or single quotes.
▶ All empty tags use the following syntax: `<br />` (note the space between the element name and the slash) or `<img src="image.gif"/>` (note that no space is between the attribute value and the slash).

If you decide to migrate from HTML to XML, consider creating valid documents. This means that you must associate a DTD with each document. Obviously, using one DTD for all of your documents is much easier than creating several DTDs. A side benefit is having one standard and the same types of output for all of your XML documents. To keep up to date with the activities of both XML and HTML development, periodically go to the HTML Activity page (**http://www.w3.org/MarkUp/Activity/**).

CROSS-REFERENCE

Chapter 3 provides information about the syntax you use to write and edit XML documents.

FIND IT ONLINE

Go to **http://www.unplug.com/great/** to link to beginning, advanced, expert, and graphics-design tips.

Listing 16-2: PART OF A PROLOG FOR THE HTML CONVERSION

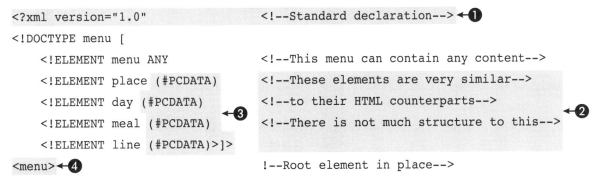

```
<?xml version="1.0"            <!--Standard declaration-->  ←❶
<!DOCTYPE menu [
    <!ELEMENT menu ANY         <!--This menu can contain any content-->
    <!ELEMENT place (#PCDATA)  <!--These elements are very similar-->
    <!ELEMENT day (#PCDATA)    <!--to their HTML counterparts-->
    <!ELEMENT meal (#PCDATA)   ←❸   <!--There is not much structure to this-->  ←❷
    <!ELEMENT line (#PCDATA)>]>
<menu>←❹                        !--Root element in place-->
```

❶ Add an XML declaration.
❷ Provide comments to document your changes.
❸ At the early stages of the conversion, declare ANY or #PCDATA.
❹ Start the document with the root element.

Listing 16-3: ANOTHER PROLOG SEGMENT FOR THE HTML CONVERSION

```
<?xml version="1.0">
<!DOCTYPE menu [
<!ELEMENT menu (place,day,meal+,service)>  ←❺
    <!--Now included in menu-->
    <!ELEMENT place (#PCDATA)        >
    <!ELEMENT day (#PCDATA)>
    <!ELEMENT meal (heading,line,foodstuff+,altbev?)>  ←❻
    <!--Now a meal is described by four elements-->
    <!ELEMENT heading (#PCDATA)>
    <!ELEMENT line (#PCDATA)>
    <!ELEMENT foodstuff (price,choice?)>  ←❼
```

❺ The root element now contains some child elements.
❻ Break the meal element into four child elements.
❼ Two elements now move under the foodstuff element.

Establishing Proper Tag Structures

Elements cause a lot of trouble during the conversion of HTML documents to XML. Not only do you need to be concerned with the overall structure of the document, but you also have to consider the format of every tag. HTML browsers are designed to be forgiving. Miss an end tag — even a required one — and the document content still appears — although it might not be formatted correctly. XML browsers are not supposed to be forgiving. Tags need to be properly constructed and nested correctly.

There are three basic considerations when you review HTML elements for conversion to XML. First, some HTML elements do not require end tags. Second, HTML empty elements are formatted in the same way as other elements: they do not have the option of combining the start tag and end tag into one. Third, HTML elements are not case-sensitive (although the unwritten standard for entering HTML elements is to use all uppercase letters).

On the other hand, all XML elements require end tags, which are formatted as `</element>`, which is identical to HTML's end-tag format.

Empty elements must either follow the rule for all elements — they must have start tags and end tags — or they may be in a special combination form in which there is a single tag that ends with a slash. Examples of empty HTML elements include `<IMG>` and `<BR>`.

Elements in XML are case-sensitive. XML parsers sense a difference between `<Body>`, `<BODY>`, and `<boDy>;`. HTML browsers don't. So even if a start tag has a matching end tag, you must be careful that they match in capitalization.

Learning About Uppercase and Lowercase in XML

As you know, case is important in XML. One reason for the program's case-sensitivity is its support of Unicode. Each Unicode character — even uppercase and lowercase versions of what you might think of as the same character — is represented by a different code. For example, uppercase *A* is `#x0041` and lowercase *a* is `#x0061`. When an XML parser processes a document, it evaluates each character or individual character code. (For more information about XML's Unicode support, refer to Chapter 4.) Another instance of case sensitivity in XML is in its keywords. Most XML keywords (such as `#PCDATA` and `NDATA`) must be all uppercase. On the other hand, reserved processing instructions (such as `<?xml?>` or `<?xml:space?>` must be all lowercase.

There are instances of case insensitivity that are expressed in certain cases as a matter of form. For example, language codes are usually entered in lowercase characters, whereas country codes are usually entered in uppercase. In addition, HTML elements are usually entered in all uppercase, and XML elements are usually entered in all lowercase.

CROSS-REFERENCE

Chapter 6 shows you how to plan an XML DTD, which should be associated with a converted HTML document.

FIND IT ONLINE

Develop your corporate intranet strategy at http://www.cio.com/WebMaster/strategy/.

CONVERTING HTML DOCUMENTS TO XML

Establishing Proper Tag Structures

Listing 16-4: ELEMENTS CONVERTED IN THE HTML DOCUMENT

```
<!—Using the structure from the second XML prolog—>
<menu>
  <place>Pat's Food Room</place>
  <day>Menu for Tuesday</day>
  <meal>
    <heading>Breakfast</heading>
    <line>Get off to a great start!</line>
    <foodstuff>Eggs, Toast, Home Fries, Small Orange Juice
 and Coffee
       <price>All for $7.95</price></foodstuff>
  </meal>
  <meal>
    <heading>Lunch</heading>
    <line>Keep your energy up!</line>
    <foodstuff>Tuna fish or roast beef sandwich, potato
Chips, choice of soda
       <price>For the low price of $9.95</price></foodstuff>
  </meal>
  <meal>
    <heading>Dinner</heading>
    <line>Keep eating, you're almost done for the day!</line>
    <foodstuff>Chicken Florentine served over rice with
assorted side veggies, choice of water
       <price>For the price of $17.95</price></foodstuff>
    <altbev>Wine available for the price of $27.95 per bottle</altbev>
  </meal>
  <meal>
    <heading>Dessert</heading>
    <line>Finish this and you can go to bed</line>
    <foodstuff>Vanilla Ice Cream
      <price>$4.95</price></foodstuff>
    <foodstuff>Cookies<choice>Ask for today's selection</choice>
      <price>$3.95</price></foodstuff>
  </meal>
  <service>All meals subject to 18% service charge</service>
</menu>
```

▲ Now, use the elements that you declared in the new XML DTD. Make sure that you match every start tag with a counterpart end tag.

Correcting Attributes

Correcting attributes for an HTML-to-XML document conversion is a matter of properly defining attributes in the XML document's DTD. In HTML, each element has a set of predefined attributes. Typically, in older versions of HTML, many attributes were devoted to the presentation of an element in its electronic or printed format — its formats and enhancements. In XML, attributes tend to contain more information about the specific content associated with an element. In many cases, you will find yourself using most of the attribute information from the converted HTML document to help define the associated style sheet and then deleting those attributes and their values from the converted XML document and making sure that they are not included in the new DTD.

Once you have declared the new elements, you must define their attributes. Because of the importance of style sheets in XML, these attributes will probably not be used for formatting. Attributes that store information passed to an application, such as the location of graphic files, are important. For elements that store graphic files, the filename is an attribute of the element.

Another important use for attributes is for element identifiers. These attributes identify the location of specific elements, which makes it easy to create extended links and extended pointers.

Remember that when you declare attributes in the DTD, you can control the values for those attributes.

The values may be required or a specific value. You can also declare a set of valid attribute values.

Reviewing XML's Attribute Declarations and Types

When you declare an attribute in an XML DTD, follow this format:

```
<!ATTLIST elementname
     AttributeName     AttributeType
Default
```

In this example, ATTLIST is a reserved keyword, elementname is the name of the element to which the attribute applies, AttributeName represents the name of the attribute, AttributeType represents the name of a supported attribute type, and Default is a default keyword or value (#REQUIRED, #IMPLIED, #FIXED value, or a default value).

XML follows its parent, SGML, in providing a set of attribute types from which you can choose: CDATA, which indicates that the attribute is character data; ID, which is a unique identifier for the element; IDREF, which is a reference to an ID that is declared in another part of the DTD; ENTITY, which is an individual entity; ENTITIES, which is a list of entities separated by one or more spaces; NMTOKEN, which is a name token; NMTOKENS, which is a list of name tokens separated by one or more spaces; NOTATION, which is the name of a notation; and enumerated notation, which is a list of values enclosed within parentheses and separated by pipe (|) symbols.

CROSS-REFERENCE

Learn how to declare elements and specify element characteristics and behavior in Chapter 8.

FIND IT ONLINE

Use Safer Site (**http://www.netlaw.com/safer.htm**) to address legal issues at your Web site.

Listing 16-5: ENTITIES CONVERTED IN THE HTML DOCUMENT

```
<!- Partial code listing. The next section is part of the internal DTD->
<!- Create these entities so that it is easier to add items to the menu->
<!ENTITY bf1 "Eggs, Toast, Home Fries, Small Orange Juice and Coffee">
<!ENTITY ln1 "Tuna fish or roast beef sandwich, potato chips, choice of soda">
<!-Or place an entire meal into another XML document->
<!-In this case all of the structure of dinner is moved to a separate file->
<!ENTITY dinner SYSTEM "dinner.xml">
<!- Sample use of one of the entities used in the XML document->
<meal>
<heading>Breakfast</heading>
<line>Get off to a great start!</line>
<foodstuff>&bf1;
<price>All for $7.95</price></foodstuff>
</meal>
<meal>
<heading>Lunch</heading>
<line>Keep your energy up!</line>
<foodstuff>&ln1;
<price>For the low price of $9.95</price></foodstuff>
</meal>
<!-Remember dinner is in a separate file->
<meal>
<heading>Dinner</heading>
&dinner;
</meal>
```

▲ *The entities make it possible to create a flexible menu so that breakfast, lunch, and dinner entries can be easily changed within the entity declaration.*

Modifying Entities

As Chapter 10 states, entities are named chunks of information. The information within an entity declaration might be changed from time to time, might be tedious to type, or might allow for a compilation of information from various external sources.

In most HTML, entities are limited to characters, except for HTML Version 4.0 and beyond. In XML, this is one of several possibilities. Certainly you will always find a need for character entities, but if you are doing a conversion, you should look for other opportunities to use entities.

As you have learned, the two primary categories of entities are general and parameter. A general entity occurs within the document — sometimes including the DTD — while the parameter entity can occur only within the DTD.

Whenever your document contains data that is subject to change, you can use general entities during the conversion. An example might be the copyright information placed on each page at a Web site. You might also define a general entity to use whenever your company name occurs in the document. Examine the HTML document for opportunities to use general entities. In some instances, you can create a file of general entities to be plugged into each document you need to convert.

Use the parameter entity to make modifications to your DTD. One of the best uses for a parameter entity is to import a section of the DTD that is common to more than one of your documents. You might be involved in converting a large number of HTML documents that have the same structure. By using a parameter entity, you can define a single DTD and use it for multiple HTML-XML conversions. If the structure changes, it's a simple matter of changing one DTD rather than several.

Using Entities to Divide Conversion Work

You can use entities to divide a conversion process into more manageable tasks. There are several reasons why the pieces may be separated. You might want to convert a section of an HTML document that is repeated in other HTML documents. This saves you the trouble of doing a conversion more than once. Another reason might be that you want more than one person to do an HTML document conversion.

Converting an HTML document in pieces greatly speeds up the conversion process. This technique does require that everyone involved in the conversion understands the structure of the finished XML document. If not, the XML document has to be reformatted. If you get involved in a document conversion process and want to split up the tasks, it is helpful to assign the same tasks to the people involved; for example, one person works exclusively on tables, while another works on the rest of the body content.

CROSS-REFERENCE

Chapter 9 provides the information for defining attributes and their characteristics and values.

FIND IT ONLINE

Make your site attractive to search engines at http://www.city-net.com/~lmann/help/tips.html.

Listing 16-6: ATTRIBUTES AND MORE COMMENTS ADDED TO THE DTD

```
<?xml version="1.0">
<!DOCTYPE menu [
<!ELEMENT menu (place,day,meal+,service)>
    <!-- The location now included in menu -->
    <!ELEMENT place (#PCDATA)>
    <!-- Add a unique identifier -->
    <!ATTLIST place
            id   ID   #REQUIRED>
    <!-- Add the day of the week from which the writer can select -->
    <!ELEMENT day (#PCDATA)>
    <!ATTLIST day
            value (Sunday|Monday|Tuesday|Wednesday|Thursday|Friday|Saturday)>   ◀❶
    <!ELEMENT meal (heading,line,foodstuff+,altbev?)>
    <!-- Now a meal is described by four elements-->
    <!-- Add a list of meals from which the writer can select -->
    <!ELEMENT heading (#PCDATA)>
    <!ATTLIST heading
            value (Breakfast|Brunch|Lunch|Dinner|Dessert)>   ◀❷
    <!-- Write a catchy line -->
    <!ELEMENT line (#PCDATA)>
    <!ELEMENT foodstuff (price,choice?)>
    <!ELEMENT price (#PCDATA)>
    <!ELEMENT altbev (#PCDATA)>
    <!ELEMENT choice (#PCDATA)>
    <!ELEMENT service (#PCDATA)>
    ]>
```

❶ *Limit the value of* day *to a day of the week.*
❷ *Allow a choice of five meals for the* heading *element.*

Personal Workbook

Q&A

1 What is the major difference in the order of development between converting an HTML document to XML and building an XML document from scratch?

_____

_____

_____

2 Why isn't it a good idea to use the HTML DTD when converting an HTML document to XML?

_____

_____

_____

3 The <HTML> and <HTML> tags of an HTML document should be replaced by which element?

_____

_____

_____

4 What are the three things to consider when converting HTML elements to XML elements?

_____

_____

5 What is wrong with the following XML start and end tag combination: <body> </Body>

_____

_____

_____

6 Why will you delete some attribute information when converting an HTML document to XML.

_____

_____

_____

7 Why would you use general entities in an HTML-to-XML document conversion?

_____

_____

_____

8 Why would you use parameter entities in an HTML-to-XML document conversion?

_____

_____

ANSWERS: PAGE 460

EXTRA PRACTICE

1. When wouldn't you want to convert HTML documents to XML?

2. Create an XML declaration for a document with a standalone DTD.

3. Go online, select a simple Web page, and develop a structure for the document for a conversion to XML.

4. Go to a commercial site on the World Wide Web and view the source of a page. How would you structure an XML document based on the source?

5. Compare the structures from the previous two exercises.

6. Create a parameter entity that can be used as part of the DTD for both of the structures developed in exercises 3 and 4.

REAL-WORLD APPLICATIONS

✔ Your company has spent a lot of money building HTML pages. Write a memo explaining the advantages and disadvantages of converting them to XML.

✔ You are trying to create an online recipe empire. As one of your goals, you need to convert all of the recipes on the Web to XML. Write a DTD to help simplify that process.

✔ You used HTML to publish your résumé on the Web. Convert your résumé to XML.

✔ You are a project leader responsible for converting your company's intranet documents to XML. In a logical way, divide the work among your team in order to convert the documents accurately but also to meet a strict deadline.

Visual Quiz

How would you convert this HTML code into an XML DTD?

_____

_____

_____

_____

_____

_____

```
W Microsoft Word - visual quiz 16                        _ B X
 File  Edit  View  Insert  Format  Tools  Table  Window  Help    _ B X

<!DOCTYPE HTML PUBLIC "-//W3C//DTD HTML 4.0//EN">
<HTML><HEAD>
<TITLE>A Sample HTML Document</TITLE></HEAD>
<BODY BGCOLOR="white">
<H1>Lists</H1>
Thanks for visiting. On this page, you'll see an <A
HREF="http://www.eddy.net/OL">ordered list</A> and an
<A HREF="http://www.eddy.net/UL">unordered list.</A>
<H3>An Ordered List</H3>
<OL><LI>Do this step.
<LI>Then do this step.
<LI>Do it all over again starting at the top.</OL>
<H3>An Unordered List</H3>
<UL><LI>Planes
<LI>Trains
<LI>Automobiles
</UL>
<CENTER><IMG SRC="scene.gif"></CENTER>
</BODY></HTML>

Page 1   Sec 1      1/1   At      Ln     Col      REC TRK EXT OVR WPH
```

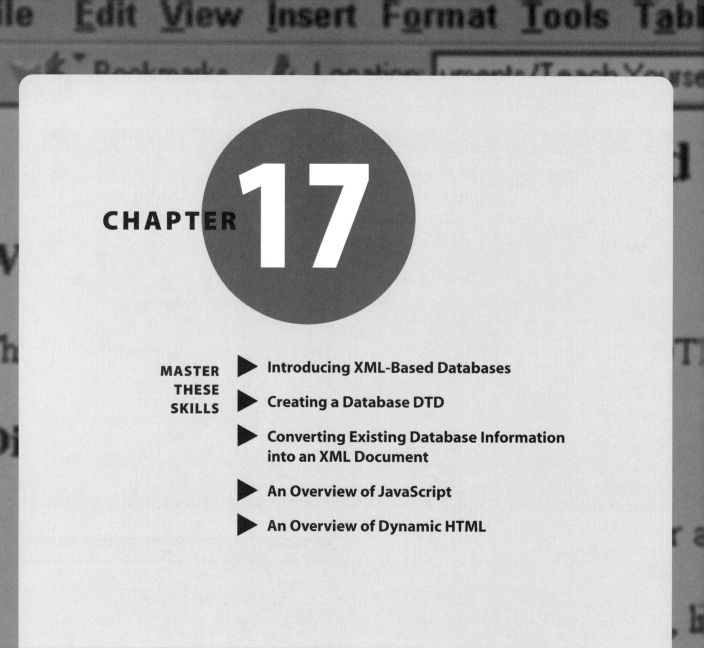

CHAPTER **17**

MASTER
THESE
SKILLS

▶ **Introducing XML-Based Databases**

▶ **Creating a Database DTD**

▶ **Converting Existing Database Information into an XML Document**

▶ **An Overview of JavaScript**

▶ **An Overview of Dynamic HTML**

Building an XML Database

This chapter provides an overview of creating XML database documents. In the first three tasks, you'll learn how to create a database DTD and convert existing database information into an XML document. The last two tasks in the chapter introduce JavaScript and Dynamic HTML — two technologies that form the basis of dynamic documents.

XML databases should be highly structured documents with which you can control the organization of your information. Electronic databases are growing in popularity. For example, online catalog companies use electronic databases to compile information about customers and inventory, and individuals can gather information about contacts and organize it into easy-to-access files.

As you have learned, XML parsers not only produce standard Web pages but also can send processed information to intermediate applications for further processing. So, XML developers can design fill-in forms into which visitors to a Web site can type information. With some programming, the information then can be placed into an XML document, which in turn can export to a database program.

When you design and create a DTD for a standard document (such as a memorandum or a computer manual), the ratio of elements to content is relatively low. For example, a single element can control a large amount of body text throughout a document. Creating a database DTD is an intense process. For every field in the database, there must be a corresponding element. Using a little forethought, you can convert the contents of a database into a text (ASCII) file and then use a word processor to modify the text file into an accurate XML document.

Finally, the last two tasks discuss JavaScript and Dynamic HTML and how both technologies work together to make Web documents dynamic. By declaring elements that are similar to HTML's STYLE or the Netscape extensions LAYER and ILAYER, you can nest JavaScript scripts, Java applets, and ActiveX objects within the XML documents that you plan to display on the Web.

Introducing XML-Based Databases

As the Web becomes more central to many enterprises, it becomes more important to use Internet-ready business applications for day-to-day business. These applications should provide the following features:

▶ They should support the standard file types for that type of application. For example, database programs should support the .dbf file type and spreadsheets should support .xls and .wk* types.

▶ They should support Internet file types, such as .xml, .htm, .html, .shtml, and so on, depending on the type of application and its purpose. This makes it easier to convert word-processing documents, spreadsheets, and databases to Web pages and Web-based forms.

▶ They should incorporate various Internet technologies, such as the ability to transfer files (such as Web pages) to and from servers. This means that some level of communications should be enabled within the applications.

▶ They should start supporting sophisticated technologies, such as scripting, and Dynamic HTML.

Databases have already become an important part of the Web. For example, any commercial site at which goods are sold should have one or more underlying databases, which include customer information as well as inventory information. The customer database produces lists of contacts for catalog mailings and e-mail contacts, and the inventory database allows for instantaneous checking for the availability of merchandise. Often, Web-based marketing sites ask prospective customers to enter information into fill-in forms. Then that information is exported into databases for later processing as mailing lists or contacts lists. Using XML, developers can not only declare elements to build a fill-in form but can also use parsers to transfer the output directly into the record. As with any other XML DTD, a fill-in form DTD can include elements that must be used in a particular order, attribute lists of valid values from which a choice is required, a set structure of root, child, and other descendant elements, and more.

Reviewing the Structure of a Database

Databases are made up of records, which are composed of fields. A *field*, which is the smallest unit of information, contains one piece of information, such as a first name or a ZIP code. A *record* consists of a group of related fields. For example, a record can contain all the desired information about a customer, an employee, or an inventory item. Use *forms*, or input forms, to enter information into the records in a database. Forms should formatted and arranged so that data entry is as easy as possible. Note that many forms are designed to include some, but not all, fields. For example, some fields contain the results of a calculation, which is performed after the information is entered into a record. Other forms are custom-made to enable only some parts of a record to be entered.

CROSS-REFERENCE

In Chapter 6, you can get information about planning a DTD for any type of XML document — even a database.

FIND IT ONLINE

Kira's Web Toolbox (**http://lightsphere.com/dev/**) contains tools for creating and maintaining Web sites.

TAKE NOTE

HOW RELATIONAL DATABASES WORK

A standard nonrelational database is self-contained: it holds all the information about a particular piece of business. A relational database consists of several standalone databases, each of which serves a unique purpose to a central database. For example, from a central database of all your employees, you could access the following databases: home address and telephone numbers, income and expenses for corporate departments, and so on. Each single-purpose database is "attached" to the central database through a common field, such as an ID number. In XML, you could use links to associate relational databases. For more about XML links, see Part IV.

Listing 17-1: ELEMENT DECLARATIONS FOR THE DATABASE DTD

```
<!ELEMENT database ← ❶

    (name, address, city, state, zip, ← ❷
        telephone, fax, email)>

    <!ELEMENT name (prefix, first_name,
        last_name, suffix)>

    <!ELEMENT address (address_1,
        address_2)>

    <!ELEMENT city (#PCDATA)>

    <!ELEMENT state (#PCDATA)>         ← ❸

    <!ELEMENT zip (#PCDATA)>

    <!ELEMENT telephone (tel_1|tel_2)>

    <!ELEMENT fax (#PCDATA)>

    <!ELEMENT cell (#PCDATA)>

    <!ELEMENT e-mail (#PCDATA)>
```

❶ Declare the root element.
❷ List the first generation of child elements.
❸ Declare each element on the list.

Listing 17-2: ADDING SOME ATTRIBUTES

```
<!ELEMENT database (name, address, city,
    state, zip, telephone, fax, email)>
<!ATTLIST database
        lang    (en|fr|es|de)      "en">
    <!ELEMENT name (prefix, first_name,
        last_name, suffix)>
    <!ATTLIST name
        id      ID              #REQUIRED>
        <!ELEMENT prefix (#PCDATA)>
        <!ELEMENT first_name (#PCDATA)>
        <!ELEMENT last_name (#PCDATA)>
        <!ELEMENT suffix (#PCDATA)>
    <!ELEMENT address (address_1,
        address_2)>
    <!ATTLIST address
        <!ELEMENT address_1 (#PCDATA)>
        <!ATTLIST address_1
            id      ID              #REQUIRED>
        <!ELEMENT address_2 (#PCDATA)>
        <!ATTLIST address_2
            id      ID              #REQUIRED>
    <!ELEMENT city (#PCDATA)>
    <!ATTLIST city
        id      ID              #REQUIRED>
```

▲ Because of the onset of style sheets, the use of attributes has declined — for styling. Thus, in this example, most of the attributes are identifiers, which will enable the use of extended links and extended pointers.

Creating a Database DTD

Planning, laying out, and creating a database DTD requires more effort than if you created a new database using a program developed specifically for that purpose: For example, you won't have the help in automatically adding or defining fields that you would have if you were using a database program. However, once you have designed one database DTD, you can probably apply it to similar types of DTDs.

Typically, each field in a database matches with an element in a database DTD. When you start compiling the list of potential elements, factor in the position of a particular element within the generations of elements. For example, in a database of name and address information, will you define a parent `name` element under which fall child elements for the first name, last name, and so on? Your other choice is to eliminate `name` altogether and just have one level of `first-name`, `last-name`, and `middle-initial` elements. You'll have to answer the same "generational" question about address elements and telephone elements. Your decision not only affects the way that the DTD is laid out but also the design of the database associated with the DTD. In addition, the way you specify generations might also affect the processing of output as well as the ease with which future developers understand the DTD's structure.

The top of a typical name-and-address DTD might look like this:

```
<?xml version="1.0"?>
<!DOCTYPE customer [
<!ELEMENT customer (name+, address*,
```

```
  city+, state+, zip+, telephone*,
  fax?, email?)>
]>
```

In this example, someone can enter any amount of information into each of the fields. In this example, someone can enter any amount of information into each of the fields.

For database DTDs, a better solution is to allow one entry per root and first-generation elements and use comma separators to set a specific order of entry. For example:

```
<!ELEMENT customer
  (name, address, city, state, zip,
  telephone, fax, email)>
```

To keep tight control of the element structure, most child elements will have children of their own. For example, let's say that a database XML document is designed to send parsed output to a database with fields that are limited in size or type. Setting strict limitations in the DTD will help prevent future problems in fitting output to particular fields.

TAKE NOTE

▶ **SPECIFYING DATA TYPES**

XML 1.0 supports only parsed character data (just letters, digits, and special characters), names, and name tokens as data types. However, databases usually include more data types, including Boolean, date, and so on. To address this discrepancy, you can declare lists of attribute values from which the individuals creating XML documents based on the DTD can choose.

CROSS-REFERENCE

Chapter 8 discusses how to declare generations of elements and to set their structure.

FIND IT ONLINE

Answer your Web security questions at **http://www. w3.org/Security/FAQ/www-security-FAQ.html.**

Planning for a Database

Before you start designing and deciding on the content of a database, ask yourself the following questions:

▶ What is the purpose of this database? Will you use it to compile information about future customers? Do you want to track your employees and changes in their status?

▶ What information will you process for output? Will you prepare monthly or weekly reports? Will you create mailing lists and form letters from the information? Will the output go to an application that processes it in some way?

▶ What formatting and enhancements will be applied to the output? Will the output be printed or displayed onscreen? Will the output be converted to a particular file format?

▶ What specific information do you need to compile? What fields does this database require?

▶ Are you planning the database for future changes and growth? Will you define reserved fields or can you add fields at a later time.

▶ How can you ensure that certain types of information belong in the fields for which they were defined?

▶ How will you sort records in this database? Will you have to pay special attention to sorting fields?

Listing 17-3: A FEW DETAILS OF AN EMPLOYEE DATABASE

```xml
<?xml version = "1.0"?>
<!DOCTYPE employee [
<!ELEMENT employee (f_name, l_name, empid,
    title, dept, location, ext, email)>
<!ATTLIST employee
    id   ID   #IMPLIED>
  <!ELEMENT f_name (#PCDATA)>
  <!ELEMENT l_name (#PCDATA)>



  <!ELEMENT location (#PCDATA)>
  <!ATTLIST location
    warehouse   CDATA   #FIXED   "Acme"
    wphone      CDATA   #FIXED
                        "800-555-5555">
```

① Declare the root and child elements for the database.
② Add an identifier attribute.
③ For convenience, add two attributes with predefined, fixed values.

Converting Existing Database Information into an XML Document

After you have completed the database DTD, turn to creating the database document. An XML document is a text (ASCII) document with no hidden formatting characters. So, even if you are working without a database program, you can move information into an XML document quite easily. First, edit the file containing the information to prepare it for conversion. Then save the file as a text file. You can now edit the text file, adding prolog lines, markup, and content until the file is an accurate XML document.

One of the most important factors in a smooth conversion operation is to prepare the material being moved. For example, if you want to move names and addresses that you have typed into a word-processing document, make sure that each field is separated from the next by a separator character and that each record is on a single line. Sometimes, you can convert the text as you edit into a table so that you can easily detect whether all fields are filled in. Another way to ensure that the information is properly prepared is to insert tabs, which add extra space between each field so that you can view it more easily. However, before you save the file, be sure to convert any tables back to text for an easier import.

When you move records from a database application — even if you convert the file to a text format — the first row may contain field labels and not the actual information. So, be prepared to check the text file for accuracy and remove the field labels, unless

you want to use them as titles — perhaps as the content of an element named `title`.

When you finally incorporate all the database information into the XML document, you'll have to continue editing. You may find that lines don't break the way you want them to, you may detect random characters that should have been removed earlier, and you may want to indent elements to show nesting. You'll also want to add attributes, entities, and other components to the document.

TAKE NOTE

► USING ACTIVE SERVER PAGES TO CONVERT DATA

Active Server Pages (ASP) is a Microsoft technology with which you can create Web pages for the Microsoft Internet Information Server (IIS) and other servers. ASP allows you to use JScript, VBScript, or PerlScript to create dynamic pages using the ActiveX interface and other components. You can use ASP to replace your CGI scripts. One advantage of using ASP is that it can render data from almost any database server. For more information about ASP, visit **http://www.microsoft. com/workshop/server/toc.htm**, **http://support. microsoft.com/support/activeserver/**, and **http:// support.microsoft.com/support/activeserver/ faq/**. Other ASP pages include What is ASP? (**http:// www.chilisoft.com/allaboutasp/main.asp**), ActiveServerPages.com (**http://activeserverpages. com/**), and the ASP Alliance (**http://www. aspalliance.com/**).

CROSS-REFERENCE

Chapter 9 discusses how to declare attributes for each of the elements in a DTD.

FIND IT ONLINE

Link to hypertext tips, techniques, and theory pages from **http://www.eastgate.com/Hypertext.html**.

Listing 17-4: AN INVENTORY DATABASE DTD

```
<?xml version="1.0"?>
<!DOCTYPE invent [
<!ELEMENT invent (name, itemno, dept, warehse, pdate, onhand)>◄❶
   <!ELEMENT name (#PCDATA)>
   <!ATTLIST name
        id              ID                      #REQUIRED>
   <!ELEMENT itemno (#PCDATA)>
   <!ATTLIST itemno
        id              ID                      #REQUIRED>
   <!ELEMENT dept (#PCDATA)>
   <!ATTLIST dept
            name        (nails|bolts|tools)         "bolts"◄❷
            id          ID                      #REQUIRED>
   <!ELEMENT warehse (#PCDATA)>
   <!ATTLIST warehse
            location    (Miami|Erie|Troy)           "Troy"◄❸
            id          ID                      #REQUIRED>
   <!ELEMENT pdate (year,month,day)>
   <!ATTLIST pdate
            id          ID                      #REQUIRED>
      <!ELEMENT year
      <!ATTLIST year
                value   CDATA                   #FIXED   "1999">◄❹
      <!ELEMENT month
      <!ELEMENT day
   <!ELEMENT onhand (#PCDATA)>
```

❶ Declare the root and list its child elements.
❷ Offer a choice of department names and a default value.
❸ Offer a choice of warehouse locations and a default value.
❹ Fix the year value to 1999. (Next year, change it to 2000.)

An Overview of JavaScript

Throughout the short history of the Web, Web site developers have wanted to make their pages unique. Along the way, developers have changed the color of page backgrounds, selected different typefaces and adjusted point sizes, and inserted graphics and animations to enhance their pages. The level of sophistication grew into professional page design. At the same time, developers took advantage of their programming talents to use Common Gateway Interface (CGI) scripts and software plug-ins and applets. However, CGI scripts, plug-ins, and applets require some programming experience.

In 1995, Netscape developed LiveScript, a programming language that enabled administrators to control Web servers, to add scripts to Web pages on client computers, and to interface with Java applets. Later that year, Netscape, in conjunction with Sun (the developer of the Java programming language) changed LiveScript's name to JavaScript. Although some people think that Java and JavaScript are closely associated, they are actually related through their syntax, which is similar to C and C++.

JavaScript enables both programmers and non-programmers to insert scripts into Web documents. You can use JavaScript to write scripts that:

- ▶ Respond to a user action, such as clicking or double-clicking.
- ▶ Control page display or the processing of Java applets.

- ▶ Control the user's movement among several frames.
- ▶ Enhance entering data into fill-in forms.
- ▶ Process information on the client computer before passing it to the server.

The HTML 4.0 DTD includes a scripting attribute that incorporates events attributes into almost every HTML element. So, in an XML DTD, you can include scripting attributes. According to the HTML 4.0 recommendation, "user agents must not evaluate script data as HTML markup but instead must pass it on as data to a script engine." Thus, an HTML browser that also supports XML will support scripting. Scripts are in the category of non-HTML data.

TAKE NOTE

▶ LEARNING ABOUT ECMASCRIPT

Microsoft has developed its own version of JavaScript, JScript. Until now, there has been no central JavaScript standard. in 1997, ECMA, a standards organization (**http://www.ecma.ch/**), released the first standard, known as ECMA-262 or ECMAScript. ECMAScript incorporates most JavaScript features. JScript fully conforms to the ECMAScript standard. Although ECMAScript is a standard, current Web browsers do not fully support it. You can downlo9ad ECMA Script manuals from **ftp://ftp.ecma.ch/ecma-st/e262-doc.exe** (Word fromat) or **ftp://ecma.ch/ecma-st/e262-pdf.pdf** (Acrobat Reader format).

CROSS-REFERENCE

Learn how to modify an existing DTD to support your XML documents in Chapter 11.

FIND IT ONLINE

http://www.gooddocuments.com/homepage/homepage_m.htm explains how to write for intranets.

Table 17-1: SELECTED JAVASCRIPT RESOURCES ON THE WEB

Site Name	URL	Description
JavaScript Documentation	**http://developer.netscape.com/docs/manuals/javascript.html**	Links to many JavaScript manuals, articles, tools, and so on
JavaScript Guide	**http://developer.netscape.com/docs/manuals/communicator/jsguide4/index.htm**	A JavaScript user guide from its developer
JavaScript Reference	**http://developer.netscape.com/docs/manuals/communicator/jsref/index.htm**	A JavaScript reference guide from its developer
JavaScript Reference	**http://www.dcs.napier.ac.uk/~andrew/javascript/contents.htm**	A table of contents (links) to an online reference guide for JavaScript
JavaScript Articles, Links, and Resources	**http://www.webdeveloper.com/categories/javascript/**	Links to a variety of JavaScript resources, including frequently asked questions, references, and articles
Webmonkey: JavaScript Collection	**http://www.hotwired.com/webmonkey/javascript/**	Links to crash courses, JavaScript articles, and other Web resources
JavaScript Guide	**http://www.lucky.net/docs/java/toc.html**	A table of contents (links) to JavaScript basics, language concepts, and reference
JavaScript Tutorial	**http://www.ucsolutions.com/js/index.htm**	A four-lesson tutorial on JavaScript
Microsoft Scripting Home Page	**http://msdn.microsoft.com/scripting/**	The home page for Microsoft JScript and VBScript software and documentation

An Overview of Dynamic HTML

efore Dynamic HTML (DHTML), Web pages looked like electronic versions of printed pages: They lacked any movement except for animated GIFs. Using DHTML, a Web page developer can embed scripts, Java applets, and ActiveX objects to enable actions and processing.

Both Netscape and Microsoft provide different ways of working with DHTML, which results in difficulties in implementing DHTML on different browsers. Microsoft uses the HTML STYLE element to define its version of DHTML objects, which are defined as styles. Netscape has developed the LAYER and ILAYER elements to create windows of HTML content that are either placed or float above the current window. Of course, Netscape extensions are not "official" HTML unless the W3C accepts them for the next version of the standard. Netscape also supports the STYLE element.

DHTML uses the following technologies:

▶ The working draft on the three-dimensional positioning and visibility of HTML elements using the CSS1 standard. The current version of the working draft of cascading style sheet positioning (CSS-P) is located at **http://www.w3. org/TR/WD-positioning/**. CSS-P guides both Netscape's and Microsoft's versions of DHTML objects.

▶ Cascading style sheets (CSS), which are covered in Chapters 24 through 29 in this book. The W3C recommendation for the current standard, CSS2, is located at **http://www.w3.org/ TR/REC-CSS2/**.

▶ The Document Object Model (DOM). The W3C recommendation is located at **http:// www.w3.org/TR/REC-DOM-Level-1/**.

Under HTML, a document is a single object. Under DHTML, the document, scripts, frames, and windows are separated into several or many objects that are organized in a hierarchy. The window in which all the content is contained is at the top level, a frame within the window the next lower level, the history of pages visited before and after the current page is next, followed by the current window, then scripts, and at the lowest level the document.

For a list of some of the Dynamic HTML resources on the Web, see Table 17-2 (next page).

TAKE NOTE

▶ LEARNING ABOUT ACTIVEX

ActiveX is Microsoft's descendant of Object Linking and Embedding (OLE), which applies an object from one application to another. ActiveX controls use Component Object Model (COM) technologies to interface with other programs and computers in order to communicate, transfer files, and display documents. To learn more about ActiveX, go to Microsoft's ActiveX Controls page (**http://www. microsoft.com/com/activex.asp**).

CROSS-REFERENCE
The chapters in Part IV describe adding extended links and pointers to XML documents.

FIND IT ONLINE
Learn about designing Web access for the disabled at **http://www.ataccess.org/design.html**.

Table 17-2: SELECTED DYNAMIC HTML RESOURCES ON THE WEB

Site Name	URL	Description
Dynamic HTML Zone	http://www.dhtmlzone.com/index.html	Articles, tutorials, resources, and discussion groups
Dynamic HTML in Netscape Communicator	http://developer.netscape.com/docs/manuals/communicator/dynhtml/index.htm	A table of contents for a 15-chapter online book about Dynamic HTML
Webmonkey: Dynamic_ Html Collection	http://www.hotwired.com/webmonkey/dynamic_html/	Crash courses, discussions, articles, archives, and links to other types of Web creation resources
Dynamic HTML Sample Code	http://developer.netscape.com/docs/examples/dynhtml.html	Links to Dynamic HTML code, for Navigator and other browsers
DevEdge Online: Presentations and Tutorials — Dynamic HTML	http://developer.netscape.com/docs/presentations/dynhtml.html	Tutorials and presentations to help others learn Dynamic HTML, JavaScript, and other Web technologies
Tips, Tricks, How-To, and Beyond: Dynamic HTML	http://tips-tricks.com/dy.html	An overview of Dynamic HTML, as defined by Netscape and Microsoft, along with many other links to Web resources
Dynamic HTML Index	http://www.all-links.com/dynamic/	A very large index of Dynamic HTML links
Dynamic HTML	http://www.microsoft.com/workshop/c-frame.htm#/workshop/author/default.asp	The Microsoft home page for Dynamic HTML

Personal Workbook

Q&A

1 What features should Internet-ready business applications provide?

_____

_____

_____

2 What are the components making up a database?

_____

_____

_____

3 What is a *field*?

_____

_____

_____

4 What is a *record*?

_____

_____

_____

5 What is a *form*?

_____

_____

_____

6 What is a *relational database*?

_____

_____

_____

7 What is *JavaScript*?

_____

_____

_____

8 What does Dynamic HTML do?

_____

_____

_____

ANSWERS: PAGE 461

EXTRA PRACTICE

① Create an XML address-book database of your friends or business associates.

② Create an XML database of the inventory of your kitchen. Declare at least three generations of elements.

③ Draw a chart of the layers of management and employees at your company. Convert the chart into an XML DTD.

④ Go online and tour the site of an online retailer such as L. L. Bean, amazon.com, or Land's End. What types of databases are they using? Analyze at least one database for possible conversion to an XML document.

⑤ A grid of television shows can be converted into a database. Plan and design a DTD that does this.

REAL-WORLD APPLICATIONS

✔ You are the human resources manager of your company. Write a specification for an XML employee database.

✔ For a library, create a virtual card catalog. Each card includes the book's title, author, ISBN identification number, category number, and copyright.

✔ The library also needs to track the books that it lends. Design a DTD that includes information from the card catalog and adds appropriate customer information. (Hint: Be sure to include the dates that each book is borrowed and due back, as well as a means for indicating that the book has actually been returned.)

Visual Quiz

How would you design a DTD based on this input form? What elements would you declare? Into what generation levels would you place the declared elements?

_____

_____

_____

_____

_____

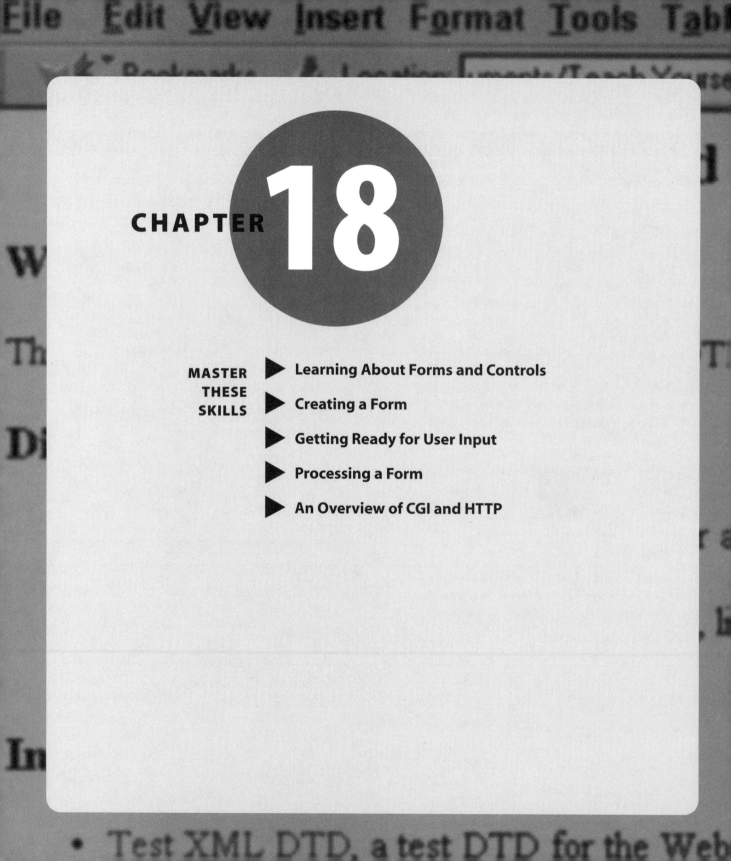

CHAPTER 18

MASTER
THESE
SKILLS

▶ Learning About Forms and Controls

▶ Creating a Form

▶ Getting Ready for User Input

▶ Processing a Form

▶ An Overview of CGI and HTTP

Using Forms in an XML Document

This chapter provides an overview of fill-in forms, starting with the concepts behind forms and concluding with overviews of the protocols that help you transfer information from forms to servers.

If you are an experienced HTML developer, you already know that HTML 4.0 includes a variety of predefined elements and attributes for creating forms and making them work. These elements and attributes enable you to design and develop good-looking forms in HTML. Creating forms in XML will require the heavy use of CSS properties to turn on borders, change background and foreground colors, set margins, change typefaces and point sizes, and so on. However, the real purpose of a form is to gather information from visitors to your site and process it in some way. This means that you want to present easy-to-use forms that will attract individuals so that they will be happy to give you information. By using Active Server Pages (ASP) or CGI scripts and the HTTP protocol, you can send the supplied information to a server for further processing.

In the first task in this chapter, you learn about forms and controls, which are the components from which forms are composed. You'll find out about the HTML elements and attributes that define individual controls, so that you can declare appropriate XML elements and attributes. Using the information in the second task, you will be able to plan and design a workable form that visitors to your Web site will find easy to use. The next step in the development of a form (and the next task in the chapter) is to prepare for user input by thorough testing. You'll also learn about JavaScript and dynamic forms and the factors that make up a successful control in a form.

The fourth task discusses how a form is processed and what happens once a user clicks on a submit button. Transferring information from a client computer to a server computer requires the use of programs and scripts to enable communications. This task will introduce both the CGI and HTTP protocols, which are covered more thoroughly in the last task of the chapter.

Learning About Forms and Controls

A form is a part of a document to which an individual can insert information using a combination of typing, selecting items from lists, clicking on buttons, checking boxes, and so on. The HTML 4.0 specification says that "users generally 'complete' a form by modifying its controls, before submitting the form to an agent for processing." In HTML, use the FORM element to mark the start and end of a form.

Controls are named components within forms. HTML 4.0 supports the following commonly used control types:

▶ The Checkbox control type is a small square box that represents an on or off status. In HTML, specify a checkbox by using the INPUT element and the TYPE="CHECKBOX" attribute and value.

▶ The File select control type is a file-uploading control. In HTML, specify the file select control type by using the INPUT element and the TYPE="FILE" attribute and value.

▶ The Menu control type is a list box or, sometimes, a pull-down menu. In HTML, specify the menu control type by using the SELECT element and either the OPTGROUP or OPTION element.

▶ The Object control type is any type of multimedia object (image, video file, or sound file) within a form. In HTML, specify the object control type by using the OBJECT element. A multimedia object can also be located outside a form.

▶ The Radio button control type is a small round button in a set of buttons from which you can select only one at a time. In HTML, specify a radio button by using the INPUT element and the TYPE="RADIO" attribute and value. Radio buttons are also known as option buttons.

▶ The Reset button control type is a push (command) button on which you click to clear a form. In HTML, specify a Reset button by using the BUTTON element or the INPUT element and the TYPE="RESET" attribute and value.

▶ The Submit button control type is a push (command) button on which you click to submit a form. In HTML, specify a Submit button by using the BUTTON element or the INPUT element and the TYPE="SUBMIT" attribute and value.

TAKE NOTE

USING THE BUTTON OR INPUT ELEMENT

The BUTTON element, which is new to HTML 4.0, is designed specifically to create buttons. In contrast, INPUT is an all-purpose element with which you can create a variety of controls. The BUTTON element was created specifically for push buttons (also known as command buttons), which are rectangular buttons on which you click to start an action. According to the HTML 4.0 recommendation, the BUTTON element "offers richer rendering capabilities than the INPUT element."

CROSS-REFERENCE

Chapter 13 discusses how to create an XML document and add elements, attributes, and entities.

FIND IT ONLINE

Build and promote Web sites using the resources at http://www.evandelay.com/freeinternet/.

Using Forms in an XML Document

Learning About Forms and Controls

HTML 4.0: THE BUTTON ELEMENT

```
<!ELEMENT BUTTON - -
     (%flow;)* -(A|%formctrl;|FORM|FIELDSET)-- push button -->
<!ATTLIST BUTTON
  %attrs;                                -- %coreattrs, %i18n, %events --
  name          CDATA         #IMPLIED ◄①
  value         CDATA         #IMPLIED  -- sent to server when submitted --
  type          (button|submit|reset) submit  -- for use as form button --◄②
  disabled      (disabled)    #IMPLIED  -- unavailable in this context --◄③
  tabindex      NUMBER        #IMPLIED  -- position in tabbing order --
  accesskey     %Character;   #IMPLIED  -- accessibility key character --
  onfocus       %Script;      #IMPLIED  -- the element got the focus --
                                                                       ◄④
  onblur        %Script;      #IMPLIED  -- the element lost the focus --
  %reserved;>                            -- reserved for possible future use --
```

① *You can name a button for later identification.*
② *The* type *attribute provides three choices:* button, submit, *and* reset.
③ *Use the* disabled *attribute to prevent user action.*
④ *A script runs when the control is active or becomes inactive.*

Listing 18-1: A SAMPLE HTML FORM CONVERTED TO XML

```
<form action="cgi-bin/form-example" method="post">
<para>Type your name:◄①
 ②<input type="text" name="name" size="40"></para>
<para>Type your email address:
   <input type="text" name="email" size="30"></para>
<para>Type your password:            ④
 ③<input type="hidden" name="pswd" size="10"><maxlength="8"></para>
<para><input type="submit"><input type="reset"></para></form>
```

① *Specify a label to prompt the user.*
② *Define a text box that will contain typed information.*
③ *The* hidden *type is not displayed on the form.*
④ *Specify a submit button and a reset button.*

Creating a Form

Before you create a form, you should plan and design it. As you know, forms are made up of controls. Designing a form layout is very similar to designing page layout for an entire document. You want to make sure that users enter information in a logical order and understand the meaning of each control. In addition, controls shouldn't be too far apart or too close together. Select easy-to-read fonts and don't vary point sizes too much. Let your eyes and those of colleagues be the judge.

Using the HTML model, create a form by inserting a start tag to mark the beginning of the form and an end tag to mark the end. Embed controls and optional text labels for those controls within the form tags. For guidance in declaring elements and attributes that are appropriate for forms, refer to the HTML 4.0 recommendation.

For forms developers using HTML, the INPUT element sets the type of user input: characters that are typed, buttons that are clicked, and boxes and buttons that are selected. (See the INPUT element and the attribute-list declarations on the facing page.) The last type of control, the list box, is controlled by the SELECT, OPTGROUP, and OPTION elements. (The SELECT, OPTGROUP, and OPTION element declarations are not shown in this book.)

In XML, you can declare elements similar to those that you use to create a form in HTML. However, you may have to incorporate some programming or scripts in order to submit the form and its information to the server. In HTML, use the METHOD attribute to specify the HTTP method by which the form is submitted to a server that contains a form-handling program. Your choices are METHOD="GET" and METHOD="POST". METHOD="GET" appends the submitted information to a newly created URI named by the ACTION attribute using an environment variable. According to the HTML 4.0 specification, this method is deprecated. METHOD="POST" specifies the form to be sent to a server. This method, which is recommended, is difficult to use according to some form experts. For more information about HTTP, see the final task in this chapter.

TAKE NOTE

CREATING LIST BOX CONTROLS

In some ways, you can compare a typical form to a dialog box. In fact, some dialog boxes are forms. Both forms and dialog boxes contain a variety of controls, from command buttons to lists and checkboxes to radio buttons. Forms and dialog boxes can contain lists of items from which you can select one and sometimes more than one option. To create a list box in a form, use the SELECT (selection list) element. Then, use the OPTGROUP and OPTION child elements to specify groups of options and individual options, respectively. The OPTION element provides the SELECTED attribute with which you can highlight the option that you wish to set as the default.

CROSS-REFERENCE
Chapter 14 instructs you in adding tables, creating table sections, and formatting table components.

FIND IT ONLINE
Look up terms and link to other Internet resources at http://www.pcwebopaedia.com/.

HTML 4.0: THE FORM AND LABEL ELEMENTS

```
<!ELEMENT FORM - - (%block;|SCRIPT)+ -(FORM) -- interactive form -->
<!ATTLIST FORM
  %attrs;                             -- %coreattrs, %i18n, %events --
  action         %URI;          #REQUIRED -- server-side form handler --  ←❶
  method         (GET|POST)     GET       -- HTTP method used to submit the form--  ←❷
  enctype        %ContentType;  "application/x-www-form-urlencoded"  ←❸
  onsubmit       %Script;       #IMPLIED  -- the form was submitted --
  onreset        %Script;       #IMPLIED  -- the form was reset --         ←❹
  accept-charset %Charsets;     #IMPLIED  -- list of supported charsets --
>


<! - Each label must not contain more than ONE field -->
<!ELEMENT LABEL - - (%inline;)* -(LABEL) —form field label text -->
<!ATTLIST LABEL
  %attrs;                             -- %coreattrs, %i18n, %events --
  for          IDREF          #IMPLIED  -- matches field ID value --
  accesskey    %Character;    #IMPLIED  -- accessibility key character --
  onfocus      %Script;       #IMPLIED  -- the element got the focus --
  onblur       %Script;       #IMPLIED  -- the element lost the focus --
>
```

❶ Use the action *attribute to specify the server's form handler.*
❷ *Specify the HTTP method for submitting the form.*
❸ *The encoding type specifies the content.*
❹ *Run a script when the form is submitted or reset.*

Getting Ready for User Input

Once you have completed a form, you should thoroughly test it by entering information into each text box and evaluating each of the other controls. Make sure that every control works as you think it should. Also, test the form using as many XML browsers as you can find. (Some browsers will work a little differently than others.)

Check the forms by asking the following questions:

▶ Is each of the text boxes the proper dimensions? In your judgment, can you see enough of the text that you enter? Have you allowed for the greatest amount of information that will be entered?

▶ Do checkboxes alternately clear and check with each click under every browser?

▶ How many radio buttons can you select in any of the browsers with which you test? No more than one button in a group can be filled at any particular time.

▶ Are pre-selected options the proper choices?

▶ Are labels spelled correctly? Do labels appear in the selected font and point size?

TAKE NOTE

▶ MAKING DYNAMIC FORMS

You can use JavaScript to create scripts that cause forms to become dynamic. For example, the HTML 4.0 forms elements declarations include scripting attributes that can be triggered when a user activates a control (onfocus), inactivates an element by activating another (onblur), submits a form (onsubmit), resets a form (onreset), selects text (onselect), or changes the value of an element (onchange). You might actually declare an XML element dedicated to running JavaScript scripts.

▶ JUDGING CONTROLS

The measure of a control is whether it can be submitted to an application. In HTML, a control always has a name (use the name attribute), an initial value (usually set with the value attribute), and a current value (which a user might have set). A control whose content can be submitted to an application is successful or valid. The HTML 4.0 recommendation states that a control is successful or unsuccessful under one or more of these circumstances:

▶ If it is outside the form, it is unsuccessful.

▶ A control with its name paired with its current value is successful.

▶ If the value of the disabled attribute is "disabled", it is unsuccessful.

▶ If a form has more than one submit button, the activated button is successful.

▶ If a checkbox is checked, it is probably successful.

▶ If one radio button is filled, it is the successful radio button in the set.

▶ If a menu option is selected, it is successful.

▶ Reset buttons are not successful.

CROSS-REFERENCE

In Chapter 15, you learn how to define framesets and to display parts of your documents in frames.

FIND IT ONLINE

You'll find a long guide to Web style at **http://wwwwseast2.usec.sun.com/styleguide/**.

HTML 4.0: THE INPUT ELEMENT

```
<!ENTITY % InputType
  "(TEXT | PASSWORD | CHECKBOX |
    RADIO | SUBMIT | RESET |
    FILE | HIDDEN | IMAGE | BUTTON)"        ❶
<!—attribute name required for all but submit & reset -->
<!ELEMENT INPUT - O EMPTY            -- form control -->  ❷
<!ATTLIST INPUT
  %attrs;                            -- %coreattrs, %i18n, %events --
  type       %InputType;  TEXT       -- what kind of widget is needed --  ❸
  name       CDATA        #IMPLIED   -- submit as part of form --
  value      CDATA        #IMPLIED   -- required for radio and checkboxes --  ❹
  checked    (checked)    #IMPLIED   -- for radio buttons and check boxes --
  disabled   (disabled)   #IMPLIED   -- unavailable in this context --
  readonly   (readonly)   #IMPLIED   -- for text and passwd --  ❹
  size       CDATA        #IMPLIED   -- specific to each type of field --
  maxlength  NUMBER       #IMPLIED   -- max chars for text fields --  ❹
  src        %URI;        #IMPLIED   -- for fields with images --
  alt        CDATA        #IMPLIED   -- short description --
  usemap     %URI;        #IMPLIED   -- use client-side image map --
  tabindex   NUMBER       #IMPLIED   -- position in tabbing order --
  accesskey  %Character;  #IMPLIED   -- accessibility key character --
  onfocus    %Script;     #IMPLIED   -- the element got the focus --
  onblur     %Script;     #IMPLIED   -- the element lost the focus --
  onselect   %Script;     #IMPLIED   -- some text was selected --
  onchange   %Script;     #IMPLIED   -- the element value was changed --
  accept     %ContentTypes; #IMPLIED -- list of MIME types for file upload --
  %reserved;>                        -- reserved for possible future use --
```

❶ *The entity declaration incorporates all the input types.*
❷ *The INPUT element is empty.*
❸ *Specify the type of input with the type attribute*
❹ *Certain attributes apply to only some input types.*

Processing a Form

Once you have created a fill-in form, you have to provide a means of transferring the form information that a visitor to your site enters to an application that will process that information — perhaps load it into a database, send it to someone as an e-mail message, or reformat it for displaying online.

When a user clicks on a submit button, a program or script should be activated. The browser with which the user is viewing the form transfers the information from the client computer to the URI specified in the `ACTION` attribute:

```
<FORM
ACTION="http://x.com/cgi-bin/pgm123
   METHOD="post">
```

The target resource is located on a server named `x.com`. The server takes over and searches for the `pgm123` program in the `cgi-bin` folder. Furthermore, the server communicates by using the `post` method, which identifies the form and does not append it to the URI. Once the server locates `pgm123`, it transmits the information in the form to the program. The program then processes the information and sends a message back to the server.

In the example, remember that `cgi-bin` was a folder. It is also a reserved word for a folder that stores one or more cgi-bin programs. Applications that are categorized as cgi-bin use the Common Gateway Interface (CGI) protocol to create HTML in response to user requests. In addition, the program

that you use to send a form from a client to a server uses the HyperText Transport Protocol (HTTP) as its transfer protocol. HTTP is programmed to understand the hypertext links in the documents that it transfers. In fact, you can use an HTTP script to process forms. You'll learn more about both CGI and HTTP in the following task.

TAKE NOTE

HTML ACTION ATTRIBUTE RULES

In HTML, the `ACTION` attribute sets the action taken when an individual clicks a submit button. The value of `ACTION` is a URI for a program that will process the information. The basic rules controlling the `ACTION` attribute are:
- ▶ The form-handling program must support the type of data in the submitted form.
- ▶ The URI for the processing program is either absolute or relative.
- ▶ When you send the form to an HTTP URI, the form is submitted to a program, which can be processed by a cgi-bin program or an HTTP script, known as a server-side form handler.

SCRIPTS VS. PROGRAMS

A *program* is a set of instructions executed by a computer to accomplish one or more tasks. For example, a spreadsheet program enables you to calculate data, sort data, store data in a system of rows and columns, produce output, and so on. A *script* is also a set of instructions. However, a script usually instructs a program to perform some type of operation.

CROSS-REFERENCE

Chapter 16 discusses how to convert your current HTML documents to accurate XML documents.

FIND IT ONLINE

http://www.software.ibm.com/xml/ has a page with links to tutorials, standards, tools, DTDs, and samples.

Listing 18-2: AN HTML FORM

```
<FORM ACTION="/cgi-bin/form-example" METHOD="post"><FIELDSET>
<LEGEND ALIGN="top"><B><FONT SIZE="+1">Name Information</FONT></B></LEGEND>
First Name:<INPUT TYPE="text" NAME="fname" SIZE="28">  
Last Name:<INPUT TYPE="text" NAME="lname" SIZE="29"><BR></FIELDSET>
<P><FIELDSET>
<LEGEND ALIGN="top"><B><FONT SIZE="+1">Address Information</FONT></B></LEGEND>
Address:<INPUT TYPE="text" NAME="addr1" SIZE="72"><BR>    
          <INPUT TYPE="text"
NAME="addr2" SIZE="72"><BR>
City:    <INPUT TYPE="text" NAME="city" SIZE="40">
State:<INPUT TYPE="text" NAME="state" SIZE="2">
Zip:<INPUT TYPE="text" NAME="zip" SIZE="9"><BR></FIELDSET>
<INPUT TYPE="submit" ALIGN="left"><INPUT TYPE="reset" ALIGN="right">
</FORM>
```

❶ *The* ALIGN *attribute and* FONT *element apply alignment and formatting.*
❷ *Add the*   *entity to insert a non-breaking space.*
❸ *The*
 tag inserts a line break.
❹ *The* INPUT *element does not need an end tag.*

Listing 18-3: AN HTML FORM ADAPTED TO XML

```
<form action="/cgi-bin/form-example" method="post">
<fieldset><legend>Name Information</legend>
<field>First Name:<input type="text" name="fname" size="28"/></field>
<field>Last Name:<input type="text" name="lname" size="29"/></field></fieldset>
<fieldset><legend>Address Information</legend>
<field>Address:<input type="text" name="addr1" size="72"/></field>
<field><input type="text" name="addr2" size="72"/></field>
<field>City:<input type="text" name="city" size="40"/></field>
<field>State:<input type="text" name="state" size="2"/></field>
<field>Zip:<input type="text" name="zip" size="9"/></field></fieldset>
<input type="submit"/><input type="reset"/></form>
```

▲ *This XML version is easier to read because every start tag has a matching end tag. Style sheet properties will replace most formatting elements and attributes.*

An Overview of CGI and HTTP

As you learned in the prior task, HyperText Transport Protocol (HTTP) is a transfer protocol that is programmed to understand the hypertext links in the documents that it transfers.

A *protocol* is a set of rules and regulations that control communications between two computers that may or may not run under the same operating system or have the same microprocessor. A protocol enables the connection and transfer of information between the computers.

The Common Gateway Interface (CGI) is a protocol that creates HTML in response to a user request in the form of a URI. Working together, both protocols service requests from client computers. This task provides an overview of these protocols. Table 18-2 lists selected CGI resources on the Web.

Learning About CGI

CGI is a platform-independent interface (a gateway) between a client and server, which is sometimes known as the HTTP server. A gateway can be written in any language that results in an executable file: C, C++, Perl, Python, and so on.

A CGI program runs when it is requested — in real time. This means that you can use the program to output up-to-date information immediately. CGI is executed on the server, so the client computer's resources are not used (as opposed to Java, which is executed on the client). A CGI program cannot make requests of users. The best that a user can do is to let XML or HTML provide the instructions for using a form, enter valid information in the form, click a submit button, and let submission instructions trigger the CGI program.

Learning About HTTP

HTTP is a protocol that allows client computers and server computers to communicate. Thus, if a browser program on a client computer requests a document from a program on the server, HTTP allows both events to occur. The markup language that you use to create the document is an important factor. For example, HTTP understands HTML and can interpret its elements, attributes, attribute values, and other document components and "explain" them to the server. Tim Berners-Lee, who is credited with developing the World Wide Web, also put HTTP into effect.

CROSS-REFERENCE
Find out how to build XML database DTDs and create or convert documents in Chapter 17.

FIND IT ONLINE
At **http://idm.internet.com/ifaq.html**, you'll find answers to intranet questions and links to other Web resources.

Table 18-1: SELECTED CGI RESOURCES ON THE WEB

Site Name	URL	Description
CGI Programming FAQ	http://htmlhelp.com/FAQ/cgifaq.html	A long detailed list of questions and answers about using CGI and related technologies
The Common Gateway Interface	http://hoohoo.ncsa.uiuc.edu/cgi/	Links to information about CGI from major players
CGI: The Common Gateway Interface for Server-Side Processing	http://WDVL.com/Authoring/CGI/	A paper and examples on using CGI
CGI Tutorial	http://www.bobsplace.com/cgi-tutorial/	Links to an online tutorial on CGI and Web forms
Adam Stanislav's CGI Programming Tutorial	http://www.geocities.com/Silicon Valley/Heights/7394/cgi.html	A user-friendly tutorial on CGI programming for programmers
JemTek CGI Tutorial	http://www.jemtek.com.au/jemtek/cgi/tutorial.htm	An online tutorial on CGI, including security and environmental variables
CGI Tutorial	http://www.sanford.com/intro.cgi/start.html	Links to an online tutorial on CGI and forms
Form Processor	http://www.freescripts.com/html/form_main.shtml	A script that processes HTML forms
BigNoseBird.Com	http://www.bignosebird.com/	Links to free CGI scripts and tutorials and other Web building resources
The CGI Resource Index	http://www.cgi-resources.com/	Many links to CGI programs, scripts, documentation, and more
CGI Reference Guide	http://shore.net/techtalk/reference/cgi.html	Links to CGI tutorials and other CGI resources

Personal Workbook

Q&A

1 What is a *control*? What are some examples of control types?

_____

_____

_____

2 To what other design process can you compare designing a form layout?

_____

_____

_____

3 What's the best method for submitting a form to a server?

_____

_____

_____

4 What is a *successful control*?

_____

_____

_____

5 What kind of radio button is successful?

_____

_____

_____

6 What should happen when a user clicks on a submit button?

_____

_____

_____

7 What is *CGI*?

_____

_____

_____

8 What is *HTTP*?

_____

_____

_____

ANSWERS: PAGE 462

EXTRA PRACTICE

① Go online and find a form that you like. See if you can design and create a similar form.

② Go online and find a badly designed form. What makes the form unattractive?

③ Create a DTD with form elements for a simple address book.

④ Create a form into which you can insert name and address information for the address book.

⑤ Create a To Do list form that combines text boxes for tasks to be completed and checkboxes to signal that a task is complete.

⑥ For your company's intranet, create a form for the football pool. What controls would you use? How would you process and calculate the data from each form?

REAL-WORLD APPLICATIONS

✔ You run an online catalog company. Design and create an order form that contains customer name and address information and secure credit data.

✔ Your market research firm polls prospective and existing clients about worldwide trends. Design and create a form that serves as a template for a new monthly survey.

✔ Your employees must report on projects and time spent on all projects each week. Design and create short form that includes a slot for every day of the week and a large text for comments.

✔ Your weekly newspaper must prequalify its group of free subscribers every six months by gathering three pages of information. Design a form that is easy for your subscribers to fill in. (Hint: Use radio buttons and checkboxes as often as possible.)

Visual Quiz

You saw this input form in Chapter 17. How would you re-create its design with help from the DTD that you wrote in Chapter 17?

_____

_____

_____

_____

_____

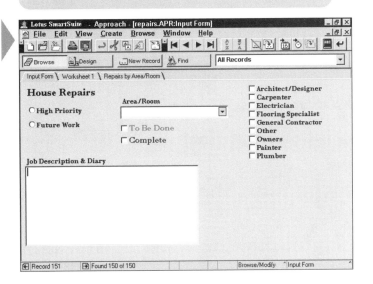

PART

IV

Using Links and Extended Pointers

This part discusses XML's sophisticated linking features, which go well beyond the simple links available in HTML documents. A *link* forms a relationship between two documents or two sections of one document. A simple link, which is the standard in HTML, enables a user to jump ahead to a new location. XML supports both extended links and extended pointers in your documents. Using extended links, you can link to several locations at once and can form a link from any of its linking resources to another. Using extended pointers, you can link to particular elements, attributes, and other components of a document.

W3C is developing the XML Linking Language (XLink) to support the use of extended links, and the XML Pointer Language (XPointer) to support extended pointers. Currently, both the XLink and XPointer languages are in the working-draft stage of development. This means they have not yet reached the stable specification stage. A working draft is subject to updates and even replacement with a completely new specification.

CHAPTER **19**

MASTER
THESE
SKILLS

▶ **Learning How Links Work**

▶ **Understanding XML Links**

▶ **Using Inline vs. Out-of-Line Links**

▶ **Using Link Semantics**

▶ **Specifying Types of Link Behaviors**

XLink and XPointer Building Blocks

This chapter provides an overview of XML links, which you can apply to the topics covered in Chapters 20 to 23. The first task in this chapter describes how links work, introduces terms that are unique to XML linking, and discusses each type of XML link: simple, extended, and extended link group. In addition, you can compare how the code for each of the links looks and works in HTML documents versus XML documents. You'll also see the syntax of the HTML A element so that you can use it as a guideline for defining XML attributes. And you can view the XLink productions and a table that lists predefined XLink attributes.

The remaining tasks in the chapter build on the basic knowledge presented in this first task. As you browse through the rest of the chapter, you'll learn the differences — sometimes substantial, often subtle — between types of links and their attributes and between one related attribute and another. You'll find out about inline links versus out-of-line links, remote titles and roles versus local titles and roles,

single-direction links versus multiple-direction links, and so on.

This chapter also shows you some of the differences in link behavior, which you can specify by setting two attribute values, separately or in tandem. The basic link behavior is traversal — the act of jumping from the link to the link resource. The show attribute specifies whether a link resource is displayed or processed when the link is traversed, and the actuate attribute starts traversal automatically or at a user's request.

As you read through the chapter, you'll discover that several of the Take Notes discuss how you can cross-reference in SGML, which does not include linking in its specification. You can use some of these discussions to plan your XML documents — particularly the long ones that are composed of smaller documents.

You can apply what you learn in this chapter to the use of simple links, extended links, extended link groups, and extended pointers — all of which will be covered in Chapters 20 to 23.

Learning How Links Work

The centerpiece of a link is the URI, which states the absolute or relative address of the resource that is the target of the link. An *absolute URI* starts with the name of an Internet protocol, such as `http:`, `ftp:`, `gopher:`, `file:`, `mailto:`, and so on. The next part of the syntax represents the *host name*, the actual address of the resource (such as `www.eddygrp.com`), which specifies (from left to right) the computer on which the server software is located, the registered name of the company or institution that owns the computer, and the domain of the computer. The URI usually concludes with a filename (such as `sample.xml`, `index.htm`, or `site.html`). If you use extended links and extended pointers in your documents, that information is tacked onto the filename.

A *relative URI* does not contain the complete Internet address. For example, if the current document and the document to which it links are located on the same computer, you don't need to enter an absolute URI. You can use the filename alone if the two documents share the same folder. You can add a folder name if the two documents are stored on the same drive in separate folders. If the two documents are stored on separate drives, add the drive name. The bottom line is that you should write URIs that ensure that the link works — that you can jump from the source document to the target.

In HTML, URIs of both types can include *fragment identifiers*, which are pound-sign symbols (#)

that match the value of the `NAME` attribute of the target resource's `A` element. Fragment identifiers are relatives of the connector that indicates the link-retrieval method for extended links as specified in the XLink language working draft.

Cross-Referencing in SGML Documents

SGML does not have an "official" standard for linking. However, you can use several methods to cross-reference other locations in the current document or an external document. You can add the predefined `ID`, `IDREF`, or `IDREFS` attributes (also available in XML) and unique values to elements at either end of a cross-reference. You can also define your own identifying attributes (such as `name` or `title`). In addition, you can declare an element specifically used for cross-referencing, or you can call an external document by using a parameter entity. Sometimes you must code a link manually, and sometimes you can depend on an SGML-supported browser to automatically form a link. If you work in a group, you can maintain a list of cross-referencing attributes and elements as well as a list of values used for particular instances. As this chapter continues, you can read more Take Notes that discuss SGML cross-referencing and linking. You can use some of these concepts in your XML documents.

CROSS-REFERENCE

In Chapter 3, you learn about EBNF notation and how to use it to enter valid characters and code.

FIND IT ONLINE

The W3C XML Linking Language working draft is located at **http://www.w3.org/TR/WD-xlink**.

HTML 4: THE A ELEMENT AND ITS ATTRIBUTE LIST

```
<!ELEMENT A - - (%inline;)* -(A)        -- anchor --> ◄❶
<!ATTLIST A
  %attrs;                              -- %coreattrs, %i18n, %events --
  charset      %Charset;      #IMPLIED -- char encoding of linked resource --
  type         %ContentType;  #IMPLIED -- advisory content type --
  name         CDATA          #IMPLIED -- named link end --
  href         %URI;          #IMPLIED -- URI for linked resource -- ◄❷
  hreflang     %LanguageCode; #IMPLIED -- language code --
  rel          %LinkTypes;    #IMPLIED -- forward link types -- ◄❸
  rev          %LinkTypes;    #IMPLIED -- reverse link types -- ◄❹
  accesskey    %Character;    #IMPLIED -- accessibility key character --
  shape        %Shape;        rect     -- for use with client-side image maps --
  coords       %Coords;       #IMPLIED -- for use with client-side image maps --
  tabindex     NUMBER         #IMPLIED -- position in tabbing order --
  onfocus      %Script;       #IMPLIED - the element got the focus --
  onblur       %Script;       #IMPLIED -- the element lost the focus -->
```

❶ *The inline* A *element anchors a simple HTML link.*
❷ *Use the* href *keyword to indicate a URI.*
❸ *The* rel *keyword indicates the forward relationship from URI to anchor.*
❹ *The* rev *keyword indicates the backward relationship from anchor to URI.*

Listing 19-1: A SAMPLE HTML A LINK

```
❶                    ❷              ❸
<A href="http://www.sample.com/test.xml">
Sample Document</A> ◄❹
```

❶ *Enter the* A *start tag.*
❷ *Add the* href *attribute and a URI.*
❸ *End the start tag.*
❹ *Insert the text of the link and the end tag.*

Listing 19-2: A SAMPLE HTML LINK LINK

```
<LINK REL="x-doc" TITLE="Companies
Starting with X"
HREF="http://www.eddygrp.com/x_cos.htm">
```

▲ *Use the HTML* LINK *element, a link that is independent of the type of media, to show a link from the current document to another, primarily to provide internal documentation.*

Understanding XML Links

XLinks — in conjunction with XPointers — establish hyperlinks in XML documents. The W3C XLink working draft defines two categories of links: simple links and extended links. Use the `xml:link` attribute to specify a link or location term, following this syntax:

```
xml:link="simple"|"extended"|"locator"
         |"group"|"document"
```

Simple links (`"simple"`) are analogous to the links formed by the A element in HTML. Insert a simple link in a document to be able to jump from its location in the source document to a destination in either the same document or another document. Simple links always move in one direction, from the source location to the target location. For more information, read this chapter and Chapter 20. In the XLink working draft, see Section 4.2.

Extended links (`"extended"`) enable you to define many links in one or more XML documents. When you use extended links, you can jump from any link in any document to a link resource in any document. You can identify the content associated with a particular link so that if the content changes but the identifier remains the same, you can still access the link.

Extended links can be inline or out-of-line. An *inline link* is an internal link within the current document. An *out-of-line* link specifies the location of the link in an external file. Because it's not a local resource, an application must be able to find it easily; out-of-line links are particularly useful for *extended link groups* (`"group"`), which are a particular type of extended link. Whatever their location — in the current document or in an external document — inline links and out-of-line links follow the same syntax. To learn more about extended links and extended link groups, read this chapter and Chapters 21 and 22, as well as Sections 4.3 and 5 in the XLink working draft (**http://www.w3.org/TR/WD-xlink/**).

The `xml:link` attribute supports the use of two other keywords: `locator` and `document`. `locator` indicates that a URI — and no other attributes — will follow. `document` indicates that an extended link that is an entire document follows.

TAKE NOTE

USING THE ID, IDREF, AND IDREFS ATTRIBUTES AS CROSS-REFERENCES

You can use cross-references in almost the same way that you use links. Especially in SGML, whose specification includes no means of linking, cross-references are one of the ways to establish a relationship of one element to another within a single document. In both SGML and XML, the ID, IDREF, and IDREFS are predefined attributes (and keywords) that allow you to associate identifying information with an element. The ID keyword indicates that a valid XML identifier follows. The IDREF keyword indicates that a valid XML identifier used as a cross-reference follows. The IDREFS keyword indicates that a list of identifier cross-references follow.

CROSS-REFERENCE

Chapter 4 discusses the Unicode characters and character sets that are valid within XML documents.

FIND IT ONLINE

Go to **http://www.w3.org/TR/NOTE-xlink-principles** to learn about the principles of XLink design.

Table 19-1: XLINK ATTRIBUTES

Attribute Name	Purpose	Syntax
actuate	Actuates link traversal with or without a request	actuate (auto|user)
behavior	Specifies detailed link behavior	behavior CDATA
content-role	Specifies the role of a local link resource	content-role CDATA
content-title	Specifies the title of a local link resource	content-title CDATA
href	Names a remote resource locator	href CDATA
inline	Identifies an inline or out-of-line link	inline (true|false)
role	Specifies the role of a remote link resource	role CDATA
show	Shows whether a link resource is displayed or processed	show (embed|replace|new)
steps	Specifies the number of steps that extended link group processing continues through other groups	steps CDATA
title	Specifies the title of a remote link resource	title CDATA
xml:attributes	Maps user-chosen attribute names for a linking element	xml:attributes CDATA
xml:link	Processes one or more XLink linking elements that follow.	xml:link CDATA

XML 1.0: THE XLINK PRODUCTIONS

❶

```
[1]    Locator ::= URI
                    | Connector ( XPointer | Name)
                    | URI Connector (XPointer | Name)
[2] Connector ::= '#' | '|'  ←❷
[3]       URI ::= URIchar*  ←❸
[4]     Query ::= 'XML-XPTR=' ( XPointer | Name)  ←❹
```

❶ Use the Locator production to write the link.
❷ The Connector symbol indicates the link-retrieval method.
❸ The URI specifies the resource that contains the link.
❹ The Query formulates a query to find an XPointer.

Using Inline vs. Out-of-Line Links

An inline link is a link specified within a linking element in the current document. It is considered to be a local resource of the link. Note that child elements are not considered part of the local resource; they are part of the link. On the other hand, an out-of-line link is *not* a local resource. The out-of-line link specifies the location of the link so that a target application can find it. However, both types of links are coded in the same way. Use the following attribute syntax to express whether a link is inline or out-of-line:

```
inline                  ('true' | 'false')
```

The value for an inline link is `true` (the default) and for an out-of-line link is `false`.

The HTML `A` element specifies an inline link because its attributes and their values are completely contained within, and therefore are dependent on, the `<A>` start tag. So, all simple links are inline links. On the other hand, an out-of-line link is completely outside the link element. Instead, it is in a document consisting of links only. When you have to change a link because one of its attribute values changed, you don't have to modify the document that refers to the link. Instead, you edit the document in which the links are stored. Out-of-line links are particularly useful when you work with documents that should not be edited, such as contracts and other similar legal documents, or those that cannot be edited, such as read-only Adobe Acrobat (`pdf`) files. Out-of-line links also lend themselves to use in extended link groups, which are discussed in Chapter 22.

TAKE NOTE

▶ CROSS-REFERENCING DOCUMENT INSTANCES

You can use individual document-instances to form a long document and ultimately to cross-reference the entire document. For example, a group co-authoring a business-plan proposal can split the document into standalone segments. Each member of the group works on a segment, checks it for accuracy, keeps a list of identifiers for the segment, and inserts identifiers that cross-reference other parts of the segment. He or she can insert `#PCDATA` placeholders for identifiers that cross-reference elements in other segments. When the segments are merged into the final document, the placeholders are converted to identifiers, the document is tested, and it is produced.

▶ USING HYTIME TO LINK IN SGML DOCUMENTS

HyTime, a standard that uses SGML-like code to insert `ID` and `IDREF` links to documents, works in about the same way as the placeholder methods discussed in the prior Take Note. However, when individuals work on segments of a document, they don't have to insert the placeholders; HyTime creates a temporary `IDREF` target within the segment. For more information about HyTime, read the online document "A Reader's Guide to the HyTime Standard" (**http://www.hytime.org/ papers/ htguide.html**). The paper "Internet and the Humanities: The Promises of Integrated Open Hypermedia (**http://www.nada.kth.se/cid/publikationer/cid_1. html**) discusses using SGML, HyTime, and DSSSL to create, link, and style documents.

CROSS-REFERENCE

In Chapter 9, you learn how to add attributes, attribute types, and default values to an XML DTD.

FIND IT ONLINE

Go to **http://www.cimi.org/products/tagging_guide/ tg5-4-5.htm** to read about SGML cross-referencing.

Listing 19-3: A SAMPLE INLINE LINK DECLARATION

```
<!ENTITY % link-semantics.att ←❶
   "inline          (true|false) ←❷    'true' ←❸
    role ←❹         CDATA              #IMPLIED"
>
```

❶ *Declare the* `link-semantics.att` *parameter entity.*
❷ *The inline attribute can have a value of* true *or* false.
❸ *The default value is* true.
❹ *The* role *attribute specifies the role of a remote link resource.*

Listing 19-4: A SIMPLE INLINE LINK DECLARATION

```
<!ENTITY % simple-link-semantics.att ←❶
   "inline            (true|false)             'true'"
>
                        ❷                        ❸
```

❶ *For a simple link, declare the* `simple-link-semantics.att`
  parameter entity.
❷ *The inline attribute can have a value of* true *or* false.
❸ *The default value is* true.

Listing 19-5: AN EXAMPLE OF OUT-OF-LINE LINKS

```
              ❶
<tracings xml:link="group"  ❷
   title="Trace" inline="false">
   <locator href="right_wing1.5" ←❸
❹→ role="criticism"/>
   <locator href="left_wing3.1"
       role="counter"/>
   <locator href="professor8.3"
       role="analysis"/>
   <locator href="spin_doctor2.2"
       role="spin"/>
   <locator href="extremist10.12"
       role="distort"/>
</tracings>
```

❶ *Declare a group of extended links.*
❷ *A value of* false *makes this an out-of-line link.*
❸ *The* locator *attribute specifies a URI.*
❹ *The* role *attribute specifies the role of a remote link resource.*

Listing 19-6: OUT-OF-LINE LINKS FOR A BOOK

```
               ❶
<book xml:link="group"        ❷
   title="Online Book" inline="false">
   <locator href="chap1.xml" ←❸
   ❹ title="Chapter 1"/>
   <locator href="chap2.xml"
       title="Chapter 2"/>
   <locator href="chap3.xml"
       title="Chapter 3"/>
   <locator href="chap4.xml"
       title="Chapter 4"/>
   <locator href="apxa.xml"
       title="Appendix A"/>
</book>
```

❶ *Declare a group of extended links.*
❷ *A value of* false *makes this an out-of-line link.*
❸ *The* locator *attribute specifies a URI.*
❹ *The* title *attribute specifies the title of a remote link resource.*

Using Link Semantics

L ink semantics are simply the unique terms that you use to describe your links, their attributes, and attribute values. For example, xml:link="simple", xml:link= "group", and inline="true" are all forms of link semantics in which each attribute and value has a distinct meaning. However, beyond the definition of these individual terms, the semantics change subtly: pairs of similar attribute names indicate major differences in how they are treated by XML parsers.

In XML, the location of link resources are signaled by slightly different attribute names. These name variations tell an XML parser what type of link it is processing. For example, XLink provides the role and content-role attributes. As you have learned in preceding tasks, the role attribute specifies the role of a remote link resource. The role attribute is a string that specifies the metadata of a link — the author, creation or edit date, comments, and even documentation of the link, for those who will edit the link in the future. The counterpart attribute name for local link resources is content-role. Each of these attributes uses the same syntax:

```
role        CDATA
content-role  CDATA
```

However, the name of each of the attributes tells the XML parser that it can find one link in an external document and the other link within the current document. The parser then uses the remaining information associated with the link to accurately process the link.

The attribute name for a document title also provides the same clue to the XML parser: title specifies the title of a remote link resource, and content-title names the title of a local link resource. Each of these attributes use the same syntax:

```
title        CDATA
content-title  CDATA
```

Once again, the difference in names is a signal to the XML parser. However, the current XLink working draft states that it does not require an application to use a title in a particular way.

TAKE NOTE

▶ TRAVERSING LINKS

An important term in the XLink language is traverse. When you click on a link or trigger it in some other way, the link is activated and you are accessing a resource. This entire process is called *traversing* the link.

▶ LEARNING ABOUT ONE-DIRECTIONAL AND MULTIDIRECTIONAL LINKING

Links in HTML and all simple links in XML operate in one direction — from the link to the link resource. XML links can also be *multidirectional*, which means that you can jump to several locations simultaneously via a single link. Note that multidirectional does *not* mean that you can jump from a link resource back to its link. With multidirectional linking, you can establish links throughout a document, and you can also associate several documents at once — using inline and out-of-line links.

CROSS-REFERENCE

In Chapter 10, you can learn how to use both parameter entities in your DTDs and general entities elsewhere.

FIND IT ONLINE

At **http://www.stg.brown.edu/~sjd/xlinkintro.html**, get an XLink briefing from one of its authors.

Listing 19-7: DECLARING A LOCAL ROLE AND TITLE

```
<!ENTITY % local-resource-semantics.att ◄①

  "content-role    CDATA      #IMPLIED ◄②

  content-title    CDATA      #IMPLIED"
                      ③
```

① *Declare the* `local-resource-semantics.att` *parameter entity.*
② *Specify the* `content-role` *attribute for a local resource.*
③ *Specify the* `content-title` *attribute for a local resource.*

Listing 19-8: AN EXAMPLE OF A LOCAL, SIMPLE LINK

```
<anchor xml:link="simple" ◄①

  content-title="Local Link Example"

  href="/r/abc.xml" ◄②

  show="new" content-role="Example">
  to show a simple link</anchor>
     ③                        ④
```

① *Specify a simple, local link.*
② *Add a relative URI.*
③ *Create a new link resource.*
④ *Specify the role of the local link.*

Listing 19-9: DECLARING A REMOTE ROLE AND TITLE

```
                        ①
<!ENTITY % remote-resource-semantics.att ②

  "role      CDATA                    #IMPLIED

  title      CDATA                    #IMPLIED

  show       (embed|replace|new) ③    #IMPLIED

  actuate    (auto|user)              #IMPLIED

  behavior   CDATA                    #IMPLIED"

>
```

① *Declare the* `remote-resource-semantics.att` *parameter entity.*
② *Specify the* `role` *attribute for a remote resource.*
③ *Specify the* `title` *attribute for a remote resource.*

Listing 19-10: AN EXAMPLE OF A REMOTE, SIMPLE LINK

```
<anchor xml:link="simple" ◄①

  title="Remote Link Example" ②

  href="http://www.eddygrp.com/r/abc.xml"

  show="new" role="Example">
  to show a simple link</anchor>
     ③                ④
```

① *Specify a simple, remote link.*
② *Add an absolute URI.*
③ *Create a new link resource.*
④ *Specify the role of the remote link.*

Specifying Types of Link Behaviors

The show and `actuate` attributes affect link behavior during traversal and can work in tandem. The current XLink working draft states, "Behavior focuses on what happens when the link is traversed, such as opening, closing, or scrolling windows or panes; displaying the data from various resources in various ways; testing, authenticating, or logging user and context information; or executing various programs.

The show attribute, which determines whether a link resource is displayed or processed, uses the following syntax:

```
show          (embed|replace|new)
```

The embed keyword embeds the new link resource in the current resource at the location at which traversal originated. The `replace` keyword replaces the current resource with the new link resource at the location at which traversal originated. The new keyword creates a new link resource without replacing the current resource.

The `actuate` attribute, which starts link traversal with or without a request, uses the following syntax:

```
actuate       (auto|user)
```

The auto keyword retrieves the specified linking resource when any resources of that link are encountered. The user keyword does not retrieve the specified linking resource until the user explicitly asks for it. If the value of `actuate` is auto, all auto

resources must be retrieved and are retrieved in the order in which they were specified. Note that Listing 19-11 appears in the current XLink working draft.

CROSS-REFERENCE

In Chapter 13, you can find out how to create an XML document in which you can insert links.

Listing 19-11: THE SHOW AND ACTUATE ATTRIBUTES

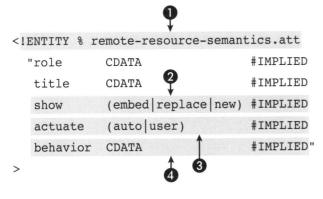

```
<!ENTITY % remote-resource-semantics.att

   "role       CDATA                   #IMPLIED
   title       CDATA                   #IMPLIED
   show        (embed|replace|new)     #IMPLIED
   actuate     (auto|user)             #IMPLIED
   behavior    CDATA                   #IMPLIED"

>
```

❶ *Enter the entity declaration.*
❷ *Present the* show *attribute and its list of values.*
❸ *Type the* actuate *attribute and its two value choices.*
❹ *Use the* behavior *attribute to specify other traversal instructions.*

Listing 19-12: AN EXAMPLE OF THE SHOW ATTRIBUTE

```
<saylink xml:link="simple" title="Work"
    href="http://www.twain.com/xml/dog.xml"
    show="new" ←❶
    content-role="author">Mark Twain ←❷
</saylink>
```

❶ *When you activate the link, the target resource appears in a new window.*
❷ *The role of this link is to specify the author's name.*

Listing 19-13: AN EXAMPLE OF THE SHOW AND ACTUATE ATTRIBUTES

```
<saylink xml:link="simple" title="Work"
    href="http://www.twain.com/xml/dog.xml"
    actuate="auto" show="replace" ←❷
    content-role="author">Mark Twain
</saylink>
```

❶ *The link is automatically activated.*
❷ *The resource is replaced with new information.*

Listing 19-14: A MAPPING EXAMPLE

```
<!ATTLIST TEXT-BOOK
    xml:link        CDATA   #FIXED      "simple"
    xml:attributes  CDATA   #FIXED
                    "title a-title role a-role"
>
```

❶ *The* title *attribute is mapped to the unique* a-title.
❷ *The* role *attribute is mapped to* a-role.

Personal Workbook

Q&A

1 What do *extended links* do?

_____

_____

_____

2 According to the W3C XLink working draft, what are the two categories of links?

_____

_____

_____

3 What attribute do you use to specify a link in an XML document?

_____

_____

_____

4 Which type of XML link is similar to links formed by the HTML A element?

_____

_____

_____

5 What is an *inline link*?

_____

_____

_____

6 What is an *out-of-line link*?

_____

_____

_____

7 How do you express that a link is inline or out-of-line?

_____

_____

_____

8 What title attribute do you use for a local link resource?

_____

_____

_____

ANSWERS: PAGE 463

EXTRA PRACTICE

1 Examples in this chapter include a link that refers to a Mark Twain quotation. Develop an XML DTD and document that includes the links with which you can link to other quotations and cite their authors.

2 Write a frequently-asked questions (FAQ) page. Next to each question, insert a link to its answer at the bottom of the current page.

3 For the FAQ page, modify the links so that each goes to a separate answer page at your Web site.

4 Create a Web page featuring a list of your favorite books. Include links to author bios and to an online bookstore from which others can order these titles.

5 For each item on a personal or business inventory list, write a link that jumps to an expanded description of the item.

REAL-WORLD APPLICATIONS

✔ Your company publishes a series of user guides. To publish the guides on the Web, write a Web page table of contents that lists and links to each chapter, each of which is composed of a set of XML pages.

✔ For the user guides in the previous exercise, write a Web page table of contents that lists and links to chapters, each of which is a paramter entity.

✔ You are a college professor who must research, write, and publish a series of papers. Prepare a DTD and a dummy document that includes links to footnotes, a bibliography, and external citations.

✔ You run an online catalog. Rather than present pages that show full-size slow-loading photographs of your goods, include thumbnail pictures that link to the full-size photographs.

Visual Quiz

How would you code the inline links on this Web page? (Hint: You can find many of the URLs in Chapter 11.)

_____

_____

_____

_____

_____

_____

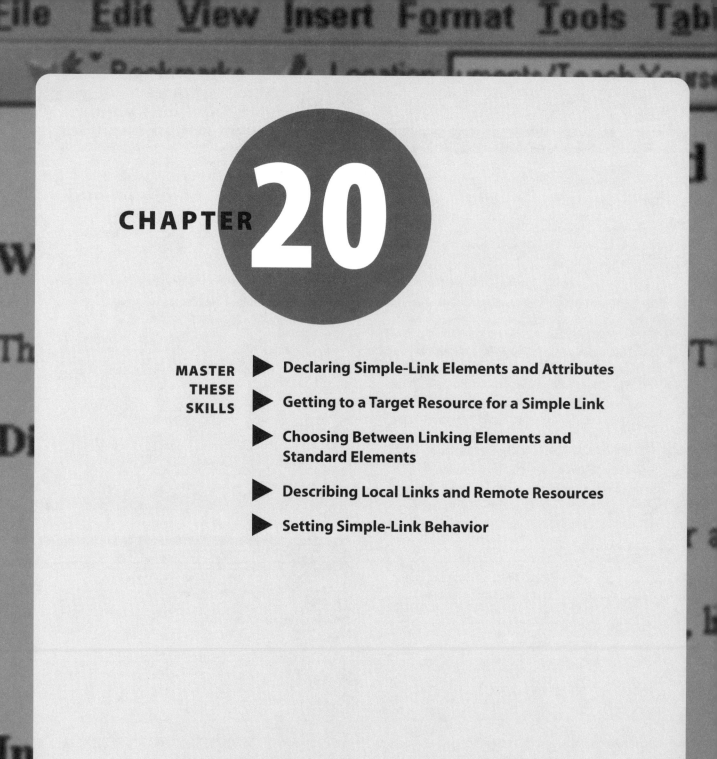

CHAPTER **20**

MASTER
THESE
SKILLS

▶ **Declaring Simple-Link Elements and Attributes**

▶ **Getting to a Target Resource for a Simple Link**

▶ **Choosing Between Linking Elements and Standard Elements**

▶ **Describing Local Links and Remote Resources**

▶ **Setting Simple-Link Behavior**

Using Simple Links

In this chapter, you learn more about using simple links. You can also use this information for the two other types of links: extended and extended link groups. The information here ranges from the beginning to the end of XML document creation—from the DTD with which you specify link-related attributes and values to the XML document that includes the links with which users will traverse target resources.

This chapter also features a continuing discussion on the advantages and disadvantages of using elements specifically dedicated to linking versus elements that serve a variety of purposes, including linking. Also throughout the chapter, you'll see how certain HTML attributes with which you are probably familiar compare with certain XLink counterparts. If you have a working knowledge of HTML, these comparisons will enable your XML erudition.

In the first task in this chapter, you learn how to declare XLink-related attributes and values in an XML DTD. The first task also reviews the element types that allow the use of linking attributes and those that do not. The task ends with a list of characteristics of a simple link,

according to the current W3C XLink working draft.

In the second task, you'll find out more about the use of URIs in forming links to local and remote target resources. Also included is a continuation of the discussion about building links within elements dedicated to linking or within standard all-purpose elements.

The third task is dedicated to the discussion of building links by using elements dedicated to linking versus using all-purpose elements. In addition, you'll find out the two ways of using the `xml:link` and `xml:attributes` attributes in your DTDs and XML documents.

The following task expands on the use of the `content-role`, `role`, `content-title`, and `title` attributes that were introduced in Chapter 19. You'll also learn why it is important to include even optional link attributes in your link statements.

The final task in the chapter covers the `behavior` attribute, which provides instructions for traversal between the link and the target resource. Also included in this task is a discussion of using entities in DTDs to include commonly used attribute declarations.

Declaring Simple-Link Elements and Attributes

Before you can use any type of link in an XML document, you must follow two steps in the DTD: declare an element and then specify the type of link and other linking characteristics in the element's attribute list.

To declare an element that can create simple links, use the following syntax:

```
<!ELEMENT simp_link ANY>
```

Remember that the ANY keyword indicates that the element can contain any type of content — both markup and character data.

Then, declare an attribute list for the element. Be sure to include an xml:link attribute value and a href attribute is required:

```
<!ATTLIST simp_link
     xml:link    CDATA    #FIXED "simple"
```

The xml:link declaration ensures that only simple links are allowed within any document associated with the DTD.

You can list other attributes as you would for any other element. Then, signal the end of the declaration by using a greater-than (>) symbol. For example:

```
        href       CDATA           #REQUIRED
        id         ID              #REQUIRED
        inline     (true|false)    "true"
        role       CDATA           #IMPLIED
        title      CDATA           #IMPLIED
>
```

As you read through the rest of this chapter, you'll find examples of element declarations in XML DTDs and links in XML documents on the facing pages.

Should you declare elements specifically for links or should you declare the xml:link attribute in selected elements? In most cases, it's up to you. The reasons behind your decisions don't relate to the XML specification or the current XLink working draft. For example, you can choose to dedicate specific elements to linking in order to document or organize your DTD. On the other hand, if you don't declare linking elements, you have to make sure that *all* the elements that might eventually contain links include the xml:link attribute and the most appropriate attribute value. With very long and complex DTDs, you might forget.

XML's contentspec production sets the allowable types of content for elements that you declare in an XML DTD. You can choose from one of the two following element types:

▶ Use the EMPTY keyword to specify an empty element. Remember that an empty element can contain attributes — especially links. So, you can use an empty element to contain a link. Just make sure to include xml:link in the element's attribute list.

▶ Use the ANY keyword to specify an element with any content, including a link. Again, declare the xml:link attribute in the attribute list.

CROSS-REFERENCE

In Chapter 1, you can learn about the differences between character data and markup in XML documents.

FIND IT ONLINE

At **http://www.texcel.no/se97talk.htm**, see why you should care about document management system links.

Simple-Link Characteristics

Simple links in XML must have the following characteristics, as stated in the XLink working draft:

▶ The link is expressed at one of its ends (similar to the A element in some documents)

▶ Users can only initiate travel from that end to the other.

▶ The link's effect on windows, frames, go-back lists, stylesheets in use, and so on is mainly determined by browsers, not by the link itself. For example, traversal of A links normally replaces the current view, perhaps with a user option to open a new window.

▶ The link goes to only one destination (although a server may have great freedom in finding or dynamically creating that destination).

❶ *The* xml:link *attribute specifies a simple link.*
❷ *A link must include an absolute or relative URI.*
❸ *By default, the link must be inline.*
❹ *The declaration allows for an internal or external role or title.*

Listing 20-2: ADDING LINK ATTRIBUTES TO A TYPICAL ELEMENT

```
<!ELEMENT text ANY>
<!ATTLIST text
  xml:link       (simple|extended)      "simple"
  href           CDATA                  #REQUIRED
  id             ID                     #REQUIRED
  name           CDATA                  #IMPLIED
  language       (en|fr|es)             "en"
  inline         (true|false)           "true"
  content-role   CDATA                  #IMPLIED
  content-title  CDATA                  #IMPLIED
  show           (embed|replace|new)    #IMPLIED
  actuate        (auto|user)            #IMPLIED
  behavior       CDATA                  #IMPLIED
>
```

❶ *By default,* xml:link *is a simple link.*
❷ content-role *and* content-title *refer to the link.*
❸ *Both* show *and* actuate *are optional attributes.*
❹ *The* behavior *attribute contains instructions.*

Listing 20-1: A SIMPLE LINKING ELEMENT AND ITS ATTRIBUTES

```
<!ELEMENT anchor ANY>
<!ATTLIST anchor
  xml:link       CDATA                  #FIXED "simple"
  href           CDATA                  #REQUIRED
  id             ID                     #REQUIRED
  inline         (true|false)           "true"
  role           CDATA                  #IMPLIED
  title          CDATA                  #IMPLIED
  content-role   CDATA                  #IMPLIED
  content-title  CDATA                  #IMPLIED
  show           (embed|replace|new)    "replace"
  actuate        (auto|user)            #IMPLIED
>
```

291

Getting to a Target Resource for a Simple Link

As you learned in the prior chapter, you can build a simple link to a target resource by using two types of URIs. You can enter an absolute URI to link to a remote or local resource. Remember that the absolute URI contains the complete address of the target resource starting with the protocol and ending with an extended link or extended pointer. For example:

```
http://www.sample.com/docs/x.doc#ID(x135)
```

You can also jump to a local resource by entering a relative URI. However, a relative URI does not contain all the address information of an absolute URI. The only requirement for linking success is that you provide enough information to get to the target resource. At its smallest, a relative URI is composed of the fragment identifier (#) and an extended pointer. (For more on extended pointers, see Chapter 23.) For example:

```
#ID(x135)
```

As the target resource gets farther away from the current document (in another file, in another sub-folder or folder, on another drive, on another computer in a network, and so on), you add another piece of information to the URI — until the address is complete and absolute. For example:

```
x.doc#ID(x135)
    or
docs/x.doc#ID(x135)
```

Comparing the show Attribute with the HTML TARGET Attribute

When you compare XML (or XLink or XPointer) with HTML, you will find many similarities beyond their relationships as SGML-based markup languages. For example, the XLink show attribute serves approximately the same purpose as the TARGET attribute in HTML — although show provides fewer choices as well as one important new choice.

The TARGET attribute controls the window into which a new page is loaded. TARGET offers a choice of five values: *window*, _blank, _parent, _self, _top. The *window* value represents the name of a window into which the page is loaded. The other four values are reserved keywords that load the page into a blank window, the parent window that is one level above the current window, the current window, or the original window at the site, respectively.

XLink's show attribute controls the location and processing of a link resource (the other end of a link). You can choose from three possible values: replace, new, and embed. The replace keyword replaces the current resource with the new link resource in the same way a new page is loaded into the current window (i.e., TARGET's _self keyword). The new keyword creates a new link resource without replacing the current resource (i.e., the _blank keyword). The embed keyword is entirely new. It embeds the new link resource in the current resource; a link is maintained between the link resource and the application in which it was developed.

CROSS-REFERENCE

In Chapter 6, you can learn how to plan and outline DTDs for single documents and document sets.

FIND IT ONLINE

For several pages of XML linking resources, go to **http://www.oasis-open.org/cover/xll.html**.

Listing 20-3: A SIMPLE LINK TO A LOCAL RESOURCE

```
<linker xml:link="simple" ❶
href="/hello.xml" ❷
title="greeting" show="replace">
Howdy</linker>
❹                              ❸
```

❶ Specify that the link is simple.
❷ Enter a relative URI for a file in the same folder.
❸ The target resource replaces the content of the current window.
❹ Enter the text that indicates the link location.

Listing 20-4: ANOTHER SIMPLE LINK TO A LOCAL RESOURCE

```
<linker xml:link="simple" ❶
href="/hi/hello.xml" ❷
title="greeting" show="replace"
actuate="user"> ❸
Howdy</linker>
        ❹
```

❶ Specify that the link is simple.
❷ Enter a relative URI for a file in a different folder.
❸ The user must start the linking process.
❹ Conclude the link with an end tag.

Listing 20-5: A SIMPLE LINK TO A REMOTE RESOURCE

```
          ❶
<linker xml:link="simple"        ❷
href="http://www.eddygrp.com/hi/hello.xml"
title="greeting" show="replace" ❸
actuate="auto"> ❹
Howdy</linker>
```

❶ Specify that the link is simple.
❷ Enter an absolute URI for a remote file.
❸ The target resource appears in the current window.
❹ The linking process is automatic.

Listing 20-6: ANOTHER SIMPLE LINK TO A REMOTE RESOURCE

```
          ❶
<picture xml:link="simple" ❷
href="http://www.eddygrp.com/figs/ace.jpg"
id="acecard" show="new" ❸
inline="true"/> ❹
```

❶ Specify that the link is simple.
❷ Enter an absolute URI for a remote file.
❸ The target resource appears in a new window.
❹ End the empty element with a slash and greater-than symbol.

Choosing Between Linking Elements and Standard Elements

As you know, simple links and the HTML A element are coded in approximately the same way. For example, a typical HTML A element statement looks like this:

```
<A href="http://www.sample.com/note003.xml"
title="Citation 3" target="_blank">
The Adventures of Tom Sawyer</A>
```

Its counterpart XML link code looks like this:

```
<lelem xml:link="simple" role="endnote"
href="http://www.sample.com/note003.xml"
title="note003" show="new">
The Adventures of Tom Sawyer</lelem>
```

The HTML A element is dedicated to linking: It serves no other purpose. In HTML, you *must* construct links by using the A element (and to a limited extent, the LINK element) whose attributes are also predefined for you. However, when you develop an XML DTD, you have a choice: You can declare elements that link and perform no other function — in the same tradition as A — or you can add the xml:link attribute and its values to any element that may ever include a link.

Declaring XLink attributes for an element means that one instance of the element might include a link and the next instance might not. For example, look at these two coded paragraphs in an XML document:

```
<para xml:link="simple" role="endnote"
href="http://www.sample.com/note003.xml"
title="note003" show="new">
The Adventures of Tom Sawyer</para>
```

```
<para>When he moved to Hartford, in an
area in which other writers and artists
lived, Twain lived in a wonderful house.
</para>
```

Because of the inclusion of the xml:link attribute, the purpose of the first para element will be quite obvious to those who will maintain the document in the future. Of course, remember that you can (and should) always add comments throughout your documents.

Associating the xml:link and xml:attributes Attributes

The current XLink working draft states that you can associate the attributes xml:link and xml:attributes with your documents in two distinct ways. The first method is to declare xml:link and xml:attributes and their values in the DTD; the second is to include them in the link statements in your current document. Using xml:link as an example, say you include the following declaration in a DTD:

```
xml:link    CDATA    #FIXED    "simple"
```

Because of the presence of the #FIXED keyword, this declaration states that all xml:links *must* be simple ones: they are "fixed" as simple. If all xml:links are simple, there is no reason to include them in link statements. Conversely, if you include an xml:link attribute and value in the XML document, the working draft states that the attribute-list declaration is not needed in the DTD.

CROSS-REFERENCE

Chapter 9 instructs you on how to declare attributes, their types, values, and choices of values.

FIND IT ONLINE

The site at **http://www.cen.com/ng-html/xml/xml-timeline.html** provides a detailed XML timeline.

Listing 20-7: A SIMPLE LINKING ELEMENT AND ITS ATTRIBUTES

```
<anchor id="qst991203"  ①
href="http://www.sample.com/quest.xml"  ②
title="question" show="replace">
Today's Question:          ④
Why is the sky blue?
</anchor>
```

① The identifier allows an extended pointer to point to this link.
② The absolute link implies a remote target resource.
③ The title attribute names the target resource.
④ The target resource replaces the current resource.

Listing 20-8: A SIMPLE LINK ADDED TO AN ELEMENT

```
<text id="para503" xml:link="simple"
href="/names/adams.xml" show="new"
title="prez">The Second</text>
```

▲ The xml:link attribute is in this example but not in the prior one. Note also that you can place the attributes in any order, and you can break the lines into long or short lengths.

Listing 20-9: AN EMPTY ELEMENT WITH A SIMPLE LINK

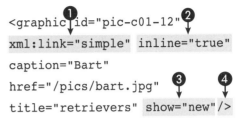

```
<graphic id="pic-c01-12"  ① ②
xml:link="simple" inline="true"
caption="Bart"
href="/pics/bart.jpg"      ③   ④
title="retrievers" show="new"/>
```

① The xml:link attribute specifies a simple link.
② The value of the inline attribute is inline.
③ The end of an empty element is marked with />.
④ The show attribute creates a new resource.

Listing 20-10: SIMPLE LINKS TO DESCRIPTIONS

```
<project id="991213001" xml:link="simple"
    href="/projects/991213001.xml"
    show="replace">12-13-99_001
</project>
<project id="991213003" xml:link="simple"
    href="/projects/991213003.xml"
    show="replace">12-13-99_003
</project>
<project id="991215003" xml:link="simple"
    href="/projects/991215003.xml"
    show="replace">12-15-99_003
</project>
```

▲ These links jump to documents that describe projects. The links now display a project code but can show a summary or lengthy and detailed narrative. When a project is completed, its link can be moved to another "Done" document.

Describing Local Links and Remote Resources

Chapter 19 introduced you to the `content-role`, `role`, `content-title`, and `title` attributes, which pass information about links or target elements to the application processing the XML document — in the same way that a processing instruction works. A side benefit of using these optional attributes is that they provide metadata or comment information to individuals viewing the document. Although these attributes have similar meanings, the `content-role`/`role` and `content-title`/`title` pairs are not completely in sync because links and target resources are completely different objects.

The `content-role` attribute provides information about how to process the content of the link (that is the local resource) to the processing application.

The `role` attribute provides information about how to process the target resource at the other end of a link to the processing application. For example, `role` can describe how to process the target resource when the link activates the resource.

The `content-title` attribute provides title information for the local resource. Processing applications are not required to process the title information in any way.

The `title` attribute provides title information for the target resource. Processing applications are not required to process the title information in any way.

TAKE NOTE

LEARNING ABOUT LOCATORS

A *locator* is the character-string part of a linking element. It is probably an abbreviation of Uniform Resource Locator (URL), which is now incorporated into Uniform Resource Identifier (URI). To find the locator in a linking element, look for the characters within the quotation marks or single quote marks.

INCLUDING ATTRIBUTES THAT ARE NOT REQUIRED IN LINK STATEMENTS

Earlier in this chapter, you learned how to declare link elements in an XML DTD. Look at the following segment of link-related attributes in a DTD:

```
<!ELEMENT jump ANY>
<!ATTLIST jump
 xml:link (simple|extended)  "simple"
 href            CDATA       #REQUIRED
 id              ID          #REQUIRED
 show (embed|replace|new)    "replace"
 actuate    (auto|user)      #IMPLIED
```

Only two of the attributes, `href` and `id`, are required. The other two give default values. A "non-required" attribute need not appear when its element is used in a document: after all, it is optional. And you can accept a default value without entering it. However, there is no reason why you should not incorporate optional attributes and default values in your documents. One advantage of entering optional attributes and their values is that those who maintain your documents in the future will understand your code. Also, some XML processors and target applications need to process both required and optional attributes and values.

CROSS-REFERENCE

In Chapter 11, you can find out how to modify a DTD that you find online or stored elsewhere.

FIND IT ONLINE

At **http://www.xml.com/xml/pub/98/06/xlink/av.html**, link to many XLink articles, guides, and columns.

Listing 20-11: A SIMPLE LINK WITH A TITLE AND ROLE

```
<meta id="infoses" xml:link="simple"
href="/bios/seddy.xml" show="replace"
content-title="author"
content-role="biographical information">
Sandra E. Eddy
</meta>
```

❶ Specify a simple link.
❷ Enter a local URI.
❸ Provide a title for the link and its element.
❹ Specify the role of the link.

Listing 20-12: A SIMPLE LINK WITH A TITLE AND ROLE

```
<meta id="tyxcyc" xml:link="simple"
href="/grpinfo/tyxcyc.xml"
show="replace"
content-title="editcycle"
content-role="Teach Yourself XML
editorial cycle"
</meta>
```

▲ This occurrence of the meta element and its link provides information about an editing cycle. The target resource could include an annotated outline or a list of landmark dates.

Listing 20-13: A SIMPLE LINK WITH TWO TITLES AND TWO ROLES

```
<meta id="infoses" xml:link="simple"
href="/bios/seddy.xml" show="replace"
content-title="author link"
content-role="link to bio"
title="author"
role="biographical information">
Sandra E. Eddy
</meta>
```

❶ The content-title attribute labels the link.
❷ The content-role attribute instructs about the link.
❸ The title attribute labels the target resource.
❹ The role attribute specifies the role of the target.

Listing 20-14: A SIMPLE LINK WITH TWO TITLES AND TWO ROLES

```
<project id="991213001" xml:link="simple"
   href="/projects/991213001.xml"
   content-title="991213001 project link"
   content-role="link to a project file"
   title="Project 12-13-99_001 Info"
   role="project information">
   show="replace">12-13-99_001
</project>
```

▲ This example demonstrates the use of titles and role instructions for a link and its target resource.

Setting Simple-Link Behavior

The behavior attribute is another relative of `role`, `content-role`, `title`, and `content-title`. However, `behavior` provides information and instructions about the traversal between the link and the target resource to the XML parser or other processing application. According to the current XLink working draft, "behavior focuses on what happens when the link is traversed, such as opening, closing, or scrolling windows or panes; displaying the data from various resources in various ways; testing, authenticating, or logging user and context information; or executing various programs."

The XLink working draft also discusses the fact that link behavior during traversal is also closely connected with link formatting before, during, and after traversal. The best example of this is from HTML's `BODY` element. `BODY` controls the look of the entire HTML document, and three of its attributes — `LINK`, `ALINK`, and `VLINK` — set the color of links before they have been clicked on, as they are clicked on, and after they have been visited, respectively. Other traversal-related XLink attributes are `actuate` and `show`, which were summarized in the prior chapter and will be covered in more detail in the following chapter.

Using Entities to Define Much-Used Attribute Lists

As you browse through the HTML 4.0 element declarations in other chapters in this book, you probably notice the frequent use of entities within attribute lists. If you look at the HTML 4.0 DTD, you'll find pages of entities that contain attribute declarations or combine related elements.

The entities in the DTD contain commonly-used attribute-list declarations so that they don't have to be entered each time an element is declared. One of the most common attributes is `%attrs;`, which contains three other entities—`%coreattrs;`, `%i18n;`, and `%events;`. Each of those popular entities contains several attribute declarations. For example, `%coreattrs;` contains four attribute declarations that are widely used throughout HTML. The core attributes are `id` (to associate an identifier with an HTML element), `class` (to specify a character or special character), `style` (to associate a style sheet), and `title` (to provide a title).

When you create your own DTDs, you can also use entities to save yourself keystrokes as well as document length. During the design or early-development phase, evaluate your planned elements. If you identify groups of attributes that will be used within several element declarations, include them in entities rather than entering them over and over. Common attributes typically include identifiers, names, titles, and language. If you use scripts to make your documents dynamic, add some scripting attributes, too.

CROSS-REFERENCE

Chapter 12 discusses how to parse a document and all its components, including links of all types.

FIND IT ONLINE

Read an overview by an XLink coauthor at **http://www.oasis-open.org/cover/xlinkMaler980402.html**.

Listing 20-15: A LINK WITH SEVERAL LINKING ATTRIBUTES

```
<linker xml:link="simple"
href="/hello.xml"
content-title="Hello Link"
content-role="linking to hello file"
title="greeting" show="replace"
role="display hello file">
Howdy</linker>
```
❶ Label the link and its element.
❷ Instruct about link processing.
❸ Label the target resource.
❹ Specify the role of the target resource.

Listing 20-16: ANOTHER LINK WITH SEVERAL LINKING ATTRIBUTES

```
<para xml:link="simple"
href="http://www.sample.com/note003.xml"
title="Go to an Endnote"
role="link to endnote"
content-title="An Endnote"
content-role="display endnote"
show="new">
The Adventures of Tom Sawyer</para>
```
❶ Label the target resource.
❷ Specify the role of the target resource.
❸ Label the link and its element.
❹ Instruct about link processing.

Listing 20-17: AN EMPTY ELEMENT WITH LINK TITLE AND ROLE

```
<picture xml:link="simple"
href="http://www.eddygrp.com/figs/ace.jpg"
content-title="Link to the Ace Picture"
content-role="link to the ace picture"
id="acecard" show="new"
inline="true"/>
```
❶ Label the link and its element.
❷ Instruct about link processing.

Listing 20-18: AN EMPTY ELEMENT WITH LINK, TRAVERSAL, AND RESOURCE ROLES

```
<picture xml:link="simple"
href="http://www.eddygrp.com/figs/ace.jpg"
content-title="Link to the Ace Picture"
content-role="link: ace picture"
behavior="load: ace.jpg"
title="The Ace"
role="show: ace.jpg"
id="acecard" show="new"
inline="true"/>
```
❶ Send a processing instruction about the link.
❷ Send a processing instruction about traversal.
❸ Send a processing instruction about the target resource.

Personal Workbook

Q&A

1 What two steps do you need to do to use any type of link in an XML document?

_____

_____

_____

2 What does the ANY keyword mean in an element declaration?

_____

_____

_____

3 What attribute is always required in an attribute list for a linking element?

_____

_____

_____

4 Does a simple link ever traverse from the target resource to the link?

_____

_____

5 Can a simple link ever go to more than one destination?

_____

_____

_____

6 What are the two ways that you can associate the xml:link attribute with a document?

_____

_____

_____

7 What does the #FIXED keyword indicate?

_____

_____

_____

8 What does the behavior attribute do?

_____

_____

_____

ANSWERS: PAGE 464

EXTRA PRACTICE

1 Go online and find XLink papers written by Eve Maler and Steve DeRose, the coauthors of XLink.

2 Go online and get a copy of the XLink working draft. Find and read the section about locator syntax.

3 Design and construct an online greeting card that displays a popup message in a new window.

4 Write a timeline of important events in your life. In a separate document, create a separate timeline of the important worldwide events that occurred during your lifetime. Add links between your personal timeline and the world-events timeline.

5 Write a grocery list. Link each item on the list with its aisle in your supermarket. When the aisle number displays, keep both the grocery list and aisle number onscreen.

REAL-WORLD APPLICATIONS

✔ Research and write a paper on your favorite subject. Include footnotes. Then, construct links between locations in the paper and footnotes. Make sure that the page layout includes room for footnotes at the bottom of each page and that footnotes are in a font that is at least two points smaller than body text.

✔ You have decided to help a relative who is writing a family history, which includes separate biography files for every family member. Plan and construct a family tree with links to the biography files.

✔ In Chapter 19, you worked on a series of troubleshooting guides. For each document, create an index with links to the actual page on which the indexed item appears.

Visual Quiz

How would you create this table of links to nine pages?

_____

_____

_____

_____

_____

_____

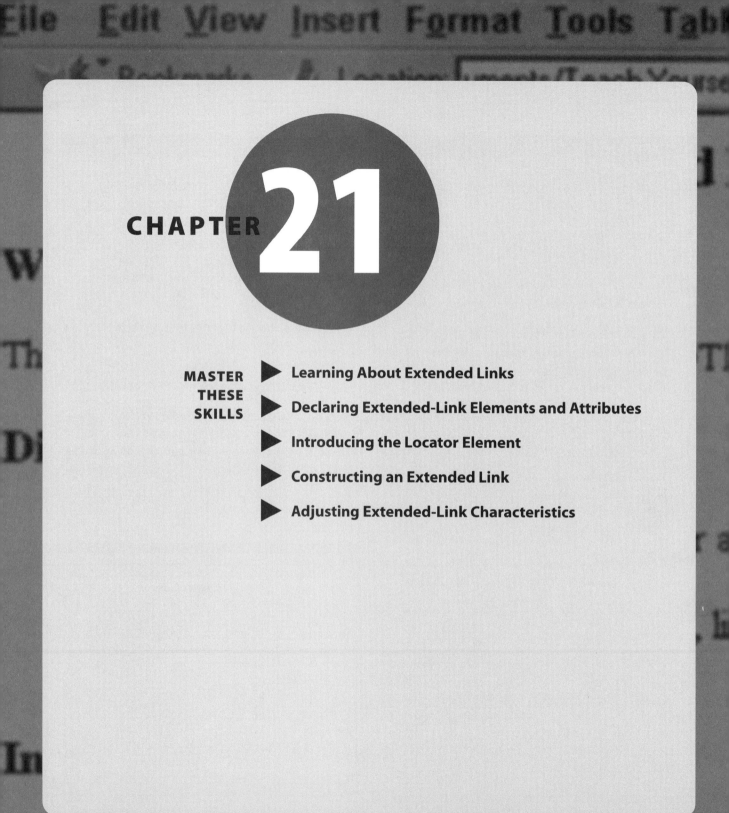

CHAPTER 21

MASTER
THESE
SKILLS

▶ Learning About Extended Links

▶ Declaring Extended-Link Elements and Attributes

▶ Introducing the Locator Element

▶ Constructing an Extended Link

▶ Adjusting Extended-Link Characteristics

Using Extended Links

In the prior chapter, you found out how to use the simple link, which is very similar to the HTML A element. Use a simple link to link to a single target resource in the current document or in a remote document. As you know, XML's simple links include new and sophisticated attributes that expand upon and enhance the power of your links. Now, it's time to go to a higher level of link. This chapter covers extended links, which enables a user to use a link to choose from several locations. The starting point of the link might be a drop-down list or a pop-up menu.

An extended link is made up of a parent element and one or more child elements, which are nested within the parent. These child elements, known as locator elements, contain the link, target resource information, and other attributes. The parent element, known as the extended element, serves two purposes: it contains the locator elements and its attributes can set characteristics of the entire extended link. The first task in this chapter discusses and demonstrates the extended element-locator element structure.

Before you include an extended link in an XML document, you must declare both the extended element and the locator element and list their attributes. In the second task, you will find out about these element and attribute-list declarations. The task also includes a table that lists all the linking attributes that are supported within each XLink link type.

The third task discusses the locator element and its attributes. Along the way, you will find out why certain linking attributes are supported and others are not—for both the locator element and the extended-element parent. Also included are the rules for designated resources, which is part of the XLink working draft. The fourth task demonstrates how to build an extended link and examines multidirectional linking. The final task discusses how the show and actuate attributes work under extended links.

In addition, throughout the chapter, you will find many examples illustrating the use of extended links.

Learning About Extended Links

As you learned in Chapter 20, a simple link in XML includes two components: the linking element and the target resource. The linking element is made up of an element, a link attribute (which includes the URI of the target resource), other optional linking attributes, and other attributes. The target resource, either local or remote, is composed of the information that will be displayed or processed when the linking element is activated. An extended link is structured in a different way: The extended element encloses one or more nested locator elements using the following structure:

```
<extended_element linking_attributes
    other_attributes>
<locator element URI
    linking_attributes other_attributes/>
<locator element URI
    linking_attributes other_attributes/>
<locator element URI
    linking_attributes other_attributes/>
<locator element URI
    linking_attributes other_attributes/>
</extended_element>
```

Notice that the extended element itself does not include a URI but can incorporate optional linking attributes and other attributes. The locator elements are the home of the URI. In addition, each of the locator elements can hold other linking and non-linking attributes. This nested extended-element and locator-element(s) structure allows for multiple links.

It's important to note that both the extended element and locator element can contain many of the same linking and nonlinking attributes. If you create a list of locator elements, each of which will contain the same attribute having the same value, you can usually move the attribute and its value into the extended element start tag. The nested locator elements will inherit the attributes and values of their parent extended element.

Noticing the Fluid XML Technologies

At the time of this writing, XML 1.0 is an official W3C recommendation. As you will learn in Part 5, CSS2 (for cascading style sheets) is also a W3C recommendation. According to W3C, a recommendation is "a stable document and may be used as reference material or cited as a normative reference from another document."

Most of the other technologies related to XML are at various levels of development and have not reached the recommendation stage. For example, XSL is still a future style sheet standard, which is currently at the working draft stage. XLink is a working draft, and XPointer, which is covered in Chapter 24, is also a working draft. According to W3C, a working draft is "a draft document and may be updated, replaced, or obsoleted by other documents at any time. It is inappropriate to use W3C Working Drafts as reference material or to cite them as other than 'work in progress.'" In fact, some of the topics in working drafts are absent: they will be included in a later draft.

CROSS-REFERENCE

Chapter 2 reviews an XML document and discusses the role that internal and external DTDs play.

FIND IT ONLINE

To read about active links, go to **http://nestroy. wi-inf.uni-essen.de/Forschung/Publikationen/ WWW7/**.

Listing 21-1: AN EXAMPLE OF AN EXTENDED LINK

```
<messages xml:link="extended"   ①
                    ②  inline="true">
  <locator href="adams001.txt"
                  role="premise"/>
  <locator href="jefferson001.txt"
                  role="reply"/>   ③
  <locator href="adams002.txt"
                  role="response"/>
</messages>   ④
```

① *Define the extended link.*
② *Specify that this is an inline link.*
③ *Add empty locator elements and URIs.*
④ *Conclude the extended link with an end tag.*

Listing 21-2: ANOTHER EXAMPLE OF AN EXTENDED LINK

```
<farmer xml:link="extended"   ①
                    ②  inline="true">
  <locator href="plowman.doc"   ③
                  title="plowman"/>   ④
  <locator href="sodbuster.doc"
                  title="sodbuster"/>
  <locator href="yeoman.doc"
                  role="yeoman"/>
</farmer>
```

① *Define the extended link.*
② *Specify that this is an inline link.*
③ *Insert a locator element and a URI.*
④ *Provide the title for the target resource.*

Listing 21-3: AN EXAMPLE OF AN IN-LINE EXTENDED LINK

```
<extended xml:link="extended"   ①
  inline="true" show="replace"   ③
Biographies of Famous Composers   ②
  <locator title="Bach" href="bach.xml"/>
  <locator title="Brahms"
     href="brahms.xml"/>
</extended>   ④
```

① *Define the extended link.*
② *Specify that this is in-line link.*
③ *Display the target resource in the current window.*
④ *Add empty locator elements and relative URIs.*

Listing 21-4: AN EDITED EXAMPLE OF AN IN-LINE EXTENDED LINK

```
<extended inline="true"   ①
     xml:link="extended" show="new"   ②
title="Biographies of Famous Composers"   ③
content-role="load file">
  <locator title="Bach" href="bach.xml"
    ④  behavior="sound: bach.au"/>
  <locator title="Brahms"
     href="brahms.xml"
    ④  behavior="sound: brahms.au"/>
  </extended>
```

① *Define the extended link.*
② *Display the target resource in a new window.*
③ *Move the title to a* title *attribute.*
④ *In each locator element, add sound-file* behavior.

Declaring Extended-Link Elements and Attributes

In Chapter 20, you learned that before you can use a link in an XML document, you must edit its DTD — to declare linking attributes under elements that will serve as linking elements. First, make sure that the element declaration is included. Then, specify the type of link and other linking characteristics in the element's attribute list. Whether a link is simple or extended, use the following element declaration:

```
<!ELEMENT ext_link ANY>
    or
<!ELEMENT graf EMPTY>
```

Then, declare an attribute list for the element, and be sure to include an xml:link attribute value:

```
xml:link    CDATA    #FIXED    "extended"
```

Remember that the attribute list for the extended element enclosing extended links does *not* include a href attribute. The attribute list of the locator element, which is the child of the extended element, takes care of that.

You can list other attributes as you would for any other element — but make sure that you include a set of link-related attributes. Note that all the following attributes are optional: You need not include them for a particular element.

```
inline          (true|false)        "true"
content-role    CDATA               #IMPLIED
content-title   CDATA               #IMPLIED
role            CDATA               #IMPLIED
```

```
title           CDATA                   #IMPLIED
show            (embed|replace|new)     "new"
actuate         (auto|user)             "user"
behavior        CDATA                   #IMPLIED
```

However, as Chapter 20 states, it's wise to add all optional XLink attributes to your documents to help certain processing applications and to provide informal comments for future maintainers of this DTD.

As you learned earlier in this task, not every type of link supports every linking attribute. Table 21-1 lists each element type and linking attribute. A *yes* in a table cell indicates that a particular type supports a particular linking attribute. A *no* indicates that the type does not support the attribute.

TAKE NOTE

ADDING CAPABILITIES TO EXTENDED LINKS

Extended links have all the capabilities of simple links plus four more, as stated in the current XLink working draft:

▶ Enabling outgoing links in documents that cannot be modified to add an inline link
▶ Creating links to and from resources in formats with no native support for embedded links (such as most multimedia formats)
▶ Applying and filtering sets of relevant links on demand
▶ Enabling other hypermedia capabilities

CROSS-REFERENCE
In Chapter 3, you can find out about entering proper XML declarations and supported characters.

FIND IT ONLINE
Review an XML-compliant DTD at **http://www. oasis-open.org/cover/xmlspec-19980323-dtd.txt**.

Table 21-1: SUPPORTED LINKING ATTRIBUTES FOR LINK ELEMENT TYPES

Link Type Attribute	simple	extended	locator	group	document
actuate	yes	yes	yes	no	no
behavior	yes	yes	yes	no	no
content-role	yes	yes	no	no	no
content-title	yes	yes	no	no	no
href	yes	no	yes	no	yes
inline	yes	yes	no	no	no
role	yes	yes	yes	no	no
show	yes	yes	yes	no	no
steps	no	no	no	yes	no
title	yes	yes	yes	no	no
xml:link	yes	yes	yes	yes	yes

Listing 21-5: A DECLARATION FOR AN EXTENDED-LINK ELEMENT

```
<!ELEMENT multilnks ANY> ❶

<!ATTLIST multilnks
  xml:link ◀❷    CDATA      #FIXED   "extended" ❸
  inline          (true|false)        'true'
  role            CDATA              #IMPLIED
  title           CDATA              #IMPLIED
  show            CDATA     ❹▶       #IMPLIED
  actuate         CDATA              #IMPLIED
>
```

❶ An extended linking element does not have to be named extended.
❷ Add an xml:link attribute.
❸ The value for an extended link is "extended".
❹ The remaining attributes are optional.

Listing 21-6: AN EXAMPLE OF AN EXTENDED LINK

```
<multilnks xml:link="extended" ◀❶
      inline="true" show="new"> ❷
  <locator href="home.xml"
           title="Home Page"/>
  <locator href="sitemap.xml"
           title="Site Map"/>                ◀❸
  <locator href="copyrt.xml"
           title="Copyright Page"/>
</multilnks> ◀❹
```

❶ Specify the extended link.
❷ Open each target resource in a new window.
❸ Specify a set of locator elements.
❹ End the extended link.

Introducing the Locator Element

In the previous chapter, you learned that the locator is the name for the address string that is within the URI and that is enclosed within the quotation marks or single quote marks. Obviously, it follows that the locator element might be a good identifier for an element that includes a URI.

As you learned in the first task of this chapter, an extended-link element is actually a shell that contains one or more locator elements, each of which define a link and target resource. The set of locator elements is nested within their parent extended element start tag and end tag. Since the locator-element set is associated with a single starting point, it should link to related target resources. As you can see in Table 21-1, extended and locator elements share many linking attributes. However, each of these elements supports some linking attributes that are not supported by the other. For example:

▶ Extended elements do not include links, so they do not need nor support the use of the `href` attribute. However, locator elements do support `href`.

▶ An extended element should not contain a mix of inline and out-of-line locators. Therefore, a locator element should not support the `inline` attribute. Because the parent element, in this case, should control whether its child elements are inline or out-of-line, the extended element supports `inline`.

▶ A locator element does not support the `content-role` and `content-title` attributes, which define the role and title of the local resource, respectively. The parent element should control the entire content of an extended link, so the extended element supports `content-role` and `content-title`.

The current XLink working draft sets rules for designating resources using the locator. You'll find the text of the rules in the Take Note on the facing page.

Inline and Out-of-Line Links

An inline link is an internal link; that is, it is completely within the current document. An out-of-line link refers to an external file that contains the link and target resource information. Basically, you can compare an inline link with an internal DTD subset: Both are entirely enclosed within the current document and do not have any external components. An out-of-line link is analogous to an external DTD subset. Both are composed of a reference within the current document and an external document that contains important information — in the case of the DTD, all the element, attribute, and other declarations that support the current document; and in the case of the out-of-line link, the link and target resources. When the XLink recommendation appears — in the near future — it will probably include instructions on setting up an external out-of-line link document and referring to it from within the current document.

CROSS-REFERENCE

Chapter 8 provides detailed information about declaring elements and controlling order and content.

FIND IT ONLINE

At **http://journals.ecs.soton.ac.uk/xml4j/ xlinkexperience.html**, read about a new XLink implementation.

XLink Working Draft Rules for Designated Resources

▶ The URI, if provided, locates a resource called the containing resource.

▶ If the URI is not provided, the containing resource is considered to be the document in which the linking element is contained.

▶ If an XPointer is provided, the designated resource is a sub-resource of the containing resource; otherwise the designated resource is the containing resource.

▶ If the Connector is followed directly by a Name, the Name is shorthand for the XPointer "id(Name)"; that is, the sub-resource is the element in the containing resource that has an XML ID attribute whose value matches the Name. This shorthand is to encourage use of the robust id addressing mode.

▶ If the connector is "#", this signals an intent that the containing resource is to be fetched as a whole from the host that provides it, and that the XPointer processing to extract the sub-resource is to be performed on the client, that is to say on the same system where the linking element is recognized and processed.

▶ If the connector is "|", no intent is signaled as to what processing model is to be used for accessing the designated resource.

Listing 21-7: A DECLARATION FOR A LOCATOR ELEMENT

❶

```
<!ELEMENT loclink ANY>
<!ATTLIST loclink
  xml:link ←❷  CDATA   #FIXED   "locator"  ❸
  href         CDATA            #REQUIRED
  actuate      CDATA            #IMPLIED
  behavior     CDATA            #IMPLIED
  role         CDATA       ❹→   #IMPLIED
  show         CDATA            #IMPLIED
  title        CDATA            #IMPLIED>
```

❶ *A locator element does not have to be named* locator.
❷ *Add an* xml:link *attribute.*
❸ *The value for an extended link is* "locator".
❹ *All but one of the remaining attributes are optional.*

Listing 21-8: AN EDITED EXAMPLE OF AN EXTENDED LINK

```
<family xml:link="extended"
    title="Family Ties" ←❶
    inline="true" show="replace">
  <loclink href="tom.jpg"
    title="Tom"     ❷
    behavior="play:tom.au"/>
  <loclink href="gerry.jpg"
    title="Gerry"/> ❷
    behavior="play:gerry.au"/>
  <loclink href="sally.jpg"
    title="Sally"/> ❷
    behavior="play:sally.au"/>
</multilnks>
```

❶ *Add a title to the extended link.*
❷ *Play a sound file during traversal.*

Constructing an Extended Link

Throughout this chapter, you have seen several examples of extended links. Now, you'll learn how to construct an extended link, element by element and attribute by attribute. To begin an extended link, enter the start tag for the extended element. Make sure that you include all the appropriate attribute-value pairs within the start tag. For example:

```
<extend xml:link="extended" inline="true"
    show="replace" actuate="user"
    id="el256"
    title="A Sample Extended Link"
    content-title="Bug Reports - 1999">
```

All the attributes in the extended element control the characteristics of the extended element and the locator elements. Note that the id attribute is the only non-linking attribute in this example. (Remember that you can give the extended element any valid XML name; it's not necessary to give it the name extended.) Then, add the first locator element, making sure to include an absolute or relative URI and other linking and non-linking attributes. For example:

```
<locator id="el256a"
    href="http://www.eddygrp.com/bug.doc"
    title="Bug Report 12/3/99"/>
```

The /> combination indicates that the locator element is empty: Although the locator element can contain attributes and values, you cannot include any type of content. The reason that a locator element is empty is that its sole purpose is to link to a target resource. Remember, though, that an empty element usually serves as a placeholder for future content — a graphic, sound file, or even a document. However, the locator element supports a title, so you can use that attribute to label or describe the element in some way.

Add the remaining locator elements, using the same format. Finally, close the extended element by inserting an end tag:

```
</extend>
```

Multidirectional Linking

XML extended links are *multidirectional*, which means that you are not limited to jumping in one direction — from the link to the target resource — as you do with the HTML A element and the simple link in XML. At their most simple configuration, multidirectional links and extended links are one and the same. Both offer the choice of jumping to several locations from a single location — in a linear way. True multidirectional complexity occurs when you establish links throughout a document, and create extended links starting at the target resources. At this point, you no longer have to jump repeatedly from one link to one of its target resources. You might be able to jump from a menu or list of locator choices to another target resource. Multidirectional linking can cause a great deal of chaos in which users won't know exactly where they are when they display target resources. In addition, some links might actually be placed in other people's target resources.

CROSS-REFERENCE

In Chapter 10, you can find out how to use entities to insert content into XML DTDs and other documents.

FIND IT ONLINE

Learn some XLink technical details at http://www.oasis-open.org/cover/xmlExtendedLink.html.

Listing 21-9: LINKED MAPS

```
<regions xml:link="extended"     ①
    title="New York Regions"
②→inline="true" show="replace">     ③
 <locator href="/regions/nyc.gif"
    title="New York City"/>
<locator href="/regions/li.gif"
    title="Long Island"/>
<locator href="/regions/hudson.gif"
    title="The Hudson Valley"/>
<locator href="/regions/catskills.gif"
    title="The Catskills"/>
<locator href="/regions/cap.gif"
    title="The Capital Region"/>
<locator href="/regions/adiron.gif"
    title="The Adirondacks"/>
<locator href="/regions/thous.gif"
    title="The Thousand Islands"/>
<locator href="/regions/leather.gif"
    title="The Leatherstocking District"/>
<locator href="/regions/finger.gif"
    title="The Finger Lakes"/>
<locator href="/regions/niagara.gif"
    title="The Niagara Frontier"/>
 <locator href="/regions/chautal.gif"
    title="Chautauqua & Allegheny"/>
</regions>     ④
```

① Specify that this link is extended.
② Insert attributes whose values are inherited by the locator elements.
③ Enter locators, each with a URI and title.
④ Complete the extended link with an end tag.

Listing 21-10: CHANGING LINKS

```
<regions xml:link="extended"
    title="New York Regions"
    inline="true" show="replace">
  <locator href="/regions/nyc.xml"←⑤
    title="New York City"
⑥→behavior="load:nyc.gif"/>
 <locator href="/regions/li.xml"←⑤
    title="Long Island"
⑥→behavior="load:li.gif"/>
  <locator href="/regions/hudson.xml"←⑤
    title="The Hudson Valley"
⑥→behavior="load:hudson.gif"/>
  <locator href="/regions/catskills.xml"←⑤
    title="The Catskills"
⑥→behavior="load:catskills.gif"/>
  <locator href="/regions/cap.xml"←⑤
    title="The Capital Region"
⑥→behavior="load:cap.gif"/>
  <locator href="/regions/adiron.xml"←⑤
    title="The Adirondacks"
⑥→behavior="load:adiron.gif"/>
  <locator href="/regions/thous.xml"←⑤
    title="The Thousand Islands"
⑥→behavior="load:thous.gif"/>
  <locator href="/regions/leather.xml"←⑤
    title="The Leatherstocking District"
⑥→behavior="load:leather.gif"/>
</regions>
```

⑤ Change the link from a graphic to a document.
⑥ Use the behavior attribute to load the graphic.

Adjusting Extended-Link Characteristics

You first learned about the `show` and `actuate` attributes in the "Specifying Types of Link Behaviors" task at the end of Chapter 19.

The `show` attribute controls whether the target resource is displayed or processed. The main purpose of `show` is to determine whether the contents of the current window are replaced by that of the target resource, whether a new window opens to hold the target resource contents, or whether the contents are embedded in the current window.

An actuator is a person or application that activates a process such as a link traversal or the start of a program. The `actuate` attribute controls whether link traversal is automatic or whether the user must explicitly request traversal. Note that an *actuator* can be a person or application.

For simple links, the `show` and `actuate` attributes determine the response of one link. So, even if you do not think about how certain values affect the traversal, you won't encounter clashing windows or sudden automatic linking. However, for an extended link consisting of several locators, the effects could be quite bizarre. In fact, until you test these attributes a few times, consider placing the `show` and `actuate` attributes and their values with the extended element. This enables all the locator elements to work in the same way.

With careful planning and possibly some programming, you can set some spectacular `show` and `actuate` effects. For example, you could set several locators to `show="new"` to open several target resources simultaneously in preprogrammed small windows on your Desktop. If properly controlled, this could be an interesting way to display a home page. To enhance the effect, the delay of certain small windows could be timed through a bit of programming. You could dynamically open the same windows by selectively setting `actuate="auto"`. You could automate an online presentation by setting `actuate="auto"` and specifying a series of target resources (presentation pages), each with links to the next page. You could change the way that each target resource appeared onscreen by specifying `show="new"` or `show="replace"`.

TAKE NOTE

USING THE BACK BUTTON IN WEB BROWSERS

As you have learned, XML's extended links can move in one direction or be multidirectional. Note that multidirectional does *not* mean that you can jump from a link resource back to its link. Although clicking on a Back button in popular browsers causes you to return to a previous page, that process is not a multidirectional one: You are not jumping from a link resource back to its link, as you might think. Your browser is actually displaying an older page on a list of previous pages saved in your browser cache.

CROSS-REFERENCE

In Chapter 12, you can learn how to test your documents for accuracy and validity by using an XML parser.

FIND IT ONLINE

http://www.developer.com/directories/pages/dir.xml.html links to XML categories and resources.

Listing 21-11: ELEMENT DECLARATIONS AND SAMPLE CODE FOR AN EXTENDED LINK

```
<!ELEMENT extended ANY>
<!ATTLIST extended
    xml:link        CDATA                   #FIXED          "extended"
    inline          (true|false)            "true"
    role            CDATA                   #IMPLIED
    content-role    CDATA                   #IMPLIED
    content-title   CDATA                   #IMPLIED
    title           CDATA                   #IMPLIED
    show            (replace|new|embed      "replace"
    actuate         (actuate|user)          "user"
    behavior        CDATA                   #IMPLIED
>
<!ELEMENT locator ANY>
<!ATTLIST locator
    xml:link        CDATA                   #FIXED          "locator"
    href            CDATA                   #REQUIRED
    behavior        CDATA                   #IMPLIED
    role            CDATA                   #IMPLIED
    title           CDATA                   #IMPLIED
>

<extended xml:link="extended">
    <locator href="home.xml" title="Home Page"/>
    <locator href="sitemap.xml" title="Site Map"/>
    <locator href="products.xml" title="Products"/>
    <locator href="services.xml" title="Services"/>
    <locator href="about.xml" title="About Frammis"/>
    <locator href="copyrt.xml" title="Copyright Page"/>
</extended>
```

▲ *This example of element declarations and the extended and locator links in an XML documents demonstrates that you do not have to include default attribute values.*

Personal Workbook

Q&A

1 What is the structure of an extended link?

_____

_____

_____

2 Where do you find the link and target information in an extended link?

_____

_____

_____

3 If all your locator elements contain the same attribute having the same value, what do you do?

_____

_____

_____

4 Why doesn't the locator element support the inline attribute?

_____

_____

5 Do locator elements inherit the attributes of the extended element in which they are nested?

_____

_____

_____

_____

6 Why is the locator element empty?

_____

_____

_____

7 What is an *actuator*?

_____

_____

_____

_____

8 How do you place a target resource in a new window?

_____

_____

_____

ANSWERS: PAGE 466

EXTRA PRACTICE

❶ For an online newsletter, create a table of contents of links from any article to any other article, and from any article to the top page.

❷ Your baseball card collection is overflowing. Organize it by creating an XML document to serve as a database. Add extended links to the document to organize your collection by date, player, and position.

❸ In Chapter 19, you created a Web page that listed your favorite books. Change the simple links that display author and bookstore information to extended links to other books by the author.

REAL-WORLD APPLICATIONS

✔ You publish music CDs. You would like to have visitors to your Web site listen to samples of your artists' works. For each of your CDs, create an extended link to sample files for each track.

✔ On your personal page on your corporate intranet, you would like to compile a list of your contacts with links to their home and business address information, telephone and e-mail information, and so on. Many of your contacts work at two or three companies. Streamline the contact list by building extended links to centralized corporation pages.

Visual Quiz

This organization chart shows three levels of management. How would you link from any box to the top box? How would you link from the top box to the three boxes representing the second layer simultaneously? How would you link simultaneously from the second-level boxes to the levels that report to them?

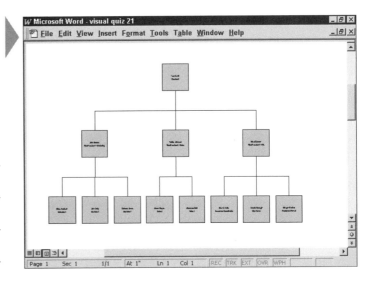

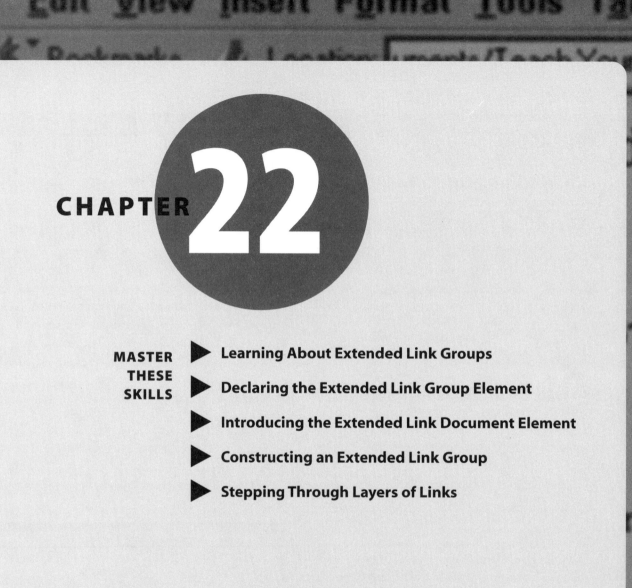

CHAPTER 22

MASTER
THESE
SKILLS

▶ **Learning About Extended Link Groups**

▶ **Declaring the Extended Link Group Element**

▶ **Introducing the Extended Link Document Element**

▶ **Constructing an Extended Link Group**

▶ **Stepping Through Layers of Links**

Employing Extended Link Groups

In this chapter, you learn about the final type of XML link, the extended link group. An extended link group, which has a similar structure to the extended link and is a special kind of extended link, refers a set of related documents that can contain links to all the other documents in the set and to other documents outside the set. Each of the five tasks in this chapter covers a particular aspect of the extended link group and its child element, the extended link document.

An extended link group is made up of nested extended link document elements, each referring to a single document in the document set. Each document in the set may or may not include simple, extended, or other extended link groups.

Like other XML elements or XML-type elements, you declare the extended link group element and the extended link document and their attributes in the DTD before using them in an XML document with which the DTD is associated. The extended link group element and the extended link document elements each have two link-related attributes but can use other nonlink attributes as well as CSS or XSL styles.

The extended link document element, which is nested within an extended link group element, contains the linking information for one related document in the set. Unlike its relative, the locator element, which can accept any content, the extended link document element is empty. Thus, it cannot presently hold content; it is a placeholder for the contents of the future target resource.

The extended link group element supports a unique attribute, `steps`. When a linked-to document contains an extended link group that leads to another extended link group, and so on, the `steps` attribute prevents a processor or application from processing more layers than you desire. Simply set a numeric value beyond which you don't want the processor to go.

Finally, remember that the XLink language is still at the working-draft stage. According to W3C, a working draft is "a draft document and may be updated, replaced, or made obsolete by other documents at any time." Until XLink becomes a W3C recommendation, which is the actual standard, you should periodically visit the W3C (**http://www.w3.org/**) to check on the status of XLink.

Learning About Extended Link Groups

In the prior chapter, you learned about extended links, which are new to XML. Remember that an extended link is composed of an extended element under which is nested one or more locator elements. An extended link jumps from one link location to one or more target resources. For example, using a menu or drop-down list containing a set of target resources, a user can choose a particular link in the same way that he or she could select one menu command or a list option.

As you might guess by looking at its name, an extended link group is another form of extended link that is structured in the same way as an extended link: Within the parent element is one or more nested child elements. However, instead of the extended link's one linking element and several target resources, an extended link group contains several linking elements to a group of related documents. According to the current XLink working draft, "an extended link group element may be used to store a list of links to other documents that together constitute an interlinked group. Each such document is identified by means of an extended link document element, a special kind of locator element."

The extended link group element encloses one or more nested extended link document elements using the following structure:

```
<extended_group steps_attributes
   <document element URI_attribute/>
   <document element URI_attribute/>
   <document element URI_attribute/>
```

```
   <document element URI_attribute/>
   <document element URI_attribute/>
</extended_group>
```

As with the extended element, the extended link group element does not include a URI. However, note that it contains the `xml:link` attribute and another attribute, `steps`, which you will learn about in the last task in this chapter.

Extended link document elements work in much the same way as the extended link's locator elements. Within an extended link document element is a URI. Remember that the URIs in locator elements refer to a target resource in the current document or in an external document. However, URIs in extended link document elements refer to target documents in an related group of documents.

TAKE NOTE

▶ **APPLYING ATTRIBUTES AND STYLES TO XML LINKS**

Like any other XML-like elements, XML link elements support the use of attributes and styles. For example, you can use identifier attributes to name a specific element for processing or styling actions. You also have the full benefit of applying CSS or XSL styles. For example, the title of a link or other content (where content is allowed) can be formatted as any selected text is. You can change its color, typeface, point size, and so on.

CROSS-REFERENCE

In Chapter 1, you can get an overview of all the components that make up an XML document.

FIND IT ONLINE

Café con Leche (**http://metalabl.unc.edu/xml/**) features up-to-date XML news and resources.

Listing 22-1: THE FIRST STEP IN BUILDING AN EXTENDED LINK GROUP

```
❶          ❷              ❸
<group xml:link="group" steps="2">
</group>◄❹
```

❶ *Begin with an extended link group element start tag.*
❷ *Insert the* xml:link *attribute and use a value of "* group*".*
❸ *Set a value for the* steps *attribute.*
❹ *Insert the end tag so that you don't forget it.*

Listing 22-2: THE SECOND STEP

```
         ❺
<group xml:link="group" steps="2">
                               ❼
   <document xml:link="document"◄❻
      href="http://www.eddygrp.com/doc1.doc"
      />◄❽
</group>
```

❺ *Indent and add the first extended link document start tag.*
❻ *Insert the* xml:link *attribute and use a value of "document".*
❼ *Enter the* href *attribute and the URL of the document.*
❽ *Insert the empty-element end tag characters.*

Listing 22-3: THE THIRD STEP

```
<group xml:link="group" steps="2">
   <document xml:link="document"
      href="http://www.eddygrp.com/doc1.doc"
   />
   <document xml:link="document"
      href="http://www.eddygrp.com/doc2.doc"
   />           ❾
</group>
```

❾ *Add the next extended link document element using the same format.*

Listing 22-4: THE FINAL STEP

```
<group xml:link="group" steps="2">
   <document xml:link="document"
      href="http://www.eddygrp.com/doc1.doc"
   />           ❿
   <document xml:link="document"
      href="http://www.eddygrp.com/doc2.doc"
   />
   <document xml:link="document"
      href="http://www.eddygrp.com/doc3.doc"
   />
   <document xml:link="document"
      href="http://www.eddygrp.com/doc4.doc"
   />
</group>
```

❿ *Complete the extended link group by adding the remaining extended link document elements.*

Declaring the Extended Link Group Element

In Chapter 20, you learned that before you can use a link in an XML document, you must edit the DTD associated with the document — to declare linking attributes under elements that will serve as linking elements. First, you must make sure that the desired element declaration is included in the DTD. Then, specify the type of link and other linking characteristics in the element's attribute list following the specifications in the current XLink working draft or the future recommendation. Regardless of the type of link, the element declaration and attribute-list declaration follow the same format used by other XML-like elements. According to the current XLink working draft, a typical extended link group element will look something like this:

```
<!ELEMENT group (document*)>
```

As you know, this means that the extended link document element is a declared child element of the extended link group element. Next, declare an attribute list for the group element. Include an `xml:link` attribute value:

```
xml:link    CDATA    #FIXED    "group"
```

Now you can add an optional `steps` attribute:

```
steps    CDATA    #IMPLIED
```

The `steps` attribute limits the layers of links (and associated documents) that a processor will go through in order to process the current document. The `steps` attribute eliminates the possibility of a processor finding a link in a document and, if that link contains a link, jumping to that link, and so on.

Note that the short attribute list for the extended link group element does *not* include a `href` attribute. The only supported link-related attributes are `xml:link` and `steps`. (You'll find the default element declaration and the default attribute list for the extended link group element on the facing page.)

Even if you don't plan to use a particular attribute for the documents associated with a particular DTD, it's a good idea to declare it. As Chapter 20 states, it's a good idea to add optional XLink attributes to your documents to help certain processing applications and also to provide informal comments for future developers and maintainers of this DTD. If you have any questions about link types and their supported attributes, refer to Table 21-1.

The following task examines the extended link document element and continues the discussion of using extended link groups.

TAKE NOTE

EXAMINING OUT-OF-LINE EXTENDED LINK GROUPS

Since extended link groups are composed of external documents, they are out-of-line links. So, there is no need for the extended link group element or the extended link document element to support the use of the `inline` attribute: There is no choice between inline and out-of-line values.

CROSS-REFERENCE

Chapter 3 presents EBNF notation with which you can code XML markup in DTDs and in documents.

FIND IT ONLINE

A paper at **http://journals.ecs.soton.ac.uk/~lac/ht98/ohs.htm** discusses XML and open hypermedia.

Listing 22-5: A DECLARATION FOR AN EXTENDED-LINK GROUP ELEMENT

```
❶ <!ELEMENT group (document*)>
   <!ATTLIST group                        ❸
❷ xml:link    CDATA    #FIXED    "group"
❹ steps       CDATA    #IMPLIED
   >
```

❶ *An group linking element does not have to be named* group.
❷ *Add an* xml:link *attribute.*
❸ *The value for an extended link group is "*group*".*
❹ *The* steps *attribute is optional.*

Listing 22-6: A WEB SITE EXAMPLE

```
    ❶        ❷
<site xml:link="group" steps="2">     ❸
   <page xml:link="document"
     href="http://www.eddygrp.com/home.xml"
   />
   <page xml:link="document"
     href="http://www.eddygrp.com/site.xml"
   />
   <page xml:link="document"
     href="http://www.eddygrp.com/prod.xml"
   />
   <page xml:link="document"
     href="http://www.eddygrp.com/abt.doc"
   />
</site> ◄❹
```

❶ *Begin with the extended link group element start tag.*
❷ *Insert the* xml:link *attribute and use a value of "*group*".*
❸ *Insert a set of extended link document elements.*
❹ *Complete the extended link group with an end tag.*

Listing 22-7: AN EXPANDED WEB SITE EXAMPLE

```
                                    ❶
<site xml:link="group" steps="2">
<!--The home page link -->
   <page xml:link="document" id="home"
❷ href="http://www.eddygrp.com/Ł
     home.xml"
   />
<!--The site map link -->
   <page xml:link="document" id="site"
❷ href="http://www.eddygrp.com/Ł
     site.xml"
   />
<!--The products page link -->
   <page xml:link="document" id="prod"
     href="http://www.eddygrp.com/Ł
     prod.xml"
   />
<!--The services page link -->
   <page xml:link="document" id="serv"
     href="http://www.eddygrp.com/Ł
     serv.xml"
   />
<!--The financials link -->
   <page xml:link="document" id="finan"
     href="http://www.eddygrp.com/Ł
     finc.xml"
   />
<!--The management page link -->
   <page xml:link="document" id="mgmt"
     href="http://www.eddygrp.com/Ł
     mgmt.xml"
   />
</site>
```

❶ *Restrict linking to two steps deep.*
❷ *The* href *attribute refers to an extended link document.*

321

Introducing the Extended Link Document Element

As you learned earlier in this chapter, an extended link group element is actually a shell that contains one or more extended link document elements, each of which include a link to a particular document in an interlinked set of documents. The set of extended link document elements is nested within their parent extended link group element start tag and end tag.

The extended link group element and the extended link document element share one attribute (`xml:link`). However, each element contains its own short list of unique attributes.

▶ Extended link group elements do not include links, so they do not need nor support the use of the `href` attribute. However, extended link document elements do support `href`.

▶ Extended link group elements have the optional `steps` attribute, which controls the processing of the entire set of interconnected documents. Individual extended link document elements specify one of the set of documents; thereby eliminating the need for a `steps` attribute.

According to the current XLink working draft, a typical extended link document element will look something like this:

```
<!ELEMENT document xml:link="document
    href="http://www.eddygrp.com/doc1.doc>
```

The extended link document element is empty, which means that it is a placeholder for future content — in this case, a linked-to resource — and cannot contain any character data. To illustrate, Table 21-1 shows that the extended link document element does not support the use of any of the attributes that would add content to the element. The extended link document element exists solely to refer to a document that might or might not contain a link.

TAKE NOTE

▶ ### EVOLVING THROUGH THE XLINK DRAFTS

Although earlier versions of the XLink language supported the same underlying structure as the current working draft, they varied in many details. For example, the language itself was known as XLL, and the `xml:link` attribute was `XML-LINK`. Most programmers know that entering even one incorrect punctuation mark can causes processing errors and days of debugging. This evolution of the XLink specification emphasizes the importance of periodically checking its current status at W3C (**http://www.w3.org/**).

▶ ### EXTENDED LINKS VERSUS EXTENDED LINK GROUPS

When you compare the element declarations for the extended link element and the extended link group element in the current XLink working draft, notice the difference:

```
<!ELEMENT extended ANY>
<!ELEMENT group (document*)>
```

The extended element can contain any content, including the locator element. However, the extended element group is restricted to including the extended link document element.

CROSS-REFERENCE

Chapter 8 covers the process of declaring elements and specifying their structure and type of content.

FIND IT ONLINE

Browse through XML, DSSSL, and SGML resources and tools at **http://www.cogsci.ed.ac.uk/~ht/**.

Listing 22-8: THE EXTENDED LINK DOCUMENT ELEMENT DECLARATION

❶

```
<!ELEMENT document EMPTY>
<!ATTLIST document
❷→ xml:link    CDATA   #FIXED          "document"  ❸
    href         CDATA   #REQUIRED
>                              ❹
```

❶ A document linking element does not have to be named document.
❷ Add an xml:link attribute.
❸ The value for a document link is "document".
❹ The href attribute is required.

Listing 22-9: BUILDING LINKS TO CHAPTERS

❶   **❷**

```
<book xml:link="group" steps="1">
  <chapter xml:link="document"
❸   href="http://www.x.com/book/ch01.xml"
  />                              ❹
  <chapter xml:link="document"
    href="http://www.x.com/book/ch02.xml"
  />
  <chapter xml:link="document"
    href="http://www.x.com/book/ch03.xml"
  />
</book>
```

❶ Begin the extended link group with a start tag.
❷ The xml:link attribute equals "group".
❸ Begin the first extended link document with a start tag.
❹ Insert the URL of a chapter file.

Listing 22-10: A LONGER BOOK EXAMPLE

```
<book xml:link="group" steps="1">
  <chapter id="toc" xml:link="document"
    href="http://www.x.com/book/toc.xml"  ←❺
  />
  <chapter id="intro" xml:link="document"
    href="http://www.x.com/book/intr.xml"
  />                        ❻
  <chapter id="ch01" xml:link="document"
    href="http://www.x.com/book/ch01.xml"
  />
  <chapter id="ch02" xml:link="document"
    href="http://www.x.com/book/ch02.xml"
  />
  <chapter id="ch03" xml:link="document"
    href="http://www.x.com/book/ch03.xml"
  />
  <chapter id="glos" xml:link="document"
    href="http://www.x.com/book/glos.xml"
  />
  <chapter id="apxa" xml:link="document"
    href="http://www.x.com/book/apxa.xml"
  />
  <chapter id="index" xml:link="document"
    href="http://www.x.com/book/indx.xml"
  />
</book>              ❼
```

❺ Add a table of contents document to the group.
❻ Insert an identifier attribute in each extended link document.
❼ Add a glossary, an appendix, and the index to the end.

Constructing an Extended Link Group

Throughout this chapter, you have seen several examples of extended link groups. Now you'll learn how to build an extended link group step by step. To begin an extended link group, enter the start tag for the group element. Make sure that you include the one or two appropriate attribute-value pairs within the start tags. For example:

```
<group xml:link="group" steps="1"
```

Then add the first extended link document element, making sure to include a URI. (Remember that you can give the group and document elements any valid XML name; it's not necessary to give the the name group and document, respectively.)

For example:

```
<document id="10001" xml:link="document"
/>href="http://www.eddygrp.com/bug1.doc"
```

The /> characters indicate that the extended link document element is empty, as it is declared in the DTD. The /> combines the start tag and the end tag. The reason that a extended link document element is empty is that its sole purpose is to name the URL of one of the documents in the interconnected link group. Remember that an empty element can include attributes such as the non-linking id attribute, which enables you to identify this particular occurrence of the element for future processing.

Add the remaining extended link document elements using the same format:

```
<document id="10002" xml:link="document"
```

```
  href="http://www.eddygrp.com/bug2.doc"
/>
<document id="10003" xml:link="document"
  href="http://www.eddygrp.com/bug3.doc"
/>
<document id="10004" xml:link="document"
  href="http://www.eddygrp.com/bug4.doc"
/>
<document id="10005" xml:link="document"
  href="http://www.eddygrp.com/bug5.doc"
/>
```

Finally, close the group element by inserting an end tag, as follows:

```
</group>
```

For examples of simple, extended, and group link declarations, see Section 4, "Linking Elements," in the W3C's XML Linking Language (XLink) working draft, located at **http://www.w3.org/TR/WD-xlink**.

TAKE NOTE

LINKING TO "FOREIGN" DOCUMENTS FROM WITHIN YOUR EXTENDED LINK GROUPS

When you use extended link groups, sometimes you'll link to documents that you "own" on your computer or your local network only. Since you are responsible for updating your own documents, you can ensure that all the links remain viable. However, if you link to documents outside your control, plan on spending extra time verifying the links and reviewing the complete documents to make sure that you still want to include them in your group.

CROSS-REFERENCE

In Chapter 13, you find out how to start an XML document and enter elements and other components.

FIND IT ONLINE

A paper at **http://www.texcel.no/sgml97.htm** discusses XML and modern software architectures.

Listing 22-11: AN EXTENDED LINK GROUP FOR PROJECT SCHEDULING

```
<sched xml:link="group" steps="1">
  <doc xml:link="document"
    href="/startup.doc"/>
  <doc xml:link="document"
    href="/planning.doc"/>
  <doc xml:link="document"
    href="/design.doc"/>
  <doc xml:link="document"
    href="/staff.doc"/>
  <doc xml:link="document"
    href="/kickoff.doc"/>
  <doc xml:link="document"
    href="/phase1.doc"/>
  <doc xml:link="document"
    href="/phase2.doc"/>
  <doc xml:link="document"
    href="/phase3.doc"/>
  <doc xml:link="document"
    href="/phase4.doc"/>
  <doc xml:link="document"
    href="/windup.doc"/>
</sched>
```

▲ *This extended link group consists of links to a set of documents that follow a project from beginning to end. Links in each document enable you to jump from one document to another.*

Listing 22-12: AN EXTENDED LINK GROUP FOR TABLES OF CONTENTS

❶

```
<site xml:link="group" steps="2">
<!--The home page link -->
  <page xml:link="document" id="home"
❷  href="http://www.eddygrp.com/Ł
   home.xml"
  />
<!--The site map link -->
  <page xml:link="document" id="site"
❷  href="http://www.eddygrp.com/Ł
   site.xml"
  />
<!--The products page link -->
  <page xml:link="document" id="prod"
   href="http://www.eddygrp.com/Ł
   prod.xml"
  />
<!--The services page link -->
  <page xml:link="document" id="serv"
   href="http://www.eddygrp.com/Ł
   serv.xml"
  />
<!--The financials link -->
  <page xml:link="document" id="finan'
   href="http://www.eddygrp.com/Ł
   finc.xml"
  />
<!--The management page link -->
  <page xml:link="document" id="mgmt"
   href="http://www.eddygrp.com/Ł
   mgmt.xml"
  />
```

❶ *The* href *goes to a table of links to every chapter.*
❷ *The* href *goes to a chapter's sub-table of contents.*

Stepping Through Layers of Links

As you have learned, when you construct an extended link group, the extended link document's href attribute jumps to a document that may or may not have links. Clearly, you won't always know the contents of the documents to which you link—especially if you link to "foreign" documents that are beyond your control.

If an XML document contains links, they may be simple, extended, or extended link groups. In the last case, it is possible for a link in an extended link group to go through layers of documents, each containing other extended link groups. In the future, when XML documents cover the Web, visitors to your site may easily get lost in a tangle of links.

The current XLink working draft contains an answer to this dilemma—the steps attribute. In all the examples in this chapter, you have seen the steps attribute in use. The steps attribute, which is part of the extended link group element's attribute list, sets a limit on the number of layers of extended link groups that can be processed. Simply give steps a value that instructs a processor or other application the number of layers that it can go through.

An example used in the current XLink working draft states: "Should a group of documents be organized with a single 'hub' document containing all the out-of-line links, it might make sense for each non-hub document to contain an extended link group containing only one reference to the hub document. In this case, the best value for steps would be 2."

Organizing Linked Documents

You can use various types of Web site organizations to demonstrate how pages are arranged — either in an organized or disorganized way:

▶ A site can have a top-down, organization-chart arrangement. At the top is a single home page, under that is the first layer of pages, and each of those pages can have subsidiary pages.

▶ A site may start with a home page, but after that follow a different organization: Pages are arranged sequentially with a single page linking to the page before it and to the page after it. All pages usually link back to the home page and sometimes link to a table of contents, site map, or index page.

▶ A site may start with a home page, which is merely the entrance to the site. Then, the pages can be linked in a random manner. This type of site is so disorganized that it's bound to have pages that don't link to any other pages — especially if the site has gone through many changes and additions. Some of the older or obsolete pages may still exist but link only to other obsolete pages that have been deleted.

▶ A site may look like a wheel composed of pages that are all linked to a hub page.

Obviously, the best Web site is the most organized. This fact also applies to external link groups.

CROSS-REFERENCE

In Chapter 19, you can learn the basics of XML links so that you can identify the best link for a purpose.

FIND IT ONLINE

Go to an XLink information page (**http://www.xmlinfo.com/xlink/**) to link to several resources.

Listing 22-13: THE LARGEST WEB SITE EXAMPLE AND ITS ELEMENT DECLARATIONS

```
<!ELEMENT site (page*)>
<!ATTLIST site
   xml:link   CDATA   #FIXED      "group"
   steps      CDATA   #IMPLIED
>
<!ELEMENT page EMPTY>
<!ATTLIST page
   xml:link   CDATA   #FIXED         "document"
   href       CDATA   #REQUIRED
>


<site xml:link="group" steps="2">
<!--The home page link -->
  <page xml:link="document" id="home" href="http://www.eddygrp.com/home.xml"/>
<!--The site map link -->
  <page xml:link="document" id="site" href="http://www.eddygrp.com/site.xml"/>
<!--The products page link -->
  <page xml:link="document" id="prod" href="http://www.eddygrp.com/prod.xml"/>
<!--The services page link -->
```

❶ *Declare the optional* steps *attribute.*
❷ *Specify that you cannot go more than two layers down.*
❸ *Add comments to explain the markup of the document.*

Personal Workbook

Q&A

1 What is an *extended link group*?

_____

_____

_____

2 What is the difference between a URI in an extended link and in an extended link group?

_____

_____

_____

3 How do you prepare to use an extended link group in an XML document?

_____

_____

_____

4 Why do the extended link group element and the extended link document element not support the inline attribute?

_____

_____

_____

5 What is the declared content of the extended link document element?

_____

_____

_____

6 What is the value of the `xml:link` attribute for an extended link group element?

_____

_____

_____

7 What does the `steps` attribute do?

_____

_____

_____

8 Is `steps` an attribute of the extended link group element or the extended link document element?

_____

_____

_____

ANSWERS: PAGE 467

EXTRA PRACTICE

1 Write a presentation about the five most important parts of your job. Then, plan and prepare an extended link group that displays all the pages in order.

2 Edit the extended link group that you just wrote. Now display the pages from back to front.

3 As you know, there are 52 cards in a typical deck. How would you write an extended link group to link to one randomly chosen card at a time?

4 For your first European trip, you want to travel light. Instead of carrying an itinerary with you, you have decided to post pages for each part of your trip to your Web site. Construct one or more extended link groups and documents that contain links that enable you to link to a page devoted to a particular date or to move through the pages sequentially.

REAL-WORLD APPLICATIONS

✔ You publish a weekly newspaper. Now you want to post your archives at your Web site. Allow access to each document under the year in which it was published.

✔ You have prepared your college thesis by writing each section in its own particular document. Insert links to footnotes within each document. Then, use an extended link group to link from file to file sequentially.

✔ You have posted a large collection of recipes, each in its own file, on your Web site. For better organization, plan and implement an extended link group that encompasses the entire collection.

Visual Quiz

Convert this list of document links to an extended link group. How would you link to the first page? How would you jump to the last page? How would you move from page to page?

_____

_____

_____

_____

_____

Teach Yourself XML - Netscape

File Edit View Go Communicator Help

Bookmarks Location: uments/Teach Yourself XML/Ch22 Employing Extended Link Groups/xmlchaps.htm

Teach Yourself XML

- Chapter 1: XML Building Blocks
- Chapter 2: Examining an XML Document
- Chapter 3: The Anatomy of XML Syntax
- Chapter 4: Supported Characters and Character Sets
- Chapter 5: An Overview of XML Software
- Chapter 6: Planning a DTD
- Chapter 7: Starting a DTD
- Chapter 8: Declaring Elements
- Chapter 9: Defining Attributes
- Chapter 10: Using Entities
- Chapter 11: Modifying an Existing DTD
- Chapter 12: Parsing an XML Document
- Chapter 13: Creating a Basic XML Document

You are offline. Choose "Go Online..." to connect

CHAPTER **23**

MASTER
THESE
SKILLS

▶ **Learning About Extended Pointers**

▶ **Pointing to an Absolute Location**

▶ **Pointing to a Relative Location**

▶ **Pointing to a Node**

▶ **Using Other Location Terms**

Making the Most of Extended Pointers

In this chapter, you learn about extended pointers (XPointers) and the current version of the XPointer language. XPointers enable those using extended links to further pinpoint the location of their target resources by using such criteria as elements, attributes, attribute values, and other components within XML documents. Using a combination of extended pointers and extended links, you can even locate a span of components in a document.

XPointers use location terms to find a specific target. A location term is a name or keyword for a specific place or component in a target document. You can use one or more absolute location terms, relative location terms, spanning location terms, attribute location terms, and string location terms — separately or in combination — to pinpoint a particular location to which to link. To specify an XPointer, simply add a fragment identifier, which starts with the pound sign (#) symbol, to a URI.

▶ An *absolute location term* is analogous to an absolute URI. Its address is a complete reference to the final target location.

▶ A *relative location term* is analogous to a relative URI. Its address starts with the current location and uses a partial reference to link to the next location on the way to the target. The *argument* (the value or expression used to find the location in the document) for a relative location term can include an instance number, node name or type, attribute name and/or value, several keywords, and string.

▶ A *spanning location term* locates a span of document components starting at the first character of one XPointer and ending at the last character of another XPointer.

▶ An *attribute location term* locates a particular attribute by name.

▶ A *string-match location term* simply matches a string or a location between strings.

Finally, remember that the XPointer language is still at the working draft stage. According to W3C, a working draft is "a draft document and may be updated, replaced, or obsoleted by other documents at any time."

Learning About Extended Pointers

Pointers work with extended links to refine linking. When you use an extended pointer, your target resource could be a particular occurrence of an element, attribute, attribute value, or other markup or character-data component of a document. As you know, XML supports two types of links: simple and extended as well as a special kind of extended link, the extended link group. Simple links, which are analogous to HTML links, do not support extended pointers. Extended links and extended link groups, both of which are new to XML, enable you to jump from any link to any other link using link statements that are either inline or out-of-line. For extended links, you can add XPointer fragment identifiers to refine the desired link location even further. For example, you can link to the seventh child of the third child of the fifth element — if it exists in the target XML document.

XPointers use one location term or a series of location terms to point to a particular link. A *location term* simply refers to a target location in a document. The first location term in an XPointer is usually absolute (that is, it is an entire URI and fragment identifier, which begins with a pound sign (#) symbol and which points to a particular starting location. The fragment identifier, which is the actual XPointer, is composed of any combination of absolute, relative, and string-match location terms.

Each location term builds on the previous one, using the hierarchical structure (root element/child element/child of child, and so on) of XML documents to point to a distinct location in a document. (The facing page shows the XPointer productions, which define the basic categories of location terms. In some of the remaining tasks in this chapter, you'll see particular location-term productions.)

For XPointers, the most important part of the URI is the fragment identifier, which starts with a pound sign symbol (#) and includes one or more location terms. Each argument that you add to a location term refines the search for the specific document component even more.

XPointers can also point to a span from one location term to another in a document. You'll find out about several varieties of XPointers and their location terms in the tasks that follow.

CROSS-REFERENCE

Chapter 19 explores the basic building blocks of simple links and extended links.

FIND IT ONLINE

Go to **http://www.w3.org/TR/WD-xptr** at W3C to browse through the current XPointer working draft.

XML 1.0: XPOINTER PRODUCTIONS

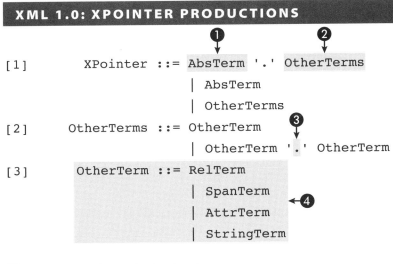

```
[1]        XPointer ::= AbsTerm '.' OtherTerms
                      | AbsTerm
                      | OtherTerms

[2]     OtherTerms ::= OtherTerm
                      | OtherTerm '.' OtherTerm

[3]      OtherTerm ::= RelTerm
                      | SpanTerm
                      | AttrTerm
                      | StringTerm
```

1 An XPointer can be an absolute location term...
2 ...and/or another type of location term.
3 Separate two terms with a period.
4 Another term can be relative, span, attribute, or string-match.

Listing 23-1: AN EXAMPLE OF AN ABSOLUTE XPOINTER

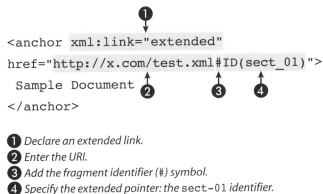

```
<anchor xml:link="extended"
href="http://x.com/test.xml#ID(sect_01)">
  Sample Document
</anchor>
```

1 Declare an extended link.
2 Enter the URI.
3 Add the fragment identifier (#) symbol.
4 Specify the extended pointer: the sect-01 identifier.

Listing 23-2: AN EXAMPLE OF AN RELATIVE XPOINTER

```
<anchor xml:link="extended"
href="/test.xml#child(3,#element,art,5)">
  Sample Document
</anchor>
```

1 Enter the fragment identifier symbol.
2 Choose the third child of the current element.
3 The element's art attribute must have a value of 5.

Pointing to an Absolute Location

An absolute location term is a specific location. When you use an absolute location term, you don't need to go through any intermediate locations first. An absolute location term enables you to set a specific starting point for a containing resource. Then, you can add other types of location terms to further refine the link. You can combine absolute location terms and relative location terms in a single argument. In fact, when you use relative location terms, you usually start the argument with an absolute location term. To specify an absolute location term, you can choose from four reserved keywords — named or otherwise:

▶ The `root()` keyword, the default, indicates the root location. This is the top location on the drive on which the target resource is located. The root is analogous to the `c:` folder on a Windows computer. Note that the keywords `root()` and `origin()` have empty argument lists to set them apart from identifiers that might be called `root` or `origin`. The empty parentheses are required.

▶ The `origin()` keyword indicates the containing resource — the document in which the link is located. Do not use `origin()` in conjunction with a locator that specifies a different containing resource. A prior name for this keyword was `here()`.

▶ The `id(name)` keyword and named identifier refers to a location within the current document that contains an `ID` attribute with a name that matches the keyword. This keyword-name combination works best when the XML document is associated with a DTD in which the ID attribute was specified.

▶ The `html(namevalue)` keyword and name value specifies an absolute HTML address for the containing resource. A match occurs when a `name` attribute whose value is the same as *namevalue* is found.

TAKE NOTE

▶ **THE ORIGINS OF XPOINTERS**

The XPointer language is based on the Text Encoding Initiative's (TEI) extended pointers. Because XML supports XPointers and SGML applications support TEI extended pointers, there are bound to be both similarities and differences between the two types of pointers. To learn more about TEI extended pointers, start at the Text Encoding Initiative Guidelines page (**http://etext.virginia.edu/TEI.html**). This page contains a table of contents for the Guidelines as well as a search index. It also has links to other TEI and SGML pages.

CROSS-REFERENCE

Chapter 13 covers the creation of a basic XML document, including its elements, attributes, and more.

FIND IT ONLINE

XLink and XPointer support and resource links are located at **http://www.drmacro.com/hyprlink/xlink/**.

XML 1.0: XPOINTER ABSOLUTE LOCATION TERM PRODUCTIONS

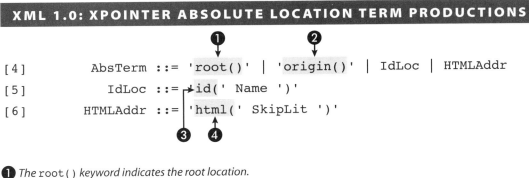

```
[4]      AbsTerm ::= 'root()' | 'origin()' | IdLoc | HTMLAddr
[5]        IdLoc ::= 'id(' Name ')'
[6]     HTMLAddr ::= 'html(' SkipLit ')'
```

❶ *The* root() *keyword indicates the root location.*
❷ *The* origin() *keyword indicates the containing resource.*
❸ *The* id *keyword indicates that a named ID attribute will follow.*
❹ *The* html *keyword indicates that an absolute URI will follow.*

Listing 23-3: EXAMPLES OF ABSOLUTE LOCATION TERMS

```
<anchor xml:link="extended"
    href="http://x.com/test.xml#html(code)">    ❶
    Sample Document
</anchor>
```

```
<anchor xml:link="extended"
    href="http://x.com/test.xml#root().ID(sect_01)">    ❷
    Sample Document
</anchor>
```

```
<anchor xml:link="extended"
    href="http://x.com/test.xml#HTMLAddr(linker)">    ❸
    Sample Document
</anchor>
```

❶ *This XPointer jumps to the section named* code *of* test.xml.
❷ *This jumps to the root and to the* sect_01 ID *attribute.*
❸ *This looks for an element whose* name *attribute equals* linker.

Pointing to a Relative Location

X Pointers generally start with one absolute location term followed by one or more relative location terms. Relative location terms either point to a target location in the hierarchy of locations or to an element that appears in a particular processing order. To specify a relative location term, you can choose from seven reserved keywords:

- ▶ The `child` keyword indicates a child of the current target.
- ▶ The `descendant` keyword is a child, grand-child, or other offspring of the current target.
- ▶ The `ancestor` keyword is a parent, grandparent, or other forebear of the current target.
- ▶ The `preceding` keyword is any element, related or not, processed properly before the current target is processed.
- ▶ The `following` keyword is any element, related or not, processed properly after the current target is processed.
- ▶ The `psibling` keyword is any element that has the same parent as the current target and is processed before the current target is processed.
- ▶ The `fsibling` keyword is any element that has the same parent as the current target and is processed after the current target is processed.

After typing a keyword, enter one or more arguments, which can be composed of a variety of input: instances of a targeted element, a node type, an attribute, or a value. Wildcards are accepted as attributes and values.

The following example selects the next-to-last following (`-2`) sibling of an element (`#element`) for which the attribute `LAST` has any value:

```
fsibling(-2,#element,"LAST",#IMPLIED)
```

The following example fetches all `mix` elements that descend from the `ID(2489)` resource:

```
<anchor xml:link="extended"
   href="http://www.sample.com/test.xml
   #ID(2489).descendant(all,mix)">
Sample Document</anchor>
```

The period in the third line marks the end of one location term and the beginning of the next.

This example starts at the root and traverses through subdirectories until it reaches the second instance of the `RECIPE` element:

```
root().descendant(2,"RECIPE")
```

TAKE NOTE

▶ **LEARNING ABOUT LOCATION TERMS FROM THE SOURCE**

According to the current XPointer working draft, "an XPointer consists of a series of location terms, each of which specifies a location, usually relative to the location specified by the prior location term. Each location term has a keyword (such as `id`, `child`, `ancestor`, and so on) and can have arguments such as an instance number, element type, or attribute."

CROSS-REFERENCE

In Chapter 15, you can go through the steps used to convert standard HTML documents to XML.

FIND IT ONLINE

Review an introduction to TEI extended pointers at **http://users.ox.ac.uk/~lou/papers/XR/**.

XML 1.0: XPOINTER RELATIVE LOCATION TERM PRODUCTIONS

```
[7]          RelTerm ::= Keyword? Arguments

[8]          Keyword ::= 'child'
                       | 'descendant'
                       | 'ancestor'
                       | 'preceding'
                       | 'following'
                       | 'psibling'
                       | 'fsibling'

[9]        Arguments ::= '(' InstanceOrAll
                         (',' NodeType
                         (',' Attr ',' Val)*)? ')'

[10] InstanceOrAll ::= 'all' | Instance

[11]        Instance ::= ('+' | '-')? [1-9] Digit*


[13]            Attr ::= '*'                /* any attribute name */
                       | Name

[14]             Val ::= '#IMPLIED'         /* no value specified, no defau
                       | '*'                /* any value, even defaulted */
                       | Name
                       | SkipLit            /* exact match */
```

1 *A relative term is made up of a keyword and arguments.*
2 *You can choose from seven keywords.*
3 *Select all or one instance of an element and...*
4 *...choose a node type, attribute, and value.*

337

Pointing to a Node

As you know, each XML document is made up of nodes, which are junctions at which one generation of elements or other document components meets its parent generation or its child generation. In the XPointer language, you can point to a node in order to link to it or to move through it toward another location term. You can either name a node or use a reserved keyword. A node name is a valid XML name, which starts with a letter or underscore character. The reserved keywords that you can use to point to a node are the following:

- ▶ The #element keyword, the default, specifies an XML element.
- ▶ The #pi keyword specifies an XML processing instruction.
- ▶ The #comment keyword specifies a comment in a document.
- ▶ The #text keyword specifies text within an XML element or a CDATA section.
- ▶ The #cdata keyword specifies text within a CDATA section.
- ▶ The #all keyword enables you to specify all node types.

The #pi, #comment, #text, and #cdata node types ignores constraints set within attributes. However, each of these node types allow the use of the StringTerm location term; that is, string matches. However, the #element node types allow attribute constraints. If attribute constraints exist, the #all node type is identical to the #element type. If you use the #all keyword, matches may be contiguous or noncontiguous nodes.

Learning About Nodes in the XPointer Language

In Chapter 30, you will discover that the Extensible Stylesheet Language (XSL) also uses a structure of nodes in determining that elements to which a particular style is applied. The XPointer language also refers to nodes. The current XPointer working draft states the following (with authors' comments within parentheses):

1. The string location term generally returns only part of a node, but if the matched content had markup within it, the result may include portions of multiple elements. (To learn about the string location term, refer to the "Pointing to a String," later in this chapter.)
2. The string location term, when used with the all instance value, returns a list of typically discontiguous portions of string data.
3. The relative location terms may specify the instance argument as all, meaning that all candidate nodes are included in the result. The result is thus a vector of possibly non-adjacent nodes, rather than a subtree. (The argument all appears within the XML 1.0: XPointer Relative Location Term Productions listing in the "Pointing to a Relative Location" task.)
4. A spanning XPointer may include various elements only partially.

CROSS-REFERENCE
Chapter 21 teaches you how to use extended links to reach certain target resources.

FIND IT ONLINE
http://www.wotsit.org/ has information about programmer's file and data formats.

XML 1.0: THE NODETYPE PRODUCTION

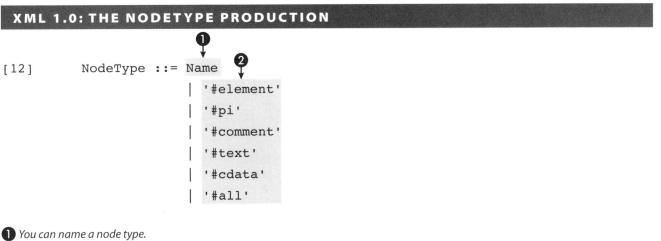

```
[12]        NodeType ::= Name
                       | '#element'
                       | '#pi'
                       | '#comment'
                       | '#text'
                       | '#cdata'
                       | '#all'
```

❶ *You can name a node type.*
❷ *Enter one of these keywords to select a node type.*

Listing 23-4: NAMING A NODE

```
id(chap05).child(2,section,"intro")
```

❶ *Enter the* id *keyword to identify a particular identifier,* chap05.
❷ *Select the second occurrence of the* section *child element.*
❸ *Find the first occurrence of the* intro *attribute.*

Listing 23-5: LOCATING AN ELEMENT AND ATTRIBUTE

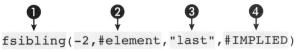

```
fsibling(-2,#element,"last",#IMPLIED)
```

❶ *Enter a keyword to identify a sibling following this node.*
❷ *Select the next-to-last following sibling.*
❸ *Identify the* last *attribute.*
❹ *The last attribute has an unspecified value.*

Using Other Location Terms

The XPointer language supports three other relative location terms: spanning terms, attribute-match terms, and string-match terms.

You can locate a span of information that starts at the first character of one location term and stops at the last character of another location term. To enter a spanning statement, type the span reserved keyword immediately followed by a left parenthesis (( ), enter the first combination of absolute location terms and/or relative location terms, insert a comma, enter the second combination of location terms, and end with a right parenthesis ( )).

Depending on how a processing application is programmed and how the XPointer statement is written, SpanTerm may or may not find complete elements or other document components. If SpanTerm finds incomplete elements or components, an XML document may not be accurate enough to qualify as being well-formed.

Use the attr keyword to locate an attribute by name and return the value of the attribute. The attribute name must be a valid XML name, starting with a letter or underscore character.

You can combine three productions — StringTerm, Position, and Length — to locate one or more strings or places between strings.

Ensuring the Integrity of Links

The current XPointer working draft discusses methods for ensuring that the integrity of links persists as far into the future as possible. Obviously, this is one reason why XPointers are used with extended links. According to the working draft, the longest-lasting locators use only an ID attribute. If the developer does not have control over the development of a particular target-resource document and it does not include IDs, a developer can include an XPointer that points to the nearest ID and then uses the relative location term child to find the desired element. The working draft states that this approach is "relatively robust" for two reasons:

▶ "It has a good probability of withstanding editing; for example, no edit outside the element with the ID can harm the reference."

▶ "It will fail obviously rather than quietly if the link does break."

The working draft also says that when you use a relative location term, specify a name attribute and value for the element to which you want to link. If you use this approach, the working draft states:

▶ It is more clear because people typically refer to things by type: "the second section," "the third paragraph," and so on.

▶ It is more robust because it increases the chance of detecting breakage if the original target no longer exists.

CROSS-REFERENCE

Chapter 22 talks about using extended link groups to find links in sets of related documents.

FIND IT ONLINE

http://www.oasis-open.org/cover/maler980331.html discusses XML and broken links.

XML 1.0: OTHER LOCATION-TERM PRODUCTIONS

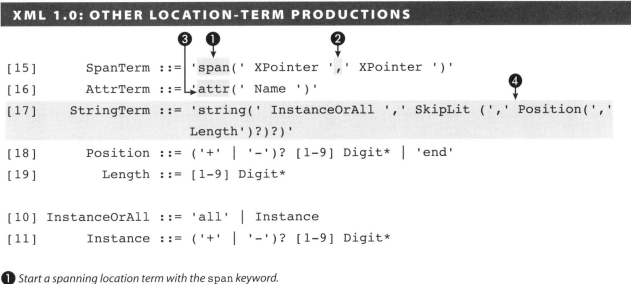

```
[15]        SpanTerm ::= 'span(' XPointer ',' XPointer ')'
[16]        AttrTerm ::= 'attr(' Name ')'
[17]      StringTerm ::= 'string(' InstanceOrAll ',' SkipLit (',' Position(','
                         Length')?)?)'
[18]        Position ::= ('+' | '-')? [1-9] Digit* | 'end'
[19]          Length ::= [1-9] Digit*

[10] InstanceOrAll ::= 'all' | Instance
[11]        Instance ::= ('+' | '-')? [1-9] Digit*
```

❶ Start a spanning location term with the span keyword.
❷ Separate two XPointers with a comma.
❸ Start an attribute location term with the attr keyword.
❹ A string location term includes instances, a string, position, and length.

Listing 23-6: A SPANNING LOCATION TERM EXAMPLE

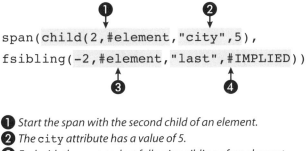

```
span(child(2,#element,"city",5),
fsibling(-2,#element,"last",#IMPLIED))
```

❶ Start the span with the second child of an element.
❷ The city attribute has a value of 5.
❸ End with the next-to-last following sibling of an element.
❹ The last attribute has any value.

Listing 23-7: STRING AND ATTRIBUTE LOCATION TERM EXAMPLES

```
root().string(3,"Section",4)
```
←❶

```
id(chap1).string(4,'!',1,8)
```
←❷

```
attr(value)
```
←❸

❶ Select the fourth position in the third occurrence of Section.
❷ Select the fourth exclamation point and eight characters following.
❸ Choose the attribute named value.

Personal Workbook

Q&A

1 What do XPointers enable you to do with extended links?

_____

_____

_____

2 What is a *location term*?

_____

_____

_____

3 What part of a URI makes up an XPointer?

_____

_____

_____

4 What is an *absolute location term*?

_____

_____

_____

5 What is a *relative location term*?

_____

_____

_____

6 What is a *spanning location term*?

_____

_____

_____

7 What is an *attribute location term*?

_____

_____

_____

8 What is a *string-match location term*?

_____

_____

_____

ANSWERS: PAGE 468

EXTRA PRACTICE

1 Write a location term that starts at the root and goes to the chap element.

2 Write a location term that finds the 12345 identifier in the current document.

3 Write a location term that finds the second child of the mark element.

4 Write a location term that finds the first occurrence of the mark element whose name attribute has a value of brown.

5 Write a location term that spans from the frompage element to the third occurrence of the topage element.

6 Write a location term that finds the element that is processed immediately after the mark element is processed.

REAL-WORLD APPLICATIONS

✔ For a computer manual, you want to add links to each of the introductory and summary paragraphs in every chapter.

✔ For any document, you want to build links that point to all the revision text and text that is marked as deleted.

✔ For an inventory database, you want to add links to all negative data. (Hint: Use an attribute to specify a positive or negative value.)

✔ For a document that contains many quotations, you want to link to the span of each quotation ending with the name of the quotation author.

Visual Quiz

You can find this example and the following XPointers in the current XPointer working draft. What target does id(a27).child(2,DIRECTION) locate? What target does id(a27).child(2,#element) locate? What target does id(a27).child(2,#text) locate?

_____

_____

_____

_____

```
W Microsoft Word - visual quiz 23                            _ 8 X
📖 File  Edit  View  Insert  Format  Tools  Table  Window  Help    _ 8 X

    <!DOCTYPE SPEECH [
    <!ELEMENT SPEECH (#PCDATA|SPEAKER|DIRECTION)*>
    <!ATTLIST SPEECH
           ID       ID        #IMPLIED>
    <!ELEMENT SPEAKER (#PCDATA)>
    <!ELEMENT DIRECTION (#PCDATA)>
    ]>
    <SPEECH ID="a27"><SPEAKER>Polonius</SPEAKER>
    <DIRECTION>crossing downstage</DIRECTION>
    You go to seek Lord Hamlet? There he is.</SPEECH>

Page 1   Sec 1       1/1      At 4.3"   Ln 19  Col 1      REC TRK EXT OVR WPH
```

PART

V

Styling XML Output

In 1996, the World Wide Web Consortium (W3C) announced *cascading style sheets* (CSSs) — sets of document style sheets that enable HTML developers, and now developers of XML documents, to change the appearance of documents. For HTML, style sheets mean that styling elements and attributes (such as the FONT and CENTER elements and ALIGN attribute) are now less important than they were in the early days of HTML. Two cascading style sheet standards exist: CSS1 and CSS2. CSS1, the first standard, was a set of rules to format and enhance text, paragraphs, and documents. CSS2, the current standard, adds to the CSS1 base a set of styles for visual browsers, aural devices, printers, Braille devices, and so on, as well as styles for table layout, internationalization features, and more. Because most browsers still do not support CSS2, using CSS1 presently is the best choice. However, it is important to test all your style sheets; not all properties are fully supported by all browsers.

As you know, XML documents separate content and format. Thus, using style sheets for documents to be output to the computer screen or printer is imperative.

In this part, you learn about cascading style sheets and how to style your XML documents.

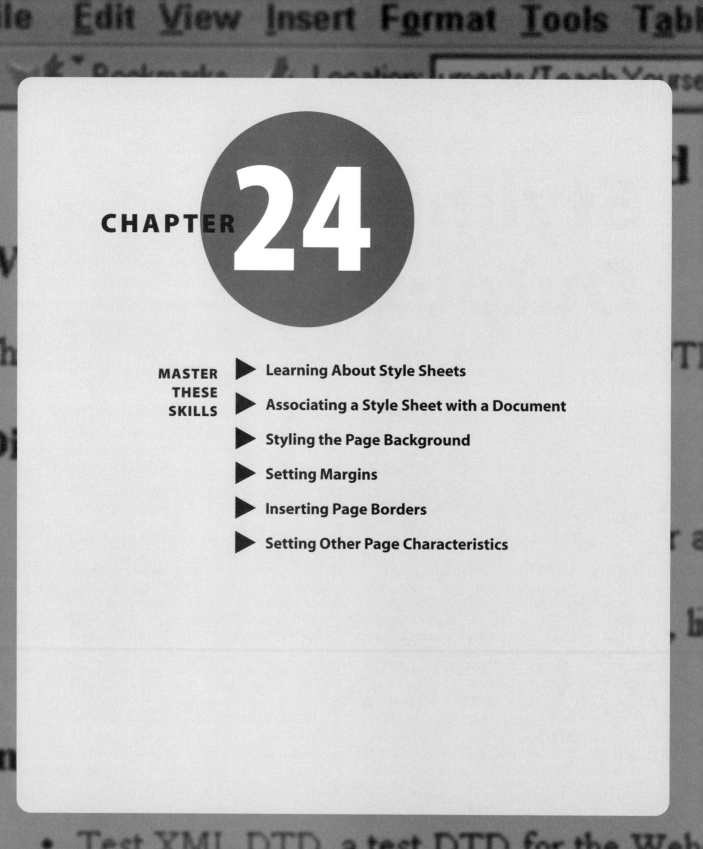

CHAPTER **24**

MASTER
THESE
SKILLS

▶ **Learning About Style Sheets**

▶ **Associating a Style Sheet with a Document**

▶ **Styling the Page Background**

▶ **Setting Margins**

▶ **Inserting Page Borders**

▶ **Setting Other Page Characteristics**

Laying Out and Styling Pages

As you have learned in previous chapters, XML elements control document structure and content. Style sheets enable you to control the appearance of XML documents when the documents are to be printed or displayed electronically. Unlike HTML, XML does not include predefined elements for formatting and enhancing documents. XML documents to be printed or displayed must have associated style sheets.

Most people who use word processing programs know that each document they create is associated with a style sheet — default or custom-made. The default style sheet automatically applies standard formats (such as left alignment, the Times New Roman font, and a point size of 10) to each paragraph of body text in a document, and applies a font such as Helvetica, a boldface enhancement, and a higher point size to headings.

Most individuals with intermediate or advanced word-processing skills have learned how to create their own style sheets so they can apply custom styles — to various levels of headings, lists, and so on. Style sheets enable them to develop well-formatted documents using a set of standards, thereby controlling the look of each type of document. Style sheets also enable users to apply several styles at once to one or more paragraphs, which saves a great deal of time in document creation This feature enables all press releases to use the same fonts and point sizes for headings and body text, and all employee manuals to use a different set of fonts and point sizes — assuming that the people who create and edit the documents follow the style-sheet standards.

In addition to using style sheets for text formatting and enhancements in XML documents, you can use them to set document-wide margins, add white space before and/or after paragraphs, align paragraphs, and much more. Users can instantly change the look of a document by attaching a different style sheet. Or they can make a single change to a style sheet to change one format for all the documents to which the style sheet is attached.

Learning About Style Sheets

Use style sheets to define *rules* (formats and enhancements) for selected text, paragraphs, or entire documents. After attaching a style sheet to a document (see the following task), a user can apply a rule to selected text simply by choosing the element with which that particular rule is associated.

A style-sheet rule is composed of two parts: The *selector* is the element to which the rule applies, and the *declaration* consists of the property (similar to an attribute) and the value—both within brackets. Look at the following example:

```
PARA { FONT: 12pt "Century Schoolbook" }
```

In the example, PARA is the selector (the element), FONT is the property, and both 12pt and "Century Schoolbook" are values.

Note that in the example, the font size value of 12pt is an approximation. The font size probably depends on the editor with which you create the paragraph, the browser with which you view the paragraph, or the printer with which you print it.

A style sheet enables an XML developer to define universal formats for all identical elements in a document. For example, all top-level headings should always look the same, and lower-level headings should vary so that each descending level has a gradually reduced point size and different enhancements (through using varying combinations of boldface, italics, bold italics, and such) to make the organization more distinct. Using a style sheet, a writer can change the font, font size, and color of all level-one headings by using a single style rule. Without a style sheet, a writer must use the default styles or redefine the look of every level-one heading.

You can attach multiple cascading style sheets to a single document and define several styles for a single element; in general, the style that is closest to a particular element affects that element. Currently, some browsers support style sheets—completely or partially—and many other browsers will support style sheets soon.

TAKE NOTE

▶ FORMATTING WITH SGML'S FOSI

Formatting Output Specification Instance (FOSI) is an SGML specification (that is, an actual SGML document) that describes the appearance, or styles, of a printed document. However, if you use an SGML publishing system to create documents, you will find that the system formats documents in almost the same way word processors do. In addition, if you use style sheets to add formats and enhancements, FOSIs are superfluous. Therefore, FOSIs are less common than they used to be.

▶ THE SGML CALS DECLARATION

The Continuous Acquisition and Life Cycle Supports (CALS) declaration is a U.S. Department of Defense standard for SGML documents. CALS is a DTD that incorporates FOSI for formats. Also included in the CALS DTD are elements and attributes for creating and formatting tables.

CROSS-REFERENCE

In Chapter 2, you learn about XML documents, including DTDs — both internal and external DTD subsets.

FIND IT ONLINE

The current official cascading style-sheet specification is located at **http://www.w3.org/TR/REC-CSS2/**.

Listing 24-1: TWO STYLES FOR PARAGRAPHS

```
PARA { color: red; font-family: Arial,
      "Century Gothic", sans-serif;
      font-style: italic }
PARA {
   color: red;
   font-family: Arial, "Century Gothic",
      sans-serif;
   font-style: italic
}
```

▲ *Both examples include the same styles: red italicized text and the Arial, Century Gothic, or other sans serif typeface. Enclose strings with embedded spaces (for example, "Century Gothic") within quotation marks.*

Listing 24-2: HEADING AND ORDERED-LIST STYLES

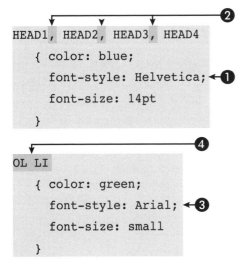

❶ *List all the elements and the rules that apply to them.*
❷ *Separate similar elements with commas.*
❸ *Define properties for parent and child elements.*
❹ *Separate parent and child elements with spaces.*

Listing 24-3: PART OF A MEMO DTD

```
<?xml version="1.0"?>                          ❶
<!DOCTYPE MEMO [
<!ELEMENT MEMO (TO, FROM, SUBJECT, BODY)>
<!ELEMENT TO      (#PCDATA)>
<!ELEMENT FROM    (#PCDATA)>
<!ELEMENT SUBJECT (#PCDATA)>
<!ELEMENT BODY    (#PCDATA)>
]>
```

```
<!doctype style-sheet SYSTEM "-//Sandra      ❷
Eddy//DTD  CSS Style Sheet//EN">
MEMO { font-family: "Times New Roman",
 "Book Antigua", serif;
        font-size: 12pt;                      ❸
        margin: 1in }
TO, FROM, SUBJECT { font-weight: bold }      ❹
```

❶ *The DTD declares elements for a memo.*
❷ *Start the style sheet with a document type declaration.*
❸ *Specify fonts, a font size, and margins for the root element.*
❹ *Make the child elements* TO, FROM, *and* SUBJECT *bold.*

Associating a Style Sheet with a Document

You associate a style sheet with an XML document in the same way you use the LINK element to associate an external style sheet document in an HTML document.

Note that this task uses information based in part on a W3C working draft, "Associating Stylesheets with XML Documents" (**http://www.w3.org/TR/WD-xml-stylesheet**). To obtain up-to-date information, browse the W3C Technical Reports page (**http://www.w3.org/TR**).

To associate a style sheet with an XML document, insert the xml-stylesheet processing instructions (PI) anywhere within the XML document prolog, using the following productions:

```
[1]    StylesheetPI ::= '<?xml-stylesheet'
                        (S PseudoAtt)* S '?>'
[2]       PseudoAtt ::= Name S '=' S
                               PseudoAttValue
[3]  PseudoAttValue ::= '"' ([^"<&]
                        |CharRef
                        |PredefEntityRef)* '"'
                            "'" ([^'<&]
                        |CharRef
                        |PredefEntityRef)* "'"
[4] PredefEntityRef ::= '&amp;'|'&lt;'
                        |'&gt;'|'&quot;
                        |'&apos;'
```

The keyword xml-stylesheet indicates that the attached external document is a style sheet. The following pseudo attributes are supported:

```
href       CDATA      #REQUIRED
type       CDATA      #REQUIRED
title      CDATA      #IMPLIED
media      CDATA      #IMPLIED
charset    CDATA      #IMPLIED
alternate  (yes|no)   "no"
```

The attribute href specifies a URI link to the style sheet. The attribute type specifies that the document is a cascading style sheet (css). You can also use xsl style sheets (see Chapter 30). The attribute title specifies a title name of the external style-sheet document; media indicates the type of destination; charset names the character set used in the style sheet. If alternate="no" is used, this processing instruction (the default) associates the main style sheet with the document. If alternate="yes" is used, this processing instruction associates an alternate style sheet.

TAKE NOTE

STYLE-SHEET HELP FROM *WEB REVIEW*

The online magazine *Web Review* has articles about style sheets and other valuable information. (The home page is at **http://webreview.com/wr/pub/guides/style/style.html**.) You can obtain an overview of the CSS specification at **http://webreview.com/wr/pub/guides/style/glossary.html** and a master list of properties at **http://webreview.com/wr/pub/guides/style/mastergrid.html**. *Web Review* also presents a list of properties that have been tested against the Netscape Navigator and Microsoft Internet Explorer browsers.

CROSS-REFERENCE

In Chapter 3, you find out how to use Extended Backus-Naur Form (EBNF) notation to write all types of XML documents.

FIND IT ONLINE

Validate your style sheet by downloading the W3C CSS Validation Service (**http://jigsaw.w3.org/css-validator/**).

Exploring Style-Sheet Resources

The W3C offers several style-sheet resources — mostly oriented to HTML writers but very helpful to XML developers. The home page is located at **http://www.w3.org/style/**. You can visit the W3C Core Styles site (**http://www.w3.org/StyleSheets/Core/**), which offers several predefined style sheets. Use them in your documents or, at the very least, use them as aids when you construct your own style sheets. You can also go to **http://www.w3.org/MarkUp/Guide/style/** to view Dave Raggett's article, "Adding a Touch of Style," which is an introductory guide to styling Web pages.

Listing 24-4: A SAMPLE PROCESSING INSTRUCTION

```
<?xml-stylesheet href="memo.css"
 title="block" type="text/css" ?>
```

▲ You can run the xml-stylesheet *processing instruction on one or two lines.*

Listing 24-5: AN INDENTED PROCESSING INSTRUCTION

```
<?xml-stylesheet
    href="memo.css"
    title="block"
    type="text/css" ?>
```

▲ Alternatively, you can format and indent parts of the instruction to make it easier to read.

Listing 24-6: AN EXAMPLE OF ALTERNATE STYLE SHEETS

```
<?xml-stylesheet
    href="letter1.css"
    title="block"
    type="text/css"
    alternate="no"?>
<?xml-stylesheet
    href="letter2.css"
    title="indent"
    type="text/css"
    alternate="yes"?>
```

❶ → `alternate="no"?>`

❷ → `alternate="yes"?>`

❶ *Use* alternate="no" *to identify the main style sheet.*
❷ *Use* alternate="yes" *to identify the alternate.*

Listing 24-7: ANOTHER ALTERNATE STYLE SHEET EXAMPLE

```
<!—default memo style sheet—>
<?xml-stylesheet
            href="memo.css"
            type="text/css"
            alternate="no" ?>

<!—formal memo style sheet—>
<?xml-style-sheet
            href="memof.css"
            type="text/css"
            alternate="yes" ?>
```

▲ This example shows another way to associate style sheets. Note that the comments state the type of style sheet.

Styling the Page Background

You can specify five individual background properties or use one property to combine one to five background properties for the pages in your document.

The `background-attachment` property enables you to scroll or fix the background image: the `scroll` value moves the background image as the user moves up and down the page, and `fixed` freezes the background image.

The `background-color` property specifies a background color using the following: the default `transparent` keyword; a valid name (red, maroon, yellow, green, lime, teal, olive, aqua, blue, navy, purple, fuchsia, black, gray, silver, or white); a three-digit hexadecimal color code (ranging from 0 to F, where succeeding digits represent red, green, and blue); a six-digit hexadecimal color code (where red, green, and blue are represented by two digits each); and the keyword `rgb`, followed either by three-digit absolute decimal red-green-blue values (ranging from 000 to 255), or by relative red-green-blue values (each ranging from 0.0% to 100.0%).

Use the `background-image` property to specify the URI of a background image, or enter `none` (the default), which indicates no background image.

The `background-position` property specifies a starting position for a background image using coordinates for the upper-left or lower-right corner of the image, a vertical position (`top`, `center`, and `bottom`). Set a horizontal position with the `left`, `center`, or `right` value followed by a two-letter unit-of-measure abbreviation, or with a percentage followed by a percent sign.

The `background-repeat` property repeats a background image a set number of times, depending on your choice of keywords: `repeat` (the default) fills the page with the image, `repeat-x` fills the page horizontally, `repeat-y` fills the page vertically, and `no-repeat` does not repeat the image.

This example shows typical background styles:

```
BODY { background-image: url(pattern.gif);
       background-color: silver;
       background-repeat: repeat-x; }
```

You can use the `background` property to combine the individual background properties: `background-attachment`, `background-color`, `background-image`, `background-position`, and `background-repeat` — in that order:

```
BODY {background: url(pattern.gif)
             silver repeat fixed }
```

You don't need to specify the property name. The browser should interpret the unique values for each property.

TAKE NOTE

ADDING COMMENTS TO A STYLE SHEET

If you want to add comments to a style sheet, enclose them within /* and */; for example:

```
UL { font-style: Arial}
 /* A font for unordered lists */
```

CROSS-REFERENCE

Chapter 7 describes how to start a DTD, which includes an XML declaration and other declarations.

FIND IT ONLINE

Go to **http://www.w3.org/TR/NOTE-xml-stylesheet** to learn how to refer to style sheets in XML documents.

Table 24-1: SELECTED COLORS AND THEIR HEXADECIMAL VALUES

Color	Hexadecimal Value
black	#000000
bright cyan	#00FFFF
bright fuchsia	#FF00FF
bright medium-yellow	#FFFF00
dark blue-green	#006666
dark lime-green	#00AA00
dark red	#AA0000
light rose	#FFB6C1
medium blue	#0000CC
medium cyan	#00CCCC
medium gold	#FFFFAA
medium lime-green	#00CC00
medium peach	#FAAAAC
medium red	#CC0000
medium rose	#FFADDA
navy blue	#0000FF
off-white	#F0F7F7
pale blue	#AAADEA
pale cyan	#C0FFEE
pale gold	#FFFFCC
pumpkin	#FF8127
reddish brown	#550000
strong blue	#0000FF
strong lime-green	#00FF00
strong red	#FF0000
white	#FFFFFF

Listing 24-8: THE BACKGROUND PROPERTIES

```
background: { background-attachment_value
            | background-color_value
            | background-image_value
            | background-position_value
            | background-repeat_value }

background-attachment:{ scroll|fixed }

background-color: { color-name|#rgb
                  |#rrggbb
                  |rgb(rrr,ggg,bbb)
                  |rgb(rrr%,ggg%,bbb%)
                  |transparent }

background-image: { url(url_name)|none }

background-position:{ [+|-]percent%
                    |[+|-]length|{1,2}
                    |[0%|[+|-]vert_pos]
                    |[0%|[+|-]horiz_pos] }

background-repeat: { repeat|repeat-x
                   |repeat-y |no-repeat }
```

▲ *The* background *property combines values from the other background properties:* background-attachment, background-color, background-image, background-position, *and* background-repeat.

Setting Margins

To set page margins, specify four specific margin properties or use one property that combines one to four margin properties. A margin is outside the content of the page, borders, and padding but within the page edges.

The `margin-bottom` property turns on or off the bottom margin and/or specifies the bottom-margin size. The `margin-left` property turns on or off the left margin and/or sets the left-margin size. The `margin-right` property turns on or off the right margin and/or sets the right-margin size. The `margin-top` property turns on or off top margins and/or sets the top-margin size.

All four margin properties accept the same values: 0 (the default), which represents the parent element's current margin value; an absolute measurement, followed by a two-letter unit-of-measure abbreviation (see Table 24-2); a percentage of the parent element's margin, followed by the percent sign; and the `auto` keyword, which automatically calculates a minimum margin value.

The `margin` property combines the individual margin properties: `margin-top`, `margin-right`, `margin-bottom`, and `margin-left` — in that order. To specify an absolute measurement for one, two, three, or four margins, specify a value followed by a two-letter unit-of-measure abbreviation. To specify a percentage of the parent element's margins, enter a value followed by the percent sign. To automatically calculate a minimum value for one, two, three, or four margins, enter the `auto` keyword. If you supply one value for the `margin` property, all margins are set to that value. If you supply two values, the browser supplies values for the opposite sides of the element: top and bottom, right and left. If you supply three values, the browser sets values for the top, right, and bottom margins. The remaining margin, left, obtains its value from its opposite, the right margin.

For example:

```
BIGPAGE {margin: 0.5in}
```

is equivalent to

```
BIGPAGE {margin: 0.5in 0.5in 0.5in 0.5in }
```

The following example shows three values:

```
BIGPAGE {margin: 1in 0.5in 0.75in}
```

The example sets the top margin to 1in, the right margin to 0.5in, and the bottom margin to 0.75in. The only margin that remains is the left margin; it automatically takes its value from the right-margin setting.

TAKE NOTE

THE DOCUMENT STYLE SEMANTICS AND SPECIFICATION LANGUAGE

The Document Style Semantics and Specification Language (DSSSL) is a comprehensive and complex standard for SGML and XML documents. DSSSL (ISO/IEC 10179: 1996) describes both the transformation of a document from one DTD to another and styling — regardless of the platform.

CROSS-REFERENCE

In Chapter 11, you learn how to match existing DTDs to your XML documents and revise your documents to fit DTDs.

FIND IT ONLINE

An Introduction to DSSSL, located at **http://itrc. uwaterloo.ca/~papresco/dsssl/tutorial.html**, is a DSSSL overview.

Listing 24-9: THE MARGIN PROPERTIES

```
margin: { [length_top|percent_top%|auto]
       [length_right|percent_right%|auto]
       [length_bottom|percent_bottom%|auto]
       [length_left|percent_left%|auto] }


margin-bottom: { 0|length|percent%|auto }

margin-left: { 0|length|percent%|auto }

margin-right: { 0|length|percent%|auto }

margin-top: { 0|length|percent%|auto }
```

▲ *The* margin *property combines the* margin-bottom, margin-left, margin-right, *and* margin-top *properties.*

Listing 24-10: MARGIN EXAMPLES

```
BIGPAGE { margin-bottom: 18pt } ←❶

BIGPAGE { margin-right: 0.5in;
          margin-top: 1.0in;
          margin-bottom: 1.0in; ←❷
          margin-left: 0.5in
        }
BODY
    { margin-right: 18pt; ←┐
      margin-top: 36pt;    ├ ❸
      margin-bottom: 18pt; ←┘
      margin-left: 18pt }
BODY { margin-top: 36cm } ←❹
```

❶ This example sets a bottom margin of 18 points.
❷ This example sets two values for different margins.
❸ This example sets three of four margins to 18 points.
❹ This example sets the top margin to 36 centimeters.

Table 24-2: XML-SUPPORTED UNITS OF MEASURE

Unit of Measure	Description	Absolute or Relative
cm	centimeters	absolute
em	the height of the current font	relative
ex	the height of the letter *x* in the current font	relative
in	inches	absolute
mm	millimeters	absolute
pc	picas	absolute
pt	points	absolute
px	pixels, relative to the size of the window	relative

Inserting Page Borders

To set the width of borders, you can specify four specific border-width properties or use one property that combines one to four border-width properties. Note that you can use other border properties that set the color, style, and width.

The `border-bottom-width`, `border-left-width`, `border-right-width`, and `border-top-width` properties set the width of the bottom, left, right, and top borders, respectively. You can set each of the border-width properties with a keyword or with an absolute measurement.

Note that a border is outside the content of the page but within the page edges and within the top, left, right, and bottom margins. The width of borders varies from browser to browser.

▶ Use the `thin` keyword to set a width that is narrower than either a `medium` or `thick` width.

▶ Use the `medium` keyword to set a width that is wider than a `thin` one but narrower than a `thick` one. This is the default border width.

▶ Use the `thick` keyword to set a width that is wider than a `thin` or `medium` one.

▶ To set an absolute border width, enter a positive value followed by a two-letter abbreviation representing the unit of measure (see Table 24-2).

Use the `border-width` property to set the width of one, two, three, or four borders. To specify a width, you can use the `thin`, `medium`, and `thick` keywords or set a length in the same way you set individual border widths.

The `border-width` property recognizes specified widths in the following order: `border-width-top`, `border-width-right`, `border-width-bottom`, and `border-width-left`. If you supply one width, all borders are set to that width. If you supply two or three widths, the browser supplies widths from the opposite sides of the element. Elements are paired as follows: top and bottom, left and right.

TAKE NOTE

▶ LEARNING ABOUT DSSSL-ONLINE

DSSSL Online (or DSSSL-O) comprises a subset of DSSSL characteristics (see the previous Take Note) especially dedicated to styling electronic documents so they can be read by SGML, XML, and HTML browsers.

▶ STRUCTURING A DSSSL OR DSSSL-O STYLE SHEET

DSSSL-O style sheets are similar to DTDs in that they are made up of hierarchies of elements. Both DSSSL and DSSSL-O are made up of elements, known as *characteristics*, with which you can apply many types of styles to *flow objects* — objects that fill a defined area in document output. Typical flow objects include hyperlinks, characters, paragraphs, pages, groups of adjacent pages, graphics, and tables. *Flow-objects classes*, which are groups of related flow objects, include both named formatting attributes and named *ports* — locations to which ordered lists of flow objects are attached.

CROSS-REFERENCE

In Chapter 13, you learn how to insert elements, attributes, and more in an XML document.

FIND IT ONLINE

Learn about DSSSL-O at **http://sunsite.unc.edu/pub/ sun-info/standards/dsssl/dssslo/do960816.htm.**

Listing 24-11: THE BORDER WIDTH PROPERTIES

```
border-width:{ [thin|medium|thick|length]
               [thin|medium|thick|length]
               [thin|medium|thick|length]
               [thin|medium|thick|length] }

border-bottom-width:{ thin|medium|thick
                      |length }

border-left-width:{ thin|medium|thick
                    |length }

border-right-width:{ thin|medium|thick
                     |length }

border-top-width:{ thin|medium|thick
                   |length }
```

▲ *The* border-width *property combines values from the individual border-width properties:* border-bottom-width, border-left-width, border-right-width, *and* border-top-width.

Listing 24-12: EXAMPLES OF BORDER PROPERTIES

```
TEXT { border-bottom-width: thick;
     font-family: "Times New Roman",
          serif;
     color: red
   }

HEAD1 { border-left-width: 0.25in; }
       font-family: "Helvetica",
            "Arial Bold", sans-serif;
       font-weight: bold
     }
```

▲ *These examples apply border-width properties as well as setting font attributes and text color for four elements.*

Listing 24-13: STYLES FOR A MEMO

```
<!doctype style-sheet SYSTEM "-//Sandra
Eddy//DTD  CSS Style Sheet//EN">
MEMO { border-width: thick; ◀①
      font-family: "Times New Roman",
      "Book Antigua", serif;
      font-size: 12pt; margin: 1in }
```

① *This style adds a thick border to each page of a memo.*

Listing 24-14: HEADINGS AND TITLE STYLES

```
<!doctype style-sheet SYSTEM
     "-//Sandra Eddy//DTD
     CSS Style Sheet//EN">
MANUAL { font-family: "Times New Roman",
         "Book Antigua", serif;    ◀①
         font-size: 12pt; margin: 1in }
TITLE { font-family: Helvetica,
        Arial Black, sans-serif;
        font-size: 24pt; font-weight: bold;
    ②▶ margin: 2in }
HEADING1 { font-family: Helvetica,
           Arial Black, sans-serif;
           font-size: 16pt; font-weight: bold}
HEADING2 { font-family: Helvetica,
           Arial Black, sans-serif; ◀③
           font-size: 14pt; font-weight: bold;
      ④▶ font-style: italic }
```

① *Style the entire manual under the* MANUAL *root element.*
② *Change all the title page margins to 2in.*
③ *The font styles for the* HEADING1 *element override* MANUAL *styles.*
④ *Add italics to the* HEADING2 *element.*

357

Setting Other Page Characteristics

The clear, float, height, and width properties apply to page and other elements.

The clear property displays a floating element next to or below the current element. You can choose one of four keywords to control the display of the element. If you use the none keyword (the default), the floating element display ignores the position of the current element; the display does not wait for the margins to be clear and floats at the current alignment setting. Use the left or right keyword to float an element after the left margin or the right margin, respectively, is clear. Use the both keyword to float an element after both the left and right margins are clear.

The float property floats or inserts the element in the document. Use the left keyword to float the element on the left side and wrap text on its right side. Use the right keyword to float the element on the right side and wrap text on its left side. Use the none keyword (the default) to display the element as inserted on the page.

The height property specifies the height of the selected element. You can set a positive absolute value by entering the value, followed by a two-letter abbreviation representing the unit of measure (see Table 24-2). Or you can enter the auto keyword (the default) to have the user's browser automatically calculate the value. If the height of the element is equal to auto, the aspect ratio (that is, the current proportions of the element) is maintained. If both the height and width of the element are equal to auto, the browser does not change the element's dimensions.

The width property specifies the width of the selected element. You can set a positive absolute value by entering the value, followed by a two-letter abbreviation representing the unit of measure. You can enter a positive relative value by entering the value, followed by a percent sign. Or you can enter the auto keyword (the default) to have the user's browser automatically calculate the value. If the element is wider than the specified width, the browser will scale the element. If the height of the element is equal to auto, the aspect ratio (proportions of the element) is maintained. If both the height and width of the element are equal to auto, the browser does not change the element's dimensions.

TAKE NOTE

MAKING A STYLE MORE IMPORTANT

Add the ! important keyword to the end of a declaration to make the current property declaration more important than others. There are two categories of CSS declarations: *author-defined* and *user-defined*. An author-defined declaration that is *not* important overrides a user-defined declaration that is *not* important. An author-defined important declaration overrides a user-defined important declaration. A user-defined important declaration overrides an author declaration that is *not* important.

CROSS-REFERENCE

Chapter 30 introduces XSL, a new styling language that is designed especially for XML documents.

FIND IT ONLINE

Go to **http://www.ornl.gov/sgml/WG8/ wg8home.htm** for links to style sheet resources and SGML and language information.

Listing 24-15: THE HEIGHT AND WIDTH PROPERTIES

```
height: { length|auto }
```
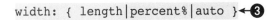 ❶

```
IMG.bigpics { height: 400px;
              width: 250px }
```
❷

```
width: { length|percent%|auto }
```
❸

```
IMG.bigpics { width: 85% }
```
❹

❶ The height *syntax enables you or the browser to set the* *height.*

❷ *The example sets* height *and* width *for an image.*

❸ *The* width *syntax also supports a percentage value.*

❹ *The* width *value is a percentage of the imported image's* *width.*

Listing 24-16: THE CLEAR AND FLOAT PROPERTIES

```
clear: { none|left|right|both }
```
❺

```
IMG.clearex.gif { clear: left }
```
❻

```
float: { left|right|none }
```
❼

```
IMG.float.gif { float: left }
```
❽

❺ *The* clear *property floats an element before or after margins* *clear.*

❻ *The example floats a graphic after the left margin is clear.*

❼ *The* float *property sets the floating element-text relationship.*

❽ *The image floats on the left and text is on the right.*

Listing 24-17: STYLES FOR A MEMO

```
<!doctype style-sheet SYSTEM
  "-//Sandra Eddy//DTD
   CSS Style Sheet//EN">
MEMO { border-width: thick;
       font-family: "Times New Roman",
                 "Book Antigua", serif;
       font-size: 12pt;
       margin: 1in }
TO, FROM, SUBJECT { font-weight: bold }
LOGO { height: 100px; width: 60px }
```
❾

❾ *The logo will measure 100 pixels by 60 pixels.*

Listing 24-18: OTHER STYLES FOR A MEMO

```
<!doctype style-sheet SYSTEM
  "-//Sandra Eddy//DTD
   CSS Style Sheet//EN">
MEMO { border-width: thick;
       font-family: "Times New Roman",
         "Book Antigua", serif;
       font-size: 12pt;
       margin: 1in }
TO, FROM, SUBJECT { font-weight: bold }
LOGO { height: 100px;
       width: 60px;
       float: left }
```
❿

❿ *The logo will float on the left side of the page, and text will* *wrap on the right side.*

Personal Workbook

Q&A

1 What do style sheets do to XML documents?

_____

_____

_____

2 What happens when you attach a different style sheet to a document?

_____

_____

_____

3 What happens when you change part of a style sheet that is attached to several documents?

_____

_____

_____

4 What are _style-sheet rules_?

_____

_____

_____

5 Name and describe the two parts of a style sheet rule.

_____

_____

_____

6 How can you attach more than one style sheet to a single document?

_____

_____

_____

7 Name the style-sheet properties the `background` property includes.

_____

_____

_____

8 Name the border-width properties. What do they do?

_____

_____

_____

ANSWERS: PAGE 469

EXTRA PRACTICE

❶ Find the Chocolate style sheet at the W3C.

❷ Write styles to do the following: make the background silver, add a fixed image to a page, and center the image horizontally and vertically. Then, write a single statement that incorporates all these styles.

❸ Write styles that set the left and right margins to 8 points and the top and bottom margins to 1.5 inches. Incorporate these settings into one statement.

❹ Write styles that set thick bottom and right borders and medium top and left borders. Incorporate these settings into one statement.

❺ Omit the left and right borders of a page element and set the top and bottom borders to 10 picas.

REAL-WORLD APPLICATIONS

✔ Your corporate intranet is composed of unstyled XML documents. Using the styles you learned in this chapter, add margins and borders that will apply to all types of pages. Attach the style sheet to each of your documents.

✔ You have been assigned to write a style-sheet reference. Make a table of the properties and values from this chapter. As you continue through the remaining CSS chapters, continue to fill in the table.

✔ You are in charge of converting your documents to XML. The first set of documents you will work on are corporate letters. Create a DTD that will contain all elements of a letter, including a corporate logo. Add appropriate attributes that will control the use of each element. Finally, style the template document with margins and borders.

Visual Quiz

Identify the bad syntax in this style sheet.

_____

_____

_____

_____

_____

_____

```
W Microsoft Word - visual quiz 24
File  Edit  View  Insert  Format  Tools  Table  Window  Help

<!doctype sytle-sheet SYSTEM "-//Sue D. Nimm//DTD
  CSS Style Sheet//EN">
MANUAL { background-image: url(funny.doc)
        border: big;
        margin: 80%
TITLE { font-family: Helvetica, Arial Black, sans-serif;
        font-size: 24pt;
        font-weight: bold;
        margin: 2in 1in 0.5in 1in 1in }
```

Page 1   Sec 1   1/1   At 3"   Ln 12 Col 1   REC TRK EXT OVR WPH

CHAPTER 25

MASTER
THESE
SKILLS

▶ **Setting Border Colors**

▶ **Selecting Border Styles**

▶ **Working with Padding and Whitespace**

▶ **Vertically Aligning Paragraphs**

▶ **Spacing Lines**

Styling Paragraphs and Page Elements

This chapter continues to cover the styling of XML documents using cascading style sheets. Remember that the previous chapter emphasized page-based properties. This chapter turns to properties that style paragraphs and related document elements.

Many CSS properties serve more than one purpose. For example, the border properties discussed in the prior chapter set the width of borders — primarily page borders. However, you can also use these properties to specify the border width of other document elements such as tables and imported images. Be aware that many CSS properties can style all ranges of document components — from the entire document to individual characters. For example, in this chapter, you find out about other border properties that add color and other border enhancements that also set widths.

You also learn about two types of properties that add white space to your XML documents. *Whitespace* is any area on a page that does not contain text or graphics. Adding whitespace to a page highlights the text-and-graphics content and separates areas of content, thereby temporarily resting the viewers' eyes. As you lay out a document, you should plan the locations of text, graphics, and white space.

When you lay out the contents of a page, you can adjust paragraphs by aligning them vertically. When you vertically align an element, you can control its position on a page — especially in respect to the element you previously placed on the page. You can align an element along, above, or below the currently active text line; at the top, bottom, or middle of the previously inserted element; or you can align the element relative to its parent element.

This chapter also explains how to set spaces between text lines — specifically, the space between the current text line and the line that follows — in the same way you space lines with a word processor. Cascading style sheets enable you to enter a number that is multiplied by the current font size, or set an absolute or relative space.

Setting Border Colors

In the previous chapter, you learned how to use one set of border properties — for the widths of borders. In this task and the next, you find out how to specify other border properties as well as use other properties to set the widths of one, two, three, or four borders — of pages as well as page elements (such as tables and images). You can specify six individual border properties or use one property to combine one to six border styles. Remember that a border is outside the content of the page but within the page edges and within the top, bottom, left, and right margins.

The `border-color` property sets colors of one, two, three, or four borders with a choice of five types of color options:

▶ Name a color using a valid name (red, maroon, yellow, green, lime, teal, olive, aqua, blue, navy, purple, fuchsia, black, gray, silver, or white).

▶ Specify a three-digit hexadecimal color code (ranging from 0 to F, where one digit represents red, the next green, and the last blue).

▶ Enter a six-digit hexadecimal color code (where red, green, and blue are represented by two digits — 00 to FF — each).

▶ Type the keyword `rgb`, followed by a three-digit absolute decimal red-green-blue value (ranging from 000 to 255).

▶ Type the keyword `rgb`, followed by a relative red-green-blue value (each ranging from 0.0% to 100.0%, the equivalent of an absolute value of 000 to 255, respectively).

The initial color value is set within the user's browser. Table 24-1 (in Chapter 24) lists selected colors and their six-digit hexadecimal values.

Learning About RGB Colors

RGB (red-green-blue) colors combine red, green, and blue values from your video card. Colors range from the blackest black (with an RGB value of 0-0-0 or 000-000-000) to the whitest white (255-255-255) and include many colors between — including shades of red, green, and blue. For example, the strongest version of red is 255-0-0, blue is 0-255-0, and green is 0-0-255. Combinations of colors such as purple, which mixes red and blue, might have the value of 255-255-0. Grays combine three similar values, such as 100-100-100, which is a medium gray, or 180-180-180, which is a darker gray. RGB colors are the basis for Web color palettes.

Colors vary according to the graphics board and the software installed on a computer, so you should view all colors and see how they work together before making a color choice. Regardless of your color choices, there is a very good chance that some browser will interpret your colors in a strange way.

CROSS-REFERENCE

In Chapter 1, you learn about XML building blocks, including attributes, which help style documents.

FIND IT ONLINE

The XML Resource Guide (**http://www.xml.com/ xml/pub/listrescat**) lists a variety of valuable XML links.

Listing 25-1: SELECTED BORDER COLOR PROPERTIES

```
border-color: { [color-name_t|#rgb_t
    |#rrggbb_t|rgb(rrr_t,ggg_t,bbb_t)
    |rgb(rrr_t%, ggg_t%, bbb_t%)]
    [color-name_rt|#rgb_rt|#rrggbb_rt
    |rgb(rrr_rt,ggg_rt,bbb_rt)
    |rgb(rrr_rt%, ggg_rt%, bbb_rt%)]
    [color-name_b|#rgb_b|#rrggbb_b
    |rgb(rrr_b,ggg_b,bbb_b)
    |rgb(rrr_b%, ggg_b%, bbb_b%)]
    [color-name_l|#rgb_l |#rrggbb_l
    |rgb(rrr_l,ggg_l,bbb_l)
    |rgb(rrr_l%, ggg_l%, bbb_l%)] }
```

▲ *The* border-color *property includes five color options repeated four times, one set for each border — top, right, bottom, and left — in a clockwise order.*

Listing 25-2: STYLES FOR FOUR PARAGRAPHS

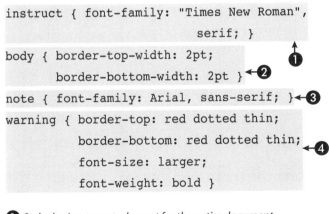

```
instruct { font-family: "Times New Roman",
                          serif; }
body { border-top-width: 2pt;
       border-bottom-width: 2pt }
note { font-family: Arial, sans-serif; }
warning { border-top: red dotted thin;
          border-bottom: red dotted thin;
          font-size: larger;
          font-weight: bold }
```

❶ Style the instruct *element for the entire document.*
❷ Apply borders above and below the body *element.*
❸ Change the font for the note *element.*
❹ Emphasize the warning *element using both border and enhanced text.*

Listing 25-3: STYLES FOR A DOCUMENT AND THREE HEADINGS

```
document { font-family: "Times New Roman",
                "Book Antigua", serif;
           font-size: 12pt }
head1 { font-family: Helvetica, "Britannic
              Bold", sans-serif;
        border-color: red;
        border-style: solid;
        font-weight: bold;
        font-size: 24pt }
head2 { font-family: Helvetica, "Britannic
              Bold", sans-serif;
        border-color: blue;
        border-style: dashed;
        font-weight: bold;
        font-style: italic;
        font-size: 20pt }
head3 { font-family: Helvetica, "Britannic
              Bold", sans-serif;
        border-color: green;
        border-style: dotted;
        font-weight: bold;
        font-size: 16pt }
```

▲ *Each level of heading has a bottom border that varies in color and, for the two lower headings, in size. The headings, which are all bold, are sometimes italicized. The font size decreases as the heading level decreases.*

Selecting Border Styles

The `border-style` property turns on or off (or formats) one, two, three, or four borders, using the following syntax:

```
border-style:{ [none|dotted|dashed|solid
            |double|groove|ridge|inset
            |outset][none|dotted|dashed
            |solid|double|groove|ridge
            |inset|outset][none|dotted
            |dashed|solid|double|groove
            |ridge|inset|outset][none
            |dotted|dashed|solid|double
            |groove|ridge|inset|outset] }
```

Notice that the keyword list in the syntax repeats four times — once per border (top, right, bottom, and left) in a clockwise order. If you supply one style, all borders are set to that style. If you supply two or three styles, the browser supplies styles for the opposite sides of the element. Elements are paired as follows: top and bottom, left and right. If you supply four styles, the browser treats each border individually.

The `none` keyword omits a border altogether and overrides any `border-width` value. The `dotted`, `dashed`, and `solid` keywords draw a dotted-, dashed-, and solid-line border, respectively. The `double` keyword draws a double-solid-line border. The `groove` and `ridge` keywords draw a three-dimensional grooved or ridged border, respectively, using the `border-color` value (see the previous task). The `inset` or `outset` keyword draws a three-dimensional inset or outset, using the `border-color` value. Examples of border styles are on the facing page.

Note that some browsers can't interpret most `border-style` values, so they draw a solid line instead.

TAKE NOTE

SETTING COLOR, STYLE, AND/OR WIDTH OF SPECIFIC BORDERS

The `border-bottom`, `border-left`, `border-right`, and `border-top` properties specify the color, style, and/or width of the bottom, left, right, and top borders, respectively.

These properties specify multiple properties for a border in the same way you can individually set rules for the `border-color`, `border-style`, and `border-bottom-width` properties. You do not need to specify the property name; the browser should be programmed to recognize and interpret the unique values for each property. Table 24-1 (Chapter 24) lists selected colors and their six-digit hexadecimal values. The `border-bottom`, `border-left`, `border-right`, and `border-top` properties accept only one style, in contrast to `border-style`, which accepts as many as four.

SETTING COLOR, STYLE, AND/OR WIDTH OF ALL BORDERS

The `border` property enables you to specify the color, style, and/or width of all four borders simultaneously. This property works on all four borders in the same way the individual border properties work on individual borders.

CROSS-REFERENCE

In Chapter 5, you can read about XML software, including programs for styling your documents.

FIND IT ONLINE

Go to **http://www.htmlhelp.com/reference/css/** to access The Guide to Cascading Style Sheets.

Listing 25-4: SELECTED BORDER PROPERTIES — COLOR, STYLE, AND WIDTH

```
border: {[border-color_value]|[border-style_value] | [border-width_value] }

border-bottom: {[border-color_value] | [border-style_value]
              |[border-bottom-width_value] }

border-left: {[border-color_value] | [border-style_value]
             |[border-left-width_value] }

border-right: {[border-color_value] | [border-style_value]
             | [border-right-width_value] }

border-top: { [border-color_value] | [border-style_value]
            | [border-top-width_value] }
```

▲ The border *property enables you to set color, style, and width for all borders. The* border-bottom, border-left, border-right, *and* border-top *properties apply color, style, and width to individual borders.*

Listing 25-5: DOCUMENT STYLES

```
document { font-family: "Times New Roman",
 "Book Antigua", serif;
            font-size: 12pt }
head1 { font-family: Helvetica,
 "Britannic Bold", sans-serif;
        border-color: red;
        border-style: groove;
        font-weight: bold;
        font-size: 24pt }
head2 { font-family: Helvetica,
 "Britannic Bold", sans-serif;
        border-color: blue;
        border-style: inset outset;
        font-weight: bold;
        font-style: italic;
        font-size: 20pt }
```

▲ *This version of the heading styles eliminates the* border-bottom *style and replaces it with* border-color *and* border-style *properties.*

Listing 25-6: A VARIATION OF THE DOCUMENT STYLES EXAMPLE

```
document { font-family: "Times New Roman",
 "Book Antigua", serif;
            font-size: 12pt; }
head1 { font-family: Helvetica,
 "Britannic Bold", sans-serif;
        border-bottom: black solid thick;
        font-weight: bold;
        font-size: 24pt }
head2 { font-family: Helvetica,
 "Britannic Bold", sans-serif;
        border-bottom: black solid thick;
        line-height: 1.2;
        font-weight: bold;
        font-style: italic;
        font-size: 20pt }
```

▲ *This version of the heading styles changes the values of the* border-style *property for each heading.*

Working with Padding and Whitespace

Padding applies whitespace to an area between the optional borders or margins and the edge of the text on a page. It's different from whitespace in that padding adds whitespace around the *peripheral* areas of a page, between the margins and optional borders and the content of the page. You can use CSS productions to set both padding and whitespace.

You can specify four individual padding properties or use one property to combine one to four padding properties. Padding is above the content of the page, within the page edges, and below margins and borders.

The `padding-bottom`, `padding-left`, `padding-right`, and `padding-top` properties turn on or off padding and/or set padding size for the bottom, left, right, and top sides, respectively. You can set padding in three ways: enter 0 (the default) to accept the parent element's current padding; enter an absolute measurement, followed by a two-letter abbreviation for the unit of measure (see Table 24-2 in Chapter 24); or specify a percentage of the parent element's padding, followed by the percent sign.

You can use the `padding` property to combine the individual padding properties: `padding-bottom`, `padding-left`, `padding-right`, and `padding-top`. The `padding` property turns on or off one, two, three, or four paddings and/or sets padding size. You can specify a positive or negative length, followed by a two-letter abbreviation representing the unit of measure. You can also specify a percentage of the parent element's padding. Follow the entered value with the percent sign. If you supply one value, all paddings are set to that value. If you supply two or three values, the browser supplies values from the opposite sides of the element. Elements are paired as follows: top and bottom, left and right.

Use the `white-space` property to turn on or off whitespace. You have the choice of three keywords: `normal` (the default) doesn't add whitespace to an element, `pre` treats the element as preformatted content in the same way as the HTML `PRE` element, and `nowrap` doesn't wrap text.

Using the xml:space Processing Instruction

The `xml:space` processing instruction either preserves or turns off the whitespace in an XML document, using the following syntax:

`xml:space (default|preserve)`

The `default` keyword enables a target application to set its own whitespace values; the `preserve` keyword keeps the whitespace values (as the `PRE` element preserves whitespace in an HTML document). Use `xml:space` in a DTD as follows:

```
<!ATTLIST pre_type   xml:space
(default|preserve)      "preserve">
```

The example shows the `xml:space` attribute for the `pre-type` element.

CROSS-REFERENCE

In Chapter 9, you learn about writing attribute declarations and setting characteristics.

FIND IT ONLINE

CSS Structure and Rules is located at **http://www. htmlhelp.com/reference/css/structure.html**.

STYLING PARAGRAPHS AND PAGE ELEMENTS
Working with Padding and Whitespace

Listing 25-7: THE PADDING AND WHITESPACE PROPERTIES

❶

```
padding: { [length_top|percent_top%]
           [length_right|percent_right%]
           [length_bottom|percent_bottom%]
           [length_left|percent_left%] }
padding-bottom: { 0|length|percent% }
padding-left: { 0|length|percent% }
padding-right: { 0|length|percent% }      ←❷
padding-top: { 0|length|percent% }
white-space: { normal|pre|nowrap }        ←❸
```

❶ Use the padding *property to specify an absolute or relative size.*

❷ Use the individual padding properties to set values for sides.

❸ The white-space *property provides three choices of values.*

LISTING 25-8: SAMPLE PADDING STYLES

```
BIGPAGE { padding-bottom: 8pt }

BIGPAGE { padding-right: 0.75in;
          padding-top: 0.5in;
          padding-bottom: 0.5in;
          padding-left: 0.75in }

BIGPAGE { padding-right: 6pt;
          padding-top: 6pt;
          padding-bottom: 6pt;
          padding-left: 6pt }

BIGPAGE { padding: 6pt }

PARA { padding: 6pt 4pt }

HEAD1 { white-space: pre }
```

▲ *These six examples show padding and whitespace settings. Note that the third and fourth examples actually produce the same values.*

Listing 25-9: STYLES FOR LISTS AND LIST ITEMS

```
<STYLE type="text/css">
   UL { background: green; margin: 12px 12px 12px 12px;
      padding: 3px 3px 3px 3px;      /* No borders set */  }
   LI { color: black;                /* text color is black */
      background: gray;              /* Content, padding will be gray */
      margin: 12px 12px 12px 12px;   /* No borders set */
      padding: 12px 0px 12px 12px;   /* Note 0px padding right */
      list-style: none               /* no glyphs before a list item */
      border-style: dashed;          /* sets border style on all sides */
      border-width: medium;          /* sets border width on all sides */
      border-color: black;           /* sets border color on all sides */  }
</STYLE>
```

▲ *This HTML example based on an example from the CSS2 specification styles unordered lists and list items. The padding for UL separates the content from the margin. The padding for LI separates the border from the content.*

Vertically Aligning Paragraphs

Use the `vertical-align` property to set the up-and-down alignment of the selected element. You can choose from several keywords, or you can enter a percentage value, using the following syntax:

```
vertical-align: { baseline|sub|super|top
                 |text-top|middle|bottom
                 |text-bottom|percent% }
```

Enter the `baseline` (the default) keyword to vertically align the element with the baseline of the current element, or with the baseline of the parent element if the current element has no baseline. (For information about how characters fit on a line of text and how one line of text is related to the preceding and following lines, see the "Learning the Fine Points of Line Spacing" sidebar in the next task.) The `sub` and `super` keywords make the element a subscript and superscript, respectively. The `top` keyword aligns the top of the element with the top of the highest element on the current line. The `bottom` keyword aligns the bottom of the element with the lowest element. The `middle` keyword aligns the element with the middle of the element, computed by starting with the baseline and adding half the x-height of the parent element's typeface. The `text-top` and the `text-bottom` keywords align the element with the top and bottom of the parent element's typeface, respectively. You can also specify a percentage, followed by a percent sign, of the text's line height.

Note that if you use the `top` or `bottom` keywords, an inadvertent loop in the display of the element may occur.

Learning the Fine Points of Character Size

Measuring the height and vertical position of a printed or displayed character is not always as simple as you might think. New terms and measurements enable you to differentiate the parts of a character and the line to which it is related. For example, the invisible line on which a nonsubscript or nonsuperscript character sits is the *baseline*. If a character is above the baseline, it is a superscript; if it is below the baseline, it is a subscript.

You can also analyze the character section by section. The *x-height* is the measurement of the body of a lowercase character from the top of the character down to the baseline. The *cap height* marks the difference between lowercase (for example, *w*) and uppercase (for example, *W*) characters; it is the measurement from the top of the x-height to the top of the uppercase character. If you add the x-height and cap height (in other words, all parts of the character above the baseline), the result is the *ascender*. If part of a character falls below the baseline (for example, a lowercase *p* or *q*), it is the *descender*. You learn the terminology for measuring the spaces between lines in the following task.

CROSS-REFERENCE

Chapter 13 introduces you to creating a basic XML document, which may be displayed onscreen or printed.

FIND IT ONLINE

Find the Cascading Style Sheets Guide at **http://www. europa.com/~bloo/html/style/styleindex.htm**.

Listing 25-10: SEVERAL STYLES

```
BODY {
    margin-left: 8em
}
TABLE {
    margin-left: auto;
    margin-right: auto
}
CAPTION {
    margin-left: -8em;
    width: 8em;
    text-align: right;
    vertical-align: bottom
}
```

▲ *This example from the CSS2 specification shows how to align the caption text with the lowest element on the current line.*

Listing 25-11: VERTICAL ALIGNMENT AND OTHER STYLES

```
SUB { vertical-align: sub }        ◄❶
SUP { vertical-align: super }
SUB { vertical-align: text-bottom; ◄❷
     color: red }
SUP { vertical-align: text-top;    ◄❸
     color: teal }
SIGNAT { vertical-align: text-bottom; ◄❹
        font-style: italic }
```

❶ *The HTML SUB and SUP elements produce subscript and superscript.*
❷ *This aligns with the bottom of the parent's typeface.*
❸ *This aligns with the top of the parent's typeface.*
❹ *This also aligns with the bottom of the parent's typeface.*

Listing 25-12: MEMO STYLES

```
<?xml version="1.0"?>
<!DOCTYPE MEMO [
<!ELEMENT MEMO (TO, FROM, SUBJECT,
 BODY)>
<!ELEMENT TO      (#PCDATA)>
<!ELEMENT FROM    (#PCDATA)>
<!ELEMENT SUBJECT (#PCDATA)>
<!ELEMENT BODY    (#PCDATA)>
]>

<!doctype style-sheet SYSTEM "-//Sandra
 Eddy//DTD  CSS Style Sheet//EN">
MEMO { border-width: thick;
      font-family: "Times New Roman",
 "Book Antigua", serif;
      font-size: 12pt;
      margin: 1in }
TO, FROM { font-weight: bold }
SUBJECT {font-weight: bold;
        vertical-align: sub }
```

▲ *This version of the memo uses a subscript value to separate the* subject *element from the preceding element.*

Listing 25-13: STYLES FOR CHEMICAL FORMULAS

```
<!doctype style-sheet SYSTEM "-//Sandra
 Eddy//DTD  CSS Style Sheet//EN">
chemist { font-family: Arial, sans-serif;
        font-size: 12pt;
        margin: 1in;
        padding: 0.5in }
superscript {font-size: 9pt;
           vertical-align: sup }
subscript { font-size: 9pt;
           vertical-align: sub }
```

▲ *These style examples enable a writer to specify chemical formulas and use both superscript and subscript vertical alignment.*

Spacing Lines

The `line-height` property specifies the height of the text line from baseline to baseline. You can either use a keyword or enter a value using the following syntax:

```
line-height: {
normal|number|length|percent% }
```

Use the `normal` keyword (the default) to accept the parent element's line height. (Note that the suggested numeric value for `normal` should range between 1.0 and 1.2.) You can enter a number by which the current font size is multiplied to result in a new line height. You can set the length, which is a positive value followed by a two-letter unit-of-measure abbreviation (see Table 24-2 in Chapter 24). You can enter a positive percentage, followed by a percent sign, to specify a value relative to the current line height. Note that negative values are not valid. The initial `line-height` value is set by the user's browser.

Before computers, printed materials were set using wood or metal blocks — all with the same vertical height — set in a shallow box, which represented all the lines on a single page. Each block contained a character with space above and below to align it with its fellow characters within its line. So, uppercase characters were greater in height and had less space above, lowercase characters without pronounced ascenders and descenders had more-or-less equal space above and below, and lowercase characters with descenders had less space below. To measure the point size of a particular character, you actually look at the virtual block in which it is "carved."

Certain typefaces take up more vertical space than others. For example, the characters in the Helvetica typeface, which is commonly used for headings, are higher (thereby leaving less space above and below) than characters in the Times Roman typeface, which is usually used for body text. This is one reason it's not a good idea to combine typefaces (à la ransom notes) on a single line or use more than one or two fonts per page. In general, characters in modern, less ornate typefaces are "shorter" than older, fancier typefaces.

TAKE NOTE

▶ LEARNING ABOUT LEADING

In the printing lexicon, *leading* (pronounced *ledding*) is the space between the baseline of one text line to the baseline of the previous or next text line, measured in points. So, leading includes the vertical height of the character plus any space above and below. However, in desktop publishing (including electronic publishing), leading is now the measurement from the top of the highest uppercase character on one line to the top of the highest uppercase character on the prior or next line. By default, the proportion of space to actual character is 20%, but in general, the greater the point size of the typeface, the less the leading should be.

CROSS-REFERENCE

In Chapter 16, you can find out how to convert HTML documents, including elements and attributes, to XML.

FIND IT ONLINE

The page at **http://tips-tricks.com/stylesheet.html** is loaded with style sheets and Web links.

Listing 25-14: THREE LINE HEIGHT STYLES

```
DIV { line-height: 1.2;
      font-size: 10pt }     /* number */

DIV { line-height: 1.2em;
      font-size: 10pt }     /* length */

DIV { line-height: 120%;
      font-size: 10pt }     /* percentage */
```

▲ *In these three examples from the CSS2 specification, each* line-height *value results in the same line spacing measurement.*

Listing 25-15: STYLES FOR THE P ELEMENT

```
BUTTON P {
  font-style: normal;
  font-variant: normal;
  font-weight: 600;
  font-size: 9pt;
  line-height: normal;
  font-family: Charcoal
}
```

▲ *This example from the CSS2 shows the properties of the* P *child element of the* BUTTON *element used to open drop-down menus.*

Listing 25-16: EXAMPLES OF BODY AND HEADING STYLES

```
BODY { padding: 8px;
       line-height: 1.33 }
H1   { font-size: 2em;
       margin: .67em 0 }
H2   { font-size: 1.5em;
       margin: .83em 0 }
H3   { font-size: 1.17em;
       margin: 1em 0 }
H4   { margin: 2.33em 0 }
H5   { font-size: .83em;
       line-height: 1.17em;
       margin: 1.67em 0 }
H6   { font-size: .67em;
       margin: 2.33em 0 }
```

▲ *The line height for the HTML* BODY *element is 1.33 times the normal font size. All heading elements are children of* BODY. *The line height of* H5 *is 1.17em. All other heading elements have inherited the value of 1.33.*

Listing 25-17: EXAMPLES OF STYLES FOR A DOCUMENT

```
document { font-family: "Times New Roman",
 "Book Antiqua", serif; font-size: 12pt }
head1 { font-family: Helvetica,
"Britannic
 Bold", sans-serif;
      border-color: red;
      font-weight: bold;
      font-size: 24pt }
head2 { font-family: Helvetica,
"Britannic Bold", sans-serif;
      border-color: blue;
      font-weight: bold;
      font-style: italic;
      font-size: 20pt }
```

Personal Workbook

Q&A

1 What is *whitespace*? What is its purpose?

_____

_____

_____

2 What does *RGB* represent?

_____

_____

_____

3 What are the five ways in which you can set border colors?

_____

_____

_____

4 What does the `border-style` property do?

_____

_____

_____

5 What border properties combine color, style, and width?

_____

_____

_____

6 What is *padding*?

_____

_____

_____

7 What is the processing instruction that also controls whitespace in a document?

_____

_____

_____

8 What is the *baseline*?

_____

_____

_____

ANSWERS: PAGE 470

EXTRA PRACTICE

1 Write a style sheet that applies four separate colors to a border around an element named `dogpic`.

2 Go online and find a chart of hexadecimal color codes.

3 Write a style sheet that places solid black borders above and below the `world` element.

4 Change the preceding style sheet so that green ridged borders appear on the left and right of the `world` element.

5 For a page that is 8.5 by 11 inches, add margins that are 1.5 inches on the top and bottom and 0.75 on the left and right.

6 For a manuscript, write two short style sheets. One, for rough drafts, uses double-space lines. The second, for final drafts, uses single-spacing.

REAL-WORLD APPLICATIONS

✔ Your company's management has decided to create custom scratch pads for informal intra-office correspondence. You must design a simple form that includes the left-aligned corporate logo, the left-aligned title NOTE at the top of the page, and a dotted red border around the entire page.

✔ You work for a toy manufacturer whose customers have complained about its poorly formatted and difficult-to-understand instructions. As the new instruction-sheet designer and writer, you want to combine border color and styles to highlight headings and important notes.

✔ Your company has asked you to design a one-page employment application form, which includes fields surrounded by borders. You have discovered that you must squeeze the fields on the form by using vertical alignment and line-spacing properties.

Visual Quiz

How would you style this page? Use border properties and separate the three lines by setting appropriate line heights.

_____

_____

_____

_____

_____

_____

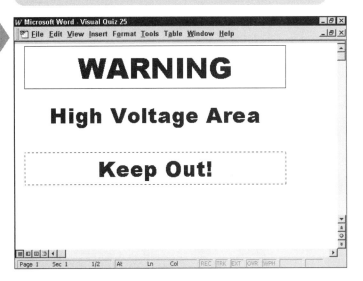

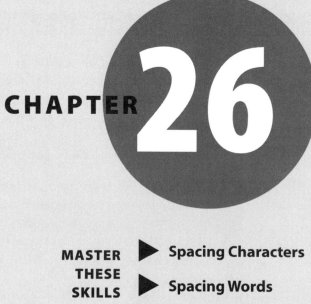

CHAPTER **26**

MASTER THESE SKILLS

▶ **Spacing Characters**

▶ **Spacing Words**

▶ **Indenting Text**

▶ **Aligning Text**

▶ **Changing Case**

Styling Text

In the previous chapter, you learned about cascading style sheet properties that were used primarily for paragraph formatting. As you found out, many CSS properties serve more than one purpose. You can use some properties to apply formats to entire documents, paragraphs, and document elements, and sometimes to all three. This chapter shows that this trend continues; you can also use some of the properties you learned in previous chapters to format and enhance *selected text*. In addition, in this chapter you are introduced to some properties that are unique to styling text.

In this chapter, you find out about compressing and expanding the spaces between characters as well as words. For example, if you want to fit a 57-line document on a 55-line page, you can not only decrease the spacing between the lines (as you learned in Chapter 25) or reduce the size of the margins (as discussed in Chapter 24), but you can also compress overflowing words to move them to the end of the previous line.

You also learn about indenting and aligning text in this chapter. When you plan a document, you want your readers to have a particular feeling about it. You can design a document to look modern or classical, formal or informal. The way the document is laid out and how it is styled enhance the contents. Generally, indented text is more formal and traditional than block text for which there is no indention. Most formal documents have text that is either aligned with the left margin or *justified* (that is, aligned with both the left margin and the right margin). When you center some text or align it with the right margin, you introduce a an up-to-date look. When you add well-placed graphics to the mix of indention and alignment, your documents will shine.

Finally, you learn how to change the case (upper and lower) of selected text. You might do this for emphasis or to make sure all headings are a particular case.

Spacing Characters

In the prior chapter, you learned how to adjust text vertically — above, on, or below the baseline. In this first task, you find out how to arrange characters on a line horizontally. *Kerning* enables you to adjust the space between two adjacent letters. Typically, the larger the size of a particular typeface, the farther apart some characters appear onscreen or on the printed page. At some point, the characters are so far apart that the reader sees them as separate rather than part of a word (see the first example on the facing page).

The `letter-spacing` property sets spacing between characters using the following syntax:

`letter-spacing: { normal|[+|-]length }`

You can enter the `normal` keyword (the default) to represent the normal spacing between characters. You can also specify a positive or negative value for the length of the space between the characters, followed by a two-letter abbreviation representing the unit of measure (see Table 24-2 in Chapter 24). If the value is positive, it represents an increase in the spacing between characters. If the value is negative, it is usually a decrease in spacing.

Learning About Serif and Sans Serif Typefaces

Typefaces are categorized as serif or sans serif. To understand the difference between the two categories, you have to understand the meaning of the word serif. A *serif* is a decorative line or embellishment at the top or bottom of a character. The word *sans* means without, so sans serif basically means without decorations. Typically, body text, such as that in this book, is composed of serif characters. According to experts, serif typefaces (such as Times Roman or Times New Roman, Book Antigua, Bookman Old Style, Garamond, and Palatino) are easier to read. The serifs — especially at the baseline — cause the reader's eyes to move from one character to another. On the other hand, headings, headlines, and signs are usually composed of sans serif characters, which are considered to be more legible; they get the reader's attention. Note that sans serif characters are usually bolder and larger than body text characters. Commonly used sans serif typefaces include Helvetica, Gill Sans, Univers, News Gothic, Century Gothic, Letter Gothic, and Verdana. The first example on the facing page is in the Arial sans serif typeface. Note that the most conservative approach is to limit yourself to one serif typeface and one sans serif typeface per page — and even better, per document.

CROSS-REFERENCE

In Chapter 4, you learn about the international characters and character sets supported by XML.

FIND IT ONLINE

Find answers to all your CSS questions at the very large **http://www.zeldman.com/faq1c.html** site.

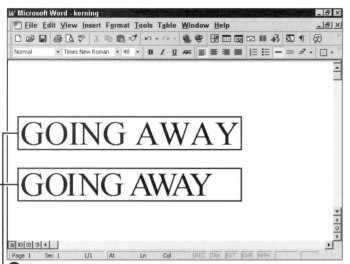

① This is an unkerned headline.
② Some pairs of letters have been compressed and others expanded.

Listing 26-1: EXAMPLE OF TABLE CAPTION STYLES

```
BODY {
    margin-left: 8em
}
TABLE {
    margin-left: auto;
    margin-right: auto
}
CAPTION {
    margin-left: -8em;
    width: 8em;
    text-align: center;
    letter-spacing: 0.1em;
    vertical-align: bottom
}
```

▲ *The table caption in this example is centered, and the spacing between each of its characters is slightly increased from the default 0.0em.*

Listing 26-2: EXAMPLES OF PARAGRAPH STYLES

```
PARA1 { letter-spacing: 4mm;
        font-weight: bolder }
PARA2 { letter-spacing: 3mm;
        font-weight: bold }
PARA3 { letter-spacing: 2mm;
        font-weight: normal }
PARA4 { letter-spacing: 1mm;
        font-weight: lighter }
```

▲ *Styles for four types of paragraphs gradually decrease both the spacing between letters and the boldness of characters.*

Listing 26-3: EXAMPLES OF CHANGING HEADING STYLES

```
document { font-family: "Times New Roman",
 "Book Antigua", serif;
        font-size: 12pt }
head1 { font-family: Helvetica,
 "Britannic Bold", sans-serif;
        border-bottom: black solid medium;
        font-weight: bold;
        font-size: 24pt;
        letter-spacing: -2pt }
head2 { font-family: Helvetica,
 "Britannic Bold", sans-serif;
        border-bottom: black solid medium;
        font-weight: bold;
        font-style: italic;
        font-size: 20pt;
        letter-spacing: -1.5pt }
head3 { font-family: Helvetica,
 "Britannic Bold", sans-serif;
        border-bottom: black solid medium;
        font-weight: bold;
        font-size: 16pt;
        letter-spacing: -1pt }
```

▲ *The styles for these three levels of headings gradually decrease spacing between characters as the font size is reduced.*

379

Spacing Words

In the previous task, you learned how to compress and expand spaces between letters. Cascading style sheets also enable you to compress and expand spacing between words. This enables you to fit more words on a single line (for example, to force the last word of a heading to join all the other words on a single line), to space out the words on a line (for example, to have text take up more room on a page), or to simulate justification — if you are prepared to spend a great deal of time on the task. (Note that you can use the `text-align` property to justify text.) You can also combine word spacing and line spacing to control the position of every character in a paragraph.

The `word-spacing` property sets spacing between words, using the following syntax:

`word-spacing: { normal|[+|-]length }`

You can enter the `normal` keyword (the default) to represent the normal spacing between words. You can also specify a value for the length of the space, followed by a two-letter abbreviation representing the unit of measure (see Table 24-2 in Chapter 24). If the value is positive, it is usually an increase in the spacing between words. If the value is negative, it is usually a decrease in spacing.

Publishing Properly

Whether you intend to print a document or publish it electronically, you should consider the following tips from professionals:

▶ When emphasizing a word, don't underscore it. Italics are a gentle emphasis, and boldface is stronger.

▶ After using your spell checker, do a visual check. For example, a spell checker does not know the difference between words such as *it's* and *its* or *their* and *there*. Some spell checkers also do not look for double words such as *the the*.

▶ Don't overuse styles such as kerning, word spacing, and line spacing.

▶ Text lines should not be too short. Your readers expect a certain range of characters on each page. One suggestion is to use no more than 13 words or 65 characters per line.

▶ If you increase line spacing, don't automatically go to double-spacing (for example, for a 10-point font with 8-point line spacing, don't increase the line spacing to 16 points). Instead, increase the line spacing by about 50%. Then, once again, visually check the result.

▶ Use *curly* quotation marks rather than inch marks to enclose quotations. The Unicode code for a curly quotation marks are as follows: a left double quotation mark is “ or “, a right double quotation mark is ” or ”, a left single quotation mark is ‘ or ‘ and a right single quotation mark is ’ or ’.

CROSS-REFERENCE

Chapter 18 covers how to create and enhance forms and group controls in XML documents.

FIND IT ONLINE

Learn about CSS and HTML authoring at http://www.microsoft.com/workshop/author/default.asp.

Listing 26-4: CHANGED TABLE CAPTION STYLES

```
BODY {
    margin-left: 8em
}
TABLE {
    margin-left: auto;
    margin-right: auto
}
CAPTION {
    margin-left: -8em;
    width: 8em;
    text-align: center;
    letter-spacing: 0.1em;
    word-spacing: 1em;
    vertical-align: bottom

}
```

▲ *The table caption from the last task now includes a* word-spacing *value that adds space between words.*

Listing 26-5: CHANGED PARAGRAPH STYLES

```
PARA1 { letter-spacing: 4mm;
        word-spacing: 3mm;
        font-weight: bolder }


PARA2 { letter-spacing: 3mm;
        word-spacing: 2mm;
        font-weight: bold }


PARA3 { letter-spacing: 2mm;
        word-spacing: 1mm;
        font-weight: normal }


PARA4 { letter-spacing: 1mm;
        font-weight: lighter }
```

▲ *The four sample paragraphs from the previous task now decrease character spacing, word spacing, and boldness.*

Listing 26-6: AN EXAMPLE OF DECREASED SPACING

```
document { font-family: "Times New Roman",
 "Book Antigua", serif;
            font-size: 12pt }
head1 { font-family: Helvetica,
 "Britannic Bold", sans-serif;
        border-bottom: black solid medium;
        font-weight: bold;
        font-size: 24pt;
        letter-spacing: -2pt;
        word-spacing: 2pt }
head2 { font-family: Helvetica,
 "Britannic Bold", sans-serif;
        border-bottom: black solid medium;
        font-weight: bold;
        font-style: italic;
        font-size: 20pt;
        letter-spacing: -1.5pt;
        word-spacing: 1.5pt }
head3 { font-family: Helvetica,
 "Britannic Bold", sans-serif;
        border-bottom: black solid medium;
        font-weight: bold;
        font-size: 16pt;
        letter-spacing: -1pt;
        word-spacing: 1pt }
head4 { font-family: Helvetica,
 "Britannic Bold", sans-serif;
        border-bottom: black solid medium;
        font-weight: bold;
        font-style: italic;
        font-size: 14pt;
        letter-spacing: -0.5pt
        word-spacing: 0.5pt }
```

▲ *The styles for these four levels of headings gradually decrease spacing between both characters and words as the font size is reduced.*

Indenting Text

ocuments that are produced by desktop publishing professionals often follow a specific paragraph format: The first paragraph after a heading is not indented and all other paragraphs are. You can use the `text-indent` property to indent the first line of text from the left margin.

The `text-indent` property indents the first line of text in a paragraph using the following syntax:

```
text-indent: { length|percent% }
```

This property specifies the first-line indention of the text, measured from the left margin or as a percentage of change from the original indent. You can indent in the following two ways:

▶ To set an absolute text indent, enter a positive value followed by a two-letter abbreviation representing one of the supported units of measure.

▶ To set a relative text indent, enter a percentage value relative to the width of the parent element followed by a percent sign.

When you write and lay out documents, widows and orphans will inevitably crop up. Both widows and orphans result from an undesirable line break within a paragraph. Depending on the publishing expert you cite, a *widow* is either one word making up the last word of a paragraph or the last short line of a paragraph whose other lines are on the preceding page. An *orphan* is the single short line or few words starting a paragraph whose other lines are on the following page.

Often, you can use a combination of kerning and word spacing styles to fit the entire paragraph on one page. Experiment with margin settings; however, margin settings affect an entire document. Adjusting settings to lay out one paragraph can have undesired effects on other pages. Also consider deleting words from the paragraph or breaking a long paragraph into two short paragraphs.

TAKE NOTE

▶ HYPHENATING TEXT

To lessen wide variations in line lengths and ragged left-aligned paragraphs, hyphenate body text.

Most, if not all, word processors have an automatic hyphenation feature. If you create your documents using this type of editor, turn on automatic hyphenation and then manually adjust the hyphenation when you perform your final edits. Look for the following problems:

▶ If three successive lines end with hyphenated words, edit to eliminate some of those words.

▶ Don't hyphenate the names of people or businesses.

▶ Don't hyphenate short words.

▶ Some automatic hyphenation features don't always break words properly. When in doubt, consult a dictionary.

CROSS-REFERENCE

In Chapter 19, you are introduced to using extended links and extended pointers in XML documents.

FIND IT ONLINE

The CSS Gallery (**http://www.microsoft.com/ truetype/css/gallery/entrance.htm**) has demos of style sheets.

Listing 26-7: EXAMPLE OF TWO PARAGRAPH ELEMENTS

```
<!ELEMENT DOCUMENT (PARAIND|PARABLK)
  <!ELEMENT PARAIND (#PCDATA)>   ❶
  <!ELEMENT PARABLK (#PCDATA)>   ❷
                                        ❸
DOCUMENT { font-family: "Times New Roman",
 "Bookman Old Style", serif;
              font-size: 12pt; margin: 1in }
PARAIND  { text-indent: 0.5in }   ❹
```

❶ One child element is PARAIND (paragraph indent).
❷ The other child element, PARABLK (paragraph block), isn't indented.
❸ Declare the typeface, font size, and margin for the root element.
❹ Indent the PARAIND (paragraph indent) element.

Listing 26-8: MEMO EXAMPLE

```
<?xml version="1.0"?>
<!DOCTYPE MEMO [
<!ELEMENT MEMO (TO, FROM, SUBJECT, BODY)>
<!ELEMENT TO      (#PCDATA)>
<!ELEMENT FROM    (#PCDATA)>
<!ELEMENT SUBJECT (#PCDATA)>
<!ELEMENT BODY    (#PCDATA)> ]>
<!doctype style-sheet SYSTEM "-//Sandra
 Eddy//DTD  CSS Style Sheet//EN">
MEMO { border-width: thick;
       font-family: "Times New Roman",
 "Book Antigua", serif; font-size: 12pt;   ❺
  margin: 1in;  text-indent: 0in }
TO, FROM, SUBJECT { font-weight: bold }
BODY {text-indent: 1in }   ❻
```

❺ The MEMO root element has no indention.
❻ The indented BODY element controls body text.

Listing 26-9: AN EXAMPLE OF TWO BODY TEXT STYLES

```
<?xml version="1.0"?>
<!DOCTYPE CHAPTER [
<!ELEMENT CHAPTER
(INTRO,(H1|H2|H3|BODY1ST|BODYREST),
   SUMMARY>
 <!ELEMENT INTRO     (#PCDATA)>
 <!ELEMENT H1        (#PCDATA)>
 <!ELEMENT H2        (#PCDATA)>
 <!ELEMENT H3        (#PCDATA)>
 <!ELEMENT BODY1ST   (#PCDATA)>
 <!ELEMENT BODYREST  (#PCDATA)>
 <!ELEMENT SUMMARY   (#PCDATA)>
]>

CHAPTER  { font-family: "Times New Roman",
"Book Antigua", serif;
          font-size: 12pt }
H1       { 18pt Helvetica bold }
H2       { 16pt Helvetica italic bold }
H3       { 14pt Helvetica bold }
BODYREST { text-indent: 1in }
SUMMARY  { font-style: italic }
```

▲ This example shows element declarations and styles for a chapter document. The developer can choose from two paragraph types: BODY1ST and BODYREST. BODY1ST inherits styles from the root element, CHAPTER. Each BODYREST paragraph is indented one inch.

Aligning Text

If you are an HTML developer, you know that HTML provides the `align` attribute for many elements. The `align` attribute, which serves the same purpose as the `text-align` property featured in this task, is very popular for aligning selected text and objects with the left margin and/or right margin or centering between the margins. In the latest HTML specification, HTML 4.0, `align` is *deprecated*, which means it will eventually be omitted from a future HTML specification. Rather than use a predefined `align` attribute in HTML, or define and use an `align` attribute in XML, use the `text-align` property instead.

One reason for aligning text is to call attention to it. For example, you can align headings with the right margin to spotlight them as well as to modernize the look of the document. Or you can center an important quotation, also leaving plenty of white space above and below for further emphasis.

The `text-align` property sets horizontal alignment of selected text using the following syntax:

`text-align: { left|right|justify|center }`

You have a choice of four keywords:

▶ The `left` keyword (the default) aligns text within the element with the left margin.

▶ The `right` keyword aligns text within the element with the right margin.

▶ The `justify` keyword aligns text within the element with both the left and right margins. Note that justification can result in large spaces between words. You may be able to correct these gaps by using the `letter-spacing` and/or `word-spacing` properties.

▶ The `center` keyword centers text within the element between the left and right margins.

The initial alignment value depends on the user's browser and the direction in which the language is displayed.

Selecting the Best Typeface for Body Text

As you learned in a sidebar earlier in this chapter, a serif typeface (such as Times Roman or Times New Roman, Book Antigua, Bookman Old Style, Garamond, or Palatino) is your best choice for body text. In addition, medium and light typeface weights — rather than boldface — are much easier to read. Use italics to emphasize a few selected words, such as new terms; italicizing standard body text makes it difficult to read. Most experts suggest that body text range from 9- to 11-point size. However, if you want to attract readers over the age of 35 to your documents, select an 11- or 12-point size. If you plan to break your documents into multiple columns, reduce the point size and test column widths very carefully. Avoid narrow columns that result in a great deal of hyphenation. If you justify text, make sure the gaps between words are not excessive.

CROSS-REFERENCE

In Chapter 22, you discover how to write extended-link-group statements in XML documents.

FIND IT ONLINE

The site at **http://desktoppublishing.com/ stylesheets.html** provides many CSS and styling links.

Listing 26-10: ALIGNING AND STYLING A CENTERED HEADING

```
<H1 align="center">How to Carve Wood
</H1>
<HEAD>
  <TITLE>How to Carve Wood</TITLE>
    <STYLE type="text/css">
    H1 {text-align: center }
    </STYLE>
</HEAD>
<BODY>
<H1>How to Carve Wood</H1>
</BODY>
```

▲ *This HTML example from the CSS2 specification first uses the* align *attribute to center a top-level heading and then shows how to style it.*

Listing 26-11: AN EXAMPLE OF QUOTATION STYLES

```
BODY   { margin: 1in;
            font-family: "Book Antiqua",
  Centaur, serif;
            font-size: 12pt }
QUOTE  { text-align: center;  ←①
            font-style: italic }
QUOTER { text-align: right;  ←②
            font-size: 10pt }
```

① *Specify that each quotation is centered.*
② *Right-align the name of the individual being quoted.*

Listing 26-12: EXAMPLES OF PARAGRAPH ALIGNMENT STYLES

```
BODY   { font-family: Arial, "Courier New",
  sans-serif }
PARALEFT { text-align: left }
PARACENT { text-align: center }
PARART   { text-align: right }
PARAJUST { text-align: justify }
```

▲ *This example provides four choices of paragraph alignment: left, center, right, and justify.*

Listing 26-13: AN EXAMPLE OF STYLING A TABLE

```
BODY     { margin: 8pt }
TABLE    { margin-left: auto;
            margin-right: auto }
CAPTION { font-family: "Times New Roman",
  "Book Antiqua", serif;
            text-align: center;
            vertical-align: bottom }
```

▲ *This table caption is centered under its table.*

Changing Case

Sometimes, you will want to force selected text to be uppercase or lowercase. For example, to ensure that some headings are always capitalized, add the `text-transform` property to those headings' list of styles.

The `text-transform` property uses the following syntax:

```
text-transform: { capitalize|uppercase
                |lowercase|none }
```

This property transforms text to initial uppercase, all uppercase, or all lowercase, or turns off the case inherited from its parent, using the following keywords:

- ▶ The `capitalize` keyword applies initial uppercase to the selected text.
- ▶ The `uppercase` keyword applies all uppercase to the selected text.
- ▶ The `lowercase` keyword applies all lowercase to the selected text.
- ▶ The `none` keyword (the default) turns off the value inherited from the parent.

Inheriting Styles

As you know, XML uses an element tree to set the structure of a document. The position of a certain element on the tree shows its place in the generation of elements. A parent element's properties determine the properties of its children.

A few CSS properties are automatically inherited by a child element — unless the author, a user, or a browser or other processor explicitly restates the property for the child. Inheritance is determined by those who wrote the CSS specification. In general, a property that explicitly affects an element and any nested elements should be inherited. For example, the CSS2 specification uses the HTML `H1` top-level heading with an emphasizing element (`EM`) to illustrate that emphasized text within a heading will inherit the color of its parent. This prevents the author, user, or processor from changing the emphasized text too much. However, some children should not inherit every property. For example, a table might be surrounded by a border, but you may not want every table cell surrounded.

The following properties are automatically inherited: `border-color`, `color`, `font`, `font-family`, `font-size`, `font-style`, `font-variant`, `font-weight`, `letter-spacing`, `line-height`, `list-style`, `list-style-image`, `list-style-position`, `list-style-type`, `text-align`, `text-indent`, `text-transform`, `white-space`, and `word-spacing`.

The following properties are not inherited: `background`, `background-attachment`, `background-color`, `background-image`, `background-position`, `background-repeat`, `border`, `border-bottom`, `border-bottom-width`, `border-left`, `border-left-width`, `border-right`, `border-right-width`, `border-style`, `border-top`, `border-top-width`, `border-width`, `clear`, `display`, `float`, `height`, `margin`, `margin-bottom`, `margin-left`, `margin-right`, `margin-top`, `padding`, `padding-bottom`, `padding-left`, `padding-right`, `padding-top`, `text-decoration`, `vertical-align`, and `width`.

CROSS-REFERENCE

In Chapter 30, you get an overview of the XSL styling language, which works hand in hand with XML.

FIND IT ONLINE

Learn how CSS and dynamic HTML work together at http://www.dhtmlzone.com/articles/dhtmlcss.html.

Listing 26-14: STYLING FOUR TYPES OF PARAGRAPHS

```
<!ELEMENT body (para|note|caution|tip)
  <!ELEMENT para (#PCDATA)>
  <!ELEMENT note (#PCDATA)>
  <!ELEMENT caution (#PCDATA)>
  <!ELEMENT tip (#PCDATA)>


body { margin: 1in;
      font-size: 12pt }
para { font-family: "Times New Roman",
  "Century Schoolbook, serif }
note { border: black solid thin
      font-family: Arial, sans-serif }
caution { border: black solid thick;
          text-transform: uppercase;
          font-family: Arial, sans-serif;
          font-weight: bolder }
tip { border: red solid thin
      font-family: Arial, sans-serif }
```

▲ *This example shows four types of paragraphs. The styles for the* caution *element emphasize the importance of that type of paragraph. The contents of each instance of the* caution *element are all uppercase, more bold, and surrounded by a thick border.*

Listing 26-15: ANOTHER EXAMPLE OF STYLED QUOTATIONS

```
BODY    { margin: 1in;
          font-family: "Book Antigua",
            Centaur, serif;
          font-size: 12pt }
HEADING {font-family: Helvetica, Arial,
            sans-serif;
          font-size: 14pt;
          font-weight; bold;
          text-transform: uppercase;
          text-align: left;
          border-top: black inset medium }
```

```
QUOTE  { text-align: center;
         font-style: italic }
QUOTER { text-align: right;
         font-size: 10pt }
```

▲ *An enhanced version of the quotations example from the previous task now includes a heading, which is all uppercase.*

Listing 26-16: ANOTHER VERSION OF HEADING STYLES

```
document { font-family: "Times New Roman",
  "Book Antigua", serif; font-size: 12pt }
head1 { font-family: Helvetica,
  "Britannic Bold", sans-serif;
        border-bottom: black solid medium;
        font-weight: bold;
        font-size: 24pt;
        text-transform: uppercase }
head2 { font-family: Helvetica,
  "Britannic Bold", sans-serif;
        border-bottom: black solid medium;
        font-weight: bold;
        font-style: italic;
        font-size: 20pt;
        text-transform: uppercase }
head3 { font-family: Helvetica,
  "Britannic Bold", sans-serif;
        border-bottom: black solid medium;
        font-weight: bold;
        font-size: 16pt;
        text-transform: uppercase }
head4 { font-family: Helvetica,
  "Britannic Bold", sans-serif;
        border-bottom: black solid medium;
        font-weight: bold;
        font-style: italic;
        font-size: 14pt;
        text-transform: uppercase }
```

▲ *Yet another version of the heading styles forces the text of all headings to be uppercase.*

Personal Workbook

Q&A

1 What is *kerning*?

_____

_____

_____

2 Why would you kern selected text?

_____

_____

_____

3 Describe the main difference between serif and sans serif characters.

_____

_____

_____

4 Why would you adjust spaces between words?

_____

_____

_____

5 What does the `text-indent` property do?

_____

_____

_____

6 What is the difference between a widow and an orphan?

_____

_____

_____

7 What choices of alignment does the `text-align` property offer?

_____

_____

_____

8 How do you change the case of selected text?

_____

_____

_____

ANSWERS: PAGE 470

EXTRA PRACTICE

1 Write a style sheet that gradually decreases the spaces between each of the letters in the English alphabet. You should write at least eight styles for eight separate lines, each containing all the letters.

2 Using the previous exercise as a guide, gradually increase the spaces between the words in the text line *I'm learning how to style XML documents.*

3 Using the previous exercise as a starting point, write the styles that increase the indention of the text line *I'm learning how to style XML documents.* Start with no indention, and increase the indention value in each style by 3 points.

REAL-WORLD APPLICATIONS

✔ You designed a no-trespassing poster in the prior chapter. Add styles that adjust character and line spacing and force the characters of the main heading to be all uppercase.

✔ Your company's newsletter, which was previously printed, will now be completely redesigned and posted on your corporate Web site. Evaluate the existing design and declare appropriate elements. Then, style each of the elements using all the styles you have learned in this and previous chapters.

✔ In the prior chapter, you designed a one-page employment application form. You have been told that you must make room for two more fields at the bottom of the form. Space characters and words so one line is subtracted from the form.

Visual Quiz

How would you style this memo template? Make sure you include styles for two levels of headings, the To, From, CC, Date, and Subject elements, and body text. (Note that the border is associated with the Subject element.)

_____

_____

_____

_____

Frammis Widgets

Memo

To:

From:

CC:

Date:

Subject:

The first line of every paragraph in the body text is indented one-half inch from the left margin. The rest of the lines in each paragraph hug the left margin.

CHAPTER **27**

MASTER
THESE
SKILLS

▶ **Specifying Font Families and Point Size**

▶ **Working with Font Styles, Variants, and Weights**

▶ **Styling Headings**

▶ **Styling Body Text**

▶ **Decorating Text**

Enhancing Text

Throughout the previous chapters in this part, you have seen many examples that have included text-styling properties. In this chapter you see the syntax for each of these properties and learn about the valid values for each.

The first two tasks in this chapter focus on the six cascading style sheet font properties with which you can set or modify almost any aspect of the text in your documents. You can select one or more particular font families (typefaces) or generic family names to apply to selected text. Note that if you name a particular font family, it must be installed on your computer. (This is the reason you should always include a generic family name when you write a font family statement.) You can also use a property to change the font size (point size) of selected text, ranging from the smallest body text to the largest headings or headlines, from a single character to all the characters in an entire document. Be aware that your font-size choice must be supported by the selected typeface. (Some fonts support a wide range of point sizes, and others support only a limited number of point sizes.) Also note

that many browsers do not support style sheets in any way; other browsers support a limited number of style sheet properties.

The CSS specification supports the use of text-enhancement and text-decoration properties as well. For example, you can specify the level of italics as well as the level of boldness. You can also style selected text by using small caps, which are a smaller version of uppercase letters. Finally, you can combine all font properties into one. When you use the font property, you can specify as many as six font properties using a single style statement.

The next two tasks in the chapter offer advice and rules for styling headings and body text, respectively. You will want to distinguish headings from body text by using the font properties, but it's a good idea to abide by the recommendations of publishing experts when doing so.

Finally, the last task in the chapter describes how to decorate selected text with lines above, below, or through it, and how to blink the text — if a browser supports it.

Specifying Font Families and Point Size

You can categorize the six font properties in the same way you do some of the other properties in the CSS specification (namely for borders and margins): You can specify five individual font properties or combine each of these properties under one. In this task, you learn about specifying fonts and point sizes. In the next task, you learn about additional font properties.

The `font-family` property specifies a typeface by one or more particular names (such as "Times New Roman" or Arial), a generic family name (such as `serif`, `sans-serif`, `cursive`, `fantasy`, and `monospace`), or a combination of both. You can list more than one typeface name. Ending a list of typeface names with at least one generic typeface is a good idea. This ensures that a font family will be defined if a specific font is not available. The initial `font-family` value is set by the user's browser. Use quotation marks to enclose family names of two or more words that are separated by spaces (for example, "Courier New" or "Bookman Old Style").

The `font-size` property specifies an absolute or relative point size for selected text. You can set the point size by entering a value or a keyword. You can enter an absolute measurement, followed by a two-letter abbreviation for the unit of measure (see Table 24-2 in Chapter 24), or you can specify a percentage of the parent element's point size, followed by the percent sign. You can type a keyword that represents a size relative to the current point size: `larger` or `smaller`. Finally, you can type a keyword that represents an absolute size. Valid keywords are `xx-small`, `x-small`, `small`, `medium`, `large`, `x-large`, and `xx-large`. These sizes are determined by the browser.

Many experienced style sheet users recommend using relative, rather than absolute, font sizes. When a user sets an *absolute* font size, he or she specifies an actual size (for example, 12pt); however, when the user sets a *relative* font size, he or she indicates how much larger or smaller the new size is from the current size.

TAKE NOTE

USING TABLES OF CONTENTS AND SITE MAPS

Tables of contents can serve a valuable purpose — for large books and even for smaller publications. Whether your documents end up onscreen or as printed material, a table of contents can introduce and attract readers to a document or to particular chapters or sections.

If you produce electronic documents for a Web site, consider a site map, which can range from a simple list to a very graphical map of all the pages at your site. Site maps provide a valuable service to your visitors; they should contain links to every page as well as a link to your home page.

CROSS-REFERENCE

In Chapter 24, you learn all about attaching cascading style sheets to your XML documents.

FIND IT ONLINE

For many links to desktop publishing and Web design sites, go to **http://ideabook.com/links.htm**.

Listing 27-1: THE FONT-FAMILY AND FONT-SIZE PROPERTIES

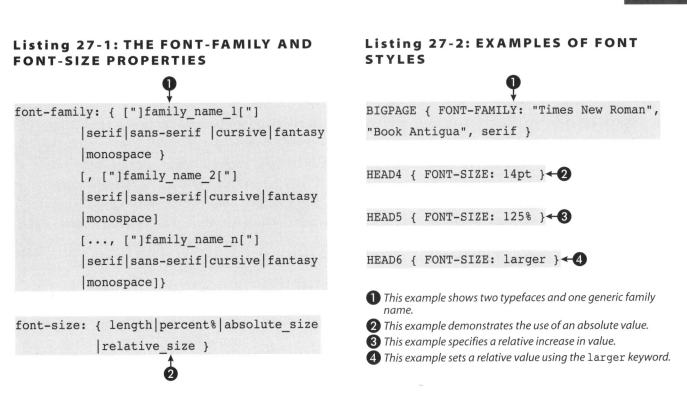

❶

```
font-family: { ["]family_name_1["]
        |serif|sans-serif |cursive|fantasy
        |monospace }
        [, ["]family_name_2["]
        |serif|sans-serif|cursive|fantasy
        |monospace]
        [..., ["]family_name_n["]
        |serif|sans-serif|cursive|fantasy
        |monospace]}
```

```
font-size: { length|percent%|absolute_size
        |relative_size }
```

❷

❶ The font-family *property specifies one or more typefaces or families.*

❷ The font-size *property sets the size of selected text.*

Listing 27-2: EXAMPLES OF FONT STYLES

❶

```
BIGPAGE { FONT-FAMILY: "Times New Roman",
"Book Antigua", serif }
```

```
HEAD4 { FONT-SIZE: 14pt }  ← ❷
```

```
HEAD5 { FONT-SIZE: 125% }  ← ❸
```

```
HEAD6 { FONT-SIZE: larger }  ← ❹
```

❶ *This example shows two typefaces and one generic family name.*

❷ *This example demonstrates the use of an absolute value.*

❸ *This example specifies a relative increase in value.*

❹ *This example sets a relative value using the* larger *keyword.*

HTML 4.0: THE FONT ELEMENT

```
<!ELEMENT FONT - - (%inline;)*        — local change to font —>
<!ATTLIST FONT
  %coreattrs;                         — id, class, style, title —
  %i18n;                              — lang, dir —
  size            CDATA    #IMPLIED   — [+|-]nn e.g. size="+1", size="4"
  color           %Color;  #IMPLIED   — text color —
  face            CDATA    #IMPLIED   — comma separated list of font names —
>
```

▲ *Use the deprecated HTML 4.0* FONT *element as a guide for your own custom font element. Note that this DTD uses entities to declare most attributes. Note also that this SGML DTD encloses comments within double dashes.*

Working with Font Styles, Variants, and Weights

The font-style property enables you to enter a keyword to specify the degree of "lean" to the selected text. Valid keywords are normal (the default), which is unitalicized text; oblique, which is slightly italicized text; and italic, which is italicized. If you choose italic and the current typeface does not offer italics, text may be oblique instead. When you evaluate a typeface for italic or oblique properties, you can look for the following synonyms: *slanted* and *incline* can represent oblique, and *cursive* can represent italic.

Use the font-variant property to specify normal text (in this case, non-small caps) or small caps. Enter the normal keyword for normal text or the small-caps keyword, respectively. Small caps are uppercase characters that are smaller in size than standard uppercase characters. If a particular typeface does not include smaller uppercase characters, standard uppercase characters may be scaled down or may replace small caps.

Enter a keyword or number to specify the font-weight, which is the degree of boldness or lightness of selected text. You can choose from normal, which is the standard, nonbold, nonlight text weight; bold, which is the standard boldface text; bolder, which is a relative value that is bolder than standard boldface and the equivalent of ultrabold or heavy text; or lighter, which is a relative value that is the equivalent of light text. Valid numbers range from 100 to 900, where 100 is the lightest weight, 200 and 300

are somewhere between light and normal, 400 is the equivalent of normal weight, 500 and 600 are somewhere between normal and bold, 700 is the equivalent of bold, and 800 and 900 are bolder than bold.

Use the font property to specify up to six types of properties for fonts: the point size, font family, style, variant, weight, and line height (which was covered in the last task in Chapter 25). The font property specifies multiple properties for fonts in the same way you can individually set rules for the font-size, font-style, font-variant, font-weight, and line-height properties (for an example, see the facing page). You do not need to specify the name for a particular font property. The browser should interpret the unique values for each property. If you do not specify a particular value, the browser uses the initial value.

TAKE NOTE

USING INDEXES

Indexes are very important tools — especially for long reference and nonfiction books. Before adding an index to a book, make sure your document is thoroughly edited and ready to publish. The best way to build an index is to open your document in a word processor that contains an indexing feature. Once you create the index, you'll probably have to correct your document several times, rebuilding the index after each set of corrections.

CROSS-REFERENCE

Chapter 25 covers cascading style sheet properties for styling paragraphs and other page elements.

FIND IT ONLINE

http://www.truetype.demon.co.uk/links.htm has nine categories of typography links.

Listing 27-3: THE FONT-STYLE, FONT-VARIANT, FONT-WEIGHT, AND FONT PROPERTIES

```
font-style: { normal|italic|oblique }
```
❶

```
font-variant: { normal|small-caps }
```
❷

❸

```
font-weight: { normal|bold|bolder|lighter

|100|200|300|400|500|600|700|800|900 }
```

❹

```
font: { font-size_value |font-family_value
   |[[ font-style_value ]
   |[ font-variant_value ]
   |[ font-weight_value ]]
   |[ line-height_value ]}
```

❶ The font-style property sets the level of italics.
❷ The font-variant property enables you to apply small caps.
❸ The font-weight property sets levels of boldness or lightness.
❹ The font property mixes five font properties and line spacing.

Listing 27-4: FONT STYLE EXAMPLES

```
PARANOTE { font-variant: small-caps;
            font-weight: bolder }
```
❶

```
HEAD2, HEAD4 { font-style: italic;
                font-weight: bold}
```
❷

```
PARAWARN { font-weight: 800 }
```
❸

```
PARA {font: small-caps/90%
 "times new roman", serif }
```
❹

❶ This example sets small caps that are bolder than bold.
❷ These two headings will be in bold italics.
❸ This element's text will be extremely bold.
❹ The font property selects typefaces and sets 90% line height.

LISTING 27-5: PROVIDING DIFFERENT STYLES

```
handout { font-family: Braggadocio, Impact,
            sans-serif }
line1   { font-size: 24pt;
          font-weight: 600 }
line2   { font-size: 36pt;
          font-weight: 700 }
line3   { font-size: 48pt;
          font-weight: 800 }
line4   { font-size: 72pt;
          font-weight: 900 }
```

▲ This example provides styles for four lines of text. The text in each line is larger and bolder.

Listing 27-6: ADAPTING AN EARLIER HTML EXAMPLE

```
<!— This was adapted from the HTML
    example in Chapter 26 and then
    improved. —>

HEAD1 { text-align: center;
        font-family: Helvetica,
      "Arial Black", sans-serif;
        font-weight: bolder;
        font-size: 24pt }



<HEAD1>How to Carve Wood</HEAD1>
```

▲ This example is adapted from an earlier example. Additions include font-family, font-weight, and font-size statements.

Styling Headings

When a document includes both headings and body text, you need to treat each type of element distinctly. Both deserve careful treatment. This task suggests ways of dealing with heading styles and body-text styles using the CSS properties that have been covered in this chapter and the previous two. The first part of this task discusses headings.

Here are some rules that should guide your styling of headings:

▶ Select a headings typeface that is distinctly different from your body-text typeface. Generally, a headings typeface should come from the sans serif family. Use the same typeface for all headings.

▶ Experts state that the point size of top-level headings should be no more than three times larger than the point size of body text. This means that if the body text is 10 points, the top-level headings should be no greater than 30 points. Another more conservative way of calculating point size for headings is to make the lowest-level heading two points greater than the body text size. Then, add two more points to the next higher heading, and so on. So, if your body text is 10 points and you have five levels of headings, their point sizes should be 12, 14, 16, 18, and 20.

▶ Add whitespace above and below headings to further emphasize them.

▶ If your headings will be longer than a few words, don't use all uppercase characters. To test whether you should use uppercase or a mix of case, find your longest heading and view it both ways.

▶ If heading text overflows to two lines, the length of both lines should not be identical. The first line should be longer than the second.

▶ Consider reducing the spacing between headings composed of two lines.

▶ Align headings consistently. For example, if one heading is centered, all should be centered.

TAKE NOTE

▶ USING SUBHEADS

When you use several levels of headings in a document, each lower-level heading is nested under the one above. All the lower headings are considered to be *subheads* of the headings under which they are nested. Use a subhead to introduce a new section, to break the body text into readable sections, and to summarize a particular section's contents. However, don't use too many subheads on a single page. Excessive subheads break up the body text too much and may distract your readers.

You can also use a subhead to further explain the meaning of its parent heading. For example, a book title (such as *The Story of Benedict Arnold*) is often followed by a subhead (e.g., *Misunderstood Revolutionary*). This subhead calls attention to the author's opinion.

CROSS-REFERENCE

Chapter 26 discusses how to move individual characters on a text line and in paragraphs.

FIND IT ONLINE

Find design, typography, computer, and many other links at **http://www.will-harris.com/**.

Listing 27-7: THE HTML H1 ELEMENT ADAPTED FOR XML

```
<!ELEMENT H1 (#PCDATA)>
<!ATTLIST H1
    id       ID                   #IMPLIED
    align    (left|center|right)  #IMPLIED
    title    CDATA                #IMPLIED
>
```

▲ *The top-level* H1 *element includes an identifier and title. The* align *attribute should probably be omitted and the* text-align *property used instead. Using a style sheet, you can also specify the font family and size.*

Listing 27-8: EXAMPLES OF DOCUMENT STYLES

```
document { font-family: "Times New Roman",
    "Book Antigua", serif; font-size: 12pt }
head1 { font-family: Helvetica,
    "Britannic Bold", sans-serif;
    font-size: 24pt }
head2 { font-family: Helvetica,
    "Britannic Bold", sans-serif;
    font-size: 20pt }
head3 { font-family: Helvetica,
    "Britannic Bold", sans-serif;
    font-size: 16pt }
head4 { font-family: Helvetica,
    "Britannic Bold", sans-serif;
    font-size: 14pt }
```

▲ *Declare a default font family and font size for a document. Then specify the* font-family *and* font-size *for four headings.*

Listing 27-9: ADDING MORE STYLES

```
document { font-family: "Times New Roman",
    "Book Antigua", serif; font-size: 12pt }
head1 { font-family: Helvetica,
    "Britannic Bold", sans-serif;
    border-bottom: black solid medium;
    font-weight: bold;
    font-size: 24pt }
head2 { font-family: Helvetica,
    "Britannic Bold", sans-serif;
    border-bottom: black solid medium;
    font-weight: bold;
    font-style: italic;
    font-size: 20pt }
head3 { font-family: Helvetica,
    "Britannic Bold", sans-serif;
    border-bottom: black solid medium;
    font-weight: bold;
    font-size: 16pt }
head4 { font-family: Helvetica,
    "Britannic Bold", sans-serif;
    border-bottom: black solid medium;
    font-weight: bold;
    font-style: italic;
    font-size: 14pt }
```

▲ *Then, specify a* font-weight *for the four headings and a* font-style *for two headings. Finally, add a bottom border for each of the headings.*

Styling Body Text

Body text is almost the reverse of headings. While a heading points to a particular section of a document, body text *is* that section. A heading gets attention, and body text is deliberately part of the background. Here are some guidelines for styling body text:

▶ Select a body-text typeface that is distinctly different from your headings typeface. Generally, a body-text typeface should come from the serif family. Use the same typeface for most body text. If you want to emphasize certain paragraphs, you can use a different typeface—perhaps the same sans serif typeface that you use for headings—but in a medium or light version.

▶ Typefaces vary widely in look and quality. Before committing to a typeface, experiment with it. Is it the correct weight? Is every character (in both uppercase and lowercase), numbers, and special characters readable? Be sure to test the boldface and italics versions, too.

▶ When you need to fit more words on a page, consider reducing the overall point size.

▶ When a page contains quite a bit of body text, try to insert whitespace, graphics, or subheads—if appropriate.

▶ Try both left-aligned and justified paragraphs. If you want your readers to view your document as traditional or formal, justification might be the better choice. However, if justification causes long spaces between words, either switch to left alignment or experiment with the `letter-spacing` and `word-spacing` properties.

▶ As a rule, don't vary point size. However, you can change size occasionally to emphasize a word. The following Take Note features other choices for emphasizing words and phrases.

▶ Align body text consistently. For example, if one paragraph is left-aligned, all should be left-aligned. Exceptions include special-use paragraphs (for example, quotations).

TAKE NOTE

▶ EMPHASIZING TEXT

Use various styles (boldface, italics, small caps/uppercase, and color) for emphasis. Generally, boldface is the best choice, but too many bold words on a page can look spotty. Italics is a good alternate; however, if your document contains many book titles (which typically are italicized) your readers may be confused by the dual purpose of italics. Combining boldface with italics is one alternative. The size of uppercase (even small caps) and lowercase characters varies a great deal in some typefaces, so don't overuse small caps and all uppercase for emphasis. Color is a good alternative to boldface, but it has the same "spottiness" problem. Also, when you underline words for emphasis in electronic documents, readers may confuse those words for Internet links.

CROSS-REFERENCE

In Chapter 28, you find out about applying new and previously learned styles to various types of lists.

FIND IT ONLINE

Read an article on typography and typesetting at http://www.pbtweb.com/typostyl/typostyl.htm.

Listing 27-10: EXAMPLES OF TEXT-ENHANCEMENT ELEMENTS AND STYLES

```
<?xml version="1.0"?>
<!DOCTYPE document [
<!ELEMENT document (normal|bold|ital)>
   <!ELEMENT normal (#PCDATA)>
   <!ELEMENT bold (#PCDATA)>
   <!ELEMENT ital (#PCDATA)>
]>

document { font-family: "Times New Roman",
   "Book Antigua", serif;
            font-size: 12pt }
normal { font-weight: normal;
         font-style: normal }
bold { font-weight: bold }
ital { font-style: italic }
```

▲ *This example contains four elements (the root and three child elements), each of which can style selected body text.*

Listing 27-11: AN ENHANCED DOCUMENT

```
<document>
<normal>Do</normal>
<bold>not</bold>
<normal> shake the can of soda before you
</normal>
<ital>open</ital>
<normal> it.</normal>
</document>
```

▲ *This part of an XML document shows how to apply the elements to the text.*

Listing 27-12: IMPROVED TEXT-ENHANCEMENT ELEMENTS AND STYLES

```
<?xml version="1.0"?>
<!DOCTYPE document [
<!ELEMENT document (bold|ital)>
   <!ELEMENT bold (#PCDATA)>
   <!ELEMENT ital (#PCDATA)>
]>

document { font-family: "Times New Roman",
   "Book Antigua", serif;
   font-size: 12pt;
   font-weight: normal;
   font-style: normal }
bold { font-weight: bold }
ital { font-style: italic }
```

▲ *This example shows a better way to define elements and styles. The* normal *element no longer exists and its properties are now the default for the entire document.*

Listing 27-13: A BETTER ENHANCED DOCUMENT

```
<document>
Do <bold>not</bold> shake the can of soda
before you
<ital>open</ital> it.
</document>
```

▲ *Now the document segment is much easier to read and maintain.*

Decorating Text

The text-decoration property enhances text by inserting lines over, under, or through it, or by blinking it. Use the following syntax to decorate selected text:

```
text-decoration: { none|[underline|overline
                  |line-through|blink] }
```

You can decorate text in various ways by choosing from the following keywords: none (the default), which does not decorate the selected text; underline, which underlines the selected text; overline, which draws a line over the selected text; line-through, which strikes through the selected text; and blink, which turns on and off the display of selected text. Although browsers should recognize blink, not all browsers are programmed to "blink" selected text.

Before you use text decorations, think about the ramifications. For example, most users think of underlined text as a link. Many people think of strikethrough text as deleted. In fact, the only practical use for the line-through keyword is to indicate text that has been deleted and will be removed at the end of an editing cycle.

USING PSEUDO-ELEMENTS

CSS *pseudo-elements* enable you to specify styles for first line or letter of a paragraph. Style the first line:

```
<PARA:first-line>
first_line_text
</PARA:first-line>
```

The following CSS properties support first-line: background-attachment, background-color, background-image, background-position, background-repeat, clear, color, font, font-family, font-size, font-style, font-variant, font-weight, letter-spacing, line-height, text-decoration, text-transform, vertical-align, and word-spacing.

Use the first-letter pseudo-element to style the first letter of a paragraph:

```
<PARA:first-letter>
first_character
</PARA:first-letter>
```

The following CSS properties support first-letter: background-attachment, background-color, background-image, background-position, background-repeat, border, border-bottom, border-bottom-width, border-color, border-left, border-left-width, border-right, border-right-width, border-style, border-top, border-top-width, border-width, clear, color, float, font, font-family, font-size, font-style, font-variant, font-weight, line-height, margin, margin-bottom, margin-left, margin-right, margin-top, padding, padding-bottom, padding-left, padding-right, padding-top, text-decoration, text-transform, vertical-align (if the value of float is none), and word-spacing.

CROSS-REFERENCE

In Chapter 29, you find out about applying new and previously learned styles to tables and table components.

FIND IT ONLINE

See an online typography and typesetting museum at http://www.slip.net/~graphion/museum.html.

Listing 27-14: STYLES FOR A DOCUMENT AND FOR ONE ELEMENT

```
document { font-family: "Times New Roman",
  "Book Antigua", serif;
          font-size: 12pt }
bignote { white-space: pre; ◄❶
          text-decoration: underline; ◄❷
          text-decoration: overline; ◄❸
          font-weight: bold
          font-size: 14pt;
          color: red }
```

❶ Use the pre value to keep the content's format.
❷ The underline appears under the text.
❸ The overline is over the text.

Listing 27-15: AN EXAMPLE OF DELETED TEXT

```
document { font-family: "Times New Roman",
  "Book Antigua", serif;
          font-size: 12pt }
delete
    {   text-decoration: line-through }

<document>To install this program, double-
click on the setup icon.
<!— Everyone should know the following
  information. —>
<delete>To be able to click, you must have
a mouse and proper software
installed on your computer.</delete>

<document>Then, let the installation program
take over. Follow the directions.</document>
```

▲ You can use line-through to mark deleted text in a draft copy. Be sure to delete the strikethrough text before you publish the document.

Listing 27-16: AN EXAMPLE OF UNDERLINED TEXT

```
document { font-family: "Times New Roman",
"Book Antigua", serif; font-size: 12pt }
under     { text-decoration: underline }

<document>Don't confuse this underlined
URL,
<under>http://www.false.com/linkless/
</under>
, with a real link.
```

▲ Don't emphasize text by underlining it. If the underlined text is in an electronic document, your readers might mistake the text for a link.

Listing 27-17: AN EXAMPLE OF BLINKING TEXT

```
document { font-family: "Times New Roman",
"Book Antigua", serif; font-size: 12pt }
blinkhead     { font-family: Helvetica,
  Arial, sans-serif;
  text-decoration: blink;
  font-weight: bold;
  font-size: 14pt;
  text-transform: uppercase;
  text-align: center }
blinktext     { text-decoration: blink }

<blinkhead>IMPORTANT</blinkhead>
<document>This is an
<blinktext>important</blinktext>
  announcement.
```

▲ This document contains two pieces of blinking text. Remember that not all browsers support the text-decoration: blink style.

Personal Workbook

Q&A

1 Why is it important to add a generic family name to a font family statement?

_____

_____

_____

2 When you name a font family name that includes spaces, what punctuation do you use?

_____

_____

_____

3 What does the `font-style` property do to selected text?

_____

_____

_____

4 What does the `font-weight` property do?

_____

_____

_____

5 What sort of typeface should you use for headings? What sort of typeface should you use for body text?

_____

_____

_____

6 When your headings are composed of two lines, what case (upper or lower) should you avoid?

_____

_____

_____

7 When you want your readers to perceive a document as formal or traditional, what is the best text alignment choice?

_____

_____

_____

8 What are the five keywords for the `text-decoration` property?

_____

_____

_____

ANSWERS: PAGE 472

EXTRA PRACTICE

1 Create a document that announces this week's NFL football results. Each of the winning teams and its score should be emphasized with boldface. Each pair of teams should be separated by a horizontal line as well as line spacing.

2 Research Zapf Dingbats and other dingbats online.

3 Find free fonts to download online.

4 Design and write a Web resource page that lists at least five links to an important subject. At the top of the page, enter a heading. Then, emphasize the name of each of the resources.

5 Using the font properties you learned in this chapter and those featured in previous chapters, come as close as you can to re-creating the cover of your favorite book.

REAL-WORLD APPLICATIONS

✔ Your small company is ready to produce its first Web site. You can't afford to hire a graphic designer. Plan, design, and build a home page that includes at least one heading, a brief introduction, and links to the five other pages at your site.

✔ You are writing an illustrated family history. Plan a cover, pages that introduce your grandparents' families, and pages dedicated to each of the last three generations. Design a template for each of these three types of pages.

✔ Each year, your company must take an inventory of all its equipment. Design a form that names each type of equipment at the top and leaves plenty of space on the rest of the page for columns of serial numbers, names, locations, and descriptions. (Hint: Use styles from other chapters as well.)

Visual Quiz

This is a page from *XML in Plain English*, also by Sandra E. Eddy and published by IDG Books Worldwide, Inc. How do you style the headings on this page? How do you style the body text? How do you indent body text? How do you set spaces between the lines? (Hint: Use styles from other chapters as well.)

W Microsoft Word - visual quiz 27

File Edit View Insert Format Tools Table Window Help

letter-spacing

Purpose
Sets spacing between characters.

Syntax
`letter-spacing: {normal|[+|-]length}`

Where
normal represents the normal spacing between characters. This is the default.

length is a positive value followed by a two-letter abbreviation representing the unit of measure. *length* is usually an increase in the spacing between characters, but can be a decrease (a negative value).

Notes
Valid relative units of measure are em (the height of the current font), ex (the height of the letter x in the current font), and px (pixels, relative to the size of the window). Valid absolute units of measure are in (inches), cm (centimeters), mm (millimeters), pt (points), and pc (picas).

Page 1   Sec 1   1/1   At   Ln   Col   REC TRK EXT OVR WPH

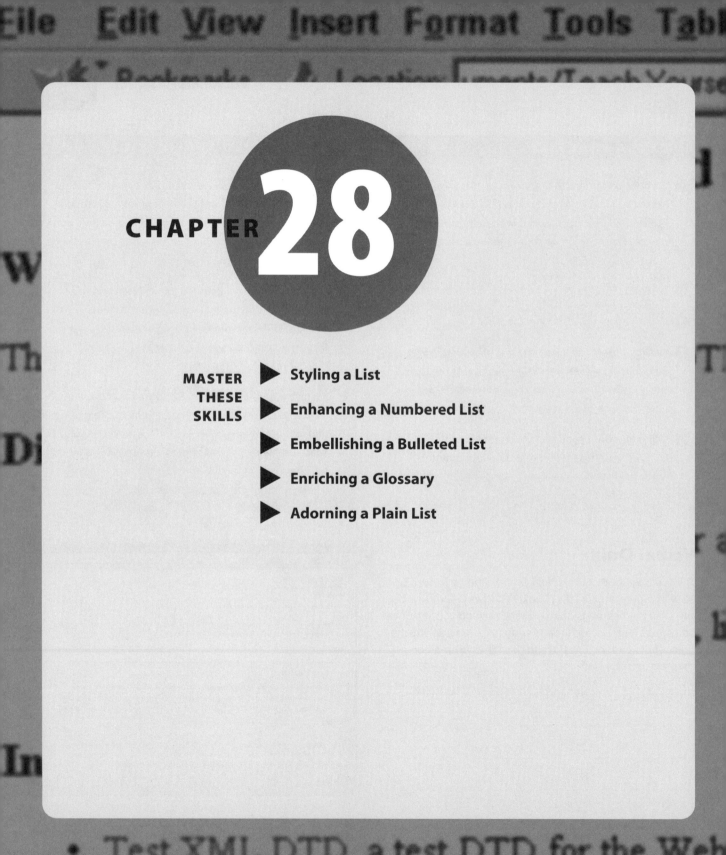

CHAPTER **28**

MASTER
THESE
SKILLS

▶ Styling a List

▶ Enhancing a Numbered List

▶ Embellishing a Bulleted List

▶ Enriching a Glossary

▶ Adorning a Plain List

Styling Lists

As you learned in Chapter 14, you can use various types of lists to present steps that you want your readers to follow, to emphasize important facts, to summarize information, or to present a formal list of terms and definitions. If you use HTML as a basis for defining elements for your XML documents, remember that HTML supports ordered (numbered) lists, unordered (bulleted) lists, definition lists, and two types of plain lists.

The first type of list featured in this chapter is the *ordered list*. Typically, you use an ordered list to present a list of steps that should be followed in the order in which they are presented. For example, when you want to tell a user how to install a program or lead a customer through an online purchase, your audience must follow your instructions step by step in a specific order. *Unordered lists*, in contrast, list items that you wish to emphasize. Your readers can look at unordered-list items in any sequence. For example, you might use an unordered list to name each member of a group of politicians on one side of a particular issue, or to cite some of the books in your library. Although you might want to present items in both lists in alphabetical or some other order, it's not critical to do so. A glossary, or *definition list*, is an altogether different type of list. A definition list is made up of terms, typically in boldface, and the definition of each term, typically in the typeface used for body text. Note that a *plain list*, which is also covered at the conclusion of this chapter, is an unordered list without the bullets.

In this chapter, you learn how to apply styles — either specific to lists or to text in general — to lists. The CSS specification provides four properties especially designed for styling lists. You can use a property to import images to use as bullets, change the alignment of list items, and declare the type of bullet or number used to precede list items. In addition, you can use other properties to style lists just as you would other types of text. For example, you can change the color, typeface, point size, and other enhancements for selected list items. Or you can select an entire list and change its alignment, add borders, and so on.

Styling a List

To style lists, you can specify four specific list-style properties or use one property that combines one to four list-style properties.

The `list-style-image` property specifies a list-item marker, which is the image preceding items on an ordered or unordered list. To import an image, specify a URL. If you enter the `none` keyword, no image will be imported.

The `list-style-position` property specifies the position of the items on an ordered or unordered list. You can choose from two keywords: `inside` aligns the second line of the list-item text with the left margin (that is, under the list-item marker); `outside` (the default) displays the second line of the list-item text under the first line (that is, it creates a hanging indent).

The `list-style-type` property specifies the number or bullet type preceding items on an ordered (numbered) or unordered (bulleted) list. You can select from several keywords. Use the `none` keyword to omit any preceding items from either type of list. For unordered lists, choose from the `disc` keyword (the default), which uses filled bullets; the `circle` keyword, which uses unfilled circles; and the `square` keyword, which uses filled square bullets. For ordered lists, you can use the `decimal` keyword, which uses Arabic numerals (1, 2, 3); the `lower-roman` keyword, which uses small Roman numerals (i, ii, iii); the `upper-roman` keyword, which uses large Roman numerals (I, II, III); the `lower-alpha` keyword, which uses lowercase alphabetic letters (a, b, c); and the `upper-alpha` keyword, which uses uppercase alphabetic letters (A, B, C).

Use the `list-style` property to combine the individual list-style properties: `list-style-image`, `list-style-position`, and `list-style-type` — in that order. Simply choose the keywords supported by the individual list-style property. You do not need to specify the property name. The browser should interpret the unique values for each property.

Selecting Typefaces and Point Sizes for Presentations

Most presentations consist of bulleted lists that identify the main topics. Whether you give a presentation in front of a class using a projector or display it on a series of Web pages, use the same general guidelines for your selection of typefaces and point sizes. Typefaces should be simple and easy to read. You can select almost any sans serif family or one of the less ornate serif fonts. The weight of characters should range from medium weight to bold. Choose a point size that you would normally use for a heading. For example, bulleted items can range from 16 to 18 points and page titles two to four points greater. However, if you are preparing an online presentation, scale the point size down. Instead of selecting for the observers in the last row of a classroom, realize that your online audience will be sitting approximately 20 inches from their monitors.

CROSS-REFERENCE

In Chapter 7, you'll learn how to start a DTD, define the root element, and list the first child elements.

FIND IT ONLINE

Learn about XML and link to resources at Textuality's XML home page (**http://www.textuality.com/xml/**).

Listing 28-1: THE LIST-STYLE PROPERTIES

```
list-style-image: { url(url_name)|none }
```
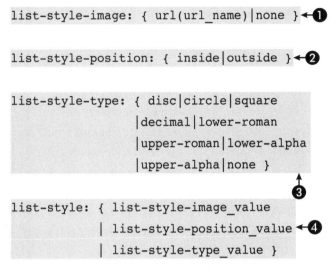
❶

```
list-style-position: { inside|outside }
```
❷

```
list-style-type: { disc|circle|square
                   |decimal|lower-roman
                   |upper-roman|lower-alpha
                   |upper-alpha|none }
```
❸

```
list-style: { list-style-image_value
            | list-style-position_value
            | list-style-type_value }
```
❹

❶ Use `list-style-image` to import an image as a bullet.
❷ Set the position of a list using `list-style-position`.
❸ Use `list-style-type` to specify the type of bullet or number.
❹ The `list-style` property incorporates the three list styles into one.

Listing 28-2: AN EXAMPLE OF TWO LIST STYLE PROPERTIES

```
ulist { list-style-position: outside }
ulist { list-style-type: square }

<ulist>Citrus</ulist>
<ulist>Tangerines</ulist>
<ulist>Grapefruits</ulist>
<ulist>Oranges</ulist>
<ulist>Limes</ulist>
</ulist>
```

▲ *This example shows a list whose second through fifth items will be indented under the first item. The bullets for all five list items will be square.*

Listing 28-3: AN EXAMPLE OF AN IMPORTED BULLET IMAGE

```
unorder { list-style-image: url(button.gif)
}

<unorder>
<item>Home Page</item>
<item>Previous Page</item>
<item>Next Page</item>
<item>Site Map</item>
</unorder>
```

▲ *Each of the items in this sample list is preceded by a button image.*

Listing 28-4: AN EXAMPLE OF COMBINED LIST STYLE PROPERTIES

```
ul { list-style: url(leaf.gif) outside }

<ul>
<li>New England</li>
<li>Maine</li>
<li>New Hampshire</li>
<li>Vermont</li>
<li>Massachusetts</li>
<li>Rhode Island</li>
<li>Connecticut</li>
</ul>
```

▲ *This example uses an imported graphic as a bullet and indents all items under the first item farther away from the left margin.*

Enhancing a Numbered List

Ordered, or numbered, lists enable you to present information in a particular order. The most common use for numbered lists is giving instructions. For example, you can tell how to install a program step by step, or how to prepare a recipe. The primary difference between ordered and unordered lists is the importance of the order: For the instructions to be valid, one step in a list must be done before the next step is started.

When you declare the element that represents a numbered list, consider following the lead of the HTML OL element declaration. The declarations for entities and elements for all types of lists appear on the facing pages of this chapter. Most lists, including numbered lists, are composed of individual list items, which must be embedded within a list-item element (think about using the HTML LI element as a template).

When you style a numbered list, use any properties that change the appearance of text. For example, you can change the font or point size, the case, and the weight. You can also add borders and decorations.

Remember that you can apply some of the list-style properties to ordered lists. In particular, the list-style-type property provides the following values that affect ordered lists:

▶ When the value of list-style-type is decimal, numbering is in Arabic characters (for example, 1, 2, 3, 4, 5, and so on).

▶ When the value of list-style-type is lower-alpha, numbering is in lowercase alphabetic characters (a, b, c, d, e, and so on).

▶ When the value of list-style-type is upper-alpha, numbering is in uppercase alphabetic characters (A, B, C, D, E, and so on).

▶ When the value of list-style-type is lower-roman, numbering is in lowercase Roman characters (i,ii,iii, iv, v, and so on).

▶ When the value of list-style-type is upper-roman, numbering is in uppercase Roman characters (I, II, III, IV, V, and so on).

▶ When the value of list-style-type is none, the list is not preceded by any type of numbers.

Note that you can also precede a numbered list with a graphic image. Simply use the list-style-image property described in the prior task.

TAKE NOTE

▶ USING GRAPHICAL NUMBERS AS DESIGN ELEMENTS

Standard ordered lists are preceded by number characters that are the same font and point size as the list-item text. If all the items in a list are long enough to support a number that is two or three lines high, consider importing a graphical number instead. This enables you to use color, size, and professional design to enhance your documents. On most occasions, use a design that simulates a sans serif typeface to get the best effect.

CROSS-REFERENCE

Chapter 8 covers how to declare elements in DTDs and how to list descendant elements.

FIND IT ONLINE

Get free programming source code for all your Internet pages at **http://www.freecode.com/**.

HTML 4.0: THE OL AND LI ELEMENT DECLARATIONS

```
<!ENTITY % OLStyle "CDATA">              — constrained to: "(1|a|A|I|I)"  —>
<!ELEMENT OL - - (LI)+                    — ordered list —>
<!ATTLIST OL
  &attrs;                                 — %coreattrs, %i18n, %events —>
  type            %OLStyle;  #IMPLIED  — numbering style —-
  compact         (compact)  #IMPLIED  — reduced interitem spacing —-
  start           NUMBER     #IMPLIED  — starting sequence number —>

<!ENTITY % LIStyle "CDATA">         — constrained to: "(%ULStyle;|%OLStyle;)" —>
<!ELEMENT LI - O (%flow;)                 — list item —>
<!ATTLIST LI
  &attrs;                                 — %coreattrs, %i18n, %events —
  type            %LIStyle;  #IMPLIED  — numbering style —-
  value           NUMBER     #IMPLIED  — reset sequence number —>
```

▲ The OL and LI elements incorporate attributes from the OLStyle and LIStyle entities. Other catchall entities for both elements are %coreattrs, %i18n, and %events (which are shown in the following listing and later in this chapter).

HTML 4.0: LIST-RELATED ENTITIES

```
<!ENTITY % coreattrs
 "id       ID            #IMPLIED  — document-wide unique id —
  class    CDATA         #IMPLIED  — space separated list of classes —
  style    %StyleSheet;  #IMPLIED  — associated style info —
  title    %Text;        #IMPLIED  — advisory title/amplification —-">

<!ENTITY % i18n
 "lang     %LanguageCode;  #IMPLIED  — language code —
  dir      (ltr|rtl)       #IMPLIED  — direction for weak/neutral text —"
```

▲ The coreattrs entity includes core attributes that are used by almost all HTML elements. Note the inclusion of the StyleSheet and Text entities. The i18n entity specifies the language code and the display or print direction of selected text.

Embellishing a Bulleted List

Unordered, or bulleted, lists enable you to provide information in no particular order. For example, you can list the basic requirements for installing a program; it doesn't matter if you check the amount of storage on your hard drive or the presence of a mouse in any particular order. Use a bulleted list to emphasize the importance of a few related phrases or sentences before moving on to standard body text or a new topic.

As pointed out in the prior task, you can use HTML as a guide to declaring many XML elements. For example, when you declare the element that represents an unordered list, browse through the HTML UL element declaration.

When you style a bulleted list, use any properties that change the appearance of text. For example, you can change the font or point size, the case, and the weight. You can also add borders and decorations. Just make sure that the styles that you apply do not clash with the bullets, which are significant design elements.

As you learned in the prior task, you can apply some of the list-style properties to unordered lists. The list-style-type property values for unordered lists are as follows:

▶ When the value of `list-style-type` is `disc`, the character that precedes the list is a filled bullet. This is the default.

▶ When the value of `list-style-type` is `circle`, the character that precedes the list is an unfilled circle.

▶ When the value of `list-style-type` is `square`, the character that precedes the list is a square bullet.

▶ When the value of `list-style-type` is `none`, no character precedes the list.

CROSS-REFERENCE

Chapter 9 covers how to define attributes, which control the values and behavior of elements.

FIND IT ONLINE

The HTML Goodies page (**http://www.htmlgoodies. com/**) provides help for styling documents and more.

HTML 4.0: THE UL ELEMENT

```
<!ENTITY % ULStyle "(disc|square|circle)">

<!ELEMENT UL - - (LI)+                — unordered list —>
<!ATTLIST UL
  &attrs;                             — %coreattrs, %i18n, %events —
  type           %ULStyle;  #IMPLIED  — bullet style —
  compact        (compact)  #IMPLIED  — reduced interitem spacing —>
```

▲ *The HTML* UL *element declaration resembles the declaration of both the* OL *and* LI *elements. Obviously, the only change is within the type attribute, which provides a bullet style rather than a number style.*

Listing 28-5: STYLING AN ORDERED LIST

```
litem { font-family: "Times New Roman",
          "Book Antigua", serif;
        font-size: 9pt;
        font-weight: bold;
        color: red }
<head2>Install the Program</head2>
<olist>
<litem>Load the CD-ROM disk.</litem>
<litem>Close the player door.</litem>
<litem>Open Windows Explorer.</litem>
<litem>Go to the CD-ROM drive.</litem>
<litem>Open the setup folder.</litem>
<litem>Double-click on setup.exe.</litem>
</olist>
```

▲ *An ordered list provides numbered steps that you should follow one by one. (Remember that you must refer to the style sheet as well as the DTD in the XML document.)*

Listing 28-6: STYLING AN UNORDERED LIST

```
litem { font-size: 10pt;
        font-weight: 700;
        border-width: thin }

<heading1>Today's Specials</heading1>
<bullist>
<item>Acme Widgets</item>
<item>Acme Widget Helpers</item>
<item>Acme Concrete Mix</item>
<item>Acme Shovels</item>
<item>Acme Pickaxes</item>
</bullist>
```

▲ *Use a bulleted list to emphasize the importance of a few related words or phrases.*

411

Enriching a Glossary

According to the HTML 4.0 specification, a *glossary* is known as a definition list. A definition list is made up of definition terms and definition descriptions.

You can use three elements to create a definition list. For example, in HTML, DL signals the start and end of the list, DT specifies the start and end of the definition term, and DD sets the start and end of the definition description.

As you can see, the following code looks like the text beneath it:

```
<dl>
<dt>Null Modem Cable</dt>
<dd>A special cable used to connect two
computers that are in close proximity for
the purpose of communications.</dd>
<dt>Object</dt>
<dd>A piece of information that has been
identified for embedding or linking in
applications.</dd></dl>
```

Null Modem Cable A special cable used to connect two computers that are in close proximity for the purpose of communications.

Object A piece of information that has been identified for embedding or linking in applications.

As with both ordered and unordered lists, you can style a definition list using any properties that affect the appearance of text or enhance it. For example, you can change its color, font, or font size. You can also add borders and decorations. Also note that you can apply one list-style property — `list-style-position` — to definition lists. However, it's best to avoid using this property. Keep each definition term–definition description pair aligned with the same invisible vertical line.

TAKE NOTE

▶ **INLINE ELEMENTS VS. BLOCK ELEMENTS**

The HTML specification states that the content of the DT element is inline and the DD content is block-level. The content of an *inline element* flows from the previous element to the following element without a break to a new line, depending on whether there is enough room on the current line. The content of a *block element* starts on a new line and triggers another break at the end of its display. Remember that the inline DT and block DD elements are paired. Thus, the end of the definition description causes a break after which the next definition term occurs.

▶ **USING THE CSS DISPLAY PROPERTY**

The `display` property inserts the current element in a box, which is formatted in one of three ways depending on your selection of a keyword. The syntax of the `display` property is the following:

```
display: { inline|block|list-
item|none }
```

If you select `inline`, the current element is displayed in an inline box on the current line. If you select `block` (the default), a break is triggered and the element is displayed in a box on a new line. If you select `list-item`, the element is contained in a box that is preceded by a bullet. If you select `none`, the element is not displayed.

CROSS-REFERENCE

Chapter 14 presents the details of adding lists and tables to the content of your XML documents.

FIND IT ONLINE

Go to **http://www.insidedhtml.com/home.asp** to learn about dynamic HTML and link to Web resources.

HTML 4.0: THE DL, DT, AND DD ELEMENTS

```
<!ELEMENT DL - - (DT|DD)+              -- definition list -->
<!ATTLIST DL                                                    ←❶
  &attrs;                             -- %coreattrs, %i18n, %events -->


<!ELEMENT DT - ) (%inline;)*          -- definition term -->
<!ELEMENT DD - ) (%flow;)*            -- definition description -->   ←❷
<!ATTLIST DT|DD)
  &attrs;                             -- %coreattrs, %i18n, %events -->


<!ENTITY % inline "#PCDATA | %fontstyle; | %phrase; | %special; | %formctrl;">  ←❸


<!ENTITY % flow "%block; | %inline; ">  ←❹
```

❶ The DL element encloses all the term-definition pairs.
❷ The DT and DD elements specify terms and definitions, respectively.
❸ The % inline entity applies to inline (or text-level) elements.
❹ The % flow entity encompasses both block and inline elements.

Listing 28-7: STYLING A DEFINITION LIST

```
term { font-family: Arial, Helvetica,
      sans-serif; font-weight: bold }
describe { font-family: Arial, Helvetica,
      sans-serif; font-weight: normal }
<dlist>
<term>antimacassar</term>
<describe>A cloth that prevents macassar
oil from staining a chair.</describe>
<term>macassar</term>
<describe>Oil used for men's hairdressing.
</describe></dlist>
```

▲ Definition lists are typically used for formatting glossaries.

Listing 28-8: STYLING A NARRATIVE DEFINITION LIST

```
player { font-family: Arial, Helvetica,
      sans-serif; font-weight: bold }
says { font-family: "Times New Roman",
      "Book Antigua", serif;
      font-weight: normal }
<play><player>John</player>
<says>Marcia</says>
<player>Marcia</player>
<says>John</says>
<player>John</player>
<says>Marcia</says></play>
```

▲ You can also use a definition list to write a narrative.

Adorning a Plain List

HTML provides two deprecated elements, DIR and MENU, for plain lists, which are lists of words and phrases *not* preceded by either numbers or bullets. (Remember that a deprecated element will be omitted from a future specification.) The HTML 4.0 specification states that the DIR element is meant to be used for multiple column lists, and the MENU element produces single-column lists. The specification encourages HTML developers to use unordered lists instead of plain lists.

Those who developed HTML designed the DIR element to list short directory listings, which are lists of computer files. The MENU element originally was planned for listing short menu choices — for computers, not for restaurants.

As an XML developer, should you ever use plain lists or should you abide by the recommendation of the HTML gurus? You should probably follow the suggestion to use unordered lists to properly emphasize lists in your documents. However, if you want to use plain lists occasionally, make sure that you emphasize them by using text-enhancement properties to change the typeface, point size, weight, color, or all of these. You can also emphasize a list by surrounding it on all sides with a border or by adding a vertical line border on one side. Using list-style properties is probably not appropriate for a plain list.

Keeping Your List Items Parallel

When you create a list from items such as phrases and sentences, you should keep each item parallel to every other item. To be parallel, the order of subject and verb must agree. For example, if one item starts with a verb (such as *follow*, *start*, *open*, and so on), all the items should start with a verb.

If the sentence structure of one item is *active voice* (for example, *Put on your visor.*) rather than *passive voice* (for example, *The visor must be put on.*), reword all passive list items to make them active. (Of course, you should write in active voice anyway. Active-voice sentences are more lively and easier to read.)

Look at the following ordered list:

1. Load the CD-ROM.
2. The player door should be closed.
3. Open Windows Explorer.

The second item on the list is not parallel with the two other items; it is written in passive voice. In items 1 and 3, which are active-voice sentences, an action word starts the sentence. In item 2, the past participle *closed* ends the sentence. To form a parallel sentence, change the second item to read:

2. Close the player door.

CROSS-REFERENCE

Chapter 13 discusses how to create a basic XML document and add all its markup and character data.

FIND IT ONLINE

The HTML Station (**http://www.december.com/ html/**) contains many links that aid in Web-page development.

HTML 4.0: THE DIR AND MENU ELEMENTS

```
<!ELEMENT (DIR|MENU) - - (LI)+ -(%block;) -- directory list, menu list -->
<!ATTLIST DIR
  &attrs;                          -- %coreattrs, %i18n, %events --
  compact      (compact)  #IMPLIED -- reduced interitem spacing -->


<!ATTLIST MENU
  &attrs;                          -- %coreattrs, %i18n, %events --
  compact      (compact)  #IMPLIED -- reduced interitem spacing -->
```

❶ DIR *and* MENU *both require start tags and end tags.*
❷ DIR *and* MENU *both contain one or more list items.*
❸ DIR *and* MENU *are both block elements.*
❹ *Both elements contain the same attributes.*

Listing 28-9: STYLING A PLAIN LIST

```
item { font-family: "Times New Roman",
          "Book Antigua", serif;
       font-style: italic }
<head2>Our Other Pamphlets</head2>
<plain>
<item>Preparing Vegetarian Turkey</item>
<item>Carving a Cabbage Centerpiece</item>
<item>Decorating with Soybeans</item>
<item>Building Your Own Ski Slope</item>
<item>Dusting without Tears</item>
<item>Conestogas on the Interstate</item>
</plain>
```

▲ *Use a plain list to present a set of publications.*

Listing 28-10: STYLING ANOTHER PLAIN LIST

```
item { font-family: "Courier New",
          Courier, sans-serif }
<dir>
<item>autoexec.bat</item>
<item>cga.vid</item>
<item>command.com</item>
<item>config.sys</item>
<item>dblspace.sys</item>
<item>dosshell.vid</item>
<item>ega.vid</item>
<item>graphics.pro</item>
<item>himem.sys</item>
</dir>
```

▲ *The original* DIR *element was designed to list computer files.*

Personal Workbook

Q&A

1 Why would you use an ordered list?

_____

_____

_____

2 What is another name for an ordered list?

_____

_____

_____

3 Why would you use an unordered list?

_____

_____

_____

4 What is another name for an unordered list?

_____

_____

_____

5 Why would you use a definition list?

_____

_____

_____

6 Name the four CSS list properties.

_____

_____

_____

7 What does the `list-style-type` property do for ordered lists? What does this property do for unordered lists?

_____

_____

_____

8 What three components make up a definition list?

_____

_____

_____

ANSWERS: PAGE 473

EXTRA PRACTICE

❶ Go online and find a page that instructs you how to install a popular browser once you have downloaded it. Reformat and style the installation steps as an ordered list.

❷ Prepare a styled top-ten list of reasons why you agree or disagree with a particular opinion or philosophy.

❸ Change the style of the top-ten list so that it looks completely different.

❹ Create a glossary of terms for one of your areas of expertise. Apply boldface to the terms.

❺ Create a plain list of your five favorite books.

❻ Go online and find a glossary of printing terms. Then, define your own XML elements and recreate and style the glossary.

REAL-WORLD APPLICATIONS

✔ Make a styled shopping list. First, categorize the list under headings. Next, list items under each heading using unordered lists. Finally, style all the elements.

✔ Choose a topic and create a short presentation using different levels of headings and both ordered and unordered lists. (Hint: Make sure that you select typefaces and point sizes that your audience can see from the back of a large room.)

✔ Imagine that you run a small toy store. Create an advertising handout that contains a list of five sale items. Use other elements and apply styles to enhance the page.

✔ Using a definition list format, convert your company's current telephone list. Style the page using font and color properties.

Visual Quiz

How would you code and style the lists on this page?

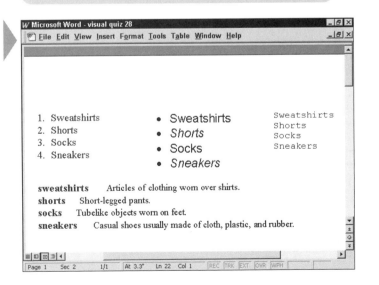

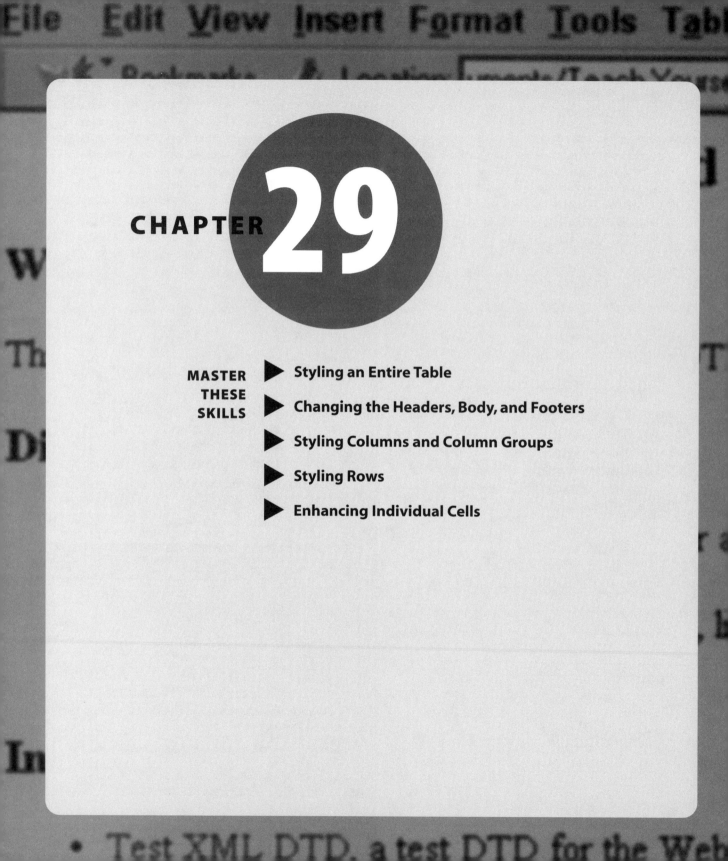

CHAPTER **29**

MASTER
THESE
SKILLS

▶ **Styling an Entire Table**

▶ **Changing the Headers, Body, and Footers**

▶ **Styling Columns and Column Groups**

▶ **Styling Rows**

▶ **Enhancing Individual Cells**

Styling Tables

As you learned in Chapter 14, a table is composed of rows and columns containing cells of data. You can consider each cell of a table a separate document whose contents you can style by using paragraph and text formats and enhancements. In this chapter, you will learn how to style an entire table and its contents, selected rows and columns and their contents, and even individual cells and their contents. In the process, you will review the structure of tables and the elements that you can use to construct a table. You'll even find out about some new elements not covered in Chapter 14. (All the table elements discussed in this chapter are based on HTML 4.0 elements.)

The first task in this chapter demonstrates how to apply cascading style sheet properties to entire tables. When you define styles for an entire table, you actually set the defaults for each of the components making up the table — down to the level of the individual cell. For example, you may select a basic typeface and point size, a font weight, a default border, and a background or text color. This, in effect, sets an overall standard for all the tables in the documents to which the current DTD is attached.

The next steps in styling a table focus on individual components. You can declare elements that enable you to separate a table into sections or feature individual parts. For example, you can split a table into three sections (the header, body, and footer), into two types of rows (heading rows and data rows), groups of columns, groups of rows, and individual cells. After you have split a table or have pinpointed a particular component, you can apply styles to differentiate one component from the others, to highlight it, or even to direct your readers' eyes toward the row dimension (if the table is row-centric), or the column dimension (if the table is column-centric). Marking parts of a table for styling enables you to enhance the whole by applying different background or text colors, by changing the weight of selected borders, or by employing other CSS properties to the separate components.

Styling an Entire Table

When you style an XML document or document set, you should focus on the big picture first. Set properties such as the base font and point size and the margin size, and apply other entire-document styles. Then concentrate on the next largest components, such as the default paragraphs, sections, and all the graphics in your document. The final step is to identify special parts, such as unique types of paragraphs (introductions, summaries, notes, warnings, tips, and so on). You want to set standards for each component of the document.

The same philosophy is true for styling tables: Start with the entire table first and work down until you reach the smallest component — the cell.

The Cascading Style Sheet specification provides no properties specifically for tables. However, you can use most CSS properties to format and enhance tables and their contents. The following example shows that you can specify typeface and point size, set border properties, and specify the background and foreground colors.

```
table { font-family: Arial,
        "Century Gothic", sans-serif;
    font-size: 9pt;
    border: black solid medium;
    background-color: yellow;
    color: navy }
```

All these formats and enhancements maintain the desired relationship between a particular type of component — the table — and the document itself. In this example, the sans serif typeface will contrast with the body text, which is probably from the serif family. In addition, the point size is probably less than that of the body text, which should range from 10 to 12 points. The background color, yellow, should also contrast with the color of the page background yet allow for readable text (black by default). When you set styles for a specific document component, you specify a standard that will apply to every like component in the document.

TAKE NOTE

▶ STYLING TABLE CAPTIONS

Table captions briefly describe a table. You can also use captions to cross-reference every table in a document. You can apply position styles as well as text enhancement styles to captions to standardize the appearance of your documents. For example, you can place all captions below every table in a document, or you can float them to the left of the tables and float the tables to the right. You can apply boldface to captions and increase their point size to make them important document components (that is, they make more of an impact on your readers' eyes), or decrease weight and point size to decrease their significance (perhaps to keep the readers' eyes on another page element such as the table itself or a graphic).

CROSS-REFERENCE

Chapter 24 introduces you to CSS properties and covers styling pages and page elements.

FIND IT ONLINE

You can find a directory of links to outstanding Web design resources at **http://html.miningco.com**.

HTML 4.0: THE TABLE ELEMENT, ITS CHILD ELEMENTS, AND THE TABLE

```
<!ELEMENT TABLE - - (CAPTION?, (COL*|COLGROUP*), THEAD?, TFOOT?, TBODY+)> ←❶

<!ELEMENT CAPTION   - - (%inline;)*          -- table caption -->←❷

<!ELEMENT THEAD     - O (TR)+                 -- table header -->

<!ELEMENT TFOOT     - O (TR)+                 -- table footer -->←❸

<!ELEMENT TBODY     O O (TR)+                 -- table body -->

<!ELEMENT COLGROUP  - O (COL)*               -- table column group -->

<!ELEMENT COL       - O EMPTY                 -- table column -->←❹

<!ELEMENT TR        - O (TH|TD)+             -- table row -->

<!ELEMENT (TH|TD)   - O (%flow;)*           -- table header cell,
                                                table data cell -->
```

```
<!ATTLIST TABLE                      -- table element --
  %attrs;                            -- %coreattrs, %i18n, %events --
  summary        %Text;    #IMPLIED  -- purpose/structure for speech output --
  width          %Length;  #IMPLIED  -- table width --
  border         %Pixels;  #IMPLIED  -- controls frame width around table --
  frame          %TFrame;  #IMPLIED  -- which parts of frame to render --
  rules          %TRules;  #IMPLIED  -- rulings between rows and cols --
  cellspacing    %Length;  #IMPLIED  -- spacing between cells --
  cellpadding    %Length;  #IMPLIED  -- spacing within cells --
>
```

```
<!ELEMENT CAPTION - - (%inline;)*
<!ATTLIST CAPTION
  %attrs;                                    -- %coreattrs, %i18n, %events --
```

❶ *The HTML* TABLE *element has six child elements.*
❷ *The* CAPTION *element specifies the characteristics of a table caption.*
❸ *The* TR *element is a child of* THEAD, *TFOOT, and* TBODY.
❹ *The* COL *element is empty.*

Changing the Headers, Body, and Footers

The HTML 4.0 specification names three elements with which you can divide a table into sets of rows — the header area, the footer area, and the main body in between — in order to style those areas in their own distinctive ways. Use these elements as a guide when you create your own custom DTDs for XML.

The HTML THEAD element marks the area at the top of the table where the rows in the table header will be located. The TFOOT element marks the area at the bottom of the table where the rows in table footer will be located. TBODY marks the nonheader, non-footer rows in the central part of the table. Typically, the THEAD section should enclose the rows that make up the data heading cells, and the TFOOT section should incorporate totals or notes. Use your own discretion when dividing a table. For example, you can use the THEAD and TBODY elements and omit the TFOOT section. Or mark the first three rows as THEAD and the last three rows as TFOOT, ensuring a symmetrical table.

The following example shows the element structure of a table divided into three parts:

```
<table><thead>
    <row><c></c><c></c><c></c></row>
</thead>
<tbody>
    <row><c></c><c></c><c></c></row>
</tbody>
<tfoot>
    <row><c></c><c></c><c></c></row>
</tfoot></table>
```

The following example demonstrates how you can style the table header rows and table footer rows:

```
table { font-family: "Book Antigua",
        "Century Schoolbook", serif;
    font-size: 10pt }
thead { font-weight: bold;
    background-color: silver }
tfoot { font-style: italic;
    background-color: silver }
```

TAKE NOTE

RECOGNIZING THE DIFFERENCE BETWEEN A HEADING AND A HEADER

Headings with headers are completely different. A *heading* is the title of a chapter or section. Typically presented in a bold, plain, and larger typeface, a heading names (and emphasizes) the topic to be discussed in the following paragraphs. Remember that HTML provides six levels of heading elements. By default, a *header* displays the same information — such as today's date or the chapter title — at the top of every page in a document. (Its counterpart is the *footer*, which repeats information at the bottom of every page.)

This points out another advantage of using XML. In HTML, the only way to produce headers (and footers) is by using frames above (and below) a large frame. In XML, you can declare specific elements to enclose header and footer information.

CROSS-REFERENCE

Chapter 5 provides an overview of the software with which you can edit and check your XML documents.

FIND IT ONLINE

http://www.w3.org/TR/WD-WAI-AUTOOLS/ gives disability guidelines for authoring tools.

HTML 4.0: THE THEAD, TBODY, AND TFOOT ELEMENTS AND RELATED ENTITIES

```
<!ELEMENT THEAD      - O (TR)+>
<!ELEMENT TBODY      O O (TR)+>  ◄━❶
<!ELEMENT TFOOT      - O (TR)+>
<!ATTLIST (THEAD|TBODY|TFOOT)            -- table section --
   %attrs;                               -- %coreattrs, %i18n, %events --
   %cellhalign;                          -- horizontal alignment in cells --◄━❷
   %cellvalign;                          -- vertical alignment in cells --◄━❸
>
```

❶ The THEAD, TBODY, and TFOOT elements include the TR child element.
❷ The %cellhalign; attribute horizontally aligns cells.
❸ The %cellvalign; attribute vertically aligns cells.

Listing 29-1: STYLES FOR A PATRIOTIC TABLE

❶

```
table { font-family: "Book Antigua",
              "Century Schoolbook", serif;
         font-size: 10pt }
thead { background-color: red }  ◄━❷
tbody ( background-color: white }◄━❸
tfoot { background-color: blue } ◄━❹
```

❶ Define the font and font size for the entire table.
❷ Make the thead background color red.
❸ Use a white background so that the body text is readable.
❹ Make the tfoot background color blue.

Listing 29-2: STYLES FOR A TWO-SECTION TABLE

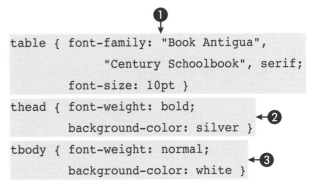

```
table { font-family: "Book Antigua",
              "Century Schoolbook", serif;
         font-size: 10pt }
thead { font-weight: bold;
        background-color: silver }  ◄━❷
tbody { font-weight: normal;
        background-color: white }   ◄━❸
```

❶ Define styles for the entire table.
❷ Make the header text bold and its background silver.
❸ Set the body text to normal weight and the background to white.

Styling Columns and Column Groups

Remember that HTML is a row-centric markup language, so manipulating table rows makes sense—in the HTML world. However, when you write XML DTDs, you can customize your tables and table elements so that they are either row-centric or column-centric.

You have just learned how to partition and style tables the HTML way—by rows and groups of rows. Now we move styling to the vertical: in this task, you'll find out how to divide and style tables by columns and groups of columns.

The HTML COLGROUP element marks the start and end of a column group. The COL element identifies one or more columns for further action—primarily alignment but also the application of other attributes and styles. As defined within the HTML specification, the COL element is an empty element: it cannot have content. On the facing page, see the COLGROUP and COL element declarations and attribute lists.

The following example shows a table divided into two column groups with individual columns explicitly specified:

```
<TABLE>
  <COLGROUP span="2" align="left">
    <COL id="100"/>
    <COL id="200"/>
  </COLGROUP>
  <COLGROUP span="3">
    <COL id="300" align="left"/>
    <COL id="400" align="center "/>
    <COL id="500" align="right"/>
  </COLGROUP></TABLE>
```

Note that the TABLE, COLGROUP, and COL elements follow the HTML model, but also note that this table does not include explicitly defined rows, as the usual HTML table would.

In XML, you can create your own column and column-group elements. For example, you could declare a COLGROUP element simply to span columns in the same way that you use the SPAN element in HTML to mark the beginning and end of a section. Then you could apply unique styles to the column span. (Of course, you could declare an XML SPAN element instead to span areas throughout a document, in body text, and within lists and tables.) You could declare a COL element to identify a column in a column-centric table (as you use the HTML ROW element to specify a row-centric table row).

CROSS-REFERENCE

Chapter 13 discusses how to enter various XML components into a basic document.

FIND IT ONLINE

The HTML Writers Guild (http://www.hwg.org/) has resources for Web page designers and developers.

HTML 4.0: THE COLGROUP AND COL ELEMENTS

```
<!ELEMENT COLGROUP  - O (COL)*>
<!ATTLIST COLGROUP
  %attrs;                            -- %coreattrs, %i18n, %events --
  span          NUMBER      1        -- default number of columns in group --  ←❶
  width         %MultiLength;  #IMPLIED -- default width for enclosed COLS --
  %cellhalign;                       -- horizontal alignment in cells --
  %cellvalign;                       -- vertical alignment in cells -->
<!ELEMENT COL       - O EMPTY>
<!ATTLIST COL                        -- column groups and properties --
  %attrs;                            -- %coreattrs, %i18n, %events --
  span          NUMBER      1        -- COL attributes affect N columns --  ←❷
  width         %MultiLength;  #IMPLIED -- column width specification --
  %cellhalign;                       -- horizontal alignment in cells --
  %cellvalign;                       -- vertical alignment in cells -->
```

❶ *The* COLGROUP *element spans a set number of columns.*
❷ *The* COL *element also spans columns, mainly to set alignment.*

LISTING 29-3: A PATRIOTIC TABLE

```
table { font-family: "Book Antigua",
           "Century Schoolbook", serif;
      font-size: 10pt }
cl { background-color: red }   ←❷          ❶
cc ( background-color: white }  ←❸
cr { background-color: blue }  ←❹
<table><cl><col>left cols</col></cl>
  <cc><col>one col of center contents</col>
     <col>one col of center contents</col>
  </cc><cr><col>right cols</col></cr></table>
```

❶ *Define the font and font size for the entire table.*
❷ *Make a red background for the leftmost columns.*
❸ *Use a white background in the center.*
❹ *Make a blue background for the rightmost columns.*

LISTING 29-4: ANOTHER TWO-SECTION TABLE

```
table { font-family: "Book Antigua",
           "Century Schoolbook", serif;
      font-size: 10pt }
lcols { font-weight: bold;
        background-color: silver }
rcols { font-weight: normal;
        background-color: white }
<table>
 <lcol><col>left contents</col></lcol>
 <rcol>
    <col>one column of body contents</col>
 </rcol></table>
```

▲ *This is the counterpart of Listing 29-2 in the previous task. In this example, the leftmost column has a silver background, and the remaining columns have a white background.*

Styling Rows

Earlier in this chapter, you found out how to group table rows into header, body, and footer sections and then style them. If you wanted to make the last row in a table a footer in order to highlight it, you could do so. However, assume that you would like to feature a row somewhere in the body. For example, you may want to bring attention to a row containing profit information about a one division of your company.

The HTML TR element marks the start and end of a single row. Use the TR element to define the row as well as to apply attributes and styles to all the rows with that same element name.

The following example shows the element structure of a simple two-column table made up of three rows:

```
<table>
<row><data></data><data></data></row>
<row><data></data><data></data></row>
<row><data></data><data></data></row>
</table>
```

The elements are defined in such a way that you cannot select a single row for different styles. The following example shows one way of featuring a row — by changing the element name:

```
<table>
<row><data></data><data></data></row>
<hrow><data></data><data></data></hrow>
<row><data></data><data></data></row>
</table>
```

Now you can specify unique properties for the hrow element. Another way to feature a row is to declare a span element to simply mark the beginning and end of a document section. Then, style the span element. For example:

```
<table>
<row><data></data><data></data></row>
<span>
<row><data></data><data></data></row>
</span>
<row><data></data><data></data></row>
</table>
```

When you style a spanning element that you might use in other parts of the document, make sure that you are willing to accept its styles wherever you place the element. If this becomes a problem, you may have to declare a few versions of the element, each styled in its own unique way.

TAKE NOTE

DEALING WITH EMPTY ROWS

Sometimes a table includes one or more rows that have no content. For example, you might want to add extra space between two groups of rows. To specify an empty row, insert a start tag and an end tag. For example:

```
<row></row>
```

As you can see, the area between the tags remains empty. What if an empty row needs to be filled in order to have any height? You can either use the line-height style to specify a height measurement, or fill a cell in the row with the Unicode character #x0020 to insert a space.

CROSS-REFERENCE

Chapter 14 instructs you how and why to use lists and tables in your XML documents.

FIND IT ONLINE

Learn and see good Web-page design at http://www.avalon.net/~librarian/bones/bones.html.

HTML 4.0: THE TR ELEMENT

```
<!ELEMENT TR           - O  (TH|TD)+
        -- table row -->
                              ❶
<!ATTLIST TR
  %attrs;
        -- %coreattrs, %i18n, %events --
  %cellhalign;
        -- horizontal alignment in cells --❷
  %cellvalign;
        -- vertical alignment in cells -->
```

❶ The TR *element has two child elements,* TH *and* TD.
❷ *You can align the contents of cells horizontally or vertically.*

Listing 29-5: STYLING A TABLE, ITS ROWS, AND A SELECTED ROW

```
table { font-family: Arial,
             "Lucia Console", sans-serif;
        font-size: 10pt }
hrow { font-weight: bold;
        background-color: silver }  ❷ ❶
<table>
    <row><data></data><data></data></row>  ❸
    <hrow><data></data><data></data></hrow>
    <row><data></data><data></data></row>
</table>
```

❶ *Style the entire table.*
❷ *Emphasize the* hrow *element with boldface and background color.*
❸ *Because of additional styling, this row will be featured.*

Listing 29-6: A LONG TABLE WITH MANY STYLES

```
table { font-family: "Times New Roman",
             "Book Antigua", serif;      ❶
        font-size: 10pt;
        font-weight: normal;             ❷
        border: black double thin;
        background-color: white
             "Lucia Console", sans-serif;
        font-size: 12pt;
        font-weight: bolder }
tfoot { font-style: italic }  ❸
hrow { font-weight: bold;
        background-color: silver }  ❹
table { font-family: "Times New Roman",
             "Book Antigua", serif; Ł
        font-size: 10ptŁ
        font-weight: normal;
        border: black double thin;Ł
        background-color: white }Ł
thead { font-family: Arial,
             "Lucia Console", sans-serif;Ł
        font-size: 12pt;
        font weight: bolder }Ł
tfoot { font-style: italic }Ł
hrow { font-weight: bold;Ł
        background-color: silver }Ł
<table><thead>
    <row><data></data><data></data></row>
    </thead><body>
    <row><data></data><data></data></row>
    <hrow><data></data><data></data></hrow>
    <row><data></data><data></data></row>
    <hrow><data></data><data></data></hrow>
    <row><data></data><data></data></row>
    </tbody><tfoot>
    <row><data></data><data></data></row>
    </tfoot></table>
```

❶ *Set the table-wide styles with a serif typeface.*
❷ *Style the header rows with a bold, larger heading typeface.*
❸ *Style the footer with italicized text.*
❹ *Emphasize special rows with boldface and a background color.*

Enhancing Individual Cells

As you learned in Chapter 14, HTML provides two cell elements that you can "borrow" from when you create the XML DTDs with which you declare table elements. The HTML TD element creates individual cells in the body of the table, and the HTML TH element defines heading cells, usually emphasizing the contents of those cells with boldface. Both the TD and TH elements are *always* nested within the TR element: You cannot define table cells without specifying a table row first.

The TH element does not require your splitting a table into sections: The element can emphasize text in one or more rows with or without the THEAD, TBODY, and TFOOT elements and their potential styles.

Defining or selecting an individual cell also enables you to emphasize it in some way — by setting a background or text color, changing font characteristics, or changing some other text-oriented style. As you found out in the prior task, you can either use a unique cell selection or creation element to identify a particular cell, or you can embed the "special" cell within a spanning element.

Because HTML is row-centric, the TD and TH elements are the only way to create columns — that is, the borders between cells. Remember that XML custom elements enable tables to be either row-centric or column-centric. As you have just learned, if a table is row-centric, the elements that set cell borders also form columns. However, if a table is column-centric, the reverse happens, and the elements that set cell borders also form rows. The listing on the facing page demonstrates a table with filled table cells.

TAKE NOTE

ENSURING THAT HEADING CELLS ARE BOLDFACE

When you identify a particular cell as a heading cell, some browsers automatically apply boldface to the cell contents; however, other browsers ignore the "boldness" of the cell contents altogether. To ensure that heading text is always displayed in boldface, apply the `font-weight` property to your heading table cell heading element. In addition, as you define styles for the heading cells, consider changing the default typeface to sans serif.

LEAVING EMPTY CELLS IN A TABLE

The previous task discussed leaving empty rows in a table. For example, when you create a mileage chart, the intersection of the row and column referring to the same city must remain blank. (The distance between Saratoga Springs and itself is 0 miles.) To leave a cell empty, use the technique that you learned for leaving a row empty. For example:

```
<cell></cell>
```

In most situations, the dimensions of the cells next to the empty cell control the empty cell's dimensions. However, if you need to fill in the cell with invisible contents to have the cell appear in the table, enter the Unicode character #x0020, which inserts a space.

CROSS-REFERENCE

Chapter 10 specifies how to write and use internal and external general and parameter entities.

FIND IT ONLINE

Learn about design for visually impaired users at http://www.rnib.org.uk/wedo/research/access.htm.

HTML 4.0: THE TH AND TD ELEMENTS

```
<!ELEMENT (TH|TD)    - O (%flow;)*      — table header cell, table data cell ->
<!ATTLIST (TH|TD)                       — header or data cell —-
   %attrs;                              — %coreattrs, %i18n, %events —
   abbr              %Text;   #IMPLIED  — default number of columns in group —-
   axis              CDATA    #IMPLIED  —- names groups of related headers —-
   headers           IDREFS   #IMPLIED  — list of ids for header cells —-
   scope             %Scope;  #IMPLIED  — scope covered by header cells —-
   rowspan           NUMBER   1         — number of rows spanned by cell —
   colspan           NUMBER   1         — number of columns spanned by cell —
   %cellhalign;                         — horizontal alignment in cells —
   %cellvalign;                         — vertical alignment in cells —
>
```

▲ *The declarations for the HTML* TH *and* TD *elements are identical. The elements have a variety of formatting attributes that you can simulate using CSS styles.*

Listing 29-7: AN EXAMPLE OF TABLE SECTION STYLES AND A TABLE SEGMENT

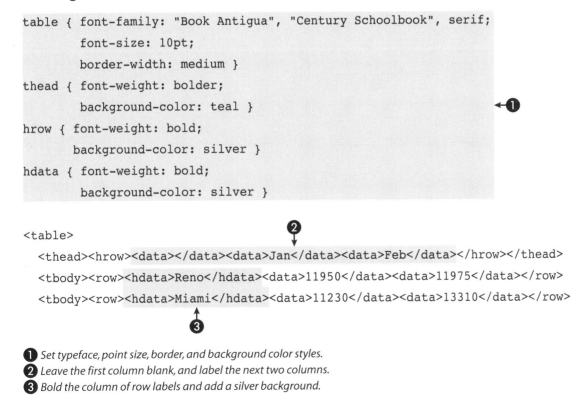

```
table { font-family: "Book Antigua", "Century Schoolbook", serif;
        font-size: 10pt;
        border-width: medium }
thead { font-weight: bolder;
        background-color: teal }              ❶
hrow { font-weight: bold;
       background-color: silver }
hdata { font-weight: bold;
        background-color: silver }
```

```
                                      ❷
<table>
   <thead><hrow><data></data><data>Jan</data><data>Feb</data></hrow></thead>
   <tbody><row><hdata>Reno</hdata><data>11950</data><data>11975</data></row>
   <tbody><row><hdata>Miami</hdata><data>11230</data><data>13310</data></row>
                    ❸
```

❶ *Set typeface, point size, border, and background color styles.*
❷ *Leave the first column blank, and label the next two columns.*
❸ *Bold the column of row labels and add a silver background.*

Personal Workbook

Q&A

1 When you define styles for an entire table, what are you doing?

_____

_____

_____

2 What are some of the ways in which you can split a table or highlight its components?

_____

_____

_____

3 Does the Cascading Style Sheet specification provide table styling properties?

_____

_____

_____

4 What is the purpose of _table captions_?

_____

_____

_____

5 What are the names of the HTML elements that form the header, footer, and body sections of a table?

_____

_____

_____

6 What are two ways to select a table row?

_____

_____

_____

7 How do you specify an empty row or empty cell?

_____

_____

_____

8 How do you break a row into columns?

_____

_____

_____

ANSWERS: PAGE 473

1 Create styles to differentiate between alternating rows in a small spreadsheet.

2 Define styles to highlight column labels and row labels in the same sheet.

3 In Chapter 14, you created a table of computer prices. Now style that table using various borders, colors, and typeface properties.

4 Design a To Do sheet of planned tasks at the office. Define styles to emphasize column labels, row labels, and top-priority tasks.

5 Create a memo template using a table as the underlying grid. Then define styles to add borders around the page and between the first two columns and set a background color to the leftmost column.

✔ Your company has assigned you to update the design of the company telephone list, which is a two-column table of names and extensions. Define styles that include the company name as a heading within a section with a background color, and the name and extension information as body text.

✔ You want to modernize an online newsletter using a table as a grid that separates the main headline, which runs from the left margin to the right margin and four columns of body text. Split the fourth column into two parts so that you can add a table of contents in the lower-right corner of the page. Then, define styles for the headline and the body text.

Visual Quiz

What styles would you use to reproduce the look of this table?

_____

_____

_____

_____

Person	Location	Distance		
		Theresa	Jim	Susan
Theresa	Main Street	-	1 mile	4 miles
Jim	Oak Lane	1 mile	-	3.5 miles
Susan	BC Way	4 miles	3.5 miles	-

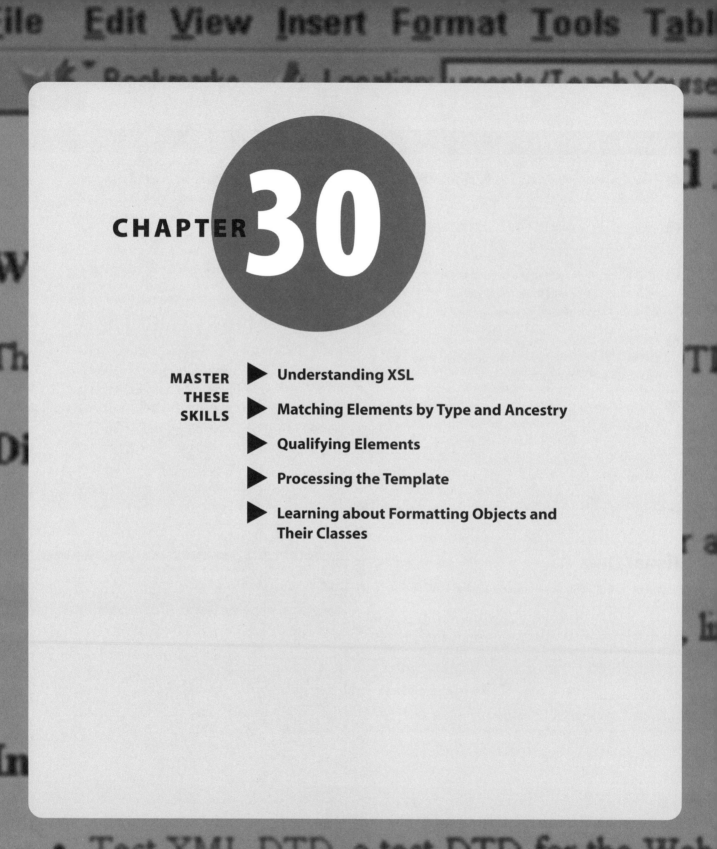

CHAPTER 30

MASTER
THESE
SKILLS

▶ **Understanding XSL**

▶ **Matching Elements by Type and Ancestry**

▶ **Qualifying Elements**

▶ **Processing the Template**

▶ **Learning about Formatting Objects and
Their Classes**

• Test XML DTD, a test DTD for the Web

Introducing XSL

This chapter provides an overview of *Extensible Stylesheet Language* (XSL) and its features. XSL enables writers and editors to write documents with which to format and enhance XML document output using nested DSSSL Online (DSSSL-O) rules and incorporating CSS and CSS-like properties. If you have read other chapters in this book, you have a good idea of how to code XSL statements and use XSL properties.

XSL is an XML grammar. XSL documents are constructed in the same way as XML documents; once you have learned how to use XML, you are well on your way to creating properly constructed XSL documents. XSL consists of two parts: a language that transforms XML documents and a vocabulary for formatting XML elements. XSL documents must be well-formed according to the rule set in the XML specification. XSL processing starts with a source tree, which includes all the generations of elements and attributes in the document and ends in a result tree. The use of trees shows the importance of the hierarchy of elements and attributes in a document.

In the first task in this chapter, many new terms are introduced as you learn about XSL as a whole. Some terms have been inherited from DSSSL, and others are unique to XSL. The following tasks go through XSL processing and styling, step by step. For example, you will learn how to write patterns to match elements by various criteria: type, ancestry, and qualifiers such as child elements, attributes and their values, position, and wildcards. Then, you will find out how to process a template, which contains the pattern and directions on producing output, new elements, and more. Along the way, you will learn about the treatment of whitespace in your output as well as writing and invoking macros. Finally, you will find out about how you can use formatting objects to affect your output. XSL formatting properties are very similar (and sometimes identical) to the CSS properties that you explored in all the other chapters in this part.

It is very important to note that XSL is currently a W3C working draft, which means that you can expect further changes to the language.

Understanding XSL

XSL is a style-sheet language that uses *declarations* (statements specifying properties and values for those properties) to create an external XSL document. In the XSL document, as in an XML document, you can set formats and enhancements for one or more XML elements — e.g., you can define all level-one headings as bold, red, in the Arial typeface, and 16-point size. You can also specify properties for families of elements: You can apply certain formats or enhancements for a parent element to its *descendant* (all generations following the target element) and *ancestor* (all the generations prior) elements. With XSL, you can also style elements by their position and value, generate text and graphics, and define formatting macros. You can write XSL documents for all types of printed and electronic output. (Note: XSL can be an internal document in an HTML or ASP document.)

When you declare an XSL style, you define a template for each format or enhancement. A *template* consists of a pattern and an action. The *pattern* is a string that uses various criteria to match one or more input element types (known as *nodes*) in the source tree. The *source tree* contains all the elements and attributes defined in the XML document's DTD — the root, child elements, and other generations and each of the element's attributes. The *action* specifies a *subtree* (that is, the elements that match the pattern) and results in the application of *formatting objects*, styled objects that fill defined areas in the output. Formatting objects include hyperlinks, pages, groups of adjacent pages,

and graphics. Note that formatting objects are known as flow objects in DSSSL.

In processing an XSL style sheet against an XML document, the XML document is first analyzed to produce a source tree. Next, the XSL style sheet is run against the source tree, which concludes with a *result tree* (a tree of elements that result from processing). Finally, the result tree is interpreted, using XSL's formatting language to produce formatted output.

XSL provides a set of predefined elements, each beginning with `xsl:`. The root element, which indicates that the current document is an XSL style sheet, is `xsl:stylesheet`.

TAKE NOTE

▶ THE XSL:STYLESHEET ELEMENT

In XML, reserved processing instructions begin with `<?xml`. `<xsl:stylesheet>` may look like a processing instruction, but it's really a start tag, so under XML rules there must be an end tag (`</xsl:stylesheet>`) at the end of the style sheet.

▶ USING XSL AND CSS TOGETHER

XSL can create new document contents and perform sophisticated selection techniques. XML sometimes sends unformatted data to applications — not for output but for further processing. Although CSS does not affect this type of data, XSL does. Thus, you can use XSL and CSS together: Use XSL to transform information, then style the information by using CSS.

CROSS-REFERENCE

Chapter 24 introduces CSS, and discusses how to attach style sheets of all types to XML documents.

FIND IT ONLINE

The official XSL home page (**http://www.w3.org/Style/XSL/**) contains more than five pages of links.

Table 30-1: SELECTED XSL ELEMENTS

Element	Action
xsl:arg	Supplies an argument for an invoked macro.
xsl:attribute-set	Names each attribute in the set.
xsl:choose	Indicates one of several choices. Elements nested within xsl:choose are xsl:when and xsl:otherwise.
xsl:attribute-set	Indicates a named set of attributes.
xsl:constant	Defines a constant.
xsl:macro	Defines a macro.
xsl:for-each	Indicates the use of the same template for several elements.
xsl:id	Indicates a unique identifier.
xsl:if	Indicates if-then conditional processing.
xsl:import	Imports an element with a URI.
xsl:include	Includes another style sheet with a URI.
xsl:invoke	Runs a macro.
xsl:macro-arg	Supplies a named argument to a macro.
xsl:number	Makes a list of numbers by level, count, or a starting position.
xsl:preserve-space	Indicates an element type that preserves whitespace.
xsl:apply-templates	Processes elements selected by a particular select pattern.
xsl:strip-space	Indicates an element type that does not preserve whitespace.
xsl:stylesheet	Indicates a style sheet — this is the root XSL element.
xsl:template	Indicates a template rule.
xsl:use	Indicates an attribute set or list of attributes to be used or not used.
xsl:value-of	Calculates generated text from the source tree or from a string constant.

Matching Elements by Type and Ancestry

In order to process and/or style an element, you must select it. One way to do so is to write one or more patterns. Remember that a pattern is a string that uses various criteria to match one or more elements in the XML document. If a match occurs, the defined XSL processing commences.

The most basic element match is specifying the element by name and processing a particular style. The facing page includes selected productions from the XSL working draft.

A very important type of pattern can also include references to ancestors and descendants of a single target element. This enables you to select some instances and ignore other instances of the same element. Using this type of selection, you can also style the same element differently, depending on the context in which it appears in a document. You can use the following criteria to select a particular element: all its ancestors; all its descendants; certain descendants or ancestors, using wildcard characters to pinpoint the selection; alternate patterns of ancestry; and one or more particular element attributes, their values, or both.

The target element is the focus of a pattern; from the target element might flow generations of ancestors and descendants and their attributes. You can use a specific path to pinpoint a particular ancestor element. For example, say you see three generations of elements, from the parent (`city`) to the lowest child generation (`house`), arranged like this:

```
city
```

```
    addr
        house
```

In this case, you can match the lowest generation as follows:

```
<xsl:template match=" city/addr/house">
action
</xsl:template>
```

If you match on a different path (for example, `city/zip/vendor/house`), you can apply styles to a completely different occurrence of the `house` element. The listing on the next page shows the current XSL alternation and ancestry production.

You can also match ancestor elements using two or more alternative matching patterns by creating an *anchor*, which only one element can match and which must be the first of a series of patterns.

TAKE NOTE

LEARNING ABOUT RECURSION

In each case of a series of nested elements, an XSL processor relies on *recursion*, in which processing of all elements is not complete until the last (and most insignificant) child element is processed. The processing for the target element relies on the processing for the child element nested immediately below it, which in turn relies on its child, and so on, until the "least" child is processed. Each processing result affects the element above it.

CROSS-REFERENCE

Chapter 25 teaches you how to style paragraphs and page elements using CSS properties.

FIND IT ONLINE

You can access the most extensive list of XSL links at **http://www.oasis-open.org/cover/xsl.html**.

XSL: SELECTED PRODUCTIONS

```
[1]          SelectExpr ::= UnionExpr                    ←①

[2]           MatchExpr ::= SelectExpr ←②

[3]           UnionExpr ::= PathExpr |(PathExpr '|' UnionExpr) ←④

[4]            PathExpr ::= AbsolutePathExpr |ComposeExpr
         ③
[5]    AbsolutePathExpr ::= '/' SubtreeExpr?

[6]          SubtreeExpr ::= '/'? ComposeExpr

[7]          ComposeExpr ::= FilterExpr
                            |(FilterExpr '/' SubtreeExpr)

[8]           FilterExpr ::= NodeExpr('['BooleanExpr']')?

[9]             NodeExpr ::= SubNodeExpr | OtherNodeExpr

[10]         SubNodeExpr ::= ElementExpr
                            |AttributeExpr
                            |TextExpr
                            |CommentExpr
                            |PiExpr

[11]       OtherNodeExpr ::= IdExpr
                            |AncestorExpr
                            |AncestorOrSelfExpr
                            |IdentityExpr
                            |ParentExpr

[12]         ElementExpr ::= QName |'*'

[13]       AttributeExpr ::= ('@' QName) |('@''*')

[14]              PiExpr ::= 'pi''('Literal?')'

[15]            TextExpr ::= 'text''('')'

[16]         CommentExpr ::= 'comment''('')'

[17]              IdExpr ::= ConstantIdExpr | VariableIdExpr
```

① *A select pattern returns a list of selected nodes.*
② *A match pattern must match a node.*
③ *This expression unites the results of the right-side expression.*
④ *The results of this expression is a node set.*

Qualifying Elements

You can write patterns that match elements by one or more qualifiers such as the presence of certain child elements, an attribute, or the position of an element among its *siblings* (other elements of the same generation). Qualifiers enable you to constrain the possible matches. For a match to occur, *all* qualifiers must be met. Listing 30-5 lists the qualifier productions from the current XSL working draft.

XSL enables you to match on a particular child element. For example:

```
<xsl:template match="city[east]">
action
</xsl:template>
```

In order to match, the `city` element must have at least one `east` child element. This enables you to limit the matches to cities on the East Coast.

You can select an element based on the presence of a particular attribute, an attribute with any value, or an attribute with a specific value. For example:

```
<xsl:template match=
"city[east]/addr[attribute (stor)]">
action
</xsl:template>
```

The match to `addr` takes place only when the `stor` attribute is present. In the following example, the `stor` attribute must have a value of 2.

```
<xsl:template match=

"city[east]/addr[attribute(stor="2")]">
action
</xsl:template>
```

You can select an element based on its position among its sibling elements. For example:

```
<xsl:template match="city/addr[only-of-
type()]">
action
</xsl:template>
```

In this example, the child element `addr` must be the only of its kind under the `city` element. Table 30-2 lists all the positional qualifiers in the current XSL working draft. Note that Listing 30-2 is an example from the current XSL working draft.

TAKE NOTE

MATCH ELEMENTS WITH WILDCARDS

To match related elements, you can use wildcards in much the same way that you use them in a search for files or text in computer programs. XSL enables you to set wildcards using a * pattern using XSL productions [32] and [33]:

```
EqualityExpr ::= SelectExpr '='
Literal
    Literal ::= '"' [^"]* '"'
               "'" [^']* "'"
```

A wildcard matches one element. When you use a wildcard to search several generations, it matches one level.

CROSS-REFERENCE

Chapter 13 discusses how to create a basic XML document on which to base XSL documents.

FIND IT ONLINE

Go to **http://www.w3.org/TR/WD-xml-names/** to read the XML namespaces working draft, which is subject to change.

Table 30-2: POSITION-MATCHING QUALIFIERS

Qualifier Syntax	Required Element Position
first-of-any()	Must be the first sibling of any type
First-of-type()	Must be the first sibling of a particular type
Last-of-any()	Must be the last sibling of any type
Last-of-type()	Must be the last sibling of a particular type
not()	Negates one of the previous tests
and	Combines two tests, both of which must be true
or	Combines two tests, one of which must be true

Listing 30-1: PART OF A SAMPLE STYLE SHEET

```
<xsl:stylesheet
  xmlns:xsl="http://www.w3.org/TR/WD-xsl"
  xmlns:fo="http://www.w3.org/TR/WD-xsl/FO"
  result-ns="fo">
  <xsl:template match="/">
    <fo:basic-page-sequence font-
family="serif">
      <xsl:apply-templates/>
    </fo:basic-page-sequence>
  </xsl:template>
```

❶ Use the xmlns (XML namespace) declaration to access a URI.
❷ The result tree uses the formatting object vocabulary.
❸ The element match is on the root.
❹ The rule specifies a page sequence formatted with a serif font.

XSL: BOOLEAN AND RELATED PRODUCTIONS

```
[24]        BooleanExpr ::= AndExpr|OrExpr|BooleanPrimaryExpr ←❶
[25] BooleanPrimaryExpr ::= BooleanGroupExpr|NotExpr|PositionalExpr
                            |TextExpr|EqualityExpr
[26]            AndExpr ::= BooleanPrimaryExpr ('and' BooleanPrimaryExpr)+ ←❷
[27]             OrExpr ::= BooleanPrimaryExpr ('or' BooleanPrimaryExpr)+ ←❸
[28]    BooleanGroupExpr ::= '(' BooleanExpr ')'
[29]            NotExpr ::= 'not''(' BooleanExpr ')' ←❹
[30]      PositionalExpr ::= 'first-of-type''('')'|'first-of-type''('')'
                            |'last-of-type''('')'|'first-of-any''('')'
                            |'last-of-any''('')'
```

❶ A Boolean expression is either true or false.
❷ The AndExpr production must combine true expressions.
❸ One OrExpr must be true.
❹ The result of NotExpr is true if BooleanExpr is false.

Processing the Template

When the template is processed, it is *instantiated* (the template allocates a structure, initializes variables, and produces objects). To process the template, XSL provides the instruction tag: `xsl:apply-templates`. The xsl:instruction processes the of child elements of the target element and character children.

The following example from the current XSL working draft creates an attribute set named `title-style` and uses it in a template rule:

```
<xsl:attribute-set name="title-style">
 <xsl:attribute name="font-size">
       12pt"</xsl:attribute>
 <xsl:attribute name= "font-weight">bold
 </xsl:attribute>
</xsl:attribute-set>
<xsl:template match="chapter/heading">
 <fo:block quadding="start">
   <xsl:use attribute-set="title-style"/>
   <xsl:apply-templates/>
 </fo:block>
</xsl:template>
```

The top several lines of the example define the attribute set (as suggested by the presence of the `xsl:attribute-set` element). The `xsl:attribute-set` element, which is a child of the xsl:attribute-set, specifies the individual attributes within the set. Notice that the attributes have the exact names as their counterpart CSS properties. The remaining lines match the `heading` child element, which is under the parent element `chapter`. The fo declaration states that the object will be styled in a block format and specifies that *quadding* (used to set the alignment of the object) should start. Note that all four listings on the facing page appear in the current XSL working draft.

TAKE NOTE

▶ PRESERVING OR STRIPPING WHITESPACE IN XSL

After a result tree has been produced, but before further processing, whitespace may be stripped from the XML document. In the template, use the `xsl:preserve-space` element to preserve whitespace, and use the `xsl:strip-space` element to strip whitespace. Other criteria that determine whether whitespace is preserved include the following: the whitespace setting for the parent element is `xml:space="preserve"`; the whitespace setting for an ancestor element is `xml:space="preserve"` with no intervening element set to `xml:space="default"`, or no whitespace character is included in its chunk of sibling characters.

▶ USING MACROS IN XSL

You can use macros within templates to perform processing that occurs regularly. To define and name a macro, use the `xsl:macro` element with the name attribute. To invoke the named macro, use the `xsl:invoke` element and the `macro` attribute. To declare a named argument for a macro, use the `xsl:macro-arg` with the name attribute. If the macro produces new contents, use the `xsl:contents` element to insert it in the macro.

CROSS-REFERENCE

Chapter 26 covers the topic of applying styles to selected document text and moving text on the page.

FIND IT ONLINE

To learn about CSS and XSL together, see the W3C note at **http://www.w3.org/TR/NOTE-XSL-and-CSS**.

Listing 30-2: A PROCESSING EXAMPLE

```
<xsl:template match="chapter/title">
    <fo:rule-graphic/> ←❶
    <fo:block space-before="2pt">
        <xsl:text>Chapter </xsl:text> ←❷
        <xsl:number/>
        <xsl:text>: </xsl:text>    ←❸
        <xsl:apply-templates/>
    </fo:block>
    <fo:rule-graphic/> ←❹
</xsl:template>
```

❶ Set a rule formatting object above the text.
❷ Specify the word Chapter as text and add a space.
❸ Calculate a chapter number and add a colon.
❹ Set a rule formatting object below the text.

Listing 30-3: AN XSL:APPLY-TEMPLATES EXAMPLE

```
<xsl:template match="chapter"> ←❶
    <fo:block> ←❷
        <xsl:apply-templates/> ←❸
    </fo:block>    ←❹
</xsl:template>
```

❶ Match the chapter element.
❷ Specify that the chapter will be placed in a block format.
❸ The xsl:apply-templates element processes child elements.
❹ End the code by inserting end tags.

Listing 30-4: ANOTHER XSL:APPLY-TEMPLATES EXAMPLE

```
<xsl:template match="author-group"> ←❶
    <fo:inline-sequence> ←❷
        <xsl:apply-templates
            select="author"/>  ←❸
    </fo:inline-sequence>
                              ←❹
</xsl:template>
```

❶ Match the author-group element.
❷ Specify grouped results that are assigned shared inherited properties.
❸ The xsl:apply-templates element processes the selected element.
❹ End the code by inserting end tags.

Listing 30-5: SAMPLE MACRO CODE

```
<xsl:macro name="warning-para"> ←❶
    <fo:block-level-box><fo:block> ←❷
        <xsl:text>Warning! </xsl:text>
        <xsl:contents/>
        </fo:block></fo:block-level-box>
</xsl:macro><xsl:template match="warning
    <xsl:invoke macro="warning-para"> ←❸
        <xsl:apply-templates/></xsl:invoke>
    </xsl:template>            ❹
```

❶ Start the macro definition with the xsl:macro element.
❷ Specify that the warning has a block format and is boxed.
❸ Invoke the macro.
❹ The xsl:apply-templates element processes the child elements.

Learning About Formatting Objects and Their Classes

Many XSL properties are based on those in the CSS and DSSSL styling languages. For example, `background-attachment`, `background-color`, and `background-image` (all CSS properties) are included in the list of XSL formatting objects. A complete list of XSL formatting objects is included in the current XSL working draft. You can also find comprehensive reference information about both CSS and DSSSL-O (the online version of DSSSL) in my book *XML in Plain English*, also published by IDG Books Worldwide.

As you have learned, formatting objects fill a defined area in document output. Typical formatting objects include hyperlinks, characters, paragraphs, pages, groups of adjacent pages, graphics, and tables. In the current XSL working draft, formatting objects are classified into the groups listed in Table 30-3 on the facing page.

Documents styled with XSL are composed of rectangles and spaces both outside and inside the rectangles. Rectangular areas can contain other rectangular areas, too. Each rectangle is analogous to a self-contained document: it has its own text direction, margins, borders, padding, and other styling properties. Spaces control the location of document content.

Some XSL properties are inherited and others are not. Before you complete an XSL style sheet, be sure to check the current working draft or recommendation for inheritance characteristics.

XSL places formatting objects in four types of rectangular areas—area-containers, block-areas, line-areas, and inline-areas:

- ▶ **Area-containers** can contain other area-containers, block-areas, and display-spaces (blank spaces inserted before and after line-areas and block-areas to control their location within the rectangle). You can set the direction of the text display in an area-container. Area-containers are located in specific places or attached within an edge in the rectangle.
- ▶ **Block-areas** can contain other block-areas, line-areas, and display-spaces. Block-areas are stacked within the rectangle.
- ▶ **Line-areas** can contain inline-areas and inline-spaces (blank spaces inserted before and after inline-areas to control their location). Line-areas are stacked in the block-areas in which they are contained.
- ▶ **Inline-areas** can contain other inline-areas and are stacked in the rectangles.

TAKE NOTE

▶ REVIEWING HTML FLOW OBJECTS

The following HTML elements are considered to be flow objects: A, AREA, BASE, BODY, BR, CAPTION, COL, COLGROUP, DIV, FORM, FRAMESET, HR, HTML, IMG, INPUT, MAP, META, OBJECT, PARAM, PRE, SCRIPT, SELECT, SPAN, TABLE, TBODY, TD, TEXTAREA, TFOOT, THEAD, TITLE, and TR.

CROSS-REFERENCE

In Chapter 28, you can read all the details about applying styles to a variety of XML list types.

FIND IT ONLINE

You'll find a technical XSL tutorial at http://www.micrsoft.com/workshop/xml/xsl.

Table 30-3: XSL FORMATTING OBJECT CLASSES

Class	Declaration	Purpose
block	`<fo:block>`	Creates a block-level area that contains lines of text
block-level-box	`<fo:block-level-box>`	Draws borders and creates backgrounds for block-level text or graphics
character	`<fo:character>`	Controls the behavior of inline characters in a document; replaces selected characters with a glyph
graphic	`<fo:graphic>`	Contains an internal or external inline or block graphic image
inline-box	`<fo:inline-box>`	Draws borders and creates backgrounds for inline text or graphics
link	`<fo:link>`	Creates and styles a link
link-end-locator	`<fo:link-end-locator>`	Gives information about a targeted linked resource; a child of `link`
list	`<fo:list>`	Groups list items in a block format
list-item	`<fo:list-item>`	Contains the bullet, number, or graphic preceding the text and list-item text
list-item-body	`<fo:list-item-body>`	Contains list-item text and sets styling
list-item-label	`<fo:list-item-label>`	Specifies the bullet, number, or graphic preceding list-item text
page-number	`<fo:page-number>`	Creates and displays a page number
page-sequence	`<fo:page-sequence>`	Defines page layout and page layout sequences
queue	`<fo:queue>`	Contains content flow objects for an area; a child of `page-sequence`
rule-graphic	`<fo:rule-graphic>`	Draws a rule line
score	`<fo:score>`	Draws a line above, through, or below text
sequence	`<fo: sequence>`	Groups flow objects and assigns inherited properties to them
simple-page-master	`<fo:simple-page-master>`	Defines a page layout; a child of `page-sequence`

Personal Workbook

Q&A

1 What is a *template*?

_____

_____

_____

2 What is a *pattern*?

_____

_____

_____

3 What is an *action*?

_____

_____

_____

4 What are *formatting objects*? What are formatting objects known as in DSSSL?

_____

_____

_____

5 What are the steps used to process an XSL style sheet against an XML document?

_____

_____

_____

6 What is the prefix for XSL's predefined elements?

_____

_____

_____

7 Is `<xsl:stylesheet>` a processing instruction?

_____

_____

_____

8 What does the `xsl:apply templates` element do?

_____

_____

_____

ANSWERS: PAGE 474

1 Write an XML DTD with elements that produce a book. Elements should include chapters, four levels of headings, paragraphs of various types specified by a `type` attribute, and text. Valid paragraph types are body, `note`, `tip`, and `warning`. (This DTD is the basis for the remaining questions.)

2 Create a pattern that formats a warning paragraph with red boldface text.

3 Create a pattern that finds a note in Chapter 3 and applies a border.

4 Create a pattern that finds any occurrence of a paragraph element with the `type` value of `tip` and gives it a black border and an aqua background.

✔ In a Real-World Application in Chapter 8, you created a letterhead DTD. Using XSL, rewrite the DTD so that you can apply an informal or formal style depending on the value of a `style` attribute.

✔ In another RWA in Chapter 8, you planned and wrote a DTD that included name, address, and grade information that could be plugged into a database program and that could also be printed in a report format. Rewrite the DTD so that you can retrieve grade information based on a student's address.

Visual Quiz

This illustration is identical to the one in Chapter 27's Visual Quiz. Using XSL, how do you style the headings on this page? How do you style the body text? How do you indent body text? How do you set spaces between the lines? (Hint: Use the styling properties from the other chapters in this part. Find their counterparts in the current XSL working draft.)

_____

_____

_____

W Microsoft Word - visual quiz 27

📑 File Edit View Insert Format Tools Table Window Help

letter-spacing

Purpose
Sets spacing between characters.

Syntax
    letter-spacing: {normal|[+|-]length}

Where
　　normal represents the normal spacing between characters. This is the default.

　　length is a positive value followed by a two-letter abbreviation representing the unit of measure. length is usually an increase in the spacing between characters, but can be a decrease (a negative value).

Notes
Valid relative units of measure are em (the height of the current font), ex (the height of the letter x in the current font), and px (pixels, relative to the size of the window). Valid absolute units of measure are in (inches), cm (centimeters), mm (millimeters), pt (points), and pc (picas).

Page 1   Sec 1   1/1   At   Ln   Col   REC TRK EXT OVR WPH

Appendix A:
Personal Workbook Answers

Chapter 1

see page 4

1 **What is the history of the term *markup*?**

A: The term *markup* comes to us from typesetting: editors "mark up" manuscripts with corrections and instructions for page and paragraph layout.

2 **What is *XML markup*?**

A: XML marks up the instructions to the programs that process and build XML documents.

3 **What is the difference between *character data* and *XML text*?**

A: Character data includes all the text and images that appear on the page. XML text is the combination of markup and character data.

4 **What are *elements*?**

A: Elements define common components of an XML document.

5 **What is the character that marks the difference between start tags and end tags?**

A: The only difference between the start tag and end tag is the slash (/), which identifies the end tag and is placed between the less-than character and the first character in the element name.

6 **How can you describe the characteristics of a particular element?**

A: You can use attributes or child elements to describe an element's characteristics. You can also use style sheets to set some elements' characteristics.

7 **Show two ways to write an empty element.**

A: `<empty_element/>` or `<empty_element></empty_element>`.

8 **What is an *entity*?**

A: An entity is one or more characters from the ISO 10646 standard that replaces an entity reference in a document.

Visual Quiz

Q: Circle the markup on this page, and underline the character data.

A: The markup on this page includes the first eight lines and all the components within the less-than symbols (<) and the greater-than (>) symbols. The character data is Charles Smith, Tess Curtis, Christmas Party, and all the text within the `<BODY>` start tag and the `</BODY>` end tag.

Appendix A: Personal Workbook Answers

Chapter 2

see page 20

❶ What is a *document type definition* (DTD)?

A: A document type definition (DTD) defines elements and their attributes, entities, and notation for one or more XML documents.

❷ What is the difference between a well-formed XML document and a valid XML document?

A: A valid document includes a document type definition (DTD).

❸ Name the possible contents of an internal DTD subset.

A: An internal DTD subset can range from a reference to an external DTD subset to an entire DTD.

❹ What components make up a document type declaration?

A: A document type declaration includes the !DOCTYPE keyword, a document type name, and an internal DTD subset or a reference to an external DTD subset.

❺ What are the rules for start tags and end tags in elements that are not empty?

A: All non-empty elements must have start tags and end tags with matching element names.

❻ What are the three categories of XML elements?

A: XML elements fall into three categories: Elements define the structure of documents, specify the content of documents, and apply formats to parts of documents.

❼ What is a *document type*?

A: A document type refers to a class of documents, such as memoranda, letters, reports, manuals, and so on.

❽ What characters do you use to "delimit" an internal DTD?

A: Use the left bracket ([) and right bracket (]) to mark the limits of an internal DTD.

Visual Quiz

Q: Identify components in this XML document. Where is the XML declaration? Where is the document type declaration? Mark the symbol that starts the DTD and the symbol that ends the DTD. What is the name of the root element? Circle the output text. Mark one start tag and one end tag. Identify the empty element and show its location in the output text.

A: The XML declaration is the first line of the document. The document type declaration starts on the second line with the DOCTYPE keyword. The left bracket ([) starts the DTD, and the right bracket (]) ends the DTD. The root element is MEMO. The output text encompasses the lines between the <BODY> start tag and the </BODY> end tag. One start tag is <TITLE>; one end tag is </TITLE>. The empty element is named LOGO. Its location in the output text is the following line: `<LOGO src="smalllogo.gif"/>`.

Chapter 3

see page 34

❶ What does *EBNF* stand for?

A: Extended Backus-Naur Form.

❷ What is a *grammar*?

A: A *grammar* comprises all of the productions in a syntax; it is the complete set of rules for a language.

❸ What is the general syntax for an XML production?

A: The general syntax for an XML production is `Symbol ::= expression` or `symbol ::= expression`.

Appendix A: Personal Workbook Answers

④ Is XML sensitive or insensitive to the case of its symbols? Why?

A: XML is a case-sensitive language. Symbols that have an initial uppercase letter indicate a *regular expression* (a way of grouping characters or options); all other symbols are completely lowercase.

⑤ What do brackets represent in XML syntax?

A: Brackets indicate that the grouped content within is optional.

⑥ Can you use a combination of quotation marks and single quote marks to delimit an expression? Within an expression?

A: Do not mix quotation marks and single quote marks in an expression. If you use quotation marks to delimit an expression, use single quote marks within the expression. If you use single quote marks to delimit an expression, use quotation marks within the expression.

⑦ What does an exclamation point mean in an XML statement?

A: An exclamation point indicates that a reserved keyword follows.

⑧ What does the *not* character mean in an XML statement?

A: The not character indicates that you *cannot* select the bracketed character or characters preceded by the not.

Visual Quiz

Q: The Language Identification productions in the XML specification enable an individual to declare the code of the language in which an XML document will be written. For the `ISO639Code`, `IanaCode`, `UserCode`, and `Subcode` productions, specify the characters that are valid and the order in which they can appear. Then combine the appropriate productions to form the three possible versions of the `LanguageID` production.

A: Valid characters for the `ISO639Code` production are two instances of any alphabetic character ranging from lowercase a to z or uppercase A to Z. The `IanaCode` production must start with lowercase i or uppercase I followed by one or more alphabetic characters ranging from lowercase a to z or uppercase A to Z. The `UserCode` production must start with lowercase x or uppercase X followed by one or more alphabetic characters ranging from lowercase a to z or uppercase A to Z. The `Subcode` production consists of one or more alphabetic characters ranging from lowercase a to z or uppercase A to Z.

The `LanguageID` production can form the three following versions:

```
LanguageID ::= ISO639Code ('-' Subcode)*
LanguageID ::= IanaCode ('-' Subcode)*
LanguageID ::= UserCode ('-' Subcode)*
```

Chapter 4

see page 48

① What is the URL of the Unicode Consortium's home page?

A: The Unicode Consortium's home page is located at **http://www.unicode.org/**.

② What is the name of the international XML-supported standard for character sets? What is its alternate name?

A: The name of the standard for character sets is the International Standard ISO 10646-1. Its alternate name is Unicode.

③ What is the main difference between `CDATA` and `#PCDATA`?

A: `CDATA` is unparsed character data, whereas `#PCDATA` is parsed character data.

APPENDIX A: PERSONAL WORKBOOK ANSWERS

4 **Name the URL of the Contents page at the Unicode site.**

A: The URL of the Contents page at the Unicode site is **http://www.unicode.org/unicode/contents.html**.

5 **What is *UTF-8*?**

A: UTF-8 is an 8-bit version of a character set specified by the Unicode Technical Committee (UTC). UTF-8 is the default encoding for XML documents.

6 **What does *UCS* represent? What does *UTF* represent?**

A: The acronym UCS represents *universal coded character set* or *Universal Character Set*, and UTF represents *UCS transformation format*.

7 **Under UTF-8, how many bytes long are common ASCII characters? How many bytes long are non-ASCII characters?**

A: The common ASCII characters are one byte long, whereas the non-ASCII characters are three bytes long.

8 **What production do you use to represent the name of an encoding?**

A: Use the `EncName` production to represent an encoding name.

Visual Quiz

Q: **This XML document is a DTD that lists 10 character references. Go to the Unicode Consortium site and identify each of the character references. Then write an XML document that includes all 10 characters.**

A: The `&#x0040;` entity represents an at sign (@).

Note that the at sign is already on your keyboard and does not appear in the `BaseChar` production. Thus, the best answer is to ignore this trick part of the question.

The `&#x00A1;` entity represents an inverted exclamation mark (¡).

The `&#x00A2;` entity represents a cent symbol (¢).

The `&#x00AE;` entity represents a registered trademark ((r)).

The `&#x00A9;` entity represents a copyright symbol ((c)).

The `&#x00D8;` entity represents a stroke or slash O (Ø).

The `&#x00F7;` entity represents a division symbol (÷).

The `&#x00B6;` entity represents a paragraph symbol (¶).

The `&#x00A7;` entity represents a section symbol (§).

The `&#x01C1;` entity represents a lateral click symbol (().

```
<?xml version="1.0"?>
<copyright>&#x00A9;, , 1999</copyright>
<title>Samples of Special
   Characters</title>
<characters>
&#x0040; is an at sign, which you can find
   on the keyboard. Will this code cause
   a parsing error?
<break/>
&#x00A1; is an inverted exclamation mark.
<break/>
&#x00A2; is a cent symbol.
<break/>
&#x00AE; is a registered trademark.
<break/>
&#x00D8; is a stroke or slash O.
<break/>
&#x00F7; is a division symbol.
<break/>
&#x00B6; is a paragraph symbol.
<break/>
&#x00A7; is a section symbol.
<break/>
&#x01C1; is a lateral click symbol.
</characters>
```

Appendix A: Personal Workbook Answers

Chapter 5

see page 62

1 **What steps do you take to download a program?**

A: Most downloads involve finding the appropriate page, selecting a platform (for example, Windows, Mac, or UNIX), and clicking on a link or a Download button. After you specify the folder in which you want the program to be stored, simply wait for the executable (.EXE) or compressed (e.g., ZIP) file to download completely.

2 **What are the three common installation options?**

A: You can usually select a default installation, customized installation, or minimum installation.

3 **If you download a file with the .ZIP extension, what do you have to do to it?**

A: If you have downloaded a compressed file, you will have to "uncompress" it.

4 **What U.S. government office provides information on copyright laws? What is the URL of its Web site?**

A: To learn about U.S. copyright law, go to the United States Copyright Office (**http://lcweb.loc.gov/copyright/**).

5 **What are the three common ways of starting a program?**

A: (1) Click the Start button, select Programs, and select the appropriate name from the list of programs; (2) Open the My Computer window or Windows Explorer, find the folder in which the application file is located, and double-click the filename of the program; (3) Double-click the program's shortcut icon.

6 **How do you get help in learning about a program?**

A: To get help, open the Help menu and select a Topics or Contents command. Then click or double-click on a topic or type a search keyword.

7 **What types of software can you use to create an XML document?**

A: You can create an XML document using a standard word processor or text editor, or you can use a program that is created specifically for editing XML documents.

8 **What is *parsing*?**

A: Parsing is the act of analyzing the text in a document, both markup and content, using the information in the document prolog as a guide.

Visual Quiz

Q: **This is a typical Adobe FrameMaker+SGML application window. Identify each of the following elements: title bar, work area, and menu bar. Identify the two buttons that resize the application window and the button that closes the application. Name the menu under which you will find a command that saves files. In what drive will you find the program files for FrameMaker+SGML?**

A: The title bar is at the top of the window. The work area is the large area encompassing the middle part of the window. The menu bar is immediately below the title bar. The two buttons that resize the application window are the Minimize button and the Restore button, which are the first and second buttons on the right side of the title bar. The buttons that closes the application is the third button on the right side of the title bar. The File menu includes two commands with which you can save files: Save and Save As.

Appendix A: Personal Workbook Answers

Chapter 6

see page 78

① Can you use an internal DTD subset to define the components of a set of documents?

A: An internal DTD subset *must* be used for the document in which it is enclosed: it cannot define elements, attributes, entities, and so on for other documents.

② What sort of planning goes into designing a DTD?

A: When you design a DTD, you must decide on the structure, content, and formats of the future document and evaluate one or more applications that will control the output.

③ What is the best way to start a DTD outline?

A: The best way to start an outline of a DTD is to enter the highest-level components first.

④ Why should you not use a component for more than one purpose?

A: If you overuse a particular component, you may have to insert styles at particular parts of the document. This means that you may defeat the purpose of spending extra time organizing the DTD and ensuring that all the pieces of the document are properly defined.

⑤ Name five ways in which information from an XML document can be output.

A: You can print information, display information onscreen, load fields into a database, send information to a program that converts text to audio, send information that updates an inventory system, or send information to control the behavior of a metalworking machine or robot.

⑥ What is a *conditional section*, and what are the two types of conditional sections for DTDs?

A: Conditional sections are portions of the document type declaration external subset that are included in, or excluded from, the logical structure of the DTD based on the keyword that governs them. The XML provides for INCLUDE and IGNORE sections.

⑦ What is the difference between an INCLUDE **section** and an IGNORE **section?**

A: An XML parser processes only INCLUDE sections.

⑧ What are the two main differences between creating DTDs for individual documents and for sets of documents?

A: You should spend more time planning standards for the document sets, and must ensure that elements and other document components work for all the documents in the set.

Visual Quiz

Q: How you would design a DTD to duplicate the structure and formats of this sample fax cover sheet? Don't forget the margins.

A:
```
<?xml version = "1.0"?>
<!DOCTYPE fax [
<!ELEMENT fax (letterhead,head,to,myphone,
   myfax,from,phone,fax,date,pages,
   comments,bodytext)>
<!ATTLIST fax
        margins CDATA "1in">
  <!ELEMENT letterhead (#PCDATA)>
  <!ELEMENT head (#PCDATA)>
  <!ELEMENT to (#PCDATA)>
  <!ELEMENT myphone (#PCDATA)>
  <!ELEMENT myfax (#PCDATA)>
  <!ELEMENT from (#PCDATA)>
  <!ELEMENT phone (#PCDATA)>
  <!ELEMENT fax (#PCDATA)>
```

```
<!ELEMENT date (#PCDATA)>
<!ELEMENT pages (#PCDATA)>
<!ELEMENT comments (#PCDATA)>
<!ELEMENT bodytext (#PCDATA)>
]>
```

Chapter 7

see page 92

1 **What are the *document prolog* and the *document instance*?**

A: The document prolog is the top of any XML document instance, which is the entire document.

2 **What is a *DTD*?**

A: A DTD is a document type definition. A DTD specifies the elements, attributes, entities, and notations for one or more XML documents.

3 **Explain the difference between a document type declaration and a document type definition.**

A: A document type declaration points to the DTD.

4 **What is the difference between an internal DTD subset and an external DTD subset?**

A: The part of a DTD that is within the source document is the internal DTD subset, whereas the part of a DTD that is stored in a separate document is an external DTD subset.

5 **What three places can you *not* put comments in an XML document?**

A: At the very top of the document, within a character data section, or within tags or declarations.

6 **What is *metadata*?**

A: Metadata is information about the XML document in which it is located.

7 **What is the *root element*?**

A: The root element is the top-level element in an XML document within which all other XML elements for the current document are nested.

8 **Write an element declaration for the root element TALK, which can hold parsed character data.**

A: `<!ELEMENT talk (#PCDATA)>`

Visual Quiz

Q: Name the eight things that are wrong with this DTD.

A: The eight things are

1 A comment cannot start a DTD.
2 The current XML version is 1.0.
3 The XML declaration should end with a greater-than symbol.
4 `ELAMENT` should be spelled `ELEMENT`.
5 A comment should not interrupt an element declaration.
6 A comment should include an exclamation point immediately after the less-than symbol.
7 The percent sign after the para element is not valid.
8 The end of a DTD should end with one greater-than symbol — not two.

Chapter 8

see page 110

1 **How do you add a list of child elements to an element declaration?**

A: A list of child elements must be enclosed within parentheses (( )), can contain any amount of white space, and must use a comma or pipe to separate one element from the next.

Appendix A: Personal Workbook Answers

2 What does a *comma symbol* indicate? What does a *pipe symbol* mean?

A: The comma symbol compels the use of the listed elements in a particular order. The pipe symbol allows the use of the listed elements in any order.

3 Name three ways to make a DTD more understandable to those who will maintain it.

A: Indent lines to indicate the level of elements and other components. Add comments throughout the DTD. Insert blank lines between sections of related markup.

4 What are the four types of content for an element?

A: Each declared element in a DTD can have one of four possible content types: EMPTY, ANY, Mixed, or children.

5 What content can the ANY type of element include?

A: ANY can include any type of content — both unparsed and parsed data as well as any type of markup.

6 What content can the Mixed type of element include?

A: The Mixed element type comprises either parsed character data or combines #PCDATA with any number of child elements.

7 What trait of an entity reference allows it to be included in #PCDATA?

A: #PCDATA can include entity references as character data because the entity has already been declared. Therefore, its markup has already been converted to character data.

8 What content can the EMPTY type of element include?

A: An empty element is either a container for future content or an element that needs no content.

Visual Quiz

Q: What elements would you write for this database input form? What would you do to convert the information in this database to a DTD that would produce printed reports?

A: Elements for this database input form should include those for the priority, the area or room, completion, those who will perform the job, and body text. The element names are up to the individual writing the DTD. To convert the information to printed reports, use an XML processor that sends the information to an application capable of printing.

Chapter 9

see page 124

1 What is an *attribute*?

A: An attribute is an option that affects the behavior of an element and further defines it.

2 What signals an attribute-list declaration?

A: The ATTLIST keyword signals an attribute-list declaration.

3 What is the most common attribute type? What is its purpose?

A: CDATA, the most common attribute type, enables you to limit the attribute value of a string to character data only.

4 Where do you place an attribute-list declaration in a DTD?

A: An attribute list is located under the element with which it is associated.

5 List the tokenized types of attributes.

A: The tokenized types of attributes are `ID`, `IDREF`, `IDREFS`, `ENTITY`, `ENTITIES`, `NMTOKEN`, and `NMTOKENS`.

6 What purpose does the default declaration serve?

A: A default declaration enables you to further control the attribute by making it required or optional; by setting a default value (which is the only allowable value); by supplying one default value (which can be changed); or by listing a set of valid values.

7 What is the basic difference between elements and attributes?

A: Elements usually specify part of the structure of a document or a type of content. Attributes usually add information about an element.

8 When you list valid values in an attribute-list declaration, what can you include in the default declaration?

A: The default declaration can include a default value or a keyword.

Visual Quiz

Q: These are the XML productions that control the syntax of attribute declarations. Using the XML specification (http://www.w3.org/XML/) and this book, evaluate each of the VC comments for the TokenizedType production. Look at the Name and Nmtoken productions in the XML specification and decide which characters are valid and invalid in each production.

A: VC represents validity constraints, which means that a DTD must be associated with the XML document.

VC: `ID` means that the `ID` attribute name must be a valid XML name and must be unique for the element with which it is associated as an attribute.

VC: `One ID per Element Type` indicates that no element type may have more than one ID attribute.

VC: `ID Attribute Default` states that an ID attribute is either `#IMPLIED` (optional) or `#REQUIRED` (required).

VC: `IDREF` means that the `IDREF` attribute name must be a valid XML name and each name on the `IDREFS` list must be a valid XML name. In addition, each name must be identical to the value of an `ID` attribute for an element in the document.

VC: `Entity Name` indicates that the `ENTITY` attribute name must be a valid XML name and each name on the `ENTITIES` list must be a valid XML name. In addition, each name must be identical to the name of an unparsed entity declared in the DTD.

VC: `Name Token` means that the `NMTOKEN` attribute must be a valid XML name token and each name on the `NMTOKENS` list must be a valid XML name token.

The `Name` production has the following format:

`Name ::= (Letter|'-'|':'|) (NameChar)*`

Thus, valid characters include the starting character, which must be a letter or symbol from the current alphabet, a dash, or a colon, followed by any number of optional characters, including letters, digits, dashes, colons, periods, underscores, combining characters, and extenders.

The `Nmtoken` production has the following format:

`Nmtoken ::= (NameChar)*`

Therefore, valid characters include any number of characters, including letters, digits, dashes, colons, periods, underscores, combining characters, and extenders.

Chapter 10

see page 140

1 What is an *entity*?

A: An *entity* is a named chunk of information — ranging from a single character to an entire book consisting of one file.

APPENDIX A: PERSONAL WORKBOOK ANSWERS

② What is an *entity reference*?

A: An *entity reference* refers to an entity from within an XML document.

③ What are the two main categories of XML entities?

A: The two main categories of XML entities are *general* and *parameter*.

④ Describe the difference between unparsed and parsed entities.

A: An *unparsed entity* contains information that has not been processed by an XML parser. A *parsed entity* contains information that has been processed and converted into replacement text.

⑤ Describe the difference between internal and external entities.

A: An *internal entity* is stored completely within the current DTD. An *external entity* has its content stored in a separate file that is completely outside the XML document.

⑥ Describe a *general entity*.

A: A *general entity* is a string usually named within the non-DTD part of a document; its replacement text will become part of the document content. If a general entity will become part of the content, it can occur in the DTD.

⑦ Describe a *parameter entity*.

A: A *parameter entity*, which is always parsed, is a string that is named in the DTD only.

⑧ What delimiters precede and succeed general entities and PEs?

A: A general entity is preceded by an ampersand, whereas a PE is preceded by both a percent sign and a space. Both types of entities are succeeded by a semicolon.

Visual Quiz

Q: This DTD includes many mistakes, not all concerning entity declarations. Identify all the errors.

A: The errors are
1 The root element must be spelled the same in the DOCTYPE and ELEMENT declarations.
2 In the element declaration, #DATA should be #PCDATA.
3 The ENTITY keyword must be uppercase.
4 The book element is not declared in the DTD. Change the `<book>` start tag to `<mistakes>`.
5 The introduction is a character reference, and the intro element is not declared in the DTD. Replace the `<intro>` and `</intro>` tags with `&intr;`.

Chapter 11

see page 156

① What are the three types of DTDs that you can convert for an XML document?

A: You can convert an XML DTD, an SGML DTD, or a DTD from a custom XML markup language.

② What parts of the Internet provide DTDs and libraries of DTDs?

A: You can find DTDs and libraries of DTDs on the World Wide Web or at FTP sites.

③ How do you search for a DTD on the Internet?

A: Start a search engine, enter a keyword or keyword phrase in the text box, and then click a Search button or press Enter.

④ When you enter a keyword phrase in a text box, how do you format it?

A: A keyword phrase should be enclosed within quotation marks or single quotes and should be all lowercase.

Appendix A: Personal Workbook Answers

⑤ How do you use multiple external DTDs in your documents?

A: Define the extra DTDs as external PEs.

⑥ What are the three ways in which a DTD should match an XML document or document set?

A: The DTD should have been designed for the particular type of document; its elements, attributes, entities, and other components should measure up to the components of (and your desires for) the document; and the DTD should be well-constructed and accurate.

⑦ How do you convert an internal DTD subset to an external DTD subset?

A: Copy the entire internal DTD subset to a new XML document, insert an XML declaration at the top of the document, and save the document as a DTD, using a valid XML name and the `.dtd` extension.

⑧ Does XML ever allow optional end tags?

A: No. XML always requires end tags.

Visual Quiz

Q: This Web page lists individual DTDs and DTD directories. Identify DTDs that you can use for weather observation. Find a file that refers to HTML 4.0. Find an electronic newsletter.

A: A DTD that you can use for weather observation is `Terminal Aerodrome Forecasts`. A file that refers to HTML 4.0 is `ibtwsh`. The electronic newsletter reference is `<TAG>`.

Chapter 12

see page 170

① What is a *parser*?

A: A parser is a program that processes some sort of input and converts that input into some form of output for another application — such as a browser — to use.

② What types of document components do parsers check?

A: XML parsers check syntax, elements, and URLs by using programmed criteria.

③ What are the two parser categories? What do they do?

A: A non-validating parser checks how well-formed a document is. A validating parser evaluates both the DTD and the document.

④ When a parser finds a problem in a DTD or document, what does it do?

A: When a parser finds problems in a document, it issues warning and error codes.

⑤ How should you run a parser for the first time?

A: Start out with a smaller XML document, whose structure you thoroughly understand. Try running the parser without any arguments.

⑥ If you have problems running a parser for the first time, what are some of the ways that you can find the problem?

A: Run your applications incrementally, with the loader program first, followed by the parser.

⑦ How do you run a command-line utility?

A: Open an MS-DOS window and issue the first command at the prompt.

⑧ What is the main advantage of using an XML editor?

A: Most editors enable you to not only create XML documents, but also check the syntax for both your DTD and document. Some editors also show the tree structure of an XML document.

Visual Quiz

Q: Find all the errors in this XML document using an XML parser. Correct the document and rerun the parser until the document is completely accurate.

A: The `<title>` start tag does not have a matching `</title>` end tag; the slash symbol is missing from the tag at the end of the line. Although one `<para>` start tag includes an ID and the other includes an `align` attribute, neither attribute is declared in the DTD. (The fact that `Align` starts with an initial uppercase character should not affect the performance of most parsers — even if the attribute were declared.) The second `para` start tag does not end with a greater-than symbol. The `</science>` end tag should end the document.

Chapter 13

see page 186

❶ What declaration needs to be placed at the beginning of an XML document?

A: Place an XML declaration at the beginning of each document.

❷ When you use elements in a valid XML document, what should determine the choice of possible elements?

A: The elements used in a valid document are declared in the DTD.

❸ What element must all XML documents have?

A: All XML documents must have the root element.

❹ What are *attributes*?

A: Attributes are name-value pairs associated with an element. They add information that can be used by other applications, not end users.

❺ Where do you place attributes?

A: Place attributes within start tags or empty tags.

❻ What are the basic types of entities to use in an XML document?

A: There are two basic types of entities: a general entity and a parameter entity.

❼ What are *external entities*?

A: External entities can be other XML documents or they may be unparsed information such as graphic files. External entities are stored outside the current document.

❽ What is the advantage of using a combined start tag and end tag for an empty element?

A: When you use a combined start tag and end tag for an empty element, other people can tell immediately that the element was meant to be empty.

Visual Quiz

Q: What is wrong with this section of an XML document?

A: On the second line, the entity should end with a semicolon (that is, `&apos;`). On the same line, the `recipe` element is not empty, so it should not end with `/>`. The `<ingredients>` start tag on the fourth line does not have a counterpart `</ingredients>` end tag. On line six, the `</quantity>` end tag is misspelled. The end tags for the `<name>` start tags on lines eight and 12 are missing. On line 14, the `<Instructions>` start tag begins with an uppercase I. (This last mistake shouldn't affect the performance of most parsers.)

Appendix A: Personal Workbook Answers

Chapter 14

see page 202

1 **What are the basic components of a list?**

A: A list has a start tag followed by a number of list items and, at the end, an end tag.

2 **Can you nest a combination of ordered and unordered lists?**

A: Yes. You can compose nested tables of ordered and unordered lists.

3 **What are the two child elements of a definition list?**

A: The child elements of a definition are the term and the term's description.

4 **What is a *cell*?**

A: A cell is the intersection of a row and a column.

5 **How is a basic table similar to a list?**

A: A basic table is composed of a set of lists.

6 **Does a table have to contain elements that represent rows?**

A: No; you can create a table that has elements representing columns instead.

7 **What is the advantage of creating a separate heading element from the main body element of a table?**

A: A separate heading allows you to create an element that holds information used at the top of each page of a table.

8 **In a table composed of rows and cells in the row, how can you visually track the column to which the cells belong?**

A: You can use attributes as part of the cell element definition, or you can rename the cells to correspond to the column.

Visual Quiz

Q: How would you structure this table in XML?

A: One way of structuring the table is as follows:

```
<table border rules="all">
<row border>
    <cell>Person</cell>
    <cell>Location</cell>
    <cell colspan="3">Distance</cell>
</row>
<row>
    <cell></cell><cell></cell>
    <cell>Theresa</cell><cell>Jim</cell>
    <cell>Susan</cell>
</row>
<row>
    <cell>Theresa</cell>
    <cell>Main Street</cell>
    <cell>-</cell><cell>1 mile</cell>
    <cell>4 miles</cell>
</row>
<row>
    <cell>Jim</cell><cell>Oak Lane</cell>
    <cell>1 mile</cell><cell>-</cell>
    <cell>3.5 miles</cell>
</row>
<row>
    <cell>Susan</cell><cell>BC Way</cell>
    <cell>4 miles</cell>
    <cell>3.5 miles</cell><cell>-</cell>
</row>
</table>
```

Appendix A: Personal Workbook Answers

Chapter 15

see page 216

1 Does the current version of XML support frames and framesets?

A: No.

2 How can you use frames now?

A: To use frames now, a developer at your company will have to write a custom frames application or applet.

3 What does the HTML FRAMESET element do?

A: Using the HTML FRAMESET element, you can specify the dimensions for individual frames or the percentage of the window devoted to each of the frames in the frame set.

4 What does the HTML FRAME element do?

A: The HTML FRAME element specifies the URI for the document that will appear in the frame and has attributes with which you can affect the look and content of the frame.

5 What two attributes control the splitting of a window into frames?

A: ROWS controls the number of rows of frames, and COLS determines the number of columns.

6 What does the asterisk represent in the COLS or ROWS attribute?

A: The asterisk represents the remaining space in a column or row.

7 What attribute do you use to control the content of a particular frame?

A: Use the TARGET attribute to name or specify a target window in which particular contents are displayed.

8 When you have a frames site, how do you deal with browsers that do not support frames.

A: Include a NOFRAMES section for browsers that do not support frames.

Visual Quiz

Q: How would you define these frames?

A: One way of defining these frames is as follows:

```
<frametest>
<title>Frames</title>
<frameset cols=50%,*>
    <frame href="frame1.xml">
    <frameset rows=50%,*>
        <frame href="frame2.xml">
        <frameset cols=50%,*>
            <frame href="frame3.xml">
            <frame href="frame4.xml">
        </frameset>
    </frameset>
</frameset>
</frametest>
```

Chapter 16

see page 230

1 What is the major difference in the order of development between converting an HTML document to XML and building an XML document from scratch?

A: The content is available for a conversion before the structure is defined. When building from scratch, the document structure is defined first.

2 Why isn't it a good idea to use the HTML DTD when converting an HTML document to XML?

A: The HTML DTD does not contain much information related to a document's structure.

Appendix A: Personal Workbook Answers

③ The `<HTML>` and `</HTML>` tags of an HTML document should be replaced by which element?

A: The `<HTML>` and `</HTML>` tags should be replaced by the root element of the XML document.

④ What are three things to consider when converting HTML elements to XML elements?

A: All XML elements including empty elements, require end tags. XML empty elements must be formatted with an ending slash (/) and greater-than symbol (>). XML elements are case-sensitive because XML supports the Unicode standard, whose characters are case-sensitive.

⑤ What is wrong with the following XML start and end tag combination: `<body>  </Body>`

A: The capitalization of the tags does not match. This is okay in HTML but not acceptable in XML

⑥ Why will you delete some attribute information when converting an HTML document to XML?

A: In HTML, many attributes define formatting. This is not the case with XML, which relies on style sheets for formatting.

⑦ Why would you use general entities in an HTML-to-XML document conversion?

A: You use a general entity to replace content that may change or that is used often.

⑧ Why would you use parameter entities in an HTML-to-XML document conversion?

A: You could use a parameter entity to share a single DTD among XML documents with similar structures. This makes it easy to change the structure of all of the documents.

Visual Quiz

Q: How would you convert this HTML code into an XML DTD?

A: You could convert this HTML code into an XML DTD as follows:

```
<?xml version = "1.0"?>
<!DOCTYPE doc [
<!ELEMENT doc (title,(head1*|head2*|head3*
      |a*|ul*|ol*))>
  <!ELEMENT title (#PCDATA)>
  <!ELEMENT head1 (#PCDATA)>
  <!ELEMENT head2 (#PCDATA)>
  <!ELEMENT head3 (#PCDATA)>
  <!ELEMENT a EMPTY>
  <!ATTLIST a
          href CDATA #REQUIRED>
  <!ELEMENT ul|ol (li)
    <!ELEMENT li (#PCDATA)>
]>
```

Chapter 17

see page 244

① What features should Internet-ready business applications provide?

A: Internet-ready business applications should support standard file types and Internet file types, incorporate Internet technologies, and start supporting technologies such as scripting and Dynamic HTML.

② What are the components making up a database?

A: A database is made up of records, which are composed of fields.

③ What is a *field*?

A: A field, which is the smallest unit of information, contains one piece of information.

4 What is a *record*?

A: A record is composed of a group of related fields.

5 What is a *form*?

A: Use forms to enter information into the records in a database.

6 What is a *relational database*?

A: A relational database consists of several standalone databases, each of which serves a unique purpose to a central database.

7 What is *JavaScript*?

A: JavaScript is a programming language that enables administrators to control Web servers, add scripts to Web pages on client computers, and interface with Java applets.

8 What does Dynamic HTML do?

A: Dynamic HTML allows a Web-page developer to embed scripts, Java applets, and ActiveX objects, all of which enable actions and processing.

Visual Quiz

Q: How would you design a DTD based on this input form? What elements would you declare? Into what generation levels would you place the declared elements?

A: A DTD for the input form could look something like this:

```
<?xml version = "1.0"?>
<!DOCTYPE repairs [
<!ELEMENT repairs (record*)>
  <!ELEMENT record (priority,area,status,
               worker,bodytext)>
  <!ATTLIST record
          jobid  ID  #REQUIRED>
  <!ELEMENT priority (#PCDATA)>
  <!ATTLIST priority
          level (high|med|low) "med">
```

```
<!ELEMENT area (#PCDATA)>
<!ATTLIST area
          ar (br1|br2|br3|br4|bth1|bth2
             |bth3|lr|dr|fam|kit|base
             |base|land|other) "other">
<!ELEMENT status (#PCDATA)>
<!ATTLIST status
          stat (comp|incomp) "incomp">
<!ELEMENT worker (#PCDATA)>
<!ATTLIST worker
          contr      (yes|no) "yes"
          arch_des   (yes|no) "no"
          carp       (yes|no) "no"
          elec       (yes|no) "no"
          floor      (yes|no) "no"
          owner      (yes|no) "no"
          paint      (yes|no) "no"
          plumb      (yes|no) "no"
          other      (yes|no) "no">
  <!ELEMENT bodytext (#PCDATA)>
]>
```

Chapter 18

see page 258

1 What is a *control?* What are some examples of control types?

A: A control is a named component within a form. Control types are checkboxes, radio buttons, push buttons, text boxes, list boxes, and other objects.

2 To what other design process can you compare designing a form layout?

A: Designing a form layout is very similar to designing page layout for an entire document.

③ What is the best method for submitting a form to a server?

A: The post method is considered best for submitting a form.

④ What is a *successful control*?

A: A control whose content can be submitted to an application is successful.

⑤ What kind of radio button is successful?

A: If a radio button is filled, it is the successful radio button in the set.

⑥ What should happen when a user clicks on a submit button?

A: When a user clicks on a submit button, a program or script should be activated.

⑦ What is *CGI*?

A: CGI is a protocol that creates HTML in response to user requests.

⑧ What is *HTTP*?

A: HTTP is a protocol that is programmed to understand the hypertext links in the documents that it transfers.

Visual Quiz

Q: You saw this input form in Chapter 17. How would you re-create its design with help from the DTD that you wrote in Chapter 17?

A: Based on the contents of the DTD, the input form would look like a plain-text database document. However, the attributes would force the user to select certain values. (Hint: To actually redesign the output, use style sheets, covered in Part V.)

Chapter 19

see page 274

① What do extended links do?

A: Extended links establish hyperlinks in XML documents.

② According to the W3C XLink working draft, what are the two categories of links?

A: The W3C XLink working draft defines two categories of links: simple links and extended links.

③ What attribute do you use to specify a link in an XML document?

A: Use the `xml:link` attribute to specify a link.

④ Which type of XML link is similar to links formed by the HTML A element?

A: Simple links are analogous to the links formed by the A element in HTML.

⑤ What is an *inline link*?

A: An inline link is an internal link within the current document.

⑥ What is an *out-of-line link*?

A: An out-of-line link specifies the location of the link in an external file.

⑦ How do you express that a link is inline or out-of-line?

A: If a link is inline, the inline attribute has a value of `'true'`. If a link is out-of-line, the inline attribute has a value of `'false'`.

⑧ What title attribute do you use for a local link resource?

A: Use the `content-title` attribute to name the title of a local link resource.

APPENDIX A: PERSONAL WORKBOOK ANSWERS

Visual Quiz

Q: How would you code the inline links on this Web page? (Hint: You can find many of the URLs in Chapter 11.)

A: You could code the inline links on the Web page as follows:

```
<head1 align="center">XML and SGML DTDs
</head1>
<head2>Welcome</head2>
<para>This page contains links to XML and
SGML DTDs.</para>
<head2>Directories</head2>
<ulist>
<item>
<a href="http://tag.sgml.com/resource.htm">
&lt;TAG&gt;</a>,
an electronic SGML newsletter and resource
directory.
</item>
<item>
<a href="http://pw2.netcom.com
/%7Ece_allen/hrxml.htm">
XML for HR</a>,
links to several DTDs
</item>
<item>
<a href="http://www.manta.ieee.org/p1484
/xml/intro.htm">
XML DTD for v2.1 LOM Specification</a>,
links to two DTDs for the Learning Object
Metadata (LOM) draft
</item>
</ulist>
<head2>Individual DTDs</head2>
<ulist>
<item>
<a href="http://www.lists.ic.ac.uk
/archives/xml-dev/9704/0061.html">
Test XML DTD</a>,
a test DTD for the Web from the Docbook
standard
```

```
</item>
<item>
<a
href="http://www.oreilly.com/davenport/">
DocBook DTD</a>,
a Docbook DTD
</item>
<item>
<a href="http://zowie.metnet.navy.mil
/~spawar/JMV-TNG/XML/OMF.dtd">
Terminal Aerodrome Forecasts</a>,
a Weather Observation Definition
Format DTD
</item>
<item>
<a href="http://www.ics.uci.edu/~ejw
/authoring/protocol/webdav3.dtd">
WebDAV Protocol</a>,
a DTD with commented links to WebDAV
protocol documents
</item>
<item>
<a href="http://www.schema.net/general">
ibtwsh</a>,
a DTD that describes a subset of HTML 4.0
</item>
</ulist>
```

Chapter 20

see page 288

❶ What two steps do you need to do to use any type of link in an XML document?

A: To use an XML link, you must add code to the DTD. First, declare the element that will include the link, and then specify the type of link and other linking characteristics in the element's attribute list.

2 **What does the `ANY` keyword mean in an element declaration?**

A: The `ANY` keyword indicates that the element can contain any type of content — both markup and character data.

3 **What attribute is always required in an attribute list for a linking element?**

A: The required attribute for a linking element's attribute list is `href`.

4 **Does a simple link ever traverse from the target resource to the link?**

A: No. Users can only initiate travel from the link to the target audience.

5 **Can a simple link ever go to more than one destination?**

A: No. A simple link goes to only one destination.

6 **What are the two ways you can associate the xml:link attribute with a document?**

A: You can declare `xml:link` in the DTD, or you can include it in the link statements in the XML document.

7 **What does the `#FIXED` keyword indicate?**

A: The `#FIXED` keyword fixes a specific value throughout an XML document.

8 **What does the `behavior` attribute do?**

A: The `behavior` attribute provides information and instructions about the traversal between the link and the target resource to the XML parser or other processing application.

Visual Quiz

Q: How would you create this table of links to nine pages?

A: One way to create the table of links to nine pages is as follows:

```
<head1 align="center">A Linking Table
</head1>
<table cellspacing="0" border="2"
 width=623px>
<row>
 <cell width="33%" vert="middle">
 <a href="http://www.sandy.com/joke1.htm">
 Chicken Jokes</a>
</cell>
<cell width="33%" vert="middle">
 <a href="http://www.sandy.com/joke2.htm">
 Mother-in-Law Jokes</a>
</cell>
<cell width="33%" vert="middle">
 <a href="http://www.sandy.com/joke3.htm">
 Shaggy Dog Jokes</a>
</cell>
</row>
<row>
<cell width="33%" vert="middle">
 <a href="http://www.sandy.com/joke4.htm">
 Star Trek Jokes</a>
</cell>
<cell width="33%" vert="middle">
 <a href="http://www.sandy.com/joke5.htm">
 Martian Jokes</a>
</cell>
<cell width="33%" vert="middle">
 <a href="http://www.sandy.com/joke6.htm">
 Space Jokes</a>
</cell>
</row>
<row>
<cell width="33%" vert="middle">
 <a href="http://www.sandy.com/joke7.htm">
 Computer Jokes</a>
```

```
</cell>
<cell width="33%" vert="middle">
 <a href="http://www.sandy.com/joke8.htm">
 Internet Jokes</a>
</cell>
<cell width="33%" vert="middle">
 <a href="http://www.sandy.com/joke9.htm">
 Knock Knock Jokes</a>
</cell>
</row>
</table>
```
Keep in mind that the XLink working draft is subject to modification as it evolves toward a W3C recommendation.

Chapter 21

see page 302

1 What is the structure of an extended link?

A: An extended link consists of a parent extended element and one or more locator elements, which are nested within the extended element.

2 Where do you find the link and target information in an extended link?

A: The locator element includes the link and target information.

3 If all your locator elements contain the same attribute having the same value, what do you do?

A: If all your locator elements contain the same attribute having the same value, move the attribute and its value into the extended element start tag.

4 Why doesn't the locator element support the inline attribute?

A: An extended element should not contain a mix of inline and out-of-line locators, so the locator element should not allow the use of the `inline` attribute.

 **5** Do locator elements inherit the attributes of the extended element in which they are nested?

A: Yes.

6 Why is the locator element empty?

A: The locator element is empty because its sole purpose is to link to a target resource.

7 What is an *actuator*?

A: An actuator is a person or application that activates a process.

8 How do you place a target resource in a new window?

A: To place a target resource in a new window, use the `show="new"` attribute and value.

Visual Quiz

Q: This organization chart shows three levels of management. How would you link from any box to the top box? How would you link from the top box to the three boxes representing the second layer simultaneously? How would you link simultaneously from the second-level boxes to the levels that report to them?

A: As you write the XML document that creates the organization chart, include an `ID` attribute and unique value for each of the boxes (for example, `<PRESBOX ID="pres">` and `<VPSALES ID="vpsales">`). To link from any box to the top box, simply add a simple link `ID(pres)` to the markup for any box. To link from the top box to the three boxes representing the second layer simultaneously, write an extended link that looks something like this:

```
<extended xml:link="extended">
  <locator href="#vpsales"/>
  <locator href="#vpmrkt"/>
  <locator href="#vphr"/>
</extended>
```

To link simultaneously from the second-level boxes to the levels that report to them, write another extended link group for each of the second-level boxes. For example, according to the organization chart, two salespersons currently report to the vice president of sales, so the extended links would look something like this:

```
<extended xml:link="extended">
  <locator href="#boyce"/>
  <locator href="#bell"/>
</extended>
```

Note that the XLink working draft is subject to modification as it evolves toward a W3C recommendation.

Chapter 22

see page 316

❶ What is an *extended link group*?

A: An extended link group contains several elements that link to a group of related documents.

❷ What is the difference between a URI in an extended link and a URI in an extended link group?

A: A URI in an extended link refers to a target resource in the current document or in an external document. A URI in an extended link group refers to a target document.

❸ How do you prepare to use an extended link group in an XML document?

A: Before you can use an extended link group, you must declare the extended link group element and its attributes and the extended link document element and its attributes.

❹ Why do the extended link group element and the extended link document element not support the inline attribute?

A: The extended link group element and the extended link document element do not support the inline attribute because extended link groups are composed of external documents and are out-of-line links.

❺ What is the declared content of the extended link document element?

A: The extended link document element is empty.

❻ What is the value of the `xml:link` attribute for an extended link group element?

A: The value of the `xml:link` attribute for an extended link group element is "group".

❼ What does the `steps` attribute do?

A: The `steps` attribute sets a limit on the number of layers of extended link groups that can be processed.

❽ Is `steps` an attribute of the extended link group element or the extended link document element?

A: The `steps` attribute is an attribute of the extended link group element.

Visual Quiz

Q: Convert this list of document links to an extended link group. How would you link to the first page? How would you jump to the last page? How would you move from page to page?

A:
```
<extended xml:link="extended">
<locator href="http://samp.com/chap1.xml"
  title="Chapter 1: XML Building Blocks">
<locator href="http://samp.com/chap2.xml"
  title="Chapter 2: Examining an XML
  Document">
<locator href="http://samp.com/chap3.xml"
  title="Chapter 3: The Anatomy of XML
  Syntax">
<locator href="http://samp.com/chap4.xml"
  title="Chapter 4: Supported Characters
```

```
and Character Sets">
<locator href="http://samp.com/chap5.xml"
  title="Chapter 5: An Overview of XML
  Software">
<locator href="http://samp.com/chap6.xml"
  title="Chapter 6: Planning a DTD">
<locator href="http://samp.com/chap7.xml"
  title="Chapter 7: Starting a DTD">
<locator href="http://samp.com/chap8.xml"
  title="Chapter 8: Declaring Elements">
<locator href="http://samp.com/chap9.xml"
  title="Chapter 9: Defining Attributes">
<locator href="http://samp.com/chap10.xml"
  title="Chapter 10: Using Entities">
<locator href="http://samp.com/chap11.xml"
  title="Chapter 11: Modifying an Existing
  DTD">
<locator href="http://samp.com/chap12.xml"
  title="Chapter 12: Parsing an XML
  Document">
<locator href="http://samp.com/chap13.xml"
  title="Chapter 13: Creating a Basic XML
  Document">
</extended>
```

Note that the XLink working draft is subject to modification as it evolves toward a W3C recommendation.

Chapter 23

see page 330

1 **What do XPointers allow you to do with extended links?**

A: XPointers enable those using extended links to pinpoint the location of their target resources by using such criteria as elements, attributes, attribute values, and other components within XML documents.

2 **What is a *location term*?**

A: A location term is a name or keyword for a specific place or component in a target document.

3 **What part of a URI comprises an XPointer?**

A: Use a fragment identifier to compose an XPointer.

4 **What is an *absolute location term*?**

A: An absolute location term is a complete reference to the final target location.

5 **What is a *relative location term*?**

A: A relative location term starts with the current location and uses a partial reference to link to the next location on the way to the target.

6 **What is a *spanning location term*?**

A: A spanning location term is a span starting at the first character of one XPointer and ending at the last character of another XPointer.

7 **What is an *attribute location term*?**

A: An attribute location term locates a particular attribute by name.

8 **What is a *string-match location term*?**

A: A string-match location term matches a string or a location between strings.

Visual Quiz

Q: You can find this example and the following XPointers in the current XPointer working draft. What target does 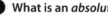`id(a27).child(2,DIRECTION)` locate? What target does `id(a27).child(2,#element)` locate? What target does `id(a27).child(2,#text)` locate?

A: According to the XPointer working draft, the answers are as follows:

Appendix A: Personal Workbook Answers

`id(a27).child(2,DIRECTION)` selects the second DIRECTION element (whose content is " To Ros.").
`id(a27).child(2,#element)` selects the second child element (that is, the first DIRECTION, whose content is "crossing downstage").
`id(a27).child(2,#text)` selects the second text region, "Fare you well, my lord." (The line break between the SPEAKER and DIRECTION elements is the first text region.)
Note that the XPointer working draft is subject to modification as it evolves toward a W3C recommendation.

Chapter 24

see page 346

❶ What do style sheets do to XML documents?

A: Style sheets enable you to control the appearance of XML documents when the documents are to be printed or displayed electronically.

❷ What happens when you attach a different style sheet to a document?

A: You can instantly change the look of a document by attaching a different style sheet.

❸ What happens when you change part of a style sheet that is attached to several documents?

A: That format changes for all the documents to which the style sheet is attached.

❹ What are *style sheet rules*?

A: Rules are formats and enhancements for selected text, paragraphs, or entire documents.

❺ Name and describe the two parts of a style sheet rule.

A: The selector is the element to which the rule applies, and the declaration consists of the property and the value.

❻ How can you attach more than one style sheet to a single document?

A: Insert the `xml:style sheet` or `xml:alternate-style` sheet processing instructions anywhere within the XML document prolog.

❼ Name the style-sheet properties that the `background` property includes?

A: The `background` property combines the `background-attachment`, `background-color`, `background-image`, `background-position`, and `background-repeat` properties.

❽ Name the `border-width` properties. What do they do?

A: The `border-bottom-width`, `border-left-width`, `border-right-width`, and `border-top-width` properties sets the width of the bottom, left, right, and top borders, respectively. Use the `border-width` property to set the width of one, two, three, or four borders.

Visual Quiz
Q: Identify the bad syntax in this style sheet.

A: The bad syntax in the style sheet is as follows: On the first line, style-sheet is misspelled. On the second line, a background image file would not have a doc extension and a semicolon is missing from the end of the line. On the third line, `border` can have a value of `thin`, `medium`, or `thick` or have a specific width. The fourth line should end with a right brace (`}`). The Arial Black font on the fifth line should be enclosed within quotation marks or single quote marks. The margin property in the last line should have four values rather than five.

469

Appendix A: Personal Workbook Answers

Chapter 25

see page 362

❶ What is *whitespace*? What is its purpose?

A: *Whitespace* is any area on a page that does not contain text or graphics. Adding whitespace to a page highlights the text-and-graphics content and separates areas of content.

❷ What does *RGB* represent?

A: RGB stands for red, green, and blue.

❸ What are the five ways in which you can set border colors?

A: Name a color by using a valid name, specifying a three-digit hexadecimal code, specifying a six-digit hexadecimal code, setting an absolute decimal red-green-blue value, or setting a relative red-green-blue value.

❹ What does the `border-style` property do?

A: The `border-style` property formats one, two, three, or four borders.

❺ What border properties combine color, style, and width?

A: The `border-bottom`, `border-left`, `border-right`, and `border-top` properties specify the color, style, and/or width of borders.

❻ What is *padding*?

A: Padding applies whitespace to an area between the optional borders or margins and the edge of the text on a page.

❼ What is the processing instruction that also controls whitespace in a document?

A: The `xml:space` processing instruction controls the whitespace in an XML document.

❽ What is the *baseline*?

A: The baseline is the invisible line on which a non-subscript or non-superscript character sits in a line of text.

Visual Quiz

Q: How would you style this page? Use border properties and separate the three lines by setting appropriate line heights.

A: Style the page using styles and values that are similar to the following:

```
doc       {font-family: "Arial Black",
           Helvetica, sans-serif;
           line-height: 105% }
warning   {font-size: 48pt;
           font-weight: bolder;
           border-style: solid}
highvolt  {font-size: 36pt;
           font-weight: bolder }
keepout   {font-size: 36pt;
           font-weight: bolder;
           border-style: dashed }
```

Chapter 26

see page 376

❶ What is *kerning*?

A: Kerning is the term used to describe the movement of one character closer to or farther away from an adjoining character.

❷ Why would you kern selected text?

A: You kern text because the larger the size of a particular typeface, the farther apart some characters appear onscreen or on the printed page. Unkerned characters are so far apart that the reader sees them as separate rather than as part of a word.

③ Describe the main difference between serif and sans serif characters.

A: Serif characters have a decorative line or embellishment at the top or bottom. A sans serif letter does not have added decorations.

④ Why would you adjust spaces between words?

A: Adjust spaces between words to fit more words on a single line, or to have text take up more room on a page.

⑤ What does the `text-indent` property do?

A: Use the `text-indent` property to indent the first line of text from the left margin.

⑥ What is the difference between a widow and an orphan?

A: A widow is either one word making up the last word of a paragraph or the last short line of a paragraph whose other lines are on the preceding page. An orphan is the single short line or few words starting a paragraph whose other lines are on the following page.

⑦ What choices of alignment does the `text-align` property offer?

A: The `text-align` property allows you to align selected text with the left margin, the right margin, or both margins, or center the text between the left and right margins.

⑧ How do you change the case of selected text?

A: Use the `text-transform` property to change the case of the selected text

Visual Quiz

Q: How would you style this memo template? Make sure that you include styles for two levels of headings, the `To`, `From`, `CC`, `Date`, and `Subject` elements, and body text. (Note that the border is associated with the `Subject` element.)

A: Style the template using styles and values that are similar to the following:

```
head1        { font-family: "Arial Black",
               Helvetica, sans-serif;
               font-size: 28pt;
               font-weight: bold }
head2        { font-family: "Arial Black",
               Helvetica, sans-serif;
               font-size: 16pt;
               text-align: right;
               font-weight: bold }
to, from,
cc, date     { font-family: "Arial Black",
               Helvetica, sans-serif;
               font-size: 14pt;
               font-weight: bold;
               margin-left: 0.5in }
subject      { font-family: "Arial Black",
               Helvetica, sans-serif;
               font-size: 14pt;
               font-weight: bold;
               margin-left: 0.5in;
               padding-bottom: 6pt;
               border-bottom-width: solid }
bodytext     { font-family: "Arial Black",
               Helvetica, sans-serif;
               font-size: 12pt;
               text-indent: 0.5in }
```

Appendix A: Personal Workbook Answers

Chapter 27

see page 390

❶ Why is it important to add a generic family name to a font-family statement?

A: Adding a generic family name ensures that a font family will be defined if a specific font is not available.

❷ When you name a font family name that includes spaces, what punctuation do you use?

A: Use quotation marks to enclose family names of two or more words that are separated by spaces.

❸ What does the `font-style` property do to selected text?

A: The `font-style` property enables you to enter a keyword to specify the degree of "lean" to the selected text.

❹ What does the `font-weight` property do?

A: The `font-weight` property sets the degree of boldness or lightness of selected text.

❺ What sort of typeface should you use for headings? What sort of typeface should you use for body text?

A: A heading's typeface should come from the sans serif family, whereas a body text typeface should come from the serif family.

❻ When your headings are composed of two lines, what case should you stay away from?

A: If your headings will be longer than a few words, don't use all-uppercase characters.

❼ When you want your readers to perceive a document as formal or traditional, what is the best text alignment choice?

A: If you want your readers to view your document as traditional or formal, justification is the best choice.

❽ What are the five keywords for the `text-decoration` property?

A: The five keywords for the `text-decoration` property are `none`, `underline`, `overline`, `line-through`, and `blink`.

Visual Quiz

Q: This is a page from *XML in Plain English*, also by Sandra E. Eddy and published by IDG Books Worldwide, Inc. How do you style the headings on this page? How do you style the body text? How do you indent body text? How do you set spaces between the lines? (Hint: Use styles from other chapters, too.)

A: Style the page using styles and values that are similar to the following:

```
doc       { margin: 1in;
            font-family: "Bookman Old Style",
              "Times New Roman", serif;
            font-size: 12pt }
termhead  { font-family: Arial,
              Helvetica, sans-serif;
            font-size: 14pt;
            font-weight: bold }
subhead   { font-family: Arial,
              Helvetica, sans-serif;
            font-size: 12pt;
            font-weight: bold;
            font-style: italic }
syntax    { font-family: "Courier New",
              "Gill Sans", sans-serif;
            margin-left: 1.5in }
where     { margin-left: 1.5in }
```

APPENDIX A: PERSONAL WORKBOOK ANSWERS

Chapter 28

see page 404

❶ Why would you use an ordered list?

A: Use an ordered list to present a list of steps that should be followed in the order in which they are presented.

❷ What is another name for an ordered list?

A: An ordered list is also known as a numbered list.

❸ Why would you use an unordered list?

A: Unordered lists list items that you wish to emphasize but can be read in any sequence.

❹ What is another name for an unordered list?

A: An unordered list is also known as a bulleted list.

❺ Why would you use a definition list?

A: Use a definition list to present a glossary of terms.

❻ Name the four CSS list properties.

A: The four CSS list properties are `list-style-image`, `list-style-position`, `list-style-type`, and `list-style`.

❼ What does the `list-style-type` property do for ordered lists? What does this property do for unordered lists?

A: The `list-style-type` property specifies the number type for ordered lists and the bullet type for unordered lists.

❽ What three components make up a definition list?

A: Use three elements to create a definition list: an element that signals the start and end of the list, an element that specifies the start and end of the definition term, and an element that sets the start and end of the definition description.

Visual Quiz

Q: How would you code and style the lists on this page?

A: Code and style the lists using styles and values similar to the following:

```
olist   { font-family: "Times New Roman",
          "Bookman Old Style", serif;
          font-size: 14pt;
          list-style-type: decimal }

ulist   { font-family: Arial,"Gill Sans",
          sans-serif;
          font-size: 16pt;
          list-style-type: disc }

list    { font-family: "Courier New",
          "Gill Sans", sans-serif;
          font-size: 12pt;
          list-style-type: none }

dlist   { font-family: "Times New Roman",
          "Book Antigua", serif }
dterm   { font-weight: bold;
          font-size: 14pt;
          padding-right: 0.5in }
ddef { font-size: 12pt }
```

Chapter 29

see page 418

❶ When you define styles for an entire table, what are you doing?

A: When you define styles for an entire table, you actually set the defaults for each of the components making up the table.

Appendix A: Personal Workbook Answers

② **What are some of the ways in which you can split a table or highlight its components?**

A: You can split a table into header, body, and footer sections; heading and data rows; column groups; row groups; and individual cells.

③ **Does the cascading-style-sheet specification provide table styling properties?**

A: No; you can use most CSS properties to format and enhance tables and their contents.

④ **What is the purpose of table captions?**

A: Table captions briefly describe or cross-reference a table.

⑤ **What are the names of the HTML elements that form the header, footer, and body sections of a table?**

A: The HTML THEAD element marks the header, the TFOOT element marks the footer, and the TBODY element marks the non-header, non-footer rows in the center of the table.

⑥ **What are two ways to select a table row?**

A: You can declare a special element to select a particular row, or you can span the selected row **using** a spanning element.

⑦ **How do you specify an empty row or empty cell?**

A: To specify an empty row or empty cell, insert a start tag and end tag without content.

⑧ **How do you break a row into columns?**

A: Nest a table-data or table-heading element within a table row.

Visual Quiz

Q: **What styles would you use to reproduce the look of this table?**

A: Code and style the table using styles and values similar to the following:

```
colhead  { font-family: "Lucida Sans",
            "Gill Sans", sans-serif;
          background-color: rgb(196,196,196);
          font-weight: bold;
          font-size: 11pt }

rowhead  { font-family: "Lucida Sans",
            "Gill Sans", sans-serif;
          background-color: rgb(196,196,196);
          font-weight: bold;
          font-size: 10pt }

subcolhead  { font-family: "Lucida Sans",
            "Gill Sans", sans-serif;
          background-color: rgb(223,223,223);
          font-weight: bold;
          font-size: 10pt }

body  { font-family: "Times New Roman",
            "Book Antiqua", sans-serif;
          background-color: rgb(223,223,223);
          font-size: 12pt }
```

Note that the red, green, and blue values for gray should be the same number or very close. Darker grays should approach black (a RGB value of 0,0,0); lighter grays should approach white (255,255,255).

Chapter 30

see page 432

① **What is a _template_?**

A: A template consists of a pattern and an action.

② **What is a _pattern_?**

A: The pattern is a string that uses various criteria to match one or more input element types.

③ **What is an _action_?**

A: The action specifies the elements that match the pattern.

④ What are *formatting objects*? What are formatting objects known as in DSSSL?

A: Formatting objects are styled objects that fill defined areas in the output. Formatting objects are known as flow objects in DSSSL.

⑤ What are the steps used to process an XSL style sheet against an XML document?

A: First, the XML document is analyzed to produce a source tree. Then, the XSL style sheet is run against the source tree, which concludes with a result tree, which is then interpreted, using XSL's formatting language, to produce formatted output.

⑥ What is the prefix for XSL's predefined elements?

A: XSL's predefined elements are prefixed with `xsl:`.

⑦ Is `<xsl:stylesheet>` a processing instruction?

A: No. `<xsl:stylesheet>` is a start tag. (`</xsl:stylesheet>` is the end tag.)

⑧ What does the `xsl:apply templates` element do?

A: The `xsl:apply-templates` element processes the matched element's child elements.

Visual Quiz

Q: This illustration is identical to the Visual Quiz illustration in Chapter 27. Using XSL, how do you style the headings on this page? How do you style the body text? How do you indent body text? How do you set spaces between the lines? (Hint: Use the styling properties from the other chapters in this part. Find their counterparts in the current XSL working draft.)

A: The following is a segment of an XSL style sheet that formats and enhances the document elements shown on the Visual Quiz page.

```
xsl:stylesheet
 xmlns:xsl="http://www.w3.org/TR/WD-xsl"
 xmlns:fo="http://www.w3.org/TR/WD-xsl/FO"
 result-ns="fo">
```

```
<xsl:template match="/">
  <fo:basic-page-sequence
      page-margin-bottom="1in"
      page-margin-left="1in"
      page-margin-top="1in"
      page-margin-right="1in"
      font-family="Bookman Old Style"
      font-size="12pt">
      <xsl:apply-templates/>
  </fo:basic-page-sequence>
</xsl:template>

<xsl:template match "termhead">
 <fo:block font-family="Arial"
          font-size="14pt"
          font-weight="bold">
 </fo:block>
</xsl:template>

<xsl:template match "subhead">
 <fo:block font-family="Arial"
          font-size="12pt"
          font-weight="bold"
          font-style="italic"
          padding-after="6pt">
 </fo:block>
</xsl:template>

<xsl:template match "syntax">
 <fo:block font-family="Courier New"
          padding-left="0.5in"
          padding-after="6pt">
 </fo:block>
</xsl:template>

<xsl:template match "where">
 <fo:block padding-left="0.5in"
          padding-after="6pt">
 </fo:block>
</xsl:template>
```

Note that the XSL working draft is subject to modification as it evolves toward a W3C recommendation.

Appendix B:
CD-ROM Contents

Applications on this CD-ROM are categorized as shareware, freeware, or demonstration versions.

Shareware

These applications, which are usually developed by individuals or small companies, can contain as many features as commercial applications produced by large companies. The difference between shareware and commercial software is that the developers of commercial programs usually have large budgets for advertising their products. However, shareware programs serve as their own advertisements. After you try a shareware program for a certain number of days and like the way that it works, you are expected to license the application for a small fee. Once you register with the shareware developer, you may receive installation disks or can download a version from the Internet. You may also receive a license, manuals, information about new releases, and a certain number of free or low-price upgrades.

Freeware Programs

These applications are in the public domain (that is, they are completely free). The developer may believe in open distribution for altruistic reasons or may want to use an older version of a program to introduce the market to an updated version.

Demonstration Versions

Also known as "demos" or trial programs, these applications are usually limited in some way. For example, a trial version may have all the features of a commercial version but not allow you to save, it may be a full-featured version that expires after a few weeks, or it may demonstrate most — but not all — of the features of the commercial program.

Programs on the CD-ROM

This section, which continues to the end of the appendix, lists each program on the CD-ROM. Each entry includes a brief description, the name of the developer, and a URL for the developer or software.

Adobe Acrobat Reader

A utility that enables you to read PDF files.
Developer: Adobe Systems Incorporated (**http://www.adobe.com/**)

Adobe FrameMaker+SGML

An XML authoring and composition product.
Developer: Adobe Systems Incorporated (**http://www.adobe.com/**)

Appendix B: CD-ROM Contents

Ælfred

A validating parser for Java programmers who want to add XML support to their applets. A SAX driver is bundled with Ælfred.

Developer: Microstar (**http://www.microstar.com/**)

blox

A suite of tools for parsing, creating, and manipulating XML documents in Frontier 4 and Frontier 5.

Developer: Technology Solutions (**http://www.techsoln.com/**)

Cascade

A cascading style-sheet editor for Macintosh computers.

Developer: Media Design in*Progress (**http://www.in-progress.com/**)

CLIP!

An XML editor.

Developer: Techno2000 USA (**http://www.t2000-usa.com/product/clip_index.html**)

ColdFusion

A tool for server-side Web-based scripting, including input validation, email, and database interaction.

Developer: Allaire Corp. (**http://www.allaire.com/**)

DataChannel DOM Builder

An application with which you can create XML using Document Object Model (DOM).

Developer: DataChannel, Inc. (**http://www.DataChannel.com/**)

DataChannel RIO

An intranet publisher that organizes and distributes corporate information. DataChannel RIO requires a relational database management server.

Developer: DataChannel, Inc. (**http://www.DataChannel.com/**)

DataChannel XML Generator

An application that produces XML output from a spreadsheet or database.

Developer: DataChannel, Inc. (**http://www.DataChannel.com/**)

DataChannel XML Parser (DXP)

A validating, Java-based XML parser for existing server-side programs that integrate XML.

Developer: DataChannel, Inc. (**http://www.DataChannel.com/**)

DataChannel XML Viewer

A viewer that shows an element tree of an XML document.

Developer: DataChannel, Inc. (**http://www.DataChannel.com/**)

EXtensible markup language PArser Toolkit (expat)

A nonvalidating, C-based XML browser that will be the core of the Netscape Mozilla XML effort.

Developer: James Clark (**http://www.jclark.com/**)

HTML Always Logically Organized (HALO)

A set of rendering and site-management tools. HALO supports XML.

Developer: Technology Solutions (**http://www.techsoln.com/**)

HoTMetaL Application Server

A server for UNIX, IIS, Windows NT, and Apache.

Developer: SoftQuad Software (**http://www.sq.com/**)

Appendix B: CD-ROM Contents

HoTMetaL PRO Version 5.0

An HTML editor that supports XML.
Developer: SoftQuad Software (**http://www.sq.com/**)

Interaction

An application that enables conferencing and displays real-time information about the current status of a Web site. This is a Macintosh program.
Developer: Media Design in*Progress (**http://www.in-progress.com/**)

InternetForms Viewer

Client-side software for viewing, filling out, and submitting InternetForms. Some sample forms are also included.
Developer: UWI.Com (**http://www.uwi.com/**)

Jade

A style engine that implements DSSSL. Jade can produce the following output: RTF, TeX, and two forms of SGML.
Developer: James Clark (**http://www.jclark.com/**)

Java 2 SDK, Standard Edition v1.2

A suite of products with which you can compile, debug, and run Java applets and applications.
Note: This software underwent a name change, and is formerly known as the Java Development Kit (JDK) 1.2. At the time of this printing, Sun Microsystems had not yet relfected this name change to their product documentation.
Developer: Sun Microsystems (**http://www.javasoft.com/**)

Koala XSL Engine for Java

An Java-based XSL processor that uses SAX 1.0 and DOM 1.0.
Developer: Jeremy Calles (**http://www.multimania.com/jcalles/XML/**)

Lark

A nonvalidating XML parser written in Java.
Developer: Tim Bray (**http://www.textuality.com/**)

Larval

A validating XML parser that has the rest of the characteristics and features of Lark.
Developer: Tim Bray (**http://www.textuality.com/**)

LT XML

XML tools and a toolkit, all for developers. Use LT XML to process well-formed XML documents. The suite includes an XML parser, a query language, and a C-based API.
Developer: University of Edinburgh, HCRC Language Technology Group (**http://www.ltg.ed.ac.uk/**)

Microsoft Internet Explorer 5

A Web browser that supports XML.
Developer: Microsoft Corporation (**http://www.microsoft.com/**)

Near and Far Designer

A visual tool with which you can create and edit DTDs.
Developer: Microstar (**http://www.microstar.com/**)

Netscape Navigator 4

A Web browser.
Developer: Netscape Communications Corporation (**http://home.netscape.com/**)

Norbert's XML Parser (NXP)

A validating Java-based parser.
Developer: Norbert H. Mikula, DataChannel, Inc. (**http://www.DataChannel.com/**)

Prototype

An application that reads a valid XML document and shows how it will look onscreen.

Appendix B: CD-ROM Contents

Developer: Pierre Morel (**http://www.pierlou.com/ prototype/body.htm**)

PSGML

An SGML text editor with an XML patch.
Developers: Lenart Staflin and David Megginson (**http://www.lysator.liu.se/projects/about_psgml.html**)

Pypointers

A Python-based XPointer implementation that finds particular XPointers in XML and HTML documents by using a DOM locator.
Developer: Lars Marius Garshol (**http://www.stud.ifi.uio.no/~larsga/download/python/ xml/index**)

Python

A scripting language used in XML development.
Developer: Python Organization (**http://www.python.org/**)

RTF2XML

An application that trnaslates RTF to an XML document. To used this program, you must also have OmniMark LE installed (**http://www.omnimark.com/develop/index.html**).
Developer: Rick Geimer (**http://www.xmeta.com/omlette**)

Simple API for XML (SAX)

A Java-based API used for writing applications that use XML parsers but do not have to rely on a particular parser.
Developer: David Megginson (**http://www. megginson.com/**)

SAX for Python

A Python version of SAX.
Developer: Lars Marius Garshol (**http://www.stud.ifi.uio.no/~larsga/download/python/ xml/index**)

SAXON

A Java class library used for processing XML documents to produce XML or HTML transformations. You can modify the ParserManager.properties file to preselect the XML parser and/or DOM implementation that you decide to use.
Developer: Michael Kay (**http://home.iclweb.com/icl2/mhkay/saxon.html**)

SP

An C++-based SGML parser that can parse well-formed XML documents.
Developer: James Clark (**http://www.jclark.com/**)

Sparse

An XSL style-sheet processor; requires a JavaScript-compatible browser.
Developer: Jeremie Miller (**http://www.jeremie.com/**)

sxml-mode

A SAX-based utility for (X)Emacs and an XML parser. Philippe Le Hégaret (**http://www.inria.fr/koala/plh/**)

tdtd

A DTD editor.
Developer: Mulberry Technologies (**http://www. mulberrytech.com/**)

Win32 Foundation Classes

C++ class libraries that correct XML markup.
Developer: Samuel R Blackburn (**http://ourworld.com-puserve.com/homepages/sam_blackburn/homepage.htm**)

XAF

An application that processes XML documents with a Java-based SAX-conformant XML parser. XAF processes architectural forms rather than XML.
Developer: David Megginson (**http://www. megginson.com/**)

Appendix B: CD-ROM Contents

XMetaL

An XML editor.
Developer: SoftQuad Software (**http://www.sq.com/**)

XML Pro

An editor that you can use to create valid or well-formed XML documents. XML Pro includes wizards that can guide you through document creation.
Developer: Vervet Logic (**http://www.vervet.com/**)

xmlproc

A Python-based validating XML parser.
Developer: Lars Marius Garshol (**http://www.stud.ifi.uio.no/~larsga/download/python/xml/index/**)

XP

A Java-based parser that tests for well-formed documents. XP, which works under JDK version 1.1 or greater, supports UTF-8, UTF-16, and ISO-8859-1.
Developer: James Clark (**http://www.jclark.com/**)

XParse

A JavaScript-based XML parser that tests for well-formedness.
Developer: Jeremie Miller (**http://www.jeremie.com/**)

XPublish

An XML publishing system for Macintosh systems.
Developer: Media Design in*Progress (**http://www.in-progress.com/**)

xslide

A major Emacs mode for editing XSL style sheets
Developer: Mulberry Technologies (**http://www.mulberrytech.com/**)

Other CD-ROM Contents

The CD-ROM includes all examples and code from the book.

The CD-ROM also includes "Unicode Characters and Character Sets," a PDF version of an appendix from *fl⅞⅝ IN LAIN NGLISH* (also written by Sandra E. Eddy and published by IDG Books Worldwide, Inc.).

Glossary

absolute link A link to another document that uses the document's complete URL or address, including the transfer protocol, the computer or network name, the directory or folder, and a filename. (For example, `http://www.widget.com/index.html.`) See relative link.

ancestor A higher-level element, such as a parent, in a family tree of elements. See *child*, *descendant*, and *parent*.

anchor The starting link that refers to another location within the current document or within another document; the ending link to which a starting link refers; the target and/or source of a link.

ATTLIST In a document type definition (DTD), a list of attributes (that is, options or characteristics) defined for an element. An ATTLIST can also contain default values for attributes. See *DTD* and *element*.

attribute A term for an option that is a setting that affects the behavior of and further defines an element. Attributes can change or specify formats, alignments, text enhancements, paragraphs, or other parts of an SGML, HTML, or XML document. In an SGML or XML document type definition (DTD), the value of an attribute is either `#REQUIRED` (it must be entered) or `#IMPLIED` (it does not have to be entered). See *attribute value*.

attribute value The value of a particular attribute. Attribute values should be enclosed within single or double quotes. If an attributeName and attribute value are missing for an element, a default value is assigned to the attribute.

base See *absolute link*.

cascading style sheets Sets of style sheets that enable Web developers to change documents' format and appearance. See *CSS1* and *CSS2*. See also *DSSSL* and *XSL*.

CDATA Character data; a string of characters that is enclosed within delimiters. When parsed, `CDATA` is not interpreted — it is inserted as text. See *delimiter* and `#PCDATA`.

character A single unit of information; a letter, digit, or symbol. See *character class*, *character data*, and *legal characters*.

character class Character set; a grouping of related letters, digits, and symbols.

character data Any characters that are not markup. See `CDATA`, *markup*, and *text*.

child An element or other object that is nested under a parent element or object; a subelement of an element. See *ancestor*, *descendant*, *nested*, and *parent*.

combining character A character that is added above or below a letter of an alphabet, such as an accent or circumflex.

connector An operator that shows the relationship between two parts of an expression or program statement. Examples include a vertical bar (|), `OR`, comma (,), or `AND`.

construction rules A set of standards that specify how a styling application makes and formats an element.

containing resource A document in which an external link is located. See *designated resource*.

Glossary

content model In a document type definition (DTD), the description of an element's content, including subelements, connectors, and character data.

content particle One unit of the content of an element type. See *content* and *content model*.

CSS1 The first standard for cascading style sheets; a simple set of rules to format and enhance text, paragraphs, and documents. See *cascading style sheets* and *CSS2*.

CSS2 The second standard for cascading style sheets; adds to the CSS1 base a set of styles for visual browsers, aural devices, printers, Braille devices, and so on, as well as styles for table layout, internationalization features, and more. See *cascading style sheets* and *CSS1*.

data characters Nonmarkup characters that form element content.

declaration A statement that defines the elements and attributes in a document without telling the computer how to use them. In a cascading style sheet, a declaration specifies a property (such as text emphasis) and its value (italic). A declaration defines markup, constraints, and attributes. See *attributes*, *constraints*, *document type declaration*, *markup*, and *selector*.

delimiter A character that indicates the start and end of a string or other piece of information. For XML, the usual delimiters are quotation marks (") and single quotes ('). See *string*.

descendant All the elements or other objects that are nested under a parent element or object; subelements of the element. See *ancestor*, *child*, *nested*, and *parent*.

descriptive markup Semantic markup; the act of creating and using markup terms that both describe and mark up at the same time. Descriptive markup is an XML feature that differentiates XML from HTML.

designated resource A document in which an external link is defined. See *containing resource*.

document entity The entire XML document as it will be read by an XML processor. This is in contrast to a document module, which is a part of the document as it is distributed over a network.

document instance The entire SGML or XML document.

document prolog The part of an SGML or XML document that includes the introduction to the document, including the document type definition (DTD).

Document Style Semantics and Specification Language See *DSSSL*.

document type declaration A declaration within an XML document that points to an external or internal document type definition (DTD). A document type declaration is *never* known as a DTD.

document type definition See *DTD*.

DSSSL Document Style Semantics and Specification Language; ISO 10179: 1996. An international style-sheet standard. See also *cascading style sheets* and *XSL*.

DTD Document type definition. A document, written with a special syntax for declarations, that specifies the elements, attributes, entities (special or legal characters), and rules for creating one document or a set of documents using XML, HTML, or another SGML-related markup language. In an XML document, a DTD is required to parse a document and test it for validity. An XML document can access an internal DTD (stored at the beginning of the document) or an external DTD (a separate document). Within an XML document, the pointer to the DTD is known as a document type declaration. A document type declaration is *never* known as a DTD. See also *document type declaration*, *external DTD subset*, and *internal DTD subset*.

element A label with which you define part of an XML document. An element usually starts with a start tag (`<tagname>`), includes an element name, may contain subelements and contents with which you vary the results of the element, and may end with an end tag (`</tagname>`). An XML element may include certain data types or may be empty. See *end tag*, *start tag*, and *subelement*.

element declaration In the document type definition (DTD), a statement that defines a particular element, attributes, and other characteristics. See *declaration* and *element*.

element tree The element-and-attribute skeleton of an XML document. An element tree reduces the document to its underlying structure of elements and attributes so you can visually check the document's logic and flow. See *grove*.

empty element An element that has no content between the start tag and the end tag but refers to an object such as an image or a line break. In an XML document, an empty element can take the traditional format (`<element_tag></element_tag>`) or a combined format (`<element_tag/>`). See *element*, *end tag*, and *start tag*.

encoding The act of converting a letter, digit, character, or a set of characters to another character or set of characters. In programming, encoding refers to converting from one format to another (for example, decimal to hexadecimal or binary to decimal). In XML, encoding refers to converting letters, digits, or characters to the supported UTF-8 or UTF-16 format. See *UTF-8* and *UTF-16*.

end tag The part of an XML statement that indicates the end of an element and its contents. The format of an end tag is `</elementname>`, in contrast to the start tag format, `<elementname>`. An end tag does not include attributes. See *element* and *start tag*.

entity A special character; a single unit or item. *Entity* is an all-purpose term that can also refer to a specific text or graphics file. There are several categories of entities in XML: general and parameter, parsed and unparsed, and external and internal. See *general entity*, *parameter entity*, *parsed entity*, and *unparsed entity*.

enumerate To list the possible valid values for a data type.

expression An equation made up of elements, subelements, attributes, operators, subexpressions, and connectors.

extended link A link to one or more locations within the current document and/or to one or more locations in other documents. To specify an extended link, use the `xml-link` attribute with the `extended` or the `locator` value. See *extended link group* and *simple link*.

extended link group An extended link that stores a list of links to other documents. An extended link group is also known as an *interlinked group*. To specify an extended link group, use the `xml:link` attribute with the `group` value. See *extended link* and *simple link*.

extensible The ability of a user to add his or her own labels to the command set of a language, such as XML.

external DTD subset The part of a DTD that is stored in a separate document, completely outside the XML document in which it is referenced. An external DTD subset can be referred to by more than one XML document. See *DTD*, *external entity*, *internal entity*, and *internal DTD subset*.

external entity An entity with its content stored in a separate file, completely outside the XML document. See *DTD* and *internal entity*.

general entity A variable named within the text of the document instance. In contrast, a parameter entity is a variable named within markup. A general entity is preceded by an ampersand symbol (`&`) and succeeded by a semicolon (`;`). See *document instance*, *entity*, *parameter entity*, *parsed entity*, and *unparsed entity*.

glyph
A graphic that represents a character, particularly in a typeface.

GLOSSARY

grammar A set of rules governing the structure of a document that conforms to a language standard. A document type definition (DTD) specifies the grammar of a particular SGML or XML document. In markup languages such as SGML and XML, each component in the grammar is known as a *production*.

grove In a tree structure of documents, a complete set (or *forest*) of documents and nodes. See *node*.

identifier A unique name used to identify or label a variable, procedure, macro, or other object.

ideographic character An ideogram; a symbol or glyph that represents another character, a word, or other object.

IETF Internet Engineering Task Force. An organization that evaluates and sets most standards for the Internet.

inline image A graphic embedded within the content of a Web document. In contrast, a displayed image is preceded by and followed by line or paragraph breaks.

inline link A link specified within a linking element. An inline link is one of its own resources. See *linking element, out-of-line link*, and *resource*.

instance See *document instance*.

internal DTD subset The part of a DTD that is located within its source document. An internal DTD subset can be used temporarily to test a document for well-formedness or validity and then replaced later with an external DTD subset. See *DTD, external DTD subset, external entity*, and *internal entity*.

internal entity An entity with its content stored completely within the DTD. See *DTD* and *external entity*.

ISO International Standards Organization. An international standards-setting organization. ISO sets standards for computing, telecommunicating, and so on. ANSI, the American National Standards Institute, is the U.S. affiliate. See *ANSI*.

keyword (1) A reserved word; a word or phrase that is a unique part of a language, such as XML, and therefore is unavailable for other uses within the language. (2) A metadata word or phrase. Search indexes use keywords to compile and, optionally, rank lists of Web documents.

ligature A combination of two or more joined letters (for example, Æ).

link A highlighted and/or underlined word or phrase (or graphic), that, when clicked on, takes you to one or more particular places in another document or one or more sections of the current document. See *hypertext* and *World Wide Web*.

location source For an XPointer, the absolute starting point for a link. After pinpointing the location source, use relative or string-match location terms to further refine the link.

location term Part of an XPointer; the term that refers to a location in a document. XPointer location terms are absolute, relative, or string-match.

locator Within a linking element, a character string that provides information about finding a resource to which the element can link. See *linking element* and *resource*.

markup Commands that define attributes, such as formats and enhancements, and describe the document. In XML and HTML documents, the commands with which the document is marked up are known as *elements*. In XML, markup includes start tags, end tags, empty-element tags, DTDs, formal references to entities or characters, processing instructions, XML comments, and indicators at the start and end of CDATA sections. The term *markup* refers to the marks that editors make on manuscripts to be revised. See *CDATA, DTD, empty element, end tag, entity, start tag*, and *text*.

media type The type of file and its contents, formatted as *file type/file format*. Examples include text/HTML and video/MPEG.

metadata According to Netscape documentation, metadata is "information about information." To allow search tools to find a Web document, the developer must provide information about the content and history of the document. Metadata can include keywords, dates of creation and modification, and the developer's name.

model group In the document type definition (DTD), one or more collections of element names, each of which specifies the hierarchy of an XML document and is enclosed within single quotes.

multidirectional link A link that you can traverse from several of its resources. See *extended link, extended link group, link, resource, simple link,* and *traversal.*

name A valid XML name that must begin with a letter or underscore character, not including the uppercase or lowercase letters X, M, or L, which are reserved. A name can include letters, digits, periods (.), dashes (-), underscores (_), colons (:), combining characters, and extenders. See *name character* and *name token.*

name character One valid character in a name or name token. See *name* and *name token.*

name token A valid XML name that can begin with any character, including letters, digits, periods (.), dashes (-), underscores (_), colons (:), combining characters, and extenders. See *name* and *name character.*

nested A command line (including attributes) that is inserted completely within another command line.

node A point of connection. In a tree structure of documents, a node connects a group of documents to the tree. See *grove.*

notation A system of defining a means of communication using a formalized set of symbols or an alphabet. For example, notation can identify Braille, musical notes, and even computer file formats. In XML, a notation names the format of an unparsed entity or an element that contains a notation attribute, or names the target application of a processing instruction.

occurrence indicator In XML syntax, a symbol specifying how often a subelement may occur within a particular element. For example, an asterisk (*) indicates that a subelement can occur from none to any number of times, a question mark (?) indicates that a subelement can occur none or one time, and a plus sign (+) indicates that a subelement can occur one or more times.

out-of-line link A link specified outside a linking element, as part of a group of multidirectional links. An out-of-line link is not one of its own resources. See *inline link, linking element, multidirectional link,* and *resource.*

parameter entity PE; a variable named within markup in the prolog of a document, document type definition (DTD), and the document instance. A parameter entity is parsed, is preceded by a percent symbol (%), and is ended with a semicolon (;). See *document instance, entity,* and *general entity.*

parent An element or other object under which other elements or objects are nested. In XML, an element is a parent of a subelement. See *ancestor, child, descendant,* and *nested.* See also *root.*

parse The process of translating binary or textual data into language that can be read by a particular computer program. In XML, a validating parser produces ESIS output, including error and warning messages.

parsed entity An entity that contains parsed data, which is replacement text. A parsed entity has a name and is called by an entity reference. See *general entity, parameter entity, parse, unparsed data,* and *unparsed entity.*

#PCDATA Parsable Character Data or Parsed Character Data. Mixed content; character data that can include CDATA, entities, and valid subelements. #PCDATA is any nonmarkup data. See *CDATA.*

Glossary

pointer An element containing an attribute that refers to one or more other elements in the same or a different document.

processing instructions PI; in an XML document, part of the markup that tells the XML processor or browser how to handle the following statement. In XML, a PI is preceded by a `<?` delimiter and ended by a `?>` delimiter. See *document prolog*.

recursive A repetitive operation that includes some or all of the results of previous operations.

relative link A link to a resource within the current document, directory/folder, or computer/network, using a partial URL or address (for example, `/subdoc.xml`). If your browser reads a partial URL or address, it will attempt to go to a relative link. See *absolute link*.

reserved word A word or term used by a program or language for its own statements, declarations, and so on. Those using XML must not use reserved words to name files, variables, elements, and attributes. Examples of reserved words in XML are `CDATA`, `PCDATA`, `DTD`, `ENTITY`, `AND`, and `OR`.

root The document element; the ultimate parent element; an XML element within which all other XML elements are nested. In other words, all nonroot elements are child elements of the root. See *valid document* and *well-formed document*. See also *parent*.

rule (1) A horizontal line that is inserted in a document to separate sections or highlight text. (2) A statement that defines the behavior of an element, subelement, entity, or other object. (3) A single standard in *construction rules*, which specify how a selected component in a document is formatted or enhanced. See *grammar*.

selector A string that identifies an element to which a declaration applies. An element that affects a specific font is a selector on which type size, text color, and typeface families can apply. See *declaration*.

semantic markup See *descriptive markup*.

simple link A unidirectional link, usually inline but sometimes out-of-line, to another location within the current document or to a location in another document. XML simple links are similar to HTML links, which use the `<A>` tag. To specify a simple link in XML, use the `xml-link` attribute with the `simple` value. See *extended link* and *extended link group*.

start tag The part of an XML statement that indicates the start of an element and its contents. The format of a start tag is `<elementname>`, in contrast to the end tag format, `</elementname>`. See *element* and *end tag*.

string A group of one or more characters, usually text, enclosed within delimiters and sometimes given a unique name as identification. See *delimiter* and *identifier*.

style One property or instruction in a style sheet. See *style sheet*.

style sheet A set of instructions with which a word-processing or Web document is laid out or formatted. Style sheets format characters, paragraphs, pages, documents, and sets of documents. See *cascading style sheets*, *DSSSL*, *style*, and *XSL*.

tag See *element*. See also *end tag* and *start tag*.

token A basic unit that cannot be broken down further. In XML, a token is a reserved word, operator, entity, symbol, punctuation mark, or variable name.

traversal The process of linking to a resource by a user or by programming code. See *linking element* and *resource*.

unparsed data Data that may or may not be valid but has not been validated by being processed through a parser. See *general entity*, *parameter entity*, *parse*, *parsed entity*, and *unparsed entity*.

unparsed entity An entity that contains unparsed data. An unparsed entity has a named notation, which the XML processor sends to the target application. See *general entity*, *notation*, *parameter entity*, *parse*, *parsed entity*, and *unparsed data*.

URI Uniform Resource Identifier. The Internet address of an anchor. A URI can be either a URL (absolute link) or a partial address (relative link), or a URN (Uniform Resource Name). See *URL* and *URN*.

URL Uniform Resource Locator. An Internet address composed of the protocol type (such as `http:`, `ftp:`, or `gopher:`), the name of the server to be contacted (say, `www.w3.org`), the directories or folders (such as `/pub/WWW/Provider/`), and the optional filename (for example, `homepage.xml`). See *URI* and *URN*.

URN Uniform Resource Name. An identifier that can contain a variety of information, including one or more URLs. See *URI* and *URL*.

valid document An XML document that is associated with a recognized document type declaration and complies with all the rules and constraints defined in the DTD. See *root* and *well-formed document*.

W3C World Wide Web Consortium — the organization that develops standards for the World Wide Web and contributes to XML, HTML, and style-sheet standards.

well-formed document An XML document that is created within XML standards but is not necessarily associated with a document type definition (DTD). A well-formed document must include at least one root XML element within which other XML elements are nested and must follow all the defined rules in the current XML specification. See *root* and *valid document*.

whitespace The "empty" sections of a document that do not include text or graphics. Use style sheets to add whitespace to a document to highlight headings and certain text and graphics, to improve the look of the document, and to make its text easier to read. See *cascading style sheets* and *style sheets*. See also *padding*.

XLink Extensible Linking Language; a set of elements and attributes that define the linking behavior of XML documents.

XML Extensible Markup Language; a "child" or subset of SGML and a markup language that coexists with both SGML and HTML. XML enables complex hyperlinks, supports long documents, and allows users to define their own elements.

XPointer XML Pointer Language; an extended pointer; an absolute, relative, or string-match location that, along with XLink, targets a specific location within a document. See *XLink*.

XSL Extensible Stylesheet Language. A style sheet language based on DSSSL and designed specifically for XML. XSL is currently under development. See *cascading style sheets* and *DSSSL*.

A

INDEX

Index

Continued

Index

INDEX

INDEX

Continued

Index

INDEX

Index

Index

Index

Index

X

XAF, 173
XED, 68
XLink, 292, 304, 306
    behavior attributes, 298
    behavior types, specifying, 284
    extended link group element, 318, 320, 322
    in-line vs. out-of-line, 280
    link attributes, 294
    locator rules, 308
    overview, 275
    semantics, 282
    steps attribute, 326
    technical details web site, 310
    traverse, 282
    understanding, 278
    Working Draft Rules for Designated Resources, 309
    workings, 276
XLinks, 24
XLL, 322
XML, 49, 433
    adding frames to documents, 217–229
    attributes, 10–11, 125–139
    basic documents, creating, 187–201
    browsers, 188, 264
    characters and character sets, 14-15, 49–61
    converting HTML documents to, 180, 231–243
    database building, 245–257
    declaration, understanding, 94–95
    document prolog, 93–109
    documents, 21–33
    DTD modifications, 79-91, 157-169
    editors, 176
    electronic document styles, 356
    elements, 6–7, 12-13, 111-123
    entities, 16–17, 141–155
    extended links, 303, 317–329
    extended pointers, 331–343
    forms, 259–271
    history, 7
    introduction, 5
    lists and tables, 203–215
    markup, 14–15
    page layout and style, 347–361
    parsed. *See* XML parsers

replace with root elements, 234
reserved entities, 17
simple links, 289–301
software, 63–75
start tags and end tags, 8–9
styling paragraphs and page elements, 125, 363–375
syntax, 35–47
tables, 419–431
text styling, 377–389, 391–403
validator, 178
XLink and XPointer building blocks, 275–287
XSL (Extensible Stylesheet Language), 433–446
XML Parser for Java, 173, 176
    error correction, 180
    message interpretation, 178
XML parsers, 50, 171-183
    behavior attributes, 298
    case-sensitivity, 236
    choosing, 172
    data entities, 150
    databases, 245
    directing to links, 282
    document development, 192
    entity references, 141, 142
    processing instructions, 152
    running, 174
XML Styler, 72
XML-Data, 136
XMLDecl, 83
xmlproc, 173
XP, 173
XParse, 173
XPointers, 10, 24, 278, 279, 292, 304, 309. *See* **pointers, extended**
XSL, 72, 304, 338
    described, 433, 434–435
    link elements, 318
    matching elements by type and ancestry, 436–437
    objects, formatting, 442
    qualifying elements, 438
    sample style sheet, 73, 222
    templates, processing, 440

Z

ZIP, 112

IDG BOOKS WORLDWIDE, INC.
END-USER LICENSE AGREEMENT

READ THIS. You should carefully read these terms and conditions before opening the software packet(s) included with this book ("Book"). This is a license agreement ("Agreement") between you and IDG Books Worldwide, Inc. ("IDGB"). By opening the accompanying software packet(s), you acknowledge that you have read and accept the following terms and conditions. If you do not agree and do not want to be bound by such terms and conditions, promptly return the Book and the unopened software packet(s) to the place you obtained them for a full refund.

1. **License Grant.** IDGB grants to you (either an individual or entity) a nonexclusive license to use one copy of the enclosed software program(s) (collectively, the "Software") solely for your own personal or business purposes on a single computer (whether a standard computer or a workstation component of a multiuser network). The Software is in use on a computer when it is loaded into temporary memory (RAM) or installed into permanent memory (hard disk, CD-ROM, or other storage device). IDGB reserves all rights not expressly granted herein.

2. **Ownership.** IDGB is the owner of all right, title, and interest, including copyright, in and to the compilation of the Software recorded on the disk(s) or CD-ROM ("Software Media"). Copyright to the individual programs recorded on the Software Media is owned by the author or other authorized copyright owner of each program. Ownership of the Software and all proprietary rights relating thereto remain with IDGB and its licensers.

3. **Restrictions On Use and Transfer.**
    (a) You may only (i) make one copy of the Software for backup or archival purposes, or (ii) transfer the Software to a single hard disk, provided that you keep the original for backup or archival purposes. You may not (i) rent or lease the Software, (ii) copy or reproduce the Software through a LAN or other network system or through any computer subscriber system or bulletin-board system, or (iii) modify, adapt, or create derivative works based on the Software.
    (b) You may not reverse engineer, decompile, or disassemble the Software. You may transfer the Software and user documentation on a permanent basis, provided that the transferee agrees to accept the terms and conditions of this Agreement and you retain no copies. If the Software is an update or has been updated, any transfer must include the most recent update and all prior versions.

4. **Restrictions On Use of Individual Programs.** You must follow the individual requirements and restrictions detailed for each individual program in Appendix B of this Book. These limitations are also contained in the individual license agreements recorded on the Software Media. These limitations may include a requirement that after using the program for a specified period of time, the user must pay a registration fee or discontinue use. By opening the Software packet(s), you will be agreeing to abide by the licenses and restrictions for these individual programs that are detailed in Appendix B and on the Software Media. None of the material on this Software Media or listed in this Book may ever be redistributed, in original or modified form, for commercial purposes.

END-USER LICENSE AGREEMENT

5. Limited Warranty.

(a) IDGB warrants that the Software and Software Media are free from defects in materials and workmanship under normal use for a period of sixty (60) days from the date of purchase of this Book. If IDGB receives notification within the warranty period of defects in materials or workmanship, IDGB will replace the defective Software Media.

(b) IDGB AND THE AUTHOR OF THE BOOK DISCLAIM ALL OTHER WARRANTIES, EXPRESS OR IMPLIED, INCLUDING WITHOUT LIMITATION IMPLIED WARRANTIES OF MERCHANTABILITY AND FITNESS FOR A PARTICULAR PURPOSE, WITH RESPECT TO THE SOFTWARE, THE PROGRAMS, THE SOURCE CODE CONTAINED THEREIN, AND/OR THE TECHNIQUES DESCRIBED IN THIS BOOK. IDGB DOES NOT WARRANT THAT THE FUNCTIONS CONTAINED IN THE SOFTWARE WILL MEET YOUR REQUIREMENTS OR THAT THE OPERATION OF THE SOFTWARE WILL BE ERROR-FREE.

(c) This limited warranty gives you specific legal rights, and you may have other rights that vary from jurisdiction to jurisdiction.

6. Remedies.

(a) IDGB's entire liability and your exclusive remedy for defects in materials and workmanship shall be limited to replacement of the Software Media, which may be returned to IDGB with a copy of your receipt at the following address: Software Media Fulfillment Department, Attn.: *Teach Yourself XML,* IDG Books Worldwide, Inc., 7260 Shadeland Station, Ste. 100, Indianapolis, IN 46256, or call 1-800-762-2974. Please allow three to four weeks for delivery. This Limited Warranty is void if failure of the Software Media has resulted from accident, abuse, or misapplication. Any replacement Software Media will be warranted for the remainder of the original warranty period or thirty (30) days, whichever is longer.

(b) In no event shall IDGB or the author be liable for any damages whatsoever (including without limitation damages for loss of business profits, business interruption, loss of business information, or any other pecuniary loss) arising from the use of or inability to use the Book or the Software, even if IDGB has been advised of the possibility of such damages.

(c) Because some jurisdictions do not allow the exclusion or limitation of liability for consequential or incidental damages, the above limitation or exclusion may not apply to you.

7. U.S. Government Restricted Rights. Use, duplication, or disclosure of the Software by the U.S. Government is subject to restrictions stated in paragraph (c)(1)(ii) of the Rights in Technical Data and Computer Software clause of DFARS 252.227-7013, and in subparagraphs (a) through (d) of the Commercial Computer — Restricted Rights clause at FAR 52.227-19, and in similar clauses in the NASA FAR supplement, when applicable.

8. General. This Agreement constitutes the entire understanding of the parties and revokes and supersedes all prior agreements, oral or written, between them and may not be modified or amended except in a writing signed by both parties hereto that specifically refers to this Agreement. This Agreement shall take precedence over any other documents that may be in conflict herewith. If any one or more provisions contained in this Agreement are held by any court or tribunal to be invalid, illegal, or otherwise unenforceable, each and every other provision shall remain in full force and effect.

Sun Microsystems, Inc., Binary Code License Agreement

READ THE TERMS OF THIS AGREEMENT AND ANY PROVIDED SUPPLEMENTAL LICENSE TERMS (COLLECTIVELY "AGREEMENT") CAREFULLY BEFORE OPENING THE SOFTWARE MEDIA PACKAGE. BY OPENING THE SOFTWARE MEDIA PACKAGE, YOU AGREE TO THE TERMS OF THIS AGREEMENT. IF YOU ARE ACCESSING THE SOFTWARE ELECTRONICALLY, INDICATE YOUR ACCEPTANCE OF THESE TERMS BY SELECTING THE "ACCEPT" BUTTON AT THE END OF THIS AGREEMENT. IF YOU DO NOT AGREE TO ALL THESE TERMS, PROMPTLY RETURN THE UNUSED SOFTWARE TO YOUR PLACE OF PURCHASE FOR A REFUND OR, IF THE SOFTWARE IS ACCESSED ELECTRONICALLY, SELECT THE "DECLINE" BUTTON AT THE END OF THIS AGREEMENT.

1. LICENSE TO USE. Sun grants you a non-exclusive and non-transferable license for the internal use only of the accompanying software and documentation and any error corrections provided by Sun (collectively "Software"), by the number of users and the class of computer hardware for which the corresponding fee has been paid.

2. RESTRICTIONS. Software is confidential and copyrighted. Title to Software and all associated intellectual property rights is retained by Sun and/or its licensors. Except as specifically authorized in any Supplemental License Terms, you may not make copies of Software, other than a single copy of Software for archival purposes. Unless enforcement is prohibited by applicable law, you may not modify, decompile, reverse-engineer Software. Software is not designed or licensed for use in on-line control of aircraft, air traffic, aircraft navigation or aircraft communications; or in the design, construction, operation or maintenance of any nuclear facility. You warrant that you will not use Software for these purposes. You may not publish or provide the results of any benchmark or comparison tests run on Software to any third party without the prior written consent of Sun. No right, title or interest in or to any trademark, service mark, logo or trade name of Sun or its licensors is granted under this Agreement.

3. LIMITED WARRANTY. Sun warrants to you that for a period of ninety (90) days from the date of purchase, as evidenced by a copy of the receipt, the media on which Software is furnished (if any) will be free of defects in materials and workmanship under normal use. Except for the foregoing, Software is provided "AS IS." Your exclusive remedy and Sun's entire liability under this limited warranty will be at Sun's option to replace Software media or refund the fee paid for Software.

4. DISCLAIMER OF WARRANTY. UNLESS SPECIFIED IN THIS AGREEMENT, ALL EXPRESS OR IMPLIED CONDITIONS, REPRESENTATIONS AND WARRANTIES, INCLUDING ANY IMPLIED WARRANTY OF MERCHANTABILITY, FITNESS FOR A PARTICULAR PURPOSE, OR NON-INFRINGEMENT, ARE DISCLAIMED, EXCEPT TO THE EXTENT THAT THESE DISCLAIMERS ARE HELD TO BE LEGALLY INVALID.

5. LIMITATION OF LIABILITY. TO THE EXTENT NOT PROHIBITED BY LAW, IN NO EVENT WILL SUN OR ITS LICENSORS BE LIABLE FOR ANY LOST REVENUE, PROFIT OR DATA, OR FOR SPECIAL, INDIRECT, CONSEQUENTIAL, INCIDENTAL OR PUNITIVE DAMAGES, HOWEVER CAUSED REGARDLESS OF THE

THEORY OF LIABILITY, ARISING OUT OF OR RELATED TO THE USE OF OR INABILITY TO USE SOFTWARE, EVEN IF SUN HAS BEEN ADVISED OF THE POSSIBILITY OF SUCH DAMAGES. In no event will Sun's liability to you, whether in contract, tort (including negligence), or otherwise, exceed the amount paid by you for Software under this Agreement. The foregoing limitations will apply even if the above-stated warranty fails of its essential purpose.

6. **Termination**. This Agreement is effective until terminated. Youmay terminate this Agreement at any time by destroying all copies of Software. This Agreement will terminate immediately without notice from Sun if you fail to comply with any provision of this Agreement.Upon Termination, you must destroy all copies of Software.

7. **Export Regulations**. All Software and technical data delivered under this Agreement are subject to U.S. export control laws and may be subject to export or import regulations in other countries. You agree to comply strictly with all such laws and regulations and acknowledge that you have the responsibility to obtain such licenses to export, re-export, or import as may be required after delivery to you.

8. **U.S. Government Restricted Rights**. Use, duplication, or disclosure by the U.S. Government is subject to restrictions set forth in this Agreement and as provided in DFARS 227.7202-1 (a) and 227.7202-3 (a) (1995), DFARS 252.227-7013 (c)(1)(ii)(Oct 1988), FAR12.212 (a) (1995), FAR 52.227-19 (June 1987), or FAR 52.227-14(ALTIII) (June 1987), as applicable.

9. **Governing Law**. Any action related to this Agreement will be governed by California law and controlling U.S. federal law. No choice of law rules of any jurisdiction will apply.

10. **Severability**. If any provision of this Agreement is held to be unenforceable, this Agreement will remain in effect with the provision omitted, unless omission would frustrate the intent of the parties, in which case this Agreement will immediately terminate.

11. **Integration**. This Agreement is the entire agreement between you and Sun relating to its subject matter. It supersedes all prior or contemporaneous oral or written communications, proposals, representations and warranties and prevails over any conflicting or additional terms of any quote, order, acknowledgment, or other communication between the parties relating to its subject matter during the term of this Agreement. No modification of this Agreement will be binding, unless in writing and signed by an authorized representative of each party.

For inquiries, please contact Sun Microsystems, Inc., 901 San Antonio Road, Palo Alto, CA 94303.
JAVA™ DEVELOPMENT KIT (JDK™) VERSION 1.2

SUPPLEMENTAL LICENSE TERMS

These supplemental terms ("Supplement") add to the terms of the Binary Code License Agreement ("Agreement"). Capitalized terms not defined herein shall have the same meanings ascribed to them in the Agreement. The Supplement terms shall supersede any inconsistent or conflicting terms in the Agreement.

1. **Limited License Grant**. Sun grants to you a non-exclusive, non-transferable limited license to use the Software without fee for evaluation of the Software and for development of Java(tm) applets and applications provided that you: (i) may not re-distribute the Software in whole or in part, either separately or included with a product; (ii) may not create, or authorize your licensees to create, additional classes, interfaces, or subpackages that are contained in the "java" or "sun" packages or similar as specified by Sun in any class file naming convention; and (iii) agree to the extent Programs are developed that utilize the Windows 95/98 style graphical user interface or components contained therein, such applets or applications may only be developed to run on a Windows 95/98 orWindows NT platform. Refer to the Java Runtime Environment Version 1.2 binary code license

JDK License Agreement

(**http://java.sun.com/products/JDK/1.2/index.html**) for the availabilityof runtime code that may be distributed with Java applets and applications.

2. **Java Platform Interface.** In the event that Licensee creates an additional API(s) that (i) extends the functionality of a Java Environment, and (ii) is exposed to third-party software developers for the purpose of developing additional software that invokes such additional API, Licensee must promptly publish broadly an accurate specification for such API for free use by all developers.

3. **Trademarks and Logos.** This Agreement does not authorize Licensee to use any Sun name, trademark or logo. Licensee acknowledges as between it and Sun that Sun owns the Java trademark and all Java-related trademarks, logos and icons, including the Coffee Cup and Duke ("JavaMarks") and agrees to comply with the Java Trademark Guidelines at **http://java.sun.com/trademarks.html.**

4. **High-Risk Activities.** Notwithstanding Section 2, with respect to high-risk activities, the following language shall apply: the Software is not designed or intended for use in on-line control of aircraft, air traffic, aircraft navigation or aircraft communications; or in the design, construction, operation or maintenance of any nuclear facility. Sun disclaims any express or implied warranty of fitness for such uses.

5. **Source Code.** Software may contain source code that is provided solely for reference purposes pursuant to the terms of this Agreement.

GNU General Public License

Version 2, June 1991
Copyright © 1989, 1991 Free Software Foundation, Inc.
675 Mass Ave., Cambridge, MA 02139, USA
Everyone is permitted to copy and distribute verbatim copies of this license document, but changing it is not allowed.

Preamble

The licenses for most software are designed to take away your freedom to share and change it. By contrast, the GNU General Public License is intended to guarantee your freedom to share and change free software — to make sure the software is free for all its users. This General Public License applies to most of the Free Software Foundation's software and to any other program whose authors commit to using it. (Some other Free Software Foundation software is covered by the GNU Library General Public License instead.) You can apply it to your programs, too.

When we speak of *free software*, we are referring to freedom, not price. Our General Public Licenses are designed to make sure that you have the freedom to distribute copies of free software (and charge for this service if you wish), that you receive source code or can get it if you want it, that you can change the software or use pieces of it in new free programs, and that you know you can do these things.

To protect your rights, we need to make restrictions that forbid anyone to deny you these rights or to ask you to surrender the rights. These restrictions translate to certain responsibilities for you if you distribute copies of the software, or if you modify it.

For example, if you distribute copies of such a program, whether gratis or for a fee, you must give the recipients all the rights that you have. You must make sure that they, too, receive or can get the source code. And you must show them these terms so they know their rights.

We protect your rights with two steps: (1) copyright the software, and (2) offer you this license, which gives you legal permission to copy, distribute, and/or modify the software.

Also, for each author's protection and ours, we want to make certain that everyone understands that there is no warranty for this free software. If the software is modified by someone else and passed on, we want its recipients to know that what they have is not the original, so that any problems introduced by others will not reflect on the original authors' reputations.

Finally, any free program is threatened constantly by software patents. We wish to avoid the danger that redistributors of a free program will individually obtain patent licenses, in effect making the program proprietary. To prevent this, we have made it clear that any patent must be licensed for everyone's free use or not licensed at all.

The precise terms and conditions for copying, distribution and modification follow.

Terms and Conditions for Copying, Distribution, and Modification

0. This License applies to any program or other work that contains a notice placed by the copyright holder saying it may be distributed under the terms of this General Public License. The "Program," below, refers to any such program or work, and a "work based on the Program" means either the Program or any derivative work under copyright law: that is to say, a work containing the Program or a portion of it, either verbatim or with modifications and/or translated into another language. (Hereinafter, translation is included without limitation in the term "modification.") Each licensee is addressed as "you."

GNU License Agreement

Activities other than copying, distribution, and modification are not covered by this License; they are outside its scope. The act of running the Program is not restricted, and the output from the Program is covered only if its contents constitute a work based on the Program (independent of having been made by running the Program). Whether that is true depends on what the Program does.

1. You may copy and distribute verbatim copies of the Program's source code as you receive it, in any medium, provided that you conspicuously and appropriately publish on each copy an appropriate copyright notice and disclaimer of warranty; keep intact all the notices that refer to this License and to the absence of any warranty; and give any other recipients of the Program a copy of this License along with the Program.

    You may charge a fee for the physical act of transferring a copy, and you may at your option offer warranty protection in exchange for a fee.

2. You may modify your copy or copies of the Program or any portion of it, thus forming a work based on the Program, and copy and distribute such modifications or work under the terms of Section 1 above, provided that you also meet all of these conditions:

    (a) You must cause the modified files to carry prominent notices stating that you changed the files and the date of any change.

    (b) You must cause any work that you distribute or publish, that in whole or in part contains or is derived from the Program or any part thereof, to be licensed as a whole at no charge to all third parties under the terms of this License.

    (c) If the modified program normally reads commands interactively when run, you must cause it, when started running for such interactive use in the most ordinary way, to print or display an announcement including an appropriate copyright notice and a notice that there is no warranty (or else, saying that you provide a warranty) and that users may redistribute the program under these conditions, and telling the user how to view a copy of this License. (Exception: If the Program itself is interactive but does not normally print such an announcement, your work based on the Program is not required to print an announcement.)

These requirements apply to the modified work as a whole. If identifiable sections of that work are not derived from the Program, and can be reasonably considered independent and separate works in themselves, then this License, and its terms, do not apply to those sections when you distribute them as separate works. But when you distribute the same sections as part of a whole that is a work based on the Program, the distribution of the whole must be on the terms of this License, whose permissions for other licensees extend to the entire whole, and thus to each and every part regardless of who wrote it. Thus, it is not the intent of this section to claim rights or contest your rights to work written entirely by you; rather, the intent is to exercise the right to control the distribution of derivative or collective works based on the Program.

In addition, mere aggregation of another work not based on the Program with the Program (or with a work based on the Program) on a volume of a storage or distribution medium does not bring the other work under the scope of this License.

3. You may copy and distribute the Program (or a work based on it, under Section 2) in object code or executable form under the terms of Sections 1 and 2 above provided that you also do one of the following:

    (a) Accompany it with the complete corresponding machine-readable source code, which must be distributed under the terms of Sections 1 and 2 above on a medium customarily used for software interchange; or,

    (b) Accompany it with a written offer, valid for at least three years, to give any third party, for a charge no more than your cost of physically performing source distribution, a complete, machine-readable copy of the corresponding

GNU License Agreement

source code, to be distributed under the terms of Sections 1 and 2 above on a medium customarily used for software interchange; or,

(c) Accompany it with the information you received as to the offer to distribute corresponding source code. (This alternative is allowed only for noncommercial distribution and only if you received the program in object code or executable form with such an offer, in accord with Subsection (b) above.)

The source code for a work means the preferred form of the work for making modifications to it. For an executable work, complete source code means all the source code for all modules it contains, plus any associated interface definition files, plus the scripts used to control compilation and installation of the executable. However, as a special exception, the source code distributed need not include anything that is normally distributed (in either source or binary form) with the major components (compiler, kernel, and so forth) of the operating system on which the executable runs, unless that component itself accompanies the executable.

If distribution of executable or object code is made by offering access to copy from a designated place, then offering equivalent access to copy the source code from the same place counts as distribution of the source code, even though third parties are not compelled to copy the source along with the object code.

4. You may not copy, modify, sublicense, or distribute the Program except as expressly provided under this License. Any attempt otherwise to copy, modify, sublicense, or distribute the Program is void, and will automatically terminate your rights under this License.

However, parties who have received copies, or rights, from you under this License will not have their licenses terminated so long as such parties remain in full compliance.

5. You are not required to accept this License, since you have not signed it. However, nothing else grants you permission to modify or distribute the Program or

its derivative works. These actions are prohibited by law if you do not accept this License. Therefore, by modifying or distributing the Program (or any work based on the Program), you indicate your acceptance of this License to do so, and all its terms and conditions for copying, distributing or modifying the Program or works based on it.

6. Each time you redistribute the Program (or any work based on the Program), the recipient automatically receives a license from the original licensor to copy, distribute, or modify the Program subject to these terms and conditions. You may not impose any further restrictions on the recipients' exercise of the rights granted herein. You are not responsible for enforcing compliance by third parties to this License.

7. If, as a consequence of a court judgment or allegation of patent infringement or for any other reason (not limited to patent issues), conditions are imposed on you (whether by court order, agreement or otherwise) that contradict the conditions of this License, they do not excuse you from the conditions of this License. If you cannot distribute so as to satisfy simultaneously your obligations under this License and any other pertinent obligations, then as a consequence you may not distribute the Program at all. For example, if a patent license would not permit royalty-free redistribution of the Program by all those who receive copies directly or indirectly through you, then the only way you could satisfy both it and this License would be to refrain entirely from distribution of the Program.

If any portion of this section is held invalid or unenforceable under any particular circumstance, the balance of the section is intended to apply and the section as a whole is intended to apply in other circumstances.

It is not the purpose of this section to induce you to infringe any patents or other property right claims or to contest validity of any such claims; this section has the sole purpose of protecting the integrity of the free software distribution system, which is implemented by public license practices. Many people have made generous contributions to the

GNU License Agreement

wide range of software distributed through that system in reliance on consistent application of that system; it is up to the author/donor to decide if he or she is willing to distribute software through any other system and a licensee cannot impose that choice.

This section is intended to make thoroughly clear what is believed to be a consequence of the rest of this License.

8. If the distribution and/or use of the Program is restricted in certain countries either by patents or by copyrighted interfaces, the original copyright holder who places the Program under this License may add an explicit geographical distribution limitation excluding those countries, so that distribution is permitted only in or among countries not thus excluded. In such case, this License incorporates the limitation as if written in the body of this License.

9. The Free Software Foundation may publish revised and/or new versions of the General Public License from time to time. Such new versions will be similar in spirit to the present version, but may differ in detail to address new problems or concerns. Each version is given a distinguishing version number. If the Program specifies a version number of this License which applies to it and "any later version," you have the option of following the terms and conditions either of that version or of any later version published by the Free Software Foundation. If the Program does not specify a version number of this License, you may choose any version ever published by the Free Software Foundation.

10. If you wish to incorporate parts of the Program into other free programs whose distribution conditions are different, write to the author to ask for permission. For software which is copyrighted by the Free Software Foundation, write to the Free Software Foundation; we sometimes make exceptions for this. Our decision will be guided by the two goals of preserving the free status of all derivatives of our free software and of promoting the sharing and reuse of software generally.

No Warranty

11. BECAUSE THE PROGRAM IS LICENSED FREE OF CHARGE, THERE IS NO WARRANTY FOR THE PROGRAM, TO THE EXTENT PERMITTED BY APPLICABLE LAW. EXCEPT WHEN OTHERWISE STATED IN WRITING, THE COPYRIGHT HOLDERS AND/OR OTHER PARTIES PROVIDE THE PROGRAM "AS IS" WITHOUT WARRANTY OF ANY KIND, EITHER EXPRESSED OR IMPLIED, INCLUDING, BUT NOT LIMITED TO, THE IMPLIED WARRANTIES OF MERCHANTABILITY AND FITNESS FOR A PARTICULAR PURPOSE. THE ENTIRE RISK AS TO THE QUALITY AND PERFORMANCE OF THE PROGRAM IS WITH YOU. SHOULD THE PROGRAM PROVE DEFECTIVE, YOU ASSUME THE COST OF ALL NECESSARY SERVICING, REPAIR, OR CORRECTION.

12. IN NO EVENT UNLESS REQUIRED BY APPLICABLE LAW OR AGREED TO IN WRITING WILL ANY COPYRIGHT HOLDER, OR ANY OTHER PARTY WHO MAY MODIFY AND/OR REDISTRIBUTE THE PROGRAM AS PERMITTED ABOVE, BE LIABLE TO YOU FOR DAMAGES, INCLUDING ANY GENERAL, SPECIAL, INCIDENTAL, OR CONSEQUENTIAL DAMAGES ARISING OUT OF THE USE OR INABILITY TO USE THE PROGRAM (INCLUDING BUT NOT LIMITED TO LOSS OF DATA OR DATA BEING RENDERED INACCURATE OR LOSSES SUSTAINED BY YOU OR THIRD PARTIES OR A FAILURE OF THE PROGRAM TO OPERATE WITH ANY OTHER PROGRAMS), EVEN IF SUCH HOLDER OR OTHER PARTY HAS BEEN ADVISED OF THE POSSIBILITY OF SUCH DAMAGES.

End of Terms and Conditions

GNU License Agreement

How to Apply These Terms to Your New Programs

If you develop a new program, and you want it to be of the greatest possible use to the public, the best way to achieve this is to make it free software that everyone can redistribute and change under these terms.

To do so, attach the following notices to the program. It is safest to attach them to the start of each source file to most effectively convey the exclusion of warranty; and each file should have at least the "copyright" line and a pointer to where the full notice is found:

<One line to give the program's name and a brief idea of what it does.>
Copyright c 19yy (name of author)

This program is free software; you can redistribute it and/or modify it under the terms of the GNU General Public License as published by the Free Software Foundation; either Version 2 of the License or (at your option) any later version.

This program is distributed in the hope that it will be useful, but WITHOUT ANY WARRANTY; without even the implied warranty of MERCHANTABILITY or FITNESS FOR A PARTICULAR PURPOSE. See the GNU General Public License for more details.

You should have received a copy of the GNU General Public License along with this program; if not, write to the Free Software Foundation, Inc., 675 Mass Ave., Cambridge, MA 02139, USA.

Also add information on how to contact you by electronic and paper mail.

If the program is interactive, make it output a short notice like this when it starts in an interactive mode:

```
Gnomovision version 69, Copyright (c) 19yy
name of author
Gnomovision comes with ABSOLUTELY NO WARRANTY;
for details type 'show w'
This is free software, and you are welcome to
redistribute it under certain conditions; type
'show c' for details.
```

The hypothetical commands show w and show c should show the appropriate parts of the General Public License. Of course, the commands you use may be called something other than show w and show c; they could even be mouse-clicks or menu items — whatever suits your program.

You should also get your employer (if you work as a programmer) or your school, if any, to sign a "copyright disclaimer" for the program, if necessary. Here is a sample; alter the names:

Yoyodyne, Inc., hereby disclaims all copyright interest in the program "Gnomovision" (which makes passes at compilers) written by James Hacker.

(signature of Ty Coon), 1 April 1989
Ty Coon, President of Vice

This General Public License does not permit incorporating your program into proprietary programs. If your program is a subroutine library, you may consider it more useful to permit linking proprietary applications with the library. If this is what you want to do, use the GNU Library General Public License instead of this License.

Installing the
CD-ROM

This book's CD-ROM is cross-platform: you can mount it on a PC (using Windows 95, Windows 98, or Windows NT 4.0), Macintosh, or UNIX. To view the contents of the CD-ROM, insert it in your computer's CD-ROM drive and then do the following:

1. Open Windows Explorer (or the equivalent) on your platform of choice.
2. Double-click the icon for your CD-ROM drive.
3. To select a folder containing a particular application, click it.
4. If needed, click subfolder icons until you find the subfolder in which the installation program is located. The installation program is usually named install.
5. If the subfolder contains a readme file, click the file and read it before starting the installation.
6. To install the program, double-click the icon representing the installation program.
7. After installing the program, close all the windows associated with the installation.